A Teacher's Treasury of Quotations

A Teacher's Treasury of Quotations

Compiled by
Bernard E. Farber

McFarland & Company, Inc., Publishers
Jefferson, North Carolina, and London

Library of Congress Cataloguing-in-Publication Data

Farber, Bernard E., 1914– .
   A teacher's treasury of quotations.

   Includes indexes.
   1. Quotations, English.   2. Education – Quotations,
maxims, etc.   I. Title.
PN6081.F34   1985   082   84-43218

ISBN 0-89950-150-8 (alk. paper)

Printed in the United States of America

McFarland   Box 611   Jefferson NC 28640

To Carmyle

To me faire friend you never can be old,
For as you were when first your eye I eyde,
Such seemes your beautie still.

— Shakespeare

Preface

The quotations in this book represent many countries, cultures and periods of history. They were selected because they are profound, provocative or witty, and were written (or said) in an engaging style. Some were included for their historical interest; others for their insight into contemporary education and today's world.

This collection attempts to present a balance between differing viewpoints. The fact that a quotation has been selected for inclusion in this anthology does not necessarily signify the compiler's agreement with its sentiments. It means only that it deserves to be included.

The process of compilation is inescapably selective and consequently cannot avoid a point of view and bias of taste. Strive as one will for objectivity, the hard fact remains that the self inevitably intrudes in the selection process and what results is a work which bears the indisputable stamp of the anthologist's personality.

The number of quotations chosen from an author should not be construed as an indication of that writer's merit. Some authors—Shakespeare, Pope, Emerson, Twain, Shaw, to name only a few—wrote in a form that lends itself well to quotation, while others, equally or more praiseworthy, lacked the intangible quality of quotability. In addition, the exigency of limiting the size of the book unavoidably resulted in the omission of many worthwhile quotations.

Bernard E. Farber
Longboat Key, Florida
September 1985

Table of Contents

Table of Contents

Table of Contents

Table of Contents

A Teacher's Treasury
of Quotations

Ability

See also Competence; Skill; Talent

I think that knowing what you can *not* do is more important than knowing what you can do. In fact, that's good taste.
— Lucille Ball, in Eleanor Harris, *The Real Story of Lucille Ball*, vii (1954).

There is hardly anybody good for everything, and there is scarcely anybody who is absolutely good for nothing.
— Lord Chesterfield, *Letters to His Son*, Jan 2, 1748.

By different methods different men excel;
But where is he who can do all things well? — Charles Churchill, *An Epistle to William Hogarth*, ln.573 (1763).

Natural ability without education has more often raised a man to glory and virtue than education without natural ability. — Cicero, *Pro Archia* (62 B.C.).

Let him sing to the flute, who cannot sing to the harp. — Cicero, *Pro Murena*, xiii.29 (63 B.C.).

In a world as empirical as ours, a youngster who does not know what he is good *at* will not be sure what he is good *for*. — Edgar Z. Friedenberg, *The Vanishing Adolescent: Emotional Development in Adolescence* (1959).

It is impossible for the average boy to grow up and use the remarkable capacities that are in every boy, unless the world is for him and makes sense. And a society makes sense when it understands that its chief wealth *is* these capacities.
— Paul Goodman, *Growing Up Absurd* (1960).

You can't beat oil out of chaff.
— H.H. Hart, *Seven Hundred Chinese Proverbs*, no.625 (1937).

If anyone thinks that those who have not good natural ability cannot to some extent make up for the deficiencies of nature by right training and practice, let such a one know that he is very wide of the mark, if not out of it altogether.
— Plutarch, *Moralia: The Education of Children* (c. A.D. 95).

I can't carry a goat, and you are loading me with an ox. — Plutarch, *ibid.: On Avoidance of Lending*, 830A.

One man excels in one thing, another in another. — Publilius Syrus, *Sententiae*, no.332 (c.43 B.C.).

If thou canst dive, bring up pearls. If thou canst not dive, collect amber.
— Christina Rossetti, *The Face of the Deep*, preface (1892).

Education is the same, but capacities differ. — Saadi, *Gulistän (Rose Garden)*, vii (1258).

Capacity without education is pitiful; education without capacity is thrown away. — Saadi, *ibid.*, viii, Maxim 56.

In all classes we find men possessed of high intellectual qualities, though often without mental cultivation. For natural abilities can almost compensate for the want of every kind of cultivation, but no cultivation of the mind can make up for the want of natural abilities.
— Arthur Schopenhauer, *Will in Nature*, II.84 (1836).

If you cannot drive an ox, drive a donkey. — Suidas, *Lexicon* (c.975).

Abstraction

Abstractions are frequently attractive, ingenious, and valuable. But ever so often abstract thinking borders on mysticism. Whenever that happens I have a feeling that reason rests and imagination takes over. —Louis D. Brandeis, in Solomon Goldman, *The Words of Justice Brandeis*, 26 (1953).

A little more of the abstract and we'd both have gone potty. What is there to bite on in the abstract? You might as well eat triangles and go to bed with a sewing machine. —Joyce Cary, *The Horse's Mouth*, xxxi (1965).

An American will tinker with anything he can put his hands on. But how rarely can he be persuaded to tinker with an abstract idea. —Leland Stowe, *They Shall Not Sleep* (1944).

Absurdity

Absurdity, *n*. A statement or belief manifestly inconsistent with one's own. —Ambrose Bierce, *The Devil's Dictionary* (1911).

People who cannot recognize a palpable absurdity are very much in the way of civilization. —Agnes Repplier, *In Pursuit of Laughter*, i (1936).

There is no absurdity so palpable but that it may be firmly planted in the human head if you only begin to inculcate it before the age of five, by constantly repeating it with an air of great solemnity. —Arthur Schopenhauer *Studies in Pessimism: Psychological Observations* (1890).

Academe

The green retreats of Academus. —Mark Akenside, *Pleasures of the Imagination*, I.i.591 (1744).

But how I longed As a boy for the groves and grooves of Academe. —Christopher Fry, *Venus Observed*, I (1950).

'Mongst all these stirs of discontented strife,
O, let me lead an academic life;
To know much, and to think for nothing, know
Nothing to have, yet think we have enow. —Joseph Hall (1574–1656), *Poetical Works* (1793): *Discontent of Men with their Condition*.

And seek for truth in the groves of Academe. —Horace, *Epistles*, II.ii.45 (20 B.C.).

Thy solitary Academe should be Some shady grove upon the Thames' fair side. —Henry Peacham, *Emblems* (1603–08).

Academicism

Academism results when the reasons for the rule change, but not the rule. —Igor Stravinsky (and Robert Craft), *Conversations with Igor Stravinsky: Some Musical Questions* (1980).

This is the great vice of academicism, that it is concerned with ideas rather than with thinking. —Lionel Trilling, *The Liberal Imagination: The Sense of the Past* (1950).

Academy

See also School

Academy, *n*. (from academe.) A modern school where football is taught. —Ambrose Bierce, *The Devil's Dictionary* (1911).

They [academies] commit their pupils to the theatre of the world with just taste enough of learning to be alienated from

industrious pursuits and not enough to
do service in the ranks of science.
— Thomas Jefferson,
letter to John Adams, July 5, 1814.

Our court shall be a little academe.
— William Shakespeare,
Love's Labour's Lost, I.i.13 (1594)
[academe = academy].

Achievement

See also Success

It is not the going out of port, but the
coming in that determines the success of
a voyage.   — Henry Ward Beecher,
Proverbs from Plymouth Pulpit: Success
(1887).

Satisfaction does not come from indulgence or satiety; it comes from
achievement.   — Calvin Coolidge,
address at University of Vermont,
June 28, 1920.

It is not enough to aim, you must hit.
— Italian proverb.

There is no penalty for overachievement.
— George William Miller,
Time, July 17, 1978.

Action

See also Activity

The end of man is an action and not a
thought, though it were the noblest.
— Thomas Carlyle,
Sartor Resartus, II.vi (1833).

Action is with the scholar subordinate,
but it is essential. Without it he is not yet
man. Without it thought can never ripen
into truth.   — Ralph Waldo Emerson,
The American Scholar,
Phi Beta Kappa address at Harvard,
Aug. 31, 1837.

If you did not learn your lesson to display
it in action, what did you learn it for?
— Epictetus,
Discourses, I.xxix (c. A.D. 100).

Action is the proper Fruit of Knowledge.
— Thomas Fuller (1654–1734),
Gnomologia, no.760 (1732).

A little knowledge that acts is worth infinitely more than much knowledge that
is idle.   — Kahlil Gibran,
The Treasured Writings: The Words of
the Master, viii (1980).

The great end of life is not knowledge
but action.   — T.H. Huxley,
Technical Education (1877).

Action and not knowledge is man's
destiny and duty in this life; and his
highest principles, both in philosophy
and in religion, have reference to this
end.   — Henry Longueville Mansel,
The Limits of Religious Thought
Examined (1859).

Action takes precedence over study.
— Jerusalem Talmud: Pesahim, 3.7
(before A.D. 400).

Action will remove the doubt that theory
cannot solve.   — Tehyi Hsieh,
Chinese Epigrams Inside Out and
Proverbs (1948).

We cannot think first and act afterwards.
From the moment of birth we are immersed in action, and can only fitfully
guide it by taking thought.
— Alfred North Whitehead,
Science and the Modern World, xii
(1925).

Life does not consist in thinking, it consists in acting.   — Woodrow Wilson,
speech in New York City,
Sept. 28, 1912.

Activity

See also Action

Activity with mistakes is better than indolence without mistakes.
— Henry Ward Beecher,
*Proverbs from Plymouth Pulpit:
Human Life* (1887).

Activity is the only road to knowledge.
— George Bernard Shaw,
Maxims for Revolutionists (1903).

Adaptability

See also Adjustment

The weather-cock on a church-spire, though made of iron, would soon be broken by the storm-wind if it ... did not understand the noble art of turning to every wind. — Henrich Heine,
English Fragments, xi (1828).

The most amazing thing about little children, Elgar decided ... was their fantastic adaptability. — Kristin Hunter,
The Landlord (1966).

Adjustment

See also Adaptability

There is little or no intellectual challenge or discipline involved in merely learning to adjust. — Betty Friedan,
The Feminine Mystique, vii (1963).

Every new adjustment is a crisis of self-esteem. — Eric Hoffer,
The Ordeal of Change (1963).

Adjustment, that synonym for conformity that comes more easily to the modern tongue, is the theme of our swan song, the piper's tune to which we dance on the brink of the abyss, the siren's melody that destroys our senses and paralyzes our wills. — Robert M. Lindner,
Must You Conform? (1956)

You must adjust.... This is the legend imprinted in every schoolbook, the invisible message on every blackboard. Our schools have become vast factories for the manufacture of robots.
— Robert M. Lindner, *ibid.*

Adjustment as an educational goal is a pricked balloon. To adjust to the twentieth century is to come to terms with madness. What is needed is the adjustment of our environment to ourselves, or rather to what we would like ourselves to be. — Max Rafferty,
Suffer Little Children (1962).

The reasonable man adapts himself to the world: the unreasonable one persists in trying to adapt the world to himself. Therefore all progress depends on the unreasonable man.
George Bernard Shaw,
Maxims for Revolutionists (1903).

Administration

See also Administrator; Authority (i.e., Power); Leadership

As a general proposition, colleges are best administered by administrators, next by faculty, and most worst by students.
— William F. Buckley, Jr.,
Quotations from Chairman Bill (1970).

It is the essence of our educational system that whatever part of the institution is not run by the inmates is reserved for the parents of the inmates.
— Murray Kempton,
New York Post, Mar. 31, 1960.

I find the three major administrative problems on a campus are sex for the students, athletics for the alumni, and parking for the faculty.
— Clark Kerr, in *Time*, Nov. 17, 1958.

An administration, like a machine, does not create. It carries on.
— Antoine de Saint-Exupéry,
Flight to Arras, x (1942).

Bad administration, to be sure, can destroy good policy; but good administration can never save bad policy.
— Adlai E. Stevenson, speech in Los Angeles, Sept. 11, 1952.

I cannot give you the formula for success, but I can give you the formula for failure — which is: Try to please everybody.   — Herbert Bayard Swope, address at dinner in his honor, Dec. 20, 1950.

The buck stops here.
— Harry S Truman, hand-lettered sign on his desk when president (1945–52).

What a man dislikes in his superiors, let him not display in the treatment of his inferiors.   — Tsang Sin, *The Great Learning*, X.ii (5th cent. B.C.).

Administrator

See also Administration; Bureaucrat; Leader; Principal

Good administrators are frequently accused of wanting to keep everything tidy. The charge is correct, and so are the administrators. That is what they are there for — to contain natural chaos.
— Jacques Barzun, *The American University*, iv (1968).

The mobilizing of the mind to meet and sway the minds of other men, involved in the conduct of affairs, blunts a sense of fine truth. The administrator is the death of the artist.
— Charles Horton Cooley, *Life and the Student* (1931).

Some school officials have fogotten the reason they are there. Expediency and efficiency in administration have somehow become more important than educating children.
— Marian Wright Edelman, in Margie Casady, "Society's Pushed-Out Children," *Psychology Today*, June 1975.

That the Rector [of the proposed academy] be a Man of good Understanding, good Morals, diligent and patient, learn'd in the Languages and Sciences, and a correct pure Speaker, and Writer of the English Tongue; to have such Tutors under him as shall be necessary.
— Benjamin Franklin, *Proposals Relating to the Education of Youth in Pensilvania* (1751).

The presidency of a large university is an anachronism. The public demands that the president be everywhere at all times. He is thought to be omniscient, omnipresent, and Mr. Chips all rolled into one.
— A. Whitney Griswold, in *Yale Daily News*, 1955.

An official is always an official man, and he has a wild belief in the value of reports.   — Arthur Helps, *Conversation in a Railway Carriage* (1871).

There's no reason why the University should be stuck with me at 51 because I was a promising young man at 30.
— Robert M. Hutchins, announcing his resignation as chancellor of University of Chicago, *Time*, Jan. 8, 1951.

He who is unable to rule over himself is surely unfit to rule over others.
— Solomon Ibn Gabirol, *Choice of Pearls*, no.194 (c.1050).

Who seeks to please all men each way,
And not himself offend,
He may begin his work to-day,
But God knows where he'll end.
— Samuel Rowlands, *Epigrams* (1600).

Adolescence

See also Adolescent; Youth

Until the eighteenth century, adolescence was confused with childhood. In school Latin the word *puer* and the word *adolescens* were used indiscriminately ... there were no terms in French to distinguish between *pueri* and *adolescentes*. There was virtually only one word in use: *enfant*. — Phillipe Aries, *Centuries of Childhood* (1965).

To every period of history, there corresponded a privileged age and a particular division of human life: "youth" is the privileged age of the seventeenth century, "childhood" of the nineteenth, "adolescence" of the twentieth.
— Phillipe Ariès, *ibid.*

I was between
A man and a boy,
A hobble-de-hoy,
A fat, little, punchy concern of sixteen.
— Richard Harris Barham, *The Ingoldsby Legends: Aunt Fanny* (1910).

The age we call awkward and the growing pains it inflicts on young bodies exact occasional sacrifices.   — Colette, *Sido: The Savages* (1929).

I think what is happening to me is so wonderful, and not only what can be seen on my body, but all that is taking place inside. I never discuss myself or any of these things with anybody; that is why I have to talk to myself about them.
— Anne Frank, *The Diary of a Young Girl*, July 6, 1944 (1952).

I'm awfully scared that everyone who knows me as I always am will discover that I have another side, a finer and better side. I'm afraid they'll laugh at me, think I'm ridiculous and sentimental, not take me seriously.   — Anne Frank, *ibid.*, July 15, 1944.

Juvenile appraisals of other juveniles make up in clarity what they lack in charity.   — Edgar Z. Friedenberg, *The Vanishing Adolescent: Emotional Development in Adolescence* (1959).

Adolescence is a kind of emotional seasickness. Both are funny, but only in retrospect.   — Arthur Koestler, *Arrow in the Blue*, 82 (1952).

Of all the curable illnesses that afflict mankind, the hardest to cure, and the one most likely to leave its victim a chronic invalid, is adolescence.
— Bonaro W. Overstreet, *Understanding Fear* (1951).

Age seventeen is the point in the journey when the parents retire to the observation car; it is the time when you stop being critical of your eldest son and he starts being critical of you.
— Sally and James Reston, *Saturday Evening Post*, May 5, 1956.

Not yet old enough for a man nor young enough for a boy: as a squash is before 'tis pescod, or a codling when 'tis almost an apple. 'Tis with him in standing water, between boy and man.
— William Shakespeare, *Twelfth Night*, I.v.158 (1601)
[squash = *unripe pea pod*; pescod = *peascod, ripe pea pod*; codling = *unripe apple*; standing water = *the tide at ebb or flood when it flows neither way*].

In no order of things is adolescence the time of the simple life.
— Janet Erskine Stuart, in Maud Monahan, *Life and Letters of Janet Erskine Stuart* (1922).

Adolescent

See also Adolescence; Youth

An adolescent in his round of joyless promiscuity is no more a revolutionary than a pickpocket is a socialist; he is merely taking adult prerogatives without taking adult responsibility, taking without earning.   — Donald Barr, *Who Killed Humpty Dumpty?* (1971).

It confuses the sprouting adolescent to wake up every morning in a new body. It confuses the mother and father to find a new child every day in a familiar body.
— Donald Barr, *New York Times*, Nov. 26, 1967.

The adolescent, though given to aggression and lust, is emotionally cold, and ratiocination can be a substitute for feeling.   — Anthony Burgess, *Urgent Copy* (1968).

Every sixteen-year-old is a pornographer.... We had to know what was open to us.   — Hortense Calisher, *Queenie*, I (1971).

As for boys and girls, it is one of the sorriest mistakes to talk down to them: almost always your lad of fifteen thinks more simply, more fundamentally than you do; and what he accepts as good coin is not facts or precepts, but feelings and convictions.   — David Grayson, *The Friendly Road* (1913).

It is hard to convince a high-school student that he will encounter a lot of problems more difficult than those of algebra and geometry.   — Edgar W. Howe, *Country Town Sayings* (1911).

Tne teenagers ain't all bad. I love 'em if nobody else does. There ain't nothin' wrong with young people. Jus' quit lyin' to 'em.   — Jackie "Moms" Mabley, in *Newsday*, Apr. 6, 1967.

What I like in my adolescents is that they have not yet hardened. We all confuse hardening with strength. Strength we must achieve, but not callousness.
          — Anaïs Nin, *Diaries*, IV (1974).

As a result of all his education, from everything he hears and sees around him, the child absorbs such a lot of lies and foolish nonsense mixed in with essential truths, that the first duty of the adolescent who wants to be a healthy man is to disgorge it all.   — Romain Rolland, *Jean Christophe* (1904–12).

A Jewish man with parents alive is a fifteen-year-old boy, and will remain a fifteen-year-old boy till they die.
          — Philip Roth, *Portnoy's Complaint* (1969).

To grown people a girl of fifteen and a half is a child still; to herself she is very old and very real; more real, perhaps, than ever before or after.
          — Margaret Widdemer, *The Boardwalk: The Changeling* (1919).

And all things that were true and fair
Lay closely to my loving eye,
With nothing shadowy between —
I was a boy of seventeen.
          — Nathaniel Parker Willis, *Melanie*, I (1835).

How do you go about becoming a 17-year-old philosopher king when thoughts of screwing keep interrupting your reveries of the nature of man?
          — Carey Winfrey, *Starts and Finishes* (1975).

At seventeen years old I was already an old-fashioned brass cannon full of shot, and nothing had kept me from going off but a doubt as to my capacity to shoot straight.   — William Butler Yeats, *Autobiography*, 77 (1916).

Adult

Adults are obsolete children and the hell with them.   — Theodor Geisel, *Time*, May 7, 1979.

Grown people were always on the edge of telling you something valuable and then withdrawing it, a form of bully-teasing.
          — Lillian Hellman, *Pentimento* (1973).

Adults can learn most things better than children, though it may take them longer.   — Cyril O. Houle, *Continuing Your Education* (1964).

One of the most obvious facts about grownups to a child, is that they have forgotten what it is like to be a child.
          — Randall Jarrell, *The Third Book of Criticism* (1969).

And grownups have to act as if they know. That's how they show they love you, by knowing more stuff; it makes you feel secure.   —Jill Robinson,
Bed/Time/Story, II (1974).

Grown-ups never understand anything for themselves, and it is tiresome for children to be always and forever explaining things to them.
          —Antoine de Saint-Exupéry,
The Little Prince, i (1943).

A child becomes an adult when he realizes that he has a right not only to be right but also to be wrong.
          —Thomas Szasz,
The Second Sin: Childhood (1973).

Advice

See also Counseling

What is the supreme happiness down here below?
Listening to the song of a little girl as she goes down the road after she has asked me the way.   —Anon.,
from an ancient Chinese poem.

Listen to advice and accept instruction, that you may gain wisdom for the future.
          —*Bible: Proverbs* 19:20.

Advice is seldom welcome; and those who want it the most, always like it the least.   —Lord Chesterfield,
Letters to His Son, Jan. 29, 1748.

We ask advice, but we mean approbation.   —Charles Caleb Colton,
Lacon, 116 (1820–22).

He who builds according to every man's advice will have a crooked house.
          —Danish proverb.

Advice is less necessary to the wise than to fools, but the wise derive most advantage from it.   —Francesco Guicciardini,
Storia d'Italia (1564).

The advice of the elders to young men is very apt to be as unreal as a list of the hundred best books.
          —Oliver Wendell Holmes, Jr.,
speech, Boston, Jan. 8, 1897,
in *The Mind and Faith of Justice Holmes*,
ed. Max Lerner (1943).

Advice is not disliked because it is advice; but because so few people know how to give it.   —Leigh Hunt,
The Indicator, LI (1821).

Advice, as it always gives a temporary appearance of superiority, can never be very grateful, even when it is most necessary or the most judicious. —Samuel Johnson,
The Rambler, Jan. 15, 1751.

You ask, Lupus, to what master you should entrust your son: this has been worrying you for a long time. My advice: steer shy of grammarians and rhetoricians: your son has no business with Cicero and Vergil.... If you catch him writing poetry, disinherit him.... If you think the boy isn't very bright, make him an auctioneer or an architect.
          —Martial,
Epigrammata, V.xlii.56 (A.D. 93).

Please give me some good advice in your next letter. I promise not to follow it.
          —Edna St. Vincent Millay,
Letters, ed. Alan R. Macdougall (1952).

People who have what they want are fond of telling people who haven't what they want that they really don't want it.
          —Ogden Nash,
Kansas City Times, Jan. 22, 1977.

Only when a man is safely ensconced under six feet of earth, with several tons of enlauding granite upon his chest, is he in a position to give advice with any certainty, and then he is silent.
          —A. Edward Newton,
*The Amenities of Book-Collecting
and Kindred Affections*, iv (1918).

I pray theee, cease thy counsel,
Which falls into mine ears as profitless
As water in a sieve.
— William Shakespeare,
Much Ado About Nothing, V.i.3
(1598–99).

Since I have given you all this advice, I add this crowning precept, the most valuable of all: NEVER TAKE ANYONE'S ADVICE.
— George Bernard Shaw,
Advice to a Young Critic, 13 (1956).

When you get a bit of advice, don't bolt it. Chew it fortyseven times; and then it will digest all right.
— George Bernard Shaw,
letter to Molly Tompkins, Jan. 11, 1922.

Good advice is one of those injuries which a good man ought, if possible, to forgive, but at all events to forget at once.
— Horace Smith,
The Tin Trumpet: Advice (1836).

How is it possible to expect that mankind will take advice, when they will not so much as take warning?
— Jonathan Swift,
Thoughts on Various Subjects (1706).

Age, Old

See also Ages; Youth and Age

Education is the best provision for an old age. — Aristotle, in Diogenes Laërtius,
Lives of Eminent Philosophers, V.21
(A.D. 200's).

Wisdom is with the aged, and understanding in length of days.
— *Bible: Job* 12:12.

Many a man that couldn't direct you to the drugstore on the corner when he was thirty will get a respectful hearing when age has further impaired his mind.
— Finley Peter Dunne,
Mr. Dooley Remembers: Some Observations by Mr. Dooley (1963).

We are never too old to be instructed.
— Oliver Goldsmith, *The Citizen of the World*, let.123 (1762).

An oldtimer is someone who can remember when a naughty child was taken to the woodshed instead of to a psychiatrist.   — David Greenberg,
American Opinion, Nov. 1975.

The white locks of age were sometimes found to be the thatch of an intellectual tenement in good repair.
— Nathaniel Hawthorne,
The Scarlet Letter: Introductory (1850).

It is hard to make an olde dog stoupe.
— John Heywood,
Proverbs, II.vii. (1546).

When, if not now?   — Lacydes, in
Diogenes Laërtius, *Lacydes*, IV.viii.60
(3rd cent.), when asked why he had begun the study of geometry in old age.

Old age, to the unlearned, is winter; to the learned, it is harvest time.
— Judah Leib Lazerov,
Enciklopedie fun Idishé Vitzen,
no.499 (1928).

The older I grow the more I distrust the familiar doctrine that age brings wisdom.
— H.L. Mencken,
Prejudices, Third Series (1922).

Solon was under a delusion when he said that a man when he grows old may learn many things—for he can no more learn much than he can run much; youth is the time for any extraordinary toil.
— Plato, *Republic*, VII
(c.375–368 B.C.).

Sir, I am too old to learn.
— William Shakespeare,
King Lear, II.ii.130
(1605–06).

Hard is to teach an old horse amble true.
— Edmund Spenser,
The Faerie Queen, III.viii.xxvi (1596).

The best teachers are the aged. To the old our mouths are always partly closed; we must swallow our obvious retorts and listen. They sit above our heads, on life's raised daïs, and appeal at once to our respect and pity.
— Robert Louis Stevenson
Virginibus Puerisque: Talk and Talkers (1881).

Ages

See also Adolescence; Age, Old; Childhood; Youth

Youth is a blunder; Manhood a struggle; Old Age a regret. — Benjamin Disraeli, *Coningsby*, III.i (1844).

At twenty years of age the Will reigns; at 30, the Wit; at 40 the Judgment.
— Benjamin Franklin,
Poor Richard's Almanack, June 1741.

The old believe everything: the middle-aged suspect everything: the young know everything. — Oscar Wilde,
Chameleon, I, Dec. 1894.

At *Thirty* Man *suspects* himself a Fool;
Knows it at *Forty*, and reforms his Plan;
At *Fifty* chides his infamous Delay,
Pushes his prudent Purpose to *Resolve*;
In all the Magnanimity of Thought
Resolves; and re-resolves; then dies the
    same.   — Edward Young,
Night Thoughts, I.416 (1742).

Aim of Education

See also Means and Ends;
Objective; University, Aim of;
Woman, Education of

From cradle to grave this problem of running order through chaos, direction through space, discipline through freedom, unity through multiplicity, has always been, and must always be, the task of education.   — Henry Adams,
The Education of Henry Adams, i (1907).

That education should be regulated by law and should be an affair of the state is not then to be denied; but what should be the character of this public education, and how young persons should be educated, are questions yet to be considered. For men are by no means agreed about the things to be taught.... [and] about method there is no agreement.
— Aristotle,
Politics, VIII.ii.1 (before 322 B.C.).

My object will be, if possible, to form Christian men, for Christian boys I can scarcely hope to make.
— Thomas Arnold,
on being appointed headmaster of Rugby, 1828.

It is not necessary that this should be a school of three hundred, or fifty boys, but is is necessary that it should be a school of Christian gentlemen.
— Thomas Arnold,
address to students of Rugby after he had expelled several students for rule infractions, (c.1828–41).

Real education should educate us out of self into something far finer—into selflessness which links us with all humanity. — Nancy Astor,
My Two Countries, vii:
America (1923).

She knows what is the best purpose of education: not to be frightened by the best but to treat it as part of daily living.
— John Mason Brown,
tribute to Edith Hamilton,
Publishers' Weekly, Mar. 17, 1958.

It [education] cannot be compared to filling up an empty pot, but rather to ... lighting a fire. The proper test of an education is whether it teaches the pupil to think and whether it awakens his interest in applying his brain to the various problems and opportunities life presents.
— Geoffrey Browther,
"English and American Education,"
Atlantic, Apr. 1960.

I am convinced that we must train not only the head, but the heart and hand as well.   — Madame Chiang Kai-shek, *This Is Our China*, I.i (1940).

Our first wish is that all men should be educated fully to full humanity ... men of all ages, all conditions, both sexes and all nations. Our second wish is that every man should be wholly educated, rightly formed not only in one single matter or in a few or even in many, but in all things which perfect human nature.
          —John Amos Comenius, *The Great Didactic* (1628–32).

The primary concern of American education today is not the development of the appreciation of the "good life" in young gentlemen born to the purple.... Our purpose is to cultivate in the largest possible number of our future citizens an appreciation of both the responsibilities and the benefits which come to them because they are Americans and are free.
          —James Bryant Conant, *Annual Report to the Board of Overseers*, Harvard University, 1943.

Education is for the purpose of bringing to bear the experiences of the past in finding solutions of the problems of the present.   Calvin Coolidge, address at College of the Holy Cross, June, 1920.

The real object of education is to leave a man in the condition of continually asking questions.   Mandell Creighton, in C.A. Alington, *Things Ancient and Modern*. xi (1936).

The school is essentially a time- and laborsaving device, created—with us—by democracy to serve democracy's needs. To convey to the next generation the knowledge and the accumulated experience of the past is not its only function. It must equally prepare the future citizen for the tomorrow of our complex life.   — Ellwood P. Cubberley, *Changing Conceptions of Education* (1909).

The end of study should be to direct the mind towards the enunciation of sound and correct judgments on all matters that come before it. — René Descartes, *Rules for the Direction of the Mind*, I (1637).

The educational process has no end beyond itself; it is its own end.
          —John Dewey. *Democracy and Education*, iv (1916).

An aim implies an orderly and ordered activity, one in which the order consists in the progressive completing of a process.
          —John Dewey, *ibid.*, viii.

It is well to remind ourselves that education as such has no aims. Only persons, parents, and teachers, etc., have aims, not an abstract idea like education.
          —John Dewey, *ibid.*, viii.

The primary business of school is to train children in co-operative and mutually helpful living; to foster in them the consciousness of mutual interdependence.
          —John Dewey, *The School and Society* (1899).

Childher shuddn't be sint to school to larn, but to larn how to larn.
          —Finley Peter Dunne, *Mr. Dooley's Philosophy: What I Larned in Colledge* (1900).

The true and proper end of Schooling is to teach and Exercise Children and Youths in the Grounds of all Learning and Virtues, so far as either their capacitie in that age will suffer them to come, or is requisite to apprehend the principles of useful matters, by which they may bee made able to exercise themselves in everie good Employment afterwards by themselves.   —John Dury, *The Reformed School* (1649?).

The aim [of education] must be the training of independently acting and thinking individuals, who, however, see in the service of the community their highest life problem. — Albert Einstein, *Out of My Later Years*, ix: *On Education* (1950).

The end of learning is the formation of character. —Kaibara Ekken, *Ten Kun (Ten Precepts)*, II (1710).

The worthy fruit of academic culture is an open mind, trained to careful thinking, instructed in the methods of philosophic investigation, acquainted in a general way with the accumulated thought of past generations, and penetrated with humility. —Charles W. Eliot, inaugural address, Harvard University, Oct. 19, 1869.

The ultimate aim of the human mind, in all its efforts, is to become acquainted with Truth. Eliza Farnham, *Woman and Her Era*, I.i (1864).

Education ... should concern itself primarily ... with the liberation, organization, and direction of power and intelligence, with the development of taste, with *culture*. —Abraham Flexner, *Universities*, 53 (1930).

Education should lead and guide man to clearness concerning himself and in himself, to peace with nature, and to unity with God. Friedrich Froebel, *The Education of Man* (1826).

To give firmness to the will, to quicken it, and to make it pure, strong, and enduring, in a life of pure humanity, is the chief concern, the main object in the guidance of the boy, in instruction and the school. —Friedrich Froebel, *ibid.*

The ability to think straight, some knowledge of the past, some vision of the future, some skill to do useful service, some urge to fit that service into the well-being of the community—these are the most vital things education must try to produce. —Virginia Gildersleeve, *Many a Good Crusade* (1954).

No one has yet fully realized the wealth of sympathy, kindness and generosity hidden in the soul of the child. The effort of every true educator should be to unlock that treasure—to stimulate the child's impulses and call forth the best and noblest tendencies. —Emma Goldman, *Living My Life*, I.409 (1931).

The philosophic aim of education must be to get one out of his isolated class and into one humanity. —Paul Goodman, *Compulsory Mis-education* (1964).

Every citizen of this country, whether he pounds nails, raises corn, designs rockets or writes poetry, should be taught to know and love his American heritage; to use the language well; to understand the physical universe, and to enjoy the arts. The dollars he gains in the absence of enlightenment like this will be earned in drudgery and spent in ignorance. —Calvin Gross, *New York Times*, Apr. 27, 1963.

If education doesn't prepare the young to educate themselves throughout their lives, then it is a failure, no matter what else it may seem to accomplish. —Sydney Harris, syndicated column, *Detroit Free Press*, Aug. 1, 1980.

The whole end of education ... is found in burning into the heart and brain of the youth entrusted to it an instinctive and comprehended sense of race. —Adolf Hitler, *Mein Kampf* (1925–27).

The main part of intellectual education is not the acquisition of facts, but learning how to make facts live. —Oliver Wendell Holmes, Jr., oration, Harvard Law School Association, Cambridge, Nov. 5, 1886, on 250th anniversary of Harvard University, in M.D. Howe, *Occasional Speeches of Justice Oliver Wendell Holmes* (1962).

The object of teaching a child is to enable him to get along without his teacher. —Elbert Hubbard, *Note Book*, 217 (1927).

The aim of education is the knowledge not of facts but of values.
—William Ralph Inge,
The Church in the World, Oct. 1932.

I have always regarded the development of the individual as the only legitimate goal of education.   —Susan Jacoby,
Inside Soviet Schools (1974).

What is really important in education is not that the child learns this and that, but that the mind is matured, that energy is aroused. —Søren Kierkegaard,
Either/Or, II (1843).

The most important function of education at any level is to develop the personality of the individual and the significance of his life to himself and to others. This is the basic architecture of a life; the rest is ornamentation and decoration of the structure.
—Grayson Kirk,
Quote, Jan. 27, 1963.

Children go to school, ultimately, to find out who they are and what a human life is for.   —George F. Kneller,
Existentialism and Education, 31 (1958).

What, then, is the purpose, the goal of education? ... *the achievement of moments of ecstasy*.
—George B. Leonard,
Education and Ecstasy, 17 (1968).

If the school sends out children with a desire for knowledge and some idea of how to acquire and use it, it will have done its work.   —Richard Livingstone,
On Education (1944).

The great work of a governor is to fashion the carriage and form the mind; to settle in his pupil good habits, and the principles of virtue and wisdom; to give him, by little and little, a view of mankind; and work him into a love and imitation of what is excellent and praiseworthy; and, in the prosecution of it, to give him vigor, activity, and industry.
—John Locke, *Some Thoughts concerning Education* (1693).

That which every gentleman (that takes any care of his education) desires for his son, besides the estate he leaves him, is contained, I suppose, in these four things, *virtue, wisdom, breeding* and *learning*.   —John Locke, *ibid*.

The great desideratum of human education is to make all men aware that they are gods in the making, and that they can walk upon water if they will.
—Don Marquis,
The Almost Perfect State (1927).

Our chief aim of any true system of education must be to impart to the individual the courage to play the game against any and all odds, the nerve to walk into the ambushes of existence, the hardiness to face the most despicable truth about himself and not let it daunt him permanently; it must armour him with an ultimate carelessness.
—Don Marquis, *ibid*.

Education must have an end in view, for it is not an end in itself.
—Sybil Marshall,
An Experiment in Education, iv (1963).

Primitive education was a process by which continuity was maintained between parents and children.... Modern education includes a heavy emphasis upon the function of education to create discontinuities—to turn the child of the peasant into a clerk, the farmer into a lawyer, of the Italian immigrant into an American, of the illiterate into the literate.   —Margaret Mead,
Our Education Emphases in Primitive Perspective, in *Education and the Cultural Process* (1941).

We are in pain to make them scholars, but no men; to talk, rather than to know; which is true canting.
—William Penn,
Some Fruits of Solitude, I. no.4
(1693).

Education consists essentially in preparing man for what he must do here below in order to attain the sublime end for which he was created. — Pope Pius XI, *On the Christian Education of Youth*, Dec. 31, 1929.

If you are planning for a year, sow rice. If you are planning for a decade, plant trees. If you are planning for a lifetime, educate a person. — Chinese proverb.

Whether my pupil be destined for the army, the church, or the bar, matters little to me. Before he can think of adopting the vocation of his parents, nature calls upon him to be a man. How to live is the business I wish to teach him.
— Jean Jacques Rousseau, *Émile* (1762).

Education has for its object the formation of character. — Herbert Spencer, *Social Statics*, II.xvii.4 (1850).

To prepare us for complete living is the function which education has to discharge. — Herbert Spencer, *What Knowledge Is of Most Worth?* (1859).

The highest education is that which does not merely give us information but makes our life in harmony with all existence.
— Rabindranath Tagore, *Personality* (1917).

The object of education is to give man the unity of truth.
— Rabindranath Tagore, *ibid*.

The true meaning of education is to draw out the natural essence [original nature] of the individual. This leads also to the perfecting of the personality and the awakening of the soul.
— Okada Torajiro, in Peter Copen, "Walkabout Lives!," *Phi Delta Kappan*, June 1980.

Art. 26.2. Education shall be directed to the full development of the human personality and to the strengthening of respect for human rights and fundamental freedoms, it shall promote understanding, tolerance, and friendship among all nations, racial or religious groups, and shall further the activities of the United Nations for the maintenance of peace.
— United Nations, *Universal Declaration of Human Rights*, Dec. 6, 1948.

America

From the first ... education was the American religion. It was — and is — in education that we put our faith; it is our schools and colleges that are the peculiar objects of public largess and private benefaction; even in architecture we proclaim our devotion, building schools like cathedrals. — Henry Steele Commager, *Living Ideas in America*, 546 (1951).

No people ever demanded so much of schools and of education as have the American. None other was ever so well served by its schools and its educators.
— Henry Steele Commager, *ibid*.

And you America,
Cast you the real reckoning for your present?
The lights and shadows of your future, good or evil?
To girlhood, boyhood look, the teacher and the school.
— Walt Whitman, *Leaves of Grass: An Old Man's Thought of School: For the Inauguration of a Public School*, Camden, New Jersey, 1874 (1891–92).

Analysis

See also Consideration; Deliberation; Inquiry; Investigation; Research

Analysis kills spontaneity. The grain once ground into flour springs and germinates no more. — Henri Frédéric Amiel, *Journal*, Nov. 7, 1878.

Examine carefully, and re-consider all your notions of things; analyse them, and discover their component parts and see if habit and prejudice are not the principal ones; weigh the matter, upon which you are to form your opinion, in the equal and impartial scales of reason.
— Lord Chesterfield,
Letters to His Son, Sept. 13, 1748.

To fear examination of any proposition appears to me an intellectual and moral palsy that will ever hinder the firm grasping of any substance whatever.
— George Eliot, *The George Eliot Letters*, ed. Gordon S. Haight (1954).

For, as Socrates bade men "not live a life without examination," so you ought not to accept an impression without examination, but say, "Wait, let me see who you are and whence you come," just as the night-watch say, "Show me your token."
— Epictetus, *Discourses*,
III.xii (c. A.D. 100).

Intelligent people ought to examine all different opinions. — Maimonides, *Guide for the Perplexed*, III.xiii (1190).

Nothing is so productive of elevation of mind as to be able to examine methodically and truly every object which is presented to thee in life.
— Marcus Aurelius,
Meditations, III.11 (c. A.D. 174).

Look within. Let neither the peculiar quality of anything nor its value escape thee. — Marcus Aurelius,
ibid., VI.3.

The habit of analysis has a tendency to wear away the feelings.
— John Stuart Mill,
Autobiography, v (1873).

I do not understand; I pause; I examine.
— Michel de Montaigne (1533–92),
inscription for his library.

All progress of mind consists for the most part in differentiation, in the resolution

of an obscure and complex object into its component aspects. — Walter Pater,
Appreciations: Style (1889).

Our system of education turns young people out of the schools able to read, but for the most part unable to weigh evidence or to form an independent opinion. — Bertrand Russell,
The Will to Doubt: Free Thought and Official Propaganda (1958).

The unexamined life is not worth living.
— Socrates, in Plato,
Apology 38a (before 389 B.C.).

Now I re-examine philosophies and religions,
They may prove well in lecture-rooms, yet not prove at all under the spacious clouds and along the landscape and flowing currents.
— Walt Whitman, *Leaves of Grass*,
VII: *Song of the Open Road*,
sec.6 (1855).

Anger

Who was ever taught the art of music or of steering by anger? — Epictetus,
Discourses, I.xxvi (c. A.D. 100).

The teacher should never lose his temper in the presence of the class. If a man, he may take refuge in profane soliloquies; if a woman, she may follow the example of one sweet-faced and apparently tranquil girl — go out in the yard and gnaw a post.
— William Lyon Phelps, *Teaching in School and College* (1912).

Answer

Abbott's Laws. (1) If you have to ask, you're not entitled to know. (2) If you don't like the answer, you shouldn't have asked the question.
— Charles C. Abbott,
in Paul Dickson, ed.,
The Official Rules (1978).

Every answer given arouses new questions. The progress of science is matched by an increase in the hidden and mysterious. —Leo Baeck, *Judaism and Science*, 6 (1949).

If one gives answer before he hears, it is his folly and shame. *Bible: Proverbs* 18:13.

Who answers speedily errs easily. —Judah Bonsenyor, *Dichos y Sentencias*, no.284 (14th cent.).

Whatever skeptic could inquire for,
For every *why* he had a *wherefore*. —Samuel Butler (1612–1680), *Hudibras*, I.i.131 (1663).

And his answer trickled through my head,
Like water through a sieve. —Lewis Carroll, *Through the Looking-Glass*, viii (1872).

It is natural and beautiful that childhood should inquire and maturity should teach; but it is time enough to answer questions when they are asked. —Ralph Waldo Emerson, *Essays, First Series: Spiritual Laws* (1841).

The answer is very simple. I don't mean easy, but simple. —William Faulkner, address to graduating class, Pine Manor Junior College, June 8, 1953.

It isn't very intelligent to find answers to questions which are unanswerable. —Bernard de Fontennelle, *Conversations on the Plurality of Worlds*, v (1686).

A correct answer is like an affectionate kiss. —Johann Wolfgang von Goethe, *Proverbs in Prose* (1819).

The shortest answer is doing. —George Herbert, *Outlandish Proverbs*, no.552 (1640).

If we really understand the problem, the answer will come out of it, because the answer is not separate from the problem. —Krishnamurti, *The Penguin Krishnamurti Reader: Questions and Answers* (1970).

He had a way of meeting a simple question with a compound answer—you could take the part you wanted, and leave the rest. —Eva Lathbury, *Mr. Meyer's Pupil* (early 1900's).

Never answer a question until it is asked. —Vincent S. Lean, *Collectanea*, iv.56 (1902–04).

I am not bound to please thee with my answer. —William Shakespeare, *The Merchant of Venice*, IV.i.65 (1596).

I can never give a "yes" or a "no." I don't believe everything in life can be settled by a monosyllable. —Betty Smith, *Maggie—Now*, i (1958).

Presently, Mr. Bixby turned on me and said: "What is the name of the first point above New Orleans?"
I was gratified to be able to answer promptly, and I did. I said I didn't know. —Mark Twain, *Life on the Mississippi*, vi (1883).

No answer is also an answer. —Marcus Weissmann-Chajes, *Hokma UMusar* (1875). Also a German proverb.

Appearance

See also Dress

Under that uncouth outside are hidden vast gifts of mind. —Horace, *Satires*, I.iii.33 (c.35 B.C.).

An ox with long horns, even if he does not butt, will be accused of butting. —Malay proverb.

A good exterior is a silent recommendation.   —Publilius Syrus,
Sententiae (c.43 B.C.).

Approbation

See also Praise

We thirst for approbation, yet cannot forgive the approver.
—Ralph Waldo Emerson,
Essays, First Series: Circles (1841).

The desire for approbation is perhaps the most deeply seated instinct of civilized man.   —W. Somerset Maugham,
The Moon and Sixpence (1919).

Argument

See also Controversy; Debate;
Disputation

Most of the arguments to which I am a party fall somewhat short of being impressive, owing to the fact that neither I nor my opponent knows what we are talking about.   —Robert Benchley,
Benchley—or Else! (1947).

We arg'ed the thing at breakfast, we
    arg'ed the thing at tea,
And the more we arg'ed the question, the
    more we didn't agree.   —Will Carleton, *Betsey and I Are Out*, in Michael R. Turner, ed., *Parlour Poetry* (1969).

People are more willing to be convinced by the calm perusal of an argument than in a personal discussion.
—Emily Collins,
letter to Sarah C. Owen, Oct. 23, 1848.

When a man, worsted in argument, becomes hardened like a stone, how can one reason with him any more?
—Epictetus, *Discourses*,
I.v. (c. A.D. 100).

I find you want me to furnish you with argument and intellects too.
—Oliver Goldsmith,
The Vicar of Wakefield, vii (1766).

Never from Obstinacy take the Wrong Side because your Opponent has anticipated you in taking the Right One. You begin the fight already beaten.... With bad weapons one can never win.
—Balthasar Gracián,
The Art of Worldly Wisdom,
cxlii (1647).

The best way I know of to win an argument is to start by being in the right.
—Lord Hailsham (Quintin Hogg),
New York Times, Oct. 16, 1960.

Be calm in arguing: for fierceness makes Errour a fault, and truth discourtesie.
—George Herbert,
The Temple: The Church-porch,
lii (1633).

The beginning of thought is in disagreement—not only with others but also with ourselves.   —Eric Hoffer,
The Passionate State of Mind,
no.266 (1954).

You cannot argue with your neighbor, except on the admission for the moment that he is as wise as you, although you may by no means believe it.
—Oliver Wendell Holmes, Jr., in
The Mind and Faith of Justice Holmes,
ed. Max Lerner (1943).

If a man will stand up and assert, and repeat, and re-assert that two and two do not make four, I know of nothing in the power of argument that can stop him.
—Abraham Lincoln, speech in Peoria,
Ill., Oct. 16, 1854.

There were always two sides to every argument—his and the wrong side.
—M.S. Michel,
The X-ray Murders, 51 (1942).

There is no squabbling so violent as that between people who accepted an idea

yesterday and those who will accept the same idea tomorrow.
— Christopher Morley,
Religio Journalistici (1924).

What renders the least flicker of an argument so profitless, so sterilizing, is that the minds of both the disputants are turned towards something quite different from either's authentic inner truth.
— John Cowper Powys,
The Meaning of Culture (1930).

There is no sense having an argument with a man so stupid he doesn't know you have the better of him.
— John W. Raper,
What This World Needs (1945).

The same arguments which we deem forcible as applied to others, seem feeble to us when turned against ourselves.
— Joseph Roux,
Meditations of a Parish Priest (1886).

Your reasons at dinner have been sharp and sententious; pleasant without scurrility, witty without affection, audacious without impudency, learned without opinion, and strange without heresy.
— William Shakespeare,
Love's Labour's Lost, V.i.2 (1594)
[reasons = *arguments, discourse*;
opinion = *self-conceit*; strange = *novel, original*].

Arguments should be avoided; they are always vulgar and often convincing.
— Oscar Wilde,
The Importance of Being Earnest,
II (1895).

When an arguer argues dispassionately he thinks only of the argument.
— Virginia Woolf,
A Room of One's Own, ii (1929).

Art

See also below; Artist

Art is I; science is we.
— Claude Bernard, *Introduction to the Study of Experimental Medicine* (1865).

The art of one period cannot be approached through the attitudes (emotional or intellectual) of another.
— Louise Bogan,
"Reading Contemporary Poetry,"
College English, Feb. 1953.

Art is meant to disturb. Science reassures.
— Georges Braque,
(1882–1963), *Pensées sur l'art.*

Art, it seems to me, should simplify. That, indeed, is very nearly the whole of the higher artistic process; finding what conventions of form and what details one can do without and yet preserve the spirit of the whole.   Willa Cather,
On the Art of Fiction (1920).

To me it seems as if when God conceived the world, that was Poetry; He formed it, and that was Sculpture; He colored it, and that was Painting; He peopled it with living beings, and that was the grand, divine, eternal Drama.
— Charlotte Saunders Cushman,
in Emma Stebbins,
Charlotte Cushman (1879).

Perpetual modernness is the measure of merit in every work of art.
— Ralph Waldo Emerson,
Representative Men: Plato (1850).

True art is eternal, but it is not stationary.
— Otto H. Kahn,
Of Many Things, 67 (1926).

Art does not reproduce the visible; rather, it makes visible.   — Paul Klee,
The Inward Vision (1959).

Art is not a special sauce applied to ordinary cooking; it is the cooking itself if it is good.   — W.R. Lethaby,
*Form in Civilization:
Art and Workmanship* (1922).

There is nothing but art. Art is living. To attempt to give an object of art life by dwelling on its historical, cultural, or archaeological associations is senseless.
— W. Somerset Maugham,
The Summing Up (1938).

Art, if it is to be reckoned as one of the great values of life, must teach men humility, tolerance, wisdom and magnanimity. The value of art is not beauty, but right action.
　　　　— W. Somerset Maugham,
　　　　A Writer's Notebook (1949).

The grandeur of man lies in song, not in thought.　　　— François Mauriac,
　　　Second Thoughts: The Poet's Pride
　　　　　　　　　　　　(1961).

Art is much less important than life, but what a poor life without it!
　　　　— Robert Motherwell,
　　　　letter to Frank O'Hara, 1965.

I am for an art that is political-erotical-mystical, that does something other than sit on its ass in a museum.
　　　　— Claes Oldenburg,
　　　　Store Days (1967).

The function of all art lies in fact in breaking through the narrow and tortuous enclosure of the finite, in which man is immersed while living here below, and in providing a window on the infinite for his hungry soul.　　— Pope Pius XII,
　　　　address, Apr. 8, 1952.

You must treat a work of art like a great man: stand before it and wait patiently till it deigns to speak.
　　　　— Arthur Schopenhauer,
　　　　Note-Books (c.1850).

The art of our era is not art, but technology. Today Rembrandt is painting automobiles; Shakespeare is writing research reports; Michelangelo is designing more efficient bank lobbies.
　　　　— Howard Sparks,
　　　　The Petrified Truth (1969).

There is no great art without reverence.
　　　　— Gerald Vann,
　　　　The Heart of Man (1944).

There is a great deal to be said for the Arts. For one thing they offer the only career in which commercial failure is not necessarily discreditable.
　　　　— Evelyn Waugh,
　　A Little Order: Careers for Our Sons:
　　　　Literature (1977).

An authentic work of art must start an argument between the artist and his audience.　　　　— Rebecca West,
　　　　The Count and the Castle,
　　　　　　　　I.i (1957).

Art, Definition and Description of

See also Art

Art distills sensation and embodies it with enhanced meaning in memorable form — or else it is not art.
　　　　— Jacques Barzun,
　　　　The House of Intellect,
　　　　　　　　vi (1959).

What was any art but a mould in which to imprison for a moment the shining elusive element which is life itself — life hurrying past us and running away, too strong to stop, too sweet to lose.
　　　　— Willa Cather,
　　　　The Song of the Lark (1915).

Art is the stored honey of the human soul, gathered on wings of misery and travail.　　　　— Theodore Dreiser,
　　　　Life, Art and America (1917).

Art *is* an act of attempted justice and its responsible exercise stirs the ultimate issues when it cannot decide them.
　　　　— William Ernest Hocking,
　　　Strength of Men and Nations (1959).

Art is not a thing: it is a way.
　　　— Elbert Hubbard, *Epigrams* (1910).

Great art is an instant arrested in eternity.
　　　　— James G. Huneker,
　　　　Pathos of Distance (1913).

Art is the desire of a man to express himself, to record the reactions of his personality to the world he lives in.
　　　　— Amy Lowell, *Tendencies in*
　　　Modern American Poetry (1917).

All art is a revolt against man's fate.
    —André Malraux,
    Voices of Silence (1953).

Art is always and everywhere the secret confession and, at the same time, the immortal movement, of its time.
    —Karl Marx, *A Critique of Political Economy* (1859).

Art is a reaching out into the ugliness of the world for vagrant beauty and the imprisoning of it in a tangible form.
    —George Jean Nathan,
    The Critic and the Drama (1922).

All art is a kind of subconscious madness expressed in terms of sanity.
    —George Jean Nathan, *ibid.*

Art is the difference between seeing and just identifying.   —Jean Mary Norman,
    Art: Of Wonder and the World.

Art is a form of catharsis.
    —Dorothy Parker,
    Sunset Gun: Art (1928).

Art is a human activity consisting in this, that one man consciously, by means of certain external signs, hands on to others feelings he has lived through, and that other people are infected by these feelings, and also experience them.
    —Leo Tolstoy,
    What Is Art?, v (1896).

Art is not a handicraft; it is the transmission of feeling the artist has experienced.
    —Leo Tolstoy, *ibid.*, xix.

Art is the imposing of a pattern on experience, and our esthetic enjoyment in recognition of the pattern.
    —Alfred North Whitehead,
    Dialogues, as recorded by
    Lucien Price, 228 (1953).

Art is communication spoken by man for humanity in a language raised above the everyday happening.   —Mary Wigman,
    "The New German Dance," in Virginia Stewart, ed., *Modern Dance* (1935).

Artist

See also Art

The great artist is the simplifier.
    —Henri Frédéric Amiel,
    Journal, Nov. 25, 1861.

Any man with a vital knowledge of the human psychology ought to have the most profound suspicion of anybody who claims to be an artist, and talks a great deal about art.   —G.K. Chesterton,
    Heretics, xvi (1905).

The artistic temperament is a disease that afflicts amateurs.   —G.K. Chesterton,
    ibid., xvii.

The artist must say it without saying it.
    —Duke Ellington,
    Music Is My Mistress (1973).

Scratch an artist and you surprise a child.
    —James G. Huneker,
    Chopin: The Man and His Music (1900).

Nothing can come out of an artist that is not in the man.   —H.L. Mencken,
    Prejudices, Fifth Series, v (1926).

Every child is an artist. The problem is how to remain an artist once he grows up.
    —Pablo Picasso,
    in *Reader's Digest*, May 1977.

An artist is a dreamer consenting to dream of the actual world.
    —George Santayana,
    The Life of Reason (1905–06).

The artist, like the idiot or clown, sits on the edge of the world, and a push may send him over it.   —Osbert Sitwell,
    The Scarlet Tree, IV.ii (1945).

Aspiration

See also Goal, Personal

The ambitious climbs up high and perilous stairs, and never cares how to

come down; the desire of rising hath swallowed up his fear of a fall.
— Thomas Adams, *Diseases of the Soul* (1616).

There is always need for a man to go higher, if he has the capacity to go.
— Henry Ward Beecher, *Proverbs from Plymouth Pulpit: Man* (1887).

A man without ambition is worse than dough that has no yeast in it to raise it.
— Henry Ward Beecher, *ibid.*

Ah, but a man's reach should exceed his grasp,
Or what's a heaven for?
— Robert Browning, *Men and Women: Andrea del Sarto*, ln.97 (1855).

If you aspire to the highest place it is no disgrace to stop at the second, or even the third.
— Cicero, *De Oratore*, I. (c.55 B.C.).

He who would leap high must take a long run.
— Danish proverb.

He that stays in the valley shall never get over the hill.
— Henry Davidoff, *A World Treasury of Proverbs* (1946).

First say to yourself, what manner of man you want to be; when you have settled this, act upon it in all you do.
— Epictetus, *Discourses*, III.xxiii (c. A.D. 100).

If you wish in the world to advance,
Your merits you're bound to enhance;
You must stir it and stump it,
And blow your own trumpet,
Or, trust me, you haven't a chance!
— W.S. Gilbert, *Ruddigore*, I (1887).

God, give me hills to climb,
And strength for climbing! — Arthur
Guiterman, *Hills*, in Louis Untermeyer, ed., *Yesterday and Today* (1926).

It takes a certain level of aspiration before one can take advantage of opportunities that are clearly offered.
— Michael Harrington, *The Other America* (1962).

To him that will, waies are not wanting.
— George Herbert, *Outlandish Proverbs*, no.730 (1640).

Who aimeth at the sky,
Shoots higher much than he that means a tree. — George Herbert, *The Temple: The Church-porch*, lvi (1633).

I would sooner fail than not be among the greatest. — John Keats, letter to James Hessey, Oct. 9, 1818.

If you would hit the mark, you must aim a little above it;
Every arrow that flies feels the attraction of earth.
— Henry Wadsworth Longfellow, *Elegiac Verse*, xxi (1881).

Greatly begin! though thou have time
But for a line, be that sublime, —
Not failure, but low aim, is crime.
— James Russell Lowell, *Under the Willows and Other Poems: For an Autograph* (1868).

Do not think that what is hard for thee to master is impossible for man; but if a thing is possible and proper to man, deem it attainable by thee.
— Marcus Aurelius, *Meditations*, VI.611 (c. A.D. 174).

They that soar too high often fall hard; which makes a low and level dwelling preferable. — William Penn, *More Fruits of Solitude*, II. no.96 (1718).

Be always displeased at what thou art, if thou desire to attain to what thou art not; for where thou hast pleased thyself, there thou abidest. — Francis Quarles, *Emblems*, IV. no.3 (1635).

I worked for a menial's hire,
Only to learn, dismayed,
That any wage I had asked for life,
Life would have paid.
— Jessie Rittenhouse, *My Wage*, in H. Felleman, ed., *The Best Loved Poems of the American People* (1936).

'Tis but a base ignoble mind
That mounts no higher than a bird can
soar.   —William Shakespeare,
II Henry VI, II.i.13 (1590–91).

Who shoots at the midday Sunne,
though he be sure, he shall never hit the
marke; yet as sure he is, he shall shoot
higher than who ayms but at a bush.
—Philip Sidney,
The Countess of Pembroke's Arcadia,
II (1580–81).

The youth gets together his materials to
build a bridge to the moon, or perchance
a palace or temple on the earth, and at
length the middle-aged man concludes to
build a wood-shed with them.
—Henry David Thoreau,
Journal, July 14, 1852.

In the long run men hit only what they
aim at. Therefore, though they should
fail immediately, they had better aim at
something high.
—Henry David Thoreau,
Walden, i: *Economy* (1854).

Too low they build who build beneath
the stars.   —Edward Young,
Night Thoughts, VIII.225 (1744).

Athletics

[Athletic scholarships are] one of the
greatest educational swindles ever
perpetuated on American youth.
—A. Whitney Griswold,
in *New York Times*, Apr. 20, 1963.

The apologists of athleticism have created
a collection of myths to convince the
public that biceps is a substitute for
brains.   —Robert M. Hutchins,
"Gate Receipts and Glory,"
The Saturday Evening Post,
Dec. 3, 1938.

Gymnastic as well as music should begin
in early years; the training in it should be
careful and should continue through life.
—Plato, *The Republic*, III
(c.375–368 B.C.).

As I empathically disbelieve in seeing
Harvard or any other college turn out
mollycoddles instead of vigorous men, I
may add that I do not in the least object
to a sport because it is rough.
—Theodore Roosevelt,
speech in Cambridge, Mass.,
Feb. 23, 1907.

Footeball ... causeth fighting, brawling,
contention, quarrel picking, murder,
homicide and great effusion of bloode, as
daily experience teacheth.
—Philip Stubbes,
Anatomie of Abuses (1583).

Attempt

See also Effort

They fail, and they alone, who have not
striven.   —Thomas Bailey Aldrich,
Enamored Architect of Airy Rhyme
(c.1880).

Attempt easy Tasks as if they were
difficult, and difficult as if they were easy.
In the one case that confidence may not
fall asleep, in the other that it may not be
dismayed.   —Balthasar Gracián,
The Art of Worldly Wisdom, cciv (1647).

No one knows what he can do till he tries.
—Publilius Syrus,
Sententiae, no.586 (c.43 B.C.).

You must do the thing you think you
cannot do.   —Eleanor Roosevelt,
You Learn by Living (1960).

It is hard to fail; but it is worse never to
have tried to succeed.
—Theodore Roosevelt,
address in Chicago, Apr. 10, 1899.

Attention

See also Listening

Attention is like a narrow-mouthed
vessel; pour into it what you have to say

cautiously, and, as it were, drop by drop.   —Joseph Joubert,
Pensées (1810).

Accustom thyself to attend carefully to what is said by another, and as much as possible, be in the speaker's mind.
            —Marcus Aurelius,
Meditations, VI.53 (c. A.D. 174).

Direct thy attention to what is said. Let thy understanding enter into the things that are doing and the things which do them.   —Marcus Aurelius,
ibid., VII.30.

Authority (i.e., Power)

See also Administration

The man whose authority is recent is always stern.   —Aeschylus,
Prometheus Bound, ln.35 (c.490 B.C.).

Authority without wisdom is like a heavy axe without an edge, fitter to bruise than polish.   —Anne Bradstreet,
Meditations Divine and Moral (1664?).

Authority is never without hate.
—Euripides, *Ion* (c.417 B.C.).

He that cannot obey, cannot command.
            —Benjamin Franklin,
Poor Richard's Almanack, Aug. 1734.

The scars left from the child's defeat in the fight against irrational authority are to be found at the bottom of every neurosis.   —Erich Fromm,
Man for Himself (1947).

There's few men that can bear authority if they haven't been born with the shoulders for it. If you gave a man a nose who never had one, he would be blowing it all day.   —John Oliver Hobbes,
A Study in Temptations (1892).

Some single mind must be master, else there will be no agreement in anything.
            —Abraham Lincoln, letter to
William M. Fishback, Feb. 17, 1864.

The weaker a man in authority ... the stronger his insistence that all his privileges be acknowledged.
            —Austin O'Malley,
Keystones of Thought (1914–15).

Mix kindness with authority; and rule more by discression than rigour.
            —William Penn,
Some Fruits of Solitude,
I. no.195 (1693).

To expect to rule others by assuming a loud tone is like thinking oneself tall by putting on high heels.
            —J. Petit-Senn,
Conceits and Caprices (1869).

Authority in education is to some extent unavoidable, and those who educate have to find a way of exercising authority in accordance with the *spirit* of liberty.
            —Bertrand Russell,
*Principles of Social Reconstruction:
Education* (1916).

A teacher should have maximal authority, and minimal power.
            —Thomas Szasz,
The Second Sin: Education (1973).

Authority (for Knowledge)

You, however captivated by ... authority, follow your halter. For what else should authority be called than a halter? Those who are now counted authorities gained their reputation by following reason, not authority.   —Pierre Abélard,
Quaestiones Naturales (c.1130).

Authority sometimes proceeds from reason, but reason never from authority. For all authority that is not approved by true reason seems weak. But true reason, since it rests on its own strength, needs no reinforcement by any authority.
            —Johannes Scotus Erigena,
De Divisione Naturae (c.865–870).

Every great advance in natural knowledge has involved the absolute rejection of authority. —T.H. Huxley, *Lay Sermons, Addresses, and Reviews*, (1870).

In theology we must consider the predominance of authority; in philosophy the predominance of reason. —Johannes Kepler, *Astronomia Nova* (1609).

Anyone who conducts an argument by appealing to Authority is not using his intelligence; he is just using his memory. —Leonardo da Vinci, *Notebooks* (c.1500).

Authority has every reason to fear the skeptic, for authority can rarely survive in the face of doubt. Robert Lindner, *Must You Conform?: Education for Maturity* (1956).

A truth, established by proof, does not gain in force from the support of scholars; nor does it lose certainty because of popular dissent. —Maimonides, *Guide for the Perplexed*, II. introd. (1190).

It is not by a perpetual Amen to every utterance of a great authority that truth or literature gains anything. —Solomon Schechter, *Studies in Judaism*, I.164 (1896).

Autobiography

See also Biography

No British autobiography has ever been frank, and consequently no British autobiography has ever been good. Of all forms of literature it is the one least adapted to the national genius. You could not imagine a British Rousseau, still less a British Benvenuto Cellini. —A. Conan Doyle, *Through the Magic Door* (1908).

I am able to declare that thus far my autobiography has no more pure fiction in it than my fiction has pure autobiography. —A.E. Coppard, *It's Me, O Lord!* (1957).

An autobiography is an obituary in serial form with the last instalment missing. —Quentin Crisp, *The Naked Civil Servant*, xxix (1966).

Autobiographies ought to begin with Chapter Two. —Ellery Sedgwick, *The Happy Profession*, i (1946).

The best autobiographies are confessions; but if a man is a deep writer all his works are confessions.—George Bernard Shaw, *Sixteen Self Sketches*, 19 (1949).

Actually, I don't believe that the story of any human life can be written. It is beyond the power of literature. —Isaac Bashevis Singer, *Lost in America*, author's note (1981).

Average

There must be such a thing as a child with average ability, but you can't find a parent who will admit that it is his child.... Start a program for gifted children, and every parent demands that his child be enrolled. —Thomas D. Bailey, *Wall Street Journal*, Dec.17, 1962.

I abhor averages. I like the individual case. A man may have six meals one day and none the next, making an average of three per day, but that is not a good way to live. —Louis D. Brandeis, in Osmond K. Fraenkel, ed., *The Curse of Bigness*, 41 (1934).

The average child is an almost nonexistent myth. To be normal one must be peculiar in some way or another. —Heywood Broun, *Sitting in the World* (1924).

If some of us were not so far behind,
The rest of us were not so far ahead.
— Edwin Arlington Robinson,
The Three Taverns: Inferential (1920).

Beard

If Providence did beards devise,
To prove the wearers of them wise,
A fulsome Goat would then by Nature
Excel each other human Creature.
— Thomas D'Urfey,
Collin's Walk, iii.120 (1690).

I could never yet like a Scholar the worse
for having a long Beard.
— Oswald Dykes,
English Proverbs, 256 (1709).

If that ornamental excrement which
groweth beneath the chin be the standard
of wisdom, they [goats] carry it from
Aristotle himself.   — Thomas Fuller,
(1608–61), *The History of the Worthies
of England: Wales*, iii.484 (1662).

Having a beard and wearing a shabby
cloak does not make philosophers.
— Plutarch, *Moralia:
Isis and Osiris*, sec.352c (c. A.D. 95).

Beginning

Begin; to begin is half the work. Let half
still remain; again begin this, and thou
wilt have finished.   — Ausonius,
Epigrams, lxxxi.1 (A.D. 300's).

A journey of a thousand miles must
begin with a single step.
— Chinese proverb.

It is better to begin in the evening than
not at all.   — English proverb.

He that well his warke beginneth
The rather a good ende he winneth.
— John Gower,
Confessio Amantis (c.1393).

Well begun is half done.
— Horace, *Epistles*,
I.ii (20 B.C.).

He that climbs a ladder must begin at the
first round.   — Walter Scott,
Kenilworth, vii (1821).

Belief

See also Conviction; Credulity;
Dogma; Idea; Opinion

The human understanding is no dry
light, but receives an infusion from the
will and affections; whence proceed
sciences which may be called "sciences as
one would." For what a man had rather
were true he more readily believes.
— Francis Bacon,
Novum Organum, I. Aphor. 49 (1620).

No one finds any serious difficulty in at-
tributing the origin of other people's
beliefs, especially if he disagrees with
them, to causes which are not reasons.
— Arthur James Balfour,
The Foundations of Belief, iii (1900).

People only think a thing's worth believ-
ing in if it's hard to believe.
— Armiger Barclay,
The Kingmakers (1907).

It is always a relief to believe what is pleasant, but it is more important to believe
what is true.   — Hilaire Belloc,
The Silence of the Sea (1941).

When you want to believe in something
you also have to believe in everything
that's necessary for believing in it.
— Ugo Betti,
Struggle Till Dawn (1949).

It is always easier to believe than to deny.
Our minds are naturally affirmative.
— John Burroughs,
The Light of Day (1900).

What we desire we readily believe, and
what we ourselves think we expect others
to think.   — Caesar, *De Bello Civili*,
II.xxvii (before 44 B.C.).

No iron chain, or outward force of any kind, could ever compel the soul of man to believe or to disbelieve.
— Thomas Carlyle,
Heroes and Hero-Worship (1840).

We do everything by custom, even believe by it; our very axioms, let us boast of freethinking as we may, are oftenest simply such beliefs as we have never heard questioned. — Thomas Carlyle,
Sartor Resartus (1833).

About 999 in 1000 believe everything; the other one believes nothing — except that it is a good thing for human society that the 999 believe everything.
— Michael J. Dee,
Conclusions, v (1917).

So that nothing is so easy as to deceive one's self; for what we wish, that we readily believe; but such expectations are often inconsistent with the real state of things. — Demosthenes,
Third Olynthiac, xix (349 B.C.).

I make it a rule to believe only what I understand. — Benjamin Disraeli,
Infernal Marriage, I.iv (1828).

All you've got to do is believe what you hear, and if you do that enough, after a while you'll hear what you believe.
— Finley Peter Dunne,
Mr. Dooley Remembers: Some Observations by Mr. Dooley (1963).

A man must not swallow more beliefs than he can digest. — Havelock Ellis,
The Dance of Life, v (1923).

For, dear me, why abandon a belief
Merely because it ceases to be true.
Cling to it long enough, and not a doubt
It will turn true again, for so it goes.
— Robert Frost, *North of Boston: The Black Cottage*, ln.105 (1914).

There is no fury like that against one who, we fear, may succeed in making us disloyal to beliefs we hold with passion, but have not really won.
— Learned Hand, address, Harvard University, June 22, 1932.

Some things have to be believed to be seen. — Ralph Hodgson,
The Skylark and Other Poems (1958).

Men to a great extent believe what they want to — although I see no basis for a philosophy that tells us what we should want to want.
— Oliver Wendell Holmes, Jr.,
in *The Mind and Faith of Justice Holmes*, ed. Max Lerner (1943).

As a rule we believe as much as we can. We would believe everything if we could.
— William James,
The Principles of Psychology,
II.299 (1890).

Belief cannot be commanded.
— Samuele David Luzzatto (1800–65),
Igrot, 252.

It is easier to believe than to doubt.
— Everett Dean Martin,
The Meaning of a Liberal Education,
v (1926).

A man may be a heretick in the truth; and if he beleeve things only because his Pastor sayes so, or the Assembly so determins, without knowing other reason, though his belief be true, yet the very truth he holds, becomes his heresie.
— John Milton,
Areopagitica, sec.26 (1644).

The greatest danger against which most men have warned us is that which comes from communicating intellectual secrets to minds become subservient to the authority of an inveterate habit, for such is the power of a long-lasting observance, that most men prefer death to giving up their way of life. — Nicholas of Cusa,
De Docta Ignorantia (Learned Ignorance) (15th cent.).

Doublethink means the power of holding two contradictory beliefs in one's mind simultaneously, and accepting both of them.   — George Orwell, *1984*, II.ix (1949).

So far from making it a rule to believe a thing because you have heard it, you ought to believe nothing without putting yourself into the position as if you had never heard it.   — Blaise Pascal, *Pensées*, IV.260 (1670).

To be forced by desire into any unwarrantable belief is a calamity.
        — I.A. Richards, *Principles of Literary Criticism* (1924).

If we are told that we are wrong we resent the imputation and harden our hearts…. It is obvious not the ideas themselves that are dear to us, but our self-esteem, which is threatened. We are by nature stubbornly pledged to defend our own from attack, whether it be our person, our family, our property, or our opinion.
        — James Harvey Robinson, *The Mind in the Making* (1921).

Man is a credulous animal, and must believe *something*; in the absence of good grounds for belief, he will be satisfied with bad ones.
        — Bertrand Russell, *Unpopular Essays: An Outline of Intellectual Rubbish* (1950).

The brute necessity of believing something so long as life lasts does not justify any belief in particular.
        — George Santayana, *Scepticism and Animal Faith* (1923).

I confused things with their names: that is belief.   — Jean-Paul Sartre, *The Words*, II (tr. 1964).

It is not disbelief that is dangerous to our society; it is belief.
        — George Bernard Shaw, *Androcles and the Lion*, preface (1912).

The moment we want to believe something, we suddenly see all the arguments for it, and become blind to the arguments against it.
        — George Bernard Shaw, *The Intelligent Woman's Guide to Socialism and Capitalism*, lxxxiv (1928).

To believe in something not yet proved and to underwrite it with our lives: it is the only way we can leave the future open. Man, surrounded by facts, permitting himself no surprise, no intuitive flash, no great hypothesis, no risk, is in a locked cell. Ignorance cannot seal the mind and imagination more securely.
        — Lillian Smith, *The Journey* (1954).

Biography

See also Autobiography

The art of Biography
Is different from Geography.
Geography is about maps,
But Biography is about chaps.
        — Edmund Clerihew Bentley, *Biography for Beginners* (1905).

In writing biography, fact and fiction shouldn't be mixed. And if they are, the fictional points should be printed in red ink, the facts printed in black ink.
        — Catherine Drinker Bowen, in *Publisher's Weekly*, Mar. 24, 1958.

Biography is the only true history.
        — Thomas Carlyle, *Journal*, Jan. 13, 1832.

Read no history, nothing but biography, for that is life without theory.
        — Benjamin Disraeli, *Contarini Fleming* (1832).

Biography, like big game hunting, is one of the recognized forms of sport, and it is as unfair as only sport can be.
        — Philip Guedalla, *Supers and Supermen* (1920).

Biography broadens the vision and allows us to live a thousand lives in one.
—Elbert Hubbard, *Note Book* (1927).

Biography is, of the various kinds of narrative writing, that which is most eagerly read and most easily applied to the purposes of life.   —Samuel Johnson, *The Idler*, no.84 (1758–60).

It is perhaps as difficult to write a good life as to live one.   —Lytton Strachey, *Time*, July 2, 1979.

Biographies are but the clothes and buttons of the man—the biography of the man himself cannot be written.
—Mark Twain, *Autobiography*, I.2 (1906?).

What is biography? Unadorned romance. What is romance? Adorned biography. Adorn it less and it will be better than it is.   —Mark Twain, *Notebook*, Dec. 11, 1885 (1935).

Book

See also below; Classic; Fiction; Novel; Library; Literature; Textbook

Through and through th' inspirèd leaves, Ye maggots, make your windings; But O, respect his lordship's taste, And spare the golden bindings!
—Robert Burns, *Poetical Works* (1974): *The Book-Worms*, said to have been written in a beautifully bound but worm-eaten volume of Shakespeare in a nobleman's library.

I go to books and to nature as a bee goes to the flower, for a nectar that I can make into my own honey. —John Burroughs, *The Summit of the Years* (1913).

Next to the author of a good book is the man who makes a good commentary on it.   —Chang Chao, *Yumengying* (before 1693), in Lin Yutang, *The Importance of Understanding*, 72 (1960).

There are many books that owe their success to two things, the good memory of those who write them, and the bad memory of those who read them.
—Charles Caleb Colton, *Lacon*, 160 (1820–1822).

Contemporary books do not keep. The quality in them which makes for their success is the first to go; they turn overnight.   —Cyril Connolly, *Enemies of Promise*, ii (1938).

This, books can do—nor this alone: they give
New views to life, and teach us how to live;
They soothe the grieved, the stubborn they chastise;
Fools they admonish, and confirm the wise.   —George Crabbe, *The Library*, ln.41 (1781).

Books should to one of these four ends conduce,
For wisdom, piety, delight, or use.
—John Denham, *Of Prudence* (1650).

There is no Frigate like a Book
To take us Lands away
Nor any Coursers like a Page
Of prancing Poetry. —Emily Dickinson, *Complete Poems*, no.1263 (c.1873), ed. Thomas H. Johnson (1960).

Who, without books, essays to learn, Draws water in a leaky urn.
—Austin Dobson, *A Bookman's Budget* (1885).

Books are the best things, well used; abused, among the worst.
—Ralph Waldo Emerson, *The American Scholar*, Phi Beta Kappa address at Harvard, Aug. 31, 1837.

Women are by nature fickle, and so are men.... Not so with books, for books cannot change. A thousand years hence they are what you find them today, speaking the same words, holding forth the same comfort.   —Eugene Field, *Love Affairs of a Bibliomaniac* (1896).

The foolishest book is a kind of leaky
boat on a sea of wisdom; some of the
wisdom will get in anyhow.
— Oliver Wendell Holmes, Sr.,
The Poet at the Breakfast-Table,
xi (1872).

It is just those books which man
possesses, but does not read, which constitute the most suspicious evidence
against him.   — Victor Hugo,
The Toilers of the Sea, I.i.iv. (1866).

The proper study of mankind is books.
— Aldous Huxley,
Chrome Yellow (1921).

When a man travels and finds books
which are not known in his hometown, it
is his duty to buy them, rather than
anything else, and bring the books back
home with him.— Judah of Regensburg,
Book of the Righteous (before 1217).

A book is a friend whose face is constantly
changing. If you read it when you are
recovering from an illness, and return to
it years after, it is changed surely, with
the change in yourself. — Andrew Lang,
The Library, i (1881).

Books, nowadays, are printed by people
who do not understand them, sold by
people who do not understand them,
read and reviewed by people who do not
understand them, and even written by
people who do not understand them.
— Georg Christoph Lichtenberg,
Reflections (1799).

The pleasant books, that silently among
  Our household treasures take familiar
    places,
And are to us as if a living tongue
  Spake from the printed leaves or pic-
    tured faces.
— Henry Wadsworth Longfellow,
*The Seaside and the Fireside:
Dedication*, vi (1849).

So books give up the all of what they
  mean
Only in a congenial atmosphere,

Only when touched by reverent hands,
  and read
By those who love and feel as well as
  think.   — Amy Lowell,
The Boston Athenaeum, ln.37 (1912).

All books are either dreams or swords,
You can cut, or you can drug, with
  words.   — Amy Lowell,
Sword Blades and Poppy Seed,
ln.291 (1914).

What a sense of security in an old book
  which
Time has criticised for us!
— James Russell Lowell,
*My Study Windows:
Library of Old Authors* (1871).

We profit little by books we do not enjoy.
— John Lubbock,
The Pleasures of Life, iii (1887).

What nonsense! no one ever seduced by
books? Since the invention of writing,
people have been seduced by the power
of the word into all kinds of virtues,
follies, conspiracies and gallantries. They
have been converted to religion, urged
into sin and lured into salvation.
— Phyllis McGinley,
Ladies' Home Journal, July 1961.

There are books one needs maturity to
enjoy just as there are books an adult can
come on too late to savor.
— Phyllis McGinley,
The Province of the Heart (1959).

He fed his spirit with the bread of books,
And slaked his thirst at the wells of
  thought.   — Edwin Markham,
Young Lincoln, in T.C. Clark, ed.,
1000 Quotable Poems (1937).

A book ought to be like a man or a
woman, with some individual character
in it, though eccentric, yet its own; with
some blood in its veins and speculation in
its eyes and a way and a will of its own.
— John Mitchel,
Jail Journal (1854).

A book is the only place in which you can examine a fragile thought without breaking it, or explore an explosive idea without fear it will go off in your face.... It is one of the few havens remaining where a man's mind can get both provocation and privacy.
—Edward P. Morgan,
Clearing the Air (1963).

When you sell a man a book you don't sell him just twelve ounces of paper and ink and glue—you sell him a whole new life. —Christopher Morley,
Parnassus on Wheels, iv (1917).

Books are a part of man's perogative;
In formal ink they thoughts and voices hold,
That we to them our solitude may give,
And make time present travel that of old.
—Thomas Overbury,
A Wife (1614).

Wear the old coat and buy the new book.
—Austin Phelps,
The Theory of Preaching (1881).

The best of mural decorations is books; they are more varied in color and appearance than any wall-paper, they are attractive in design.
—William Lyon Phelps,
radio address, Apr. 6, 1933.

There is no reason why the same man should like the same books at eighteen and at forty-eight. —Ezra Pound,
ABC of Reading, I.viii (1934).

Men do not understand BOOKS until they have had a certain amount of life. Or at any rate no man understands a deep book, until he has seen and lived at least part of its contents. —Ezra Pound,
ibid., II.

Books, I say, are truly alchemical agents; for they, more than other of man's creations, have the power of transforming something common (meaning you and me as we are most of the time) into something precious (meaning you and me as God meant us to be).
—Lawrence Clark Powell,
The Alchemy of Books (1954).

The peace of great books be for you,
Stains of pressed clover leaves on pages,
Bleach of the light of years held in
leather. —Carl Sandburg, *Smoke and Steel* (1920): *For You.*

You cannot open a book without learning something. —William Scarborough,
Chinese Proverbs, no.545 (1875).

Of making many books there is no end, and one often wishes that all save the greatest were consigned to oblivion. For that matter, in a sense they are.
—Vida D. Scudder,
The Privilege of Age (1939).

A book? O rare one!
Be not, as is our fangled world, a garment
Nobler than that it covers.
—William Shakespeare,
Cymbeline, V.iv.133 (1610).
[fangled = *fond of finery*].

The lesson intended by an author is hardly ever the lesson the world chooses to learn from his book.
—George Bernard Shaw,
Man and Superman:
Epistle Dedicatory (1903).

The generall end therefore of all the book is to fashion a gentleman or noble person in vertuous and gentle discipline.
—Edmund Spenser,
The Faerie Queen, preface (1596).

Books are good enough in their own way, but they are a mighty bloodless substitute for life. —Robert Louis Stevenson,
Virginibus Puerisque:
An Apology for Idlers (1881).

Books, like proverbs, receive their chief value from the stamp and esteem of ages through which they have passed.
—William Temple (1628–99),
Miscellanea, II:
Of Ancient and Modern Learning (1692).

My books are water; those of the great
geniuses are wine. Everybody drinks
water.   —Mark Twain,
Notebook, Dec. 11, 1885 (1935).

People may think as they like about well-
thumbed favourites, but there is
something incomparably thrilling in first
opening a brand-new book.
—Evelyn Waugh,
Decline and Fall, III.iv (1928).

Ignorant asses visiting stationers' shops,
their use is not to inquire for good books,
but new books.   —John Webster,
The White Devil, preface (1612).

Camerado, this is no book,
Who touches this touches a man,....
It is I you hold and who holds you,
I spring from the pages into your arms.
—Walt Whitman,
Leaves of Grass, XXXIII:
So Long! (1855).

Book, Bad

Books treating of light subjects are
nurseries of wantonness; they instruct the
loose reader to become naught, whereas,
before touching naughtiness, he knew
naught.   —Richard Brathwaite,
The English Gentlewoman (1631).

There is no worse robber than a bad
book.   —Selwyn Gurney Champion,
Racial Proverbs, 201 (1938).
An Italian proverb.

It deserves not to be read in schools,
But to be freighted in the Ship of Fools.
—Edward Coke, when Francis Bacon
presented him with a copy of his
Novum Organum (1620), on the title
page of which appeared the device of
a ship sailing through the Pillars
of Hercules.

There are books of which the backs and
covers are by far the best parts.
—Charles Dickens,
Oliver Twist, xiv (1837–39).

Even bad books are books and therefore
sacred.   —Günter Grass,
The Tin Drum, I:
Rasputin and the Alphabet (1963).

Book, Best-Seller

A best-seller was a book which somehow
sold well simply because it was selling
well.   —Daniel J. Boorstin,
The Image, iv (1962).

A best-seller is the gilded tomb of a
mediocre talent. —Logan Peasall Smith,
Afterthoughts, v: Art and Letters
(1931).

Book, Borrowing

A little known law of physics postulates
that the number of books you have borrowed and failed to return equals the
number of books you are owed. This law
is called the Conservation of Literature.
—Martin F. Kohn,
"Make Abe happy: Return a book,"
Detroit Free Press, Feb. 12, 1982.

I mean your borrowers of books—those
mutilators of collections, spoilers of the
symmetry of shelves, and creators of odd
volumes.   —Charles Lamb,
The Essays of Elia:
The Two Races of Man (1823).

Perhaps this book holds precious lore,
And you may best discern it.
If you appreciate it more
Than I—why don't return it!
—Christopher Morley,
The Rocking Horse: Lines for an
Eccentric's Book Plate (1919).

Friends
To borrow my books and set wet glasses
on them.
—Edward Arlington Robinson,
Captain Craig, III (1902).

Book, Care

Child! do not throw this book about;
Refrain from the unholy pleasure
Of cutting all the pictures out!
Preserve it as your chiefest pleasure.
—Hilaire Belloc,
The Bad Child's Book of Beasts,
dedication (1896).

Does it afflict you to find your books
wearing out? I mean literally.... The
mortality of all inanimate things is terrible to me, but that of books most of all.
—William Dean Howells,
letter to Charles Eliot Norton,
Apr. 6, 1903.

Take particular care of thy books. Cover
the book-cases with rugs of fine quality;
and preserve them from damp and mice,
and from all manner of injury, for thy
books are thy good treasure. If thou
lendest a volume make a memorandum
before it leaves thy house, and when it is
returned, draw thy pen over the entry.
—Judah Ibn Tibbon, to his son,
Ethical Will (c.1190).

Book, Collecting

Collecting books is like collecting other
people's minds, like having people on the
shelves—only, you can just put them
away when you want to.
—John Prizeman,
Esquire, Feb. 1978.

After love, book collecting is the most ex-
hilerating sport of all.
—A.S.W. Rosenbach,
A Book Hunter's Holiday (1936).

Book, Dispraise of

Some books are lies frae end to end.
—Robert Burns,
Death and Dr. Hornbook, ln.1 (1787).

Books tell me so much that they inform
me of nothing.
—Michel de Crèvecoeur,
Letters from an American Farmer,
XII (1782).

Books are made not like children but like
pyramids ... and they are just as useless!
and they stay in the desert!... Jackals piss
at their foot and the bourgeois climb up
on them.   —Gustave Flaubert,
letter to Ernest Feydeau,
Nov./Dec. 1857.

Learning hath gained most by those
books by which the Printers have lost.
—Thomas Fuller (1608–61), *The Holy
State and the Profane State*, III.xviii:
Of Books (1642).

I hate books; they only teach us to talk
about things we know nothing about.
—Jean Jacques Rousseau,
Émile, III (1762).

And deeper than did ever plummet
sound
I'll drown my book.
—William Shakespeare,
The Tempest, V.i.56 (1611).

Book, Good

Some books are undeservedly forgotten;
none are undeservedly remembered.
—W.H. Auden,
The Dyer's Hand: Reading (1962).

No good Book, or good thing of any sort,
shows its best face at first.
—Thomas Carlyle, *Critical and
Miscellaneous Essays: Novalis* (1838).

A good book, a good friend.
—Selwyn Gurney Champion,
Racial Proverbs, 201 (1938).
An Italian proverb.

It is chiefly through books that we enjoy
intercourse with superior minds.... In the
best books, great men talk to us, give us

their most precious thoughts, and pour their souls into ours.
—William Ellery Channing (1780–1842), *On Self-Culture* (1838).

Only two classes of books are of universal appeal: the very best and the very worst.
—Ford Madox Ford, *Joseph Conrad* (1924).

Spend your money on good books, and you'll find its equivalent in gold of intelligence.   —Immanuel of Rome, *Mahberot*, xiv (c.1300).

The greatest book is not the one whose message engraves itself on the brain ... but the one whose vital impact opens up other viewpoints, and from writer to reader spreads the fire that is fed by the various essences, until it becomes a vast conflagration from forest to forest.
—Romain Rolland, *The Journey Within* (tr. 1947).

The impact of even one good book on a child's mind is surely an end in itself, a valid experience which helps him form standards of judgment and taste at the time when his mind is most sensitive to impressions of every kind.
—Lillian H. Smith, *The Unreluctant Years* (1953).

A good book is the best of friends, the same to-day and for ever.
—Martin Farquhar Tupper, *Proverbial Philosophy*, I: *Of Reading* (1838).

Good books are the most precious blessings to a people; bad books are among the worst of curses.
—Edwin Percy Whipple, *Essays and Reviews*, II (1848–49): *Romance of Rascality*.

Book, Importance of

No man has a right to bring up his children without surrounding them with books, if he has the means to buy them.
—Henry Ward Beecher, *Proverbs from Plymouth Pulpit: The Family* (1887).

Books we must have though we lack bread.   —Alice Williams Brotherton, (fl. 1800's–1930), *Ballade of Poor Bookworms*.

This will never be a civilized country until we expend more money for books than we do for chewing gum.
—Elbert Hubbard, *The Philistine*, XXV (1895–1915).

Book, Lending

Ever'thing comes t' him who waits but a loaned book.
—Frank McKinney Hubbard, *Abe Martin's Primer* (1914).

The lending of books, as well the smaller without pictures as the larger with pictures, is forbidden under the penalty of excommunication.
—*The Croyland History* (14th or 15th cent.; tr. 1947). Monastic libraries were very sparse.

Those who refuse to lend their books ... shall be fined.
—Minutes of the Latvian Jewish Community Council, 1736.

Book, Love of

Whosoever therefore acknowledges himself to be a zealous follower of truth, of happiness, of wisdom, of science, or even of faith, must of necessity make himself a lover of books.
—Richard de Bury, *Philobiblon* (1473).

But al that he mighte of his freendes hente,
On bookes and on lerning he it spente.
—Geoffrey Chaucer, *Canterbury Tales: Prologue*, ln.299 (c.1386) [hente = *take*].

How pure the joy when first my hands unfold
The small, rare volume, black with tarnished gold.
—John Ferriar, *Bibliomania* (1809).

My son! Make thy books thy companions, and let thy cases and shelves be thy pleasure-grounds and gardens. Bask in their paradise, gather their fruit, pluck their roses, take their spices and their myrrh. If thy soul be satiate and weary, change from garden to garden, from furrow to furrow, and prospect to prospect. Then will thy desire renew itself, and thy soul be filled with delight!
        —Judah Ibn Tibbon,
        Ethical Will (c.1190).

I cannot live without books.
        —Thomas Jefferson,
letter to John Adams, June 10, 1815.

The love of books is a love which requires neither justification, apology, nor defence.   —John Alfred Langford, *The Praise of Books: Preliminary Essay* (1880).

A good book makes my nostrils quiver. In all other respects, I like to think, I am a clean, wholesome American boy.
        —Leo Rosten, *The Many Worlds of L*E*O R*O*S*T*E*N: A Book Was a Book* (1964).

Knowing I lov'd my books, he furnish'd me
From mine own library with volumes that I prize about my dukedom.
        —William Shakespeare,
        The Tempest, I.ii.166 (1611).

Book, Praise for

Books are delightful when prosperity happily smiles; when adversity threatens, they are inseparable comforters. They give strength to human compacts, nor are grave opinions brought forward without books. Arts and sciences, the benefits of which no mind can calculate, depend upon books.   —Richard de Bury,
        Philobiblon, i (1473).

These [books] are the masters who instruct us without rods and ferules, without hard words and anger, without clothes or money. If you approach them, they are not asleep; if, investigating, you interrogate them, they conceal nothing; if you mistake them, they never grumble; if you are ignorant, they cannot laugh at you.   —Richard de Bury, *ibid.*

In the highest civilization, the book is still the highest delight. He who has once known its satisfactions is provided with a resource against calamity.
        —Ralph Waldo Emerson,
        Letters and Social Aims: Quotation and Originality (1876).

There are books ... which take rank in our life with parents and lovers and passionate experiences.
        —Ralph Waldo Emerson,
        Society and Solitude: Books (1870).

Books are delightful society. If you go into a room and found it full of books,— even without taking them from their shelves, they seem to speak to you, to bid you welcome. They seem to tell you that they have something inside their covers that will be good for you, and that they are willing and desirous to impart to you. Value them much.
        —William E. Gladstone,
address at the opening of new reading and recreation rooms at Saltney, Oct. 26, 1889.

What a convenient and delightful world is this world of books!—if you bring to it not the obligations of the student, or look upon it as an opiate for idleness, but enter it rather with the enthusiasm of the adventurer.   —David Grayson, *Adventures in Contentment*, xii (1907).

A book is the most delightful companion.... An inanimate thing, yet it talks.... It stimulates your latent talents. There is in the world no friend more faithful and attentive, no teacher more proficient.... It will join you in solitude, accompany you in exile, serve as a candle in the dark, and entertain you in your loneliness. It will do you good, and ask no favor in return. It gives, and does not take.   —Moses Ibn Ezra,
        Shirat Yisrael, 93 (12th cent.).

Have you noticed, after many heartaches and disillusionments, that in recommending a book to a friend the less said the better? The moment you praise a book too highly you awaken resistence in your listener.   —Henry Miller, *The Books in My Life* (1969).

Just the knowledge that a good book is waiting one at the end of a long day makes that day happier.
            —Kathleen Norris, *Hands Full of Living* (1931).

Books never pall on me. They discourse with us, they take counsel with us, and are united to us by a certain living chatty familiarity. And not only does each book inspire the sense that it belongs to its readers, but it also suggests the name of others, and one begets the desire of the other.   — Petrarch, letter to Giovanni dell'Incisa (c.1346).

While you converse with lords and dukes, I have their betters here—my books.
            —Thomas Sheridan, *My Books* (c.1730).

Book, Reading

See also Reading

Some books are to be tasted, others to be swallowed, and some few to be chewed and digested; that is, some books are to be read only in parts; others to be read, but not curiously; and some few to be read wholly, and with diligence and attention.   —Francis Bacon, *Essays: Of Studies* (1597) [curiously = *with great care*].

If time is precious, no book that will not improve by repeated readings deserves to be read at all.   —Thomas Carlyle, *Critical and Miscellaneous Essays: Goethe's Helena* (1838).

Many books require no thought from those who read them, and for a very sim-

ple reason; — they made no such demand upon those who wrote them.
            —Charles Caleb Colton, *Lacon*, 464 (1820-22).

The first time I read an excellent book, it is to me just as if I had gained a new friend. When I read over a book I have perused before, it resembles the meeting with an old one.   —Oliver Goldsmith, *The Citizen of the World*, let.83 (1762).

The book which you read from a sense of duty, or because for any reason you must, does not commonly make friends with you.   —William Dean Howells, *My Literary Passions* (1895).

We find little in a book but what we put there. But in great books, the mind finds room to put many things.
            —Joseph Joubert, *Pensées* (1810).

For reading new books is like eating new bread,
One can bear it at first, but by gradual steps he
Is brought to death's door of a mental dyspepsy.   —James Russell Lowell, *A Fable for Critics* (1848).

It is not all books that are as dull as their readers.   —Henry David Thoreau, *Walden*, iii: *Reading* (1854).

Book, Respect for

If a drop of ink fell at the same time on your books and on your coat, clean first the book and then the garment.
            —*Sefer Hasidim (Book of the Righteous)*, no.653 (13th cent.).

If you drop gold and books, pick up first the books and then the gold.
            —*Ibid.*, no.655.

Books must be treated with respect.
            —*Ibid.*, no.1741.

Book—What It Is

Books are the legacies that a great genius leaves to mankind, which are delivered down from generation to generation, as presents to the posterity of those who are yet unborn.   —Joseph Addison, *The Spectator*, no.166, Sept. 10, 1711.

Books are the most mannerly of companions, accessible at all times, in all times, in all moods, frankly declaring the author's mind, without offence.
          —A. Bronson Alcott,
          Concord Days (1872).

A book is a garden; a book is an orchard; a book is a storehouse; a book is a party. It is company by the way; it is a counselor; it is a multitude of counselors.
          —Henry Ward Beecher,
          Proverbs from Plymouth Pulpit:
          The Press (1887).

Books are the compasses and telescopes and sextants and charts which other men have prepared to help us navigate the dangerous seas of human life.
          —Jesse Lee Bennett,
          Books as Guides (1923).

Books are the blessed chloroform of the mind.   —Robert W. Chambers (1865–1933), *What English Literature Gives Us.*

A book is like a garden carried in the pocket.   —Selwyn Gurney Champion,
          Racial Proverbs, 330 (1938).
          An Arabic proverb.

God be thanked for books. They are the voices of the distant dead and make us heirs of the spiritual life of past ages.
—William Ellery Channing (1780–1842),
          On Self-Culture (1838).

Books are the true levellers. They give to all, who will faithfully use them, the society, the spiritual presence, of the best and greatest of our race.
          —William Ellery Channing, *ibid.*

Books are the quietest and most constant of friends; they are the most accessible and wisest of counsellors, and the most patient of teachers. With his daily work and his books, many a man whom the world thought forlorn has found life worth living.   —Charles W. Eliot,
          The Happy Life (1896).

My books, the best companions, is to me
A glorious court, where hourly I converse
With the old sages and philosophers;
And sometimes, for variety, I confer
With kings and emperors, and weigh
  their counsels.
—John Fletcher and Philip Massinger?,
          The Elder Brother (1625?, publ.1637).

A book's an Inn whose patron's praise
Depends on seasons and on days,
On dispositions, and—in fine—
Not wholly on the landlord's wine.
          —Richard R. Kirk (1877–1951),
          A Book's an Inn.

Books are sepulchres of thought;
The dead laurels of the dead.
          —Henry Wadsworth Longfellow,
          The Wind Over the Chimney,
          viii (1864).

For books are more than books, they are
  the life,
The very heart and core of ages past,
The reason why men lived, and died,
The essence and quintessence of their
  lives.   —Amy Lowell,
          The Boston Athenaeum, ln.41 (1912).

The intellect is a dioecious plant, and books are the bees which carry the quickening pollen from one to another mind.   —James Russell Lowell,
          Nationality in Literature (1849).

Books are not absolutely dead things, but doe contain a potencie of life in them to be as active as that soule was whose progeny they are: nay they do preserve as in a violl the purest efficacy and extraction of that living intellect that bred them.
          —John Milton,
          Areopagitica, sec.4 (1644) [violl = *vial*].

A good Booke is the pretious life-blood of a master spirit, imbalm'd and treasur'd up on purpose to a life beyond life.
— John Milton, *ibid.*

Teachers of wisdom, who could once beguile
My tedious hours, lighten every toil,
I now resign to you.   — William Roscoe, *Poetical Works* (1853): *To my Books on Parting with Them.*

Books are the treasured wealth of the world and the fit inheritance of generations and nations.
— Henry David Thoreau, *Walden*, iii: *Reading* (1854).

They are for company the best friends, in Doubt's Counsellors, in Damps Comforters, Time's Perspective, the Home Traveller's Ship or Horse, the busie Man's best Recreation, the Opiate of idle Weariness the Mindes best Ordinary, Nature's Garden and Seed-plot of Immortality.   — Bulstrode Whitelocke, *Zoötomia* (1654).

Bore

See also Boredom

Perhaps the world's second worst crime is boredom; the first is being a bore.
— Cecil Beaton, *Time*, Jan. 28, 1980.

There are those who need more time to tell than it took the event to happen. They are the farmer-generals of boredom.
— Ludwig Boerne, *Aus Meinem Tagebuche*, May 25, 1830.

Everyone is a bore to someone. That is unimportant. The thing to avoid is being a bore to oneself.   — Gerald Brenan, *Thoughts in a Dry Season* (1978).

A healthy male adult bore consumes each year one and a half times his own weight in other people's patience.
— John Updike, *Assorted Prose: Confessions of a Wild Bore* (1965).

Boredom

See also Bore; Dullness

Ennui, felt on proper occasions, is a sign of intelligence.   — Clifton Fadiman, *Reading I've Liked* (1941).

Man is the only animal that can be bored.
— Erich Fromm, *The Sane Society*, iii (1955).

Nobody is bored when he is trying to make something that is beautiful, or to discover something that is true.
— William Ralph Inge, *Our Present Discontents* (1938).

To be bored by essentials is characteristic of small minds.   .
— Robert Underwood Johnson, *Poems of Fifty Years*, preface (1930).

We forgive people who bore us; never those we bore.
— François de La Rochefoucauld, *Maxims*, no.304 (1665).

It is as cruel to bore a child as to beat him.   — George B. Leonard, *Education and Ecstasy* (1968).

The human capacity for being bored, rather than man's social or natural needs, lies at the root of man's cultural advance.
— Ralph Linton, *The Study of Man* (1936).

The capacity of human beings to bore one another seems to be vastly greater than that of any other animals. Some of their most esteemed inventions have no apparent purpose, for example, the dinner party of more than two, the epic poem, and the science of metaphysics.
— H.L. Mencken, *Minority Report: Notebooks*, no.67 (1956).

For the healthy, a monotonous environment eventually produces discomfort, irritation and attempts to vary it.
— Susanna Millar, *The Psychology of Play*, iv (1968).

The bore of all bores was the third. His subject had no beginning, middle, nor end. It was education. Never was such a journey through the desert of the mind, the Great Sahara of intellect. The very recollection makes me thirsty.
— Thomas Love Peacock,
in Jacques Barzun,
The Teacher in America, 9 (1944).

Boredom, after all, is a form of criticism.
— William Phillips,
A Sense of Present (1967).

Every normal child will kick if you bore or tire him more than is legally permissible. Only idiots don't care. — Fritz Redl,
"Discipline in the Classroom,"
Child Study, Summer 1944.

Miss Searle had always considered boredom an intellectual defeat.
— Mary Renault,
North Face, i (1948).

Oh! the old swimmin'-hole! In the long, lazy days
When the humdrum of school made so many run-a-ways.
— James Whitcomb Riley,
Complete Poetical Works (1937):
The Old Swimmin'-Hole.

Boredom is a vital problem for the moralist, since at least half of the sins of mankind are caused by the fear of it.
— Bertrand Russell,
The Conquest of Happiness (1930).

Boredom is a condition which makes men as susceptible to disgust and irritation as headache makes them to noise and glare.
— George Bernard Shaw,
Three Plays for Puritans,
preface (1901).

Boy

See also Boyhood; Child

Oh running stream of sparkling joy
To be a soaring human boy!
— Charles Dickens,
Bleak House (1852–53).

A boy has two jobs. One is just being a boy. The other is growing up to be a man. — Herbert Hoover,
speech marking the 50th anniversary of the Boys' Clubs of America,
May 21, 1956.

I do be thinking God must laugh
The time he makes a boy,
All element the creatures are,
And devilment and joy.
— Winifred M. Letts, *Boys*,
in B.E. Stevenson, *The Home Book of Modern Verse* (1925).

When I was a beggarly boy
And lived in a cellar damp,
I had not a friend nor a toy,
But I had Aladdin's lamp.
— James Russell Lowell,
*Under the Willows and Other Poems:
Aladdin* (1868).

Has any child psychologist ever noted that the talk of small boys among themselves consists almost entirely of boasting? — H.L. Mencken,
Minority Report: Notebooks,
no.142 (1956).

Of all animals the boy is the most unmanageable, inasmuch as he has the fountain of reason in him not yet regulated; he is the most insidious, sharp-witted, and insubordinate of animals. Wherefore he must be bound with many bridles. — Plato,
Laws, VII.808 (c.367–347 B.C.).

O happy boy with untaught grace!
What is there in the world to give
That can buy one hour of the life you live
Or the trivial cause of your smiling face!
— James Whitcomb Riley,
Complete Poetical Works (1937):
To a Boy Whistling.

One of the best things in the world to be is a boy; it requires no experience, but needs some practice to be a good one.
— Charles Dudley Warner,
Being a Boy, i (1878).

Blessings on thee, little man,
Barefoot boy, with cheek of tan!
With thy turned-up pantaloons,
And thy merry whistled tunes.
　　　　　—John Greenleaf Whittier,
　　　　　　The Barefoot Boy, i (1855).

The sweetest roamer is a boy's young
heart.　　　—George E. Woodberry,
North Shore Watch: Agathon (1890).

Boyhood

See also Boy; Childhood

Boyhood is a most complex and incom-
prehensible thing. Even when one has
been through it, one does not understand
what it was. A man can never quite
understand a boy, even when he has been
the boy.　　　—G.K. Chesterton,
　　　　　　Autobiography (1936).

Then here's to our boyhood, its gold and
　its gray,
The stars of its winter, the dews of its
　May!　—Oliver Wendell Holmes, Sr.,
　　　　　Poems of the Class of '29:
　　　　　　The Boys (1859).

Oh would I were a boy again,
　When life seemed formed of sunny
　years,
And all the heart then knew of pain
　Was wept away in transient tears.
　　　—Mark Lemon, *Prose and Verse:*
Oh Would I Were a Boy Again (1852).

Brain

See also Intellect; Intelligence;
Mind; Wit

The price of your hat ain't the measure of
your brain.　—American Negro proverb.

Brain, *n.* An apparatus with which we
think that we think. —Ambrose Bierce,
The Devil's Dictionary (1911).

The Modern Man's highly developed
brain has made him what he is and you
know what he is.　　　—Will Cuppy,
　　　　　　How to Tell Your Friends
　　　　　　from the Apes (1931).

We know that the human brain is a
device to keep the ears from getting on
one another.　　　—Peter De Vries
　　　　　(with Joseph Fields),
　　　Comfort Me with Apples, i (1956).

It is not the brains that matter most, but
that which guides them—the character,
the heart, generous qualities, progressive
ideas.　　　—Fëdor Dostoevsky,
　　　The Insulted and the Injured (1861).

The brains don't lie in the Beard.
　　　—Thomas Fuller (1654–1734),
　　　Gnomologia, no.4431 (1732).

Our brains are seventy-year clocks. The
Angel of Life winds them up once for all,
then closes the case, and gives the key in-
to the hand of the Angel of the
Resurrection.
　　　—Oliver Wendell Holmes, Sr.,
　　　The Autocrat of the Breakfast-Table,
　　　　　　viii (1858).

What we need now in this nation, more
than atomic power, or air-power, or
financial, industrial, or even manpower,
is brain power. The dinosaur was bigger
and stronger than anyone else—he may
even have been more pious—but he was
also dumber. And look what happened
to him.　　　—John F. Kennedy,
　　　　　address in Washington, D.C.,
　　　　　　Apr. 16, 1959.

Most brains reflect but the crown of a hat.
　　　—James Russell Lowell,
　　　A Fable for Critics, ln.704 (1848).

There's different sorts of brains....
There's brains for doing things and brains
for explaining things, and one's as good
as the other. Some do things, and others
explain what's what.
　　　—Vladimir Maximov,
The Seven Days of Creation, 188 (1975).

His brain,
Which is as dry as the remainder biscuit
After a voyage.   —William Shakespeare,
As You Like It, II.vii.38 (1600)
[remainder biscuit = stale hardtack].

Breeding

What is bred in the bone will never come
out of the flesh.   —Bidpai,
Fables: The Two Fishermen (c.300 B.C.).

The scholar, without good breeding, is a
pedant; the philosopher, a cynic.
          —Lord Chesterfield,
Letters to His Son, Oct. 9, 1747.

Men are generally more careful of the
breed of their horses and dogs, than of
their children.   —William Penn,
Some Fruits of Solitude,
I. no.85 (1693).

Better were it to be unborn than illbred.
          —Walter Ralegh (1552?–1618),
Instructions to His Son, sec.2 (1616).

Brevity

The composing room has an unlimited
supply of periods available to terminate
short, simple sentences.
          —Turner Catledge, managing editor,
New York Times. Memo to his staff,
in Time, Dec. 20, 1954.

The brevity of a pointed answer to a question worth our while gives us artistic
pleasure.   —Ernest Dimnet,
What We Live By (1932).

Well said is soon said.
          —Balthasar Gracián,
The Art of Worldly Wisdom, cv (1647).

It is nothing short of genius that uses one
word when twenty will say the same
thing.   —David Grayson,
The Friendly Road (1913).

When you've got a thing to say,
Say it! Don't take half a day.
When your tale's got little in it,
Crowd the whole thing in a minute!
          —Joel Chandler Harris (1848–1908),
Advice to Writers for the Daily Press.

Whatever you teach, be brief, that your
readers' minds may readily comprehend
and faithfully retain your words.
Everything superfluous slips from the full
heart.   —Horace,
Ars Poetica, ln.335 (20 B.C.).

The fewer thy words the fewer thine
errors.   —Solomon Ibn Gabirol,
Choice of Pearls, no.354 (c.1050).

As it is the mark of a great mind to say
much in a few words, so is it the mark of
a little one to talk much and say little.
          —François de La Rochefoucald,
Maxims, no.142 (1665).

It is my ambition to say in ten sentences
what other men say in whole books—
what other men do not say in whole
books.   —Friedrich Nietzsche,
The Twilight of the Idols (1889).

I have made this letter longer than usual,
only because I have not had time to make
it shorter.   —Blaise Pascal,
Provincial Letters, xvi (1656-7).

Therefore, since brevity is the soul of wit,
And tediousness the limbs and outward
flourishes,
I will be brief.
          —William Shakespeare,
Hamlet, II.ii.90 (1600–01)
[wit = judgment, understanding;
flourishes = embellishments].

What! so brief?
'Tis better, sir, than to be tedious.
          —William Shakespeare,
Richard III, I.iv.88 (1592–93).

Not that the story need be long, but it
will take a long while to make it short.
          —Henry David Thoreau,
letter to Mr. B., Nov. 16, 1857.

An average English word is four letters and a half. By hard, honest labor I've dug all the large words out of my vocabulary and shaved it down till the average is three letters and a half.... I never write 'metropolis' for seven cents, because I can get the same money for 'city.' I never write 'policeman,' because I can get the same price for 'cop.'   —Mark Twain, *Spelling and Pictures*, address to Associated Press, New York, Sept. 18, 1906, in Albert Bigelow Paine, ed., *Mark Twain's Speeches*, 317 (1923).

It is much easier to write a long book than a short one.   —Isaac Mayer Wise, "World of My Books," *Deborah*, Jan. 7, 1897.

Bureaucrat

The perfect bureaucrat is the man who manages to make no decisions and escapes all responsibility.
  —Brooks Atkinson, *Once Around the Sun: September 9* (1951).

Bureaucrats are the only people in the world who can say absolutely nothing and mean it.   —Hugh Sidey, *Time*, Nov. 29, 1976.

When a bureaucrat makes a mistake and continues to make it, it usually becomes the new policy. —Hugh Sidey, *ibid.*

Censor

See also Censorship

In some respects the life of a censor is more exhilarating than that of an emperor. The best the emperor can do is to snip off the heads of men and women, who are mere mortals. The censor can decapitate ideas which but for him might have lived forever. —Heywood Broun, *Pieces of Hate* (1922).

Persons who undertake to pry into, or cleanse out all the filth of a common sewer, either cannot have nice noses, or will soon lose them.
  —William Hazlitt, *Political Essays: On the Clerical Character* (1819).

The censor-moron does not really hate anything but the living and growing human consciousness. —D.H. Lawrence, *Selected Letters*, ed. Diana Trilling (1978).

Censors are necessary, increasingly necessary, if America is to avoid having a vital literature.   —Don Marquis, *Prefaces: Foreword to a Literary Censor's Autobiography* (1919).

Heresy hunters are intolerant not only of unorthodox ideas; worse than that, they are intolerant of ideas—of any ideas which are really alive and not empty cocoons.   —Philip Lee Ralph, *The Story of Our Civilization* (1954).

Censorship

See also Censor; Suppression

Only the suppressed word is dangerous.
  —Ludwig Boerne, *Ankündigung der Wage* (1818).

Like the course of the heavenly bodies, harmony in national life is a resultant of the struggle between contending forces. In frank expression of conflicting opinion lies the greatest promise of wisdom in governmental action; and in suppression lies ordinarily the greatest peril.
  —Louis D. Brandeis, U.S. Supreme Court decision, *Gilbert v. Minnesota* (1928).

To suppress the freedom of the arts is not only to cut off knowledge of the actual movements of human feeling but also, and more disastrously, contact with the realities of life. For those contacts can be

renewed only by the continually new in-
tuition of the artist.   —Joyce Cary,
Art and Reality: Ways of the
Creative Process (1958).

We shouldn't tolerate the double standard that calls something "textbook
review" when it is done by school professionals and "censorship" when it is re-
quested by parents.
— Council for Basic Education,
Bulletin, June 1975.

Restriction of free thought and free
speech is the most dangerous of all
subversions. It is the one un-American
act that could most easily defeat us.
—William O. Douglas,
address to the Authors' Guild on
receiving the Lauterbach Award,
Dec. 3, 1952.

Of all the Tyrannies of human kind
The worst is that which Persecutes the
mind.
Let us but weigh at what offence we
strike,
'Tis but because we cannot think alike.
—John Dryden,
The Indian Emperor, II.ii (1665).

Don't join the book burners. Don't think
you're going to conceal faults by conceal-
ing evidence that they ever existed. Don't
be afraid to go in your library and read
every book, as long as any document does
not offend our own ideas of decency.
That should be our only censorship.
—Dwight D. Eisenhower,
remarks at Dartmouth College
commencement, June 14, 1953.

Every burned book enlightens the world.
—Ralph Waldo Emerson,
Essays, First Series: Compensation (1841).

To command the professors of astronomy
to confute their own observations is to en-
join an impossibility, for it is to command them not to see what they do see,
and not to understand what they do

understand, and to find what they do not
discover. —Galileo Galilei (1564–1642),
The Authority of Scripture in
Philosophical Controversies (condemned
by the Inquisition).

Books won't stay banned. They won't
burn. Ideas won't go to jail. In the long
run of history, the censor and the in-
quisitor have always lost. The only sure
weapon against bad ideas is better ideas.
The source of better ideas is wisdom. The
surest path of wisdom is a liberal
education.   —A. Whitney Griswold,
Essays on Education (1954).

If we restrict the reading of certain books
until minds are prepared for them, the
minds will never be prepared for them.
—Sydney Harris, syndicated column,
Detroit Free Press, Aug. 26, 1982.

To limit the press is to insult a nation; to
prohibit reading of certain books is to
declare the inhabitants to be either fools
or slaves. —Claude Adrien Helvétius,
De l'Homme, I. sec.4 (1773).

I am … mortified to be told that, in the
United States of America … a question
about the sale of a book can be carried
before the civil magistrate.... Are we to
have a censor whose imprimatur shall say
what books may be sold, and what we
may buy?... Whose foot is to be the
measure to which ours are all to be cut or
stretched?   —Thomas Jefferson,
letter to M.G. Dufief, a Philadelphia
bookseller, Apr. 19, 1814, who was
prosecuted for selling DeBecourt's
Sur le Création du Monde.

It is most unworthy to suppress books or
silence teachers.   —Judah Loew,
Beer HaGola, vii (1598).

It is wrong to suppress the views of an opponent; it is more fitting to ponder their
meaning.   —Judah Loew,
Geburot HaShem, xix (1582).

The burning of an author's books, im-
prisonment for opinion's sake, has always

been the tribute that an ignorant age pays for the genius of its time.
—Joseph Lewis, *Voltaire: The Incomparable Infidel* (1929).

At present our notion of preserving what we think to be the truth is to gag all who do not think it's the truth. We win our arguments by forbidding argument.
—Ben B. Lindsey and Wainwright Evans, *The Revolt of Modern Youth*, 280 (1925).

Censorship, like charity, should begin at home; but unlike charity, it should end there.
—Clare Boothe Luce, (1903–), *Nuggets*.

If all mankind minus one were of one opinion, and only one person were of the contrary opinion, mankind would be no more justified in silencing that one person, than he, if he had the power, would be justified in silencing mankind.
—John Stuart Mill, *On Liberty*, ii (1859).

If any opinion is compelled to silence, that opinion may, for aught we can certainly know, be true. To deny this is to assume our own infallibility.
—John Stuart Mill, *ibid*.

We can never be sure that the opinion we are endeavoring to stifle is a false opinion; and even if we were sure, stifling it would be an evil still.
—John Stuart Mill, *ibid*.

As good almost kill a man as kill a good Book; who kills a Man kills a reasonable creature, Gods Image; but hee who destroyes a good Booke, kills reason itselfe, kills the Image of God, as it were in the eye.
—John Milton, *Areopagitica*, sec.4 (1644).

We must not think to make a staple commodity of all knowledge in the Land, to mark and license it like our broad cloath and our wooll packs.
—John Milton, *ibid.*, sec.23.

Though all the windes of doctrin were let loose upon the earth, so Truth be in the

field, we do injuriously by licensing and prohibiting to misdoubt her strength. Let her and Falsehood grapple; who ever knew Truth put to the wors, in a free and open encounter..
—John Milton, *ibid.*, sec.35 [wors = *worse*].

The first thing will be to establish a censorship of the writers of fiction, and let the censors receive any tale of fiction which is good, and reject the bad; and we will desire mothers and nurses to tell their children the authorized ones only.
—Plato, *Republic*, II (c.375–368 B.C.).

Give me six lines written by the most honorable of men, and I will find an excuse in them to hang him.
—*attr.* Cardinal de Richelieu, *Mirame* (1641).

We all know that books burn—yet we have the greater knowledge that books cannot be killed by fire. People die, but books never die…. No man and no force can put thought in a concentration camp forever.
—Franklin D. Roosevelt, message to American Booksellers Association, Apr. 23, 1942, on anniversary of the Nazi book-burning.

Assassination is the extreme form of censorship.
—George Bernard Shaw, *The Rejected Statement*, i, preface to *The Shewing-Up of Blanco Posnet* (1909).

What is at stake here is the right to read and be exposed to controversial thoughts, a valuable right subject to First Amendment protection. The most effective antidote to the poison of mindless orthodoxy is ready access to a broad sweep of ideas. There is no danger in such exposure; the danger is in mind control.
—Joseph Tauro, U.S. District Court judge, denying the right of the Chelsea, Mass., board of education to remove a poem written by a 15-year-old girl from the school library, "New Court Decisions," *United States Law Week*, Aug. 1, 1978.

If there is an Unexpurgated in the Children's Department won't you please help that young woman remove Huck from that questionable companionship.
— Mark Twain (1835–1910), letter to a librarian. "Questionable companionship" refers to Biblical characters.

If there had been a censorship of the press in Rome we should have had today neither Horace nor Juvenal, nor the philosophical writings of Cicero.
— Voltaire, letter to the Commissioner of Police of Paris, June 20, 1733.

God forbid that any book should be banned. The practice is as indefensible as infanticide. — Rebecca West, *The Strange Necessity: The Tosh Horse* (1928).

Certainty

See also Uncertainty

Oh, let us never, never doubt
What nobody is sure about!
— Hilaire Belloc,
More Beasts (for Worse Children): The Microbe (1897).

I have lived in this world just long enough to look carefully the second time into things that I am most certain of the first time. — Josh Billings, *Complete Works* (1888).

Love of certainty is a demand for guarantees in advance of action.
— John Dewey,
Human Nature and Conduct (1922).

In fact confine yourself to words; one goes
On safely then, till through that door he reaches
The very temple of all certitude.
— Johann Wolfgang von Goethe,
Faust, I: Study (1808).

We can be absolutely certain only about things we do not understand.
— Eric Hoffer,
The True Believer (1951).

Certitude is not the test of certainty. We have been cocksure of many things that were not so.
— Oliver Wendell Holmes, Jr., "Natural Law," *Harvard Law Review*, 1918.

Certainty is generally an illusion, and repose is not the destiny of man.
— Oliver Wendell Holmes, Jr., *The Path of the Law* (1897).

A reasonable probability is the only certainty. — Edgar W. Howe, *Country Town Sayings* (1911).

There is no certainty without some doubt. — Elijah Levita, *Tishbi* (1541).

The public, with its mob yearning to be instructed, edified and pulled by the nose, demands certainties; ... but there *are* no certainties. — H.L. Mencken, *Prejudices, First Series*, iii.46 (1919).

Man cannot accept certainties; he must discover them. — John Middleton Murry, *The Necessity of Art* (1924).

Among these things but one thing seems certain — that nothing certain exists, and that nothing is more pitiable or more presumptuous than man.
— Pliny the Elder, *Natural History*, II.v.25 (A.D. 77).

Certainties are arrived at only on foot.
— Antonio Porchia, *Voces* (1968).

The desire to have knowledge which can not be challenged, the certainty of final truth is not likely to lead so much to objectivity as to rigidity and arrogant dogma. — Bertrand Russell, letter to Mr. Choudhury, Oct. 20, 1962.

The certainties of one age are the problems of the next. — R.H. Tawney, *Religion and the Rise of Capitalism*, v. (1926).

Doubt is not a pleasant condition, but certainty is an absurd one.   — Voltaire, letter to Frederick the Great, Apr. 6, 1767.

Change

See also Innovator; Reform

In Change ... lies ... the very essence of our lot and life in this world. To-day is not yesterday: we ourselves change, how can our Works and Thoughts, if they are always to be the fittest, continue always the same? Change, indeed, is painful; yet ever needful.   — Thomas Carlyle, *Characteristics* (1831).

To remain young one must change. The perpetual campus hero is not a young man but an old boy.
    — Alexander Chase, *Perspectives* (1966).

The whole secret of the teacher's force lies in the conviction that men are convertible.   — Ralph Waldo Emerson, *Journals*, 1834.

If there is anything that we wish to change in the child, we should first examine it and see whether it is not something that could better be changed in ourselves.   — Carl Gustav Jung, *Psychological Reflections*, ed. Jolanda Jacobi and R.F. Hull (1970).

The dogmas of the quiet past are inadequate to the stormy present.... As our case is new, so must we think anew and act anew. We must disenthrall ourselves.   — Abraham Lincoln, second annual message to Congress, Dec. 1, 1862.

It is no evil for things to undergo change, and no good for things to subsist in consequence of change. — Marcus Aurelius, *Meditations*, IV.42 (c. A.D. 174).

If you want to make enemies, try to change something. — Woodrow Wilson, speech in Detroit, July 10, 1916.

Character

During my eighty-seven years I have witnessed a whole succession of technological revolutions. But none of them has done away with the need for character in the individual or the ability to think.   — Bernard M. Baruch, *Baruch: My Own Story*, xxii (1957).

Knowledge has outstripped character development, and the young today are given an education rather than an upbringing.   — Ilya Ehrenburg, "What I Have Learned," *Saturday Review*, Sept. 30, 1967.

Character is higher than intellect.
    — Ralph Waldo Emerson, *The American Scholar*, Phi Beta Kappa address at Harvard, Aug. 31, 1837. Also *Journals*, May 1, 1837.

Character and Intellect: the two poles of our capacity; one without the other is but halfway to happiness. Intellect sufficeth not, character is also needed.
    — Balthasar Gracián, *The Art of Worldly Wisdom*, ii (1647).

It is not book-learning young men need, nor instruction about this and that, but a stiffening of the vertebrae which will cause them to be loyal to a trust, to act promptly, concentrate their energies, do a thing—"carry a message to Garcia."
    — Elbert Hubbard, *A Message to Garcia* (1899).

Child

See also Boy; Girl

Children should be seen and not heard.
    — Aristophanes, *The Clouds*, ln.963 (423 B.C.).

Being constantly with children was like wearing a pair of shoes that were expensive and too small. She couldn't bear to throw them out, but they gave her blisters.   —Beryl Bainbridge,
Injury Time, iv (1978).

A babe is nothing but a bundle of possibilities.   —Henry Ward Beecher,
Proverbs from Plymouth Pulpit:
Children (1887).

That energy which makes a child hard to manage is the energy which afterward makes him a manager of life.
—Henry Ward Beecher, ibid.

The passionate belief in the superior worthwhileness of our children. It is stored up in us as a great battery charged by the accumulated instincts of uncounted generations.   —Ruth Benedict,
in Margaret Mead,
An Anthropologist at Work (1951).

There is no end to the violations committed by children on children, quietly talking alone.   —Elizabeth Bowen,
The House in Paris, I.ii (1935).

Children's as good as 'rithmetic to set you findin' out things.   —Francis Hodgson Burnett, The Secret Garden, ix (1909).

I am fond of children (except boys).
—Lewis Carroll,
letter to Kathleen Eschwege, in S.D. Collingwood, The Life and Letters of Lewis Carroll, 416 (1898).

As soon as I stepped out of my mother's womb on to dry land, I realized that I had made a mistake—that I shouldn't have come, but the trouble with children is that they are not returnable.
—Quentin Crisp,
The Naked Civil Servant, i (1966).

Better to be driven out from among men than to be disliked of children.
—Richard Henry Dana (1787–1879),
The Idle Man: Domestic Life (1821).

All children under nine or ten years of age are poets and philosophers.
—Ernest Dimnet,
The Art of Thinking, I.iv (1928).

All children are by nature children of wrath, and are in danger of eternal damnation in Hell.   —Jonathan Edwards,
Sermon to Children (1740).

Children are completely egoistic; they feel their needs intensely and strive ruthlessly to satisfy them.
—Sigmund Freud,
The Interpretation of Dreams:
Dreams of the Death of Beloved Persons
(1900).

For we like children who are a little afraid of us, docile, deferential children, though not, of course if they are so obviously afraid that they threaten our image of ourselves as kind, lovable people whom there is no reason to fear.
—John Holt,
How Children Fail (rev. ed. 1982).

Children are remarkable for their intelligence and ardor, for their curiosity, their intolerance of shams, the clarity and ruthlessness of their vision.
—Aldous Huxley,
Collected Essays (1959).

It might as well be admitted that children irritate us; and this means that we are no longer capable of entering into their kingdom. We revenge ourselves by teaching them all sorts of worthless knowledge.   —Holbrook Jackson,
Southward Ho! and Other Essays (1915).

I don't look for defects in children ... neither in mine nor in others. I know that a child is not born with sense.
—Carolina Maria de Jesus,
Child of the Dark: The Diary of
Carolina Maria de Jesus,
July 15, 1955 (1962).

All children are potential victims, dependent upon the world's good will.
—Sally Kempton, "Cutting Loose,"
Esquire, July, 1970.

Children have neither a past nor a future;
they enjoy the present, which very few of
us do.   —Jean de La Bruyère,
Les Caractères, xi (1688).

When I forget thy thousand ways
Then life and all shall cease.
                —Mary Lamb, A Child,
in A. Quiller-Couch, ed., The Oxford
Book of English Verse (1900).

The tears of childhood fall fast and easily,
and evil be to him who makes them flow.
                —Stephen Leacock,
The Leacock Roundabout: Softening
the Stories for the Children (1945).

The little rare-ripe sort that are smarter at
about five than ever after.
                —Abraham Lincoln,
letter to Joshua F. Speed, Oct. 22, 1846.

Ye are better than all the ballads
That ever were sung or said;
For ye are living poems,
And all the rest are dead.
                —Henry Wadsworth Longfellow,
Children, ix (1849).

In determining whether a person is a
child, the prime consideration is his age.
                —Ministry of Pensions and National
Insurance, instructions quoted in
Sunday Times, London, Dec. 22, 1957.

The greatest poem ever known
Is one all poets have outgrown:
The poetry, innate, untold,
Of being only four years old.
                —Christopher Morley,
Hide and Seek: To a Child (1920).

The difficult child is the child who is
unhappy. He is at war with himself; and
in consequence, he is at war with the
world. —A.S. Neil, Summerhill (1960).

When you are dealing with a child, keep
all your wits about you, and sit on the
floor.   —Austin O'Malley,
Keystones of Thought (1914–15).

Children … constitute man's eternity.
—Isaac Leibush Peretz, Der Dichter(1910).

Nature makes boys and girls lovely to
look upon so they can be tolerated until
they acquire some sense.
                —William Lyon Phelps,
Essays on Things (1930).

Children are entitled to their otherness,
as anyone is; and when we reach them, as
we sometimes do, it is generally on a
point of sheer delight, to us so
astonishing, but to them so natural.
                —Alastair Reid, Passwords,
Places, Poems, Preoccupations (1964).

I believe all childern's good,
    Ef they're only understood,—
Even bad ones, 'pears to me,
'S jes' as good as they kin be!
                —James Whitcomb Riley,
Complete Poetical Works (1937):
The Hired Man's Faith in Children.

Children, after being limbs of Satan in
traditional theology and mystically il-
luminated angels in the minds of educational reformers, have reverted to being
little devils—not theological devils inspired by the Evil One, but scientific
Freudian abominations inspired by the
Unconscious.   —Bertrand Russell,
Unpopular Essays: The Virtue of
the Oppressed (1950).

Some of my best friends are children. In
fact, all of my best friends are children.
—J.D. Salinger, Time, July 16, 1951.

    And children know,
Instinctive taught, the friend and foe.
                —Walter Scott,
The Lady of the Lake, II.xiv (1810).

What is a child? An experiment. A fresh
attempt to produce the just man made
perfect: that is, to make humanity
divine.   —George Bernard Shaw,
Parents and Children, preface to
Misalliance (1914).

Every child comes with the message that
God is not yet discouraged of man.
                —Rabindranath Tagore,
Stray Birds (1916).

Children's griefs are little, certainly; but so is the child.... Grief is a matter of relativity; the sorrow should be estimated by its proportion to the sorrower; a gash is as painful to one as an amputation to another.   — Francis Thompson, "Shelley," *Dublin Review*, July 1908.

The touch of children is a delight of the body. The delight of the ear is the hearing of their speech.   — Tiruvalluvar, *Kural*, vii (c.100 B.C.–A.D. 300).

The Child is father of the Man.
          — William Wordsworth,
          My Heart Leaps Up, ln.7 (1802).

Child and Parent

See also Childhood; Child Rearing; Discipline

Is is not a bad thing that children should occasionally, and politely, put parents in their place.   — Colette,
          My Mother's House:
          The Priest on the Wall (1922).

The children despise their parents until the age of 40, when they suddenly become just like them — thus preserving the system.   — Quentin Crewe,
          in study of British upper class,
          Saturday Evening Post, Dec. 1, 1962.

You may give them your love but not your thoughts,
For they have their own thoughts.
          — Kahlil Gibran,
          The Prophet: On Children (1923).

With their teeth half-shown in causeless laughter,
and their efforts at talking so sweetly uncertain,
when children ask to sit on his lap
a man is blessed even by the dirt on their bodies.   — Kalidasa, *Sakuntala*,
          vii.17 (5th cent.), in A.L. Basham,
The Wonder That Was India, 162 (1968).

When I consider how little of a rarity children are, — that the poorest people commonly have them in most abundance, — ... how often they turn out ill, and defeat the fond hopes of their parents, ... I cannot for my life tell what cause for pride there can possibly be in having them.   — Charles Lamb,
          The Essays of Elia: A Bachelor's
          Complaint of the Behaviour of Married
          People (1823).

Children, when they are little, they make parents fools; when great, mad.
          — John Ray,
          English Proverbs (1670).

Childhood

See also Boyhood; Child and Parent; Growing Up

Blessed be childhood, which brings down something of heaven into the midst of our rough earthliness.
          — Henri Frédéric Amiel,
          Journal, Jan. 26, 1868.

A happy childhood can't be cured. Mine'll hang around my neck like a rainbow, that's all, instead of a noose.
          — Hortense Calisher,
          Queenie, I (1971).

What was wonderful about childhood is that anything in it was a wonder. It was not merely a world full of miracles, it was a miraculous world. — G.K. Chesterton,
          Autobiography (1936).

Childhood is the most basic human right of children.   — David Elkind,
          "The Hurried Child," *Instructor*,
          Jan. 1982.

There is in most men's minds a secret instinct of reverence and affection towards the days of their childhood. They cannot help sighing with regret and tenderness when they think of it.
          — Saint Ethelred of Rievaulx,
          Christian Friendship (before 1167).

Childhood is something so close, so special.... It's something you ought to keep to yourself. The way you keep back tears.   —Françoise Giroud, *I Give You My Word* (1974).

Childhood, whose very happiness is love. —Letitia Elizabeth Landon, *Poetical Works* (1844): *Erinna*.

It is my belief that we are trying to eliminate childhood, and *that* is what is so terrible about being a child today. Whatever agonies children have ever lived through before, it was never so clearly childhood itself that was felt to be the enemy.   —Eda J. LeShan, *The Conspiracy Against Childhood*, i (1967).

In all our efforts to provide "advantages" we have actually produced the busiest, most competitive, highly pressured and over-organized generation of youngsters in our history—and possibly the unhappiest. We seem hell-bent on eliminating much of childhood.   —Eda J. LeShan, *ibid.*

It is customary, but I think it is a mistake, to speak of a happy childhood. Children are often overanxious and acutely sensitive. Man ought to be man and master of his fate; but children are at the mercy of those around them. —John Lubbock, *The Pleasures of Life*, i (1887).

Children without childhood are a dreadful sight.   —Mendele Mokher Seforim, *BeSeter Raam*, 4 (1913).

The childhood shows the man,
As morning shows the day.
    —John Milton,
Paradise Regained, IV.220 (1671).

To children childhood holds no particular advantage.   —Kathleen Norris, *Hands Full of Living* (1931).

That very season of childhood, when the soul, on the rainbow bridge of fancy, glides along, dry-shod, over the walls and ditches of this lower earth.
    —Jean Paul Richter,
Titan, x (1803).

You are troubled at seeing him spend his early years in doing nothing. What! is it nothing to be happy? Is it nothing to skip, to play, to run about all day long? Never in all his life will he be so busy as now.   —Jean Jacques Rousseau, *Émile* (1762).

The barb in the arrow of childhood's suffering is this—its intense loneliness, its intense ignorance. —Olive Schreiner, *The Story of an African Farm* (1883).

Childhood is a prison sentence of twenty-one years.   —Thomas Szasz, *The Second Sin: Childhood* (1973).

That great Cathedral space which was childhood. —Virginia Woolf, *Moments of Being* (1976).

Sweet childish days, that were as long
As twenty days are now.
    —William Wordsworth,
To a Butterfly (1802).

Child Rearing

See also Child and Parent; Discipline; Kindness; Parent; Punishment; Reprimand; Severity

You mustn't say anything that won't be perfectly true when he's grown up, you see. It's learning two sets of things that makes a child distrust you.
    —Josephine Dodge Bacon,
The Memoirs of a Baby, ii (1904).

Education commences at the mother's knee, and every word spoken within the hearsay of little children tends towards the formation of character.
    —Hosea Ballou,
MS. Sermons (1834?).

Fathers, do not provoke your children, lest they become discouraged.
— *Bible: Colossians* 3:21.

Train up a child in the way he should go; and when he is old, he will not depart from it.   — *Ibid., Proverbs* 22:6.

Bring thy children up in learning and obedience, yet without outward austerity. Praise them openly, reprehend them secretly.   — William Cecil, Lord Burghley, from 10 precepts to his son Robert (c.1570–80).

All children are by nature evil, and while they have none of the natural evil principle to guide them, pious and prudent parents must check their naughty passions in any way that they have in their power, and force them into decent and proper behavior and into what are called good habits.   — Martha Mary Butt, *The Fairchild Family* (1818).

Speak roughly to your little boy,
  And beat him when he sneezes:
He only does it to annoy,
  Because he knows it teases.
— Lewis Carroll, *Alice's Adventures in Wonderland*, vi (1865).

You can't make children the plaything of your mood, now kissing them tenderly, then stamping your feet at them in a frenzy. It is better not to love than to love with a despotic love. Hatred is considerably more honest than the love of a Nasser-Eddin, now appointing his fervidly beloved Persians as satraps, then impaling them on stakes.
— Anton Chekhov, letter to his eldest brother, Aleksandr, Jan. 2, 1889.

A young branch takes on all the bends that one gives it.   — Chinese proverb.

It is not strange that he who has no children brings them up so well?
— Confucius, *Analects* (c.500 B.C.).

Children have to be educated, but they have also to be left to educate themselves.
— Ernest Dimnet, *The Art of Thinking*, II.i.a (1928).

Thou shalt not belittle your child.
— Fitzhugh Dodson, *How to Parent* (1973).

The greatest gift you can give your child is the freedom to actualize his unique potential self.   — Fitzhugh Dodson, *ibid*.

"Ye know a lot about [raising children]," said Mr. Hennessy.
"I do," said Mr. Dooley. "Not bein' an author, I'm a gr-great critic."
— Finley Peter Dunne, *Dissertations by Mr. Dooley: The Bringing Up of Children* (1906).

Where parents do too much for the children, the children will not do much for themselves.   — Elbert Hubbard, *Note Book* (1927).

As longe as the twygge is gentell and plyent, ... With small force and strength it may be bent.   — Thomas Ingelend, *The Disobedient Child* (c.1560).

You Americans do not rear children, you incite them; you give them food and shelter and applause.   — Randall Jarrell, *Pictures from an Institution*, IV.x (1954).

A child is a butterfly over the seething whirlpool of life. How can one give it steadiness without weighing down its flight; how can it be tempered without tying its wings?   — Janusz Korczak, in E.P. Kulawiec, "Janusz Korczak: A Unique Educator," *Women's American ORT Reporter*, Jan./Feb. 1981.

I am determined my children shall be brought up in their father's religion, if they can find out what it is.
— Charles Lamb, letter to John Chambers, 1818.

Train children in their youth, and they won't train you in your old age.
— Judah Leib Lazerov, *Enciklopedie fun Idishē Vitzen*, no.504 (1928).

Give me a child for the first seven years, and you may do what you like with him afterwards.   —Vincent Lean, *Collectanea*, iii.472 (1902–04). Quoted as a Jesuit maxim.

Give us the child for eight years, and it will be a Bolshevist forever.
—Nikolai Lenin,
speech to the
Commisars of Education,
Moscow, 1923.

The great mistake I have observed in people's breeding their children has been, that this has not been taken care enough of in its due season; that the mind has not been made obedient to discipline, and pliant to reason, when at first it was most tender, most easy to be bowed.
—John Locke,
*Some Thoughts
concerning Education*
(1693).

If we would amend the world, we should mend ourselves; and teach our children to be, not what we are, but what they should be.   —William Penn, *Some Fruits of Solitude*, I.no.214 (1693).

My father had always said that there are four things a child needs—plenty of love, nourishing food, regular sleep, and lots of soap and water—and after those, what he needs most is some intelligent neglect.
—Ivy Baker Priest,
Green Grows Ivy, i (1958).

Best to bend while 'tis a twig.
—John Ray,
English Proverbs, 61 (1670).

Take heed your children speak no words of villainy, nor show them much familiarity, and see that they use honest sports and games. Mark well what vice they are specially inclined to, and break it betimes.   —Hugh Rhodes, *The Book of Nurture* (1554).

Bringing up a family should be an adventure, not an anxious discipline in which everybody is constantly graded for performance.   —Milton R. Sapirstein, *Paradoxes of Everyday Life*, iii (1955).

The colt that's back'd and burthen'd be ing young
Loseth his pride and never waxeth strong.
—William Shakespeare,
Venus and Adonis, ln.419 (1593).

The vilest abortionist is he who attempts to mould a child's character.
—George Bernard Shaw,
Maxims for Revolutionists (1903).

I have a morbid horror of any ill treatment of children; but I believe that love and the more touching sorts of happiness are wasted on them: they are really not capable of them. Nobody is until they've earned them.   —George Bernard Shaw, letter to Ellen Terry, Nov. 4, 1896.

It seems to me that we are doing things we do not want to do for kids who do not really want to have them done.
—Robert Paul Smith,
"Let Your Kids Alone," *Life*,
Jan. 27, 1958.

Give a child his will and a whelp his fill, Both will surely turn out ill.
—Charles Haddon Spurgeon,
John Ploughman's Pictures (1880).
See also H.G. Bohn, *Handbook of
Proverbs*, 360 (1855).

One should not promise a child to give him something and then not give it to him, because he will thereby teach him lying.   —*Talmud: Sukkah*, 46b (before A.D. 500).

I think it more prudent, to hold children to their duty by the ties of kindness and honor, than by the restraints of fear.
—Terence, *Adelphi*, I.i (160 B.C.).

When you lead your sons and daughters in the good way, let your words be tender

and caressing, in terms of disciplines that win the heart's assent.
— Elijah ben Solomon Zalman, letter to his family, *Alim LiTerufa* (1836).

Church and State, Separation of

Encourage free schools, and resolve that not one dollar of money shall be appropriated to the support of any sectarian school.... Leave the matter of religion to the family altar, the church and the private schools supported entirely by private contributions. Keep the church and state forever separated.
— Ulysses S. Grant, speech before Army of the Tennessee in Des Moines, 1875.

That to compel a man to furnish contributions of money for the propagation of opinions which he disbelieves and abhors, is sinful and tyrannical: that even the forcing him to support this or that teacher of his own religious persuasion, is depriving him of the comfortable liberty of giving his contributions to the particular pastor whose morals he would make his pattern, and whose powers he feels most persuasive to righteousness.
— Thomas Jefferson, *A Bill for Establishing Religious Freedom*, 1779; adopted Jan. 16, 1786. "and abhors" was deleted from the final bill.

The loathsome combination of Church and State. — Thomas Jefferson, letter to Charles Clay, Jan. 29, 1815.

A wall of separation between Church and State. — Thomas Jefferson, reply to the Danbury Baptist Association, Jan. 1, 1802. This was the origin of the phrase.

The fatal theory of the separation of church and state. — Pope Leo XIII, *Libertas Praestantissimum*, June 20, 1888.

Clarity

Praised be he who can state a cause in a clear, simple and succinct manner, and then stop. — Harry H. Belt, Judge, Oregon Supreme Court, *Jungwirth v Jungwirth*, 1925.

What is conceived well is expressed clear ly,
And the words to say it with arrive with ease. — Nicolas Boileau, *L'Art Poetique*, i.153 (1674).

In language clearness is everything.
— Confucius, *Analects*, XV.xl (c.500 B.C.).

The chief virtue that language can have is clearness, and nothing detracts from it so much as the use of unfamiliar words.
— Galen, *On the Natural Faculties*, I (c.175 A.D.).

Some experience of popular lecturing had convinced me that the necessity of making things plain to uninstructed people was one of the best means of clearing up the obscure corners in one's own mind.
— T.H. Huxley, *Man's Place in Nature*, preface to 1894 ed.

A thinker who cannot set forth weighty thoughts in simple and clear language should be suspected, primarily, of lacking talent for thought.— Jacob Klatzkin, *In Praise of Wisdom*, 307 (1943).

Whatever is clearly expressed is well wrote. — Mary Wortley Montagu, letter to James Steuart, July 19, 1759.

The very first lesson that we have a right to demand that logic shall teach us is, how to make our ideas clear; and a most important one it is, depreciated only by minds who stand in need of it.
— Charles S. Peirce, "How to Make Our Ideas Clear," *Popular Science Monthly*, Jan. 1878.

Making something perfectly clear only confuses everybody. — George Rockwell, *Down East*, Jan. 1976.

Perspicuity is the framework of profound thought. — Marquis de Vauvenargues, *Reflections and Maxims* (1746).

Lucidity adds beauty to profound thoughts. — Marquis de Vauvenargues, *ibid.*

Class Size

The number of pupils to be assigned to each teacher is twenty-five. If there are fifty, we appoint two teachers. If there are forty, we appoint an assistant, at the expense of the town. — *Talmud: Baba Bathra*, 21a (before A.D. 500); also Maimonides, *Mishneh Torah*, I.ii.5 (1180).

Classic

See also Book; Literature

Books that have become classics — books that have had their day and now get more praise than perusal — always remind me of retired colonels and majors and captains who, having reached the age limit, find themselves retired on half pay. — Thomas Bailey Aldrich, *Ponkapog Papers: Leaves from a Notebook* (1903).

The classics should be read by oneself alone (for reflection). History should be read together with friends (for discussion of opinions). — Chang Chao, *Yumengying* (before 1693), in Lin Yutang, *The Importance of Understanding*, 71 (1960).

I would by no means have you disown your acquaintance with the ancients, but still less would I have you brag of an exclusive intimacy with them. Speak of the moderns without contempt, and of the ancients without idolatry; judge them all by their merits, but not by their age. — Lord Chesterfield, *Letters to His Son*, Feb. 22, 1748.

When you reread a classic you do not see more in the book than you did before; you see more in *you* than there was before. — Clifton Fadiman, *Any Number Can Play* (1957).

Another odd thing about classics is that when their authors are writing them, they don't know what they're doing. — Clifton Fadiman, *Selected Writings* (1955).

If there are no classicists — who will interpret the mottoes of most of our States, not to mention the mottoes of dozens of colleges and universities? — Harry Golden, *You're Entitle': Pity the classicist* (1962).

The idea of the classics, so far as living, are our commonplaces. It is the modern books that give us the latest and most profound conceptions. It seems to me rather a lazy makeshift to mumble over the familiar. — Oliver Wendell Holmes, Jr., letter to John C. Wu, Mar. 26, 1925, *Book Notices, Uncollected Letters and Papers*, ed. Harry C. Shriver (1936).

Our erroneous notion of progress has thrown the classics and the liberal arts out of the curriculum ... The heart of any course of study designed for the whole people will be, if education is rightly understood, the same at any time, in any place, under any ... conditions.... The permanent studies are in the first place those books which have through the ages attained the dimensions of classics. — Robert M. Hutchins, *The Higher Learning in America*, 65 (1936).

My friend the professor of Greek tells me that he truly believes the classics made him what he is. This is a very grave statement, if well founded. — Stephen Leacock, *Laugh with Leacock: Homer and Humbug, an Academic Discussion* (1930).

Every man with a bellyful of classics is an enemy of the human race.
—Henry Miller,
Tropic of Cancer: Dijon (1934).

A classic is classic not because it conforms to certain structural rules, or fits certain definitions (of which its author probably never heard). It is classic because of a certain eternal and irrepressible freshness.
—Ezra Pound,
ABC of Reading: Warning (1934).

The adventurous student will always study classics in whatever language they may be written and however ancient they may be. For what are the classics but the noblest recorded thoughts of man? They are the only oracles which are not decayed.
—Henry David Thoreau,
Walden, iii: *Reading* (1854).

"*Classic.*" A book which people praise and don't read.
—Mark Twain,
Pudd'nhead Wilson's New Calendar, I.xxv (1897); also somewhat different version in *The Disappearance of Literature*, address in New York, Nov. 20, 1900, in Albert Bigelow Paine, ed., *Mark Twain's Speeches*, 210 (1923).

The classics have scarcely lost in absolute value as a voucher of scholastic respectability, since for this purpose it is only necessary that the scholar should be able to put in evidence some learning which is conventionally recognized as evidence of wasted time.
—Thorstein Veblen,
The Theory of the Leisure Class, xiv (1899).

Cleanliness

Every time a boy shows his hands, someone suggests that he wash them.
—Edgar W. Howe,
Country Town Sayings (1911).

Wash your hands always before you come to school.
—William Mather,
The Young Man's Companion (1681).

The charge of the want of cleanliness is universal and may be well maintained against every room in both buildings, as well those occupied by students as those reserved for purposes of recitation. In many instances this want of cleanliness is extended to a want of decency, and filth is found to have accumulated of such sort in such quantities as to be offensive and doubtless injurious to health.
—Report of trustees on conditions at Franklin College, University of Georgia, 1826, quoted in Christian Gauss, *How Good Were the Good Old Times?*, in A.C. Spectorsky, ed., *The College Years* (1958).

Soap and education are not as sudden as a massacre, but they are more deadly in the long run.
—Mark Twain,
The Facts Concerning the Recent Resignation (1867).

Cleverness

I always did think that cleverness was the art of hiding ignorance.
—Shelland Bradley,
An American Girl in India (1907).

The Athenians do not mind a man being clever, so long as he does not impart his cleverness to others.
—Plato,
Euthyphro, iii (c.399 B.C.).

Ignorance is not so terrible or extreme an evil, and is far from being the greatest of all; too much cleverness and too much learning, accompanied with an ill bringing up, are far more fatal.
—Plato,
Laws, VII.819 (c.367–347).

Closemindedness

See also Belief; Dogmatism; Mind; Rigidity

He hears but half who hears one party only.
—Aeschylus,
Eumenides, ln.428 (458 B.C.).

The worst thing about stubbornness of mind, about prejudices, is that they arrest development; they shut the mind off from new stimuli. Open-mindedness means retention of the childlike attitude; close-mindedness means premature intellectual old age.   — John Dewey, *Democracy and Education*, xiii (1916).

A closed mind is a dying mind.
— Edna Ferber,
radio broadcast, 1947.

None so deaf as he that will not hear.
— Thomas Fuller (1654–1734), *Gnomologia*, no.3657 (1732); also Matthew Henry, *Commentaries*, Psalm LVIII. See also John Heywood, *Proverbs*.

The fact seems to be that we are least open to precise knowledge concerning the things we are most vehement about.
— Eric Hoffer,
The Passionate State of Mind,
no.60 (1954).

I trust not him who tends to judge from a set point of view; as I mistrust him who, being the ambassador of a worthy cause, lets it master his discretion and puts himself in blinkers.
— Antoine de Saint-Exupéry,
The Wisdom of the Sands, lxvii (1950).

Never forget that the old law of the natural philosophers, that Nature abhors a vacuum, is true of the human head. There is no such thing as an empty head, though there are heads so impervious to new ideas that they are for all mental purposes solid, like billiard balls.
— George Bernard Shaw,
The Intelligent Woman's Guide to Socialism and Capitalism, i (1928).

Comedy

Comedy is criticism.
— Louis Kronenberger,
The Thread of Laughter (1952).

Comedy, we may say, is society protecting itself — with a smile. — J.B. Priestley,
George Meredith (1926).

Comedy is the last refuge of the nonconformist mind.   — Gilbert Seldes,
The New Republic, Dec. 20, 1954.

Commencement

The commencement speaker represents the continuation of a barbaric custom that has no basis in logic. If the state of oratory that inundates our educational institutions during the month of June could be transformed into rain for Southern California, we should all be happy awash or waterlogged.
— Samuel Gould,
Time, June 27, 1960.

The world is always upside down to a baccalaureate speaker.... Things have got to be wrong in order that they may be deplored.   — A. Whitney Griswold,
in *New York Times*, Apr. 20, 1963.

I am not unmindful of the appalling fact that countless middle-aged moralists like me are rising these days on countless platforms all over the world to tell thousands of helpless young captives the score — and I suspect that all of those commencement orators are almost as uncomfortable as I am!   — Adlai E. Stevenson,
Smith College commencement address,
June 6, 1955.

The adoption of the cap and gown is one of the striking atavistic features of modern college life. — Thorstein Veblen,
The Theory of the Leisure Class,
xiv (1899).

The typical college graduation is a riot of medievalism — from the Latin guild titles to the hieratically colored hoods.
— Garry Wills,
"No diploma for this administration,"
Detroit Free Press, June 3, 1982.

Committee

See also Conference

We always carry out by committee anything in which any one of us alone would be too reasonable to persist.
— Frank Moore Colby,
The Colby Essays: Subsidizing Authors,
I (1926).

I find it very useful to be a member of plenty of committees; I can point to the list whenever I am asked to do anything which might involve real work, and ask how can I be expected to shoulder any new duties?   — Robertson Davies,
The Table Talk of Samuel Marchbanks (1949).

A foolish consistency is the hobgoblin of small committees.
— William A. Emerson,
Wilson Library Bulletin, Mar. 1978, paraphrasing Ralph Waldo Emerson.

What is a committee? A group of the unwilling, picked from the unfit, to do the unnecessary.   — Richard Harkness,
New York Herald Tribune,
June 15, 1960.

I hate being placed on committees. They are always having meetings at which half are absent and the rest late.
— Oliver Wendell Holmes, Sr.,
in *Life and Letters of Oliver Wendell Holmes*, I, ed. John T. Morse, Jr. (1896).

A committee is an animal with four back legs.   — John Le Carré,
Tinker, Tailor, Soldier, Spy,
III.xxxiv (1974).

Nothing is ever accomplished by a committee unless it consists of three members, one of whom happens to be sick and the other absent.
— Hendrik van Loon,
in *Reader's Digest*, June 1934.

Common Sense

Common sense is the measure of the possible; it is composed of experience and prevision; it is calculation applied to life.
— Henri Frédéric Amiel,
Journal, Dec. 26, 1852.

If a man can have only one kind of sense, let him have common sense. If he has that and uncommon sense, too, he is not far from genius. — Henry Ward Beecher,
Proverbs from Plymouth Pulpit: The Human Mind (1887).

Common sense is the most widely shared commodity in the world, for every man is convinced that he is well supplied with it.
— René Descartes,
Discourse on Method, I (1637).

State a moral case to a ploughman and a professor. The former will decide it as well, and often better than the latter, because he has not been led astray by artificial rules.   — Thomas Jefferson,
letter to his nephew Peter Carr,
Aug. 10, 1787.

Good-sense is something very distinct from knowledge.   — William Melmoth,
Fitzosborne's Letters on Several Subjects, 240 (1739).

Fine sense and exalted sense are not half so ueful as common sense.
— Alexander Pope,
Thoughts on Various Subjects (1727).

Common sense cannot be taught.
— Quintilian, *Institutio Oratoria*,
VI.v.2 (A.D. 95 or 96).

Solid good sense is often nonsense solidified.   — Leo Stein,
Journey into the Self, 256 (1950).

What is known as common sense, whose virtue, uniquely among virtues, is that everybody has it.   Tom Stoppard,
Jumpers, II (1974).

Why level downward to our dullest perception always and praise that as common sense? The commonest sense is the sense of men asleep, which they express by snoring.   —Henry David Thoreau, *Walden*, x: *Conclusion* (1854).

Common sense is not so common.
          —Voltaire,
          Philosophical Dictionary:
          Self-Love (1764).

Communication

Extremists think "communication" means agreeing with them.   —Leo Rosten, *A Trumpet for Reason* (1970).

Precision of communication is important, more important than ever, in our era of hair-trigger balances, when a false, or misunderstood word may create as much disaster as a sudden thoughtless act.
          —James Thurber,
          Lanterns and Lances: Friends,
          Romans, Countrymen, Lend Me Your
          Muffs (1961).

Comparison

If you compare yourself with others, you may become vain & bitter; for always there will be greater & lesser persons than yourself.   —Max Ehrmann, *Desiderata* (1927).

Take heed that thou make no comparisons, and if any body happen to be praised for some brave act, or virtue, praise not another for the same virtue in his presence, for every comparison is odious.   —Francis Hawkins, *Youth's Behaviour*, vi (1663).

We throw all our attention on the utterly idle question whether A has done as well as B, when the only question is whether A has done as well as he could.
          —William Graham Sumner,
          Essays, I, ed. Albert G. Keller
          and Maurice R. Davies (1934).

Competence

See also Ability; Incompetence; Skill; Talent

Competence, like truth, beauty and contact lenses, is in the eye of the beholder.
          —Laurence J. Peter and Raymond Hull,
          The Peter Principle, iii. p.43 (1969).

He who can't write says the pen is bad.
          —Yiddish proverb.

Competition

Competitions are for horses, not artists.
          —Béla Bartók,
          Saturday Review, Aug. 25, 1962.

Thou shalt not covet, but tradition Approves all forms of competition.
          —Arthur Hugh Clough,
          Poems (1849): *The Latest Decalogue*.

The only competition worthy a wise man is with himself.
          —Anna Brownell Jameson,
          Memoirs and Essays: Washington Allston
          (1846).

Conceit

Do you see a man who is wise in his own eyes? There is more hope for a fool than for him.   —*Bible: Proverbs* 26:12. See also *Proverbs* 12:15.

Frivolity is inborn, conceit acquired by education.   —Cicero, *Pro Flacco* (before 59 B.C.).

Intellectual pride ... might be described as Original Sin in an academic hood and gown.   —John Hutchison, *Faith, Reason and Existence* (1956).

The usual education of young people results only in new forms of conceit.
          —François de La Rochefoucauld,
          Maxims, no.261 (1665).

Very few people can stand the strain of being educated without getting superior over it. — Stephen Leacock, *My Remarkable Uncle: Who Canonizes the Classics?* (1942).

Knowledge that puffs up the possessor's mind
Is ever more of a pernicious kind.
— William Mather, *The Young Man's Companion*, preface (1681).

Fools dwelling in darkness, wise in their own conceit, and puffed up with vain knowledge, go round and round, staggering to and fro like men led by the blind. — *Katha Upanishad: Adhyaya* (c.700–300 B.C.).

Conclusion

Only on the edge of the grave can man conclude anything. — Henry Adams, *The Education of Henry Adams*, vi (1907).

I knew a wise man that had it for a byword, when he saw men hasten to a conclusion, *Stay a little, that we may make an end sooner.* — Francis Bacon, *Essays: Of Dispatch* (1612).

Life is the art of drawing sufficient conclusions from insufficient premises. — Samuel Butler (1835–1902), *Note-Books: Lord, What Is Man?* (1912).

I am no athlete— but at one sport I used to be an expert. It was a dangerous game, called "jumping to conclusions." — Eddie Cantor, *The Way I See It* (1959).

Conference

See also Committee

No grand idea was ever born in a conference, but a lot of foolish ideas have died there. — F. Scott Fitzgerald, *The Crack-Up* (1936).

Creativity always dies a quick death in rooms that house conference tables. — Bruce Herschensohn, *New York Times*, Apr. 2, 1975.

Confidence

They can conquer who believe they can. It is he who has done the deed once who does not shrink from attempting it again. — Ralph Waldo Emerson, *Society and Solitude: Success* (1870).

He who knows nothing is confident in everything.— Charles Haddon Spurgeon, *John Ploughman's Talks*, ii (1869).

They are able because they think they are able. — Virgil, *The Aeneid*, V.231 (19 B.C.).

Conformity

See also Adjustment;
Nonconformity

Conformity ... becomes the criterion by which the pupil is judged in spite of the fact that initiative, originality and independence are precious qualities in life. — John Dewey, "The Need for a Philosophy of Education," *The New Era in Home and School*, Nov. 1934.

Conform and be dull. — J. Frank Dobie, *The Voice of the Coyote*, introd. (1949).

But everybody wants you
To be just like them. — Bob Dylan, *Writings and Drawings of Bob Dylan (1973): Maggie's Farm* (song) (1965).

Even as a teacher has the right and the duty to resist undue pressures towards conformity to views of ignorant or partisan community organizations, so the child under that teacher's guidance has the right to be himself, and not be subject to undue pressure toward conformity by narrow-minded or thoughtless teachers. — Henry Ehlers and Gordon C. Lee, *Crucial Issues in Education*, 3rd ed., 52 (1964).

Conformity is the ape of harmony.
— Ralph Waldo Emerson, *Journals*, 1840.

Our society cannot have it both ways: to maintain a conformist and ignoble system *and* to have skillful and spirited men to man that system.
— Paul Goodman, *Growing Up Absurd* (1960).

Woe to him inside a nonconformist clique who does not conform with nonconformity. — Eric Hoffer, *Reflections on the Human Condition* (1973).

Life cannot exist without a certain conformity to the surrounding universe — that conformity involves a certain amount of happiness in excess of pain. In short, as we live we are paid for living.
— T.H. Huxley, letter to Charles Kingley, Sept. 23, 1860.

Conformity is the jailer of freedom and the enemy of growth.
— John F. Kennedy, address to United Nations General Assembly, Sept. 25, 1961.

Every society honors its live conformists and its dead troublemakers.
— Mignon McLaughlin, *The Neurotic's Notebook* (1963).

Conformism is the philosophy of indifference. — Dagobert D. Runes, *Treasury of Thought*, 70 (1966).

To think for himself! Oh, my God, teach him to think like other people!
— Mary Wollstonecraft Shelley, when advised to send her son to a school where he would be taught to think for himself, c.1825, in Matthew Arnold, *Essays in Criticism* (1865).

The race of men, while sheep in credulity, are wolves for conformity.
— Carl Van Doren, *Why I Am an Unbeliever*, in *Twelve Modern Apostles, and Their Creeds* (1926).

We are half ruined by conformity, but we should be wholly ruined without it.
— Charles Dudley Warner, *My Summer in a Garden: Eighteenth Week* (1871).

To require conformity in the appreciation of sentiments or the appreciation of language, or uniformity of thought, feeling, or action, is a fundamental error in human legislation — a madness which would be only equalled by requiring all to possess the same countenance, the same voice or the same stature.
— Josiah Warren, *Equitable Commerce* (1846).

Conservatives

When a nation's young men are conservative, its funeral-bell is already rung.
— Henry Ward Beecher, *Proverbs from Plymouth Pulpit: Political* (1887).

In the matter of belief, we are all extreme conservatives. — William James, *Pragmatism* (1907).

I do not know which makes a man more conservative — to know nothing but the present, or nothing but the past.
— John Maynard Keynes, *The End of Laissez-Faire*, I (1926).

Generally young men are regarded as radicals. This is a popular misconception. The most conservative persons I ever met are college undergraduates.
— Woodrow Wilson, address in New York City, Nov. 19, 1905; also similar statement in speech at YMCA, Pittsburgh, Oct. 24, 1914.

Consideration

See also Analysis; Deliberation

Do not answer before you have heard, nor interrupt a speaker in the midst of his words.   —*Apocrypha: Ecclesiasticus* 11:8 (c.180 B.C.).

Read, mark, learn, and inwardly digest.
—*Book of Common Prayer: Collect for the Second Sunday in Advent* (1548).

Examine each opinion: if it seems true, embrace it; if false, gird up thy mind to withstand it.   —Lucretius, *On the Nature of Things*, II (c.45 B.C.).

Seek not to know who said this or that, but take note of what has been said.
—Thomas à Kempis,
The Imitation of Christ,
I.v.1 (1426).

Consistency

See also Inconsistency

A foolish consistency is the hobgoblin of little minds, adored by little statesmen and philosophers and divines. With consistency a great soul has simply nothing to do.   —Ralph Waldo Emerson,
Essays, First Series: Self-Reliance (1841).

The world is quite right. It does not have to be consistent.
—Charlotte Perkins Gilman,
Women and Economics, vi (1898).

Too much consistency is as bad for the mind as it is for the body. Consistency is contrary to nature, contrary to life. The only completely consistent people are the dead.   —Aldous Huxley,
Do What You Will: Wordsworth in the Tropics (1929).

The consistent thinker, the consistently moral man, is either a walking mummy or else, if he has not succeeded in stifling all vitality, a fanatical monomaniac.
—Aldous Huxley, *ibid.*

Consistency is only a negative test of truth; it is possible, however unlikely, to be consistently in error. Consistency would be a sufficient test only if we should suppose that there is nothing external to our logic which we must be true to.   —Clarence I. Lewis,
The Mind and the World-Order (1929).

The wise man does not expect consistency or harmony ... for he sees that man is a mosaic of characteristics and qualities that only rarely achieve an internal and intrinsic harmony. —Abraham Myerson,
Speaking of Man, 9 (1950).

In all things reason should prevail: it is quite another thing to be stiff, than steady in an opinion. —William Penn,
More Fruits of Solitude, II. no.155 (1718).

Consistency is a jewel; and, as in the case of other jewels, we may marvel at the price that some people will pay for it.
—George Santayana,
Character and Opinion in the United States (1920).

Contradiction

Luckily boys accept contradictions as readily as their elders do, or this boy might have become prematurely wise.
—Henry Adams,
The Education of Henry Adams,
iii (1907).

Contradiction should awaken Attention, not Passion.   —Thomas Fuller (1654–1734), *Gnomologia*, no.1157 (1732).

Do not nourish the Spirit of Contradiction.... To find difficulties in everything may prove you clever, but such wrangling writes you down a fool.
—Balthasar Gracián,
The Art of Worldly Wisdom,
cxxxv (1647).

Truth consists of paradoxes and a paradox is two facts that stand on opposite

hilltops and across the intervening valley call each other liars.
— Carl Sandburg, *Incidentals* (1904).

Contradiction is the salt which keeps truth from corruption.
— John Lancaster Spalding, *Means and Ends of Education* (1895).

In formal logic, a contradiction is the signal of a defeat; but in the evolution of real knowledge it marks the first step in progress towards a victory. This is one great reason for the utmost toleration of variety of opinion.... A clash of doctrines is not a disaster — it is an opportunity.
— Alfred North Whitehead, *Science and the Modern World* (1925).

Controversy

See also Argument; Debate; Disputation

As a fact — a mere fact of history — nearly everything we hold to be truth, save what comes immediately from the evidence of our senses, has been established by controversy.
— Hilaire Belloc, *The Silence of the Sea* (1941).

Conflict is the gadfly of thought. It stirs us to observation and memory. It instigates to invention. It shocks us out of sheep-like passivity, and sets us at noting and contriving.... [C]onflict is a *sine qua non* of reflection and ingenuity.
— John Dewey, *Human Nature and Conduct: Morals Are Human* (1922).

Both teachers and learners go to sleep at their post, as soon as there is no enemy in the field.
— John Stuart Mill, *On Liberty*, ii (1859).

The most savage controversies are those about matters as to which there is no good evidence either way.
— Bertrand Russell, *Unpopular Essays: An Outline of Intellectual Rubbish* (1950).

Conversation

Conversation teaches more than meditation.— Thomas Fuller (1654–1734), *Gnomologia*, no.1158 (1732).

Education begins a Gentleman, Conversation completes him. — Thomas Fuller, *ibid.*, no.1359.

Conversing with children is a unique art with rules and meanings of its own. Children are rarely naive in their communication. Their messages are often in a code, that requires deciphering.
— Haim G. Ginott, *Between Parent and Child*, 17 (1965).

Let friendly intercourse be a school of knowledge, and culture be taught through conversation: thus you make your friends your teachers and mingle the pleasures of conversation with the advantages of instruction.— Balthasar Gracián, *The Art of Worldly Wisdom*, xi (1647).

Conversation is the beginning and end of knowledge. — Stefano Guazzo, *Civil Conversation*, I.39 (1574).

Conversation is the full perfection of learning. — Stefano Guazzo, *ibid.*, I.43.

The best kind of conversation is that which may be called *thinking aloud*.
— William Hazlitt, *Characteristics*, no.180 (1823).

Conclusions ... are not often reached by talk any more than by private thinking. That is not the profit. The profit is in the exercise, and above all in the experience.
— Robert Louis Stevenson, *Virginibus Puerisque: On Talk and Talkers* (1881).

Conversation, the commerce of minds.
— Cyril Tourneur, *A Funerall Poeme* (1609).

Learned conversation is either the affectation of the ignorant or the profession of the mentally unemployed.
—Oscar Wilde,
Intentions: The Critic as Artist (1891).

Conviction

See also Belief; Dogma; Opinion

He who holds convictions, respects convictions. —Leo Baeck,
The Essence of Judaism, 286 (1936).

Conviction, were it never so excellent, is worthless till it convert itself into Conduct. —Thomas Carlyle,
Sartor Resartus (1833).

At eighteen our convictions are hills from which we look; at forty-five they are caves in which we hide. —F. Scott Fitzgerald,
Flappers and Philosophers: Bernice Bobs Her Hair (1920).

Every fool is fully convinced, and every one fully persuaded is a fool: the more erroneous his judgment the more firmly he holds it. —Balthasar Gracián,
The Art of Worldly Wisdom,
clxxxiii (1647).

The important thing is not that two people should be inspired by the same convictions, but rather that each of them should hold his or her convictions in a high and worthy spirit. —John Morley,
On Compromise (1874).

He who begins life by stifling his convictions is in a fair way for ending it without any convictions to stifle. —John Morley,
ibid.

What was a lie in the father becomes a conviction in the son.
—Friedrich Nietzsche,
The Antichrist, lv (1888).

Convictions are more dangerous to truth than lies. —Friedrich Nietzsche,
Human, All Too Human, I (1878).

Our firmest convictions are apt to be the most suspect, they mark our limitations and our bounds. Life is a petty thing unless it is moved by the indomitable urge to extend its boundaries.
—José Ortega y Gasset,
The Dehumanization of Art (1925).

Nearly all our disasters come from a few fools having the "courage of their convictions." —Coventry Patmore,
The Rod, the Root and the Flower (1895).

Every man is encompassed by a cloud of conforting convictions, which move with him like flies on a summer day.
—Bertrand Russell,
Sceptical Essays (1928).

Correspondence

Even if you have nothing to write, write and say so. —Cicero,
Letters to Atticus, IV.viii.4 (56 B.C.).

All letters, methinks, should be as free and easy as one's discourse, not studied as an oration, nor made up of hard words like a charm. —Dorothy Osborne,
letter to Sir William Temple, Oct. 1653.

Counseling

See also Advice

Every boy wants someone older than himself to whom he may go in moods of confidence and yearning. The neglect of this child's want by grown people ... is a fertile source of suffering.
—Henry Ward Beecher,
Eyes and Ears (1862).

Where there is no guidance, a people falls; but in an abundance of counselors there is safety. *Bible:*
—*Proverbs* 11:14.

I want to feel that boys can discuss things with me anytime. The problem is important now, not later. It may disappear after a good lunch, but he doesn't know that now. —Frank Boyden, *Life*, Nov. 30, 1962.

He who will not be counselled cannot be helped. —John Clarke, *Paroemiologia Anglo-Latina* (1639); also Benjamin Franklin, *Poor Richard's Almanack*, Aug. 1747.

It is just as important, perhaps more important, for the teacher to have the benefit of personal counseling when he needs it as it is for the student. —William C. Menninger, address to National Association of Secondary School Principals, Feb. 24, 1954.

Creativity

See also Innovator; Originality

Without creative personalities able to think and judge independently, the upward development of society is as unthinkable as the development of the individual personality without the nourishing soil of the community. —Albert Einstein, *Ideas and Opinions* (1954).

Creativity varies inversely with the number of cooks involved in the broth. —Bernice Fitz-Gibbon, *Macy's, Gimbel's and Me* (1967).

All men are creative but few are artists. —Paul Goodman, *Growing Up Absurd*, ix.3 (1960).

Invention is a curious faculty. It is an attribute of youth and with age it is lost. —W. Somerset Maugham, *Points of View* (1958).

Creativity is more than just being different. Anybody can play weird; that's easy. What's hard is to be as simple as Bach. Making the simple complicated is commonplace; making the complicated simple, awesomely simple, that's creativity. —Charles Mingus, quoted by Bob Talbert, *Detroit Free Press*, July 27, 1980.

'Tis wise to learn; 'tis God-like to create. —John Godfrey Saxe, *The Library* (1860).

Credulity

See also Belief; Opinion

The simple believes everything, but the prudent looks where he is going. —*Bible: Proverbs* 14:15.

They do not know how they stumble, those pious fools, when they rely on everything found in print without knowing its nature, root and origin. —Jacob Emden, *Mitpahat Sefarim*, 78 (1769).

He that takes up conclusions on the trust of authors, ... loses his labour, and does not know anything, but only believeth. —Thomas Hobbes, *Leviathan*, I.v (1651).

If you believe everything you read, better not read. —Japanese proverb.

There are two ways to slice easily through life; to believe everything or to doubt everything. Both ways save us from thinking. —Alfred Korzybski, *Manhood of Humanity* (1921).

Believe not all, or if you must believe, Stomach not all.—William Shakespeare, *Antony and Cleopatra*, III.i.11 (1607).

Our credulity is not to be measured by the truth of the things we believe. When men believed the earth was flat, they were not credulous: they were using their common sense, and, if asked to prove that the earth was flat, would have said simply, "Look at it." —George Bernard Shaw, *Androcles and the Lion*, preface (1912).

The fact that a believer is happier than a sceptic is no more to the point than the fact that a drunken man is happier than a sober one. The happiness of credulity is a cheap and dangerous quality of happiness, and by no means a necessity of life.   — George Bernard Shaw, *ibid.*

Every fool believes what his teachers tell him, and calls his credulity science or morality as confidently as his father called it divine revelation.
— George Bernard Shaw, *Maxims for Revolutionists* (1903).

Critic, Artistic

See also below

The critic who admires all kinds of things simultaneously cannot love any of them.
— Max Beerbohm, *Mainly on the Air: George Moore* (1946).

A good writer is not, *per se*, a good book critic. No more so than a good drunk is automatically a good bartender.
— Jim Bishop, *New York Journal-American*, Nov. 26, 1957.

The critic, one would suppose, if he is to justify his existence, should endeavour to discipline his personal prejudices and cranks — tares to which we are all subject — and compose his differences with as many of his fellows as possible, in the common pursuit of true judgment.
— T.S. Eliot, *The Function of Criticism*, i (1923).

Reviewers are forever telling authors they can't understand them. The author might often reply: Is that my fault?
— Julius and Augustus Hare, *Guesses at Truth* (1827).

A critic is a man who expects miracles.
— James Huneker, *Iconoclasts, a Book of Dramatists*, 139 (1905).

The readers and the hearers like my books;
And yet some writers cannot them digest;
But what care I? For when I make a feast,
I would my guests should praise it, not the cooks.   — Martial, *Epigrammata*, IX.lxxxii (A.D. 93).

The dramatic critic who is without prejudice is on the plane with the general who does not believe in taking human life.   — George Jean Nathan, *Comedians All* (1919).

No chronically happy man is a trustworthy critic.   — George Jean Nathan, *The Theatre in the Fifties*, 296 (1953).

Let such teach others who themselves excel,
And censure freely who have written well.   — Alexander Pope, *An Essay on Criticism*, I.15 (1711).

Authors are partial to their wit, 'tis true, But are not Critics to their judgment too?
— Alexander Pope, *ibid.*, I.17.

Critic, Artistic — Dispraise for

Critics are brushers of other men's clothes.   — H.G. Bohn, *Handbook of Proverbs*, 341 (1855).

Praise not the critic, lest he think You crave the shelter of his ink; But pray his halo, when he dies, May tip the steelyards of the skies.
— Alice Brown (1857–1948), *The Critic.*

Critics — appall'd, I venture on the name;
Those cut-throat bandits in the paths of fame.   — Robert Burns, *To Robert Graham of Fintry, Esq.*, ln.37 (1791).

Critics in general are venomous serpents that delight in hissing.   — William Barker Daniel, *Rural Sports* (1801).

Take heed of criticks: they bite, like fish, at anything, especially at bookes.
— Thomas Dekker,
Newes from Hell (1606).

Let those find fault whose wit's so very small,
They've need to show that they can think at all.   — John Dryden,
All for Love, prologue (1677).

Nature, when she invented, manufactured, and patented her authors, contrived to make critics out of the chips that were left. — Oliver Wendell Holmes, Sr.,
The Professor at the Breakfast-Table (1860).

Certain critics are cowards and traitors, who wait to attack till unhappy authors are dead, because alive they would answer.   — Tómas de Iriarte,
Literary Fables, xxii (1782).

For critics I care the five hundred thousandth part of the tythe of a half-farthing.   — Charles Lamb,
letter to Bernard Barton, Aug. 30, 1830.

Nature fits all her children with something to do,
He who would write and can't write can surely review.   — James Russell
Lowell, *A Fable for Critics*,
conclusion (1848).

He reviews with as much nonchalance as he whistles, —
He goes through a book and just picks out the thistles.
— James Russell Lowell, *ibid.*

A man of such infinite wisdom and flawless taste that any opinion he may utter is to be accepted immediately and without question — unless you disagree with him.   — George Oppenheimer,
in George Oppenheimer, ed.,
The Passionate Playgoer, 3 (1958).

Asking a working writer what he thinks about critics is like asking a lamppost what it feels about dogs. — John Osborne,
Time, Oct. 31, 1977.

Critics, as they are birds of prey, have ever a natural inclination to carrion.
— Alexander Pope,
letter to William Wycherley,
Dec. 26, 1704.

Book reviewing is a profession in which those who flunk the course get to teach the class.   — Dagobert D. Runes,
Treasury of Thought, 40 (1966).

The critic leaves at curtain fall
To find, in starting to review it,
He scarcely saw the play at all
For watching his reaction to it.
— E.B. White, *Poems and Sketches*
(1967): *Critic*.

Criticism, Artistic

See also Critic, Artistic

When you upbraid me
For my poems,
Catch also a cricket
By the wings,
And shout at him
For chirping.   — Archilocus,
epigram, in *Satire: A Critical Anthology*,
ed. John Russell and Ashley Brown
(1967).

I am bound by my own definition of criticism: *a disinterested endeavor to learn and propagate the best that is known and thought in the world.*
— Matthew Arnold,
Essays in Criticism, I: *Functions of Criticism at the Present Time* (1865).

It is unfortunate that more and more we confuse the function of criticism with being a sort of racing tip sheet. If you work for a mass media you're going to be used as a market report, a Good Housekeeping Seal of Approval.   — Clive Barnes,
in *Newsweek*, Dec. 24, 1973.

Books should be tried by a judge and jury as though they were crimes, and counsel should be heard on both sides.
— Samuel Butler (1835–1902),
Note-Books (1912).

He wreathed the rod of criticism with roses.   — Isaac D'Israeli, *Literary Miscellanies* (1796), referring to Pierre Bayle.

One always tends to overpraise a long book, because one has got through it. — E.M. Forster, *Abinger Harvest* (1936).

To criticise is to appreciate, to appropriate, to take intellectual possession, to establish in fine a relation with the criticised thing and to make it one's own. — Henry James (1843–1916), *Prefaces: What Maisie Knew* (1897).

I have always very much despised the artificial canons of criticism. When I have read a work in prose or poetry, or seen a painting, a statue, &c., I have only asked myself whether it gives me pleasure, whether it is animating, interesting, attaching? If it is, it is good for these reasons.   — Thomas Jefferson, letter to William Wirt, 1816.

I look upon reviews as a sort of infant disease to which new-born books are subject. — Georg Christoph Lichtenberg, *Reflections* (1799).

Criticism is the art wherewith a critic tries to guess himself into a share of the artist's fame.   — George Jean Nathan, *The House of Satan* (1926).

Criticism is the art of appraising others at one's own values. — George Jean Nathan, *The World in Falseface* (1972).

Every intellectual product must be judged from the point of view of the age and the people in which it was produced. — Walter Pater, *Studies in the History of the Renaissance: Mirandola* (1873).

I lose my patience, and I own it too, When works are censur'd, not as bad but new.   — Alexander Pope, *Imitations of Horace*, II.i.115 (1737).

Criticism often strips the tree of both caterpillars and blossoms.   —Jean Paul Richter, *Titan*, cv (1803).

I never read a book before reviewing it; it prejudices a man so.   — Sydney Smith, in Lady Holland, *A Memoir of the Rev. Sydney Smith* (1855).

Criticism is properly the rod of divination: a hazel-switch for the discovery of buried treasure, not a birch-twig for the castigation of offenders. — Arthur Symons, *An Introduction to the Study of Browning*, preface (1906).

Bad and indifferent criticism of books is just as serious as a city's careless drainage. —H.M. Tomlinson, *Between the Lines* (1930).

Three questions are essential to all just criticism: What is the author's object? How far has he accomplished it? How far is that objection worthy of approbation? —Nathaniel Parker Willis, *Pencillings by the Way*, preface (1835).

Criticism, Personal

If you're out to beat a dog, you're sure to find a stick.   — Hanan J. Ayalti, *Yiddish Proverbs* (1949).

No man can tell another his faults so as to benefit him, unless he loves him. — Henry Ward Beecher, *Proverbs from Plymouth Pulpit: Love* (1887).

This shows how much easier it is to be critical than to be correct. —Benjamin Disraeli, speech in House of Commons, Jan. 24, 1860.

Criticism should not be querulous and wasting, all knife and root-puller, but guiding, instructive, inspiring, a south wind, not an east wind. —Ralph Waldo Emerson, *Journals*, 1847.

All you need is to tell a man that he is no good ten times a day, and very soon he begins to believe it himself.
—Lin Yutang,
With Love and Irony (1940).

Criticism is asserted superiority.
—Henry Edward Manning,
Pastime Papers (1903).

People ask you for criticism, but they only want praise. —W. Somerset Maugham,
Of Human Bondage, 1 (1915).

It is by admiration and not by criticism that we live, and the main purpose of criticism should be to point out something to admire which we should not have noticed. —Mark Rutherford,
More Pages from a Journal (1910).

Culture

Culture, the acquainting ourselves with the best that has been known and said in the world, and thus with the history of the human spirit. —Matthew Arnold,
Literature and Dogma,
preface to 1873 edition.

The acquiring of culture is the developing of an avid hunger for knowledge and beauty.   —Jesse Lee Bennett,
On Culture and a Liberal Education (1922).

Without culture, and the relative freedom it implies, society, even when perfect, is but a jungle, This is why any authentic creation is a gift to the future.
—Albert Camus, *The Myth of Sisyphus and Other Essays: The Artist and His Time* (1955).

I think one possible definition of our modern culture is that it is one in which nine-tenths of our intellectuals can't read any poetry.   —Randall Jarrell,
on receiving the National Book Award for Poetry, *New York Herald Tribune*,
Mar. 19, 1961.

Culture itself is neither education nor lawmaking: it is an atmosphere and a heritage…. The average American college, by teaching its students to be ashamed of their fathers, does not actually elevate them in the scale of culture. All it does is to make hollow snobs of them.
—H.L. Mencken,
Minority Report: Notebooks,
no.360 (1956).

Culture is what your butcher would have if he were a surgeon.
—Mary Pettibone Poole,
A Glass Eye at the Keyhole (1938).

Culture is an instrument wielded by professors to manufacture professors, who when their turn comes will manufacture professors.   —Simone Weil,
The Need for Roots (1949).

Culture is activity of thought, and receptiveness to beauty and humane feeling. Scraps of information have nothing to do with it. A merely well-informed man is the most useless bore on God's earth.
—Alfred North Whitehead,
The Aims of Education, i (1929).

Culture is not a thing produced in classrooms, but by the subtler influences of life and association among men of the finer sort of taste and the higher kind of learning.   —Woodrow Wilson,
letter in the New York *Evening Post*,
Apr. 23, 1910.

Cultured Person

Most fathers would rather see their sons dead than either cultivated or devout.
—Louis Auchincloss,
The Rector of Justin, iii (1964).

The civilized are those who get more out of life than the uncivilized, and for this the uncivilized have not forgiven them.
—Cyril Connolly,
The Unquiet Grave (1945).

Curiosity

See also Questioning; Wonder

This disease of curiosity.
— St. Augustine,
Confessions, X (c.400).

Too much curiosity lost Paradise.
— Aphra Behn,
Lucky Chance, III.iii (1686).

A sense of curiosity is nature's original school of education. — Smiley Blanton,
Love or Perish (1956).

I loathe that low vice — curiosity.
— Lord Byron, Don Juan,
I.xxiii.181 (1819).

He that pryeth in the clouds may be struck with a thunderbolt. — John Clarke,
Paroemiologia Anglo-Latina, 31 (1639).

Every man ought to be inquisitive through every hour of his great adventure down to the day when he shall no longer cast a shadow in the sun. For if he dies without a question in his heart, what excuse is there for his continuance?
— Frank Moore Colby,
The Colby Essays, I (1926).

Curiosity is free-wheeling intelligence....
It endows the people who have it with a generosity in argument and a serenity in their own mode of life which springs from the cheerful willingness to let life take the forms it will. — Alistair Cooke,
"The Art of Curiosity," Vogue, Jan. 1953.

Children are notoriously curious about everything — everything except...the things people want them to know. It then remains for us to refrain from forcing any kind of knowledge upon them, and they will be curious about everything.
— Floyd Dell,
Were You Ever a Child? (1919).

It is nothing short of a miracle that the modern methods of instruction have not yet entirely strangled the holy curiosity of

inquiry.... It is a very grave mistake to think that the enjoyment of seeing and searching can be promoted by means of coercion and a sense of duty.
— Albert Einstein,
in George B. Leonard,
Education and Ecstacy (1969).

Desire to know why, and how, curiosity;
... which is a lust of the mind, that by perseverance of delight in the continual and indefatigable generation of knowledge, exceedeth the short vehemence of any carnal pleasure.
— Thomas Hobbes,
Leviathan, I.vi (1651).

Four be the things I'd been better without:
Love, curiosity, freckles, and doubt.
— Dorothy Parker, Enough Rope:
Inventory (1926).

Love of learning is by nature curious and inquisitive, ... prying into everything, reluctant to leave anything, material or immaterial, unexplored.   — Philo,
On the Migration of Abraham,
xxxix (before A.D. 50).

I think, at a child's birth, if a mother could ask a fairy godmother to endow it with the most useful gift, that gift would be curiosity.   — Eleanor Roosevelt,
quoted in Today's Health,
in Quote, Oct. 2, 1966.

Curiosity may have killed the cat, but it has never been detrimental to the doctor.
— Peter J. Steinchrohn,
More Years for the Asking, 17 (1940).

Curiosity, that spur in the side, that bridle in the mouth, that ring in the nose, of a lazy, an impatient, and a grunting reader.   — Jonathan Swift,
A Tale of a Tub, xi (1704).

He that breaks a thing to find out what it is has left the path of wisdom.
— J.R.R. Tolkien,
The Fellowship of the Ring (1954).

Disinterested intellectual curiosity is the life blood of real civilisation.
—G.M. Trevelyan,
English Social History,
I, preface (1942).

It is true that a child is hungry all over; but he is also curious all over, and his curiosity is excited about as early as his hunger. —Charles Dudley Warner,
My Summer in a Garden: Seventeenth Week (1871).

Curriculum

See also Studies

The customary branches of an education are four, namely, (1) reading and writing, (2) gymnastic exercises, (3) music, to which is sometimes added (4) drawing.
—Aristotle, *Politics*,
VIII.ii.3 (before 322 B.C.).

"I only took the regular course."
"What was that?" inquired Alice.
"Reeling and Writhing, of course, to begin with," the Mock Turtle replied; "and then the different branches of Arithmetic—Ambition, Distraction, Uglification, and Derision."
—Lewis Carroll,
Alice's Adventures in Wonderland,
ix (1865).

Educational writers are always blaming subjects instead of men, looking for some galvanic theme or method which when applied by a man without any gift for teaching to a mind without any capacity for learning will somehow produce intellectual results. —Frank Moore Colby,
The Colby Essays, II (1926).

The forcing of Latin, geometry, and algebra in a certain kind of manner into a certain kind of head is not education; it is persecution. —Frank Moore Colby,
ibid.

We cannot establish a hierarchy of values among studies. It is futile to attempt to arrange them in an order, beginning with one having least worth and going on to that of maximum value. In so far as any study has a unique or irreplaceable function in experience, in so far as it marks a characteristic enrichment of life, its worth is intrinsic or incomparable.
—John Dewey,
Democracy and Education, xviii (1916).

I believe that the true center of correlation on the school subjects is not science, nor literature, nor history, nor geography, but the child's own social activities. —John Dewey,
"My Pedagogic Creed,"
The School Journal, Jan. 16, 1897.

There *is* only one curriculum, no matter what the method of education: what is basic and universal in human experience and practice, the underlying structure of culture. —Paul Goodman,
Growing Up Absurd, iv.6 (1960).

The quality of a department is inversely proportional to the number of courses it lists in its catalogue.—John Hildebrand, in Paul Dickson, ed., *The Official Rules* (1978).

The world no doubt is the best or most serviceable schoolmaster; but the world's curriculum does not include Latin and Greek. —E.V. Lucas,
Reading, Writing, and Remembering (1932).

There is a profusion of some things being taught which are supposed necessary because everybody learns them.... But what is given is, for the most part, passively received; and what is obtained is, chiefly, by means of the memory.
—Harriet Martineau,
Society in America, III: *Women* (1837).

It is a foremost university. There are thirty-two hundred courses. You spend your first two years in deciding what course to take, the next two years in finding the building that these courses

are given in, and the rest of your life in wishing you had taken another course.
—Will Rogers, speech before alumni of Columbia University in New York City, Dec. 4, 1924.

Before there can be a rational *curriculum*, we must settle which things it would most concern us to know; or to use a word of Bacon's now unfortunately obsolete, we must determine the relative values of knowledge.   —Herbert Spencer, *What Knowledge Is of Most Worth?* (1859).

Custom

See also Tradition

Customs constitute moral standards.
—John Dewey, *Human Nature and Conduct* (1922).

Old custom without truth is but an old error.   —Thomas Fuller (1654–1734), *Gnomologia*, no. 3710 (1732).

A long habit of not thinking a thing *wrong*, gives it a superficial appearance of being *right*, and raises at first a formidable outcry in defense of custom.
—Thomas Paine, *Common Sense* (1776).

Cynicism

See also Skepticism

Cynicism is, after all, simply idealism gone sour.   —Will Herberg, *Judaism and Modern Man*, 177 (1951).

The so-called sophisticated who prides himself on cynicism, is only seeking to escape his own inadequacies.
—Edgar F. Magnin, *How to Lead a Richer and Fuller Life*, 11 (1951).

Cynicism is intellectual dandyism.
—George Meredith, *The Egoist*, vii (1879).

The only deadly sin I know is cynicism.
—Henry Lewis Stimson, *On Active Service in Peace and War*, introd. (1948).

What is a cynic? A man who knows the price of everything, and the value of nothing.   —Oscar Wilde, *Lady Windemere's Fan*, III (1892).

Daydreaming

The mind is here, but is gone away.
—Aristophanes, *The Knights*, ln.1120 (424 B.C.).

But my thoughts ran a wool-gathering; and I did like the countryman, who looked for his ass while he was mounted on his back.   —Miguel de Cervantes, *Don Quixote*, II.II.lvii (1615).

Though present, absent.
—Desiderius Erasmus, *Adagia*, II.vii.84 (1508).

Dean

See also Professor

First come I; my name is Jowett.
There's no knowledge but I know it.
I am Master of this College:
What I don't know isn't knowledge.
—Henry Charles Beeching, *The Masque of Balliol* (c.late 1870's).

I am the Dean of Christ Church, Sir:
There's my wife; look well at her.
She's the Broad and I'm the High;
We are the University.
—Cecil Arthur Spring-Rice, *ibid.*

Debate

See also Argument;
Controversy; Disputation

He that wrestles with us strengthens our
nerves, and sharpens our skill. Our an-
tagonist is our helper. — Edmund Burke,
*Reflections on the Revolution
in France* (1790).

On either [side] which he would dispute,
Confute, change hands, and still confute.
— Samuel Butler (1612–80),
Hudibras, I.i.69 (1663).

No learned disputants would take the
field,
Sure not to conquer, and sure not to
yield;
Both sides deceiv'd, if rightly under-
stood,
Pelting each other for the public good.
— William Cowper,
Charity, ln.620 (1782).

To ignorance the wise descend
When with the ignorant they contend.
— Johann Wolfgang von Goethe
(1749–1832), *Proverbs in Rhyme*.

In arguing too, the parson own'd his skill,
For e'en though vanquish'd, he could
argue still.   — Oliver Goldsmith,
The Deserted Village, ln.211
(1770) [own'd = *showed*].

Myself when young did eagerly frequent
Doctor and Saint, and heard great argu-
ment
About it and about: but evermore
Came out by the same door as in I went.
— Omar Khayyám, *Rubáiyát*,
XXVII (c.1100), tr. Edward FitzGerald
(1859).

The venerable tradition of respectful
argumentation, based on evidence, conducted with courtesy, and leading to the
exposition of truth, is a precious part of
our heritage in this land of freedom. It is
the duty of educated men to understand, appreciate and perpetuate this
tradition.   — James P. Shannon,
"The Tradition of Respectful Argument,"
America, July 28, 1962.

The way to get at the merits of a case is
not to listen to the fool who imagines
himself impartial, but to get it argued
with reckless bias for and against. To
understand a saint, you must hear the
devil's advocate; the same is true of the
artist.   — George Bernard Shaw,
The Sanity of Art, preface (1895).

Definition

Unless we take care to clear the first principles of knowledge from the embarrassment and delusion of words, we may
make infinite reasonings upon them to
no purpose: we may draw consequences
from consequences, and never be the
wiser.   — George Berkeley,
*A Treatise Concerning the Principles
of Human Knowledge*, sec.25 (1710).

Definitions are a kind of scratching and
generally leave a sore place more sore
than it was before.   — Samuel Butler,
(1835–1902), *Note-Books: Higgledy-
Piggledy* (1912).

"Why did you call him Tortoise, if he
wasn't one?" Alice asked.
"We call him Tortoise because he
taught us," said the Mock Turtle angrily.
"Really you are very dull!"
— Lewis Carroll,
Alice's Adventures in Wonderland,
ix (1865).

"That's the reason they're called lessons,"
the Gryphon remarked: "because they
lesson from day to day."— Lewis Carroll,
ibid.

Who is it that has written, "The beginning of education is the analysis of
terms?"   — Epictetus,
Discourses, I.xvii (c. A.D. 100).

Every definition is dangerous.
— Desiderius Erasmus, *Adagia* (1508).

It is easy for a disputant to evade facts by entrenching himself behind a definition.
—A.J. Gordon,
Ministry of Healing (1882).

The light of human minds is perspicuous words, but by exact definitions first snuffed, and purged from ambiguity.
—Thomas Hobbes,
Leviathan, I.v (1651).

For the most part we do not first see, and then define, we define first and then see. In the great blooming, buzzing confusion of the outer world we pick out what our culture has already defined for us, and we tend to perceive that which we have picked out in the form stereotyped for us by our culture.   —Walter Lippman, *Public Opinion* (1922).

I know not how men, who have the same idea under different names, or different ideas under the same name, can in that case talk to one another. —John Locke, *An Essay concerning Human Understanding*, II.iv.4 (1690).

A definition is no proof.
—William Pinckney, speech, U.S. Senate, Feb. 15, 1820.

Degree, Academic

For you have learned, not what to say, But how the saying must be said.
—James V. Cunningham,
To a Friend, on Her Examination for the Doctorate in English (1947).

The carp leaps the dragon gate.
—Justus Doolittle, *A Vocabulary and Hand-Book of the Chinese Language*, ii.181 (1872). To "leap the dragon gate" is to get an academic degree.

I had not the advantage of a classical education, and no man should, in my judgment, accept a degree he cannot read.   —Millard Fillmore, declining an honorary degree from Oxford University, 1855.

I would suggest that the B.A. be issued on paper which deteriorates in five years.
—William Haber,
in *Public Relations Journal*,
Nov. 1965.

Every Schollar that on proofe is found able to read the Originalls of the Old and New Testament into the Latin tongue, and to resolve them Logically; withall being of godly life and conversation; And at any publick Act hath the Approbation of the Overseers and Master of the Colledge, is fit to be dignified with his first Degree.   —Harvard College graduation requirements, in Solomon Goldman, *The Book of Books: An Introduction*, 154 (1948).

A college degree does not lessen the length of your ears; it only conceals it.
—Elbert Hubbard,
Epigrams (1910).

The college graduate is presented with a sheepskin to cover his intellectual nakedness.   —Robert M. Hutchins, in *Reader's Digest*, Aug. 1940.

It might be said now that I have the best of both worlds: a Harvard education and a Yale degree.   —John F. Kennedy, upon receiving an honorary degree from Yale University, June 12, 1962.

They started dropping honorary degrees all around me, but never hit me.
—John O'Hara,
on why he quit giving his manuscripts to Yale University, *Newsweek*, June 3, 1963.

A degree is not an education, and the confusion on this point is perhaps the greatest weakness in American thinking about education.
—*Prospect for America: The Rockefeller Panel Reports* (1961).

A Master of Art
Is not worth a fart.   —John Scogan, *Scogan's Jests*, compiled by Andrew Boorde (before 1549).

Many people now in commerce have a college degree but failed to get a college education.   —Stuart A. Taylor, in "College: Do You Need It?" *Parade Magazine*, May 27, 1979.

Deliberation

See also Analysis; Consideration

Deliberation, *n.* The act of examining one's bread to determine which side it is buttered on.   —Ambrose Bierce, *The Devil's Dictionary* (1911).

Deliberate with caution, but act with decision; and yield with graciousness, or oppose with firmness.
          —Charles Caleb Colton, *Lacon*, 157 (1820–22).

Mark what another sayes: for many are
Full of themselves, and answer their own notion.
Take all into thee; then with equall care
Ballance each dramme of reason; like a potion.   —George Herbert, *The Temple: The Church-porch*, liv (1633).

We ought to learn from the kine one thing: ruminating.—Friedrich Nietzsche, *Thus Spake Zarathustra*, IV.lxviii (1891).

He thinks things through very carefully before going off half-cocked.
          —Carl Spaatz, comment on Calvin Coolidge, in George E. Allen, *Presidents Who Have Known Me* (1950).

Development

See also Growth; Maturity

For everything there is a season, and a time for every matter under heaven.
          —*Bible: Ecclesiastes* 3:1.

Modern education, from the view of the psychiatrist, does not aim to free the child from all inhibitions or to lift all

repressions, but to allow him a natural development which will bring him emotional as well as intellectual maturity.
          —Karl A. Menninger, *The Human Mind* (1930).

Life is a constant becoming: all stages lead to the beginning of others.
          —George Bernard Shaw, letter the Ellen Terry, Jan. 27, 1897.

Dictionary

Dictionary, *n.* A malevolent literary device for cramping the growth of a language and making it hard and inelastic.   —Ambrose Bierce, *The Enlarged Devil's Dictionary*, ed. E.R. Hopkins (1967).

Ah! words are pictures; a dictionary is the universe in alphabetical order. Rightly considered, the dictionary is the book above all books. All the other books are in it: it is only a matter of taking them out.   —Anatole France, *On Life and Letters* (1888–92).

The responsibility of a dictionary is to record a language, not set its style.
          —Philip Gove, editor-in-chief of *Webster's Third New International Dictionary*, letter to *Life*, Nov. 11, 1961.

The writing of a dictionary ... is not a task of setting up authoritative statements about the "true meanings" of words, but a task of *recording* to the best of one's ability, what various words *have meant* to authors in the distant or immediate past. *The writer of a dictionary is a historian, not a law-giver.*   —S.I. Hayakawa, *Language in Thought and Action* (1941).

I rarely look at a dictionary, which after all is merely somebody's estimate of polite usage, a matter on which one can form one's own opinion.
          —Oliver Wendell Holmes, Jr., *Holmes-Pollock Letters*, II, ed. M.A. DeWolfe Howe (1941).

Lexicographer, a writer of dictionaries, *a harmless drudge*. —Samuel Johnson, in James Boswell, *Life of Samuel Johnson*, ix, 1755 (1791).

From the actual use I have made of my dictionary I have got little but sorrow. Many excellent words are ruined by too definite a knowledge of their meaning. —Aline Kilmer, *Hunting a Hair Shirt: And Other Spiritual Adventures* (1923).

A dictionary is but an index to the literature of a given speech; or rather it bears to language the relation which a digest bears to a series of legal reports. Neither is an authority; and he is but a sorry lawyer who cites the one, an indifferent scholar who quotes the other as such. —George Perkins Marsh, *Lectures on the English Language* (1861).

As sheer casual reading-matter, I still find the English dictionary the most interesting book in our language. —Albert Jay Nock, *Memoirs of a Superfluous Man*, IV.i (1943).

Difficulty

Difficulty is a severe instructor. —Edmund Burke, *Reflections on the Revolution in France* (1790).

A fool often fails because he thinks what is difficult is easy, and a wise man because he thinks what is easy is difficult. —John Churton Collins, (1848–1908), *Aphorisms*.

All Things are difficult before they are easy. —Thomas Fuller (1654–1734), *Gnomologia*, no.560 (1732).

Nothing is easy to the unwilling. —Thomas Fuller, *ibid.*, no.3663.

Diligence

See also Effort

Diligence is the greatest of teachers. —Arab proverb.

Whatever your hand finds to do, do it with your might. —*Bible: Ecclesiastes* 9:10.

To muche diligence is hurtfull. —Thomas Hoby, tr., *The Courtyer*, 61 (1561).

If you have great talents, industry will improve them; if you have but moderate abilities, industry will supply their deficiency. —Joshua Reynolds, lecture at the Royal Academy, London, Dec. 11, 1769.

Diligence is to the Understanding, as the Whetstone to the Razor. —Robert South, *Sermons: John* 7:17 (1692).

Disadvantaged

Any system of education that will be strong enough to take care of the poorest and the most difficult to reach, will be strong enough to take care of the intelligent classes. —Henry Ward Beecher, *Proverbs from Plymouth Pulpit: Education* (1887).

Just because a child's parents are poor or uneducated is no reason to deprive the child of basic human rights to health care, education, proper nutrition. Clearly we ignore the needs of black children, poor children, and handicapped children in the country. —Marian Wright Edelman, in Margie Casady, "Society's Pushed-Out Children," *Psychology Today*, June 1975.

By that part of our plan which prescribes the selection of youths from among the poor, we hope to avail the State of those talents which nature has sown liberally among the poor as the rich, but which perish without use, if not sought for and cultivated.   — Thomas Jefferson, *Notes on the State of Virginia* (1782).

O, teach the orphan-boy to read,
Or teach the orphan-girl to sew.
          — Alfred, Lord Tennyson,
          Lady Clara Vere de Vere, ix (1833).

In order that the opportunity of reading and making progress may not be taken from poor children … let some sufficient benefice be assigned in every cathedral church for a master who shall teach gratis the clerks of the same church, and poor scholars.   — Third Council of the Lateran, 1179.

Discipline

See also Child Rearing;
Kindness; Punishment;
Punishment, Corporal;
Reprimand; Severity

It is ominous for the future of a child when the discipline he receives is based on the emotional needs of the disciplinarian rather than on any consideration of the child's own needs.
          — Gordon W. Allport,
          Personality and Social Encounter: Prejudice in Modern Perspective (1960).

Do you have children? Discipline them, and make them obedient from their youth.   — *Apocrypha: Ecclesiasticus* 7:23 (c.180 B.C.).

Although discipline and freedom seem antithetical, each without the other destroys itself.   — Donald Barr,
Who Pushed Humpty Dumpty? (1971).

Children can stand vast amounts of sternness. They rather expect to be wrong and are quite used to being punished. It is injustice, inequity and inconsistency that kill them.   — Robert F. Capon,
Bed and Board (1965).

Discipline is a symbol of caring to a child. He needs guidance. If there is love, there is no such thing as being too tough with a child. A parent must also not be afraid to hang himself. If you have never been hated by your child, you have never been a parent.   — Bette Davis,
          The Lonely Life, xix (1962).

Discipline means power at command; mastery of the resources available for carrying through the actions undertaken. To know what one is to do and to move to do it promptly and by the use of the requisite means is to be disciplined, whether we are thinking of an army or the mind. Discipline is positive.
          — John Dewey,
          Democracy and Education (1916).

I shun discipline — mathematician's mind, narrow mind — shopkeeper's heart, dry as the wood of his counter.
          — Gustave Flaubert,
          Intimate Notebook, 1840–1841,
          24 (1967).

Neglect mending a small Fault, and 'twill soon be a great One.
          — Benjamin Franklin,
          Poor Richard's Almanack, Nov. 1755.

A fault once excused is twice committed.
          — Gabriel Harvey,
          Marginalia, 100 (1590).

Do not pursue with the terrible scourge him who deserves a slight whip.
          — Horace, *Satires*,
          I.iii.119 (c.35 B.C.).

The purpose of constructive discipline is to develop within our young people a sense of good judgment consistent with a desirable system of values, leading to proper self-control and self-direction.
          — Alvin W. Howard,
          "Discipline: Three F's for the Teacher,"
          The Clearing House, May 1965.

When a disciplinarian does something and no one responds,

He rolls up his sleeves in an attempt to enforce order.   —Lao-tse, *Tao Te Ching*, sec.38, (c.550 B.C.), tr. Gia-Fu Feng and Jane English.

If a child shows himself incorrigible, he should be decently and quietly beheaded at the age of twelve, lest he grow to maturity, marry, and perpetuate his kind.   —Don Marquis, *The Almost Perfect State* (1927).

Where does discipline end? Where does cruelty begin? Somewhere between these, thousands of children inhabit a voiceless hell.   —François Mauriac, *Second Thoughts* (1961).

Discipline must come through liberty.... If discipline is founded on liberty, the discipline itself must necessarily be *active*. We do not consider an individual disciplined only when he has been rendered as artificially silent as a mute and as immovable as a paralytic. He is an individual *annihilated*, not *disciplined*.
—Maria Montessori, *The Montessori Method* (1912).

A wilde coult the harder he is rained, the hotter he is.   —George Pettie, *A Petite Pallace*, 204 (1576).

He injures the good who spares the bad.
—Publilius Syrus, *Sententiae* (c.43 B.C.).

Administering discipline is a more laborious task than is taking refuge in a few simple punitive tricks. It is just as much more laborious and challenging as is modern medical thinking compared to the proud hocus-pocus of the primitive medicine man. The task of the teacher on his job is to translate the principles of democratic discipline into daily action in the classroom.   —Fritz Redl, *When We Deal with Children*, 254 (1966).

You cannot train a horse with shouts and expect it to obey a whisper.
—Dagobert D. Runes, *Treasury of Thought*, 368 (1966).

The severity of the master is more useful than the indulgence of the father.
—Saadi, *Gulistan (Rose Garden)* (1258).

A boy who suffers not at the hands of his teacher suffers at the hands of Time.
—Saadi, *Bustan (Fruit Garden)*, vii, Apologue 16 (1257).

Better expel one annoying pupil than ruin a whole class.   —*Sefer Hasidim (Book of the Righteous)*, no.184 (13th cent.).

I must whip my children for going into bad company instead of railing at bad company for ensnaring my children.
—Richard Steele, *The Tatler*, Oct. 4, 1709.

A good teacher is firm and active. It is important not to confuse firmness with punishment. The two are by no means identical.   —Percival M. Symonds, "Classroom Discipline," *Teachers College Record*, Dec. 1949.

Discovery

I have heard a student censured for working out his own idea before learning all that the others had done on the subject. But he was right; one may know too much, especially at first. The time for exhaustive reading is when you have worked out your own ideas with some fulness and in a spirit of discovery.
—Charles Horton Cooley, *Life and the Student* (1931).

Who learns by Finding Out has sevenfold The Skill of him who learned by Being Told.   —Arthur Guiterman, *A Poet's Proverbs*, 73 (1924).

That which we have not been forced to decipher, to clarify by our own personal effort, that which was made clear before, is not ours.   —Marcel Proust, *Remembrance of Things Past: The Sweet Cheat Gone* (1913–27).

I have come to feel that the only learning which significantly influences behavior is self-discovered, self-appropriated learning.   —Carl R. Rogers, *On Becoming a Person* (1961).

In my opinion, when once we have our understanding opened by the habit of reflection, it is always better to discover by our own exertions the things that might be found in books; it is the true secret of imprinting them on our brain, and appropriating them.
    —Jean Jacques Rousseau, *Julie*, I.xii (1761).

From the very beginning of his education the child should experience the joy of discovery.   —Alfred North Whitehead, *Dialogues*, as recorded by Lucien Price (1953).

You are also asking me questions and I hear you,
I answer that I cannot answer, you must find out for yourself.
    —Walt Whitman, *Leaves of Grass*, III: *Song of Myself*, sec.46 (1855).

Discretion

See also Judgment

An ounce of discretion is worth a pound of learning.   —Thomas Adams, *Sermons*, i.123 (1629).

There is a time to wink as well as to see.
—Thomas Fuller (1654–1734), *Gnomologia* (1732); also Benjamin Franklin, *Poor Richard's Almanack*, Mar. 1747.

Masters should be sometimes blind and sometimes deaf.   —Thomas Fuller, *ibid.*

The art of being wise is the art of knowing what to overlook. —William James, *The Principles of Psychology*, II.369 (1890).

A wise man sees as much as he ought, not as much as he can.
    —Michel de Montaigne, *Essays*, II.iii (1580): *A Custom of the Island of Cea*.

Be to her Virtues very kind,
Be to her Faults a little blind.
    —Matthew Prior, *An English Padlock* (1705).

It is not well to see everything, nor to hear everything.   —Seneca, *On Anger*, III.ii.1 (c. A.D. 55).

Discussion

Discussion, *n.* A method of confirming others in their errors. — Ambrose Bierce, *The Devil's Dictionary* (1911).

Teachers at all levels encourage the idea that you have to talk about things in order to understand them, because they wouldn't have jobs otherwise. But it's phony, you know.   — Denise Levertov, *The Craft of Poetry*, ed. William Packard (1974).

Men are never so likely to settle a question rightly as when they discuss it freely.
    —Thomas Babington Macaulay, "Southey's 'Colloquies of Society'," *Edinburgh Review*, Jan. 1830.

It is good to rub and polish our brain against that of others.
    —Michel de Montaigne, *Essays*, I.xxiv (1580): *Various Outcomes of the Same Plan*.

Discussion in class, which means letting twenty young blockheads and two cocky neurotics discuss something that neither their teacher nor they know.
    —Vladimir Nabokov, *Pnin*, iii.10 (1957).

In one case out of a hundred a point is excessively discussed because it is obscure;

in the ninety-nine remaining it is obscure because excessively discussed.
—Edgar Allan Poe,
"The Rationale of Verse,"
The Pioneer, Mar. 1843.

And friendly free discussion calling forth
From the fair jewel Truth its latent ray.
—James Thomson,
Liberty, ii.220 (1736).

Disputation

See also Argument; Debate

A good cause need not be patroned by passion, but can sustain itself upon a temperate dispute. —Thomas Browne,
Religio Medici, I.v (1643).

The tree of knowledge blasted by dispute,
Produces sapless leaves instead of fruit.
—John Denham, *The Progress of Learning*, ln.43 (1668).

It is a fault we may remark in most disputes, that, as truth is the mean between the two opinions that are upheld, each disputant departs from it in proportion to the degree in which he possesses the spirit of contradiction.
—René Descartes,
The Principles of Philosophy,
preface (1644).

Persons of good Sense, I have since observ'd, seldom fall into it [disputation], except Lawyers, University Men, and Men of all Sorts that have been bred at Edinborough. —Benjamin Franklin,
Autobiography, 19 (1868).

A disagreement may be the shortest cut between two minds. —Kahlil Gibran,
Sand and Foam (1926).

Disputation is the sifter out of the truth.
—Stefano Guazzo,
Civil Conversation,
I.41 (1574).

Scholars dispute, and the case is still before the courts. —Horace,
Ars Poetica, ln.78 (20 B.C.).

I never saw an instance of one of two disputants convincing the other by argument. I have seen many, on their getting warm, becoming rude, & shooting one another. —Thomas Jefferson,
letter to his grandson Thomas
Jefferson Randolph, 1808.

If we must disagree, let's disagree without being disagreeable.
—Lyndon B. Johnson, at
California State Democratic
Convention, Aug. 1963.

Disagreement shakes us out of our slumbers and forces us to see our own point of view through contrast with another person who does not share it.
—R.D. Laing,
The Politics of Experience (1967).

It were endless to dispute upon every thing that is disputable.
—William Penn, *Some Fruits of Solitude*, I. no.184 (1693).

O, there has been much throwing about of brains. —William Shakespeare,
Hamlet, II.ii.361 (1600–01).

When a thing is said to be not worth refuting you may be sure that either it is flagrantly stupid—in which case all comment is superfluous—or it is something formidable, the very crux of the problem.
—Miguel de Unamuno,
The Tragic Sense of Life, v (1912).

Dissent

See also Heresy; Nonconformity

We owe almost all our knowledge, not to those who have agreed, but to those who have differed. —Charles Caleb Colton,
Lacon, 379 (1820–22).

Assent—and you are sane—
Demur—you're straightway dangerous—
And handled with a Chain.
                    —Emily Dickinson,
Complete Poems, no.435 (c.1862),
ed. Thomas H. Johnson (1960).

Every scratch in the hand is not a stab to
the heart; nor doth every false opinion
make a Heretick.   —Thomas Fuller,
(1608–1661), The Holy State and the
Profane State: The Heretick (1642).

The dissenting opinions of one generation become the prevailing interpretation
of the next.   —Burton J. Hendrick,
Bulwark of the Republic (1937).

If a man is in a minority of one we lock
him up. —Oliver Wendell Holmes, Jr.,
speech in New York, Feb. 15, 1913.

Those who begin coercive elimination of
dissent soon find themselves exter-
minating dissenters. Compulsory unifica-
tion of opinion achieves only the
unanimity of the graveyard.
                    —Robert H. Jackson,
U.S. Supreme Court decision,
West Virginia State Board of
Education v Barnette, 1943. This decision
overturned the flag salute opinion in
the Gobitis case.

Mere unorthodoxy or dissent from the
prevailing mores is not to be condemned.
The absence of such voices would be a
symptom of grave illness in our society.
                    —Earl Warren,
U.S. Supreme Court opinion,
Sweezy v New Hampshire, 1957.

Dissenter

See also Nonconformity; Radical

The dissenter is every human being at
those moments of his life when he resigns
momentarily from the herd and thinks
for himself.   —Archibald Macleish,
"In Praise of Dissent," New York
Times Book Review, Dec. 16, 1956.

The liberation of the human mind has
been best furthered by gay fellows who
heaved dead cats into sanctuaries and
then went roistering down the highways
of the world, proving to all men that
doubt, after all was safe—that the god in
the sanctuary was a fraud. One horse-
laugh is worth ten thousand syllogisms.
                    —H.L. Mencken,
The American Mercury, Jan. 1924.

In this century it seems to me that we
need not just "well-adjusted," "well-
balanced" personalities, not just better
groupers and conformers ... but more
idiosyncratic, unpredicatable characters
(that rugged frontier word, "ornery," occurs to me); people who take open eyes
and open minds out with them into the
society they will share and help to
transform.   —Adlai E. Stevenson,
Smith College commencement address,
                    June 6, 1955.

Diversity

See also Individuality; Opinion,
Difference of

Tolerance of diversity is imperative,
because without it, life would lose its
savor. Progress in the arts, in the sciences,
in the patterns of social adjustments
springs from diversity and depends upon
a tolerance of individual deviations from
conventional ways and attitudes.
                    —Alan Barth,
The Loyalty of Free Men (1951).

If tolerance of diversity involves an admitted element or risk to national unity,
intolerance involves a certainty that unity
will be destroyed.   —Alan Barth, ibid.

Diversity of opinion within the
framework of loyalty to our free society is
not only basic to a university but to the
entire nation.   —James Bryant Conant,
Education in a Divided World (1948).

Differences are likely to lead to ... the
world's advancement, and add to the

charms of social intercourse. Nothing leads to boredom more than uniformity of manners and thoughts.
—Joseph Jacobs,
Jewish Contributions to Civilization,
53 (1919).

Is uniformity of opinion desirable? No more than that of face and stature.
—Thomas Jefferson,
Notes on the State of Virginia (1782).

Counting no blessing, but a flaw
That Difference is the mortal law.
—Phyllis McGinley,
"In Praise of Diversity,"
The American Scholar, 1954.

Letting a hundred flowers blossom and a hundred schools of thought contend is the policy.   —Mao Tse-tung,
On the Correct Handling of Contradictions Among the People,
Feb. 27, 1957.

There never were, in the world, two opinions alike, no more than two hairs, or two grains; the most universal quality is diversity.   —Michel de Montaigne,
Essays, II.xxxvii (1580):
Of the Resemblance of Children to Their Fathers.

If all pulled in one direction, the world would keel over.   —Yiddish proverb.

Doctrine

See also Belief; Dogma

Any doctrine that will not bear investigation is not a fit tenant for the mind of an honest man.   —Robert G. Ingersoll,
Complete Lectures: Intellectual Development (1886?).

What yesterday was fact, today is doctrine.   —Junius (pseudonym of anonymous author, believed to have been, among others, Sir Philip Francis, Lord Shelburne, Lord George Sackville, or Lord Temple), *The Letters of Junius: Dedication to the English Nation* (1769).

Dogma

See also Belief; Conviction;
Doctrine; Opinion

Man can be defined as an animal that makes dogmas.   —G.K. Chesterton,
Heretics, xx (1905).

The modern world is filled with men who hold dogmas so strongly that they do not even know that they are dogmas.
—G.K. Chesterton, *ibid.*

Men still want the crutch of dogma, of beliefs fixed by authority, to relieve them of the trouble of thinking and responsibility of directing their activity by thought.   —John Dewey,
Democracy and Education, xxv (1916).

The mind petrifies if a circle be drawn around it, and it can hardly be denied that dogma draws a circle round the mind.   —George Moore,
Confessions of a Young Man, xii (1888).

Dogmatism

See also Closemindedness;
Rigidity

It is in the uncompromisingness with which dogma is held and not in the dogma or want of dogma that the danger lies.   —Samuel Butler (1835–1902),
The Way of All Flesh, lxviii (1903).

Men possessed with an idea cannot be reasoned with. —James Anthony Froude,
Short Studies on Great Subjects
(1867–82): *Colonies*.

No man should dogmatize except on the subject of theology. Here he can take his stand, and by throwing the burden of proof on the opposition he is invincible. We have to die to find out whether he is right.   —Elbert Hubbard,
Note Book (1927).

Dogmatism is puppyism come to its full growth.   — Douglas Jerrold, *A Man Made of Money* (1849).

It is gross ignorance that produces the dogmatic spirit. The man who knows next to nothing is always eager to teach what he has just learned; the man who knows a lot scarcely believes that what he is saying can be unknown to others, and in consequence he speaks with diffidence.
— Jean de La Bruyère, *Les Caractères*, v (1688).

Doubt

See also Questioning; Skepticism

Who never doubted, never half believed. Where doubt, there truth is—'tis her shadow.   — Philip James Bailey, *Festus: A Country Town* (1839).

He who shall teach the Child to Doubt The rotting Grave shall ne'er get out.
— William Blake, *Augeries of Innocence*, ln.87 (c.1802).

Who knows most, doubts most.
— Robert Browning, *The Two Poets of Croisic*, clviii (1878).

Doubt begins only at the last frontiers of what is possible.
— Giovanni Jacopo Casanova, *Memoirs* (1826–38).

Never be afraid to doubt, if only you have the disposition to believe, and doubt in order that you may end in believing the truth.
— Samuel Taylor Coleridge, *Aids to Reflection* (1825).

Doubt is the vestibule which all must pass, before they can enter into the temple of truth.   — Charles Caleb Colton, *Lacon* (1820–22).

People who dislike doubt often get into worse trouble by committing themselves to an immature and untenable decision.
— Charles Horton Cooley, *Life and the Student* (1931).

If you would be a real seeker after truth, it is necessary that at least once in your life you doubt, as far as possible, all things.   — René Descartes, *Principles of Philosophy*, I (1644).

Freedom of speech and freedom of action are meaningless without freedom to think. And there is no freedom of thought without doubt.— Bergen Evans, *The Natural History of Nonsense*, xix (1946).

We do not know, nor can we know, with absolute certainty that those who disagree with us are wrong. We are human and therefore fallible, and being fallible, we cannot escape the *element of doubt* as to our own opinions and convictions.
— J. William Fulbright, address in Washington, D.C., Dec. 5, 1963.

With great doubts comes great understanding; with little doubts comes little understanding.   — H.H. Hart, *Seven Hundred Chinese Proverbs*, no.693 (1937).

To have doubted one's own first principles is the mark of a civilized man.
— Oliver Wendell Holmes, Jr., *Collected Legal Papers* (1920). Also in *The Mind and Faith of Justice Holmes*, ed. Max Lerner (1943).

Doubt is the beginning, not the end, of wisdom.   — George Iles, *Jottings* (1918).

Doubt everything at least once— even the proposition that two and two are four.
— Georg Christoph Lichtenberg, *Reflections* (1799).

An honest man can never surrender an honest doubt.   — Walter Malone, *The Agnostic's Creed* (1886).

But modest doubt is call'd
The beacon of the wise, the tent that
  searches
To th' bottom of the worst.
                    —William Shakespeare,
    Troilus and Cressida, II.ii.15 (1602)
    [tent = *swab for probing wounds*].

Learning learns but one lesson: doubt!
                    —George Bernard Shaw,
    The Admirable Bashville, I (1901).

The doubt of an earnest, thoughtful, patient and laborious mind is worthy of
respect. In such doubt there may be
found indeed more faith than in half the
creeds.   —John Lancaster Spalding,
    Means and Ends of Education (1895).

To believe with certainty we must begin
with doubting.   —Stanislas I,
King of Poland, *Oeuvres du Philosophe
                    Bienfaisant* (1767).

From the womb of doubt is born truth.
                    —Joshua Steinberg,
    Mishlé Yehoshua, 20.1 (1885).

For nothing worthy proving can be
  proven,
Nor yet disproven. Wherefore thou be
  wise,
Cleave ever to the sunnier side of doubt.
                    —Alfred, Lord Tennyson,
    The Ancient Sage, ln.66 (1885).

There lives more faith in honest doubt,
Believe me, than in half the creeds.
                    —Alfred, Lord Tennyson,
    In Memorium, xcvi.11 (1850).

The slow-consenting Academic doubt.
                    —James Thomson,
    Liberty, ii.240 (1736).

Dress

See also Appearance

Know, first, who you are; and then adorn
yourself accordingly.   —Epictetus,
    Discourses, III.i (c. A.D. 100).

[It is proposed] that they [students] have
peculiar Habits to distinguish them from
other Youth, if the Academy be in or
near the Town; for this, among other
Reasons, that their Behaviour may be
observed.   —Benjamin Franklin,
    *Proposals Relating to the Education
    of Youth in Pensilvania* (1751).

Wear not thy clothes foul, unsewed, dus-
ty, nor old; look that they be brushed
commonly once a day; take heed where
thou sittest or kneelest, and whom thou
approachest, for fear that there be dust or
some uncleanness.   —Francis Hawkins,
    Youth's Behaviour, iv (1663).

Dress does not give knowledge.
                    —Tómas de Iriarte,
    Literary Fables, xxvii (1782).

A man cannot dress, but his ideas get
clothed at the same time.
                    —Laurence Sterne,
    Tristram Shandy, IX.xiii (1767).

Dullness

See also Boredom

I find we are growing serious, and then
we are in great Danger of being dull.
                    —William Congreve,
    The Old Bachelor, II.ii.43 (1693).

For it is not learning that is dull. It is only
learned men who sometimes make it
so.... For it is salutary to remember ...
that the dullest, most utterly benumbing
teachers may be, and sometimes are, the
most erudite.   —John Livingston Lowes,
    "Teaching and the Spirit of Research,"
    The American Scholar, 1933.

It is the dull man who is always sure, and
the sure man who is always dull.
                    —H.L. Mencken,
    Prejudices, Second Series, i.101 (1920).

Nothing fatigues like dullness: from the weariness it begets there is no escape.
—John Lancaster Spalding,
Opportunity and Other Essays and Addresses (1900).

Economics

Once demystified, the dismal science is nothing less than the study of power.
—Richard J. Barnet,
New York Times, Sept. 16, 1973.

I have been gradually coming under the conviction, disturbing for a professional theorist, that there is no such thing as economics.   —Kenneth E. Boulding,
in Leonard Silk, *The Economists* (1976).

What we might call, by way of Eminence, the Dismal Science.   —Thomas Carlyle,
"The Nigger Question,"
Fraser's Magazine, Dec. 1849.

The Science of Political Economy *is* a Lie,—wholly and to the very root (as hitherto taught). It is also the damnedest, that is to say, the most Utterly and to the Lowest Pit condemned of God and His Angels, that the Devil, or Betrayer of Men, has yet invented, except his (the Devil's) theory of Sanctification.
—John Ruskin,
letter to John Brown, 1862.

Editing

See also Writing

You must make frequent use of the eraser if you want to write something that deserves a second reading.   —Horace,
Satires, I.x.72 (c.35 B.C.).

My son! If thou writest aught, read it through a second time, for no man can avoid slips. Let not any consideration of hurry prevent thee from revising a short epistle. Be punctillious as to grammatical accuracy, in conjugations and genders, for the constant use of the vernacular

sometimes leads to error in this regard.
—Judah Ibn Tibbon,
Ethical Will (c.1190).

I can't write five words but that I change seven.   —Dorothy Parker,
in Malcolm Cowley, ed.,
Writers at Work (1957).

There can be no doubt that the best method of correction is to put aside what we have written for a certain time, so that when we return to it after an interval it will have the air of novelty.
—Quintilian, *De Institutio Oratoria*,
X.iv.2 (A.D. 95 or 96).

I conscientiously tried [rewriting], but found that my first draft was almost always better than my second. This discovery has saved me an immense amount of time. I do not, of course, apply it to the substance, but only to the form.   —Bertrand Russell,
Portraits from Memory: How I Write (1965).

Editing is the most companionable form of education.   —Edward Weeks,
In Friendly Candor (1959).

Educated Person

See also Cultured Person;
Learned Person

No man can be well educated who has not in his intellect the color, and the inspiration, and the warmth, that the statements and emotions give.
—Henry Ward Beecher,
Proverbs from Plymouth Pulpit: The Human Mind (1887).

Respect for the fragility and importance of an individual life is still the first mark of the educated man.
—Norman Cousins,
Saturday Review, 1954.

I've over-educated myself in all the things I shouldn't have known at all.
— Noel Coward,
Collected Sketches and Lyrics
(1931): *Mild Oats.*

The educated man knows how to work, is good to work with, and is equipped not only for work but also for leisure.
— Albert Augustus David,
"Speech Day" Address, 1935.

You must not trust the multitude who say, "Only the free may be educated," but rather the philosophers who say, "Only the educated are free."
— Epictetus, *Discourses*,
II.i (c. A.D. 100).

There are a lot of completely educated people in the world and of course they will resent being asked to learn anything new.   — Robert Frost,
letter to Sidney Cox, Dec., 1914,
in Lawrance Thompson, ed., *Selected Letters of Robert Frost*, 141 (1964).

To be able to be caught up into the world of thought—that is educated.
— Edith Hamilton,
Saturday Evening Post, Sept. 27, 1958.

Why do most Americans look up to education and look down upon educated people? (Our national schizophrenia.)
— Sydney Harris, syndicated column,
Detroit Free Press, Apr. 2, 1981.

The enlightened man, is a man in his maturity, in his perfection, who is capable of pursuing his own happiness; because he has learned to examine, to think for himself, and not to take that for truth upon the authority of others, which experience has taught him examination will frequently prove erroneous.
— Paul Henry d'Holbach,
The System of Nature (1770).

An educated man is one with a universal sympathy for everything and a certain amount of Knowledge about everything that is known, and who still is on the line of evolution and is learning to the end.   — Elbert Hubbard,
Note Book, 31 (1927).

My definition of an educated man is the fellow who knows the right thing to do at the time it has to be done.... You can be sincere and still be stupid.
— Charles F. Kettering, in T.A. Boyd,
The Professional Amateur (1957).

An educated man is not necessarily a learned man or a university man, but a man with certain spiritual qualities which make him calm in adversity; happy when alone, just in his dealings, rational and sane in all the affairs of life.
— Ramsay MacDonald,
address in London, 1931.

It is a woeful mistake to suppose that the educated are kinder or more tolerant: education creates vested interests, and renders the beneficiaries acutely jealous and very vocal.   — Lewis Bernstein
Namier, *Conflicts*, 141 (1943).

We don't talk fancy grammar and eat anchovy toast. But to live under the kitchen doesn't say we aren't educated.
— Mary Norton,
The Borrowers, v (1965).

A person of bourgeois origin goes through life with some expectation of getting what he wants, within reasonable limits. Hence, the fact that in times of stress "educated" people tend to come to the front.   — George Orwell,
The Road to Wigan Pier, iii (1937).

No man is born a Master of Arts.
— Samuel Palmer,
Moral Essays on Proverbs, 285 (1710).

There is nothing as stupid as an educated man if you get off the thing that he was educated in.   — Will Rogers,
Autobiography, xvi (1926).

Those who have been taught the most know least.   — George Bernard Shaw,
Parents and Children,
preface to *Misalliance* (1914).

I'm sorry; I've never met one.
— George Bernard Shaw, when asked
for his definition of an educated man,
Ladies Home Journal, July, 1948.

I am not an educational theorist but I
think I know what an educated man looks
like. He is thoroughly inoculated against
humbug, thinks for himself and tries to
give his thoughts, in speech or on paper,
some style.   — Alan Simpson,
on becoming president of Vassar College,
Newsweek, July 1, 1963.

Education

See also below; Aim of Education; Instruction; Learning;
Schooling; Sex Education; University Education

Education is a companion which no
misfortune can depress, no crime can
destroy, no enemy can alienate, no
despotism can enslave. At home a friend,
abroad an introduction, in solitude a
solace, and in society an ornament. It
chastens vice, it guides virtue, it gives, at
once, grace and government to genius.
Without it, what is man? A splendid
slave, a reasoning savage.
              — Joseph Addison,
        The Spectator (1711–12).

Education is the result of contact. A great
people is produced by contact with great
minds.   — Calvin Coolidge,
  speech at Evanston, Ill., Jan. 21, 1923.

Anyone who has passed through the
regular gradations of a classical education, and is not made a fool by it, may
consider himself as having had a very narrow escape.   — William Hazlitt,
    *Table-Talk: On the Ignorance of
        the Learned* (1821–22).

When we talk of our political goals, we
admit the right of every man to be a
ruler. When we talk of our educational
program, we see no inconsistency in saying that only a few have the capacity to

get the education that rulers ought to
have.   — Robert M. Hutchins,
        *The Conflict in Education in a
        Democratic Society* (1953).

Any education that aims at completeness
must be at once theoretical and practical,
intellectual and moral.— Aldous Huxley,
    Words and Their Meanings (1940).

The greatest danger of traditional education is that learning may remain purely
verbal. Words are learned and placed in
dead storage in one part of the mind
while life is lived unilluminated and
unguided by this learning. Such a danger
is inherent in the very nature of
education.   — Mirra Komarovsky.
Women in the Modern World, vii (1953).

Education, at best, is ecstatic.
              — George B. Leonard,
        Education and Ecstasy, 16 (1968).

But this experiment [education] has
never yet been tried. Education has never
yet been brought to bear with one-
hundredth part of its potential force
upon the nature of children, and through
them upon the character of men and of
the race.   — Horace Mann,
        *Twelfth Annual Report of the
Massachusetts Board of Education*, 1848.

And your education! Is not that also
social, and determined by the social conditions under which you educate; by the
intervention, direct or indirect, of society
by means of the schools, etc.?
        — Karl Marx and Friedrich Engels,
        The Communist Manifesto (1848).

In large states public education will
always be mediocre, for the same reason
that in large kitchens the cooking is
usually bad.   — Friedrich Nietzsche,
        Human, All Too Human, I (1878).

My own belief is that education must be
subversive if it is to be meaningful. By
this I mean that it must challenge all the
things we take for granted, examine all
accepted assumptions, tamper with every

sacred cow, and instill a desire to question and doubt.   — Bertrand Russell, letter to "Mr. Sandbach and Friends," Mar. 18, 1962.

Almost all education has a political motive: it aims at strengthening some group, national or religious or even social, in the competition with other groups.   — Bertrand Russell, *Principles of Social Reconstruction: Education* (1916).

The perverted purposes to which education was put by totalitarian states has shattered out simple illusions about the essential goodness of education.
        — James H. Ryan, *Moral Values in American Education* (1947).

Education is not confined to children: in fact liberal education is mostly adult education, and goes on all through life in people who have active minds instead of second hand mental habits.
        — George Bernard Shaw, *Everybody's Political What's What?*, ix (1944).

One of the ultimate advantages of an education is simply coming to the end of it.   — B.F. Skinner, *The Technology of Teaching* (1968).

The people are in general inadequately educated and have little experience in philosophical and political reasoning, and so it is possible to misinform, divert, and delude them. But not forever and not about everything. They learn.
        — Bernard Smith, ed., *The Democratic Spirit*, introd. (1941).

It is scarcely possible to prevent great men from rising up under any system of education.   — Sydney Smith, *Classical Learning* (1809).

I am beginning to suspect all elaborate and special systems of education. They seem to me to be built upon the supposition that every child is a kind of idiot who

must be taught to think. Whereas, if the child is left to himself, he will think more and better.   — Anne Sullivan, letter of May 8, 1887, in Helen Keller, *The Story of My Life* (1903).

Education should be as gradual as the moonrise, perceptible not in progress but in result.— George John Whyte-Melville, *Riding Recollections* (1878).

Education has really one basic factor, a *sine qua non* — one must want it.
        — George Edward Woodberry (1855–1930), *John Goffer's Mill*.

Education, Acquisition of

I believe that the only true education comes through the stimulation of the child's powers by the demands of the social situations in which he finds himself.   — John Dewey, "My Pedagogic Creed," *The School Journal*, Jan. 16, 1897.

Abraham Flexner once remarked to me that getting education is like getting measles; you have to go where measles is. If you go where it is, unless you are by nature immune, you will get it — no need to worry about that — but if you don't go where it is, you will never get it.
        — Albert Jay Nock, *Memoirs of a Superfluous Man* (1943).

Education, Childhood

The easiest way of becoming acquainted with the modes of thinking, the rules of conduct, and the prevailing manners of any people, is to examine what sort of education they give their children; how they treat them at home, and what they are taught in their places of public worship.   — Michel de Crèvecoeur, *Letters from an American Farmer* (1782).

In my judgment there is no outward offense that in the sight of God so heavily burdens the world, and deserves such heavy chastisement, as the neglect to educate children.   — Martin Luther, *Letter to the Mayors and Aldermen* (1524), tr. F.V. Painter (1928).

Whilst that the childe is young, let him be instructed in vertue and lytterature. —John Lyly, *Euphues, the Anatomy of Wit: Of the Education of Youth* (1579).

The greatness of the human personality begins at the hour of birth. From this almost mystic affirmation there comes what may seem a strange conclusion: that education must start from birth.
— Maria Montessori, *The Absorbent Mind* (1967).

The beginning is the most important part of any work, especially in the case of a young and tender thing; for that is the time at which character is being formed and the desired impression is more readily taken.   — Plato, *Republic*, II (c.375–368 B.C.).

Above all things we must take care that the child, who is not yet old enough to love his studies, does not come to hate them and dread the bitterness which he once tasted, even when the years of infancy are left behind. His studies must be made an amusement.   — Quintilian, *Institutio Oratoria*, I.i.20 (A.D. 95 or 96).

The earliest education is most important and it undoubtedly is woman's work. If the author of nature had meant to assign it to men he would have given them milk to feed the child.   — Jean Jacques Rousseau, *Émile*, I, footnote (1762).

Education, like neurosis, begins at home.
— Milton R. Sapirstein, *Paradoxes of Everyday Life*, ii (1955).

Education, Compulsory

Material comforts should precede mental culture. I am inclined to think that we

have been precipitate in adopting universal compulsory education. It is however a step in the right direction—and it is impossible to recede now. I am therefore in support of any and every measure which tends to completing a somewhat dangerous experiment.   —Winston Churchill, 1897, in Randolph S. Churchill, *Winston S. Churchill*, I.326 (1966).

One academic phrase that has always fascinated me with its monumental inaccuracy is compulsory education. There is no such thing, and there never has been. You cannot have compulsory education—the most you can have is compulsory attendance. The body may be clamped into a seat, but there is no way of forcing the mind into gear.
— Sydney Harris, syndicated column, *Detroit Free Press*, Apr. 13, 1983.

If there is anything we want in this State, it is some measure to compel the attendance of children between the ages of six and sixteen at some school. If it is left to parents, I believe the great majority will lock up their children at home.
— Reuben G. Holmes, debate in the Constitutional Convention of South Carolina, 1868.

It was in making education not only common to all, but in some sense compulsory on all, that the destiny of the free republics of America was practically settled.   —James Russell Lowell, *Among My Books: New England Two Centuries Ago* (1870).

The state has a right to insist that its citizens shall be educated.
— *Pastoral Letter of the American Roman Catholic Hierarchy*, Feb. 1920.

The children shall come not only if their parents please, but if they do not please; there shall be compulsory education ... of all and sundry, as far as this is possible; and the pupils shall be regarded as belonging to the state rather than their parents.   — Plato, *Laws*, VII.804 (c.367–347 B.C.).

Education, Criticism of

Education tends to be diagrammatic and categorical, opening up no sluices in the human imagination on the wonder or beauty of their unique estate in the cosmos. Little wonder that it becomes so easy for our young to regard human hurt casually or to be uninspired by the magic of sensitivity.   —Norman Cousins, *Saturday Review*, 1965.

The main failure of education is that it has not prepared people to comprehend matters concerning human destiny.
—Norman Cousins, *ibid.*, 1975.

The sure foundations of the state are laid in knowledge, not in ignorance. Every sneer at education, at culture, at book learning—which is the recorded wisdom of the experience of mankind—is the demogogue's sneer at intelligent liberty, inviting national degeneracy and ruin.
—George William Curtis, in *Labor*, Aug. 14, 1954.

In alluding just now to our systems of education, I spoke of the deadness of its details.... It is a system of despair.
—Ralph Waldo Emerson, *Essays, Second Series: New England Reformers* (1844).

I am entirely certain that twenty years from now we will look back at education as it is practiced in most schools today and wonder that we could have tolerated anything so primitive.
—John W. Gardner, *No Easy Victories*, ed. Helen Rowan (1968).

We are not asking our children to do their own best but to be *the* best. Education is in danger of becoming a religion based on fear; its doctrine is to compete. The majority of our children are being led to believe that they are doomed to failure in a world which has room only for those at the top.   —Eda J. LeShan, *The Conspiracy Against Childhood*, v (1967).

Education is fatal to any one with a spark of artistic feeling. Education should be confined to clerks, and even them it drives to drink. Will the world learn that we never learn anything that we did not know before?   —George Moore, *Confessions of a Young Man*, vii (1888).

When we look at the troubled state of the present world ... one thing becomes manifest. This is the failure of recent educational practice to prepare men in terms of heart and will to prevent the strife, misunderstanding, and willfulness that now arises.   Nathan M. Pusey, *Religion and Freedom of Thought* (1954).

One of the reasons, perhaps the major reason, why education has made so little progress in comparison with other cultural endeavors over the last thousand years is that much of it has been, and still is, aloof from practical, or even intelligent, purpose.—Dagobert D. Runes, *Letters to My Teacher* (1961).

We are faced with the paradoxical fact that education has become one of the chief obstacles to intelligence and freedom of thought. —Bertrand Russell, *Sceptical Essays* (1928).

Always we need more knowledge; and this means controversial instead of dogmatic education. The schools teach only one side of their subjects; and until their graduates know both sides they had better know nothing.
—George Bernard Shaw, *Everybody's Political What's What?*, xxiv (1944).

Education, Definition and Description of

What sculpture is to a block of marble, education is to an human soul.
—Joseph Addison, *The Spectator*, no.215, Nov. 6, 1711.

Education is to get where you can start to learn. —George Aiken, in *New York Times*, Jan. 29, 1967.

To a sensible man education is like a golden ornament, and like a bracelet on the right arm.   —*Apocrypha: Ecclesiasticus* 21:21 (c.180 B.C.).

[Education] is where we decide whether we love our children enough not to expel them from our world and leave them to their own devices, nor to strike from their hands their chance of undertaking something new, something unforseen by us, but to prepare them in advance for the task of renewing a common world.
          —Hannah Arendt,
Between Past and Present, 196 (1961).

Education. From the Latin *educatio*, originally the process of nourishing or physically rearing a child or young animal. (There at one time being a distinction between a child and a young animal.)   —Richard Armour,
A Diabolical Dictionary of Education
(1969).

Education, *n*. That which discloses to the wise and disguises from the foolish their lack of understanding. — Ambrose Bierce, *The Devil's Dictionary* (1911).

The process of education is a refinement upon nature made by human nature.
          —George Boas, "The Century of the Child," *The American Scholar*, 1938.

Education is learning what you didn't know you didn't know.
          —Daniel J. Boorstin,
Democracy and Its Discontents (1974).

Education is a sieve as well as a lift.
          — Sid Chaplin,
The Day of the Sardine, ii (1961).

It is hard to get far enough away from the canvas to take any general view of such a subject as education. Education means everything.   —John Jay Chapman,
Memories and Milestones (1915).

We thus reach a technical definition of education: It is that reconstruction or reorganization of experience which adds to the meaning of experience, and which increases the ability to direct the course of subsequent experience.   —John Dewey,
Democracy and Education, vi (1916).

We state emphatically that, *upon its intelectual side education consists in the formation of wide-awake, careful, thorough habits of thinking*.
          —John Dewey, *How We Think*, v.ii: *Education in Relation to Form* (1933).

I believe that education ... is a process of living and not a preparation for future living.   —John Dewey,
"My Pedagogic Creed,"
The School Journal, Jan. 16, 1897.

I believe that education must be conceived as a continuing reconstruction of experience; that the process and the goal of education are one and the same thing.
          —John Dewey, *ibid*.

What then is education when we find actual satisfactory specimens of it in existence? In the first place, it is a process of development, of growth. And it is the *process* and not merely the result that is important.   —John Dewey,
"The Need for a Philosophy of Education," *The New Era in Home
and School*, Nov. 1934.

Education is a state-controlled manufactory of echoes.   —Norman Douglas,
How About Europe? (1930).

All education is a continuous dialogue— questions and answers that pursue every problem to the horizon. That is the essence of academic freedom.
          —William O. Douglas,
Wisdom, Oct. 1956.

Education is that which remains, if one has forgotten everything he learned in school.   — Albert Einstein,
Out of My Later Years, ix:
On Education (1950).

Education is just this—learning to frame one's will in accord with events.
— Epictetus, *Discourses*, I.xii (c. A.D. 100).

In what then does education consist? In learning to apply the natural primary conceptions to particular occasions in accordance with nature, and further to distinguish between things in our power and things not in our power.
— Epictetus, *ibid.*, I.xxii.

Education is the process of driving a set of prejudices down your throat.
— Martin H. Fischer, *Fischerisms* (1937).

Without ideals, without effort, without scholarship, without philosophical continuity, there is no such thing as education.   — Abraham Flexner, *Universities*, 97 (1930).

Education consists in leading man, as a thinking, intelligent being, growing into self-consciousness to a pure and unsullied conscious and free representation of the inner law of Divine Unity, and in teaching him ways and means thereto.
— Friedrich Froebel, *The Education of Man* (1826).

Education is the ability to listen to almost anything without losing your temper or your self-confidence.   — Robert Frost, in *Reader's Digest*, Apr. 1960.

Education is the art of making men ethical.   — Georg W.F. Hegel, *The Philosophy of Right*, Additions, par.151 (1821).

Academic education is the act of memorizing things read in books, and things told by college professors who got their education mostly by memorizing things read in books. — Elbert Hubbard, *Note Book*, 160 (1927).

Education is what you learn in books, and nobody knows you know it but your teacher.   — Virginia Cary Hudson, *O Ye Jigs and Juleps* (1962), written when she was 10 years of age.

Education is a kind of continuing dialogue, and a dialogue assumes, in the nature of the case, different points of view.   — Robert M. Hutchins, testimony before House of Representatives committee, 1952.

Education is the instruction of the intellect in the laws of Nature, under which name I include not merely things and their forces, but men and their ways; and the fashioning of the affections and the will into an earnest and loving desire to move in harmony with these laws.
— T.H. Huxley, *Lay Sermons, Addresses, and Reviews: A Liberal Education* (1870).

Man is the only creature that needs to be educated. By education we understand *nurture* (attention, food), *discipline*, and *instruction* together with culture. Accordingly man is infant, child, and pupil.
— Immanuel Kant, *Pedagogy* (1803).

To learn is to change. Education is a process that changes the learner.
— George B. Leonard, *Education and Ecstasy*, 7 (1968).

By education, I do not mean a mere capacity to read, write, and cipher; but some faithful training of the power of thought, some generous unfolding of the whole spiritual being, which shall lay a foundation for a vigorous and noble manhood.   — Horace Mann, "An Appeal to the Citizens of Massachusetts, in Behalf of their Public Schools," *The Common School Journal*, Feb. 1840.

I call therefore a compleate and generous Education that which fits a man to perform justly, skilfully and magnanimously all the offices both private and publike of peace and war.   —John Milton, *Of Education: To Master Samuel Hartlib* (1644).

And so we discovered that education is not something which the teacher does, but that it is a natural process which develops spontaneously in the human being.   —Maria Montessori, *The Absorbent Mind* (1967).

That's what education means—to be able to do what you've never done before.
          —George Herbert Palmer, *Life of Alice Freeman Palmer* (1908). Exclamation of the Palmers' cook when Mrs. Palmer baked a loaf of bread, without previous experience.

Education is nothing more than the polishing of each single link in the great chain that binds humanity together and gives it unity.   —Johann Pestalozzi (1746–1827), *The Education of Man: Aphorisms* (tr.1951).

I mean by education that training which is given by suitable habits to the first instincts of virtue in children;—when pleasure, and friendship, and pain, and hatred, are rightly implanted in souls not yet capable of understanding the nature of them, and who find them, after they have attained reason, to be in harmony with her.   —Plato, *Laws*, II.653 (c.367–347 B.C.).

The particular training in respect to pleasure and pain, which leads you always to hate what you ought to hate, and love what you ought to love from the beginning of life to the end, ... will be rightly called education. —Plato, *ibid*.

Education, properly understood, is that which teaches discernment.
          —Joseph Roux, *Meditations of a Parish Priest*, vii.7 (1886).

Always and everywhere organized education is a form of practical endeavor—a

form of social action. It is a program, deliberately conceived by some society or group, to achieve certain purposes.
          —Harold Rugg, ed., *Readings in the Foundations of Education* (1941).

Education is the leading of human souls to what is best, and making what is best out of them; and these two objects are always attainable together, and by the same means. The training which makes men happiest in themselves also makes them more serviceable to others.
          —John Ruskin, *The Stones of Venice*, iii (1851).

And what is the education of mankind if not the passage from faith in authority to personal conviction, and to the sustained practice of the intellectual duty to consent to no idea except by virtue of its recognized truth, to accept no fact until its reality has been, in one way or another, established.— Auguste Sabatier, *Religions of Authority and the Religions of the Spirit* (1903).

Education is what survives when what has been learnt has been forgotten.
          —B.F. Skinner, "Education in 1984," *New Scientist*, May 21, 1964.

Education is a private matter between the person and the world of knowledge and experience, and has little to do with school or college.   —Lillian Smith, "Bridges to Other People," *Redbook*, Sept. 1969.

To me education is a leading out of what is already there in the pupil's soul. To Miss Mackay it is a putting in of something that is not there, and that is not what I call education, I call it intrusion.   —Muriel Spark, *The Prime of Miss Jean Brodie*, ii (1961).

True goodness lies not in the negation of badness, but in the mastery of it. It is the miracle that turns the tumult of chaos into the dance of beauty. True education is that power of miracle, that ideal of creation.   — Rabindranath Tagore, *Letter to a Friend* (1928).

Education consists mainly in what we have unlearned.   — Mark Twain, *Notebook*, July 4, 1898 (1935).

Education is the acquisition of the art of the utilisation of knowledge.
     — Alfred North Whitehead, *The Aims of Education*, i (1929).

All practical teachers know that education is a patient process of the mastery of details, minute by minute, hour by hour, day by day. — Alfred North Whitehead, *Dialogues*, as recorded by Lucien Price (1953).

Education, Effect (Result) of

Education makes a greater difference between man and man, than nature has made between man and brute.
     — John Adams, letter to Abigail Adams, Oct. 29, 1776.

The roots of education are bitter, but the fruit is sweet.   — Aristotle, apothegm (before 322 B.C.).

Man can be set free from the yoke of his own nature only by education. It alone can make it possible for him to subordinate the impulses of his body to the guidance of his developing mind.
     — Mikhail A. Bakunin, *God and the State* (1882).

The test and the use of a man's education is that he finds pleasure in the exercise of his mind.   — Jacques Barzun, "Science vs. the Humanities: A Truce to the Nonsense on Both Sides," *Saturday Evening Post*, May 3, 1958.

A good education is not so much one which prepares a man to succeed in the world, as one which enables him to sustain failure.   — Bernard Iddings Bell, *Life*, Oct. 16, 1950.

I had a good education but it never went to my head, somehow. It should be a journey ending up with you at a different place. It didn't take with me. My degree was a kind of inoculation. I got just enough education to make me immune from it for the rest of my life.
     — Alan Bennett, *Getting On*, I (1972).

The grand result of schooling is a mind with just vision to discern, with free force to do: the grand schoolmaster is Practice.
     — Thomas Carlyle, *Corn-Law Rhymes* (1832).

Education makes the man.
     — James Cawthorn, *Birth and Education of Genius* (c.1750).

Give a man a fish, and you feed him for a day. Teach a man to fish, and you feed him for a lifetime.   — Chinese proverb.

By nature all men are alike, but by education widely different. — Chinese proverb.

How is it that little children are so intelligent and men so stupid? It must be education that does it.
     — Alexandre Dumas fils, in Léon Treich, *L'Esprit d'Alexandre Dumas* (1926).

One might say that the American trend of education is to reduce the senses almost to nil.   — Isadora Duncan, *My Life* (1926).

Education doesn't change life much. It just lifts trouble to a higher plane of regard.   — Robert Frost, *Quote*, July 9, 1961.

The end product of education, yours and mine and everybody's, is the total pattern of reactions and possible reactions we have inside ourselves. — S.I. Hayakawa, "How Words Change Our Lives," *Saturday Evening Post*, Dec. 27, 1958.

Education makes us what we are.
     — Claude Adrien Helvétius (1715–71), *Discours*, XXX.xxx.

We do not know what education can do for us, because we have never tried it.
— Robert M. Hutchins, *The Atomic Bomb versus Civilization* (1945).

Perhaps the most valuable result of all education is the ability to make yourself do the thing you have to do, when it ought to be done, whether you like it or not; it is the first lesson that ought to be learned; and however early a man's training begins, it is probably the last lesson he learns thoroughly.   — T.H. Huxley, *Technical Education* (1877).

I wonder whether if I had had an education I should have been more or less a fool than I am.   — Alice James, *Diary*, ed. Leon Edel (1964).

Although I do not, with some enthusiasts, believe that the human condition will ever advance to such a state of perfection as that there shall no longer be pain or vice in the world, yet I believe it susceptible of much improvement ... and that the diffusion of knowledge among the people is to be the instrument by which it is to be effected.   — Thomas Jefferson, letter to P.S. Dupont de Nemours, Apr. 24, 1816.

At the desk where I sit, I have learned one great truth. The answer for all our national problems — the answer for all the problems of the world — comes down to a single word. That word is "education."
— Lyndon B. Johnson, address to the bicentenary convocation at Brown University, Sept. 28, 1964.

Education is an art, the practice of which can become perfect only through many generations. Each generation, provided with the knowledge of the preceding one, can more and more bring about an education, which will develop man's natural gifts in due proportion and relation to their end, and thus advance the whole human race towards its destiny.
— Immanuel Kant, *Pedagogy* (1803).

Man can become man only by education. He is nothing but what education makes him. It is to be noted that man is educated only by men who themselves have been educated. — Immanuel Kant, *ibid.*

Simple as it seems, it was a great discovery that the key of knowledge could turn both ways, that it could open, as well as lock, the door of power to the many.   — James Russell Lowell, *Among My Books: New England Two Centuries Ago* (1870).

Education alone can conduct us to that enjoyment which is, at once, best in quality and infinite in quantity.
— Horace Mann, *Lectures and Reports on Education*, I (1840).

Education makes a man a more intelligent shoemaker, if that be his occupation, but not by teaching him how to make shoes; it does so by the mental exercise it gives, and the habits it impresses.   — John Stuart Mill, inaugural address as Rector of University of St. Andrews, Feb. 1, 1867.

A good education changes your judgment and conduct.
— Michel de Montaigne, *Essays*, II.xvii (1580): *Of Presumption*.

If you suffer your people to be ill educated, and their manners to be corrupted from their infancy, and then punish them for those crimes to which their first education disposed them, — you first make thieves, and then punish them.   — Thomas More, *Utopia*, 21 (1516).

Education makes a people easy to lead, but difficult to drive; easy to govern, but impossible to enslave.   — Henry Peter, Lord Brougham, speech in House of Commons. Jan. 29, 1828.

'Tis Education forms the common mind, Just as the Twig is bent, the Tree's inclin'd.   — Alexander Pope, *Moral Essays*, I.149 (1734).

The papers today say that illiteracy has decreased. The more that learn how to read the less learn how to make a living. That's one thing about a little education. It spoils you for actual work. The more you know the more you think somebody owes you a living.   —Will Rogers, *Autobiography*, xvi (1926).

Plants are fashioned by cultivation, man by education.   —Jean Jacques Rousseau, *Émile*, I (1762).

Education, which was at first made universal in order that all might be able to read and write, has been found capable of serving quite other purposes. By instilling nonsense it unifies populations and generates collective enthusiasm.   —Bertrand Russell, *Unpopular Essays: An Outline of Intellectual Rubbish* (1950).

What does education often do? It makes a straight-cut ditch of a free, meandering brook.   —Henry David Thoreau, *Journal*, Oct. 1850.

Education itself offers no ironclad guarantees against fascism, communism, or any other threat. We may hope that education will bolster the citizenry, and indeed, as the future unrolls we feel this will happen—but it will not happen strictly as cause and effect, nor will it happen if anyone relaxes and thinks that it will automatically occur.   —Ben J. Wattenberg and Richard M. Scammon, *This U.S.A.* (1965). [*Ibid.*, "Hitler's Germany was one of the best-educated nations in Europe, certainly in 1939 better-educated than the Poland it was preparing to butcher."]

Education, Financial Support of

See also Education,
Government Support of

There should be no economy in education. Money should never be weighed against the soul of a child. It should be poured out like water, for the child's intellectual and moral life.   —William Ellery Channing, (1780–1842), "Remarks on Education," *Christian Examiner*, Nov. 1833.

We now spend a good deal more on drink and smoke than we spend on education. This, of course, is not surprising. The urge to escape from selfhood and the environment is in almost everyone almost all the time. The urge to do something for the young is strong only in parents, and in them only for the few years during which their children go to school.   —Aldous Huxley, *The Doors of Perception* (1954).

Preach, my dear Sir, a crusade against ignorance; establish and improve the law for educating the common people. Let our countrymen know ... that the tax which will be paid for this purpose is not more than a thousandth part of what will be paid to kings, priests, and nobles, who will rise up among us if we keep the people in ignorance.   —Thomas Jefferson, letter to George Wythe, Aug. 13, 1786.

We are quite rich enough to defend ourselves, whatever the cost. We must now learn that we are quite rich enough to educate ourselves as we need to be educated.   —Walter Lippmann, *Citizens and Their Schools*, 25: *Education for Leadership* (1952).

There may be frugality which is not economy. A community, that withholds the means of education from its children, withholds the bread of life, and starves their souls.   —Horace Mann, "An Appeal to the Citizens of Massachusetts, in Behalf of Their Public Schools, *The Common School Journal*, Feb. 1840.

Education, Future-Oriented

One *principle of education* which those men especially who form educational schemes should keep before their eyes is this—children ought to be educated, not for the present, but for a possibly improved condition of man in the future; that is, in a manner which is adapted to the *idea of humanity* and the whole destiny of man.   —Immanuel Kant, *Pedagogy* (1803).

What can we think, then, of that barbarous method of education, by which the present is sacrificed to an uncertain future; by which a child is laid under every kind of restraint, and is made miserable, by way of preparing him for we know not what pretended happiness, which there is reason to believe he may never live to enjoy?
—Jean Jacques Rousseau,
Émile (1762).

Education, Government Support of

See also Education, Financial Support of

Aid to education in the States by the Nation ... seems to be our best chance to bring up the neglected elements in our population.   —Rutherford B. Hayes, letter to Hon. Guy M. Bryan, Nov. 13, 1884.

The constitution of Soviet Russia must ensure state aid to all students, in the forms of food, clothing, and school supplies.   —Nikolai Lenin, *Materials Relating to the Revision of the Party Programme* (1917).

In our country and in our times no man is worthy the honored name of statesman who does not include the highest prac-

ticable education of the people in all his plans of administration. —Horace Mann, *Lectures and Reports on Education*, I (1840).

Nor am I less persuaded that you will agree with me in opinion that there is nothing which can better deserve your patronage than the promotion of science and literature. Knowledge is in every country the surest basis of public happiness.   —George Washington, first annual address to Congress, Jan. 8, 1790.

Promote then, as an object of primary importance, institutions for the general diffusion of knowledge. In proportion as the structure of a government gives force to public opinion, it is essential that public opinion should be enlightened.
—George Washington, farewell address, Sept. 17, 1796.

Education, Importance of

See also Education, Importance to State of

When you commence to sow the seed of education in the vast field of the Republic, you must not count the expense of reaping the harvest. After bread, education is the first need of a people.
—George Jacques Danton, speech in the French Convention, Aug. 13, 1793.

Education has become too important to be left to educators. —Peter F. Drucker, *The Age of Discontinuity*, IV.xiv (1968).

I am now entirely absorbed in endeavors to effect the establishment of a general system of education in my native state.... My hopes however are kept in check by the ordinary character of our state legislatures, the members of which do not generally possess information enough to perceive the important truths, that knowledge is power, that knowledge is

safety, and that knowledge is happiness.
—Thomas Jefferson,
letter to George Ticknor, Nov. 25, 1817.

Our progress as a nation can be no swifter than our progress in education.... The human mind is our fundamental resource.   —John F. Kennedy, message to Congress, Feb. 20, 1961.

Upon the subject of education, not presuming to dictate any plan or system respecting it, I can only say that I view it as the most important subject which we, as a people, can be engaged in.
—Abraham Lincoln, communication to the people of Sangamon County, Ill., Mar. 9, 1832.

A good education and sound bringing-up is of the first and middle and last importance; and I declare it to be most instrumental and conducive to virtue and happiness.... Education is of all our advantages the only one immortal and divine.   —Plutarch, *Moralia: The Education of Children* (c. A.D. 95).

School children may not be made to neglect [their studies] even for the building of the Temple.   —*Talmud: Shabbath*, 119b (before A.D. 500); also Maimonides, *Mishneh Torah*, I.ii.2 (1180).

Every town in which there are no schoolchildren shall be destroyed.
—Talmud, *ibid.*

It is an axiom in political science that unless a people are educated and enlightened it is idle to expect the continuance of civil liberty or the capacity for self-government.   —Texas Declaration of Independence, Mar. 2, 1836.

Sir, in a political point of view, nothing can possibly afford greater stability to a popular government than the education of your people.   —Samuel Whitbread, speech in House of Commons, Feb. 19, 1807.

Education, Importance to State of

See also Education, Importance of

Upon the education of the people of this country the fate of this country depends.
—Benjamin Disraeli, speech in House of Commons, June 15, 1874.

A well-instructed people alone can be permanently a free people.
—James Madison, second annual message to Congress, Dec. 5, 1810.

A popular government without popular information or the means of acquiring it, is but a Prologue to a Farce or a Tragedy, or, perhaps both. Knowledge will forever govern ignorance; and a people who mean to be their own Governors must arm themselves with the power which knowledge gives.   —James Madison, letter to W.T. Barry, Aug. 4, 1822.

Education is of still greater importance to the State than to the fathers, for ... the death of the father often deprives him of the final fruits of education; but his country sooner or later perceives its effects. Families dissolve, but the State remains.   —Jean Jacques Rousseau, *Works* (1773): *Political Economy*.

On the diffusion of education among the people rests the preservation and perpetuation of our free institutions.
—Daniel Webster, address in Madison, Ind., June 1, 1837.

Education, Liberal

See also Humanities

A liberal education is mere tomfoolery.
—Aristophanes, *The Knights*, ln.334 (424 B.C.).

A young person who neglects the liberal arts may be both pious and pure; but so long as he has to live among men, I do not see how anyone can call him happy.
— St. Augustine,
De Ordine (c. A.D. 395).

A liberal-arts education is supposed to provide you with a value system, a standard, a set of ideas, not a job.
— Caroline Bird,
The Case Against College (1975).

That man ... has had a liberal education who has been so trained in youth that his body is the ready servant of his will, and does with ease and pleasure all the work that, as a mechanism, it is capable of; whose intellect is a clear, cold, logic engine, with all its parts of equal strength, and in smooth working order.
— T.H. Huxley,
Lay Sermons, Addresses, and Reviews: A Liberal Education (1870).

A liberal education is an artificial education which has not only prepared a man to escape the great evils of disobedience to natural laws, but has trained him to appreciate and to seize upon the rewards, which Nature scatters with as free a hand as her penalties.   — T.H. Huxley,
ibid.

There are other forms of culture beside physical science; and I should be profoundly sorry to see the fact forgotten, or even to observe a tendency to starve, or cripple, literary, or aesthetic, culture for the sake of science.   — T.H. Huxley,
ibid.: Scientific Education.

I want to emphasize in the great concentration which we now place upon scientists and engineers how much we still need the men and women educated in the liberal tradition, willing to take the long look, undisturbed by prejudices and slogans of the moment, who attempt to make an honest judgment on difficult events.   — John F. Kennedy,
address at University of North Carolina, Oct. 12, 1962.

How priceless is a liberal education!... It is not impaired by age, but its value increases with use.... It cannot be inherited or purchased. It must be acquired by individual effort.... It is the greatest blessing that a man or woman can enjoy, when supported by virtue, morality, and noble aims.   — William McKinley,
speech in Philadelphia, Feb. 22, 1898.

Hence it is that his education is called "Liberal." A habit of mind is formed which lasts through life, of which the attributes are, freedom, equitableness, calmness, moderation, and wisdom.... This is the main purpose of a University in its treatment of its students.
— John Henry Newman,
The Idea of a University,
Discourse V (1873).

Liberal Education makes not the Christian, not the Catholic, but the gentlemen.   — John Henry Newman,
ibid.

Liberal Education, viewed in itself, is simply the cultivation of the intellect, as such, and its object is nothing more or less than intellectual excellence.
— John Henry Newman, *ibid.*

Men derive no greater advantage from a liberal education than that it tends to soften and polish their nature, by improving their reasoning faculties and training their habits, thus producing an evenness of temper and banishing all extremes.   — Plutarch,
The Lives of Noble Grecians and Romans: Coriolanus (before A.D. 120).

The first of the liberal arts is grammar, the second rhetoric, the third dialectic, the fourth arithmetic, the fifth geometry, the sixth music, the seventh astronomy.
— Rabanus Maurus Magnentius,
De Institutione Clericorum (Education of the Clergy) (9th cent.).

I conclude that the secret of a genuine liberal education is to learn what you want to know for the sake of your own enlightenment, and not let anybody teach you anything whatever for the purpose of pulling you through an examination.   — George Bernard Shaw, *Pen Portraits and Reviews: Our Great Dean* (1919).

An ancient sentence about liberal education says it is the education worthy of a free man, and the converse is equally ancient: the free man is the one who is worthy of a liberal education. Both sentences remain true, the only difficulty being to know how many men are capable of freedom.   — Mark Van Doren, *Liberal Education* (1943).

The object of a liberal training is not learning, but discipline and the enlightenment of the mind.
                 — Woodrow Wilson, speech in Cambridge, Mass., July 1, 1909.

Education, Practical

With our technology changing so fast, what we used to call "a practical education" has totally changed: it is no longer learning how to do something, but learning to prepare for a future that does not yet exist; it is the capacity for learning, rather than the content, that is crucial in modern society.   — Sydney Harris, syndicated column, *Detroit Free Press*, Aug. 20, 1981.

Already we say, "That man is the best educated who is the most useful," and the true test of education will be in its possessor's ability to serve.
                 — Elbert Hubbard, *Note Book*, 181 (1927).

Education, Religious

All too often a religious education fails to build up anything in the soul; it merely stamps it — brands it, so to speak — with the fear of death, the last judgment and hell.   — Georges Bernanos, *La Grande Peur des Bien-Pensants* (1931).

Parochial education ... cannot be said to meet the requirements of a democracy that rests upon a community of shared education experience.
                 — William Clayton Bower, *Church and State in Education* (1944).

In educating the young it is not sufficient that religious instruction be given to them at fixed times; it is necessary also that every other subject that is taught to them be permeated with Christian piety. If this is wanting, little good can be expected from any kind of learning.
— Pope Leo XIII, *Militantis Ecclesiae*, 1897.

Education belongs pre-eminently to the Church. — Pope Pius XI, *On the Christian Education of Youth*, Dec. 31, 1929.

Every method of education founded, wholly or in part, on the denial or forgetfulness of original sin and of grace, and relying on the sole powers of human nature, is unsound.   — Pope Pius XI, *ibid.*

Education, State Responsibility for

See also State Responsibility for Education

Society possesses an original and fundamental right in the education of children. We must accordingly reject without compromise and brush aside the claim of parents to impart through family education their narrow views to the minds of their offspring.
                 — N. Bukharin and E. Preobeashensky, *The ABC of Communism* (1922).

The education of children is of far more importance to the State than to parents, since the effects of it will be felt by Society, and principally *after* these parents are dead and gone. It is because through it Society accomplishes the end of its being that all education is a public *trust*.
                 — Laurence Gronlund, *The Co-operative Commonwealth in its Outlines* (1884).

It is indeed a sin and shame that we must be aroused and incited to the duty of educating our children and of considering their highest interests, whereas nature itself should move us thereto, and the example of the heathen affords us varied instruction. — Martin Luther, *Letter to the Mayors and Aldermen* (1524), tr. F.V. Painter (1928).

The education of the people is not only a means, but the best means, of attaining that which all allow to be the chief end of government; and, if this be so, it passes my faculties to understand how any man can gravely contend that government has nothing to do with the education of the people. — Thomas Babington Macaulay, speech in House of Commons, Apr. 19, 1847.

There is but one method of preventing crimes, and of rendering a republican form of government durable, and this is, by disseminating the seeds of virtue and knowledge through every part of the state by means of proper places and modes of education, and this can be done effectively only by the interference and aid of the Legislature. — Benjamin Rush, *The Influence of Physical Causes Upon the Moral Faculty* (1788).

I hold it for indisputable, that the first duty of a State is to see that every child born therein shall be well housed, clothed, fed, and educated, till it attains the years of discretion. — John Ruskin, *Time and Tide*, xiii (1867).

If, then, education be of admitted importance to the people, under all forms of government, and of unquestioned necessity when they govern themselves, it follows, of course, that its cultivation and diffusion is a matter of public concern and a duty which every government owes to its people. — Thaddeus Stevens, speech in Pennsylvania legislature, Apr. 1835.

Education, Study of

Education, which you brought into View in one of your Letters, is a Subject so vast, and the Systems of Writers are so various and so contradictory: that human Life is too short to examine it; and a Man must die before he can learn to bring up his Children. — John Adams, letter to Thomas Jefferson, June 19, 1815.

We are only just realising that the art and science of education require a genius and a study of their own; and that this genius and this science are more than a bare knowledge of some branch of science or literature. — Alfred North Whitehead, *The Aims of Education*, i (1929).

Education, Universal

The preservation of the means of knowledge among the lowest ranks is of more importance to the public than all the property of all the rich men in the country. — John Adams, *Dissertation on the Canon and the Federal Law* (1765).

Since the whole city has one end, it is manifest that education should be one and the same for all, and that it should be public, and not private.... [T]he training in things which are of common interest should be the same for all.
— Aristotle, *Politics*, VIII.i.2 (before 322 B.C.).

Learning, to be of much use, must have a tendency to spread itself among the common people.— Henry Ward Beecher, *Proverbs from Plymouth Pulpit: Political* (1887).

We must get rid of the evil which causes our woes—ignorance whence emerge alternately despotism and demogogery! Of all the remedies which can solicit the attention of the statesman and politician to prevent such evils, there is one that excels and includes all the rest; it is universal education. — Léon Gambetta, address in Bordeaux, June 26, 1871.

Next in importance to freedom and justice is popular education, without which neither freedom nor justice can be permanently maintained.
— James A. Garfield,
letter accepting nomination for presidency, July 12, 1880.

I look for a day when education will be like the landscape, free for all. Beauty and truth should be free to every one who has the capacity to absorb. The private school, the private library, the private art gallery, the exclusive college, have got to go. We want no excellence that is not for all.
— Elbert Hubbard,
Note Book, 113 (1927).

That every man may receive at least a moderate education and thereby be enabled to read the histories of his own and other countries, by which he may duly appreciate the value of our free institutions, appears to be an object of vital importance.
— Abraham Lincoln,
communication to the people of Sangamon County, Ill., Mar. 9, 1832.

I desire to see the time when education — and by its means, morality, sobriety, enterprise, and industry — shall become much more general than at present, and should be gratified to have it in my power to contribute something to the advancement of any measure which might have a tendency to accelerate the happy period.
— Abraham Lincoln,
ibid.

Now surely nothing but universal education can counterwork this tendency to the domination of capital and the servility of labor.... If education be equally diffused, it will draw property after it by the strongest of all attractions; for such a thing never did happen, and never can happen, as that an intelligent and practical body of men should be permanently poor.
— Horace Mann,
Twelfth Annual Report of the Massachusetts Board of Education,
1848.

Free education for all children in public schools. Abolition of child factory labor in its present form. Combination of education with industrial production, etc.
— Karl Marx
and Friedrich Engels,
The Communist Manifesto (1848).

The free school is the promoter of that intelligence which is to preserve us a free nation; therefore the state or nation, or both combined, should support free institutions of learning sufficient to afford to every child growing up in the land the opportunity of a good common school education.
— Republican National
Platform, 1888.

Art. 26.1. Everyone has the right to education. Education shall be free, at least in the elementary and fundamental stages. Elementary education shall be compulsory. Technical and professional education shall be made generally available, and higher education shall be equally accessible to all on the basis of merit.
— United Nations,
Universal Declaration of Human Rights,
Dec. 6, 1948.

Education, Value of

[They] realized that education was not a thing of one's own to do with what one pleases — that it was not a personal privilege to be merely enjoyed by the possessor — but a precious treasure transmitted; a sacred trust to be held, used and enjoyed, and if possible strengthened — then passed on to others upon the same trust.
— Louis D. Brandeis,
address to the Menora Conference at Harvard University, 1914.

Idjacation is something that a man has to fight f'r an' pull out iv its hole be th' hair iv its head. That's the reason it's so precious.
— Finley Peter Dunne,
Mr. Dooley's Opinions:
Mr. Carnegie's Gift (1901).

Most Americans do value education as a business asset, but not as the entrance into the joy of intellectual experience or acquaintance with the best that has been said and done in the past. They value it not as an experience, but as a tool.
— W.H.P. Faunce,
letter to Abraham Flexner, Jan. 16, 1928.

He that at any rate procures his child a good mind, well-principled, tempered to virtue and usefulness, and adorned with civility and good breeding, makes a better purchase for him than if he laid out the money for an addition of more earth to his former acres.... 'Tis not good husbandry to make his fortune rich, and his mind poor.   — John Locke,
Some Thoughts concerning Education,
90 (1693).

Education is a treasure.   — Petronius,
Satyricon, xlvii (c. A.D. 60).

Neither must we cast a slight upon education, which is the first and fairest thing that the best of men can ever have, and which, though liable to take a wrong direction, is capable of reformation. And this work of reformation is the great business of every man while he lives.
— Plato, *Laws*,
I.643 (c.367–347 B.C.).

Effort

See also Attempt; Diligence

Wha does the utmost that he can,
   Will whyles do mair. — Robert Burns,
Epistle to Dr. Blacklock, st.viii (1789)
[whyles = *sometimes*; mair = *more*].

Education don't come by bumping against the school-house.
— Selwyn Gurney Champion,
Racial Proverbs, 625 (1938).
An American Negro proverb.

Whatever is worth doing at all is worth doing well.   — Lord Chesterfield,
Letters to His Son, Mar. 10, 1746.

And when I lie in the green kirkyard,
   With mould upon my breast,
Say not that she did well—or ill,
   Only "she did her best."
— Dinah Mulock Craik,
Obituary (1887).

He that would have the fruit must climb the tree. — Thomas Fuller (1654–1734),
Gnomologia, no.2366 (1732).

Mediocrity obtains more with application than superiority without it.
— Balthasar Gracián,
The Art of Worldly Wisdom, xviii (1647).

There is no failure except in no longer trying.   — Elbert Hubbard,
Note Book (1927).

All wish to be learned, but no one is willing to pay the price.   — Juvenal,
Satires, VII (c. A.D. 110).

The education, gentlemen, moral and intellectual of every individual must be, chiefly his own work. How else could it happen that young men, who have had precisely the same opportunities, should be continually presenting us with such different results, and rushing to such opposite destinies?   — William Wirt,
speech at the trial of Aaron Burr
in Richmond, Va., May 1807.

Eloquence

See also Oratory; Speech

Borrowed eloquence, if it contains as good stuff, is as good as our own eloquence.   — John Adams,
letter to Benjamin Rush, Aug. 28, 1811.

Eloquence may exist without a proportional degree of wisdom.
— Edmund Burke,
Reflections on the Revolution in France
(1790).

It is not what the speaker says but who he is that gives weight to eloquence.
— Euripides, *Hecuba* (c.425 B.C.).

True eloquence consists in saying all that should be, not all that could be said.
— François de La Rochefoucald, *Maxims*. no.250 (1665).

Eloquence is a painting of thought.
— Blaise Pascal, *Pensées*, I.26 (1670).

Continuous eloquence wearies.
— Blaise Pascal, *ibid.*, VI.355.

It was you rhetoricians who more than anyone else strangled true eloquence. By reducing everything to sound, you concocted this bloated puffpaste of petty drivel whose only real purpose is the pleasure of punning and the thrill of ambiguity. Result? Language lost its sinew, its nerve. Eloquence died. — Petronius, *Satyricon*, i.4 (c. A.D. 60).

Plenty of eloquence, but little wisdom.
— Sallust, *Bellum Catilinae*, v. (c.41 B.C.).

For I have neither wit, nor words, nor worth,
Action, nor utterance, nor the power of speech,
To stir men's blood.
— William Shakespeare, *Julius Caesar*, III.ii.225 (1599–1600).

Flowers of rhetoric, in sermons and serious discourses, are like blue and red flowers in corn, pleasing to them who come only for amusement, but prejudicial to him who would reap profit.
— Jonathan Swift, *Thoughts on Various Subjects* (1706).

Eloquence, smooth and cutting, is like a razor whetted with oil.
— Jonathan Swift, *ibid.*

English Language

See also Language

English is destined to be in the next and succeeding centuries more generally the language of the world than Latin was in the last or French is in the present age.
— John Adams, letter to the President of Congress, Sept. 5, 1780.

English, *n.* A language so haughty and reserved that few writers succeed in getting on terms of familiarity with it.
— Ambrose Bierce, *The Enlarged Devil's Dictionary*, ed. E.R. Hopkins (1967).

The English language is in very good shape. It is changing in its own undiscoverable way, but it is not going rotten like a plum dropping off a tree.
— Robert Burchfield, "A Conversation with Robert Burchfield," *U.S. News & World Report*, Dec. 15, 1980.

I am of this opinion, that our tongue should be written clean and pure, unmixt and unmangled with borrowing of other tongues, wherein if we take not heed betimes, ever borrowing and never paying, she shall be fain to keep her house as bankrupt. — John Cheke, letter to Thomas Hoby, 1557.

When we consider the richness, good sense and strict economy of English, none of the other living languages can be put beside it. — Jakob Grimm, *Über den Ursprung der Sprache* (1851).

The American language differs from English in that it seeks the top of expression while English seeks its lowly valleys.
— Salvador de Madariaga, *Americans* (1930).

English is the most difficult, arbitrary and careful of all languages.
— Matthew Fontaine Maury, *Scraps from the Lucky Bag* (1840).

If the English language had been properly organized ... then there would be a word which meant both "he" and "she," and I could write, "If John or Mary

comes, heesh will want to play tennis," which could save a lot of trouble.
— A.A. Milne, *The Christopher Robin Birthday Book* (1930).

Our English tongue of all languages most swarmeth with the single money of monosyllables, which are the only scandal of it. Books written in them and no other seem like shopkeepers' boxes, that contain nothing else save halfpence, three-farthings and two-pences.
— Thomas Nashe, *Christes Teares Over Jerusalem* (1593).

English is the most modern of the great languages, the most widely spoken, and the most international.... Its swiftness and transparent accuracy of expression, and especially the fact that it has shed most of the old grammatical forms which time has rendered useless and scarcely intelligible, have made English a model, pointing the way which must be followed in building the Interlanguage.
— Sylvia Pankhurst, *Delphos*, v (1926).

Good English is that form of speech which is appropriate to the purpose of the speaker, true to the language as it is, and comfortable to speaker and listener. It is the product of custom, neither cramped by rule nor freed from all restraint; it is never fixed, but changes with the organic life of the language. — Robert C. Pooley, *Teaching English Usage*, 14 (1946).

The English have no respect for their language, and will not teach their children to speak it. They spell it so abominally that no man can teach himself what it sounds like.
— George Bernard Shaw, *Pygmalion*, preface (1912).

So now they have made our English tongue a gallimaufry or hodgepodge of all other speeches. — Edmund Spenser, *The Shepherd's Calendar: Letter to Gabriel Harvey* (1579).

For the initiate ours is a cruel language, its freaky orthography and idiosyncracies never so apparent as on the printed page.
— William Styron, *Sophie's Choice*, 89 (1976).

There is no such thing as Queen's English. The property has gone into the hands of a joint stock company and we own the bulk of the shares.
— Mark Twain, *Notebook*, Apr. 13, 1897 (1935); also *Pudd'nhead Wilson's New Calendar*, xxiv (1897).

English usage is sometimes more than mere taste, judgment, and education— sometimes it's sheer luck, like getting across the street. — E.B. White, *The Second Tree from the Corner: Shop Talk* (1954).

Wondrous the English language,
    language of live men,
Language of ensemble, powerful
    language of resistance,
Language of a proud and melancholy
    stock, and of all who aspire,
Language of growth, faith, self-esteem,
    rudeness, justice, friendliness, prudence, decision, exactitude, courage.
— Walt Whitman, *As I Sat Alone* (1856).

View'd freely, the English language is the accretion of every dialect, race, and range of time, and is both the free and compacted composition of all.
— Walt Whitman, *November Boughs: Slang in America* (1888).

Enlightenment

See also Education; Learning

Light: or, failing that, lightning: the world can take its choice.
— Thomas Carlyle, *Heroes and Hero-Worship*, V: *The Hero as a Man of Letters* (1840).

A little light will dispel much darkness.
—Issachar Eilenburg,
Tzeda LaDerek (1623).

Enlightenment doesn't care how you get there.   —Thaddeus Golas,
The Lazy Man's Guide to Enlightenment (1972).

To bung up a man's eyes ain't the way to enlighten him.
—Thomas Chandler Haliburton,
Wise Saws (1843).

Enlighten the people generally, and tyranny and oppression of body and mind will vanish like evil spirits at the dawn of day.   —Thomas Jefferson,
letter to P.S. Dupont de Nemours,
Apr. 24, 1816.

I look to the diffusion of light and education as the source most to be relied on for ameliorating the condition, promoting the virtue, and advancing the happiness of man.   —Thomas Jefferson,
letter to Cornelius Camden Blatchly,
Oct. 21, 1822.

"I must really improve my mind," I tell myself, and once more begin to patch and repair that crazy structure. So I toil and toil on at the vain task of edification, though the wind tears off the tiles, the floors give way, the ceilings fall, strange birds build untidy nests in the rafters, and owls hoot and laugh in the tumbling chimneys.   —Logan Pearsall Smith,
Trivia: Edification (1902).

Their young eyes grew sudden fair
With dawning answers there.
—Francis Thompson,
The Hound of Heaven, ln.58 (1893).

There are two ways of spreading light: to be
The candle or the mirror that reflects it.
—Edith Wharton,
Vesalius in Zante (1902).

Enthusiasm

See also Zeal

You can't sweep other people off their feet, if you can't be swept off your own.
—Clarence Day,
The Crow's Nest: A Wild Polish Hero (1921).

Nothing great was ever achieved without enthusiasm.   —Ralph Waldo Emerson,
Essays, First Series: Cicles (1841).

Enthusiasm is very catching, especially when it is very eloquent.
—Mary Russell Mitford,
in A.G.K. L'Estrange, *Life*, II.i (1817).

Enthusiasm is that temper of the mind in which the imagination has got the better of the judgment.—William Warburton,
The Divine Legislation of Moses, I (1737).

Environment

In our culture teacher and student come frequently from quite different environments, while the bureaucrats who set up curricula and syllabuses inhabit yet another.   —Robert Claiborne,
God or Beast (1974).

Men   think   differently   who   live differently.   —Harold J. Laski,
An Introduction to Politics (1931).

Epigram

See also Maxim; Proverb

The epigram has been compared to a scorpion, because as the sting of the scorpion lieth in the tail, the force of the epigram is in the conclusion.
—Lilius Gyraldus,
De Poetica Historia, x (1545).

The epigram is a beautiful meaning in few and clear words.... It slings at the mark without delay.—Moses Ibn Ezra,
Shirat Yisrael, 117 (12th cent.).

Somewhere in the world there is an epigram for every dilemma.
— Hendrik Willem van Loon,
Tolerance (1925).

Equality

Equality is the result of human organization. We are not born equal.
— Hannah Arendt,
The Origins of Totalitarianism (1973).

If a man is genuinely superior to his fellows the first thing that he believes in is the equality of man.
— G.K. Chesterton,
Heretics, xvii (1905).

True equality can only mean the right to be uniquely creative. — Erik H. Erikson,
in *The Woman in America*,
ed. Robert J. Lifton (1965).

We clamor for equality chiefly in matters in which we ourselves cannot hope to obtain excellence.   — Eric Hoffer,
The Passionate State of Mind,
no.198 (1954).

Your levellers wish to level *down* as far as themselves; but they cannot bear levelling *up* to themselves.
— Samuel Johnson, in James Boswell,
Life of Samuel Johnson, xiv,
July 21, 1763 (1791).

Education then, beyond all other devices of human origin, is a great equalizer of the conditions of men, — the balance wheel of the social machinery ... and, if this education should be universal and complete, it would do more than all things else to obliterate factitious distinctions in society.   — Horace Mann,
Twelfth Annual Report of the
Massachusetts Board of Education, 1848.

There is no merit in equality, unless it be equality with the best.
— John Lancaster Spalding,
Thoughts and Theories of
Life and Education (1897).

We must recover the element of quality in our traditional pursuit of equality. We must not, in opening our schools to everyone, confuse the idea that all should have equal chance with the notion that all have equal endowments.
— Adlai E. Stevenson,
address to United Parents Association,
New York Times, Apr. 6, 1958.

Error

It is not dishonorable to commit an error.
— Aaron Abulrabi,
Sefer Matteh (c.1410).

Men make mistakes not because they think they know when they do not know, but because they think others do not know.   — Sholom Aleichem,
Yidishe Folks Tzeitung, 1902.

The best lessons a man ever learns are from his mistakes. It is not for want of schoolmasters that we are still ignorant.
— Henry Ward Beecher,
Proverbs from Plymouth Pulpit:
Man (1887).

There is nothing final about a mistake, except its being taken as final.
— Phyllis Bottome,
Strange Fruit (1928).

A man protesting error is on the way toward uniting himself with all men that believe in truth.   — Thomas Carlyle,
Heroes and Hero-Worship (1840).

Truth is a good dog; but beware of barking too close to the heels of an error, lest you get your brains kicked out.
— Samuel Taylor Coleridge,
Table Talk, June 7, 1830.

Men still preserve the errors of their childhood, of their country, and of their age long after having recognized all the truths needed to destroy them.
— Marquis de Condorcet, *Sketch for*
a Historical Picture of Progress of the
Human Spirit (1794).

What can we know, or what can we discern,
When error chokes the window of the mind? —(Sir) John Davies,
The Vanity of Human Learning, xv (1599).

The chief cause of human errors is to be found in the prejudices picked up in childhood. —René Descartes, *Principles of Philosophy*, I (1644).

Forgive, son; men are men, they needs must err. —Euripides, *Hippolytus*, ln.615 (428 B.C.).

Instruction does not prevent waste of time or mistakes; and mistakes themselves are often the best teachers of all. —James Anthony Froude, *Short Studies on Great Subjects: Education* (1867–82).

Nothing is more harmful to a new truth than an old error. —Johann Wolfgang von Goethe, *Proverbs in Prose* (1819).

Admitting Error clears the Score
And proves you Wiser than before. —Arthur Guiterman, *A Poet's Proverbs* (1924).

The road to wisdom? —
Well, it's plain
and simple to express:
Err
and err
and err again
but less
and less
and less. —Piet Hein, *Grooks: The Road to Wisdom* (1966).

The greatest mistake you can make in life is to be continually fearing that you will make one. —Elbert Hubbard, *Note Book* (1927).

Man approaches the unattainable truth through a succession of errors. —Aldous Huxley, *Do What You Will: Wordsworth in the Tropics* (1929).

An error cannot be believed sincerely enough to make it a truth. —Robert G. Ingersoll, *The Great Infidels* (1881?).

One must never confuse error and the person who errs. —Pope John XXIII, *Pacem in Terris*, Apr. 10, 1963.

When everyone is wrong, everyone is right. —Nivelle de La Chaussée, *La Gouvernante*, I.iii (1747).

It is one thing to show a man that he is an error, and another to put him in possession of truth. —John Locke, *An Essay concerning Human Understanding*, IV.vii.11 (1690).

The man who makes no mistakes does not usually make anything. —William Connor Magee, sermon, 1868; also Edward John Phelps, speech, Jan. 24, 1899.

The right to be wrong is as important as the right to be admired. —Edward R. Murrow, speech at Hamilton College, June 1954.

Good-nature and good-sense must ever join;
To err is human, to forgive divine. —Alexander Pope, *An Essay on Criticism*, II.524 (1711). Sentiment expressed also by other writers, including Plutarch, *Moralia: Against Colotes* and Seneca, *Naturales Quaestiones*.

When I have listened to my mistakes, I have grown. —Hugh Prather, *Notes to Myself* (1970).

A life spent in making mistakes is not only more honorable but more useful than a life spent doing nothing. —George Bernard Shaw, *The Doctor's Dilemma*, preface (1911).

The error which we hold inquiringly, striving to find what element of fact there be in it, is worth more to us than the

truth which we accept mechanically and retain with indifference.
—John Lancaster Spalding, *Thoughts and Theories of Life and Education* (1897).

I have learned throughout my life as a composer chiefly through my mistakes and pursuits of false assumptions, not by my exposure to founts of wisdom and knowledge.   —Igor Stravinsky, *Themes and Episodes: Contingencies* (1966).

If you shut your door to all errors truth will be shut out. —Rabindranath Tagore, *Stray Birds* (1916).

Examination

See also Intelligence Test

The system of competitive examinations is a sad necessity. Knowledge is wooed for her dowry, not for her diviner charms.
—Charles Synge Christopher Bowen (1835–94), *Lecture on Education*.

Examinations are formidable, even to the best prepared, for the greatest fool may ask, more than the wisest man can answer.   —Charles Caleb Colton, *Lacon*, 170 (1820–22).

Examinations are of use only so far as they test the child's fitness for social life and reveal the place in which he can be of the most service and where he can receive the most help.   —John Dewey, "My Pedagogic Creed," *The School Journal*, Jan. 16, 1897.

Americans are probably the most tested, measured, sorted, and classified people who ever lived.   —Bernard Feder, *The Complete Guide to Taking Tests* (1979).

As long as learning is connected with earning, as long as certain jobs can only be reached through exams, so long must we take the examination system seriously.

If another ladder to employment was contrived, much so-called education would disappear, and no one would be a penny the stupider.   —E.M. Forster, *New York Times*, Nov. 24, 1963.

I *always* get seventy-eight. No more, no less. It's nerve-wracking. I'd almost rather flunk once in a while. —Ruth Gordon, *Over Twenty-One*, I (1943).

Even superficial experience teaches us that the results of an examination are valid only for the day when it is held.
—Johann Herbart, *Collected Works* (1850–52): *Brief Encyclopedia of Practical Philosophy*.

Be patient, then, and sympathetic with the type of mind that cuts a poor figure in examinations. It may, in the long examination which life sets us, come out in the end in better shape than the glib and ready reproducer, its passions being deeper, its purposes more worthy, its combining power less commonplace, and its total mental output consequently more important.   —William James, *Talks to Teachers on Psychology* (1899).

To those who know, a written examination is far from being a true criterion of capacity. It demands too much of memory, imitativeness, and the insidious willingness to absorb other people's ideas. Parrots and crows would do admirably in examinations. Indeed the colleges are full of them.   —Stephen Leacock, *My Discovery of England: Oxford As I See It* (1922).

Examinations are harmless when the examinee is indifferent to their result, but as soon as they matter, they begin to distort his attitude to education and to conceal its purpose. The more depends on them, the worse their effect.
—Richard Livingstone, *On Education* (1944).

In an examination those who do not wish to know ask questions of those who cannot tell. — Walter Alexander Raleigh, (1861–1922), *Some Thoughts on Examinations*; also Oscar Wilde, *Chameleon*, I., Dec. 1894.

I believe that the testing of the student's achievements in order to see if he meets some criterion held by the teacher, is directly contrary to the implications of therapy for significant learning.
— Carl R. Rogers,
On Becoming a Person (1961).

The examination system, and the fact that instruction is treated mainly as training for a livelihood, leads the young to regard knowledge from a purely utilitarian point of view, as the road to money, not as the gateway to wisdom.
— Bertrand Russell,
Principles of Social Reconstruction: Education (1916).

No educational system is possible unless every question directly asked of a pupil at any examination is either framed or modified by the actual teacher of that pupil in that subject.
— Alfred North Whitehead,
The Aims of Education, i (1929).

Examinations, when the man was weighed
As in a balance! — William Wordworth,
The Prelude, III.69 (1850).

Example

See also Practice What Preach

For you are well aware that it is not only by bodily exercises, by educational institutions, or by lessons in music, that our youth are trained, but that much more effectually by public examples. — Aeschines, *Against Clesiphon*, xci (330 B.C.).

Do but set the example yourself, and I will follow you. Example is the best precept. — Aesop, *Fables: The Two Crabs* (6th cent. B.C.).

Words but direct, examples must allure.
— Williams Alexander,
Earl of Stirling, *Doomsday: The Ninth Hour*, cxiii (1614).

One example is more valuable, both to good and ill, than twenty precepts written in books. — Roger Ascham,
The Schoolmaster, I (1570).

Children have never been very good at listening to their elders, but they have never failed to imitate them.
— James Baldwin, *Nobody Knows My Name: Fifth Avenue, Uptown* (1961).

Example is the school of mankind, and they will learn at no other.
— Edmund Burke, *Letters on a Regicide Peace*, I (1796).

Example is better than precept.
— English proverb, going back to c.1400. Similar thought expressed by many writers.

A good Example is the best Sermon.
— Thomas Fuller (1654–1734),
Gnomologia, no.146 (1732); also Benjamin Franklin, *Poor Richard's Almanack*, June 1747.

Parents are Patterns. — Thomas Fuller,
ibid, no.3843.

The crab instructs its young, "Walk straight ahead — like me."
— Hindustani proverb.

The little snake studies the ways of the big serpent. — Japanese proverb.

I have ever deemed it more honorable and more profitable, too, to set a good example than to follow a bad one.
— Thomas Jefferson, letter to Correa de Serra, Dec. 27, 1814.

Children have more need of models than of critics. — Joseph Joubert,
Pensées, no.261 (1810).

Example is a dangerous lure; where the wasp got through the gnat sticks fast.
—Jean de La Fontaine,
Fables, III.16 (1668).

Nothing is so contagious as example.
—François de La Rochefoucauld,
Maxims, no.230 (1665).

If you must hold yourself up to your children as an object lesson (which is not at all necessary), hold yourself up as a warning and not as an example.
—George Bernard Shaw, *Parents and Children*, preface to *Missalliance*, (1914).

Few things are harder to put up with than the annoyance of a good example.
—Mark Twain, *Pudd'nhead Wilson's Calendar*, xix (1894).

Excellence

See also Perfection

The sad truth is that excellence makes people nervous.   —Shana Alexander,
The Feminist Eye: Neglected Kids—The Bright Ones (1970).

We expect to be inspired by mediocre appeals to "excellence," to be made literate by illiterate appeals for literacy.
—Daniel J. Boorstin,
The Image, i (1962).

The society which scorns excellence in plumbing because plumbing is a humble activity and tolerates shoddiness in philosophy because it is an exalted activity will have neither good plumbing nor good philosophy. Neither its pipes nor its theories will hold water.
—John W. Gardner, *Excellence: Can We Be Equal and Excellent Too?* (1971).

The good is the enemy of the best.
—Ralph A. Habas,
Morals for Moderns, 211 (1939).

Before the gates of excellence the high gods have placed sweat; long is the road

thereto and rough and steep at first; but when the heights are reached, then there is ease, though grievously hard in the winning.   —Hesiod,
Works and Days (8th cent. B.C.).

Every man who can be a first-rate something—as every man can be who is a man at all—has no right to be a fifth-rate something; for a fifth-rate something is no better than a first-rate nothing.
—Josiah G. Holland,
Plain Talks on Familiar Subjects, i: *Self Help* (1865).

Excellence when concealed, differs but little from buried worthlessness.
—Horace, *Odes*,
IV.ix.29 (c.20 B.C.).

Excellence costs a great deal.
—May Sarton,
The Small Room (1961).

Expectation, Learning and Role

Children who are treated as if they are uneducable almost invariably become uneducable.   —Kenneth B. Clark,
Dark Ghetto (1965).

Boys and girls are expected, also, to behave differently to each other, and to people in general—a behavior to be briefly described in two words. To the boy we say, "Do"; to the girl, "Don't."
—Charlotte Perkins Gilman,
Women and Economics, i (1898).

Our expectation of what the human animal can learn, can do, can be remains remarkably low and timorous.
—George B. Leonard,
Education and Ecstasy, 14 (1968).

Experience

All experience is an arch, to build upon.
—Henry Adams, *The Education of Henry Adams*, vi (1907).

For it is by doing what we ought to do when we study the arts we learn the arts themselves; we become builders by building and harpists by playing the harp. —Aristotle, *Nicomachean Ethics*, II.i. (before 322 B.C.).

Learning teacheth more in one year than experience in twenty, and learning teacheth safety, when experience maketh more miserable than wise. He hazardeth sore that waxeth wise by experience.... It is costly wisdom that is bought by experience. —Roger Ascham, *The Schoolmaster*, I (1570).

You cannot create experience. You must undergo it. —Albert Camus, *Notebooks 1935–1942*, I (1962).

Often a liberal antidote of experience supplies a sovereign cure for a paralyzing abstraction built upon a theory. —Benjamin N. Cardozo, *The Paradoxes of Legal Science*, 125 (1928).

You have not had thirty years' experience.... *You* have had one year's experience 30 times. —J.L. Carr, *The Harpole Report*, xxi (1970).

What I hear, I forget;
What I see, I remember;
What I do, I understand.
—Ancient Chinese proverb.

You cannot speak of ocean to a well-frog,—the creature of the narrower sphere. You cannot speak of ice to a summer insect,—the creature of a season. —Chuang-tzu, *Autumn Floods*, (4th–3rd cent. B.C.).

I was thinking that we all learn by experience, but some of us have to go to summer school. —Peter De Vries, *The Tunnel of Love*, xiv (1954).

Experience cannot deliver to us necessary truths; truths completely demonstrated by reason. Its conclusions are particular, not universal. —John Dewey, *The Quest for Certainty*, ii (1929).

Experience itself, as such, is defective, and hence default is inevitable and irremediable. The only universality and certainty is in a region above experience, that of the rational and conceptual. —John Dewey, *Reconstruction in Philosophy* (1920).

An ounce of wit that is bought,
Is worth a pound that is taught.
—Benjamin Franklin, *Poor Richard's Almanack*, Dec. 1745.

You cannot step twice into the same river; for other and ever other waters flow on. —Heraclitus, *Fragments* (c.500 B.C.).

Yeeres know more than bookes. —George Herbert, *Outlandish Proverbs*, no.928 (1640).

At every step the child should be allowed to meet the real experiences of life; the thorns should never be plucked from his roses. —Ellen Key, *The Century of the Child*, iii (1909).

Experience is a hard teacher because she gives the test first, the lesson afterwards. —Vernon Sanders Law, "How to Be a Winner," *This Week*, Aug. 14, 1960.

The world fears a new experience more than it fears anything. Because a new experience displaces so many old experiences.... The world doesn't fear a new idea. It can pigeon-hole any idea. But it can't pigeon-hole a real new experience. —D.H. Lawrence, *Studies in Classic American Literature* (1922).

One thorn of experience is worth a whole wilderness of warning. —James Russell Lowell, *Among My Books: Shakespeare Once More* (1870).

If you want knowledge, you must take part in the practice of changing reality. If you want to know the taste of a pear, you

must change the pear by eating it
yourself.   — Mao Tse-tung,
          *Quotations from Chairman
          Mao Tse-tung*, xxii (1966).

a man who is so dull
that he can learn only by personal
    experience
is too dull to learn
anything important by experience.
— Don Marquis, *Archy Does His Part:
    archy on this and that* (1935).

The word experience is like a shraphnel
shell, and bursts into a thousand
meanings.   — George Santayana,
          *Character and Opinion in the
          United States* (1920).

Philosophers have sometimes said that all
ideas come from experience; they never
could have been poets and must have
forgotten they were ever children. The
great difficulty in education is to get experience out of ideas.
— George Santayana, *The Life of Reason*,
    I: *Reason in Common Sense* (1905–06).

We learn not in the school, but in life.
— Seneca, *Letters to Lucilius*,
    CVI (c. A.D. 64).

Without living experience no person is
educated. With nothing but academic
degrees, even when overloaded by a
smattering of dead languages and two
penn'orth of algebra, the most erudite
graduates may be noodles and ig-
noramuses. The vital difference between
reading and experience is not measurable
by examination marks.
— George Bernard Shaw,
    Sixteen Self Sketches, 113 (1949).

Which would have advanced the most at
the end of a month, — the boy who had
made his own jackknife from the ore
which he had dug and smelted, reading
as much as would be necessary for this —
or the boy who had attended the lectures
on metallurgy at the Institute in the
mean while, and had received a Rogers'

penknife from his father. Which would
be most likely to cut his fingers?
— Henry David Thoreau, *Walden*,
          i: *Economy* (1854).

Experience teacheth many things, and all
    men are his scholars:
Yet is he a strange tutor, unteaching that
    which he hath taught.
          — Martin Farquhar Tupper,
          Proverbial Philosophy, I (1838).

We should be careful to get out of an experience only the wisdom that is in it —
and stop there; lest we be like the cat that
sits down on a hot stove-lid. She will
never sit down on a hot stove-lid again —
and that is well; but also she will never sit
down on a cold one any more.
— Mark Twain, *Pudd'nhead
Wilson's New Calendar*, I.xi (1897).

Expert

See also Specialist

An expert is a man who has made all the
mistakes, which can be made, in a very
narrow field.   — Niels Bohr,
in Alan L. Mackay, *Scientific Quotations:
    The Harvest of a Quiet Eye* (1977).

An expert is one who knows more and
more about less and less.
          — Nicholas Murray Butler,
          commencement address, Columbia
          University.

An expert is someone who knows some of
the worst mistakes that can be made in
his subject, and how to avoid them.
          — Werner Heisenberg,
          Physics and Beyond (1971).

The essence of the expert is that his field
shall be very special and narrow: one of
the ways in which he inspires confidence
is to rigidly limit himself to the little toe;
he would scarcely venture an off-the-
record opinion on an infected little
finger.   — Louis Kronenberger,
          Company Manners, I.iv (1954).

Explanation

Intellectual man has become an explaining creature. Fathers to children, wives to husbands ... experts to laymen ... doctors to patients, man to his own soul, explained.... For the most part, in one ear, out the other.   —Saul Bellow,
Mr. Sammler's Planet (1970).

I wish he would explain his Explanation.
        —Lord Byron, *Don Juan:*
        Dedication, ii.16 (1819).

I am an enemy of long explanations: they deceive either the maker or the hearer, and usually both.
        —Johann Wolfgang von Goethe,
        Götz von Berlichingen, I (1773).

I am master of everything I can explain.
        —Theodor Haecker,
        Journal in the Night (tr. 1950).

Explanations explanatory of things explained.   —Abraham Lincoln,
        referring to Stephen A. Douglas's explanations during the Lincoln-Douglas debates, 1858.

When you don't know much about a subject you are explaining, compliment the person you are explaining to on knowing all about it and he will think that you do, too.   —Don Marquis,
        The Almost Perfect State (1927).

You have made the steep places level.
        —Plautus, *Miles Gloriosus*,
        ln.1018 (c.200 B.C.).

Shall I tell you why?
Ay, sir, and wherefore; for they say every why hath a wherefore.
        —William Shakespeare,
The Comedy of Errors, II.ii.43 (1593).

Fact

Nothing in education is so astonishing as the amount of ignorance it accumulates in the form of inert facts.
        —Henry Adams,
        The Education of Henry Adams,
        xxv (1907).

Philosophers and theologians have yet to learn that a physical fact is as sacred as a moral principle.   —Louis Agassiz,
        Atlantic Monthly, 1874.

Every man has a right to his opinion, but no man has a right to be wrong in his facts.   —Bernard Baruch,
        in *Reader's Digest*, Mar. 1948.

A fact in itself is nothing. It is valuable only for the idea attached to it, or for the proof which it furnishes.
        —Claude Bernard,
        Introduction to the Study of
        Experimental Medicine (1865).

No statement of facts, however honest your people may be, can be relied upon until it has been subjected to the careful study and criticism of people who have a different point of view.
        —Louis D. Brandeis,
        in Alfred Lief, ed., *The Social and*
Economic Views of Mr. Justice Brandeis,
        411 (1934).

It is facts that are needed; Facts, Facts, Facts. When facts have been supplied, each of us can try to reason from them.
        —James Bryce,
        Modern Democracies (1922).

Plain matters of fact are terrible stubborn things.   —Eustace Budgell,
        Liberty and Progress, ii.76 (1732).
See also Alain René Lesage, *L'Histoire*
        de Gil Blas, x.i (1715–35).

The credibility, or the certain truth of a matter of fact does not immediately prove anything concerning the wisdom or goodness of it.   —Joseph Butler,
        The Analogy of Religion (1736).

What are facts but compromises? A fact merely marks the point where we have agreed to let investigation cease.
— Bliss Carman,
Atlantic Monthly, May 1906.

Facts are not truths; they are not conclusions; they are not even premisses, but in the nature and parts of premisses. The truth depends on, and is only arrived at, by a legitimate deduction from all the facts which are truly material.
— Samuel Taylor Coleridge,
Table Talk, Dec. 27, 1831.

The trouble with facts is that there are so many of them.
— Samuel McChord Crothers,
The Gentle Reader (1903).

Creatures whose mainspring is curiosity will enjoy the accumulating of facts, far more than the pausing at times to reflect on those facts.   — Clarence Day,
This Simian World, ix (1920).

No facts to me are sacred; none are profane.   — Ralph Waldo Emerson,
Essays, First Series: Circles (1841).

If a man will kick a fact out of the window, when he comes back he finds it again in the chimney corner.
— Ralph Waldo Emerson,
Journals, 1842.

Facts are never neutral; they are impregnated with value judgments.
— Peter Gay,
Style in History (1974).

A wise man recognizes the convenience of a general statement, but he bows to the authority of a particular fact.
— Oliver Wendell Holmes, Sr.,
The Poet at the Breakfast-Table,
x (1872).

Facts do not cease to exist because they are ignored.   — Aldous Huxley, *Proper Studies: A Note on Dogma* (1927).

Facts are ventriloquists' dummies. Sitting on a wise man's knee they may be made to utter words of wisdom; elsewhere they say nothing or talk nonsense.
— Aldous Huxley,
Time Must Have a Stop (1944).

A world of facts lies outside and beyond the world of words.   — T.H. Huxley,
Lay Sermons, Addresses, and Reviews
(1870).

Those who refuse to go beyond fact rarely get as far as fact.   — T.H. Huxley,
The Progress of Science (1887).

Sit down before fact as a little child, be prepared to give up every preconceived notion, follow humbly wherever and to whatever abyss nature leads, or you shall learn nothing.   — T.H. Huxley,
letter to Charles Kingsley,
Sept. 23, 1860.

The fatal futility of Fact.
— Henry James (1843–1916),
Prefaces: The Spoils of Poynton (1897).

People don't ask for facts in making up their minds. They would rather have one good, soul-satisfying emotion than a dozen facts.   — Robert Keith Leavitt,
Voyages and Discoveries (1939).

In science, all facts, no matter how trivial or banal, enjoy democratic equality.
— Mary McCarthy,
On the Contrary (1961).

One of the most untruthful things possible, you know, is a collection of facts, because they can be made to appear so many different ways.
— Karl A. Menninger,
A Psychiatrist's World (1959).

There are no eternal facts, as there are no eternal truths.   — Friedrich Nietzsche,
Human, All Too Human, I (1878).

Facts are carpet-tacks under the pneumatic tires of theory.
— Austin O'Malley,
Keystones of Thought (1914–15).

I'm not afraid of facts, I welcome facts *but a congeries of facts is not equivalent to an idea.* This is the essential fallacy of the so-called "scientific" mind. People who mistake facts for ideas are incomplete thinkers; they are gossips.
—Cynthia Ozick,
We Are the Crazy Lady and Other Feisty Feminist Fables, in Francine Klagsbrun, ed., *The First Ms. Reader* (1972).

Facts are the air of scientists. Without them you can never fly. —Ivan Pavlov, *Bequest to the Academic Youth of Soviet Russia*, Feb. 27, 1936.

A fact is like a sack which won't stand up when it is empty. In order that it may stand up, one has to put into it the reason and sentiment which have caused it to exist. —Luigi Pirandello, *Six Characters in Search of an Author*, I (1921).

Science is built of facts the way a house is built of bricks; but an accumulation of facts is no more science than a pile of bricks is a house. —Henri Poincaré, *Science and Hypothesis* (1901).

She always says, my lord, that facts are like cows. If you look them in the face hard enough they generally run away.
—Dorothy L. Sayers, *Clouds of Witness*, iv (1956).

Let us not underrate the value of a fact; it will one day flower into a truth.
—Henry David Thoreau, *Excursions* (1863).

The brightest flashes in the world of thought are incomplete until they have been proved to have their counterparts in the world of fact. —John Tyndall, *Fragments of Science for Unscientific People*, II: *Scientific Materialism* (1871).

It is as fatal as it is cowardly to blink facts because they are not to our taste.
—John Tyndall, *ibid.: Science and Man.*

We want the facts to fit the preconceptions. When they don't, it is easier to ignore the facts than to change the preconceptions. —Jessamyn West, *The Quaker Reader*, introd. (1962).

Failure

There is no loneliness greater than the loneliness of a failure. The failure is a stranger in his own house.—Eric Hoffer, *The Passionate State of Mind*, no.223 (1954).

There's dignity in suffering—
Nobility in pain—
But failure is a salted wound
That burns and burns again.
—Margery Eldredge Howell (1893–1946), *Wormwood.*

There is the greatest practical benefit in making a few failures early in life.
—T.H. Huxley, *On Medical Education* (1870).

I think success has no rules, but you can learn a great deal from failure.
—Jean Kerr, *Mary, Mary*, I (1960).

I would prefer even to fail with honor than win by cheating. —Sophocles, *Philoctetes* (409 B.C.).

Faith

Faith is often the boast of the man who is too lazy to investigate.
—F.M. Knowles, *A Cheerful Year Book* (1906).

Faith and doubt are both needed—not as antagonists but working side by side—to take us around the unknown curve.
—Lillian Smith, *The Journey* (1954).

There are those who scoff at the schoolboy, calling him frivolous and shallow. Yet it was a schoolboy who said:

"Faith is believing what you know ain't so."   — Mark Twain,
Notebook, Feb. 2, 1894 (1935); also Pudd'nhead Wilson's New Calendar, xii (1897).

Falsehood

Falsehood is so near to truth that a wise man would do well not to trust himself on such a narrow edge.   — Cicero, Academica, II.xxi (c.45 B.C.).

A Hair perhaps divides the False and True.   — Omar Khayyám, Rubáiyát, IL (c.1100), tr. Edward FitzGerald (1859).

Little children do not lie till they are taught to do so. — Saadia ben Joseph, in a letter, A.D. 928.

Family

[The family:] The only preserving and healing power counteracting any historical, intellectual or spiritual crisis no matter what depth.
            — Ruth Nanda Anshen, ed., The Family: Its Function (1959).

Where does the family start? It starts with a young man falling in love with a girl— no superior alternative has yet been found.   — Winston Churchill, speech in House of Commons, Nov. 6, 1950.

For individuals the breakdown of the family means the gloomy despair of a life without happiness, of a life which not even pleasure can light up. For nations it means slow death through sterility, and it can even mean this for the human race.
            — Jacques Leclercq, Marriage and the Family (1933).

Famous People

Great men are rarely isolated mountain-peaks; they are the summits of ranges.
            — Thomas Wentworth Higginson, Atlantic Essays (1871).

The world's great men have not commonly been great scholars, nor its great scholars great men.
            — Oliver Wendell Holmes, Sr., The Autocrat of the Breakfast-Table (1858).

Lives of great men all remind us
We can make our lives sublime,
And, departing, leave behind us
Footprints on the sands of time.
            — Henry Wadsworth Longfellow, A Psalm of Life, vii (1838).

Fanatic

A fanatic is a man that does what he thinks th' Lord wud do if He knew the facts iv the case. — Finley Peter Dunne, Mr. Dooley's Opinions (1901).

How wearisome is the grammarian, the phrenologist, the political or religious fanatic, or indeed any possessed mortal whose balance is lost by the exaggeration of a single topic. It is incipient insanity.
            — Ralph Waldo Emerson, Essays, First Series: Intellect (1841).

What is objectionable, what is dangerous about extremists is not that they are extreme, but that they are intolerant. The evil is not what they say about their cause, but what they say about their opponents.   — Robert F. Kennedy, The Pursuit of Justice: Extremism, Left and Right (1964).

Fanaticism

It is part of the nature of fanaticism that is loses sight of the totality of evil and rushes like a bull at the red cloth instead of at the man who holds it.
            ˒Dietrich Bonhoeffer, Ethics (1955).

If there is anything more dangerous to the life of the mind than having no independent commitment to ideas, it is having an excess of commitment to some special and constricting idea.
— Richard Hofstadter,
Anti-intellectualism in American Life,
I.ii.29 (1963).

Fanaticism consists in redoubling your effort when you have forgotten your aim.
— George Santayana,
The Life of Reason, I:
Reason in Common Sense (1905–06).

Father

See also Parent

Diogenes struck the father when the son swore.   — Robert Burton,
The Anatomy of Melancholy,
III.ii.2.5 (1621).

It is the duty of a father to train them up from their tenderest years in the paths of virtue, in good discipline and Christian principles.... But as for forcing them to this or that study, it is a thing I do not so well approve. Persuasion is all, I think, that is proper in such a case.
— Miguel de Cervantes,
Don Quixote, II.II.xvi (1615).

Who touches a father touches a son.
— Egyptian proverb.

One father is more than a hundred Schoolmasters.   — George Herbert,
Outlandish Proverbs, no.686 (1640).

What a father says to his children is not heard by the world, but it will be heard by posterity.   — Jean Paul Richter,
Levana (1807).

It doesn't matter who my father was; it matters who I remember he was.
— Anne Sexton,
A Small Journal, Jan. 1, 1972, in Howard Moss, ed., *The Poet's Story*,
(1974).

He who does not teach his son a craft, teaches him brigandage.   — *Talmud: Kiddushin*, 29a (before A.D. 500).

Whoever teaches his son teaches not only his son but also his son's son — and so on to the end of generations.   — Talmud, *ibid.*, 30a.

Fear

No passion so effectually robs the mind of all its powers of acting and reasoning as fear.   — Edmund Burke,
On the Sublime and Beautiful,
II.ii (1756).

Nothing is more despicable than respect based on fear.   — Albert Camus,
Notebooks 1935–1942, III.153 (1962).

To me the worst thing seems to be for a school principally to work with the methods of fear, force and artificial authority. Such treatment destroys sound sentiments, the sincerity and the self-confidence of the pupil. It produces the submissive subject.   — Albert Einstein,
Out of My Later Years, ix:
On Education (1950).

Fiction

See also Literature; Novel

Historical fiction is not only a respectable literary form; it is a standing reminder of the fact that history is about human beings.   — Helen M. Cam,
Historical Novel (1961).

For fiction, imaginative work that it is, is not dropped like a pebble upon the ground, as science may be; fiction is like a spider's web, attached ever so lightly perhaps, but still attached to life at all four corners.   — Virginia Woolf,
A Room of One' Own,
iii (1929).

Folly

Natural Folly is bad enough; but learned Folly is intolerable.   —Thomas Fuller (1654–1734), *Gnomologia* (1732).

There are as many fools at a university as elsewhere.... But their folly, I admit, has a certain stamp—the stamp of university training, if you like. It is trained folly.
    —William Gerhardie,
    The Polyglots, vii (1925).

Fool

See also Ignorant Person;
Stupidity; Unlearned

Nothing is more characteristic of a man than the manner in which he behaves towards fools.   —Henri Frédéric Amiel,
    Journal, Dec. 17, 1954.

He who teaches a fool is like one who glues potsherds together, or who rouses a sleeper from deep slumber.—*Apocrypha: Ecclesiasticus* 22:7 (c.180 B.C.).

Fools and intelligent people are equally harmless. It is half-fools and the half-intelligent who are the most dangerous.
    —Johann Wolfgang von Goethe,
    Proverbs in Prose (1819).

If all fooles wore white Caps, wee should seeme a flock of geese. – George Herbert,
    Outlandish Proverbs, no.513 (1640).

The right to be a cussed fool
 Is safe from all devices human,
It's common (ez a gin'l rule)
 To every critter born o' woman.
        —James Russell Lowell,
        The Biglow Papers, Ser.II:
        Latest Views of Mr. Biglow (1866).

A learned fool is a greater fool than an ig-norant fool.   —Molière,
    The Learned Women, IV.iii (1672).

Better a witty fool than a foolish wit.
        —William Shakespeare,
        Twelfth Night, I.v.36 (1601).

A well-read fool is the most pestilent of blockheads: his learning is a flail which he knows not how to handle, and with which he breaks his neighbor's shins as well as his own.   —Stanislas I,
King of Poland, *Oeuvres du Philosophe Bienfaisant* (1767).

Hain't we got all the fools in town on our side? And ain't that a big enough majori-ty in any town?   —Mark Twain,
        The Adventures of Huckleberry Finn,
        xxvi (1884).

Let us be thankful for the fools. But for them the rest of us could not succeed.
        —Mark Twain,
        Pudd'nhead Wilson's New Calendar,
        I.xxviii (1897).

Footnote

Scholarly barbed-wire.
        —Edmund Wilson, in
Princeton Alumni Weekly, Dec. 4, 1973.

Force

See also Discipline; Punish-ment; Punishment, Corporal

Boys naturally look on all force as an enemy, and generally find it so.
        —Henry Adams,
The Education of Henry Adams, i (1907).

Force is not a remedy.   —John Bright,
        speech in Birmingham, England,
        Nov. 16, 1880.

Who overcomes
By force hath overcome but half his foe.
        —John Milton,
        Paradise Lost, I.648 (1667).

Freedom

See also below

The Fourteenth Amendment, as now applied to the state, protects the citizen against the state itself and all of its creatures—boards of education not excepted.   —Robert H. Jackson, majority decision, U.S. Supreme Court, *West Virginia State Board of Education v Barnette*, 1943. This decision overturned the flag salute opinion in the *Gobitis* case.

The free man cannot be long an ignorant man.   —William McKinley, address in Pittsburgh, Nov. 3, 1897.

The greatest right in the world is the right to be wrong.   —Harry Weinberger, New York *Evening Post*, Apr. 10, 1917.

Freedom, Academic

See also Censorship; Freedom of Expression; Freedom of Thought

One condition is essential: freedom of discussion, unmolested inquiry. As in the early days of this century, we must have a spirit of tolerance which allows the expression of a great variety of opinions. On this point there can be no compromise even in days of an armed truce.
          —James Bryant Conant, *Education in a Divided World* (1948).

Studying a philosophy does not mean endorsing it, much less proclaiming it. We study cancer in order to learn how to defeat it. We must study the Soviet philosophy in our universities for exactly the same reason. No one must be afraid to tackle that explosive subject before a class.   —James Bryant Conant, *ibid.*

Men of moral and intellectual distinction could scarcely agree to teach in schools where an alien attitude was forced upon them.   —Marie Curie, *Pierre Curie* (1923).

An inviolable refuge from tyranny should be found in the university. It should be an *intellectual experiment station*, where new ideas may germinate and where their fruit, though still distasteful to the community as a whole may be allowed to ripen until finally, perchance, it may become part of the accepted international food of the nation or of the world.
          —Declaration of the First Committee on Academic Freedom of the American Association of University Professors, 1915.

A teacher should impart what's true
At least what they allow him to.
          —Irwin Edman, *Flower for a Professor's Garden of Verses* (c.1935).

By academic freedom I understand the right to search for truth and to publish and teach what one holds to be true. This right implies also a duty: one must not conceal any part of what one has recognized to be true.—Albert Einstein, letter on his 75th birthday, Mar. 13, 1954.

Anyone in a cap and gown can blast the presuppositions of life, can rob our sons and daughters of all the principles on which civilization depends—but let him as much as whisper "academic freedom, I've got my fingers crossed," and no professional educator dares say a word of criticism.   —Robert I. Gannon, *After Black Coffee* (1946).

Academic freedom is simply a way of saying that we get the best results in education and research if we leave their management to people who know something about them.
          —Robert M. Hutchins, *The Higher Learning in America*, i (1936).

A university ... is a continuing Socratic conversation on the highest level for the very best people you can think of, you can bring together, about the most important questions, and the thing that you must do to the uttermost possible limits is to guarantee those men the freedom to think and to express themselves.
— Robert M. Hutchins,
testimony before House of Representatives committee, 1952.

The right to interfere with the rights of others is no part of academic freedom.
— Grayson Kirk, "Ideas and Men,"
New York Times, June 6, 1965.

How can a man teach with autority, which is the life of teaching, how can he be a Doctor in his book as he ought to be, or else had better be silent, whenas all he teaches, all he delivers, is but under the tuition, under the correction of his patriarchial licenser to blot or alter what precisely accords not with the hidebound humour which he calls his judgement.
— John Milton, Areopagitica,
sec. 21 (1644) [Doctor = teacher].

To think that the bell does not toll for academic freedom or freedom of the press if economic freedom is shackled is a dangerous illusion.   — Walter Wriston,
Time, Aug. 13, 1979.

Freedom of Expression (Speech, Press)

See also Censorship; Freedom, Academic; Freedom of Thought

I would rather starve and rot and keep the privilege of speaking the truth as I see it, than of holding all the offices that capital has to give from the presidency down.
— Brooks Adams,
The Degradation of the Domestic Dogma (1919).

Liberty of speech inviteth and provoketh liberty to be used again, and so bringeth much to a man's knowledge.
— Francis Bacon,
The Advancement of Learning,
II.xxiii.22 (1605).

Free speech is to a great people what winds are to oceans and malarial regions, which waft away the elements of disease, and bring new elements of health. Where free speech is stopped miasma is bred, and death comes fast.
— Henry Ward Beecher,
Royal Truths (1862).

If we want truth, every man ought to be free to say what he thinks without fear. If the advocates of one side are to be rewarded with miters, and the advocates on the other with rope or stake, truth will not be heard.   — Desiderius Erasmus,
letter to Cardinal Campeggio,
Dec. 6, 1520.

Where men cannot freely convey their thoughts to one another, no other liberty is secure.   — William Ernest Hocking,
Freedom of the Press (1947).

When men have realized that time has upset many fighting faiths, they may come to believe even more than they believe the very foundations of their own conduct that the ultimate good desired is better reached by free trade in ideas — that the best test of truth is the power of the thought to get itself accepted in the competition of the market, and that truth is the only ground upon which their wishes safely can be carried out.
— Oliver Wendell Holmes, Jr.,
dissenting opinion, U.S. Supreme Court,
Abrams v United States, 1919.

The right to be heard does not automatically include the right to be taken seriously. To be taken seriously depends entirely upon what is being said.
— Hubert H. Humphrey,
address at the University of Wisconsin,
Aug. 23, 1965.

No government ought to be without censors; and, where the press is free, no one ever will.   — Thomas Jefferson, letter to George Washington, Sept. 9, 1792.

And I honor the man who is willing to sink
Half his present repute for the freedom to think,
And, when he has thought, be his cause strong or weak,
Will risk t' other half for the freedom to speak.   — James Russell Lowell, *A Fable for Critics*, ln.1067 (1848).

Complete liberty of contradicting and disproving our opinion is the very condition which justifies us in assuming its truth for purposes of action; and on no other terms can a being with human faculties have any rational assurance of being right.   — John Stuart Mill, *On Liberty*, ii (1859).

Strange it is that men should admit the validity of the arguments for free discussion, but object to their being "pushed to an extreme"; not seeing that unless the reasons are good for an extreme case, they are not good for any case.
    — John Stuart Mill, *ibid.*

If teachers of mankind are to be cognizant of all they ought to know, everything must be free to be written and published without restraint.
    — John Stuart Mill, *ibid.*

Though the silenced opinion be an error, it may, and very commonly does, contain a portion of truth; and since the general or prevailing opinion on any subject is rarely or never the whole truth, it is only by the collision of adverse opinions that the remainder of the truth has any chance of being supplied.   — John Stuart Mill, *ibid.*

Give me the liberty to know, to utter, and to argue freely, according to conscience, above all liberties.
    — John Milton, *Areopagitica*, sec.35 (1644) [utter = *publish*].

To be able to think freely, a man must be certain that no consequences will follow whatever he writes.   — Ernest Renan, *The Christian Church* (1879).

Thought is not free if the profession of certain opinions makes it impossible to earn a living.   — Bertrand Russell, *Sceptical Essays* (1928).

In general, we have as natural a right to make use of our pens as or our tongue, at our peril, risk, and hazard. I know many books which have bored their readers, but I know of none which has done real evil.   — Voltaire, *Philosophical Dictionary: Liberty of the Press* (1764).

Freedom of Thought

See also Freedom, Academic; Freedom of Expression; Freedom of Religion

Thought that is silenced is always rebellious.... Majorities, of course, are often mistaken. This is why the silencing of minorities is necessarily dangerous. Criticism and dissent are the indispensable antidote to major delusions.
    — Alan Barth, *The Loyalty of Free Men* (1951).

It is common knowledge that the thought of man shall not be tried, for the Devil himself knoweth not the thought of man.
    — Thomas Brion, Chief Justice, Common Pleas, England, 1477.

The freest possible scope should be given to all the opinions, discussions, and investigations of the learned; if frail they will fail, if right they will remain; like steam, they are dangerous only when pent in, restricted, and confined.
    — Charles Caleb Colton, *Lacon*, 312 (1820–22).

It is our attitude toward free thought and free expression that will determine our

fate. There must be no limit on the range of temperate discussion, no limits on thoughts. No subject must be taboo. No censor must preside at our assemblies.
— William O. Douglas, address to the Authors' Guild, on receiving the Lauterbach Award, Dec. 3, 1952.

I maintain that opinion is free, and that conduct alone is amenable to the law.
— Thomas Erskine, arguendo, *Trial of Thomas Paine*, 1792.

The opinions of men are not the object of civil government, nor under its jurisdiction. — Thomas Jefferson, *A Bill for Establishing Religious Freedom*, 1779; adopted Jan. 16, 1786. Deleted from the final bill.

The only real security for social well-being is the free exercise of men's minds.
— Harold J. Laski, *Authority in the Modern State* (1919).

I know but one freedom and that is the freedom of the mind. As for any other freedom, it is but a mockery and a delusion, for however free you may think yourself, you have to use the door when you go out of the room, nor are you free to make yourself young at will or to profit by the sun at night.
— Antoine de Saint-Exupéry, *The Wisdom of the Sands*, lxv (1950).

Not only is freedom of thought and speech compatible with piety and the peace of the State, but it cannot be withheld without destroying at the same time both the peace of the State and piety itself. — Baruch Spinoza, *Tractatus Theologico-Politicus* (1670).

If men's minds were as easily controlled as their tongues, every king would sit safely on his throne, and government by compulsion would cease. — Baruch Spinoza, *ibid.*, xx.

This I believe: that the free, exploring mind of the individual human is the most valuable thing in the world. And this I would fight for: the freedom of the mind to take any direction it wishes, undirected. And this I must fight against: any idea, religion, or government which limits or destroys the individual.
— John Steinbeck, *East of Eden*, xiii (1952).

If we value the pursuit of knowledge, we must be free to follow wherever that search may lead us. The free mind is no barking dog, to be tethered on a ten-foot chain. — Adlai E. Stevenson, speech at University of Wisconsin, Oct. 8, 1952.

The Future

If you do not think about the future, you cannot have one. — John Galsworthy, *Swan Song*, II.vi (1928).

We should all be concerned with the future because we will have to spend the rest of our lives there.
— Charles F. Kettering, *Seed for Thought* (1949).

Anyone who tries to draw the future in hard lines and vivid hues is a fool. The future will never sit for a portrait. It will come around a corner we never noticed, take us by surprise. — George B. Leonard, *Education and Ecstasy*, 139 (1968).

The Future is something which everyone reaches at the rate of sixty minutes an hour, whatever he does, whoever he is.
— C.S. Lewis, *The Screwtape Letters*, xxv (1942).

We send Johnny to school "to help him lead a better life in the future." But how many of us have taken the time to think seriously about what the future will be like? Most of us, teachers included, assume that today's way of life will be repeated in the future. Yet all the evidence points toward a radically

changed tomorrow. Johnny must learn to anticipate the directions and rate of change. All of this will require broad, imaginative innovations in our educational system.   —Alvin Toffler,
Future Shock (1970).

All education springs from some image of the future. If the image of the future held by a society is grossly inaccurate, its educational system will betray its youth.
          —Alvin Toffler,
Learning for Tomorrow: The Role of the Future in Education (1974).

Future Generation

These things shall be,—a loftier race
Than e'er the world hath known shall rise
With flame of freedom in their souls,
And light of knowledge in their eyes.
          —John Addington Symonds
(1840–93), *The Days That Are to Be.*

[Children will] do all we have left undone, all we have failed to do, all we might have done had we been wise enough, all we have been too weak and too stupid to do.
          —Kate Douglas Wiggin,
Marm Lisa (1896).

Generalization

See also Hypothesis;
Proposition; Theory

It being the nature of the mind of man, to the extreme prejudice of knowledge, to delight in the spacious liberty of generalities, as in a champion region, and not in the enclosure of particularity.
          —Francis Bacon, *The Advancement of Learning*, II.viii.1 (1605).

I daresay that I have worked off my fundamental formula on you that the chief end of man is to frame general propositions and that no general proposition is worth a damn.   —Oliver Wendell
Holmes, Jr., letter to Sir Frederick
Pollock, Nov. 22, 1920, *Holmes-Pollock Letters*, ed. M.A. DeWolfe Howe (1941).

Men are more apt to be mistaken in their generalizations than in their particular observations.   —Niccolò Machiavelli,
Discourses, i (1531).

General notions are generally wrong.
          —Mary Wortley Montagu, letter to
Wortley Montagu, Mar. 28, 1710.

Any general statement is like a checque drawn on a bank. Its value depends on what is there to meet it. —Ezra Pound,
ABC of Reading, I.i (1934).

Generation Gap

See also Youth and Age

The dead might as well try to speak to the living as the old to the young.
          —Willa Cather,
One of Ours, II.vi (1922).

It is a great pity that men and women forget that they have been children. Parents are apt to be foreigners to their sons and daughters. —George William
Curtis, *Prue and I*, vii (1857).

Children are all foreigners. We treat them as such. We cannot understand their speech or the mode of life, and so our Education is remote and accidental and not closely applied to the facts.
          —Ralph Waldo Emerson,
Journals, 1839.

Youth and age will never agree.
          —David Ferguson,
Scottish Proverbs, 112 (1641).

Each generation has a different language, and can't learn what former generations knew until it has been translated into their words.   —Katherine Butler
Hathaway, *The Journals and Letters of the Little Locksmith* (1946).

So long as there is life in the world, each generation will react against its predecessor, correct it, go beyond it. The house that accommodates the fathers never quite suits the children.
          —Richard Livingstone,
On Education (1944).

His father watched him across the gulf of years and pathos which always must divide a father from his son.
—John P. Marquand,
The Late George Apley, x (1937).

The minds of different generations are as impenetrable one by the other as are the monads of Leibniz.   — André Maurois,
Ariel, xii (1924).

Even very recently, the elders could say: "You know I have been young, and *you* can never have been old." But today's young people can reply: "You have never been young in the world I am young in, and you never can be...." This break between generations is wholly new: it is planetary and universal.
— Margaret Mead,
Culture and Commitment (1970).

What's happening now is an immigration in time, with people over 40 the migrants into the present age, and the children born in it the natives.— Margaret Mead,
ibid.

The commonest axiom of history is that every generation revolts against its fathers and makes friends with its grandfathers.
— Lewis Mumford,
The Brown Decades (1931).

We think our fathers fools, so wise we grow;
Our wiser sons, no doubt, will think us so.   — Alexander Pope,
An Essay on Criticism, II.438 (1711).

Generation Gap: A chasm, amorphously situated in time and space, that separates those who have grown up absurd from those who will, with luck, grow up absurd.   — Bernard Rosenberg,
Dictionary for the Disenchanted (1972).

I tell you there's a wall ten feet thick and ten miles high between parent and child.
— George Bernard Shaw, *Parents and Children*, preface to *Misalliance* (1914).

Genius

See also Gifted Person; Talent

To do easily what is difficult for others is the mark of talent. To do what is impossible for talent is the mark of genius.
— Henri Frédéric Amiel,
Journal, Dec. 17, 1856.

Genius, that power which dazzles mortal eyes,
Is oft but perseverance in disguise.
— Henry Austin,
Perseverance Conquers All (c.1613).

We define genius as the capacity for productive reaction against one's training.
— Bernhard Berenson (1865–1959),
The Decline of Art.

It is only the thrust of genius that has ever forced the inertia of Humanity to yield.
— Henri Bergson, *Two Sources of Morality and Religion*, 181 (1935).

"Genius," which means the transcendent capacity of taking trouble, first of all.
— Thomas Carlyle,
History of Frederick the Great,
IV.iii (1858–65).

Genius is reason made sublime.
— Marie Joseph de Chénier,
Épître à Voltaire (1806).

The drafts which true genius draws upon posterity, although they may not always be honoured so soon as they are due, are sure to be paid with compound interest, in the end.   — Charles Caleb Colton,
Lacon, 34 (1820–22).

It is strange that we have so few men of genius on our faculties.... Institutions and genius are in the nature of things antithetical, and if a man of genius is found living contentedly in a university, it is peculiarly creditable to both.
— Charles Horton Cooley,
Life and the Student: Roadside Notes of Human Nature, Society and Letters, 184 (1931).

Too often we forget that genius, too, depends upon the data within its reach, that even Archimedes could not have devised Edison's inventions.
—Ernest Dimnet,
The Art of Thinking, IV.i (1928).

With the stones we cast at them, geniuses build new roads for us.
—Paul Eldridge,
Maxims for a Modern Man (1965).

Every man of genius sees the world at a different angle from his fellows, and there is his tragedy. —Havelock Ellis,
The Dance of Life, iii (1923).

In every work of genius we recognize our own rejected thoughts; they come back to us with a certain alienated majesty.
—Ralph Waldo Emerson,
Essays, First Series: Self-Reliance (1841).

Colleges hate geniuses, just as convents hate saints. —Ralph Waldo Emerson,
Uncollected Lectures: Public and Private Education (1870).

Genius not only diagnoses a situation by non-logical thought but supplies the remedy. —Robert Graves,
Difficult Questions, Easy Answers: Genius (1973).

A great genius forms itself on another great genius less by assimilation than by friction. One diamond grinds another.
—Heinrich Heine,
Germany from Luther to Kant (1834).

The world is always ready to receive talent with open arms. Very often it does not know what to do with genius.
—Oliver Wendell Holmes, Sr.,
The Professor at the Breakfast-Table: Iris, Her Book (1860).

Genius is a promontory jutting out into the infinite. —Victor Hugo,
William Shakespeare (1864).

In the republic of mediocrity genius is dangerous. —Robert G. Ingersoll,
Liberty in Literature (1890).

Genius, in truth, means little more than the faculty of perceiving in an unhabitual way. —William James, *The Principles of Psychology*, II.110 (1890).

Between genius and talent there is the proportion of the whole to its part.
—Jean de La Bruyère,
Les Caractères, xii:
Des Jugements (1688).

Good sense travels on the well-worn paths; genius, never. And that is why the crowd, not altogether without reason, is so ready to treat great men as lunatics.
—Cesare Lombroso,
The Man of Genius, preface (1889).

Talk not of genius baffled. Genius is master of man;
Genius does what it must, and talent does what it can. —Owen Meredith
(1831–91), *Last Words of a Sensitive Second-Rate Poet*.

There is no genius without a touch of madness. —Seneca,
Moral Essays: On the Tranquility of the Mind, XVII.x (c. A.D. 62).

A genius is a man selected by Nature to carry on the work of building up an intellectual consciousness of her own instinctive purpose.
—George Bernard Shaw,
Man and Superman: Epistle Dedicatory (1903).

It is necessary for the welfare of society that genius should be privileged to utter sedition, to blaspheme, to outrage good taste, to corrupt the youthful mind, and, generally, to scandalize one's uncles.
—George Bernard Shaw,
The Sanity of Art (1895).

It takes a lot of time to be a genius, you have to sit around so much doing nothing, really doing nothing.
—Gertrude Stein,
Everybody's Autobiography, ii (1937).

Genius seems to be the faculty of having faith in everything, and especially one's self.   — Arthur Stringer, *The Devastator*, 116 (1944).

When a true genius appears in the world, you may know him by this sign, that the dunces are all in confederacy against him.
— Jonathan Swift,
Thoughts on Various Subjects (1706).

The function of genius is not to give new answers, but to pose new questions which time and mediocrity can solve.
— H.R. Trevor-Roper,
Men and Events (1958).

Genius is not a single power, but a combination of great powers. It reasons, but it is not reasoning; it judges, but it is not judgment; it imagines, but it is not imagination; it feels deeply and fiercely, but it is not passion. It is neither, because it is all.   — Edwin Percy Whipple,
Literature and Life: Genius (1871).

Genius is more often found in a cracked pot than in a whole one. — E.B. White,
One Man's Meat: Lime (1944).

The public is wonderfully tolerant. It forgives everything except genius.
— Oscar Wilde, *Intentions: The Critic as Artist* (1891).

Girl

See also below; Child; Woman; Youth

Young girls like the excess of any quality. Without knowing, they want to suffer, to suffer they must exaggerate; they like to have loud chords struck on them.
— Elizabeth Bowen,
The House in Paris, II.v (1935).

If girls aren't ignorant, they're cultured.... You can't avoid suffering.
— William Cooper,
Scenes from Provincial Life,
III.ii (1950).

"Boys will be boys — "
"And even that ... wouldn't matter if we could only prevent girls from being girls."   — Anthony Hope,
The Dolly Dialogues, no.16 (1894).

You may chisel a boy into shape, as you would a rock, or hammer him into it if he be of a better kind, as you would a piece of bronze. But you cannot hammer a girl into anything. She grows as a flower does.
— John Ruskin,
Sesame and Lilies, ii (1865).

Girls, Education of

See also Women, Education of

An eminent teacher of girls said, "the idea of a girl's education is, whatever qualifies her for going to Europe."
— Ralph Waldo Emerson,
The Conduct of Life: Culture (1860).

Nothing is more neglected than the education of girls.... As for girls, they say, it is not necessary that they be learned, curiosity renders them vain and affected; it is enough if they know how to govern some day their households, and to obey their husbands without question.
— François Fénelon,
The Education of Girls (1681).

In those days, people did not think it was important for girls to read. Some people thought much reading gave girls brain fever.   — Ann McGovern,
The Secret Soldier (1975).

The whole system is demoralizing and foolish. Girls study for prizes and not for learning, when "honors" are at the end. The unscholarly motive is wearying. If they studied for sound learning, the cheer which would come with every day's gain would be health-preserving.
— Maria Mitchell, Mar. 13, 1882,
in Mitchell Kendall, ed.,
Maria Mitchell, Life, Letters and Journals (1896).

If there were to be any difference between a girls' education and a boys', I should say that of the two the girl should be earlier led, as her intellect ripens faster, into deep and serious subjects: and that her range of literature should be, not more, but less frivolous.   —John Ruskin, *Sesame and Lilies*, ii (1865).

It is not to be wondered at, ma'am—all this is the natural consequence of teaching girls to read. Had I a thousand daughters, by Heaven, I'd as soon have them taught the black art as their alphabet!   —Richard Brinsley Sheridan, *The Rivals*, I.ii (1775).

I would by no means wish a daughter of mine to be a progeny of learning; I don't think so much learning becomes a young woman; for instance—I would never let her meddle with Greek, or Hebrew, or Algebra,...or such inflammatory branches of learning—neither would it be necessary for her to handle any of your mathematical, astronomical, diabolical instruments.—Richard Brinsley Sheridan, *ibid*. Mrs. Malaprop speaking.

I would send her, at nine years old, to a boarding-school, in order to learn a little ingenuity and artifice. Then, sir, she should have a supercilious knowledge in accounts;—and as she grew up, I would have her instructed in geometry, that she might know something of the catagious countries;...she should be mistress of orthodoxy, that she might not misspell, and mispronounce words;...that she might reprehend the true meaning of what she is saying.
          —Richard Brinsley Sheridan, *ibid*. Mrs. Malaprop speaking.

Give me a girl at an impressionable age, and she is mine for life.—Muriel Spark, *The Prime of Miss Jean Brodie*, I (1961).

Goal, Personal

See also Aspiration

You must keep your goal in sight, Labor toward it day and night, Then at last arriving there— You shall be too old to care.
          —Witter Bynner (1881–1968), *Wisdom*.

Slight not what's near through aiming at what's far.   —Attr. Euripides, *Rhesus* (c.455–441 B.C.).

We only lose our way when we lose our own aim.   —François Fénelon (1651–1715), *Spiritual Letters*, (tr. 1878).

It is not a very proper remark that we should above all place the goal beyond the reach of men, in order that they may at least proceed as far as is possible for their strength to carry them?
          —Georg Forster (1754–94), *Collected Works*.

Man's main task in life is to give birth to himself.   —Erich Fromm, *Man for Himself*, iv (1947).

Man's chief goal in life is still to become and stay human, and defend his achievements against the encroachments of nature.   —Eric Hoffer, *The Temper of Our Time*, v: *The Return of Nature* (1967).

No wind makes for him that hath no intended port to sail unto.
          —Michel de Montaigne, *Essays*, II.i (1580): *Of the Inconsistency of Our Actions*.

If you don't know where you are going, you will probably end up somewhere else.   —Laurence J. Peter and Raymond Hull, *The Peter Principle*, xv (1969).

Men frequently view teaching as a stepping stone to educational administration while women look to careers as classroom teachers.   —Carol Polowy, "Sex Discrimination: The Legal Obligations of Educational Institutions," *Vital Speeches*, Feb. 1, 1975.

You speak in your letter of modern education "tending toward career-oriented goals." In my day, fifty years ago, we did not tack the word "oriented" onto everything, but we were just as interested in a career, just as eager to reach our goal, as are the young students of today.   —E.B. White, letter to Mitchell Uscher, Feb. 1974, *Letters*, ed. Dorothy Lobrano Guth (1976).

Graduate, University

Why is it that the boy or girl who on June 15 receives his degree, eager, enthusiastic, outspoken, idealistic, reflective, and independent, is on the following Sept. 15, or even June 16 ... dull, uninspiring, shifty, pliable and attired in a double-breasted, blue serge suit? The answer must lie in the relative weakness of the higher education, compared with the forces that make everybody think and act like everybody else.
          —Robert M. Hutchins, farewell address at University of Chicago, *Time*, Feb. 12, 1951.

He is piping hot from the university. He smells of buttered loaves yet.
          —Thomas Middleton, *Your Five Gallants* (1608?).

When we exchanged the short undergraduate gown for the B.A.-M.A. gown and hood, we put on more than an emblem of brief scholastic achievement. We put on the mantle of humility before great learning; we put on the love of learning and belief in its significance; we put on the responsibility to us all that great teachers had given us, the duty not to let the torch go out unheeded.
          —Virginia Ridley, "American Girl at Oxford," *Christian Science Monitor*, Oct. 21, 1958.

You know it's been said that "when you graduate from Harvard or Yale it takes the next 10 years to live it down and the next 40 to try to forget it."   —Will Rogers, *Autobiography*, xi (1926).

Grammar

See also Language; Punctuation

And that my grammar go awry,
          And that my English be askew,
Sooth, I can prove an alibi—
          The Bard of Avon did it too.
                    —Franklin P. Adams,
          Erring in Company, in Carolyn Wells, ed., *The Book of Humorous Verse* (1936).

The grammar has a rule absurd
          Which I would call an outworn myth:
"A preposition is a word
          You mustn't end a sentence with!"
                    —Berton Braley (1882–1966), *No Rule to Be Afraid Of*.

—More fault of those who had the hammering
Of prosody into me and syntax,
And did it, not with hobnails but tin-tacks!   —Robert Browning, *Dramatic Romances and Lyrics: The Flight of the Duchess*, XV (1845).

The approach to English grammar in the 20th century—the move toward a kind of logical, mathematical description of the language—has been a disaster, leaving children totally at sea. Schoolmasters are also confused and don't know what to teach. The upshot is that, by some estimates, about 15 percent of all Americans are now functionally illiterate.
          —Robert Burchfield, "A Conversation with Robert Burchfield," *U.S. News & World Report*, Dec. 15, 1980.

It is not the business of grammar, as some critics seem preposterously to imagine, to give law to the fashions which regulate our speech. On the contrary, from its

conformity to these, and from that alone, it derives all its authority and value.
— George Campbell,
The Philosophy of Rhetoric (1776).

This is the sort of English up with which I will not put. — Winston Churchill (1874–1965), marginal comment addressed to the proofreader who had "corrected" a sentence of his memoirs.

French grammar cannot be made easy. Nor can Latin grammar. It can be made, and ought to be made, clear and interesting. — Ernest Dimnet, *The Art of Thinking*, II.i.b (1928).

If you are writing to your friend, when you want to know what words to write grammar will tell you; but whether you should write to your friend or should not write grammar will not tell you.
— Epictetus,
Discourses, I.i (c. A.D. 100).

You can be a little ungrammatical if you come from the right part of the country.
— Robert Frost,
The Atlantic, Jan. 1962.

I give you a new definition of a sentence: A sentence is a sound in itself on which other sounds called words are strung.
— Robert Frost, letter to John T. Bartlett, Feb. 22, 1914, in Lawrance Thompson, ed., *Selected Letters of Robert Frost*, 110 (1946).

We are almost ashamed to refer to the fact that a report has come to us that your brotherhood is teaching grammar to certain people.... If it should be clearly proved hereafter that the report we have heard is false and that you are not devoting yourself to the vanities of worldly learning, we shall render thanks to God for keeping your heart from defilement by the blasphemous praises of infamous men. — St. Gregory the Great, letter to Desiderius, Bishop of Vienne, *Epistles*, XI.54 (c.590–604).

When a thought takes one's breath away, a lesson on grammar seems an impertinence.
— Thomas Wentworth Higginson, preface to *Poems by Emily Dickinson* (1890).

Grammar is to speech what salt is to food.
— Moses Ibn Ezra,
Shirat Yisrael, 110
(12th cent.).

Where strictness of grammar does not weaken expression, it should be attended to.... But where, by small grammatical negligence, the energy of an idea is condensed, or a word stands for a sentence, I hold grammatical rigor in contempt.
— Thomas Jefferson,
letter to James Madison, 1801.

And I would fain have any one name to me that tongue, that any one can learn or speak as he should do, by the rules of grammar. Languages were made not by rules or art, but by accident and the common use of people. — John Locke, *Some Thoughts concerning Education* (1693).

It is well to remember that grammar is common speech formulated.
— W. Somerset Maugham,
The Summing Up, xiii (1938).

The greater part of the world's troubles are due to questions of grammar.
— Michel de Montaigne,
Essays, II.xii (1580):
Apology for Raymond Sebond.

A man's grammar, like Caesar's wife, must not only be pure, but above suspicion of impurity. — Edgar Allan Poe, *Marginalia* (1844–49).

If your four negatives make your two affirmatives, why then, the worse for my friends and the better for my foes.
— William Shakespeare, *Twelfth Night*, V.i.21 (1601).

There is a busybody on your staff who devotes a lot of his time to chasing split infinitives. Every good literary craftsman splits his infinitives when the sense demands it. I call for the immediate dismissal of this pedant. It is of no consequence whether he decides to go quickly or quickly to go or quickly go. The important thing is that he should go at once.   — George Bernard Shaw, letter to the London *Times*, in Blanche Eliza Patch, *Thirty Years with G.B.S.* (1951).

I am the king of the Romans, and above grammar.   — Emperor Sigismund (1368–1437), when a prelate called his attention to a mistake in grammar in his opening speech at the Council of Constance, 1414.

To go through the grammar of one language is of great use for the mastery of every other grammar; because there obtains, through all languages, a certain analogy to each other in their grammatical construction.   — Sydney Smith, *Classical Learning* (1809).

When I read some of the rules for speaking and writing the English language correctly — as that a sentence must never end with a particle — and perceive how implicitly even the learned obey it, I think:
    Any fool can make a rule
    And every fool will mind it.
          — Henry David Thoreau, *Journal*, Feb. 3, 1860.

The next grammar book I bring out I want to tell how to end a sentence with five prepositions. A father of a little boy goes upstairs after supper to read to his son, but he brings the wrong book. The boy says, "What did you bring that book that I don't want to be read to out of up for?"   — E.B. White, letter to J.G. Case, Mar. 30, 1962, *Letters*, ed. Dorothy Lobrano Guth (1976).

Growing Up

See also Boyhood; Childhood; Growth

If growing up is painful for the Southern Black girl, being aware of her displacement is the rust on the razor that threatens the throat.   — Maya Angelou, *I Know Why the Caged Bird Sings*, introd. (1970).

Growing is not the easy, plain sailing business that it is commonly supposed to be: it is hard work — harder than any but a growing boy can understand; it requires attention, and you are not strong enough to attend to your bodily growth and to your lessons too. — Samuel Butler (1835–1902), *The Way of All Flesh*, xxxi (1903).

Those parents who concern themselves with their children's problems are crazy. The problems of a nine-year-old kid cannot be solved in any way, except by becoming ten.   — Al Capp, in Lore and Maurice Cowan, *The Wit of the Jews* (1970).

If you expect a boy to be a man, the sooner you let him start practicing, the better.   — Harry Golden, *You're Entitle': Early adulthood* (1962).

Children with Hyacinth's temperament don't know better as they grow older; they merely know more.
          — Saki (1870–1916), *Hyacinth*.

Growth

See also Development; Growing Up; Maturity

Oh, the glory of growth, silent, mighty, persistent, inevitable! To awaken, to open up like a flower to the light of a fuller consciousness! —Emily Carr, *Hundreds and Thousands*, Oct. 17, 1933 (1966).

Since life means growth, a living creature lives as truly and positively at one stage as at another, with the same intrinsic fullness and the same absolute claims. Hence education means the enterprise of supplying the conditions which insure growth, or adequacy of life, irrespective of age. —John Dewey, *Democracy and Education*, iv (1916).

Education as growth or maturity should be an ever-present process.
—John Dewey, *Experience and Education*, iii (1938).

Why build these cities glorious
If man unbuilded goes
In vain we build the world, unless
The builder grows.
—Edwin Markham, *Man-Making*, in T.C. Clark, ed., *1000 Quotable Poems* (1937).

All growth is a leap in the dark, a spontaneous, unpremeditated act without the benefit of experience. —Henry Miller, *The Wisdom of the Heart: The Absolute Collective* (1941).

We do not grow absolutely, chronologically. We grow sometimes in one dimension, and not in another, unevenly. We grow partially. We are relative. We are mature in one realm, childish in another. The past, present, and future mingle and pull us backward, forward, or fix us in the present. We are made up of layers, cells, constellations.
—Anaïs Nin, *The Diaries of Anaïs Nin*, IV (1974).

A road that does not lead to other roads always has to be retraced, unless the traveller chooses to rust at the end of it.
—Tehyi Hsieh, *Chinese Epigrams Inside Out and Proverbs*, 144 (1948).

Habit

To learn new habits is everything, for it is to reach the substance of life. Life is but a tissue of habits.
—Henri Frédéric Amiel, *Journal*, Dec. 30, 1850.

'Tis easier to prevent bad habits than to break them. —Benjamin Franklin, *Poor Richard's Almanack*, Oct. 1745.

Bad habits are easier to abandon today than tomorrow. —Judah Leib Lazerov, *Encyklopedie fun Idishē Vitzen*, no.492 (1928).

We naturally like what we have been accustomed to.... This is one of the causes which prevent men from finding truth.
—Maimonides, *Guide for the Perplexed*, I.xxxi (1190).

Habit is stronger than reason.
—George Santayana, *Interpretations of Poetry and Religion* (1900).

Handwriting

Most people enjoy the sight of their own handwriting as they enjoy the smell of their own farts. —W.H. Auden, *The Dyer's Hand: Writing* (1962).

Every man has one thing he can do better than anyone else—and usually it's reading his own handwriting.
—G. Norman Collie, *Education Digest*, Apr. 1967.

In his penmanship man stands revealed—
Purest intent by chastest style is sealed.
—Joseph Ezobi, *Kaarat Kesef* (1270).

See to it that thy penmanship and handwriting is as beautiful as thy style. Keep thy pen in fine working order, use ink of good color. Make thy script as perfect as possible.... The beauty of a composition

depends on the writing, and the beauty of the writing on pen, paper, and ink; and all of these excellencies are an index to the author's worth.
　　　　　　　—Judah Ibn Tibbon,
　　　　　　　Ethical Will (c.1190),
　　　　　　　　　　　　to his son.

Men of quality are in the wrong to undervalue, as they often do, the practise of a fair and quick hand in writing; for it is no immaterial accomplishment.
　　　　　　　　　　—Quintilian,
Institutio Oritoria, I.v (A.D. 95 or 96).

Who'er writ it writes a hand like a foot.
　　　　　　　—Jonathan Swift,
　　　　　Polite Conversation (1738).

Health

See also Mental Health

I should have performed the office of but half a friend were I to confine myself to the improvement of the mind only. Knowledge indeed is a desirable, a lovely possession, but I do not scruple to say that health is more so. It is of little consequence to store the mind with science if the body be permitted to become debilitated.　　　—Thomas Jefferson, letter to Thomas Mann Randolph, Aug. 27, 1786.

Pray for a sound mind in a sound body.
　　　　　　　—Juvenal, Satires,
　　　　　　　VIII.356 (c.110).

Hearing

See also Listening

Hearing a hundred times is not as good as seeing once.
　　　　—Selwyn Gurney Champion,
　　　　　Racial Proverbs, 445 (1938).
　　　　　　　A Japanese proverb.

The sense of hearing should always be conjoined with that of sight, and the

tongue should be trained in combination with the hand. The subjects that are taught should not merely be taught orally, and thus appeal to the ear alone, but should be pictorially illustrated, and thus develop the imagination by the help of the eye.　　　—John Amos Comenius, The Great Didactic (1628-32).

Every man hears only what he understands. —Johann Wolfgang von Goethe, Proverbs in Prose (1819).

Learning is easilier gotten by the eares then by the eyes.　—Stefano Guazzo, Civil Conversation, I.40 (1574).

Less vividly is the mind stirred by what finds entrance through the ears than what is brought before the trusty eyes.
　　　　　　　—Horace, Ars Poetica,
　　　　　　　ln.180 (20 B.C.).

Heart

The heart is wiser than the intellect.
　　　　　　　—Josiah G. Holland,
　　　　　　　Kathrina (1868).

It is the heart, and not the brain,
That to the highest doth attain.
　　　—Henry Wadsworth Longfellow,
　　　The Building of the Ship, viii (1849).

The heart has eyes that the brain knows nothing of.　　—Charles H. Parkhurst, Sermons: Coming to the Truth (1921).

I trust your wisdom only when it comes from the heart, your goodness when it comes from the mind.
　　　　　　　—Arthur Schnitzler,
　　　Buch der Sprüche und Bedenken,
　　　　　　　230 (1927).

Heredity

A child's education should begin at least one hundred years before he was born.
　　　—Oliver Wendell Holmes, Sr., The Autocrat of the Breakfast-Table, i (1858).

Deep in the cavern of the infant's breast
The father's nature lurks, and lives anew.
—Horace, *Odes*,
IV.iv (23 B.C.).

Heresy

See also Dissent;
Nonconformity

They that approve a private opinion, call
it opinion; but they that mislike it,
heresy; and yet heresy signifies no more
than private opinion.—Thomas Hobbes,
Leviathan, I.xi (1651).

The heresy of one age becomes the orthodoxy of the next.   —Helen Keller,
Optimism, ii (1903).

Heresies are experiments in man's un-
satisfied search for truth. —H.G. Wells,
Crux Ansata, 14 (1944).

High School

What is learned in high school, or for
that matter, anywhere at all, depends far
less on what is taught than on what one
actually experiences in the place.
—Edgar Z. Friedenberg,
*The Dignity of Youth
and Other Atavisms* (1965).

In the Middle West, the high school is
the place where the band practices.
—Robert M. Hutchins,
in *New York Herald Tribune*,
Apr. 22, 1963.

In pursuit of an educational program to
suit the bright and the not-so-bright we
have watered down a rigid training for
the elite until we now have an educational diet in many of our public high
schools that nourishes neither the classes
or the masses.   —Agnes Meyer,
Out of These Roots, ii (1953).

Historian

See also History, Writing of

No honest historian can take part with—
or against—the forces he has to study. To
him even the extinction of the human
race should be merely a fact to be
grouped with other vital statistics.
—Henry Adams, *The Education
of Henry Adams*, xxx (1907).

What makes a good writer of history is a
guy who is suspicious. Suspicion marks
the real difference between the man who
wants to write honest history and the one
who'd rather write a good story.
—Jim Bishop,
New York Times, Feb. 5, 1955.

It has been said that though God cannot
alter the past, historians can; it is perhaps
because they can be useful to Him in this
respect that He tolerates their existence.
—Samuel Butler (1835–1902),
Erewhon Revisited, xiv (1901).

Who does not know history's first law to
be that an author must not dare to tell
anything but the truth? And its second
that he must be bold to tell the whole
truth? That there must be no suggestion
of partiality anywhere in his writings?
Nor of malice?   —Cicero,
De Oratore, II.62 (c.55 B.C.).

I don't think the historian should be a
judge in a formal sense, saying "He was
good," "He should have been sen-
tenced," "He should have been re-
prieved." The historian is not God, but I
think it's inevitable that historians use
judgment. I don't think this is a defin-
able distinction, but it is a distinction.
—Henry Steele Commager,
in Israel Shenker, *Words and Their
Masters*, 132 (1974).

The further you get away from any period
the better you can write about it. You
aren't subject to interruptions by people
that were there. —Finley Peter Dunne,
*Mr. Dooley Remembers: Some
Observations by Mr. Dooley* (1963).

Historians relate, not so much what is done, as what they would have believed.
— Benjamin Franklin,
Poor Richard's Almanack, Mar. 1739.

The historian's first duties are sacrilege and the mocking of false gods. They are his indispensable instruments for establishing the truth.   — Jules Michelet,
History of France, I (1833).

History repeats itself, says the proverb, but that is precisely what it never really does. It is the historians (of a sort) who repeat themselves. — Clement F. Rogers,
Verify Your References, 31 (1938).

History

See also below; The Past

History does not unfold: it piles up.
— Robert M. Adams,
Bad Mouth (1977).

If an historian were to relate truthfully all the crimes, weaknesses and disorders of mankind, his readers would take his work for satire rather than for history.
— Pierre Bayle,
Historical and Critical Dictionary (1697).

History is not life. But since only life makes history the union of the two is obvious.   — Louis D. Brandeis,
in Solomon Goldman, *The Words of Justice Brandeis*, 93 (1953).

Not to know what happened before one was born is to remain always a child.
— Cicero, *De Oratore*,
II.34 (c.55 B.C.).

We are never completely contemporaneous with our present. History advances in disguise; it appears on stage wearing the mask of the preceding scene, and we tend to lose the meaning of the play.   — Régis Debray,
Revolution in the Revolution?,
i (1967).

History repeats itself in the large because human nature changes with geological leisureliness. — Will and Ariel Durant,
The Lessons of History (1968).

There is properly no history, only biography. — Ralph Waldo Emerson,
Essays, First Series: History (1841).

History repeats itself, it is true, but history will not bear mimicry.
— Augustus Jessopp,
Daily Life, 163 (1885).

History must always be taken with a grain of salt. It is, after all, not a science but an art.   — Phyllis McGinley,
*Saint Watching:
Aspects of Sanctity*
(1969).

There is no history of mankind, there are only many histories of all kinds of aspects of human life. And one of these is the history of political power. This is elevated into the history of the world.
— Karl R. Popper,
The Open Society and Its Enemies
(1945).

I doubt if there is a thing in the world as wrong or unreliable as history. History ain't what it is; it's what some writer wanted it to be, and I just happened to think I remember ours is as cock-eyed as the rest.   — Will Rogers,
Autobiography (1926).

All that the historians give us are little oases in the desert of time, and we linger fondly on these, forgetting the vast tracks between one and another that were trodden by the weary generations of men.
— John Alfred Spender,
*The Comments of Bagshot,
Second Series* (1914).

The chief value of history, if it is critically studied, is to break down the illusion that peoples are very different. — Leo Stein,
Journey into the Self,
254 (1950).

The poetry of history lies in the quasi-miraculous fact that once, on this familiar spot of ground, walked other men and women, as actual as we are today, thinking their own thoughts, swayed with their own passion, but now all gone, one generation vanishing after another, gone as utterly as we ourselves shall shortly be gone like ghosts at cock-crow.
—G.M. Trevelyan,
Clio (1904).

Human history becomes more and more a race between education and catastrophe.   —H.G. Wells,
The Outline of History, xv (1920).

History has no time to be just.... She keeps her eyes fixed on the victorious, and leaves the vanquished in the shadows.   —Stefan Zweig,
The Right to Heresy, 15 (1936).

History, Definition and Description of

History is a tangled skein that one may take up at any point, and break when one has unravelled enough.—Henry Adams,
The Education of Henry Adams,
xx (1907).

History, *n*. An account mostly false, of events mostly unimportant, which are brought about by rulers mostly knaves, and soldiers, mostly fools.
—Ambrose Bierce,
The Devil's Dictionary (1911).

Histories are a kind of distilled newspapers.   —Thomas Carlyle,
Heroes and Hero-Worship, III:
The Hero as Poet (1840).

History is only a confused heap of facts.
—Lord Chesterfield,
Letters to His Son, Feb. 5, 1750.

History is the witness that testifies to the passing of time; it illumines reality, vitalizes memory, provides guidance in

daily life, and brings us tidings of antiquity.   —Cicero,
De Oratore, II.36 (c.55 B.C.).

What is history after all? History is facts which become lies in the end; legends are lies which become history in the end.
—Jean Cocteau,
The Observer, Sept. 22, 1957.

What constitutes history may be thus described: it is the act of comprehending and understanding induced by the requirements of practical life.
—Benedetto Croce,
History as the Story of Liberty (1941).

History is a post-mortem examination. It tells you what a country died of. But I'd like to know what it lived of.
—Finley Peter Dunne,
Mr. Dooley Remembers: Some Observations by Mr. Dooley (1963).

History is the transformation of tumultuous conquerors into silent footnotes.   —Paul Eldridge,
Maxims for a Modern Man (1965).

The history of the world is a farce.
—Gustave Flaubert,
Intimate Notebook, 1840–1841,
37 (1967).

History is more or less bunk.
—Henry Ford, on witness stand in *Chicago Tribune* libel case, July 15, 1919.

History is the study of other people's mistakes.   —Philip Guedalla,
Supers and Supermen, 54 (1920).

History is principally the inaccurate narration of events which ought not to have happened.   —Earnest Albert Hooten,
Twilight of Man, 194 (1939).

For what is history, but ... huge libel on human nature, to which we industriously add page after page, volume after volume, as if we were holding up a

monument to the honor, rather than the infamy of our species.
                        —Washington Irving,
                    History of New York (1809).

History is a bath of blood.
                        —William James,
                    Memories and Studies (1911).

The history of all hitherto existing society is the history of class struggles.
                —Karl Marx and Friedrich Engels,
                    The Communist Manifesto (1848).

The course of life is like the sea;
Men come and go; tides rise and fall;
And that is all of history.
                        —Joaquin Miller,
                    The Sea of Fire, IV (1873).

History is the crystallisation of popular beliefs.   —Donn Piatt,
                *Memories of Men Who Saved the
                    Union: Abraham Lincoln* (1887).

A lot of history is just dirty politics cleaned up for the consumption of children and other innocents.
                —Richard Reeves, syndicated column,
                    Detroit Free Press, Nov. 4, 1982.

History is past politics, and politics present history.   —Sir John Seeley,
                The Growth of British Policy (1895).

All history is only one long story to this effect: men have struggled for power over their fellow-men in order that they might win the joys of earth at the expense of others, and might shift the burdens of life from their own shoulders upon those of others.   —William Graham Sumner,
                    The Forgotten Man (1883).

The history of the world is the record of a man in quest of his daily bread and butter.   —Hendrik Willem van Loon,
                    The Story of Mankind (1921).

The history of the great events of this world are scarcely more than the history of crimes.   —Voltaire,
                *Essay on the Morals and the
                    Spirit of Nations* (1756).

Human history is in essence a history of ideas.   —H.G. Wells,
                    The Outline of History, xl (1920).

History, Lessons of

1. Whom the gods would destroy, they first make mad with power.
2. The mills of God grind slowly, but they grind exceedingly small.
3. The bee fertilizes the flower it robs.
4. When it is dark enough, you can see the stars.   —Charles A. Beard,
    when asked if he could summarize the lessons of history in a short book, said he could do it in four sentences,
                    Reader's Digest, Feb. 1941.

He that would know what shall be, must consider what hath been. —H.G. Bohn,
                    Handbook of Proverbs, 396 (1855).

The disadvantage of men not knowing the past is that they do not know the present. History is a hill or high point of vantage, from which alone men see the town in which they live or the age in which they are living.   —G.K. Chesterton,
                All I Survey: On St. George Revivified
                                    (1933).

To cite the examples of history, in order to animate us to virtue, or to arm us with fortitude, is to call up the illustrious dead, to inspire and to improve the living.   —Charles Caleb Colton,
                    Lacon, 18 (1820–22).

The lesson of history is rarely learned by the actors themselves.
                        —James A. Garfield,
            in William Ralston Balch, *Maxims
                of James Abram Garfield* (1880).

What experience and history teach is this—that people and governments never have learned anything from history, or acted on principles deduced from it.
                —Georg Wilhelm Friedrich Hegel,
                    The Philosophy of History,
                                introd. (1832).

History, by apprising [men] of the past, will enable them to judge of the future; it will avail them of the experience of other times and other nations.
— Thomas Jefferson, *Notes on the State of Virginia* (1782).

It is not often that nations learn from the past, even rarer that they draw the correct conclusions from it. For the lessons of historical experience, as of personal experience, are contingent. They teach the consequences of certain actions, but they cannot force a recognition of comparable situations.   — Henry Kissinger, *A World Restored* (1957).

We have need of history in its entirety, not to fall back into it, but to see if we can escape from it.
— José Ortega y Gasset, *The Revolt of the Masses*, x (1930).

The knowledge of what has gone before affords the best instruction for the direction and guidance of human life.
— Polybius, *Histories*, I.i (c.125 B.C.).

In a word, we may gather out of history a policy no less wise than eternal; by the comparison and application of other men's forepassed miseries with out own like errors and ill deservings.
— Walter Ralegh (1552?–1618), *History of the World*, preface (1614).

To know one's origins is to know one's present and to be able to create one's future.   — William Henry Schubert, *Curriculum Books: The First Eighty Years*, p. xi (1980).

History, Study of

The economic interpretation of history does not necessarily mean that all events are determined solely by economic forces. It simply means that economic facts are the ever recurring decisive forces, the chief points in the process of history.
— Eduard Bernstein, *Evolutionary Socialism* (tr. 1909).

We have not formed the right theory of History until we see History itself as a spiritual drama, moving toward a significant denouement and at the same time a process which has meaning and value as it goes on.   — Rufus Jones, *The Eternal Gospel* (1938).

Nowadays we may see the office of historical research as that of explaining, and therefore lightening, the pressure that the past must exercise upon the present, and the present upon the future. Today we study the day before yesterday, in order that yesterday may not paralyse today, and today may not paralyse tomorrow. — Frederic William Maitland, *Collected Papers*, III.439 (1911).

Let him be taught not so much the histories as how to judge them.
— Michel de Montaigne, *Essays*, I.xxvi (1580): *Of the Education of Children*.

Every student during his academic period ought to get up one bit of history thoroughly from the ultimate sources, in order to convince himself what history is not.   — William Graham Sumner, *Folkways* (1907).

To study ancient civilizations is to get a complete image of how society develops, succeeds and fades. There are few philosophical, moral or even scientific problems that have not been debated by ancient writers at one time or another. So we get a blueprint of the direction of mankind and what mankind can and cannot do under different circumstances.
— Marguerite Yourcenar, "Ancient-History Lesson: Our Problems Are Nothing New," *U.S. News & World Report*, July 28, 1980.

History, Writing of

See also Historian

It is impossible to write ancient history because we lack source materials, and impossible to write modern history because we have far too many. — Charles Péguy, *Clio* (1917).

The very ink with which history is written is merely fluid prejudice. — Mark Twain, *Pudd'nhead Wilson's New Calendar*, II.xxxiii (1897).

History can be well written only in a free country.   — Voltaire, letter to Frederick the Great, May 27, 1737.

Anybody can make history. Only a great man can write it.   — Oscar Wilde, *Intentions: The Critic as Artist* (1891).

Homework

The homework habit is disgraceful. Children loathe homework, and that is enough to condemn it.   — A.S. Neill, *Summerhill* (1960).

If they required such overtime, day in and day out all the year round, from the Prime Minister, the Lord Chief Justice or the Astronomer Royal, they would be certified for a mental hospital. It would kill me in a week. — George Bernard Shaw, in *Time*, Mar. 15, 1948.

Hope

All this drudgery will kill me if once in a while I cannot hope something, for somebody! If I cannot sometimes see a bird fly and wave my hand to it.
        — Willa Cather, *The Song of the Lark*, II (1915).

The times are nondescript; in many ways they are despairing. In education, however, we deal with new beginnings. There are risks, but there is always a degree of hope. — Christopher J. Hurn, "The Prospects for Liberal Education: A Sociological Perspective," *Phi Delta Kappan*, May 1979.

It is because modern education is so seldom inspired by a great hope that it so seldom achieves a great result. The wish to preserve the past rather than the hope

of creating the future dominates the minds of those who control the teaching of the young.   — Bertrand Russell, *Principles of Social Reconstruction: Education* (1916).

Take from me the hope that I can change the future, and you will send me mad.
        — Israel Zangwill, *The Melting Pot* (1920).

Human Nature

See also Nature and Nurture

Drive Nature from your door with a pitchfork, and she will return again and again.   — Horace, *Epistles*, I.x.24 (20 B.C.).

There is nothing that can be changed more completely than human nature when the job is taken in hand early enough.   — George Bernard Shaw, *On the Rocks*, preface (1934).

Nature has always had more power than education.   — Voltaire, *Life of Molière* (1739).

Humanities

See also Education, Liberal

It does not necessarily follow that a scholar in the humanities is also a humanist — but it should. For what does it avail a man to be the greatest expert on John Donne if he cannot hear the bell tolling?   — Milton S. Eisenhower, "The Need for a New American," *The Educational Record*, Oct. 1963.

There is always money for, there are always doctorates in, the learned foolery of research into what, for scholars, is the all-important problem: Who influenced whom to say what when? Even in this age of technology the verbal humanities are honored. The non-verbal humanities, the arts of being directly aware of the given facts of our existence, are almost completely ignored.   —Aldous Huxley, *The Doors of Perception* (1954).

In science, the total absorption of the individual event in the generalization is the goal; on the other hand, the humanities are concerned rather with providing for the special meaning of the individual event within an appropriate general system.   —Moody E. Prior, *Science and the Humanities* (1962).

The wise educator will prevent the spirit of narrow scientism from setting the norm by which all beliefs and convictions are to be gauged. He will exert his influence in giving the arts and humane subjects as high a place in students' esteem as the scientific and technological, for it is the arts and literature which honor the visions and faiths that have transformed lives and led to new truth.
          —Harold O. Soderquist, *The Person and Education*, 140 (1964).

Humility

Let not the wise man glory in his wisdom.
          —*Bible: Jeremiah* 9:23.

A prudent man conceals his knowledge, but fools proclaim their folly.   —*Bible: Proverbs* 12:23.

What is most needed for learning is an humble mind.   —Confucius, *The Book of History* IV (c.500 B.C.).

Proclaim not all thou knowest, all thou owest, all thou hast, nor all thou canst.
          —Benjamin Franklin, *Poor Richard's Almanack*, Oct. 1739.

The fuller the ear is of rice-grain, the lower it bends; empty of grain, it grows taller and taller.
          —Malay proverb.

Humor

See also Laughter; Levity

Humor is an affirmation of dignity, a declaration of man's superiority to all that befalls him.   —Romain Gary, *Promise at Dawn* (1961).

More is often taught by a jest than by the most serious teaching.
          —Balthasar Gracián, *The Art of Worldly Wisdom*, xxii (1647).

Humor very often cuts the knot of serious questions more trenchantly and successfully than severity.   —Horace, *Satires*, I.x.14 (c.35 B.C.).

Analysts have had their go at humor, and I have read some of this interpretive literature, but without being greatly instructed. Humor can be dissected, as a frog can, but the thing dies in the process and the innards are discouraging to any but the pure scientific mind.
          —E.B. White, *A Subtreasury of American Humor*, preface (1941).

Humorist

The teller of a mirthful tale has latitude allowed him. We are content with less than absolute truth.   —Charles Lamb, *The Last Essays of Elia: Stage Illusions* (1833).

If a person desires to be a humorist it is necessary that the people around him shall be at least as wise as he is, otherwise his humor will not be comprehended.
          —James Stephens, *The Demi-Gods*, ii (1914).

Hypothesis

See also Generalization; Proposition; Theory

A hypothesis is an inference based on knowledge which is insufficient to prove

its high probability.
— Frederick Barry,
The Scientific Habit of Thought,
ii (1927).

The shrewd guess, the fertile hypothesis, the courageous leap to a tentative conclusion — these are the most valuable coin of the thinker at work.... Yet in many classes in school, guessing is heavily penalized and is associated somehow with laziness. — Jerome S. Bruner,
The Process of Education, 14, 64 (1960).

The great tragedy of Science — the slaying of a beautiful hypothesis by an ugly fact.
— T.H. Huxley, *Collected Essays*,
VIII: *Biogenesis and Abiogenesis* (1894).

It is the first duty of a hypothesis to be intelligible.   — T.H. Huxley,
Man's Place in Nature,
ii (1863).

It is a good morning exercise for a research scientist to discard a pet hypothesis every day before breakfast. It keeps him young.   — Konrad Lorenz,
On Aggression, ii (1966).

It is the nature of an hypothesis, when once a man has conceived it, that it assimilates every thing to itself as proper nourishment; and from the first moment of your begetting it, it generally grows the stronger by every thing you see, hear, read, or understand. — Laurence Sterne,
Tristram Shandy, II.xix (1760).

Idea

See also below; Belief; Opinion

An idea not capable of realization is an empty soap-bubble.
— Berthold Auerbach,
Sträflinge (1846).

But the images of men's wits and knowledges remain in books, exempted from the wrong of time and capable of perpetual renovation. Neither are they fitly to be called images, because they generate still, and cast their seeds in the minds of others, provoking and causing infinite actions and opinions in succeedig ages.   — Francis Bacon,
The Advancement of Learning,
I.viii.6 (1605).

One can live in the shadow of an idea without grasping it. — Elizabeth Bowen,
The Heat of the Day, x (1949).

Hang ideas! They are tramps, vagabonds, knocking at the back-door of your mind, each taking a little of your substance, each carrying away some crumb of that belief in a few simple notions you must cling to if you want to live decently and would like to die easy! — Joseph Conrad,
Lord Jim, v (1900).

Psychologists speak of the association of ideas. It is a pleasant thought, but it is, in reality, difficult to induce ideas to associate in a neighborly way.
— Samuel McChord Crothers,
The Gentle Reader (1903).

The best university that can be recommended to a man of ideas is the gauntlet of the mob.   — Ralph Waldo Emerson,
Society and Solitude (1870).

No idea is so antiquated that it was not once modern. No idea is so modern that it will not some day be antiquated.... To seize the flying thought before it escapes us is our only touch with reality.
— Ellen Glasgow,
address to the Modern Language
Association, 1936.

The only sure weapon against bad ideas is better ideas.   — A. Whitney Griswold,
Essays on Education (1954).

Ideas move fast when their time comes.
— Carolyn Heilbrun,
Toward a Recognition of Androgyny
(1973).

Where did ideas come from? This one had leaped at him when he'd been exhausted, AWOL from his search.
—Laura Z. Hobson,
Gentlemen's Agreement, iv (1946).

An idea, to be suggestive, must come to the individual with the force of a revelation.   —William James,
The Varieties of Religious Experience, 113 (1902).

The very idea that there is another idea is something gained.   —Richard Jefferies, *The Story of My Heart* (1883).

That fellow seems to me to possess but one idea, and that is a wrong one.
—Samuel Johnson, in James Boswell, *Life of Samuel Johnson*, xix, 1770 (1791).

A word cannot pick up an idea and carry it over to another mind. Ideas become effective in a group only in so far as all the members of the group have learned forms of thought which are common.
—Charles H. Judd,
The Psychology of Social Institution, 214 (1926).

We do not sell ideas if they are not good. Ideas are not salami.
—Nikita Khrushchev, in *New York Herald Tribune*, Feb. 11, 1960.

The thinker dies, but his thoughts are beyond the reach of destruction. Men are mortal; but ideas are immortal.
—Walter Lippmann,
A Preface to Morals, I.iii.2 (1929).

A young man must let his ideas grow, not be continually rooting them up to see how they are getting on.
—William McFee,
Harbours of Memory: The Idea (1921).

An idea isn't responsible for the people who believe in it.   —Don Marquis, "The Sun Dial," *New York Sun* (1912–22).

It is one thing to study historically the ideas which have influenced our predecessors, and another thing to seek in them an influence fruitful for ourselves.
—John Morley,
Critical Miscellanies: Carlyle (1871–77).

An idea is a putting truth in checkmate.
—José Ortega y Gasset,
The Revolt of the Masses, viii (1930).

Truths that become old become decrepit and unreliable; sometimes they may be kept going artificially for a certain time, but there is no life in them.... Ideas can be too old.   —P.D. Ouspensky,
A New Model of the Universe, preface to 2nd ed. (1971).

It is terrible to see how a single unclear idea, a single formula without meaning lurking in a young man's head, will sometimes act like an obstruction of inert matter in an artery, hindering the nutrition of the brain, and condemning its victim to pine away in the fullness of his intellectual vigor and in the midst of intellectual plenty.   —Charles S. Peirce, "How to Make Our Ideas Clear," *Popular Science Monthly*, Jan. 1878.

He who resolves never to ransack any mind but his own, will be soon reduced, from mere barrenness, to the poorest of all imitations; he will be obliged to imitate himself, and to repeat what he has before often repeated.
—Joshua Reynolds,
lecture at Royal Academy, London, Dec. 10, 1774.

The fact that an idea is ancient and that it has been widely received is no argument in its favor, but should immediately suggest the necessity of carefully testing it as a probable instance of rationalization.
—James Harvey Robinson,
The Mind in the Making (1921).

General and abstract ideas are the source of the greatest errors of mankind.
—Jean Jacques Rousseau,
Émile, IV (1762).

For an idea ever to be fashionable is ominous, since it must afterwards be always old-fashioned.
— George Santayana,
Winds of Doctrine, 55 (1913).

The most effective way of shutting our minds against a great man's ideas is to take them for granted and admit he was great and have done with him.
— George Bernard Shaw,
The Quintessence of Ibsenism,
preface (rev. ed., 1913).

All erroneous ideas would perish of their own accord if given clear expression.
— Marquis de Vauvenargues,
Reflections and Maxims (1746).

The vitality of thought is in adventure. *Ideas won't keep*. Something must be done about them. When the idea is new, its custodians have fervour, live for it, and, if need be, die for it.
— Alfred North Whitehead,
Dialogues, as recorded by Lucien Price,
100 (1953).

The value of an idea has nothing whatever to do with the sincerity of the man who expresses it.   — Oscar Wilde,
The Picture of Dorian Grey (1891).

Ideas are duty free.
— Quoted in Leopold Zunz,
Nachlese zur Spruchkunde,
no.51 (1869).

Idea, Dangerous

See also Idea; Idea, New

Ideas are dangerous, but the man to whom they are least dangerous is the man of ideas.   — G.K. Chesterton,
Heretics, xx (1905).

Ideas are indeed the most dangerous weapons in the world.
— William O. Douglas,
An Almanac of Liberty
(1954).

The more subversive ideas are, the more moderate the language ought to be in expressing them.... If you look closely at most of the ideas expressed with violence, you begin to see that, once you've scraped away the terminology, you're usually left with the worst platitudes.
— Françoise Giroud,
I Give You My Word (1974).

All ideas are to some extent inevitably subversive.... Christianity was subversive to paganism.   — Albert Guérard,
Testament of a Liberal (1956).

It is said that this manifesto is more than a theory, that it is an incitement. Every idea is an incitement.
— Oliver Wendell Holmes, Jr.,
U.S. Supreme Court decision,
Gitlow v New York (1925).

You cannot put a rope around the neck of an idea; you cannot put an ideas up against a barrack-square wall and riddle it with bullets; you cannot confine it in the strongest prison cell that your slaves could ever build.   — Sean O'Casey,
Death of Thomas Ashe, iv (1918).

All great ideas are dangerous.
— Oscar Wilde,
De Profundis (1905).

Idea, New

See also Idea; Idea, Dangerous;
Opinion, New

One of the greatest pains to human nature is the pain of a new idea.
— Walter Bagehot,
Physics and Politics, v.163 (1869).

There is no adequate defense, except stupidity, against the impact of a new idea.   — Percy W. Bridgman,
The Intelligent Individual and Society,
iii (1938).

A new idea is delicate. It can be killed by a sneer or a yawn; it can be stabbed to

death by a quip and worried to death by a frown on the right man's brow.
— Charles Brower,
Advertising Age, Aug. 10, 1959.

Every new idea has something of the pain and peril of childbirth about it.
— Samuel Butler (1835–1902),
Note-Books (1912).

Every new movement or manifestation of human activity, when unfamiliar to people's minds, is sure to be misrepresented and misunderstood. — Edward Carpenter,
The Drama of Love and Death,
viii (1912).

You are never quite at ease about a new idea born in your mind, for you do not know in what storms of contradiction it may involve you. —Jean Guibert,
On Kindness (1911).

There never was an idea started that woke up men out of their stupid indifference but its originator was spoken of as a crank. — Oliver Wendell Holmes, Sr.,
Over the Teacups, vii (1891).

A new and valid idea is worth more than a regiment and fewer men can furnish the former than can command the latter.
— Oliver Wendell Holmes, Jr.,
letter to John C. Wu, July 21, 1925.

An invasion of armies can be resisted; an invasion of ideas cannot be resisted.
— Victor Hugo,
History of a Crime, x (1877).

Every new idea is obscure at first. It is or it wouldn't be new. — Robert Irwin,
in *Newsweek*, Dec. 29, 1976.

If we watch ourselves honestly, we shall often find that we have begun to argue against a new idea even before it has been completely stated. — Arthur Koestler,
The Act of Creation (1964).

Pride more often than ignorance makes us refuse to accept new ideas: finding first places taken in the intellectual parade,

we refuse to take the last.— François de La Rochefoucauld, *Maxims*, no.234 (1665).

Every advance in civilization has been denounced as unnatural while it was recent.
— Bertrand Russell,
Unpopular Essays: An Outline of Intellectual Rubbish (1950).

The vitality of a new movement in art or letters can be pretty accurately gauged by the fury it arouses.
— Logan Pearsall Smith,
Afterthoughts (1931).

The man with a new idea is a Crank until the idea succeeds. —Mark Twain,
Pudd'nhead Wilson's New Calendar, I.xxxii (1897).

Every intellectual revolution which has ever stirred humanity into greatness has been a passionate protest against inert ideas. Then, alas, with pathetic ignorance of human psychology, it has proceeded by some educational scheme to bind humanity afresh with inert ideas of its own fashioning.
— Alfred North Whitehead,
The Aims of Education, i (1929).

Ideal

An ideal is a port toward which we resolve to steer. —Felix Adler,
Life and Destiny (1903).

The ideals of yesterday are the truths of to-day. —William McKinley,
speech in Cincinnati, Sept. 1, 1901.

It is only in marriage with the world that our ideals can bear fruit: divorced from it, they remain barren.
— Bertrand Russell,
Mysticism and Logic (1917).

An ideal cannot wait for its realization to prove its validity. — George Santayana,
The Life of Reason, I:
Reason in Common Sense
(1905–06).

Idealist

Young people should remain idealistic all their lives. If you have to choose between being Don Quixote and Sancho Panza, for heaven's sake, be the Don.
—Ramsey Clark,
in *The Detroit News*, Apr. 28, 1978.

The toe of the star-gazer is often stubbed.
—Russian proverb.

When they come downstairs from their Ivory Towers, Idealists are apt to walk straight into the gutter.
—Logan Pearsall Smith,
Afterthoughts (1931).

Idleness

See also Laziness

The hardest work is to go idle.
—Hanan J. Ayalti,
Yiddish Proverbs (1949).

Expect poison from the standing water.
—William Blake,
*The Marriage of Heaven and Hell:
Proverbs of Hell* (1790).

Absence of occupation is not rest,
A mind quite vacant is a mind distress'd.
—William Cowper,
Retirement, ln.623 (1782).

A mind without occupation is like a cat without a ball of yarn.
—Samuel Willoughby Duffield,
Eric, or, The Fall of a Crown, I.i (1878).

Sloth (like Rust) consumes faster than Labour wears: the used Key is always bright.   —Benjamin Franklin,
Poor Richard's Almanack, July 1744.

If the braine sowes not corne, it plants thistles.   —George Herbert,
Outlandish Proverbs, no.1024 (1640).

To do nothing is the way to be nothing.
—Nathaniel Howe,
A Chapter of Proverbs.

Iron rusts from disuse, stagnant water loses its purity, and in cold weather becomes frozen; even so does inaction sap the vigors of the mind.
—Leonardo da Vinci,
Notebooks (c.1500).

For *Satan* finds some Mischief still
For idle Hands to do. —Isaac Watts,
Divine Songs, for the use of Children,
xx: *Against Idleness and Mischief* (1720).

Ignorance

See also below; Stupidity;
Uneducated Person

Ignorance is an evil weed, which dictators may cultivate among their dupes, but which no democracy can afford among its citizens.   —William Beveridge,
Full Employment in a Full Society,
IV (1944).

But Ignorance, the child
Of Darkness, blinding mortal men, binds down
Their souls to stupor, sloth and drowsiness.   —*Bhagavad-Gita:
The Song Celestial* (c.5th cent. B.C.).

Ignorance is not innocence but sin.
—Robert Browning,
The Inn Album, V (1875).

Gross Ignorance—144 times worse than ordinary ignorance.   —Bennett Cerf,
The Laugh's on Me (1959).

The man who confesses his ignorance shows it once; the man who tries to conceal it shows it many times.
—Selwyn Gurney Champion,
Racial Proverbs, 442 (1938).
A Japanese proverb.

A number of people who are essentially ignorant now have degrees and diplomas to certify they are educated. These people either know how ignorant they are, and thus realize education is a fraud, or they go around saying they are just as good as everybody else. Ignorance is curable. Stupidity is not.   —John Ciardi, in *Waco Tribune-Herald*, Mar. 18, 1976.

Ignorance lies at the bottom of all human knowledge, and the deeper we penetrate, the nearer we arrive unto it.
—Charles Caleb Colton, *Lacon*, 480 (1820–22).

all ignorance toboggans into know and trudges up to ignorance again.
—E.E. Cummings, *all ignorance toboggans into know* (1944).

Genuine ignorance is ... profitable because it is likely to be accompanied by humility, curiosity, and open-mindedness; whereas ability to repeat catch-phrases, cant terms, familiar propositions, gives the conceit of learning and coats the mind with varnish waterproof to new ideas.   —John Dewey, *Democracy and Education* (1916).

Ignorance gives one a large range of probabilities.   —George Eliot, *Daniel Deronda*, II.xiii (1876).

Ignorance is the root of all evil.
—Ruth Feiner, *Young Woman of Europe*, 157 (1942).

Being ignorant is not as much a shame, as being unwilling to learn.
—Benjamin Franklin, *Poor Richard's Almanack*, Oct. 1755.

While all complain of our ignorance and error, everyone exempts himself.
—Joseph Glanvill, *The Vanity of Dogmatizing* (1661).

There is nothing more frightful than ignorance in action.
—Johann Wolfgang von Goethe, *Proverbs in Prose* (1819).

Where ignorance is bliss, 'Tis folly to be wise.   —Thomas Gray, *Ode on a Distant Prospect of Eton College*, ln.99 (1747).

The little I know, I owe to my ignorance.
—Sacha Guitry, *Toutes Réflexions Faites*, v (1947).

He that knowes nothing, doubts nothing.   —George Herbert, *Outlandish Proverbs*, no.861 (1640).

The recipe for perpetual ignorance is: be satisfied with your opinions and content with your knowledge.—Elbert Hubbard, *The Philistine*, V (1897).

Most ignorance is vincible ignorance. We don't know because we don't want to know. It is our will that decides how and upon what subjects we shall use our intelligence.   —Aldous Huxley, *Ends and Means: Beliefs* (1937).

If a nation expects to be ignorant and free, in a state of civilization, it expects what never was and never will be.
—Thomas Jefferson, letter to Col. Charles Yancey, Jan. 6, 1816.

He that voluntarily continues in ignorance, is guilty of all the crimes which ignorance produces. —Samuel Johnson, letter to William Drummond, Aug. 13, 1766.

Ignorance, when it is voluntary, is criminal.   —Samuel Johnson, *Rasselas*, xxx (1759).

The greater our knowledge increases, the greater our ignorance unfolds.
—John F. Kennedy, address at Rice University, Sept. 12, 1962.

Ignorance is a voluntary misfortune.
—Nicholas Ling, ed., *Politeuphuia*, 63 (1669).

And hold there is no sin but ignorance.
—Christopher Marlowe, *The Jew of Malta*, prologue (c.1590; publ. 1633).

I can stand what I know. It's what I don't know that frightens me.
—Frances Newton,
Light, Like the Sun (1937).

Ignorance is of a peculiar nature; once dispelled, it is impossible to reëstablish it. It is not originally a thing of itself, but is only the absence of knowledge; and though man may be kept ignorant, he cannot be made ignorant.
—Thomas Paine,
The Rights of Man, I (1791).

It pays to be ignorant, for when you're smart you already know it can't be done.
—Jeno F. Paulucci,
New York Times, Nov. 7, 1976.

Our knowledge can only be finite, while our ignorance must necessarily be infinite. —Karl R. Popper,
Conjectures and Refutations (1968).

Everybody is ignorant, only on different subjects.   —Will Rogers,
The Illiterate Digest (1924).

I say there is no darkness but ignorance.
—William Shakespeare,
Twelfth Night, IV.ii.43 (1601).

If ignorance is indeed bliss, it is a very low grade of the article. —Tehyi Hsieh,
Chinese Epigrams Inside Out and Proverbs (1948).

Ignorance, my brethren, is a mist, low down into the very dark and almost impenetrable abyss of which, our fathers for many centuries have been plunged.
—David Walker,
Appeal ... to the Colored Citizens of the World, II (1829), in George Ducas, ed., *Great Documents in Black American History* (1970).

Ignorance is not bliss—it is oblivion.
—Philip Wylie,
Generation of Vipers, iv (1942).

Ignorance, Cognizance of Own

See also Ignorance; Ignorant Person

To be ignorant of one's ignorance is the malady of the ignorant.
—A. Bronson Alcott,
Table Talk: Discourse (1877).

Of all that writ, he was the wisest bard, who spoke this mighty truth—
He that knew all that ever learning writ, Knew only this—that he knew nothing yet.   —Aphra Behn,
The Emperor of the Moon, I.iii (1687).

It is the tragedy of the world that no one knows what he doesn't know—and the less a man knows, the more sure he is that he knows everything. —Joyce Cary,
Art and Reality: Ways of the Creative Process (1958).

To be conscious that you are ignorant is a great step to knowledge.
—Benjamin Disraeli, *Sybil*, I.v (1845).

Ignorance per se is not nearly as dangerous as ignorance of ignorance.
—Sydney J. Harris,
Pieces of Eight (1982).

It is worse still to be ignorant of your ignorance.   —St. Jerome,
Letters, let.53 (A.D. 370).

He doesn't know what he means, and doesn't know he doesn't know.
—F.R. Leavis, *Two Cultures?: The Significance of C.P. Snow* (1962).

For when I dinna clearly see, I always own I dinna ken, An' that's the way o' the wisest men.
—Allan Ramsay (1686–1758),
The Clock and Dial (1721).

I am better off than he is—for he knows nothing, and thinks that he knows; I neither know nor think that I know.
—Socrates, in Plato,
Apology (c.399 B.C.).

Ignorant Person

See also Fool; Ignorance;
Uneducated Person

They have neither knowledge nor
understanding, they walk about in
darkness.   —*Bible:*
                    Psalms 82:5.

I never met a man so ignorant that I
could not learn something from him.
                    —Galileo Galilei,
Dialogues concerning Two New Sciences
                    (1638).

Those which knowe nothing, think they
know all things, and holde their ignorance for wisdome.—Stefano Guazzo,
                    Civil Conversation, I.93 (1574).

The ignorant man always adores what he
cannot understand. —Cesare Lombroso,
                    The Man of Genius, III.iii (1889).

It is easier to snatch a pearl from the jaws
of a crocodile than to change the ideas of
an ignorant person.   —*Niti Sastras*
                    (Moral Stanzas) (c.1250).

Only the ignorant know everything.
                    —Dagobert D. Runes,
                    Treasury of Thought, 205 (1966).

"Illegitimate" Child

I wish I could somehow erase a single
word that has needlessly, unfairly caused
more searing human anguish, more pain
than any other. That word is
"illegitimate."   —Alex Haley,
                    "Beyond Roots," *Parade*,
                    Apr. 19, 1981.

We still put a blight on the "illegitimate"
child, though we have never defined how
he differs from ordinary children. We still
make outcasts of mothers who are not
parties to the (legal) marriage contract,
though in what respect unmarried maternity, as maternity, differs from other
maternity—especially as to the rights of

the child, is not clear.
                    —Ben B. Lindsey and Wainwright Evans,
                    The Revolt of Modern Youth (1925).

I am for children first, because I am for
Society first, and the children of today are
the Society of tomorrow. I insist,
therefore, on the right of the child to be
born, and that there be no "illegitimate"
children.   —Ben B. Lindsey
                    and Wainwright Evans, *ibid*.

A learned bastard takes precedence over
an ignorant High Priest.   —*Talmud:*
                    Horayoth, 13a (before A.D. 500).

There are no illegitimate children—only
illegitimate parents.
                    —Leon R. Yankwich,
                    U.S. District Court, *Zipkin v Mozon*,
                    June 1928, quoting columnist
                    O.O. McIntyre.

Imagination

What is now proved was once only im-
agin'd.   —William Blake,
                    The Marriage of Heaven and Hell:
                    Proverbs of Hell (1790).

Research, though toilsome, is easy; imagination, though delightful, is difficult.
                    —Andrew Cecil Bradley,
                    Oxford Lectures on Poetry (1909).

Only in men's imagination does every
truth find an effective and undeniable existence. Imagination, not invention, is
the supreme master of art as of life.
                    —Joseph Conrad,
                    A Personal Record, i (1912).

Every great advance in science has issued
from a new audacity of imagination.
                    —John Dewey,
                    The Quest for Certainty (1929).

Imagination is more important than
knowledge.   —Albert Einstein
                    (1879-1955), *On Science*.

To know is nothing at all; to imagine is everything.   — Anatole France, *The Crime of Sylvestre Bonnard*, II.ii (1881).

As a rule, indeed, grown-up people are fairly correct on matters of fact; it is in the higher gift of imagination that they are so sadly to seek.   — Kenneth Grahame, *The Golden Age: The Finding of the Princess* (1895).

For the imagination never operates in a vacuum. Its stuff is always fact of some order, somehow experienced; its product is that fact transmuted. I am not forgetting that fact may swamp imagination, and remain unassimilated and untransformed.   — John Livingston Lowes, *The Road to Xanadu* (1927).

Of all people children are the most imaginative. They abandon themselves without reserve to every illusion. No man, whatever his sensibility may be, is ever affected by Hamlet or Lear as a little girl is affected by the story of poor Red Riding-hood.
          — Thomas Babington Macaulay, "Milton," *Edinburgh Review*, Aug. 1825.

It is the extreme concreteness of a child's imagination which enables him, not only to take from each book exactly what he requires — people, or genii or tables and chairs — but literally to furnish his world with them.   — Iris Origo, *Images and Shadows*, II.vi (1970).

Imagination continually frustrates tradition; that is its function.
          — John Pfeiffer, *New York Times*, Mar. 29, 1979.

Imagination is the beginning of creation. You imagine what you desire; you will what you imagine; and at last you create what you will. — George Bernard Shaw, *Back to Methuselah*, I (1921).

Imagination is a contagious disease. It cannot be measured by the yard, or weighed by the pound, and then delivered to the students by members of the faculty. It can only be communicated by a faculty whose members themselves wear their learning with imagination.
          — Alfred North Whitehead, *The Aims of Education*, vii (1929).

Imitation

There is much difference between imitating a good man, and counterfeiting him.   — Benjamin Franklin, *Poor Richard's Almanack*, Nov. 1738.

What the child imitates he is trying to understand.   — Friedrich Froebel, *The Education of Man* (1826).

The child saies nothing, but what is heard by the fire.   — George Herbert, *Outlandish Proverbs*, no.300 (1640).

The talk of the child in the market-place, is either that of his father or of his mother.   — Talmud: *Sukkah*, 56b (before A.D. 500).

Inconsistency

See also Consistency; Opinion, Change of

When a man you like switches from what he said a year ago, or four years ago, he is a broadminded person who has courage enough to change his mind with changing conditions. When a man you don't like does it, he is a liar who has broken his promises.   — Franklin P. Adams, *Nods and Becks* (1944).

Nothing that is not a real crime makes a man appear so contemptible and little in the eyes of the world as inconsistency.
          — Joseph Addison. *The Spectator*, no.162, Sept. 5, 1711.

Behold man in his real character. He passes from white to black; he condemns in the morning what he maintained the evening before.   — Nicolas Boileau, *Satires*, viii.49 (1666).

No well-informed person has ever ...
declared that a change of mind was
inconsistency.   — Cicero, *Letters
to Atticus*, XVI.vii.3 (44 B.C.).

A wise man needes not blush for changing his purpose.   — George Herbert,
Outlandish Proverbs, no.613 (1640).

Man is so inconsistent a creature that it is
impossible to reason from his belief to his
conduct or from one part of his belief to
another. — Thomas Babington Macauley,
"Hallam's 'Constitutional History',"
Edinburgh Review, Sept. 1828.

It is also said of me that I now and then
contradict myself. Yes, I improve wonderfully as time goes on.
          — George Jean Nathan,
The Theatre in the Fifties, 296 (1953).

Some praise at morning what they blame
at night;
But always think the last opinion right.
          — Alexander Pope,
An Essays on Criticism, II.430 (1711).

Inconsistency — the only thing in which
men are consistent.   — Horace Smith,
The Tin Trumpet, I.273 (1836).

If some one finds that I contradict myself,
I reply: Because I was wrong once, I do
not intend to be wrong always.
          — Marquis de Vauvenargues,
Reflections and Maxims (1746).

Do I contradict myself?
Very well then I contradict myself.
(I am large, I contain multitudes.)
          — Walt Whitman,
Leaves of Grass, III:
Song of Myself, sec.51 (1855).

Indecision

How long will you go limping with two
different opinions?   — *Bible:
I Kings* 18:21.

With too much knowledge for the Sceptic
side,
With too much weakness for the Stoic's
pride,
He hangs between; in doubt to act, or
rest.   — Alexander Pope,
An Essay on Man, II.i.5 (1733).

Independence of Thought

See also Thought

The best compliment to a child or a
friend is the feeling you give him that he
has been set free to make his own inquiries, to come to conclusions that are
right for him, whether or not they coin-
cide with your own.   — Alistair Cooke,
"The Art of Curiosity," *Vogue*, Jan. 1953.

Index

So essential did I consider an Index to be
to every book, that I proposed to bring a
Bill into parliament to deprive an author
who publishes a book without an Index
of the privilege of copyright, and
moreover, to subject him for his offense
to a pecuniary penalty. — John Campbell,
Lives of the Chief Justices,
III, preface (1849–57).

Thus men catch knowledge by throwing
their wit on the posteriors of a book, as
boys do sparrows with flinging salt on
their tails.   — Jonathan Swift,
A Tale of a Tub, vii (1704).

Individuality

See also Diversity; Inequality

If there is any miracle in the world, any
mystery, it is individuality. — Leo Baeck,
Judaism and Ethics, 21 (1949).

Men are like trees: each one must put
forth the leaf that is created in him.
          — Henry Ward Beecher, *Proverbs from
Plymouth Pulpit: Education* (1887).

Though men are all of one composition, the several ingredients are so differently proportioned in each individual, that no two are exactly alike, and no one at all times like himself. —Lord Chesterfield, *Letters to His Son*, Dec. 19, 1749.

Each mind has its own method.
—Ralph Waldo Emerson,
Essays, First Series: Intellect (1841).

Men are born equal but they are also born different. —Erich Fromm,
Escape from Freedom, vii (1941).

For we cannot form our children as we would wish; as God has given us them, so must we accept and love, educate them as we best may, and rest content. For each has different gifts; every one is useful, but in his proper way.
—Johann Wolfgang von Goethe,
Hermann and Dorothea, iii (1798).

Commandment No. 1 of any truly civilized society is this: Let people be different. —David Grayson,
The Countyman's Year (1936).

Each student is different from all other students. He is unique, there is no one exactly like him, he is special. There has never been anyone like him, there never will be. —Herbert Greenberg,
To Educate with Love (1974).

If individuality has no play, society does not advance; if individuality breaks out of all bounds, society perishes.
—T.H. Huxley,
Administrative Nihilism (1871).

Though all men be made from one metal, yet they be not cast all in one mold. —John Lyly,
Euphues, the Anatomy of Wit (1579).

Men's features are not alike: nor are their opinions. —Maimonides,
Mishneh Torah (Second Law) (1180).

Do not measure another's coat on your own body. —Malay proverb.

At bottom every man knows well enough that he is a unique being, only once on this earth; and by no extraordinary chance will such a marvelously picturesque piece of diversity in unity as he is, ever be put together a second time.
—Friedrich Nietzsche,
Thoughts out of Season, II (tr. 1909).

They will say that you are on a wrong road, if it is your own.
—Antonio Porchia,
Voces (1968).

Let each man have the wit to go his own way. —Propertius,
Elegies, II.xxv.38 (c.25 B.C.).

I've never met an ordinary person. To me all people are extraordinary. I meet all sorts of people ... and the one thing I've learnt ... is that the word normal, applied to any human being, is utterly meaningless. In a sort of way it's an insult to our Maker, don't you think, to suppose that He could possibly work in any set pattern. —Terence Rattigan,
Separate Tables (1954).

Like the leaves on a tree, we are all alike and yet all different.
—Dagobert D. Runes,
Treasury of Thought, 20 (1966).

O the difference of man and man!
—William Shakespeare,
King Lear, IV.ii.28 (1605–06).

So many men, so many opinions; every one has his own way. —Terence,
Phormio, II.iv.454 (161 B.C.).

It were not best that we should all think alike; it is difference of opinion that makes horse races. —Mark Twain,
Pudd'nhead Wilson's New Calendar, xix (1894).

Indoctrination

See also Teaching

When I transfer my knowledge, I teach.
When I transfer my beliefs, I indoctrinate.   —Arthur Danto,
Analytic Philosophy of Knowledge
(1968).

Men had better be without education
than be educated by their rulers; for this
education is but the mere breaking in of
the steer to the yoke; the mere discipline
of the hunting dog, which by dint of
severity is made to forego the strongest
impulse of his nature, and instead of
devouring his prey, to hasten with it to
the feet of his master.
            —Thomas Hodgkin, 1823,
    in Everett Reimer, *School Is Dead:
Alternatives in Education*, 158 (1971).

Indoctrination is not an educational
crime; it is an educational necessity, in
religion as in table manners. The crime is
to indoctrinate in such a way as to destroy
the freedom and responsibility of the
pupil.   —M.V.C. Jeffreys,
        *Glaucon: An Inquiry into the
        Aims of Education* (1950).

Inequality

See also Ability; Individuality

Inequalities of mind and body are so
established by God Almighty, in his constitution of human nature, that no art or
policy can ever plane them down to a
level.   —John Adams,
letter to Thomas Jefferson, July 13, 1813.

Nature has never read the Declaration of
Independence. It continues to make us
unequal.   —Will Durant,
    New York Daily News, May 3, 1970.

Men are made by nature unequal. It is
vain, therefore, to treat them as if they
were equal.   —James Anthony Froude,
        *Short Studies on Great Subjects,
        Third Series: Party Politics* (1877).

True education makes for inequality; the
inequality of individuality, the inequality
of success; the glorious inequality of
talent, of genius; for inequality, not
mediocrity, individual superiority, not
standardization, is the measure of the
progress of the world.
                —Felix E. Schelling,
        Pedagogically Speaking (1929).

Influence

See also Parent, Influence of;
Teacher, Influence of

This learned I from the shadow of a tree,
That to and fro did sway against a wall,
Our shadow selves, our influence, may
    fall
Where we ourselves can never be.
                —Anna E. Hamilton
        (1843–75), *Influence*.

In order not to influence a child, one
must be careful not to be that child's
parent or grandparent. —Don Marquis,
        The Almost Perfect State (1927).

No star ever rose or set without influence
somewhere.   —Owen Meredith,
        Lucile, II.vi (1860).

Information

Information's pretty thin stuff, unless
mixed with experience. —Clarence Day,
    The Crow's Nest: The Three Tigers
(1921).

Information is not culture. In the mind
of a truly educated man, facts are
organized and they make up a living
world in the image of the world of reality.
                —André Maurois,
        The Art of Living (1939).

He who cares more for information than
for inspiration prefers elevators to wings.
                —J.B. Opdycke,
    Amor Vitaque: Omargrams (1912).

Initiative

See also Effort

A little ginger 'neath the tail
Will oft for lack of brains avail.
— T.F. MacManus,
Cave Sedem (1920).

An ounce of enterprise is worth a pound
of privilege.   — Frederic R. Marvin,
The Companionship of Books,
318 (1905).

An education which does not begin by
evoking initiative and end by encourag-
ing it must be wrong.
— Alfred North Whitehead,
The Aims of Education, iii (1929).

Innovator

See also Idea, New; Originality

The vast majority of human beings
dislike and even actually dread all notions
with which they are not familiar....
Hence it comes about that at their first
appearance innovators have generally
been persecuted, and always derided as
fools and madmen.   — Aldous Huxley,
Proper Studies (1927).

Innovators are inevitably controversial.
— Eva Le Gallienne,
The Mystic in the Theatre:
Eleanora Duse, i (1965).

Inquiry

See also Analysis; Investigation;
Questioning; Research

Wisdom will repudiate thee, if thou
think to enquire
WHY things are as they are or whence
they came: thy task
is first to know WHAT is.
— Robert Bridges,
The Testament of Beauty
(1929).

If a man will take his place before almost
any fact and scrounge down into it, he
will come upon something not adequately known.   — Charles Horton Cooley,
Life and the Student (1931).

Inquiry is man's finest quality.
— Solomon Ibn Gabirol,
Choice of Pearls, no.44 (c.1050).

Our reliance in this country is on the in-
quiring, individual human mind.... Not
the truth but the man: not the truth as
the state sees the truth or as the church
sees the truth or as the majority sees the
truth or as the mob sees the truth, but
the truth as the man sees it, as the man
finds it, for himself as man.
— Archibald MacLeish,
Freedom Is the Right to Choose (1951).

The spiritual perfection of man consists
in his becoming an intelligent being—
one who knows all that he is capable of
learning. And such knowledge is obtained not by virtue or piety, but through
inquiry and research.   — Maimonides,
Guide for the Perplexed, III (1190).

Truth never lost ground by inquiry:
because she is most of all reasonable.
— William Penn,
More Fruits of Solitude,
II. no.164 (1718).

The great obstacle to truth is the common
man's lethargic reluctance to make a
thorough house-cleaning of his mind.
— Dagobert D. Runes,
Treasury of Thought, 263 (1966).

The prevention of free inquiry is
unavoidable so long as the purpose of
education is to produce belief rather than
thought, to compel the young to hold
positive opinions on doubtful matters
rather than to let them see the doubt-
fulness and be encouraged to independence of mind.— Bertrand Russell,
Principles of Social Reconstruction:
Education (1916).

Instruction

See also Learning; Teaching

My son, from your youth up choose instruction, and until you are old you will keep finding wisdom.   —*Apocrypha: Ecclesiasticus* 6:18 (c.180 B.C.).

Hear, O sons, a father's instruction, and be attentive, that you may gain insight; for I give you good precepts: do not forsake my teaching.   —*Bible: Proverbs* 4:1,2. See also *Proverbs* 1:8; 5:1; 7:2; 13:1; 15:5.

Take my instruction instead of silver, and knowledge rather than choice gold; for wisdom is better than jewels and all that you may desire cannot compare with her.   —*Bible: Proverbs* 8:10, 11. See also *Job* 28:18; *Proverbs* 3:15; 16:16; 20:15.

Apply your mind to instruction and your ear to words of knowledge.   —*Bible: Proverbs* 23:12. See also *Proverbs* 2:2; 18:15; 22:17.

The effects of infantile instruction are, like those of syphilis, never completely cured.   —Robert Stephen Briffault, *Sin and Sex*, viii (1931).

Instruction increases inborn worth, and right discipline strengthens the heart.   —Horace, *Odes*, IV.iv.33 (17–13 B.C.).

Integration (Racial)

The goals of integration and quality education must be sought together; they are interdependent. One is not possible without the other. —Kenneth B. Clark, *Dark Ghetto* (1965).

We want mixed schools not because our colored schools are inferior to white schools—not because colored instructors are inferior to white instructors, but because we want to do away with a system that exalts one class and debases another.   —Frederick Douglass, *The New National Era*, 1872.

Two, four, six, eight, We won't integrate.   —Chant of white students of Central High School, Little Rock, Ark., 1957.

Intellect

See also Intelligence; Mind; Wit

Let it be clear ... that our concern is not with intelligence but with Intellect, which is the form intelligence takes in the artificial products we call learning. As knowledge is to intelligence, so learning is to Intellect.   —Jacques Barzun, *The House of Intellect*, ix (1959).

Intellect distinguishes between the possible and the impossible; reason distinguishes between the sensible and senseless. Even the possible can be senseless.   —Max Born, *My Life and My Views* (1968).

We should take care not to make the intellect our god; it has, of course, powerful muscles, but no personality.   —Albert Einstein, *Out of My Later Years*, li: *The Goal of Human Existence* (1950).

Intellectual ability without the more human attributes is admirable only in the same way as the brilliance of a child chess prodigy.   —T.S. Eliot, *Notes towards the Definition of Culture*, 23 (1948).

When the intellect seeks to understand beyond its powers, it loses even that which it understood.   —St. Gregory the Great, *Magna Moralia* (A.D. 584).

Intellect ... is the critical, creative, and contemplative side of mind. Whereas intelligence seeks to grasp, manipulate, reorder, adjust, intellect examines,

ponders, wonders, theorizes, criticizes, imagines. Intelligence will seize the immediate meaning in a situation and evaluate it. Intellect evaluates evaluations, and looks for the meanings of situations as a whole.
— Richard Hofstadter,
Anti-intellectualism in American Life, I.ii.25 (1963).

It is easier to fake intellect than virginity.
— Alexander King,
Rich Man, Poor Man, Freud and Fruit, iii (1965).

The highest intellects, like the tops of mountains, are the first to catch and reflect the dawn.
— Thomas Babington Macaulay,
"Sir James Mackintosh,"
Edinburgh Review, July 1835.

Life ... is not for the sake of the intellect, science or culture, but the reverse: intellect, science and culture have no other reality than that which belongs to them as tools for living.
— José Ortega y Gasset,
Man and Crisis (tr. 1958).

There are then two kinds of intellect: the one able to penetrate accurately and deeply into the conclusions of given premises, and this is the precise intellect; the other able to comprehend a great number of premises without confusing them, and this is the mathematical intellect. The one has force and exactness, the other comprehension.- Blaise Pascal,
Pensées, I.2 (1670).

Everyone thinks himself perfect in intellect and his child in beauty. — Saadi,
Gulistan (Rose Garden),
Maxim no.17 (1258).

Men are not narrow in their intellectual interests by nature; it takes special and vigorous training to accomplish that end.
— Jacob Viner,
Scholarship in Graduate Training (1953).

Intellect obscures more than it illumines.
— Israel Zangwill,
Children of the Ghetto, II.xv (1892).

Intellectual

See also Educated Person;
Learned Person

To the man-in-the-street, who, I'm sorry to say
Is a keen observer of life,
The word *intellectual* suggests right away
A man who's untrue to his wife.
— W.H. Auden,
*Collected Shorter Poems, 1927–1957:
Shorts* (1966).

For a long time I have hunted for a good definition of an intellectual. I wanted something simple and inclusive, not just an indirect way of bestowing my approval. But the more I tried to be fair, the more the exceptions and qualifications swamped the idea beneath them. Then one day while strap-hanging and scanning homeward-bound fellow workers, it came over me in a flash: an intellectual is a man who carries a briefcase.
— Jacques Barzun,
God's Country and Mine (1954).

The intellectual is a middle-class product; if he is not born into the class he must soon insert himself into it, in order to exist. He is the fine nervous flower of the bourgeoisie. — Louise Bogan,
Solicited Criticism: Some Notes on Popular and Unpopular Art (1955).

Intellectuals are people who believe that ideas are more important than values. That is to say, their own ideas and other people's values. — Gerald Brenan,
Thoughts in a Dry Season: Life (1978).

An intellectual is someone whose mind watches itself. I am happy to be both halves, the watcher and the watched.
— Albert Camus,
Notebooks 1935–1942 (1962).

It is always the task of the intellectual to "think otherwise." This is not just a perverse idiosyncrasy. It is an absolutely essential feature of a society.
—Harvey Cox,
The Secular City, x (1966).

I heard a definition of an intellectual that I thought was very interesting: a man who takes more words than are necessary to tell more than he knows.
—Dwight D. Eisenhower,
White House press release, "Remarks of the President at the Breakfast Given by Various Republican Groups...," Los Angeles, Sept. 24, 1954.

Scratch an intellectual and you find a would-be aristocrat who loathes the sight, the sound and the smell of common folk.
—Eric Hoffer,
First Things, Last Things (1970).

It is ironic that the United States should have been founded by intellectuals; for throughout most of our political history the intellectual has been for the most part either an outsider, a servant, or a scapegoat.   —Richard Hofstadter,
Anti-intellectualism in American Life,
III.vi.145 (1963).

A person for whom thinking fulfills at once the function of work and play.
—Christopher Lasch,
The New Radicalism in America (1965).

Swollen in head, weak in legs, sharp in tongue but empty in belly.
—Mao Tse-tung,
The Wilting of the Hundred Flowers (1963).

It's among the intelligentsia, and especially among those who like to play with thoughts and concepts without really taking part in the cultural endeavors of their epoch that we often find the glib compulsion to explain everything and to understand nothing.
—Joost A.M. Meerloo,
The Rape of the Mind (1956).

Let's face it: Intellectual achievement and the intellectual elite are alien to the main stream of American society. They are off to the side in a sub-section of esoteric isolation labeled "odd-ball," "high brow," "egghead," "double-dome."
—Elmo Roper,
"Roadblocks to Bookbuying," *Publishers Weekly*, June 16, 1958.

Intelligence

See also below; Brain; Intellect; IQ; Wisdom; Wit

I've always felt that a person's intelligence is directly reflected by the number of conflicting points of view he can entertain simultaneously on the same topic.
—Lisa Alther,
Kinflicks, vii (1977).

It is the very essence of intelligence to coordinate means with a view to a remote end, and to undertake what it does not feel absolutely sure of carrying out.
—Henri Bergson,
Two Sources of Morality and Religion, 128 (1935).

Intelligence is what intelligence tests measure.   —Edwin G. Boring,
in *The Detroit News*, July 1, 1979.

Intelligence is not to make no mistakes But quickly to see how to make them good.   —Bertolt Brecht,
The Measure Taken, III (1930).

Intelligence is not something possessed once for all. It is in constant process of forming, and its retention requires constant alertness in observing consequences, and open-minded will to learn and courage in readjustment.
—John Dewey,
Reconstruction in Philosophy (1920).

The test of a first-rate intelligence is the ability to hold two opposed ideas in the mind at the same time, and still retain the ability to function.
—F. Scott Fitzgerald,
The Crack-Up (1936).

The beginning of intelligence is discrimination between the probable and improbable, and acceptance of the inevitable.   —Solomon Ibn Gabirol,
Choice of Pearls, no.209 (c.1050).

Intelligence alone is dangerous if it is not subjected to the intuitive or rational perception of moral values. It has led, not only to materialism, but to monstrosities.
— —Pierre Lecomte du Noüy,
Human Destiny (1947).

Intelligence is the particular facility a person has to cope with a given situation.
—M.S. Michel,
Sweet Murder, 165 (1943).

One of the functions of intelligence is to take account of the dangers that come from trusting solely to the intelligence.
—Lewis Mumford,
The Transformations of Man (1956).

Intelligence is quickness in seeing things as they are.   —George Santayana,
Little Essays, 62, ed.
Logan Pearsall Smith (1920).

Intelligence is quickness to apprehend as distinct from ability, which is capacity to act wisely on the thing apprehended.
— Alfred North Whitehead,
Dialogues, as recorded by Lucien Price,
135 (1953).

Intelligence appears to be the thing that enables a man to get along without education. Education appears to be the thing that enables a man to get along without the use of his intelligence.
—Albert Edward Wiggam,
The New Decalogue of Science (1923).

Intelligence Test

See also IQ

The defect in the intelligence test is that high marks are gained by those who subsequently prove to be practically illiterate. So much time has been spent in studying the art of being tested that the candidate has rarely had time for anything else.— C. Northcote Parkinson,
Parkinson's Law, v (1957).

Intelligence tests measure how quickly people can solve relatively unimportant problems making as few errors as possible, rather than measuring how people grapple with relativity important problems, making as many productive errors as necessary with time no factor.
—Frank Riessman,
The Culturally Deprived Child (1962).

Intelligence tests: hocus-pocus used by psychologists to prove that they are brilliant, and their clients stupid. The general acceptance of this claim may not be without foundation.—Thomas Szasz,
The Second Sin: Psychology (1973).

Intelligent Person

See also Wise Person

What is an intelligent man? A man who enters with ease and completeness into the spirit of things and the intention of persons, and who arrives at an end by the shortest route.
—Henri Frédéric Amiel,
Journal, Nov. 7, 1878.

There's no guarantee that high IQ people produce better people or a better society. It is not the retarded kids of the world who produce the wars and destruction.
—Daniel Callahan,
Time, Mar. 10, 1980.

An intelligent man on one plane can be a fool on others.   —Albert Camus,
Nobebooks 1935–1942, I (1962).

The intelligent have a right over the ignorant; namely, the right of instructing them.   —Ralph Waldo Emerson, *Representative Men: Plato: New Readings* (1850).

The sign of an intelligent people is their ability to control emotions by the application of reason.   —Marya Mannes, *More in Anger* (1958).

Interest

See also Teaching

There has been much written on the role of reward and punishment in learning, but very little indeed on the role of interest and curiosity and the lure of discovery.... Good teachers know the power of this lure. Students should know what it feels like to be completely absorbed in a problem. They seldom experience this feeling in school.
          —Jerome S. Bruner, *The Process of Education*, iii (1960).

There is no such thing on earth as an uninteresting subject; the only thing that can exist is an uninterested person.
          —G.K. Chesterton, *Heretics*, iii (1905).

A teacher, like a playwright, has an obligation to be interesting or, at least, brief. A play closes when it ceases to interest audiences. Students close their minds to an over-talkative teacher.
          —Haim G. Ginott, *Teacher and Child*, 112 (1972).

No use shout at them to pay attention.... If the situations, the materials, the problems before a child do not interest him, his attention will slip off to what does interest him, and no amount of exhortation or threats will bring it back.
          —John Holt, *How Children Fail* (1982).

The test of interesting people is that subject matter doesn't matter.
          —Louis Kronenberger, *Company Manners*, III.1 (1954).

To know when one's self is interested, is the first condition of interesting other people.   —Walter Pater, *Marius the Epicurean*, iv (1885).

Interpretation

Both read the Bible day & night,
But thou read'st black where I read white.
          —William Blake, *The Everlasting Gospel*, a. ln.13 (c.1818).

It is more of a job to interpret the interpretations than to interpret the things, and there are more books about books than about any other subject: we do nothing but write glosses about each other.   —Michel de Montaigne, *Essays*, III.xiii (1588): *Of Experience*.

Intuition

The intellect has little to do on the road to discovery. There comes a leap in consciousness, call it intuition or what you will, and the solution comes to you, and you don't know how or why.
          —Albert Einstein, in *Forbes*, Sept. 15, 1974.

Intuition, the supra-logic that cuts out all routine processes of thought and leaps straight from problem to answer.
          —Robert Graves, *Five Pens in Hand* (1958).

All knowledge must be built on our intuitive beliefs; if they are rejected, nothing is left.   —Bertrand Russell, *The Problems of Philosophy* (1912).

Investigation

See also Analysis; Experiment;
Inquiry; Research

Investigate everything in the universe,
from the smallest to the largest.
— ben-Joseph ibn Paquda Bahya,
Duties of the Heart, 8.3.23 (c.1080).

We shall not cease from exploration
And the end of all our exploring
Will be to arrive where we started
And know the place for the first time.
— T.S. Eliot,
Four Quartets: Little Gidding (1943).

I must confess that a man is guilty of unpardonable arrogance who concludes,
because an argument has escaped his own
investigation, that therefore, it does not
really exist.   — David Hume,
*An Enquiry Concerning Human
Understanding*, IV.ii (1748).

The investigation of nature is an infinite
pasture-ground, where all may graze, and
where the more bite, the longer the grass
grows, the sweeter is its flavor, and the
more it nourishes.   — T.H. Huxley,
Administrative Nihilism (1871).

We should not investigate facts by the
light of arguments, but arguments by the
light of facts.   — Myson of Chen
(c.600 B.C.).

Why venture to determine the indeter-
minate?... Rather make yourself the object of your impartial scrutiny.... Before
you have investigated thoroughly your
tenement, is it not an excess of madness
to examine that of the universe? — Philo,
On Dreams, I.x (before A.D. 100).

Wisdom's task is to investigate all that
nature has to show.   — Philo,
On Providence, i (before A.D. 100).

While we are examining into everything
we sometimes find truth where we least
expected it.   — Quintilian, *Institutio
Oratoria*, XII.vii.3 (A.D. 95 or 96).

It belongs to the self-respect of intellect
to pursue every tangle of thought to its
final unravelment.
— Alfred North Whitehead,
Science and the Modern World,
xii (1925).

Those who go beneath the surface do so
at their peril.   — Oscar Wilde,
The Picture of Dorian Gray,
preface (1891).

IQ

See also Intelligence;
Intelligence Test

Gentlemen, I love and like you,
Caring little for your IQ.
— Franklin P. Adams,
The Melancholy Lute (1936):
*Lines to Three Boys, 8, 6½,
and 2 Years of Age*.

The invention of I.Q. did a great disser-
vice to creativity in education.... Individuality, personality, originality, are
too precious to be meddled with by
amateur psychiatrists whose patterns for a
"wholesome personality" are inevitably
their own.   — Joel Hildebrand,
address, "Education for Creativity in
the Sciences," *New York Times*,
June 16, 1963.

The high IQ has become the American
equivalent of the Legion of Honor,
positive proof of the child's intellectual
aristocracy.... It has become more important to be a smart kid than a good kid or
even a healthy kid.   — Sam Levenson,
Everything but Money (1966).

Ivory Tower

Those who dwell upon ivory towers
Have heads of the same material.
— Leonard Bacon,
Tower of Ivory, in David McCord,
ed., *What Cheer* (1945).

The atmosphere of libraries, lecture rooms and laboratories is dangerous to those who shut themselves up in them too long. It separates us from reality like a fog.   — Alexis Carrel,
Reflections on Life (1950).

Studying in the solitude of the mountains is not equal to sitting at the crossroads and listening to the talk of men.
          — Selwyn Gurney Champion,
Racial Proverbs, 354 (1938).
          A Chinese proverb.

Jargon

See also Language; Slang

To them the sounding jargon of the schools
Seems what it is — a cap and bells for fools.   — William Cowper,
Truth, ln.367 (1781).

Mere jargon; but, when nothing else is taught,
Men think the balderdash is food for thought.
          — Johann Wolfgang von Goethe,
Faust, I: *Witch's Kitchen*
          (1808).

Professional jargon is unpleasant. Translating it into English is a bore. I narrow-mindedly outlawed the word "unique." Practically every press release contains it. Practically nothing ever is.
          — Fred Hechinger,
          on resigning as education editor,
New York Herald Tribune, Aug. 5, 1956.

I would never use a long word where a short one would answer the purpose. I know there are professors in this country who "ligate" arteries. Other surgeons only tie them, and it stops the bleeding just as well.
          — Oliver Wendell Holmes, Sr.,
Scholastic and Bedside Teaching,
          lecture at Harvard University,
          Nov. 6, 1867.

It's the kind of language used extensively in the educational profession. Long words and complex sentences are intended to add importance to something unimportant.   — Jack Mabley,
Detroit Free Press, Nov. 2, 1981.

Much of the literature of education has been couched in language that is imprecise, cluttered with ambiguities, and generally nebulous. Such phrases as *educating for democracy*, where there is no clear understanding of what *democracy* means; *training the mind*, in the absence of a precise definition of what the *mind* is; *teaching moral and spiritual values*, when the separate terms are lacking in specific reference and content — these are examples of a vagueness in our thinking that we might do well to correct.
          — Frederick C. Neff,
Philosophy and American Education,
          94 (1966).

What's all the noisy jargon of the schools,
But idle nonsense of laborious fools,
Who fetter reason with perplexing rules?
          — John Pomfret,
Reason, ln.57 (c.1702).

Education ... is usually spoken of, and written about, in glutinous jargon of educators, guaranteed to obfuscate the issues and glaze the eye.   — *Time*.
          Sept. 28, 1981.

Journalism

Literature is the art of writing something that will be read twice; journalism what will be grasped at once. — Cyril Connolly,
Enemies of Promise, iii (1938).

But what is the difference between literature and journalism?
          Oh! journalism is unreadable, and literature is not read. That is all.
          — Oscar Wilde,
Intentions: The Critic as Artist
          (1891).

Judgment

See also Discretion

What we do not understand we have not the right to judge.
— Henri Frédéric Amiel,
Journal, Sept. 24, 1857.

For their hasty judgment has led many astray, and wrong opinion has caused their thoughts to slip.   — *Apocrypha: Ecclesiasticus* 3:24 (c.180 B.C.).

Nothing, it appears to me, is of greater value in a man than the power of judgment; and the man who has it may be compared to a chest filled with books, for he is the son of nature and the father of art.   — Pietro Aretino, letter to Fausto Longiano, Dec. 17, 1537.

Most people suspend their judgment till somebody else has expressed his own and then they repeat it.   — Ernest Dimnet, *The Art of Thinking*, III.ii.e (1928).

Everyone blames his memory; no one blames his judgment.
— François de La Rochefoucald, *Maxims*, no.89 (1665).

He that judges without informing himself to the utmost that he is capable, cannot acquit himself of judging amiss.
— John Locke, *An Essay concerning Human Understanding*, II.xxi.69 (1690).

We must not reject a proven doctrine because it is opposed to some isolated opinion of this or that great authority.... No man must surrender his private judgment. The eyes are directed forwards, not backwards.   — Maimonides, letter to Marseilles, 1195, *Responsa*, ii.26a.

The acknowledgment of ignorance is one of the surest proofs of judgment that I can find.   — Michel de Montaigne, *Essays*, II.x (1580): *Of Books*.

Knowledge is the treasure, but judgment is the treasurer, of a wise man.
— William Penn, *Some Fruits of Solitude*, I. no.162 (1693).

'Tis with our judgments as our watches, none
Go just alike, yet each believes his own.
— Alexander Pope, *An Essay on Criticism*, I.9 (1711).

Judgments too quickly formed are dangerous.   — Sophocles, *Oedipus Rex*, ln.584 (c.430 B.C.).

But as when an authentic watch is shown,
Each man winds up and rectifies his own,
So in our very judgments.
— John Suckling, *Aglaura*, epilogue (1637).

You can't depend on your judgment when your imagination is out of focus.
— Mark Twain, *Notebook*, July 4, 1898 (1935).

Justice

It is better that ten guilty persons escape than one innocent suffer.
— William Blackstone, *Commentaries on the Laws of England*, IV.27 (1765–69).

The strictest justice is sometimes the greatest injustice.   — Terence, *The Self-Tormentor*, ln.796 (163 B.C.).

Kindness

See also Child Rearing; Teaching

Compassion will cure more sins than condemnation. — Henry Ward Beecher, *Proverbs from Plymouth Pulpit* (1887).

Let me be a little kinder,
Let me be a little blinder

To the faults of those around me,
Let me praise a little more.
— Edgar A. Guest, *A Creed*,
in F. Adams and E. McCarrick,
Highdays and Holidays (1927).

A part of kindness consists in loving people more than they deserve.
— Joseph Joubert,
Pensées, no. 71 (1810).

Kindness begets kindness.
— Sophocles, *Ajax*
(c.445–440 B.C.).

We should be gentle with those who err,
not in will, but in judgment.
— Sophocles,
Trachiniae (c.413 B.C.).

If you stop to be kind, you must swerve
often from your path.
— Mary Webb,
Precious Bane, II (1924).

Knowledge

See also below; Learning; Self-
Knowledge; Understanding;
Wisdom

Man knows much more than he understands. — Alfred Adler,
Social Interest (1939).

Human knowledge and human power
meet in one; for where the cause is not
known the effect cannot be produced.
— Francis Bacon,
Novum Organum, Aphor.3 (1620).

Nam et ipsa scientia protestas est.
Knowledge itself is power.
— Francis Bacon,
*Religious Meditations:
Of Heresies* (1597).

There is no new knowledge without a
new problem. — Leo Baeck,
Judaism and Science,
6 (1949).

It behooves all of us — whether in government, in the academic world or in the
press — to avoid that most dangerous
disease, infectious omniscience.
— George W. Ball,
commencement address at
Miami University,
Oxford, Ohio,
June, 1965.

Men are called fools in one age for not
knowing what they were called fools for
averring in the age before.
— Henry Ward Beecher,
Life Thoughts (1858).

It iz better tew know nothing than tew
know what ain't so. — Josh Billings,
*Josh Billing's Encyclopedia
of Wit and Wisdom*,
286 (1874).

Knowledge is the only instrument of production that is not subject to diminishing
returns. — John Bates Clark,
"Overhead Costs in
Modern Industry,"
Journal of Political Economy,
Oct. 1927.

A man should keep his little brain attic
stocked with all the furniture that he is
likely to use, and the rest he can put away
in the lumber-room of his library, where
he can get it if he wants it.
— A. Conan Doyle,
*The Adventures of
Sherlock Holmes:
Five Orange Pips* (1891).

Knowledge is proud that he has learn'd so
much;
Wisdom is humble that he knows no
more. — William Cowper,
The Task, VI:
The Winter Walk at Noon,
ln.96 (1785).

Never try to tell everything you know. It
may take too short a time.
— Norman Ford,
Headmasters Courageous.

For remember, my friend, the son of a shepherd who possesses knowledge is of greater worth to a nation than the heir to the throne, if he be ignorant. Knowledge is your true patent of nobility, no matter who your father or what your race may be.   —Kahlil Gibran, *The Treasured Writings* (1980): *The Words of the Master*, viii.

Knowledge without sense is double folly.
—Balthasar Gracián, *The Art of Worldly Wisdom*, xvi (1647).

But Knowledge to their eyes her ample page
Rich with the spoils of time did ne'er unroll.   —Thomas Gray, *Elegy Written in a Country Churchyard*, ln.49 (1751).

Tell me what you *Know* is True;
I can *Guess* as well as you.
—Arthur Guiterman, *A Poet's Proverbs* (1924).

Knowledge fills a large brain; it merely inflates a small one.   —Sydney Harris, syndicated column, *Detroit Free Press*, Jan. 7, 1982.

Knowledge and timber shouldn't be much used till they are seasoned.
—Oliver Wendell Holmes, Sr., *The Autocrat of the Breakfast-Table*, vi (1858).

To be master of any branch of knowledge, you must master those which lie next to it; and thus to know anything you must know all.
—Oliver Wendell Holmes, Jr., lecture to undergraduates of Harvard University, Feb. 17, 1886, in M.D. Howe, *Occasional Speeches of Justice Oliver Wendell Holmes* (1962).

All knowledge resolves itself into probability.   —David Hume, *A Treatise of Human Nature*, I (1739).

If a little knowledge is dangerous, where is the man who has so much as to be out of danger?   —T.H. Huxley, *On Elementary Instruction in Physiology* (1877). Refers to Pope's famous line.

He who does not know one thing knows another.   —Kenyan proverb.

Knowledge and action are twins, each glorifying the other.
—Joseph ben Isaac Kimhi, *Shekel HaKodesh* (12th cent.).

We can add to our knowledge, but we cannot at will subtract from it.
—Arthur Koestler, *Arrow in the Blue*, 278 (1970).

What man knows is everywhere at war with what he wants.
—Joseph Wood Krutch, *The Modern Temper*, 14 (1929).

There is no common faith, no common body of principle, no common body of knowledge, no common moral and intellectual discipline.... We have established a system of education in which we insist that while every one must be educated, yet there is nothing in particular that an educated man must know.
—Walter Lippman, address, American Association for the Advancement of Science, Dec. 29, 1940.

To know is not to know, unless some one else has known that I know.
—Lucilius, *Satires*, I. frag.31 (c.123 B.C.).

The argument proceeds on the supposition that there is some line between profound and superficial knowledge similar to that which separates truth from falsehood. I know of no such line.
—Thomas Babington Macaulay, address at the opening of Edinburgh Philosophical Institution, Nov. 4, 1846.

There is no more merit in being able to attach a correct description to a picture than in being able to find out what is

wrong with a stalled motorcar. In each case it is special knowledge.
— W. Somerset Maugham,
The Summing Up, xxiv (1938).

Far better to know one thing thoroughly, Than to be superficially dressed up with many.   — Menander,
Fragments, frag.683K (c.300 B.C.).

Sin, guilt, neurosis — they are one and the same, the fruit of the tree of knowledge.
— Henry Miller,
*The Wisdom of the Heart:
Creative Death* (1941).

In expanding the field of knowledge we but increase the horizon of ignorance.
— Henry Miller,
*The Wisdom of the Heart: The
Wisdom of the Heart* (1941).

I lay it down that all knowledge forms one whole, because its subject-matter is one; for the universe in its length and breadth is so intimately knit together, that we cannot separate off portion from portion, and operation from operation, except by a mental abstraction.
— John Henry Newman,
The Idea of a University,
Discourse III (1873).

Here's my bitterness:
Would I knew a little more,
Or very much less!   — Dorothy Parker,
Death and Taxes: Summary (1931).

It is far better to know something about everything than to know all about one thing. This universality is the best. If we can have both, still better.
— Blaise Pascal,
Pensées, I.37 (1670).

Happy the sons whose fathers educate,...
The ignorant and fool will be thrown over,
But knowledge shall lift up the scholar's head.   — Ptah-hotep,
On Home Education (c.2400 B.C.).

Knowledge is not enough, unless it leads you to understanding and, in turn, to wisdom.   — David Sarnoff,
Youth in a Changing World,
June 12, 1954.

His had been an intellectual decision founded on his conviction that if a little knowledge was a dangerous thing, a lot was lethal.   — Tom Sharpe,
Porterhouse Blue, xviii (1974).

Strength exists only as the opposite of weakness, and supreme knowledge of one subject presupposes as supreme an ignorance of others.   — Alec Waugh,
On Doing What One Likes (1926).

Knowledge is always accompanied with accessories of emotion and purpose.
— Alfred North Whitehead,
Adventures of Ideas (1933).

Knowledge does not keep any better than fish.   — Alfred North Whitehead,
The Aims of Education, vii (1929).

Education is an admirable thing, but it is well to remember from time to time that nothing that is worth knowing can be taught.   — Oscar Wilde,
Intentions: The Critic as Artist (1891).

Knowledge, Acquisition of

Scholars and artists ... Both work from knowledge; but I suspect they differ most importantly in the way their knowledge is come by. Scholars get theirs with conscientious thoroughness along projected lines of logic; poets theirs cavalierly and as it happens in and out of books. They stick to nothing deliberately, but let what will stick to them like burrs where they walk in the fields.   — Robert Frost,
Collected Poems, preface:
The Figure a Poem Makes (1949).

The knowledge we have comes from our senses, and the dogmatist can go no higher for the original of his certainty.
— Joseph Glanvill, *The Vanity
of Dogmatizing*, xxii (1661).

Knowledge is acquired when we succeed in fitting a new experience into the system of concepts based upon our old experiences. Understanding comes when we liberate ourselves from the old and so make possible a direct, unmediated contact with the new, the mystery, moment by moment, of our existence.
— Aldous Huxley,
Tomorrow and Tomorrow and Tomorrow: Knowledge and Understanding (1956).

Our knowledge grows *in spots*. The spots may be large or small, but the knowledge never grows all over: some old knowledge always remains what it was.... Our minds grow in spots; and like grease-spots, the spots spread. But we let them spread as little as possible: we keep unaltered as much as our old knowledge, as many of our old prejudices and beliefs, as we can. We patch and tinker more than we renew.   — William James,
Pragmatism (1907).

It is a great nuisance that knowledge can only be acquired by hard work. It would be fine if we could swallow the powder of profitable information made palatable by the jam of fiction.
— W. Somerset Maugham,
The Art of Fiction: An Introduction to Ten Novels and Their Authors,
i. sec.1 (1955).

From contemplation one may become wise, but knowledge comes only from study.   — A. Edward Newton,
A Magnificent Farce, viii (1921).

Half of our knowledge we must snatch, not take.   — Alexander Pope,
Moral Essays, I.40 (1734).

Whatever knowledge is attainable must be attainable by scientific methods; and what science cannot discover, mankind cannot know.   — Bertrand Russell,
Religion and Science (1935).

Knowledge, Definition of

Knowledge is the conformity of the object and the intellect.   — Averroës,
Destructio Destructionum (c.1180).

Knowledge is not a loose-leaf notebook of facts.   — Jacob Bronowski,
The Ascent of Man, 436 (1973).

What is all knowledge too but recorded experience, and a product of history; of which, therefore, reasoning and belief, no less than action and passion, are essential materials?   — Thomas Carlyle,
*Critical and Miscellaneous Essays,
II* (1838): *On History*.

Knowledge is twofold, and consists not only in an affirmation of what is true, but in the negation of that which is false.
— Charles Caleb Colton,
Lacon, 114 (1820–22).

Shall I teach you what knowledge is? When you know a thing, to hold that you know it; and when you do not know a thing, to allow that you do not know it: — this is knowledge.   — Confucius,
Analects, II.xvii (c.500 B.C.).

Why, yes, as knowledge now is understood,
But who dare give the right name to the brat? — Johann Wolfgang von Goethe,
Faust, I: Night (1808).

Knowledge is the distilled essence of our intuitions, corroborated by experience.
— Elbert Hubbard,
Note Book, 112 (1927).

Knowledge ... is a product or residue of the perception-experience process. It is subjective in nature and unique to the learner. It does not exist before learning begins, or if it does, that fact does not matter.   — Earl C. Kelley
and Marie I. Rasey, *Education and the Nature of Man* (1952).

Knowledge then seems to me to be nothing but *the perception of the connexion of and agreement, or disagreement and repugnancy of any of our ideas.* In this alone it consists. Where this perception is, there is knowledge, and where it is not, there, though we may fancy, guess, or believe, yet we always come short of knowledge. —John Locke, *An Essay concerning Human Understanding*, IV.i.2 (1690).

When I speak of Knowledge, I mean something intellectual, something which grasps what it perceives through the senses; something which takes a view of things; which sees more than the senses convey; which reasons upon what it sees, and while it sees; which invests it with an idea.   —John Henry Newman, *The Idea of a University*, Discourse V (1873).

That alone is liberal knowledge, which stands on its own pretensions, which is independent of sequel, expects no complement, refuses to be *informed* ... by any end, or absorbed into any art, in order duly to present itself to our contemplation. —John Henry Newman, *ibid.*

Knowledge is recognition of something absent; it is a salutation, not an embrace. —George Santayana, *The Life of Reason*, I: *Reason in Common Sense* (1905–06).

Knowledge is nothing but the continually burning up of error to set free the light of truth.   —Rabindranath Tagore, *Sadhana* (1913).

What is most of our so-called knowledge, but a conceit that we know something which robs us of the advantage of our actual ignorance? —Henry David Thoreau, *Excursions* (1863).

This is what knowledge really is. It is finding out something for oneself with pain, with joy, with exultancy, with labor, and with all the little ticking, breathing moments of our lives, until it

is ours as that only is ours which is rooted in the structure of our lives.
        —Thomas Wolfe,
        The Web and the Rock (1939).

Knowledge, Desire for

Desire for knowledge is the path of honor; desire for wealth is the path of dishonor. Wealth is the chain that slaves wear; knowledge the kingly crown.
        —Abdullah Ansari,
        Invocations (c.1075).

All men by nature have a desire to know.
        —Aristotle, *Metaphysics*,
        I.i.1 (before 322 B.C.).

A man may be self-indulgent in books as well as in wine and pleasure. A man may be a glutton of knowledge as well as of food.   —Henry Ward Beecher,
        Proverbs from Plymouth Pulpit: Man (1887).

We are all fools, poor fools, with an eternal bandage covering our eyes, and an eternal thirst for knowledge filling our spirits.   —Karl Emil Franzos,
        Nameless Graves (1873).

If you want to know how to do a thing you must first have a complete desire to do that thing.   —Robert Henri,
        The Art Spirit (1923).

It is said that desire for knowledge lost us the Eden of the past; but whether that is true or not; it will certainly give us the Eden of the future.
        —Robert G. Ingersoll,
        Some Mistakes of Moses (1879).

It is the peculiarity of knowledge that those who really thirst for it always get it.
        —Richard Jefferies,
        Country Literature (c.1880).

A desire of knowledge is a natural feeling of mankind; and every human being, whose mind is not debauched, will be willing to give all that he has to get knowledge.   —Samuel Johnson, in James Boswell, *Life of Samuel Johnson*, xv, July 30, 1763 (1791).

Real education must ultimately be limited to men who INSIST on knowing, the rest is mere sheep-herding.
—Ezra Pound,
ABC of Reading, I.viii (1934).

The desire for knowledge, like the thirst of riches, increases ever with the acquisition of it.   —Laurence Sterne, *Tristram Shandy*, II.iii (1760).

The public have an insatiable curiosity to know everything, except what is worth knowing.   —Oscar Wilde, *The Soul of Man under Socialism* (1891).

Knowledge, Diffusion of

Knowledge is indeed as necessary as light, and in this coming age most *fairly* promises to be as common as water, and as free as air.   —Charles Caleb Colton, *Lacon*, I, preface (1820).

By far the most important bill in our whole code, is that for the diffusion of knowledge among the people. No other sure foundation can be devised for the preservation of freedom and happiness. If anybody thinks that kings, nobels, priests are good conservators of the public happiness, send him here [to Europe].
—Thomas Jefferson,
letter to George Wythe, Aug. 13, 1786.

He who receives an idea from me, receives instruction himself without lessening mine; as he who lights his taper at mine receives light without darkening me.   —Thomas Jefferson, letter to Isaac McPerson, Aug. 13, 1813.

Diffused knowledge immortalizes itself.
—James Mackintosh,
Vindiciae Gallicae (1791).

When two merchants exchange goods, each one surrenders part of his stock; but when two students exchange instruction, each one retains his own learning and acquires also the other's. Is there a bigger bargain than this?—Simeon ben Lakish, *Midrash: Tanhuma* (A.D. c.200–275).

Knowledge, Futility of

The consequences of acquiring knowledge are always incalculable and seldom beneficial.   —Edward Hyams, *William Medium* (1948).

The farther one pursues knowledge,
    The less one knows.   —Lao-tse,
The Book of Tao, sec.47,
in Lin Yutang, ed., *The Wisdom of China and India* (1942).

Pin your faith to natural knowledge, stumble through the darkness of the blind; pin your faith to supernatural knowledge, stumble through a darkness deeper still.   —*Isha Upanishad*,
(c.700–300 B.C.), in Shree Purohit Swami and W.B. Yeats, tr., *The Ten Principal Upanishads* (1937).

Knowledge, Inadequate

A smattering of everything, and a knowledge of nothing.
—Charles Dickens,
Sketches by Boz, iii: *Sentiment, Minerva House* (1836).

I have not the Chancellor's encyclopedic mind. He is indeed a kind of semi-Solomon. He *half* knows everything, from the cedar to the hyssop.
—Thomas Babington Macaulay,
letter to Macvey Napier, Dec. 17, 1830,
alluding to Henry, Lord Brougham.

Better know nothing than half-know many things.   —Friedrich Nietzsche, *Thus Spake Zarathustra: The Leech*,
IV (1891).

Knowledge, Intuitive

It is a prejudice to believe that knowledge is always rational, that there is no such thing as irrational knowledge. Actually, we apprehend a great deal more through feeling that by intellection.
—Nikolai Berdyaev,
Solitude and Society (1947).

Men can know with the heart and not only with the mind.   —Ben Zion Bokser,
From the World of Cabbalah,
189 (1954).

Knowledge, Kinds of

Knowledge is of two kinds. We know a subject ourselves, or we know where we can find information upon it.
—Samuel Johnson,
in James Boswell, *Life of Samuel Johnson*, xxvii, Apr. 11, 1775 (1791).

Francis Bacon ... asserted ... that "knowledge is power." But that is not true of *all* knowledge. Sir Thomas Browne wished to know what song the sirens sang, but if he had ascertained this it would not have enabled him to rise from being a magistrate to being High Sheriff of his county. The sort of knowledge that Bacon had in mind was that which we call scientific.
—Bertrand Russell,
The Will to Doubt:
"Useless" Knowledge (1958).

Knowledge of the lowest kind is un-unified knowledge; science is partially-unified; philosophy is completely-unified knowledge.   —Herbert Spencer,
First Principles, i (1862).

Knowledge, Lack of

It is not good for a man to be without knowledge.   —*Bible:*
Proverbs 19:2.

What man knows is not to be compared with what he does not know.
—Chuang-tzu, *Philosophy*,
i (4th–3rd cent. B.C.).

A man without knowledge is like a house without a foundation.
—Solomon Ibn Gabirol,
Choice of Pearls, no.17 (c.1050).

A man without knowledge, as I have read,
May well be compared to one who is dead.   —Thomas Ingelend,
The Disobedient Child (c.1560).

If anyone thinks nothing is known, he does not even know whether that can be known, since he declares he knows nothing.   —Lucretius, *On the Nature of Things*, IV.469 (c.45 B.C.).

Knowledge, Limited

What is all our knowledge? We do not even know what weather it will be tomorrow.   —Berthold Auerbach,
On the Heights (1865).

When my knowledge was small I swelled with pride like an elephant blinded with passion, and it seemed to me that there was nothing I did not know. But when I learned more I became aware of my foolishness, and my excitement subsided.
—Bhartrihari,
The Vairagya Sataka (c. A.D. 625).

There is no absolute knowledge. And those who claim it, whether they are scientists or dogmatists, open the door to tragedy. All information is imperfect. We have to treat it with humility.
—Jacob Bronowski,
The Ascent of Man, 353 (1973).

Spread out your knowledge, and you will see how shallow it is.   —Chuang-tzu,
Philosophy, xi
(4th–3rd cent. B.C.).

There is much that we do not know, and cannot understand—we big folks, no more than you little ones.
—Dinah Mulock Craik,
The Little Lame Prince, ii (1875).

It is in the matter of knowledge that a man is most haunted with a sense of inevitable limitation.   —Joseph Farrell,
Lectures of a Certain Professor (1877).

Actually one knows only when one knows little; with knowledge doubt increases.
—Johann Wolfgang von Goethe,
Proverbs in Prose (1819).

A wise system of education will at least teach us how little man yet knows, how much he has yet to learn.
—John Lubbock,
The Pleasures of Life (1887).

Penetrating so many secrets, we cease to believe in the unknowable. But there it sits nevertheless, calmly licking its chops.
—H.L. Mencken,
Minority Report: Notebooks,
no.364 (1956).

As soon as one begins to look deeply into any subject one realizes how very little is known, how very, very much is conjecture, hypothesis, surmise and speculation.... When it comes to vital instruction, almost everything that has been written for our edification can be junked.
—Henry Miller,
The Books in My Life (1952).

The first and wisest of them all professed
To know this only, that he nothing knew.
—John Milton,
Paradise Regained, IV.293 (1671).

You can know more and more about one thing but you can never know everything about one thing: it's hopeless.
—Vladimir Nabokov,
Strong Opinions (1981).

No man should escape our universities without knowing how little he knows. He must have some sense of the fact that not through his fault ... but inherently in the nature of things, he is going to be an ignorant man and so is everybody else.
—J. Robert Oppenheimer,
quoted by J.H. Raleigh,
Partisan Review, Summer 1967.

It takes a lot of knowledge to understand how little we know.
—Dagobert D. Runes,
Treasury of Thought, 204 (1966).

All I know is but a grain of sand picked up on the verge of the ocean of undiscovered knowledge.
—George Bernard Shaw,
Buoyant Billions, preface (1947).

We know nothing important. In the essentials we are still as wholly a mystery to ourselves as Adam was to himself.
—Booth Tarkington,
Looking Forward, 74 (1926).

A child said *What is the grass?* fetching it to me with full hands;
How could I answer the child? I do not know what it is any more than he.
—Walt Whitman,
Leaves of Grass, III:
Song of Myself, sec.6 (1855).

Knowledge, for Own Sake

Knowledge is capable of being its own end. Such is the constitution of the human mind, that any kind of knowledge, if it be really such, is its own reward.   —John Henry Newman,
The Idea of a University,
Discourse V (1873).

All knowledge has an ultimate object. Knowledge for the sake of knowledge is, say what you will, nothing but a dismal begging of the question.
—Miguel de Unamuno,
The Tragic Sense of Life, i (1912).

Knowledge, Pleasure of

For the pleasure and delight of knowledge and learning, it far surpasseth all other in nature.... We see in other pleasures there is satiety,... but of knowledge there is no satiety.
— Francis Bacon,
The Advancement of Learning,
I.viii.5 (1605).

I find that I can have no enjoyment in the World but continual drinking of Knowledge. —John Keats,
letter to John Taylor, Apr. 24, 1818.

The real animating power of knowledge is only in the moment of its being first received, when it fills us with wonder and joy; a joy for which, observe, the previous ignorance is just as necessary as the present knowledge. —John Ruskin,
The Stones of Venice, iii (1851).

Knowledge, Quest for

The pursuit of knowledge can never be anything but a leap in the dark, and a leap in the dark is a very uncomfortable thing. —Samuel Butler (1835–1902),
Note-Books (1912).

It is the appreciation of beauty and truth, the striving for knowledge, which makes life worth living.
— Morris Raphael Cohen,
A Dreamer's Journey, 166 (1949).

In the pursuit of knowledge, follow it wherever it is to be found; like fern, it is the produce of all climates, and like coin, its circulation is not restricted to any particular class. — Charles Caleb Colton,
Lacon, 126 (1820–22).

So long as the mind of man is what it is, it will continue to exult in advancing on the unknown throughout the infinite field of the universe; and the tree of knowledge will remain for ever, as it was in the beginning, a tree to be desired to make one wise. — A.E. Housman,
Introductory Lecture (1892).

Seek, therefore, knowledge; wheresoe'er Thou seekest, thou shalt find it there.
—*Mahabharata*, XII
(c.200 B.C.–c. A.D. 200).

Our souls, whose faculties can comprehend
The wondrous architecture of the world,
And measure every wandering planet's course,
Still climbing after knowledge infinite.
— Christopher Marlowe, *Tamburlaine the Great*, I.II.vii (1590).

The struggle for knowledge hath a pleasure in it like that of wrestling with a fine woman. — George Savile,
Marquis of Halifax, *Political, Moral, and Miscellaneous Thoughts and Reflections* (c.1690).

And this gray spirit yearning in desire
To follow knowledge like a sinking star,
Beyond the utmost bound of human thought. — Alfred, Lord Tennyson,
Ulysses, ln.30 (1842).

Knowledge, Resistance to

Far more crucial than what we know or do not know is what we do not want to know. — Eric Hoffer, *The Passionate State of Mind*, no.58 (1954).

We must view with profound respect the infinite capacity of the human mind to resist the introduction of useful knowledge. —Thomas R. Lounsbury,
in F.C. Lockwood, *The Freshman and His College* (1913).

Not to know is bad; not to wish to know is worse. —Nigerian proverb.

Man does not want to know. When he knows very little he plays with the possibility of knowledge, but when he finds that the pieces he has been putting together are going to spell out the answer to the riddle he is frightened and he throws them in every direction; and another civilization falls.
—Rebecca West, in Peter Wolfe, *Rebecca West: Artist and Thinker* (1971).

Knowledge, Useful

He who knows useful things, not many things, is wise.   — Aeschylus, *Fragments*, no.218 (c.458 B.C.).

The study and knowledge of the universe would somehow be lame and defective were no practical results to follow.
     — Cicero, *De Officius*, I.xliii.153 (c.43 B.C.).

A man has only so much knowledge as he puts to work.   — St. Francis of Assisi, *Mirror of Perfection* (before 1226).

'Tis not knowing much, but what is useful, that makes a wise man.
     — Thomas Fuller (1654–1734), *Gnomologia*, no.5097 (1732).

No knowledge is so easily found as when it is needed.   — Robert Henri, *The Art Spirit* (1923).

Knowledge, Useless

Many men are stored full of unused knowledge. Like loaded guns, that are never fired off, or military magazines in times of peace, they are stuffed with useless ammunition.
     — Henry Ward Beecher, *Proverbs from Plymouth Pulpit: Man* (1887).

Most of the Learning in use, is of no great Use.   — Benjamin Franklin, *Poor Richard's Almanack*, Nov. 1749.

Between falsehood and useless truth there is little difference. As gold which he cannot spend will make no man rich, so knowledge which he cannot apply will make no man wise. — Samuel Johnson, *The Idler*, no.84 (1758–60).

It is better, of course, to know useless things than to know nothing. — Seneca, *Letters to Lucilius*, LXXXVIII.vl (c. A.D. 64).

Knowledge, Value of

The lips of knowledge are a precious jewel.   — *Bible: Proverbs* 20:15. See also *Job* 28:18; *Proverbs* 3:15; 8:10; 16:16; 20:15.

There is no knowledge that is not valuable. — Edmund Burke, *Speech on American Taxation*, Apr. 19, 1774.

Knowledge is a comfortable and necessary retreat and shelter for us in an advanced age; and if we do not plant it while young, it will give us no shade when we grow old. — Lord Chesterfield, *Letters to His Son*, Dec. 11, 1747.

For there is no knowledge (seemeth it at the first of never so little moment) but it will stand the diligent observer in stead at one time or other.   — Edward Coke, (1552–1634), *Fourth Institute: Proeme*.

Amongst all things, knowledge is truly the best thing; from its not being liable ever to be stolen, from its not being purchasable, and from its being imperishable. — *Hitopadésa* (c.500).

Nothing is more excellent than knowledge.   — St. John of Damascus, *Dialectica*, I (c.730).

All knowledge is of itself of some value. There is nothing so minute or inconsiderable that I would not rather know it than not.   — Samuel Johnson, in James Boswell, *Life of Samuel Johnson*, xxvii, Apr. 14, 1775 (1791).

An extensive knowledge is needful to thinking people — it takes away the heat and fever; and helps, by widening speculation, to ease the Burden of the Mystery.   — John Keats, letter to John Hamilton Reynolds, May 3, 1818.

To an earlier age knowledge was power, merely that and nothing more; to us it is life and the *summum bonum*.
     — Charles S. Peirce, *Annual Report*, Smithsonian Instituion, June 30, 1900.

Knowledge of itself is riches. — Saadi, *Gulistan (Rose Garden)*, ii (1258).

There is only one good, that is knowledge; there is only one evil, that is ignorance. — Socrates, in Diogenes Laërtius, *Lives of Eminent Philosophers*, II. sec. 31 (3rd cent.).

He who has knowledge, has everything; he who lacks this, what has he? ... Has he not acquired this, what does he possess? — *Talmud: Nedarim*, 41a (before A.D. 500).

Any piece of knowledge I acquire today has a value at this moment exactly proportioned to my skill to deal with it. Tomorrow, when I know more, I recall that piece of knowledge and use it better. — Mark Van Doren, *Liberal Education* (1943).

He who binds
His soul to knowledge, steals the key to
heaven. — Nathaniel Parker Willis, *The Scholar of Thibêt Ben Khorat*, II (1882).

Language

See also below; Jargon; Word

Every living language, like the perspiring bodies of living creatures, is in perpetual motion and lateration; some words go off, and become obsolete, others are taken in, and by degrees grow into common use; or the same word is inverted to a new sense and notion, which in tract of time makes as observable a change in the air and features of a language as age makes in the lines and mien of a face. — Richard Bentley, *Dissertation upon the Epistles of Phalaris* (1699) [lateration = *widening*].

No grammatical rules have sufficient authority to control the firm and established usage of language. Established custom, in speaking and writing, is the standard to which we must at last resort for determining every controverted point in language and style. — Hugh Blair, *Lectures on Rhetoric and Belles Lettres* (1783).

Language is purely a species of fashion, in which by the general, but tacit, consent of the people of a particular state or country, certain sounds come to be appropriated to certain things as their signs. — George Campbell, *The Philosophy of Rhetoric*, iii (1776).

The raison-d'etre of language is an idea to be expressed. When the idea is expressed, the language may be ignored. — Chuang-tzu, *Philosophy*, xi (4th–3rd cent. B.C.).

If language is incorrect, then what is said is not meant. If what is said is not meant, then what ought to be done remains undone. — Confucius, in *Upper and Lower Case*, Dec. 1982.

Language is the archives of history....
Languge is fossil poetry. — Ralph Waldo Emerson, *Essays, Second Series: The Poet* (1844).

Language clothes nature as the air clothes the earth, taking the exact form & pressure of every object. Only words that are new fit exactly the thing, those that are old like scoriae that have been long exposed to the air & sunshine, have lost the sharpness of their mould & fit loosely. — Ralph Waldo Emerson, *Journals*, Nov. 10, 1836.

Language is a city to the building of which every human being brought a stone. — Ralph Waldo Emerson, *Letters and Social Aims: Quotation and Originality* (1876).

Words, like fashions, disappear and recur throughout English history, and one generation's phraseology, while it may seem

abominably second-rate to the next, becomes first-rate to the third.
— Virginia Graham,
Say Please, xiv (1949).

There is no such thing as good and bad (or correct and incorrect, grammatical and ungrammatical, right and wrong) in language.   — Robert A. Hall, Jr.,
Linguistics and Your Language (1950).

Language is a living thing. We can feel it changing. Parts of it become old: they drop off and are forgotten. New pieces bud out, spread into leaves, and become big branches, proliferating.
— Gilbert Highet,
Explorations: Changing Words (1971).

Never impose your language on people you wish to reach.   — Abbie Hoffman,
Revolution for the Hell of It (1968).

Many terms which have now dropped out of favor, will be revived, and those that are at present respectable will drop out, if usage so choose, with whom resides the decision and the judgment and the code of speech.   — Horace,
Ars Poetica, ln.70 (20 B.C.).

Invention in language should no more be discouraged than should invention in mechanics. Grammar is the grave of letters.   — Elbert Hubbard,
Note Book, 95 (1927).

Most of our mistakes are fundamentally grammatical. We create our own difficulties by employing an inadequate language to describe facts.
— Aldous Huxley,
Essays New and Old: Breugel (1925).

Well-chosen phrases are a great help in the smuggling of offensive ideas.
— Vladimir Jabotinsky,
The War and the Jew,
120 (1942).

The new circumstances under which we are placed call for new words, new phrases, and for the transfer of old words to new objects. An American dialect will therefore be formed.
— Thomas Jefferson,
letter to John Waldo, Aug. 16, 1813.

I am always sorry when any language is lost, because languages are the pedigree of nations.   — Samuel Johnson,
in James Boswell, *The Journal of a Tour of the Hebrides with Samuel Johnson*, Sept. 1773 (1785).

When an age is in throes of profound transition, the first thing to disintegrate is language.   — Rollo May,
Power and Innocence (1972).

The only language men ever speak perfectly is the one they learn in babyhood, when no one can teach them anything!   — Maria Montessori,
The Absorbent Mind (1967).

Language may die at the hands of the schoolmen: it is regenerated by the poets.
— Emmanuel Mounier,
Be Not Afraid (1951).

After a speech is fully fashioned to the common understanding, and accepted by the consent of a whole country and nation, it is called a language.
— George Puttenham,
The Arte of English Poesie (1589).
Also ascribed to his brother Richard.

It is quite an illusion to imagine that one adjusts to reality essentially without the use of language, and that language is merely an incidental means ... of communication or reflection. The fact of the matter is that the "real world" is to a large extent unconsciously built up on the language habits of the group.
— Edward Sapir,
in Benjamin Lee Whorf,
Language, Culture and Personality,
ed. D.G. Mandelbaum (1949).

They have been at a great feast of languages, and stolen the scraps.
— William Shakespeare, *Love's Labour's Lost*, V.i.39 (1594).

Language grows out of life, out of its needs and experiences.... *Language* and *knowledge* are indissolubly connected; they are interdependent. Good work in language presupposes and depends on a real knowledge of things.
— Anne Sullivan, address before the American Association to Promote the Teaching of Speech to the Deaf, July, 1894, in Helen Keller, *The Story of My Life* (1903).

Language is the expression of ideas, and if the people of one country cannot preserve an identity of ideas they cannot retain an identity of language.
— Noah Webster, *American Dictionary of the English Language*, preface (1828).

A language is a dialect that has an army and a navy.   — Max Weinreich, in Leo Rosten, *The Joys of Yiddish*, preface (1968).

Language, Foreign

Latin is a dead tongue,
Dead as dead can be.
First it killed the Romans —
Now it's killing me.   — Anon.

Anyone who is thoroughly familiar with the language and literature of a people cannot be wholly its enemy.
— Henri Bergson, *Two Sources of Morality and Religion*, 275 (1935).

He that is but able to express
No sense at all in several languages,
Will pass for learneder than he that's known
To speak the strongest reason in his own.
— Samuel Butler (1612–80), *Complete Works*, III (1905–28): *Satire Upon the Abuse of Learning*, I.65.

It is amazing how little of a foreign language you need if you have a passion for the thing written in it.
— John Jay Chapman, *Learning and Other Essays* (1911).

Learn a new language and get a new soul.
— Czech proverb.

Who does not know another language, does not know his own.
— Johann Wolfgang von Goethe, *Proverbs in Prose* (1819).

The Romans would never have found time to conquer the world if they had been obliged first to learn Latin.
— Heinrich Heine, *Reisebilder*, II (1827).

To be sure, languages are not to be despised or neglected; but, things are still to be preferred.   — William Penn, *Some Fruits of Solitude*, I. no.7 (1693).

I would I had bestowed that time in the tongues that I have in fencing, dancing, and bear-baiting. O, had I but followed the arts!   — William Shakespeare, *Twelfth Night*, I.iii.91 (1601) [bestowed...tongues = *spent time in learning languages*; the arts = *liberal arts*].

Nobody can say a word against Greek: it stamps a man at once as an educated gentleman.   — George Bernard Shaw, *Major Barbara*, I (1905).

Whenever the literary German dives into a sentence, that is the last you are going to see of him till he emerges on the other side of his Atlantic with his verb in his mouth.   — Mark Twain, *A Connecticut Yankee at King Arthur's Court*, xxii (1889).

Some of the German words are so long that they have a perspective. When one casts his glance along down one of these it gradually tapers to a point, like the receding lines of a railway track.
— Mark Twain, *Notebook*, May 2, 1878 (1935).

My philological studies have satisfied me that a gifted person ought to learn English (barring spelling and pro-

nouncing) in thirty hours, French in thirty days, and German in thirty years.
— Mark Twain,
A Tramp Abroad (1880).

We were taught as the chief subjects of instruction Latin and Greek. We were taught very badly because the men who taught us did not habitually use either of these languages.   — H.G. Wells,
The New Machiavelli, I.iii.5 (1911).

Language, Teaching of

Perhaps it is inevitable that the colleges which so long taught the dead languages as if they were buried should now teach the living ones as if they were dead.
— Frank Moore Colby,
The Margin of Hesitation: Confessions of a Gallomaniac (1921).

I see no sense in "faking" conversation for the sake of teaching language. It's stupid and deadening to pupil and teacher. Talk should be natural and have for its object an exchange of ideas. — Anne Sullivan, letter of Jan. 1, 1888, in *Helen Keller, The Story of My Life* (1903).

I *never taught language for the* PURPOSE *of teaching it*; but invariably used language as a medium for the communication of *thought*; thus the learning of languages was *coincident* with the acquisition of knowledge. In order to use language intelligently, one must have something to talk *about*, and having something to talk about is the result of having had experiences.— Anne Sullivan, address before the American Association to Promote the Teaching of Speech to the Deaf, July 1894, in Helen Keller, *The Story of My Life* (1903).

Laughter

See also Humor; Levity

A very wise old teacher once said: "I consider a day's teaching is wasted if we do not all have one hearty laugh." He meant

that when people laugh together, they cease to be young and old, master and pupils, workers and driver, jailer and prisoners, they become a single group of human beings enjoying its existence.
— Gilbert Highet,
The Art of Teaching (1950).

One laugh of a child will make the holiest day more sacred still.
— Robert G. Ingersoll,
The Liberty of Man, Woman and Child (1877).

Laziness

See also Idleness

The lazy mind will not take the trouble of going to the bottom of anything; but, discouraged by the first difficulties (and everything worth knowing or having is attended with some), stops short, contents itself with easy, and, consequently, superficial knowledge, and prefers a great degree of ignorance to a small degree of trouble.   — Lord Chesterfield,
Letters to His Son, July 36, 1748.

Indolence is the sleep of the mind.
— Marquis de Varvenargues,
Reflections and Maxims, (1746).

Leader

See also Administrator;
Leadership; Principal

The chief of the flock which leads it to the pasture-grounds is only an animal like the rest.   — Ani,
Teaching, no.54 (c.2000 B.C.).

A leader is best
When people barely know that he exists.
— Witter Bynner,
The Way of Life According to Laotzu (1944).

A leader should not get too far in front of his troops or he will be shot in the ass.
—Joseph Clark,
Washingtonian, Nov. 1979.

The leader is a stimulus, but he is also a response.   —Eduard C. Lindeman,
Social Discovery (1924).

In this world a man must be anvil or hammer.   —Henry Wadsworth Longfellow, *Hyperion*, IV.vi (1839).

The most important quality in a leader is that of being acknowledged as such. All leaders whose fitness is questioned are clearly lacking in force.
—André Maurois,
The Art of Living (1939).

A good leader can't get too far ahead of his followers.   —Franklin D. Roosevelt,
in Bernard M. Baruch,
The Public Years (1960).

Nothing so betrays the leader as reluctance to stand behind, defend and pay the price of the course of action he has chosen to follow. He must be willing squarely to shoulder the responsibility; and it is at this point that many people reveal deficiencies which debar them from real strength as leaders.
—Ordway Tead,
The Art of Leadership (1935).

Leadership

See also Administration; Leader

Leadership should be born out of the understanding of the needs of those who would be affected by it.
—Marian Anderson,
in *New York Times*, July 22, 1951.

Not the cry, but the flight of the wild duck, leads the flock to fly and follow.
—Chinese proverb.

People are more easily led than driven.
—David Harold Fink, *Release from Nervous Tension* (1943).

How ironic it will be if history records that the most democratic educational system in the world produced an educated class that could not lead because it could not conceal its contempt for the people who might have been its followers.   —John W. Gardner,
Recovery of Confidence (1970).

Charlatanism of some degree is indispensable to effective leadership.
—Eric Hoffer,
The True Believer (1951).

The only real training for leadership is leadership.   —Antony Jay,
Management and Machiavelli (1968).

The art of leading, in operations large or small, is the art of dealing with humanity, of working diligently on behalf of men, of being sympathetic with them, but equally, of insisting that they make a square facing toward their own problems.
—S.L.A. Marshall,
Men Against Fire (1947).

I start with the premise that the function of leadership is to produce more leaders, not more followers.   —Ralph Nader,
Time, Nov. 8, 1976.

You take people as far as they will go, not as far as you would like them to go.
—Jeannette Rankin, in Hannah Josephson, *Jeannette Rankin: First Lady in Congress*, prologue (1974).

Learned Person

See also Cultured Person;
Educated Person; Intellectual

When a learned man errs he makes a learned error.   —Arab proverb.

Who can read and write has four eyes.
—Selwyn Gurney Champion,
Racial Proverbs, 15 (1938).
An Albanian proverb.

He was naturally learn'd; he needed not the spectacles of books to read Nature; he looked inwards, and found her there.
—John Dryden,
Essay of Dramatick Poesy (1668).

Who has much learning but no good deeds is like an unbridled horse, that throws off the rider as soon as he mounts.
—Elisha ben Avuya,
Abot de R. Nathan, xxiv (2nd cent.).

The learned and the studious of thought have no monopoly of wisdom.
—Ralph Waldo Emerson,
Essays, First Series: The Over-Soul (1841).

Of learned Fools I have seen ten times ten,
Of unlearned wise men I have seen a hundred.   —Benjamin Franklin,
Poor Richard's Almanack, July 1735.

Tim was so learned, that he could name a Horse in nine Languages: So ignorant, that he bought a Cow to ride on.
—Benjamin Franklin,
ibid., Nov. 1750.

The trouble with most men of learning is that their learning goes to their heads.
—Isaac Goldberg,
Reflex, Dec. 1927.

If you want to acquire a reputation for learning at a cheap rate, it is best to ignore the dull and stupid knowledge which is everybody's posession and concentrate on something odd and out of the way.... In this way you will get the reputation of a person of profound learning and the most exquisite taste.
—Aldous Huxley,
Essays New and Old: Conxolus (1925).

Grammarian, orator, geometrician; painter, gymnastic teacher; fortune-teller, rope-dancer, physician, conjuror,—he knew everything.   —Juvenal,
Satires, III (c.110).

Two evils, of almost equal weight, may befall the man of erudition: never to be listened to, and to be listened to always.
—Walter Savage Landor,
Imaginary Conversations, 29:
Epicurus, Leontion, and Ternissa
(1824–53).

Learned men are the cisterns of knowledge, not the fountain-heads.
—James Northcote,
Table-Talk (c.1775).

Take away from our learned men the pleasure of making themselves heard, learning would be nothing to them.
—Jean Jacques Rousseau,
Julie, I. lett.xii (1761).

A day of the learned is longer than the life of the ignorant.   —Seneca,
Letters to Lucilius,
LXXVIII (c. A.D. 64).

A learned man is an idler who kills time with study. Beware of his false knowledge: it is more dangerous than Ignorance.   —George Bernard Shaw,
Maxims for Revolutionists (1903).

Very learned women are to be found, in the same manner as female warriors; but they are seldom or never inventors.
—Voltaire, *Philosophical Dictionary: Women* (1764).

Learning (i.e., Knowledge)

See *also* below; Instruction; Knowledge; Learning (i.e., Process)

There is no great concurrence between learning and wisdom. —Francis Bacon,
The Advancement of Learning,
II.xxiii.4 (1605).

Wear your learning, like your watch, in a private pocket; and do not pull it out and strike it, merely to show that you have one. If you are asked what o'clock it is,

tell it; but do not proclaim it hourly and unasked like the watchman.
— Lord Chesterfield,
Letters to His Son, Feb. 22, 1748.

Learning is like paddling a canoe against the current. It recedes if it does not advance. — Chinese proverb,
in Lin Yutang, *The Importance of Understanding*, 494 (1960).

Learning without thought is labor lost; thought without learning is perilous.
— Confucius,
Analects, II.xv (c.500 B.C.).

Here the heart
May give an useful lesson to the head,
And learning wiser grow without his
books. — William Cowper,
The Task, VI: *The Winter Walk at Noon*, ln.85 (1785).

Knowledge comes
Of learning well retain'd, unfruitful else.
— Dante, *The Divine Comedy: Paradise*, V.41 (c.1314).

Learning is the eye of the mind.
— Thomas Draxe,
Bibliotheca Scholastica Instructissima (1616).

Learning is heavy, & yet it waieth not; it is fayre, and yet fewe seeke it; sweet, but few will taste of her. — John Florio,
Firste Fruites, fo.63 (1578).

There is much more learning than knowing in the world. — Thomas Fuller (1654–1734), *Gnomologia*, no.4901 (1732).

Much learning does not teach understanding. — Heraclitus,
On the Universe, frag.16 (c.500 B.C.).

As we all know, a little learning is a dangerous thing ... But a great deal of highly specialized learning is a dangerous thing and may be sometimes even more dangerous than a little learning.
— Aldous Huxley, lecture at University of California in Santa Barbara, Feb. 9, 1959.

The road to learning is endless.
— Jacob ben Asher,
(c.1269–c.1340), *Toheka*.

Learning without wisdom is a load of books on an ass's back.
— Japanese proverb.

The advancement of learning is the highest commandment. — Maimonides, letter to Joseph Ibn Gabir, 1191.

There are three ingredients in the good life: learning, earning and yearning.
— Christopher Morley,
Parnassus on Wheels, x (1917).

Nature without learning is blind, learning apart from nature is fractional, and practice in the absence of both is aimless.
— Plutarch, *Moralia: The Education of Children* (c. A.D. 95).

A *little learning* is a dang'rous thing;
Drink deep, or taste not the Pierian spring.
There shallow draughts intoxicate the brain,
And drinking largely sobers us again.
— Alexander Pope,
An Essay on Criticism, II.215 (1711).

There are none worse than those who, as soon as they have progressed beyond a knowledge of the alphabet, delude themselves into the belief that they are the possessors of real knowledge.
— Quintilian,
Institutio Oratoria, I.i.8
(A.D. 95 or 96).

What we first learn we best ken.
— Scottish proverb.

No man is the wiser for his Learning: it may administer matter to work in, or objects to work upon; but Wit and Wisdom are born with a man. — John Selden,
Table Talk: Learning (1689).

Learning is but an adjunct to ourself,
And where we are our learning likewise is. — William Shakespeare, *Love's Labour's Lost*, IV.iii.314 (1594).

It is only when we forget all our learning that we begin to know.
— Henry David Thoreau, *Journal*, Oct. 4, 1859.

Once learning solidifies, all is over with it.   — Alfred North Whitehead, *Dialogues*, as recorded by Lucien Price (1953).

It's what you learn after you know it all that counts.   — John Wooden, *They Call Me Coach* (1973).

You must fuse at white heat the several particles of your learning into an element so ductile and so strong that nothing can destroy it without destroying you.
— Owen D. Young, address at Hendrix College, Ark., Nov. 20, 1934.

Learning, Book

Erudition, *n*. Dust shaken out of a book into an empty skull. — Ambrose Bierce, *The Devil's Dictionary* (1911).

And let a Scholler, all earths volumes carrie,
He will be but a walking dictionarie.
— George Chapman, *The Teares of Peace*, ln.266 (1609).

A scholar of the traditional text, who learns nothing else, is like a camel carrying a load of silk: silk and camel are of no use to each other.
— Abraham Ibn Ezra, *Yeshod Mora (Fountain of the Knowledge of God)* (1158).

Education should not confine itself to books. It must train executive power, and try to create that right public opinion which is the most potent factor in the proper solution of all political and social questions. Book-learning is very important, but it is by no means everything.
— Theodore Roosevelt, address in Lansing, Mich., May 31, 1907.

The learning of books that you do not make your own wisdom is money in the hands of another in time of need.
— Sanskrit proverb.

Learning, Desire for

Be eager for learning, even if it comes from the snout of a hog.
— Arab proverb.

It is impossible to withhold education from the receptive mind, as it is impossible to force it upon the unreasoning.
— Agnes Repplier, *Times and Tendencies* (1931).

Learning must be sought; it will not come of itself. — Simeon ben Lakish, *Midrash Mishlê*, (c. A.D. 200–275).

Learning, Dispraise of

Learning, that cobweb of the brain,
Profane, erroneous, and vain.
— Samuel Butler (1612–80), *Hudibras*, I.iii.1339 (1663).

Gray says, very justly, that learning never should be encouraged, it only draws out fools from their obscurity; and you know, I have always thought a running-footman as meritorious a being as a learned man. Why is there more merit in having travelled one's eyes over so many reams of papers than in having carried one's legs over so many acres of ground?
— Horace Walpole, letter to Richard Bentley, May 6, 1775.

Learning, Effect of

And it is without all controversy, that learning doth make the minds of men gentle, generous, maniable, and pliant to government; whereas ignorance makes them churlish, thwart, and mutinous.
— Francis Bacon, *The Advancement of Learning*, I.ii.8 (1605)
[maniable = *easy to handle*].

Learning makes a man fit company for himself. — Thomas Fuller (1654–1734), *Gnomologia*, no.3163 (1732).

Learning, Effort of

Learning by study must be won;
'Twas ne'er entail'd from son to son.
— John Gay, *Fables*, I:
The Pack Horse and the Carrier, ln.41 (1727).

Whence is thy learning? Hath thy toil
O'er books consum'd the midnight oil?
— John Gay, *Fables*, introd.:
The Shepherd and the Philosopher, ln.15 (1727).

Learning, Love of

Let your concern for learning
Be greater than for teaching.
By the latter you benefit others;
By the former, yourself.
— Pierre Abélard,
Astrolabius (before 1142).

Alcuin was my name: learning I loved.
— Alcuin (735–804), his own epitaph.

If you are a lover of instruction, you will be well instructed. — Isocrates, *Ad Doemonicum*. Inscribed in golden letters over his school in Athens, founded 392 B.C. Quoted in Roger Ascham, *The Schoolmaster* (1570).

If we succeed in giving the love of learning, the learning itself is sure to follow.
— John Lubbock,
The Pleasures of Life (1887).

Learning, in the Renaissance, was part of the *joie de vivre*, just as much as drinking or love-making. And this was true not only of literature, but also of sterner studies. — Bertrand Russell, *The Will to Doubt:* *"Useless" Knowledge* (1958).

Love of learning is a pleasant and universal bond, since it deals with what one *is* and not what one *has*.
— Freyda Stark,
The Journey's Echo (1963).

Learning, Value of

A little learning, indeed, may be a dangerous thing, but the want of learning is a calamity to any people.
— Frederick Douglass, address, high school commencement, Baltimore, June 22, 1894. Refers to Pope's famous line.

Learning is the only wealth tyrants cannot despoil. Only death can dim the lamp of knowledge that is within you. The true wealth of a nation lies not in its gold or silver but in its learning, wisdom, and in the uprightness of its sons.
— Kahlil Gibran,
The Treasured Writings (1980):
The Words of the Master, viii.

Of all thinge whiche wee possesse in this world, only learning is immortall.
— Stefano Guazzo,
Civil Conversation, II.216 (1574).

Learning is a name superior to beauty; learning is better than hidden treasure. Learning is a companion on a journey to a strange country; learning is strength inexhaustible. A man in this world without learning is as a beast of the field.
— *Hitopadésa*, introd. (c.500).

I have risen by my pen to a position which I would not exchange for that of the Turkish sultan, taking his wealth and giving up my learning.
— Martin Luther,
Table Talk (1566).

Learning & Knowledg is essential to the preservation of Libberty & unless we have more of it amongue us we Cannot Seporte our Libertyes Long.
— William Manning,
The Key of Libberty (1798).

When house and land are gone and
spent,
Then learning is more excellent.
        —Old English rhyme.

As when the sunne shineth, the light of
the stars is not seene: so when learning
appeareth, all other giftes are nothing to
be accounted of.   —George Pettie,
        A Petite Pallace, 229 (1576).

The desirable treasure of wisdom and
science, which all men desire by an instinct of nature, infinitely surpasses all
the riches of the world; in respect of
which precious stones are worthless; in
comparison with which silver is as clay
and pure gold is as a little sand; at whose
splendor the sun and moon are dark to
look upon; compared with whose marvel-
ous sweetness honey and manna are bitter to the taste.   —Richard de Bury,
        Philobiblon (1473).

O! this learning, what a thing it is.
        —William Shakespeare,
        The Taming of the Shrew,
        I.iv.159 (1596).

Learning (i.e., Process)

See also below; Instruction;
Learning [i.e., Knowledge];
Teaching

Incline thine ears to hear my sayings,
And apply thine heart to their comprehension.
For it is a profitable thing to put them in
thy heart.   —Amenemope,
        The Wisdom of Amenemope,
        III (c.11th cent. B.C.).

Never learn anything until you find you
have been made uncomfortable for a long
time by not knowing it.
        —Samuel Butler (1835–1902),
        The Way of All Flesh,
        xxxi (1903).

"Learning," he would say, "should be a
joy and full of excitement. It is life's

greatest adventure; it is an illustrated excursion into the mind's noble and learned
men, not a conducted tour through a jail.
So its surroundings should be as gracious
as possible to complement it."
        —Taylor Caldwell,
        The Sound of Thunder, I.ix (1957).

Learn more; then you will know how
much more you need to learn.
        —Chinese proverb, in Lin Yutang,
        The Importance of Understanding,
        489 (1960).

Personally I'm always ready to learn,
although I do not always like being
taught.   —Winston Churchill,
        speech in House of Commons,
        Nov. 4, 1952.

In order that knowledge be properly
digested, it must have been swallowed
with a good appetite. —Anatole France,
        The Crime of Sylvestre Bonnard (1881).

Children can be lured into learning. They
can be tempted and hooked on it; but
they cannot be shamed into it. When
forced to study, children use their ingenuity to get through school without
learning.   —Haim G. Ginott,
        Teacher and Child, 240 (1972).

Education is a thing of which only the
few are capable; teach as you will, only a
small percentage will profit by your most
zealous energy.   —George Gissing,
        The Private Papers of Henry Ryecroft,
        I.22 (1903).

Learning is like rowing upstream: not to
advance is to drop back.   —H.H. Hart,
        Seven Hundred Chinese Proverbs,
        no.159 (1937).

A man must *get* a thing before he can
forget it. —Oliver Wendell Holmes, Sr.,
        Medical Essays, 300 (1842–94).

I learned much from my teachers, more
from my books, and most from my troubles.   —Isaac Kaminer, *Baraitot de
        Rabbi Yitzhak* (1885), paraphrasing
        Talmud: Ta'anith, 7a (before A.D. 500).

He who would learn to fly one day must first learn to stand and walk and run and climb and dance: one cannot fly into flying.   — Friedrich Nietzsche, *Thus Spake Zarathustra*, III: *On the Spirit of Gravity* (1883–4).

We cannot know how much we learn
From those who never will return,
Until a flash of unforeseen
Remembrance falls on what has been.
            — Edwin Arlington Robinson,
            *The Man Against the Sky:
            Flammonde*, ln.89 (1916).

I am glad to learn, in order that I may teach.   — Seneca,
            Letters to Lucilius,
            VI.iv (c. A.D. 64).

An unlesson'd girl, unschool'd, unprac-
tis'd;
Happy in this, she is not yet so old
But she may learn; happier than this,
She is not bred so dull but that she can
learn.   — William Shakespeare,
            The Merchant of Venice, III.ii.160
            (1596) [happy = *fortunate*].

You cannot learn to skate without being ridiculous.... The ice of life is slippery.
            — George Bernard Shaw,
            Fanny's First Play, introd. (1911).

Only the lesson which is enjoyed can be learned well.   — Talmud:
            Aboda Zara, 19a (before A.D. 500).

The only things worth learning are the things you learn after you know it all.
            — Harry S Truman,
            Reader's Digest, Apr. 1975.

"I dunno," Arthur said, "I forget what I was taught. I only remember what I've learnt."   — Patrick White,
            The Solid Mandala, ii (1966).

Learning, Continuing

When there is nothing more to learn,
Cease learning,

And say not you must stop before then.
            — Pierre Abélard, *Astrolabius*
            (before 1142).

Furnish your mind with precepts, never stop learning; for life without learning is but an image of death.
            — Cato of Córdoba, *Catonis
            Disticha Moralia*, III.i (c. 3rd cent.).

When you're through learning, you're through.   — Vernon Sanders Law,
            "How To Be a Winner,"
            This Week, Aug. 14, 1960.

A man is never too old to learn.
            — Thomas Middleton, *The Mayor
            of Quinborough*, v (publ. 1661).

You should keep learning as long as there is anything you do not know; if we may believe the proverb, as long as you live.
            — Seneca,
            Letters to Lucilius,
            LXXVI.iii (c. A.D. 64).

When you stop learning, stop listening, stop looking and asking question, always new questions, then it is time to die.
            — Lillian Smith,
            "Bridges to Other People,"
            Redbook, Sept. 1969.

Learning, Definition of

That is what learning is. You suddenly understand something you've understood all your life, but in a new way.
            — Doris Lessing,
            The Four-Gated City (1969).

Learning is discovering that something is possible.   — Fritz Perls,
            Omni, Nov. 1979.

Effective learning means arriving at new power, and the consciousness of new things in life.
            — Janet Erskine Stuart,
            in Maud Monahan,
            *Life and Letters of Janet
            Erskine Stuart* (1922).

Learning, Futility of

Give up learning, and put an end to your
troubles.   — Lao-tse,
Tao Te Ching,
sec.20 (c.550 B.C.),
tr. Gia-Fu Feng and
Jane English (1972).

With them the seed of Wisdom did I
sow,
And with mine own hand wrought to
make it grow;
And this was all the Harvest that I
reap'd—
"I came like Water, and like Wind I go."
— Omar Khayyám,
Rubáiyát, XXVIII (c.1100),
tr. Edward FitzGerald
(1859).

Waste not your Hour, nor in vain pursuit
Of This or That endeavour and dispute;
Better be jocund with the fruitful Grape
Than sadden after none, or bitter, Fruit.
— Omar Khayyám,
ibid., LIV.

Learning, Method of

Some minds learn most when they seem
to learn least. A certain placid, unconscious, equable taking-in of knowledge suits them, and alone suits them.
— Walter Bagehot,
Literary Studies,
I (1879).

Learn as though you would never be able
to master it; hold it as though you would
be in fear of losing it.   — Confucius,
Analects,
VIII.17 (c.500 B.C.).

The perfect method of learning is
analogous to infection. It enters and
spreads.   — Leo Stein,
Journey into the Self,
231 (1950).

Learning, Youth and

What one knows is, in youth, of little
moment; they know enough who know
how to learn.   — Henry Adams,
The Education of Henry Adams,
xxi (1907).

In seed time learn, in harvest teach, in
winter enjoy.   — William Blake,
The Marriage of
Heaven and Hell:
Proverbs of Hell (1790).

Learn young, learn fair.
— David Ferguson,
Scottish Proverbs, 72 (1641).

Learning in old age is like writing on
sand; learning in youth is like engraving
on stone.   — Ibn Gabirol,
Choice of Pearls,
no.53 (c.1050).

What we first learn we best ken.
— James Kelly,
Complete Collection of Scottish
Proverbs, 340 (1721).

Lecture

Do not go lightly or casually to hear lectures; but if you do go, maintain your
gravity and dignity and do not make
yourself offensive.   — Epictetus,
Enchiridion,
no.33 (c. A.D. 110).

Most people tire of a lecture in ten
minutes; clever people can do it in five.
Sensible people never go to lecutres at all.
But the people who do go to a lecture and
who get tired of it, presently hold it as a
sort of grudge against the lecturer personally. In reality his sufferings are worse
than theirs.   — Stephen Leacock,
Laugh with Leacock:
We Have With Us Tonight
(1930).

Lecturer

See also Professor; Teacher

Lecturer, *n*. One with his hand in your pocket, his tongue in your ear, and his faith in your patience.
— Ambrose Bierce,
The Devil's Dictionary (1911).

The first duty of a lecturer — to hand you after an hour's discourse a nugget of pure truth to wrap up between the pages of your notebooks and keep on your mantlepiece for ever. — Virginia Woolf,
A Room of One's Own, i (1929).

Lesson Planning

See also Teaching

They talk much in pedagogic circles today about the duty of the teacher to prepare for every lesson in advance. To some extent this is useful.... The advice I should give to most teachers would be in the words of one who is herself an admirable teacher. *Prepare yourself in the subject so well that it shall be always on tap*: then in the class-room trust your spontaneity and fling away all further care. — William James,
Talks to Teachers on Psychology (1899).

Levity

See also Humor; Laughter

If a man insisted always on being serious, and never allowed himself a bit of fun and relaxation, he would go mad or become unstable without knowing it.
— Herodotus, *Histories*,
II. clxxiii (before 425 B.C.).

Mingle a little folly with your wisdom; a little nonsense now and then is pleasant.
— Horace, *Odes*,
IV.xii.27 (17–13 B.C.).

Fun is a good thing but only when it spoils nothing better.
— George Santayana,
*The Sense of Beauty:
The Comic* (1896).

Librarian

His work is to be a factor and trader for helps to learning, and a treasurer to keep them, and a dispenser to apply them to use or see them well used, or at least not abused. — John Dury,
letter to William Dugard,
1649.

It is the librarian's duty to distinguish between poetry and belle-litter.
— Tom Stoppard,
Travesties, I (1975).

The schools legally act *in loco parentis*, and supervision of their pupils' reading is only a part of the supervision that is assumed necessary as youngsters approach the magical age of 21. If parents have the duty to screen their daughter's boy friends and to indicate (hopefully) what time their daughters are expected home from dates, the librarian also has a duty to screen books for those daughters — and their boy friends. — Samuel Withers,
"The Library, the Child and the Censor," *New York Times Magazine*, Apr. 8, 1962.

Library

See also below; Book

Libraries are not made; they grow.
— Augustine Birrell,
Obiter Dicta: Book-Buying (1884).

These are not books, lumps of lifeless paper, but *minds* alive on the shelves. From each of them goes out its own voice, as inaudible as the streams of sound conveyed day and night by electric waves beyond the range of our physical hearing; and just as the touch of a button on our

set will fill the room with music, so by taking down one of these volumes and opening it, one can call into range the voice of a man far distant in time and space, and hear him speaking to us, mind to mind, heart to heart.
—Gilbert Highet,
The Immortal Profession (1976).

Every library should try to be complete on something, if it were only the history of pinheads.— Oliver Wendell Holmes, Sr.,
The Poet at the Breakfast-Table,
viii (1872).

Books lead us into the society of those great men with whom we could not otherwise come into personal contact. They bring us near to the geniuses of the remotest land and times. A good library is a place, a palace, where the lofty spirits of all nations and generations meet.
—Samuel Niger,
Geklibene Shriftn, I.32 (1928).

A library is thought in cold storage.
—Herbert Samuel,
A Book of Quotations (1947).

I love vast libraries; yet there is a doubt, If one be better with them or without,— Unless he use them wisely, and, indeed, Knows the high art of what and how to read.   —John Godfrey Saxe,
The Library (1860).

Library, Personal

Good as it is to inherit a library, it is better to collect one.   —Augustine Birrell,
Obiter Dicta: Book-Buying (1884).

I no sooner come into the library, but I bolt the door to me, excluding lust, avarice, and all such vices, whose nurse is idleness, the mother of ignorance, and melancholy herself, and in the very lap of eternity, amongst so many divine souls, I take my seat, with so lofty a spirit and sweet content that I pity all our great ones and rich men that know not this happiness.   —Robert Burton,
The Anatomy of Melancholy, II (1621).

It is a great thing to start life with a small number of really good books which are your very own.   —A. Conan Doyle,
Through the Magic Door (1908).

A man's library is a sort of harem, and tender readers have a great pudency in showing their books to a stranger.
—Ralph Waldo Emerson,
Society and Solitude: Books (1870).

It is vanity to perswade the world one hath much learning by getting a great library. As soon shall I believe every one is valiant that hath a well furnish'd armoury.   —Thomas Fuller (1608–61),
The Holy State and the Profane State, III.xviii: *Of Books* (1642).

He that revels in a well-chosen library, has innumerable dishes, and all of admirable flavor.   —William Godwin,
The Enquirer (1797).

What a world of wit is here packed up together! I know not whether this sight doth more dismay or comfort me: It dismays me to think that here is so much I cannot know; it comforts me to think that this variety yields so good helps to know what I should.
—Joseph Hall (1574–1656),
Occasional Meditations and Vowes
(1606).

I have honored thee by providing an extensive library for thy use, and have thus relieved thee of the necessity to borrow books. Most students must bustle about to seek books, often without finding them. But thou, thanks be to God, lendest and borrowest not. Of many books, indeed, thou ownest two or three copies.   —Judah Ibn Tibbon,
Ethical Will (c.1190), to his son.

Should a man face straitened circumstances, he should first sell his gold and jewels, then his house and estate, but not—until the very end, when he has nothing left—his library.
—Judah of Regensburg,
Book of the Righteous (13th cent.).

I don't care what a person says—I'll look at his books and I'll know what he is. If he has a gentleman's library, okay, but I'll know what he is. If he has a specialist's library, I'll want to see the variants. All good bookmen are interested in trivia. Generalizations don't mean a damn thing—anybody can make them. Trivia—not even details—trivia!
— Sol M. Malkin,
in Israel Shenker, *Words and Their Masters*, 291 (1974).

Show me his friends and I the man shall know;
This wiser turn a larger wisdom lends:
Show me the books he loves and I shall know
The man far better than through mortal friends.   — Silas Weir Mitchell,
Books and the Man (1905).

Affect not as some do that bookish ambition to be stored with books and have well furnished libraries, yet keep their heads empty of knowledge: to desire to have many books and never use them is like a child that will have a candle burning by him all the while he is sleeping.
— Henry Peacham,
The Compleat Gentleman, 52 (1622).

Library, Public

What a sad want I am in of libraries, of books to gather facts from! Why is there not a Majesty's library in every country town? There is a Majesty's gaol and gallows in every one. — Thomas Carlyle,
Journal, 1832.

The library is not a shrine for the worship of books. It is not a temple where literary incense must be burned or where one's devotion to the bound book is expressed in ritual. A library, to modify the famous metaphor of Socrates, should be the delivery room for the birth of ideas—a place where history comes to life.
— Norman Cousins,
Saturday Review, 1950.

For myself, public libraries possess a special horror, as of lonely wastes and dragon-haunted fens. The stillness and the heavy air, the feeling of restriction and surveillance, the mute presence of these other readers, "all silent and damned," combine to set up a nervous irritation fatal to quiet study.
— Kenneth Grahame,
Pagan Papers (1893).

Here is the history of human ignorance, error, superstition, folly, war and waste, recorded by human intelligence for the admonition of wiser ages still to come. Here is the history of man's hunger for truth, goodness and beauty, leading him slowly on, through flesh to spirit, from war to peace.   — Inscriptions on
library at University of Rochester.

I have often thought that nothing would do more extensive good at small expense than the establishment of a small, circulating library in every county, to consist of a few well-chosen books, to be lent to the people of the county, under such regulations as would secure their safe return in due time. — Thomas Jefferson,
letter to John Wyche, May 19, 1809.

A circulating library in a town is, as an ever-green tree of diabolical knowledge! It blossoms through the year!
— Richard Brinsley Sheridan,
The Rivals, I.ii (1775).

Books are to be call'd for, and supplied, on the assumption that the process of reading is not a half sleep, but, in highest sense, an exercise, a gymnast's struggle; that the reader is to do something for himself.... Not the book needs so much to be the complete thing, but the reader of the book does.   — Walt Whitman,
Democratic Vistas (1871).

Listening

See also Attention; Hearing

To talk to someone who does not listen is enough to tense the devil. — Pearl Bailey, *Talking to Myself* (1971).

Many men use their ears as a bolting-cloth, only to catch the bran and let the flour go. —Henry Ward Beecher, *Proverbs from Plymouth Pulpit: Man* (1887).

He listens to good purpose who takes note. —Dante, *The Divine Comedy: Inferno*, XV.99 (c.1314).

Speak your truth quietly and clearly; and listen to others, even the dull and ignorant; they too have their story. —Max Ehrmann, *Desiderata* (1927).

Many failures in academic and social growth can be traced to inability to listen than to any other single aspect of the language arts.... We must not take for granted that a person can listen because he can hear. —*Elementary English*, Apr. 1959.

The most difficult thing of all, to keep quiet and listen. —Aulus Gellius, *Attic Nights*, I.ix (c. A.D. 150).

Listen and you will learn. —Solomon Ibn Gabirol, *Choice of Pearls*, no.19 (c.1050).

No one cares to speak to an unwilling listener. An arrow never lodges in a stone: often it recoils upon the sender of it. —St. Jerome, *Letters*, let.52 (A.D. 370).

My father used to say to me: "Son, you do all right in this world if you just remember that when you talk you are only repeating what you already know—but if you listen you may learn something." —J.P. McEvoy, *Charlie Would Have Loved This* (1956).

Listening is a magnetic and strange thing, a creative force. The friends who listen to us are the ones we move forward toward, and we want to sit in their radius. When we are listened to, it creates us, makes us unfold and expand. —Karl A. Menninger, *Love Against Hate* (1942).

It is fairly well established that in a normal conversation the hearer really hears only about fifty per cent of the sounds produced by the speaker, and supplies the rest out of his own sense of the context. —Mario Pei, *The Story of Language*, 102 (1949).

The most precious thing a man can lend is his ears. —Dagobert D. Runes, *Treasury of Thought*, 225 (1966).

Give every man thy ear, but few thy voice;
Take each man's censure, but reserve thy judgment. —William Shakespeare, *Hamlet*, I.iii.68 (1600–01) [censure = *opinion*].

A good listener tries to understand thoroughly what the other person is saying. In the end he may disagree sharply, but before he disagrees, he wants to know exactly what it is he is disagreeing with. —Kenneth A. Wells, *Guide to Good Leadership* (1953).

The reason why we have two ears and only one mouth is that we may listen more and talk less. —Zeno, maxim (c.460 B.C.). Credited also to Socrates, Diogenes and Demosthenes.

Literature

See also Classic; Fiction; Novel; Poetry; Theater

Writing is not literature unless it gives to the reader a pleasure which arises not only from the things said; and that pleasure

is only given when the words are carefully or curiously or beautifully put together into sentences.
— Stopford Augustus Brooke,
Primer of English Literature (1876).

Literature is an investment of genius which pays dividends to all subsequent times.
— John Burroughs
(1837–1921), *Literary Fame.*

Every fine story must leave in the mind of the sensitive reader an intangible residuum of pleasure, a cadence, a quality of voice that is exclusively the writer's own, individual, unique.
— Willa Cather,
Not Under Forty (1936).

Literature is landscape on the desk; landscape is literature on the earth.
— Chang Chao, *Yumengying* (before 1693), in Lin Yutang,
The Importance of Understanding, 70 (1960).

Literature is a transmission of power. Text books and treatises, dictionaries and encyclopedias, manuals and books of instruction — they are communications; but literature is a power line, and the motor, mark you, is the reader.
— Charles P. Curtis,
A Commonplace Book (1957).

A people's literature is the great textbook for real knowledge of them. The Writings of the day show the quality of the people as no historical reconstruction can.
— Edith Hamilton,
The Roman Way, preface (1932).

He knew everything about literature except how to enjoy it. — Joseph Heller,
Catch-22, viii (1961).

Good literature continually read for pleasure must, let us hope, do some good to the reader: must quicken his perception though dull, and sharpen his discrimination though blunt, and mellow the rawness of his personal opinions.
— A.E. Housman,
The Name and Nature of Poetry (1933).

The thing that teases the mind over and over for years, and at last gets itself put down rightly on paper — whether little or great, it belongs to Literature.
— Sarah Orne Jewett,
letter to Willa Cather, in *The Country of the Pointed Firs and Other Stories*, preface (1896).

While the benefits of literature are very pleasant in many respects, they are especially so in this regard, that, once the annoying element of intervals of time and place is removed, they offer the presence of friends one after the other and do not allow things worth knowing to fall into decay. — John of Salisbury,
Policraticus (1159).

I doubt if anything learnt at school is of more value than great literature learnt by heart. — Richard Livingstone,
On Education (1944).

Literature exists for the sake of the people — to refresh the weary, to console the sad, to hearten the dull and downcast, to increase man's interest in the world, his joy of living, and his sympathy in all sorts and conditions of man.
— M.T. Manton, dissenting U.S.
Court of Appeals opinion, *United States v One Book Called "Ulysses,"* 1934.

And then my familiarity with literatures
Besteads me well,
Affording me always a scholarly explanation
For conduct seemingly eccentric.
— Christopher Morley,
Translations from the Chinese: Advantage of a Bookish Upbringing (1922).

Literature is news that STAYS news.
— Ezra Pound,
How to Read (1931).

Great literature is simply language charged with meaning to the utmost possible degree. — Ezra Pound,
ibid., II.

The study of literature is a necessity for boys and the delight of age, the sweet companion of our privacy, and the only branch of study which has more solid substance than display.   — Quintilian, *Institutio Oratoria*, I.v.5 (A.D. 95 or 96).

The only literature which is at the same time vital and popular is the literature of the music-hall.   — Herbert Read, *Phases of English Poetry* (1928).

Literature does its duty ... in raising our fancy to the height of what may be noble, honest, and felicitous in actual life; in giving us, though we may ourselves be poor and unknown, the companionship of the wisest fellow-spirits of every age and country.   — John Ruskin, *The Eagle's Nest* (1872).

Literature is the memory of humanity. — Isaac Bashevis Singer, *U.S. News and World Report*, Nov. 6, 1978.

The great English Universities, under whose direct authority school-children are examined in plays of Shakespeare, to the certain destruction of their enjoyment, should be prosecuted for soul murder. — Alfred North Whitehead, *The Aims of Education*, iv (1929).

The whole purport of literature ... is the notation of the heart. Style is but the faintly contemptible vessel in which the bitter liquid is recommended to the world.   — Thornton Wilder, *The Bridge of San Luis Rey*, ii (1927).

Logic

See also Rationality; Reason

The principles of logic and metaphysics are true simply because we never allow them to be anything else. — A.J. Ayer, *Language, Truth and Logic* (1936).

He was in logic a great critic, Profoundly skilled in analytic. He could distinguish and divide A hair 'twixt south and southwest side. — Samuel Butler (1612–80), *Hudibras*, I.i.65 (1663).

Of logic, and its limits, and uses and abuses ... one fact ... has long been familiar: that the man of logic and the man of insight; the Reasoner and the Discoverer, or even the Knower, are quite separable, — indeed, for the most part, quite separate characters. — Thomas Carlyle, *Characteristics* (1831).

Logic, like whiskey, loses its beneficial effect when taken in too large quantities. — Lord Dunsany, *My Ireland*, xix (1938).

The want of logic annoys. Too much logic bores. Life eludes logic, and everything that logic alone constructs remains artificial and forced.   — André Gide, *Journals*, May 12, 1927.

I am afraid you do not study logic at your school, my dear. It does not follow that I wish to be pickled in brine because I like a salt-water plunge at Nahant. — Oliver Wendell Holmes, Sr., *The Autocrat of the Breakfast-Table*, i (1858).

[L]ogic [is] the art of going wrong with confidence.   — Joseph Wood Krutch, *The Modern Temper*, 228 (1929).

A specious and fantastic arrangement of words by which a man can prove a horse chestnut to be a chestnut horse. — Abraham Lincoln, first debate with Stephen A. Douglas, Ottowa, Ill., Aug. 21, 1858.

It is because there is no logic in the course of nature that language and logic must ever be at odds. You cannot build up a tree if you have but the juices of the earth at your command; it will grow only if you sow a seed. — Antoine de Saint-Exupéry, *The Wisdom of the Sands*, lxxxix (1950).

A mind all logic is like a knife all blade. It makes the hand bleed that uses it. — Rabindranath Tagore, *Stray Birds* (1916).

One often hears the complimentary phrase "flawless logic"; and it is hard to realize that this discipline, so long considered the one kind of thinking or reasoning beyond criticism, should have this mysterious inner flaw, which consists of the fact that you can never discover whether or not it really has a flaw. — Warren Weaver, *Lady Luck: The Theory of Probability* (1982).

The fatal errors of life are not due to man's being unreasonable. An unreasonable moment may be one's finest. They are due to man's being logical. — Oscar Wilde, *De Profundis* (1905).

Love

If your basic attitude is one of loving kindness, you may yell at children and even cuff them around a bit without doing any real harm. — Smiley Blanton, *Love or Perish* (1956).

The first, the fundamental right of childhood is the right to be loved. The child comes into the world alone, defenseless, without resource. Only love can stand between his infant helplessness and the savagery of a harsh world. — Paul Hanly Furfey (1896–), *The Church and the Child*.

The love we give away is the only love we keep. — Elbert Hubbard, *Note Book* (1927).

Children need love, especially when they do not deserve it. — Harold S. Hulbert, in *Reader's Digest*, May 1949.

To cease to be loved is for the child practically synonymous with ceasing to live. — Karl A. Menninger, *A Psychiatrist's World* (1959).

To love means to communicate to the other that you are all for him, that you will never fail him or let him down when he needs you, but that you will always be standing by with all the necessary encouragements. It is something one can communicate to another only if one has it. — Ashley Montagu, *The Cultured Man* (1958).

Once you've loved a child, you love all children. You give away your love to one, and you find that by giving you have made yourself an inexhaustible treasury. — Margaret Lee Runbeck, *Our Miss Boo*, ii (1942).

Give a little love to a child, and you get a great deal back. — John Ruskin, *The Crown of Wild Olive*, xxxiv: *Work* (1866).

Loyalty Oath

I have found that men who have not even been suspected of disloyalty are very adverse to taking an oath of any sort as a condition to exercising an ordinary right of citizenship. — Abraham Lincoln, letter to William S. Rosencrans, Apr. 4, 1864.

Malapropism

See also Girl, Education of

After all, both the faculty and I are paid to be good, whereas the trustees are good for nothing. — Response of a retiring college faculty member after an introduction by the chairman of the board of trustees extrolling the professor and the faculty, in Sydney Harris, syndicated column, *Detroit Free Press*, July 21, 1982.

There, sir, an attack upon my language!
... an aspersion upon my parts of
speech!... Sure, if I reprehend anything
in this world, it is the use of my oracular
tongue, and a nice derangement of
epitaphs! — Richard Brinsley Sheridan,
    The Rivals, III.iii (1775).
    Mrs. Malaprop speaking.

Mankind, Study of

My favourite, I might say my only study,
is man.   — George Borrow,
    The Bible in Spain, v (1843).

The true science and the true study of
man is man.   — Pierre Charron,
    A Treatise on Wisdom, I.i (1601).

He that studies books alone, will know
how things ought to be; and he that
studies men, will know how things are.
    — Charles Caleb Colton,
    Lacon, I, preface (1820).

Mankind may be divided into four
classes: (1) those who know and know
that they know — of them seek knowledge; (2) those who know but do not
know that they know — awaken them; (3)
those who do not know and know that
they do not know — instruct them; (4)
those who do not know but think that
they know — they are fools, dismiss them.
    — Solomon Ibn Gabirol,
    Choice of Pearls, no.60 (c.1050).

To study, men are more profitable than
bookes.   — Thomas Overbury,
    *Newes from Any Whence:
    Answere to the Court Newes* (1613).

Trees and fields tell me nothing: men are
my teachers.   — Plato,
    Phaedrus (c.375–368 B.C.).

Know then thyself, presume not God to
scan;
The proper study of Mankind is Man.
    — Alexander Pope,
    An Essay on Man, II.i.1 (1733).

If you wish to study men you must not
neglect to mix with the society of
children.   — Jesse Torrey,
    The Moral Instructor (1819).

Manners

Manners must adorn knowledge and
smooth its way through the world.
    — Lord Chesterfield,
    Letter to His Son, July 1, 1748.

The first quality of a good education is
good manners — and some people flunk
the course.   — Hubert H. Humphrey,
    remark to hecklers at San Fernando
    Valley State College, *Connecticut
    Sunday Herald*, Jan. 1, 1967.

Self-respect is at the bottom of all good
manners. They are the expression of
discipline, of good-will, of respect for
other people's rights and comforts and
feelings. — Edward S. Martin, *A Father
    to His Freshman Son* (1917–18).

The knowledge of courtesy and good
manners is a very necessary study. It is,
like grace and beauty, that which begets
liking and an inclination to love one
another at the first sight.
    — Michel de Montaigne,
    Essays, I.xiii (1580): *The Ceremony
    of the Interviews between Kings*.

Mathematics

Multiplication is vexation,
    Division is bad;
The rule of three doth puzzle me,
    And fractions drive me mad. — Anon.,
    Elizabethan MS, traced back to 1570.

Figures — a language implying certitude.
    — Louis D. Brandeis,
    in Alfred Lief, ed., *The Social
    and Economic Views of Mr. Justice
    Brandeis*, 141 (1934).

The science of mathematics performs
more than it *promises*.... The study of

the mathematics, like the Nile, begins in minuteness, but ends in magnificence.
— Charles Caleb Colton,
Lacon, 181 (1820–22).

The way to enable a student to apprehend the instrumental value of arithmetic is not to lecture him on the benefit it will be to him in some remote and uncertain future, but to let him discover that success in something he is interested in doing depends on ability to use number.   — John Dewey,
Democracy and Education, xviii (1916).

There is no royal road to geometry.
— Euclid (fl. c.300 B.C.), reply to Ptolemy I, king of Egypt, when the latter asked if there was not some short cut to master geometry. Quoted by Proclus, *Commentaria in Euclidem* (5th cent.).

I'm very well acquainted too with matters mathematical,
I understand equations, both simple and quadradical,....
I'm very good at integral and differential calculus,
I know the scientific names of beings animalculous.   — W.S. Gilbert,
The Pirates of Penzance, I (1879).

And for mathematical sciences, he that doubts their certainty hath need of a dose of hellebore.   — Joseph Glanvill,
The Vanity of Dogmatizing, xx (1661).

In these days of conflict between ancient and modern sciences, there must surely be something to be said for a study which did not begin with Pythagoras and will not end with Einstein, but is the oldest and youngest of all.   — G.H. Hardy,
A Mathematician's Apology (1967).

Mathematics is the language of size.
— Lancelot Hogben,
Mathematics for the Million (1936).

We should drop the ideas that mathematics and what mathematics says about the world are indubitable truths. Today there is no agreement among mathemati-

cians on fundamental principles.... Mathematics is not the universally accepted, precise body of knowledge that it was thought to be 100 years ago when scholars believed that it revealed the design of the universe. — Morris Kline, "Mathematics: From Precision to Doubt in 100 Years," *U.S. News and World Report*, Jan. 26, 1981.

There are two ways to teach mathematics. One is to take real pains toward creating understanding — visual aids, that sort of thing. The other is the old British system of teaching until you're blue in the face.
— James R. Newman,
New York Times, Sept. 30, 1956.

Geometry gives us the sense of equality produced by proportion. It also heals by means of fine music all that is harsh and inharmonious or discordant in the soul, under the influence of rhythm, meter and melody.   — Philo, *On the Cherubim*, xxx (before A.D. 100).

One geometry cannot be more true than another; it can only be more *convenient*. Geometry is not true, it is advantageous.
— Robert M. Pirsig,
Zen and the Art of Motorcycle Maintenance, III.xxii (1974).

If arithmetic, mensuration, and the weighing of things be taken away from any art, that which remains will not be much.   — Plato,
Philebus, sec.55 (c.389–c.369 B.C.).

Geometry is the art of correct reasoning on incorrect figures. — Gyorgy Polya,
How to Solve It (1945).

Mathematics may be defined as the subject in which we never know what we are talking about, nor whether what we are saying is true.   — Bertrand Russell,
Mysticism and Logic (1917).

Mathematics, rightly viewed, possesses not only truth, but supreme beauty — a beauty cold and austere, like that of sculpture, without appeal to any part of

our weaker nature, sublimely pure, and capable of stern perfection such as only the greatest art can show.
— Bertrand Russell,
The Study of Mathematics (1903).

Mathematics takes us into the region of absolute necessity, to which not only the actual world, but every possible world, must conform.   Bertrand Russell,
ibid.

Arithmetic is where numbers fly like pigeons in and out of your head.
— Carl Sandburg,
Complete Poems (1950): *Arithmetic.*

Arithmetic is numbers you squeeze from you head to your hand to your pencil till you get the answer.   — Carl Sandburg,
ibid.

Maturity

See also Development; Growth

When I was a child, I spoke like a child, I thought like a child, I reasoned like a child; when I became a man, I gave up childish ways.   *Bible:*
I Corinthians 13:11.

A boy becomes an adult three years before his parents think he does, and about two years after he thinks he does.
— Lewis B. Hershey,
address, Dec. 31, 1951.

Viewing the child solely as an immature person is a way of escaping confronting him.   — Clark Moustakas,
Creativity and Conformity (1967).

It is not easy to let go the outworn life dreams of childhood. — Mildred Newman and Bernard Berkowitz, *How to Be Awake and Alive* (1975).

The maturity of man—that means, to have reacquired the seriousness that one had as a child at play.
— Friedrich Nietzsche,
Beyond Good and Evil (1886).

A mature person is one who does not think only in absolutes, who is able to be objective even when deeply stirred emotionally, who has learned that there is both good and evil in all people and in all things, and who walks humbly and deals charitably with the circumstances of life, knowing that in this world no one is all-knowing and therefore all of us need both love and charity.
— Eleanor Roosevelt,
It Seems to Me (1954).

Maxim

See also Epigram; Proverb

A good maxim is never out of season.
— H.G. Bohn,
Handbook of Proverbs, 288 (1855).

Nothing is so useless as a general maxim.
— Thomas Babington Macaulay,
"Machiavelli," *Edinburgh Review*,
Mar. 1827.

Aphorisms are salted, not sugared, almonds at Reason's feast.
— Logan Pearsall Smith,
Afterthoughts (1931).

The maxims of men reveal their character. The Indian proverb says: "Speak that I may know you."
— Marquis de Vauvenargues,
Reflections and Maxims (1746).

Meaning

See also Word, Meaning of

Meanings are discovered, not invented.
— Viktor Frankl,
The Will to Meaning (1969).

The pragmatic rule is that the meaning of a concept may always be found, if not in some sensible particular which it directly designates, then in some particular difference in the course of human experience which its being true will make.
— William James,
Some Problems of Philosophy (1911).

God and I both knew what it meant once; now God alone knows.
— Friedrich Klopstock, regarding the meaning of a passage in one of his poems, in Cesare Lombroso, *The Man of Genius*, I.ii (1889). Also attributed to Robert Browning, in reference to his *Sordello* (1840).

The meaning of things lies not in the things themselves but in our attitude towards them.
— Antoine de Saint-Exupéry, *The Wisdom of the Sands*, v (1950).

Learn, my son, to listen, not to the sounds of words that weave the wind, nor to reasonings that throw dust in your eyes. Learn to look farther.
— Antoine de Saint-Exupéry, *ibid.*, xv.

Means and Ends

See also Aim of Education; Teaching Method

You are not at liberty to execute a good plan with bad instruments.
— Henry Ward Beecher, *Proverbs from Plymouth Pulpit: Morals* (1887).

If the end is licit the means are licit.
— Hermann Busembaum, *Medulla Theologiae Moralis* (1650).

To profess to have an aim and then to neglect the means of its execution is self-delusion of the most dangerous sort.
— John Dewey, *Reconstruction in Philosophy* (1920).

Perfection of means and confusion of goals seem — in my opinion — to characterize our age.
— Albert Einstein, *Out of My Later Years*, xv: *The Common Language of Science* (1950).

Cause and effect, means and ends, seed and fruit, cannot be severed; for the effect already blooms in the cause, the end pre-exists in the means, the fruit in the seed.
— Ralph Waldo Emerson, *Essays, First Series: Compensation* (1841).

Methods and means cannot be separated from the ultimate aim.
— Emma Goldman, *My Further Disillusionment*, 174 (1924).

The end cannot justify the means for the simple and obvious reason that the means employed determine the nature of the ends produced.
— Aldous Huxley, *Ends and Means* (1937).

It is good to have an end to journey towards; but it is the journey that matters, in the end.
— Ursula K. Le Guin, *The Left Hand of Darkness*, xv (1969).

The character of the end depends on the character and functions of the means employed.
— Moses Hayyim Luzzatto, *The Path of the Upright*, i.17 (1740).

Supremacy of means over ends and the consequent collapse of all sure purpose and real efficiency seem to be the main reproach of contemporary education. The means are not bad ... the misfortune is that they are so good that we lose sight of the end.
— Jacques Maritain, *Education at the Crossroads* (1943).

There is, I think, nothing in the world more futile than the attempt to find out how a task should be done when one has not yet decided what the task is.
— Alexander Meiklejohn, *Education between Two Worlds*, 574 (1942).

The end may justify the means as long as there is something that justifies the end.
—Leon Trotsky,
in A. Pozzolini, *Antonio Gramsci: An Introduction to His Thought*, preface (tr. 1970).

The end directs and sanctifies the means.
—John Eardley Wilmot (1709–92),
Collins v Blantern, 1767.

Mediocrity

There's no such hell on earth as that of the man who knows himself doomed to mediocrity in the work he loves.
—Philip Barry,
You and I, I (1922).

Mediocre men often have the most acquired knowledge.   —Claude Bernard,
Introduction to the Study of Experimental Medicine (1865).

If every man worked at that for which nature fitted him, the cows will be well tended. —Jean Pierre Claris de Florian,
La Vacher de la Garde-chasse (1792).

In sober truth, whatever homage may be professed, or even paid, to real or supposed mental superiority, the general tendency of things throughout the world is to render mediocrity the ascendent power among mankind.
—John Stuart Mill,
On Liberty, iii (1859).

It is the American vice, the democratic disease which expresses its tyranny by reducing everything unique to the level of the herd.   —Henry Miller,
The Wisdom of the Heart: Raimu (1941).

Memory

Memory is the thing you forget with.
—Alexander Chase,
Perspectives (1966).

Our memories are card-indexes consulted, and then put back in disorder by authorities whom we do not control.
—Cyril Connolly,
The Unquiet Grave, iii (1945).

The true art of memory is the art of attention.   —Samuel Johnson,
The Idler, no.74 (1758–60).

Memory performs the impossible for man; holds together past and present, gives continuity and dignity to human life. This is the companion, this is the tutor, the poet, the library, with which you travel.   —Mark Van Doren,
Liberal Education (1943).

Mental Health

See also Health

Mental health, like dandruff, crops up when you least expect it.
—Robin Worthington,
Thinking About Marriage (1971).

Metaphor

Mr. Speaker, I smell a rat; I see him forming in the air and darkening the sky; but I'll nip him in the bud.
—Attr. Boyle Roche (1743–1807).
A classic example of mixed metaphors.

Metaphysics

See also Philosophy

Metaphysics is the finding of bad reasons for what we believe upon instinct.
—Francis Herbert Bradley,
Appearance and Reality (1893).

Metaphysics may be, after all, only the art of being sure of something that is not so, and logic the art of going wrong with confidence.   —Joseph Wood Krutch,
The Modern Temper, 228 (1929).

When you understand Physics, you have entered the hall; and when ... you master Metaphysics, you have entered the innermost court and are with the King in the same place. —Maimonides, *Guide for the Perplexed*, III.li (1190).

Metaphysics is almost always an attempt to prove the incredible by an appeal to the unintelligible. —H.L. Mencken, *Prejudices, Fifth Series* (1926).

Metaphysics, rightly shown,
But teach how little can be known.
—John Trumbull,
The Progress of Dulness (1773).

Mind

See also Brain; Intellect; Intelligence; Closemindedness; Openmindedness; Wit

The birds are moulting. If man could only moult also—his mind once a year its errors, his heart once a year its useless passions. —James Lane Allen, *A Kentucky Cardinal* (1894).

No wild thing was ever shut in a cage without wishing for freedom. And of all wild things in the world, the most uncontrollable—the least tameable—is the human mind. No king or priest or dictator has ever tamed it. It cannot rest in captivity. It cannot sleep. It has no relish for prison food.
—Maxwell Anderson,
Candle in the Wind, II (1941).

Measure your mind's height by the shade it casts! —Robert Browning, *Paracelsus*, III. ln.821 (1835).

It is not enough to have a good mind; the main thing is to use it well.
—René Descartes,
Discourse on Method (1637).

A liberal mind is a mind that is able to imagine itself believing anything.
—Max Eastman,
The Masses, Sept. 1917.

A well cultivated mind is, so to speak, made up of all the minds of preceding ages; it is only one single mind which has been educated during all this time.
—Bernard de Fontenelle,
Dialogues of the Dead, Ancient and Modern (1685).

The remarkable thing about the human mind is its range of limitations.
—Celia Green,
The Decline and Fall of Science: Aphorisms (1977).

Both Minds and Fountain Pens will work when willed,
But Minds, like Fountain Pens, must first be Filled. —Arthur Guiterman, *A Poet's Proverbs* (1924).

The mind of man is like a clock that is always running down and requires to be as constantly wound up.
—William Hazlitt,
Sketches and Essays (1839).

We have rudiments of reverence for the human body, but we consider as nothing the rape of the human mind.
—Eric Hoffer,
The Passionate State of Mind,
no.254 (1954).

The wealth of mind is the only wealth.
—Solomon Ibn Gabirol,
Choice of Pearls, no.167 (c.1050).

What is mind? No matter. What is matter? Never mind.
—Attr. Thomas Hewitt Key,
epigram published in *Punch*, 1855.

The mind can weave itself warmly in the cacoon of its own thoughts, and dwell a hermit anywhere. —James Russell Lowell, *My Study Windows: On a Certain Condescension in Foreigners* (1871).

A man's mind is known by the company it keeps. —James Russell Lowell, *ibid.: Pope* (1871).

I had no reason to doubt that brains were suitable for a woman. And as I had my father's kind of mind which was also his mother's—I learned that the mind is not sex-typed. —Margaret Mead, *Blackberry Winter* (1972).

Our minds are like crows. They pick up everything that glitters, no matter how uncomfortable our nets get with all that metal in them. —Thomas Merton, *Seeds of Contemplation* (1949).

One of the hardest things for the student to learn ... is just the simple fact that *brain-power is no guarantee for the rightness of thinking*, that ... a restlessly outreaching mind, unchecked by the humility of common sense, is more than likely to lead its owner into bogs of duplicity. —Paul Elmer More, *Humanism and America*, ed. R. Forester (1930).

Only the mind cannot be sent into exile. —Ovid, *Expistulae ex Ponto*, (c. A.D. 5).

The mind is but a barren soil—a soil which is soon exhausted, and will produce no crop, or only one, unless it be continually fertilized and enriched with foreign matter. —Joshua Reynolds, lecture at Royal Academy, London, Dec. 10, 1774.

The way the human mind ordinarily works, in apparent contempt of the logicians, is *conclusion first, premises afterwards*. —Joseph Rickaby, *An Old Man's Jottings* (1925).

A golden mind stoops not to shows of dross. —William Shakespeare, *The Merchant of Venice*, II.vii.20 (1596).

An improper mind is a perpetual feast. —Logan Pearsall Smith, *Afterthoughts* (1931).

A mind truly cultivated never feels that the intellectual process is complete until

it can reproduce in some media the thing which it has absorbed. —Ida Tarbell, *The Ways of a Woman*, v (1914).

The mind of man is more intuitive than logical, and comprehends more than it can co-ordinate. —Marquis de Vauvenargues, *Reflections and Maxims* (1746).

When people will not weed their own minds, they are apt to be overrun with nettles. —Horace Walpole, letter to Lady Ailesbury, July 10, 1779.

Mischief

Boys have a period of mischief as much as they have measles or chicken-pox. —Henry Ward Beecher, *Proverbs from Plymouth Pulpit: Children* (1887).

Misconduct

Most of what we object to as misconduct in children is a natural rebellion against the intrusion of an unimaginative adult despotism in their lives. —Floyd Dell, *Were You Ever a Child?* (1919).

Mother

See also Parent

It is to *mothers*, and to *teachers*, that the world is to look for the character which is to be enstamped on each succeeding generation, for it is to them that the great business of education is almost exclusively committed. And it will not appear by examination that neither mothers nor teachers have ever been properly educated for their profession. —Catharine Beecher, *Suggestions Respecting Improvements in Education, Presented to the Trustees of the Hartford Female Seminary* (1829).

The mother's heart is the child's school-room.   —Henry Ward Beecher, *Proverbs from Plymouth Pulpit: The Family* (1887).

What the mother sings to the cradle goes all the way to the coffin.
          —Henry Ward Beecher, *ibid.: Human Life*.

A mother is not a person to lean on but a person to make leaning unnecessary.
          —Dorothy Canfield Fisher, *Her Son's Wife* (1926).

You cannot teach every mother to be a good school educator or a good college educator. Why should you expect every mother to be a good nursery educator?
          —Charlotte Perkins Gilman, *Women and Economics*, xiii (1898).

One mother can achieve more than a hundred teachers.   —Jewish saying.

Children are what the mothers are.
No fondest father's fondest care
Can fashion so the infant heart.
          —Walter Savage Landor, *Children*, in B.E. and E.B. Stevenson, eds., *Days and Deeds* (1931).

That best academe, a mother's knee.
          —James Russell Lowell, *The Cathedral*, ln.475 (1870).

Though motherhood is the most important of all the professions—requiring more knowledge than any other department in human affairs—there was no attention given to preparation for this office.   —Elizabeth Cady Stanton (with Susan B. Anthony and Matilda Gage), *History of Woman Suffrage* (rev. ed. 1902).

Motivation

The important thing is not so much that every child should be taught as that every child should be given the wish to learn.
          —John Lubbock, *The Pleasures of Life*, x (1887).

An earnest desire to succeed is almost always prognostic of success.
          —Stanislas I, King of Poland, *Oeuvres de Philosophe Bienfaisant* (1767).

Music

Music has a power of forming the character, and should therefore be introduced into the education of the young.   —Aristotle, *Politics*, VIII.v.9 (before 322 B.C.).

The exercises of singing is delightful to nature, and good to preserve the health of man. It doth strengthen all parts of the breast, and doth open the pipes.
          —William Byrd, *Psalms, Sonnets and Songs*, preface (1588).

Musick is almost as dangerous as Gunpowder; and it may be requires looking after no less than the *Press* or the *Mint*. 'Tis possible a publick Regulation might not be amiss.   —Jeremy Collier, *A Short View of the Immorality and Profaneness of the English Stage, &c.* (1698).

Music is Love in search of a word.
          —Sidney Lanier, *The Symphony*, ln.368 (1875).

We must teach music in schools; a schoolmaster ought to have skill in music, or I would not regard him, neither should we ordain young men as preachers, unless they have well exercised in music.
          —Martin Luther, *Table Talk*, 340 (1566).

Musick, the Mosaique of the Air.
          —Andrew Marvell (1621–78), *Musicks Empire*, ln.17.

Without music life would be a mistake.
          —Friedrich Nietzsche, *The Twilight of the Idols* (1889).

Musical training is a more potent instrument than any other, because rhythm and harmony find their way into the inward places of the soul, on which they mightily fasten, imparting grace, and making the soul of him who is rightly educated graceful.   —Plato,
Republic, III (c.375-368 B.C.).

What will a Child learn sooner than a song?   —Alexander Pope,
Imitations of Horace,
II.i.205 (1737).

Music is the moonlight in the gloomy night of life.   —Jean Paul Richter,
Titan, cxxv (1803).

Music is "Ordered Sound."
—Harold Samuel,
The Mystery of Music,
ed. Walter E. Koons (1977).

Music is essentially useless, as life is.
—George Santayana,
Little Essays, 130,
ed. Logan Pearsall Smith (1920).

The trouble with music appreciation in general is that people are taught to have too much respect for music; they should be taught to love it instead.
—Igor Stravinsky,
in *New York Times Magazine*,
Sept. 27, 1964.

Nature

Go forth, under the open sky, and list
To Nature's teachings.
—William Cullen Bryant,
Thanatopsis, ln.14 (1817).

Gie me ae spark o' Nature's fire,
That's a' the learning I desire.
—Robert Burns,
Epistle to John Lapraik, ln.73 (1786).

Come forth into the light of things, let
Nature be your Teacher.
—William Wordsworth,
The Tables Turned, ln.15 (1798).

One impulse from a vernal wood
May teach you more of man,
Of moral evil and of good,
Than all the sages can.
—William Wordsworth,
ibid., ln.21.

Nature and Nurture

See also Breeding; Child
Rearing; Education, Effect
(Result) of; Human Nature

Nature passes nurture.
—David Ferguson,
Scottish Proverbs (1641).

Man is so educable an animal that it is difficult to distinguish between that part of his character which has been acquired through education and circumstance, and that which was in the original grain of his constitution.   —Francis Galton,
Inquiries into Human Faculty (1883).

Education is only second to nature. Imagine all the infants born this year in Boston and Timbuctoo to change places!
—Oliver Wendell Holmes, Sr.,
The Autocrat of the Breakfast-Table,
iv (1858).

Education altereth nature.
—John Lyly,
Euphues: The Anatomy of Wit (1579).

Newspaper

Newspapers are the schoolmasters of the common people. That endless book, the newspaper, is our national glory.
—Henry Ward Beecher,
*Proverbs from Plymouth Pulpit:
The Press* (1887).

A newspaper is a device for making the ignorant more ignorant and the crazy crazier.   —H.L. Mencken,
A Mencken Chrestomathy (1949).

Noise

For children is there any happiness which is not also noise?
— Frederick W. Faber,
Spiritual Conferences (1858).

I am sure that if people had to choose between living where the noise of children never stopped and where it was never heard, all the good-natured and sound people would prefer the incessant noise to the incessant silence.
— George Bernard Shaw, *Parents and Children*, preface to *Misalliance* (1914).

Nonconformity

See also Conformity; Dissent

For nonconformity the world whips you with its displeasure.
— Ralph Waldo Emerson,
Essays, First Series:
Self-Reliance (1841).

Whoso would be a man, must be a nonconformist.   — Ralph Waldo Emerson,
ibid.

Man is a rebel. He is committed by his biology not to conform.
— Robert M. Lindner,
Must You Conform? (1956).

If a man does not keep pace with his companions, perhaps it is because he hears a different drummer. Let him step to the music which he hears, however measured or far away.   — Henry David Thoreau,
Walden, xviii: *Conclusion* (1854).

Ever insurgent let me be,
Make me more daring than devout;
From sleek contentment keep me free,
And fill me with a buoyant doubt.
— Louis Untermeyer,
Challenge (1914): *Prayer.*

Nonsense

The learned Fool writes his Nonsense in better Language than the unlearned; but still 'tis Nonsense. — Benjamin Franklin,
Poor Richard's Almanack, July 1754.

At times a little nonsense avails more than knowledge and honor.
— Leon of Modena,
On Games of Chance, 180 (1596).

The Novel

See also Fiction; Literature

A good novel tells us the truth about its hero; but a bad novel tells us the truth about its author.   — G.K. Chesterton,
Heretics, xv (1905).

Novels (receipts to make a whore).
— Matthew Green,
The Spleen (1737).

A novel is an impression, not an argument.   — Thomas Hardy,
Tess of the D'Urbervilles,
preface (1891).

The only reason for the existence of a novel is that it does attempt to represent life.   — Henry James (1843–1916),
The Art of Fiction (1884).

Reading all these long-gone-with-the-winded novels some people are going gaga;
What this country needs is a good five-cent saga. — David McCord (b.1897),
Of Time and the Reader.

I would sooner read a time-table or a catalogue than nothing at all. They are much more entertaining than half of the novels that are written.
— W. Somerset Maugham,
The Summing Up (1938).

A novel should give a picture of common life enlivened by humour and sweetened by pathos.   — Anthony Trollope,
Autobiography (1883).

Nutrition

I certainly feel that the time is not far distant when a knowledge of the principles of diet will be an essential part of one's education.   — Fannie Farmer,
The Boston Cooking-School Cookbook, preface (1896).

Obedience

Let thy Child's first Lesson be Obedience, and the second may be what thou wilt.
— Benjamin Franklin,
Poor Richard's Almanack, May 1739.

He that obeyeth becomes one obeyed.
— Kegmeni,
Instructions (c.4000 B.C.).

Obedience stimulates subordination as fear of the police stimulates honesty.
— George Bernard Shaw,
Maxims for Revolutionists (1903).

Obedience is the primary and irremissible motive and the foundation of all morality.   — Friedrich Julius Stahl,
Die Philosophie des Rechts (1830–37).

I have thought about it a great deal, and the more I think, the more certain I am that obedience is the gateway through which knowledge, yes, and love, too, enter the mind of the child.
— Anne Sullivan,
letter of Mar. 11, 1887, in Helen Keller,
The Story of My Life (1903).

Objectivity

To tip the scales by the will to believe is childish foolishness since things will generally continue to weigh what they do despite this tipping.
— Morris Raphael Cohen,
Journal of Philosophy and Scientific Method, 1925.

There are only two ways to be quite unprejudiced and impartial. One is to be completely ignorant. The other is to be completely indifferent. Bias and prejudice are attitudes to be kept in hand, not attitudes to be avoided.
— Charles P. Curtis,
A Commonplace Book (1957).

Higher education must abandon the comfortable haven of objectivity, the sterile pinnacle of moral neutrality. In our perilous world, we cannot avoid moral judgments; that is a privilege only of the uninvolved.
— Milton S. Eisenhower,
"The Need for a New American,"
The Educational Record, Oct. 1963.

I can promise to be frank, I cannot promise to be impartial.
— Johann Wolfgang von Goethe,
Proverbs in Prose (1819).

It is only about things that do not interest one that one can give a really unbiased opinion, which is no doubt the reason why an unbiased opinion is always absolutely valueless.   — Oscar Wilde,
Intentions: The Critic as Artist (1891).

The man who sees both sides of a question, is a man who sees nothing at all.
— Oscar Wilde, *ibid.*

Observation

See also Sight

It takes little talent to see clearly what lies under one's nose, a good deal of it to know in which direction to point that organ.   — W.H. Auden,
The Dyer's Hand: Writing (1962).

He sees many things, but does not observe them; his ears are open, but he does not hear.   *Bible: Isaiah*
42:20. See also *Jeremiah* 5:21;
Matthew 13:13.

In the last analysis, we see only what we are ready to see, what we have been taught to see. We eliminate and ignore everything that is not part of our prejudices.   —Jean Martin Charcot, *De l'Expectation en Médicine* (1857).

There is no more difficult art to acquire than the art of observation, and for some men it is quite as difficult to record an observation in brief and plain language.
          —William Osler, *Aphorisms from His Bedside Teachings and Writings*, ed. William Bennett Bean (1950).

Where observation is concerned, chance favors only the prepared mind.
          —Louis Pasteur, address, University of Lille, Dec. 7, 1854.

The eyes are in the head for a reason.
          —Ad Reinhardt, *Art in America*, Mar./Apr. 1977.

The whole secret of the study of nature lies in learning how to use one's eyes.
          —George Sand, *Nouvelles Lettres d'un Voyageur* (1877).

How hast thou purchased this experience?
By my penny of observation.
          —William Shakespeare, *Love's Labour's Lost*, III.1.27 (1594).

Obvious

To spell out the obvious is often to call it in question.   —Eric Hoffer, *The Passionate State of Mind*, no.220 (1954).

We need education in the obvious more than investigation of the obscure.
          —Oliver Wendell Holmes, Jr., speech in New York, Feb. 15, 1913.

It requires a very unusual mind to undertake the analysis of the obvious.
          —Alfred North Whitehead, *Science and the Modern World*, i (1925).

Openmindedness

See also Mind; Opinion

Don't make up your mind until you have heard both sides.   —Aristophanes, *The Wasps*, ln.725 (422 B.C.).

Unfortunately I have an open mind. I let down a window in my brain about six or seven inches from the top even in the bitterest weather.   —Heywood Broun, in *Reader's Digest*, Sept. 1936.

Cursed is he that does not know when to shut his mind. An open mind is all very well in its way, but it ought not to be so open that there is no keeping anything in or out of it. It should be capable of shutting its doors sometimes, or may be found a little draughty.
          —Samuel Butler (1835–1902), *Note-Books* (1912).

The superior man is liberal toward others' opinions, but does not completely agree with them; the inferior man completely agrees with others' opinions, but is not liberal toward them.   —Confucius, in Lin Yutang, ed., *The Wisdom of China and India: The Aphorisms of Confucius* (1942).

Open-mindedness is not the same as empty-mindedness. To hang out a sign saying "Come right in; there is no one at home" is not the equivalent of hospitality.   —John Dewey, *Democracy and Education*, xiii (1916).

Who can give judgments, who can grasp arguments,
Ere from both sides he clearly learn their pleas?   —Euripides, *Heracleidae*, ln.179 (c.422 B.C.).

Without open minds there can be no open society, and if there be no open society the spirit of man is mutilated and enslaved.   —Felix Frankfurter, address at anniversary dinner in honor of John Dewey's 90th birthday, 1949.

One man's word is no man's word: we should quietly hear both sides.
　　　—Johann Wolfgang von Goethe,
　　　　　　Truth and Poetry (1811–22).

The only means of strenghtening one's intellect is to make up one's mind about nothing—to let the mind be a thorough-fare for all thoughts. Not a select party.
　　　　　　　　　—John Keats,
　　letter to George and Georgiana Keats,
　　　　　　　　　　Sept. 17, 1819.

Some minds remain open long enough for the truth not only to enter but to pass on through by way of a ready exit without pausing anywhere along the route.
　　　　　　　—Elizabeth Kenny,
　　　　　　with Martha Ostenso,
And They Shall Walk, vi (1943).

Be not lyght to follow euery mans opin-ion, nor obstinate to stande in thine owne conceipt.　　　　　—John Lyly,
　Euphues: The Anatomy of Wit,
　　　　　　　　　　40 (1579).

He was one whom in an argument woe ever betides,
Because he always thought that there was much to be said on both sides.
　　　　　　　　—Ogden Nash,
　　　　The Strange Case of Mr.
Pauncefoot's Broad Mind (1942).

If you keep your mind sufficiently open people will throw a lot of rubbish into it.
　—William Aylott Orton (b.1889),
　　Everyman Amid the Stereotype.

The open mind never acts: when we have done our utmost to arrive at a reasonable conclusion, we still, when we can reason and investigate no more, must close our minds for the moment with a snap, and act dogmatically on our conclusions. The man who waits to make an entirely rea-sonable will dies intestate.
　　　—George Bernard Shaw,
　　　　Androcles and the Lion,
　　　　　　　　preface (1912).

To state one argument is not necessarily to be deaf to all others.
　　　—Robert Louis Stevenson,
　Virginibus Puerisque: An Apology
　　　　　　　　for Idlers (1881).

A man of discernment ... knows both his own view and that of others.
　　—*Zohar (The Book of Splendor):*
　　　Exodus, 201a (c.1280–86).

Opinion

> *See also* below; Belief; Convic-
> tion; Dissent; Doctrine;
> Dogma; Idea

It is pure illusion to think that an opinion which passes down from century to cen-tury, from generation to generation, may not be entirely false.　—Pierre Bayle,
　　Thoughts on the Comet (1682).

I am sure it is one's duty as a teacher to try to show boys that no opinions, no tastes, no emotions are worth much unless they are one's own. I suffered acutely as a boy from the lack of being shown this.　　　　　—A.C. Benson,
　　　　The Upton Letters (1905).

An illogical opinion only requires rope enough to hang itself.
　　　　　—Augustine Birrell,
Obiter Dicta: The Via Media (1884).

Men get opinions as boys learn to spell,
By re-iteration chiefly.
　　—Elizabeth Barrett Browning,
　　　Aurora Leigh, VI.6 (1857).

The public buys its opinions as it buys its meat, or takes in its milk, on the princi-ple that it is cheaper to do this than to keep a cow. So it is, but the milk is more likely to be watered.　—Samuel Butler,
　(1835–1902), *Note-Books: Material for*
　　a Projected Sequel to "Alps and
　　　　　　Sanctuaries" (1912).

Opinion is that exercise of the human will which helps us to make a decision without information. —John Erskine, *The Complete Life* (1943).

A man's opinions, look you, are generally of much more value than his arguments. —Oliver Wendell Holmes, Sr., *The Professor at the Breakfast-Table*, v (1860).

With effervescing opinions, as with the not yet forgotten champagne, the quickest way to let them get flat is to let them get exposed to the air. —Oliver Wendell Holmes, Jr., U.S. Supreme Court opinion, 1920.

Next t' a fourteen-year-ole boy ther hain't nothin' as worthless as th' average opinion. —Frank McKinney Hubbard, *Abe Martin's Primer* (1914).

There is no greater mistake than the hasty conclusion that opinions are worthless because they are badly argued. —T.H. Huxley, *Aphorisms and Reflections* (1907).

For the most part, we inherit our opinions. —Robert G. Ingersoll, *Why I Am an Agnostic* (1896).

Too often we ... enjoy the comfort of opinion without the discomfort of thought. —John F. Kennedy, speech at Yale University, 1962.

Nothing is more conducive to peace of mind than not having any opinion at all. —Georg Christoph Lichtenberg, *Aphorisms* (1764–99).

Opinions cannot survive if one has no chance to fight for them. —Thomas Mann, *The Magic Mountain*, vi (1924).

Life is opinion. —Marcus Aurelius, *Meditations*, IV.3 (c. A.D. 174).

What you *see* is news, what you *know* is background, what you *feel* is opinion. —Lester Markel, *While You Were Gone* (1946).

I do not believe the people who tell me that they do not care a row of pins for the opinion of their fellows. It is the bravado of ignorance. —W. Somerset Maugham, *The Summing Up* (1938).

Where there is much desire to learn, there of necessity will be much arguing, much writing, many opinions; for opinion in good men is but knowledge in the making. —John Milton, *Areopagitica*, sec.31 (1644).

The belief that fashion alone should dominate opinion has great advantages. It makes thought unnecessary and puts the highest intelligence within the reach of everyone. —Bertrand Russell, *Unpopular Essays: On Being Modern-Minded* (1950).

Opinion is something wherein I go about to give Reason why all the World should think as I think. —John Selden, *Table Talk: Opinion* (1689).

A plague of opinion! A man may wear it on both sides, like a leather jerkin. —William Shakespeare, *Troilus and Cressida*, III.iii.265 (1602) [jerkin = *a short coat*].

To hold the same views at forty as we held at twenty is to have been stupified for a score of years and to take rank, not as a prophet, but as an unteachable brat, well birched and none the wiser. —Robert Louis Stevenson, *Virginibus Puerisque: Crabbed Age and Youth* (1881).

Opinion, Agreement of

We seldom judge a man to be sensible unless his ideas agree with ours. —François de La Rochefoucauld, *Maxims*, no.347 (1665).

"That was excellently observed," say I when I read a passage in another where his opinion agrees with mine. When we differ, then I pronounce him to be mistaken. —Jonathan Swift, *Thoughts on Various Subjects* (1706).

Opinion, Change of

See also Inconsistency

There is no state of mind, however simple, which does not change every moment. —Henri Bergson, *Introduction to Metaphysics*, 44 (1903).

If in the last few years you hadn't discarded a major opinion or acquired a new one, check your pulse. You may be dead. —Gelett Burgess, in *Forbes*, Aug. 1, 1977.

The wisest man may be wiser to-day, than he was yesterday, and to-morrow, than he is to-day. Total freedom from change, would imply total freedom from error; but this is the prerogative of Omniscience alone. —Charles Caleb Colton, *Lacon* (1820–22).

The weak-minded change their opinions because they are easily influenced by others, and the strong-minded change their opinions because they have complete mastery of their opinions. —Jacob Klatzkin, *In Praise of Wisdom*, 310 (1943).

Holding it a sound maxim that it is better to be only sometimes right than at all times wrong, so soon as I discover my opinions to be erroneous I shall be ready to renounce them. —Abraham Lincoln, communication to the people of Sangamon County, Ill., Mar. 9, 1832.

The foolish and the dead alone never change their opinion. —James Russell Lowell, *My Study Windows: Abraham Lincoln* (1871).

Remember that to change thy opinion and follow him who corrects thy error is as consistent with freedom as it is to persist in thy error. —Marcus Aurelius, *Meditations*, VIII.16 (c. A.D. 174).

Ages are no more infallible than individuals; every age having held many opinions which subsequent ages have deemed not only false but absurd; and it is certain that many opinions now general will be rejected by future ages, as it is that many, once general, are rejected by the present. —John Stuart Mill, *On Liberty*, ii (1859).

A man should never be ashamed to own he has been in the wrong, which is but saying, in other words, that he is wiser to-day than he was yesterday. —Jonathan Swift, *Thoughts on Various Subjects* (1706).

Opinion, Difference of

See also Diversity

I could never divide myself from any man upon the difference of an opinion, or be angry with his judgement for not agreeing with me in that from which, perhaps within a few days I should dissent myself. —Thomas Browne, *Religio Medici*, I.vi (1643).

Diff'ring judgements serve but to declare That Truth lies somewhere, if we knew but where. —William Cowper, *Hope*, ln.423 (1781).

The only sin in which we never forgive in each other is difference of opinion. —Ralph Waldo Emerson, *Society and Solitude: Clubs* (1870).

Every difference of opinion is not a difference of principle. —Thomas Jefferson, *First Inaugural Address*, Mar. 4, 1801.

I tolerate with the utmost latitude the right of others to differ from me in

opinion without imputing to them criminality. I know too well the weakness and uncertainty of human reason to wonder at it's [*sic*] different results.
— Thomas Jefferson,
letter to Abigail Adams,
Sept. 11, 1804.

Difference of opinion leads to inquiry, and inquiry to truth. — Thomas Jefferson, letter to P.H. Wendover, Mar. 13, 1815.

Never did two men judge alike about the same thing, and it is impossible to find two opinions exactly alike, not only in different men, but in the same man at different times. — Michel de Montaigne, *Essays*, III.xiii (1588):
Of Experience.

Whenever you find yourself getting angry about a difference of opinion, be on your guard; you will probably find, on examination, that your belief is going beyond what the evidence warrants.
— Bertrand Russell,
Unpopular Essays: An Outline of Intellectual Rubbish (1950).

Opinion, New

See also Idea, New

Every new opinion, at its starting, is precisely in a minority of one. In one man's head alone, there it dwells as yet. One man alone of the whole world believes it; there is one man against all men. — Thomas Carlyle,
Heroes and Hero-Worship, II:
The Hero as Prophet (1840).

New opinions are always suspected, and usually opposed, without any other reason but because they are not already common. — John Locke,
An Essay concerning Human Understanding: Epistle Dedicatory (1690).

New opinions often appear first as jokes and fancies, then as blasphemies and treasons, then as questions open to

discussion, and finally as established truths. — George Bernard Shaw,
Everybody's Political What's What?,
xix (1944).

Opinion, Public

Every man speaks of public opinion, and means by public opinion, public opinion minus his opinion. — G.K. Chesterton,
Heretics, viii (1905).

One should respect public opinion in so far as is necessary to avoid starvation and to keep out of prison, but anything that goes beyond this is voluntary submission to an unnecessary tyranny, and is likely to interfere with happiness in all kinds of ways. — Bertrand Russell,
The Conquest of Happiness,
ix (1930).

Opportunity

The common stock of intellectual enjoyment should not be difficult of access because of the economic position of him who would approach it. — Jane Addams,
Twenty Years at Hull House (1910).

The opportunity having passed, one may seek [in vain] to seize another. — Ani,
Teaching, no.4 (c.2000 B.C.).

That there should one Man die ignorant who had capacity for Knowledge, this I call a tragedy. — Thomas Carlyle,
Sartor Resartus, III.iv (1833).

I tasted — careless — then —
I did not know the Wine
Came once a World — Did you?
— Emily Dickinson,
Complete Poems, no.296 (c.1861),
ed. Thomas H. Johnson (1960).

Seek not fresher founts afar,
Just drop your bucket where you are.
— Sam Walter Foss
(1858–1911), *Opportunity*.

We are told that talent creates its own opportunities. But it sometimes seems that intense desire creates not only its own opportunities, but its own talents.
— Eric Hoffer,
The Passionate State of Mind,
no.18 (1954).

He who will not when he may, may not when he will.   —John of Salisbury,
Policraticus, VIII (1159); also Robert Mannyng, *Handlyng Synne* (c.1300); Thomas Percy, ed., *Reliques of Ancient English Poetry* (1765): *The Baffled Knight*, xiv.

Education is not a problem. Education is an opportunity.   —Lyndon B. Johnson,
address at William Jewell
College, Nov. 9, 1961.

All of us do not have equal talent, but all of us should have an equal opportunity to develop our talents. —John F. Kennedy,
address at San Diego State College,
June 16, 1963.

They do me wrong who say I come no
    more
  When once I knock and fail to find you
    in;
For every day I stand outside your door,
  And bid you wake, and rise to fight
    and win.   — Walter Malone,
Opportunity. First published in
Munsey's Magazine, Mar. 1905.

Opportunity has hair on her forehead, but is bald behind. If you meet her seize her, for once let slip, Jove himself cannot catch her again.   — Phaedrus,
Fabulae Aesopiae, VIII (early 1st cent.).

Salt is sold me at the same price as to you.
— Plautus, *Persa*,
ln.429 (c.200 B.C.).

The ladder was there "from the gutter to the university," and for those stalworth enough to ascend it, the schools were a boon and a path out of poverty.
— Diane Ravitch,
The Great School Wars (1974).

There is a tide in the affairs of men,
Which, taken at the flood, leads on to
    fortune;
Omitted, all the voyage of their life
Is bound in shallows and in miseries.
— William Shakespeare,
Julius Caesar, IV.iii.218 (1599–1600).

Opportunities are seldom labeled.
—John A. Shedd,
Salt from My Attic, 14 (1928).

Oratory

> *See also* Eloquence; Rhetoric;
> Speech; Voice

Why don't th' feller who says, "I'm not a speechmaker," let it go at that instead o' givin' a demonstration?
— Frank McKinney Hubbard,
Abe Martin's Primer (1914).

If you haven't struck oil in your first three minutes, *stop boring!*   — George Jessel
(1898–1981), *Dais Without End.*

The object of oratory alone is not truth, but persuasion.
— Thomas Babington Macaulay,
Essays: On the Athenian Orators (1824).

The orator is he who can speak on every question with grace, elegance, and persuasiveness, suitably to the dignity of his subject, the requirements of the occasion, and the taste of his audience. — Tacitus,
A Diologue on Oratory, xxx (c. A.D. 81).

Order

Order is a lovely thing;
On disarray it lays its wing,
Teaching simplicity to sing.
— Anna Hempstead Branch,
The Monk in the Kitchen (1927).

Good order is the foundation of all good things.   —Edmund Burke,
*Reflections on the Revolution
in France* (1790).

The graveyard is completely ordered because absolutely nothing happens there.   —C.J. Friedrich,
An Introduction to Political Theory (1967).

Order and simplification are the first steps toward the mastery of a subject — the actual enemy is the unknown.
—Thomas Mann,
The Magic Mountain, v (1924).

Order, cleanliness, seemliness make a structure that is half support, half ritual, and — if it does not create it — maintains decency.   —Florida Scott-Maxwell,
The Measure of My Days (1972).

Originality

See also Creativity; Idea, New; Innovator

For I fear I have nothing original in me — Excepting Original Sin.
—Thomas Campbell (1777–1844),
To a Young Lady who asked me to write something original for her Album.

The original writer is not he who refrains from imitating others, but he who can be imitated by none.
—François-René de Chateaubriand,
The Genius of Christianity (1802).

There is nothing mysterious about originality, nothing fantastic. Originality is merely the step beyond. —Louis Danz,
Dynamic Dissonance in Nature and the Arts (1952).

Stay at home in your mind. Don't recite other people's opinions.
—Ralph Waldo Emerson,
Letters and Social Aims: Social Aims (1876).

Everything has been said, and we are more than seven thousand years of human thought too late.
—Jean de La Bruyère,
Les Caractères: Des Ouvrages de l'Esprit (1688).

A society made up of individuals who were capable of original thought would probably be unendurable. The pressure of ideas would simply drive it frantic.
—H.L. Mencken,
Minority Report: Notebooks, no.13 (1956).

Originality and genius must be largely fed and raised on the shoulders of some old tradition.   —George Santayana,
The Life of Reason, II: *Reason in Society* (1905–06).

Eccentricity is not a proof of genius, and even an artist should remember that originality consists not only in doing things differently, but also in "doing things better."
—Edmund Clarence Stedman,
Victorian Poets, ix (1876).

What a good thing Adam had — when he said a good thing he knew nobody had said it before.   —Mark Twain,
Notebooks, July 2, 1867 (1935).

Orthodoxy

Orthodoxy: That peculiar condition where the patient can neither eliminate an old idea nor absorb a new one.
—Elbert Hubbard,
Note Book (1927).

Men insist most vehemently upon their certainties when their hold upon them has been shaken. Frantic orthodoxy is a method for obscuring doubt.
—Reinhold Niebuhr,
Does Civilization Need Religion?, 3 (1927).

Orthodoxy means not thinking—not
needing to think. Orthodoxy is uncon-
sciousness.   —George Orwell,
                                        1984 (1949).

Orthography

See also Spelling

You have made, sir, three faults in
orthography.   —Marquis de Favras,
       remark to the clerk of the court after
the reading of his death sentence, 1790.

As our alphabet now stands, the bad
spelling, or what is called so, is generally
the best, as conforming to the sound of
the letters and the words.
                           —Benjamin Franklin,
                 letter to Mrs. Jane Mecom,
                                      July 4, 1786.

The heart of our trouble is with our
foolish alphabet. It doesn't know how to
spell, and can't be taught. In this it is like
all other alphabets except one—the pho-
nographic. That is the only competent
alphabet in the world.   —Mark Twain,
      Essays: A Simplified Alphabet (1917).

English orthography satisfies all the requirements of the canons of reputability
under the law of conspicuous waste. It is
archaic, cumbrous, and ineffective; its acquisition consumes much time and
effort; failure to acquire it is easy of
detection.   —Thorstein Veblen,
        The Theory of the Leisure Class,
                                    xiv (1899).

Paperwork

The man whose life is devoted to paper-
work has lost the initiative. He is dealing
with things that are brought to his notice,
having ceased to notice anything for
himself. He has been essentially defeated
by his job   —C. Northcote Parkinson,
          In-Laws and Outlaws, ix (1962).

Parent

See also below; Child Rearing;
Discipline; Father; Mother

Children hold cheap the life of parents
who would rather be feared than respected.   —Afranius,
           Consobrini (1st cent. B.C.).

A parent is the most important teacher a
child ever has.   —Joan Beck,
       How to Raise a Bright Child (1975).

There is no one who fails in teaching the
members of his own family and yet is
capable of teaching others.
                     —Confucius, in Lin Yutang,
       The Wisdom of Confucius, 146 (1938).

Parents have become so convinced that
educators know what is best for children
that they forget that they themselves are
really the experts.
                    —Marian Wright Edelman,
             in Margie Casady, "Society's
        Pushed-Out Children," *Psychology
                           Today*, June 1975.

I believe the most stirring moment in the
experience of a parent comes on the day
he leaves the child in school for the first
time. This can be so so sharp an experience that, where there are two or
three children, this ritual has to be alter-
nated between parents.—Harry Golden,
            *Only in America: First day
                         of school* (1950).

The real menace in dealing with a five-
year-old is that in no time at all you begin
to sound like a five-year-old.
                               —Joan Kerr,
           *Please Don't Eat the Daisies:
          How to Get the Best of Your
                           Children* (1957).

The schoolmaster learns to know people
as "parents" and in this respect, I say it
without hesitation, they are all more or
less insane.   —Stephen Leacock,
       Essays and Literary Studies (1916).

When I meet a parent who tells me that his child loves school and is doing beautifully, pleasing everyone with his work, I am reminded of the sign I saw on someone's desk which read, "Anybody who feels relaxed and confident doesn't understand the situation!"
— Eda J. LeShan, *The Conspiracy Against Childhood*, vi (1967).

I am constantly amazed at the parents who can't control their children and who expect us to exert the authority they don't.   — Jane Mace, "Teaching May Be Hazardous to Your Health," *Phi Delta Kappan*, Mar. 1979.

People are always rather bored with their parents. That's human nature.
— W. Somerset Maugham, *The Bread-Winner*, II (1930).

The secret cruelties that parents visit upon their children are past belief.
— Karl A. Menninger, *A Psychiatrist's World* (1959).

Oh, what a tangled web do parents weave When they think their children are naïve.
— Ogden Nash, *The Face Is Familiar: Baby, What Makes the Sky Blue?* (1941).

It is not enough for parents to understand children. They must accord children the privilege of understanding them.
— Milton R. Sapirstein, *Paradoxes of Everyday Life*, iii (1955).

Parents must not so exasperate a child that he cannot constrain himself from rebelling against them.
— *Sefer Hasidim (Book of the Righteous)*, no.954 (13th cent.).

Parentage is a very important profession; but no test of fitness for it is ever imposed in the interest of children.
— George Bernard Shaw, *Everybody's Political What's What?*, ix.74 (1944).

If parents would only realize how they bore their children.
— George Bernard Shaw, *Parents and Children*, preface to *Misalliance* (1914).

Children begin by loving their parents; after a time they judge them; rarely, if ever, do they forgive them.
— Oscar Wilde, *The Picture of Dorian Gray*, v (1891).

Parent, Duty of

What is the grossest form of neglect? If a man does not ... devote every effort toward the education of his children.
— *Apocrypha: Aristeas*, 248 (c. 130 B.C.–A.D. 64).

Parents deserve reproof when they refuse to benefit their children by severe discipline.   — Petronius, *Satyricon*, iv (c. A.D. 60).

Parent, Expectations of

Parents who expect miracles worked upon their children must be reminded of the limitations imposed by nature. In athletics, at least, the coaches are expected to develop only promising material. No one complains if his undersized son with awkward legs does not become a football hero. Some fathers, however, seem to demand the intellectual equivalent of such a miracle.
— James Bryant Conant, Charter Day address at the University of California, Mar. 28, 1940.

All they wished for her was that she should turn herself into a little replica of them.   — Midge Decter, *Liberal Parents / Radical Children*, i (1975).

For parents to hope everything from the good education they bestow on their children is an excess of confidence, and it

is an equally great mistake to expect
nothing, and to neglect it.
                    —Jean de La Bruyère,
                    Les Caractères, xii (1688).

Parent, Influence of

That we are what we are is due to these
two factors, mothers and fathers.
                    —Charlotte Perkins Gilman,
                    The Home (1903).

He only dies half who leaves an image of
himself in his sons.   —Carlo Goldoni,
                    Pamela Nubile, II.ii (1756).

Behind almost every great man there
stands either a good parent or a good
teacher.   —Gilbert Highet,
                    Man's Unconquerable Mind (1954).

Parent, Rights of

We are opposed to state interference with
parental rights and rights of conscience in
the education of children as an infringe-
ment of the fundamental Democratic
doctrine that the largest individual liberty consistent with the rights of others in-
sures the highest type of American citizenship and the best government.
                    —Democratic National Platform,
                                    1892.

The God-given rights of parents are not
understood or are ignored by our secu-
larist educators and by many school administrators who, in a delusion of
sovereignty, act as though they, not the
parents, have complete control of the
education of the child.
                    —John T. McNicholas,
                    No Wall Between God and Child
                                    (1947).

Art. 26.3. Parents have a prior right to
choose the kind of education that shall be
given to their children.
                    —United Nations,
                    *Universal Declaration of Human
                    Rights*, Dec. 6, 1948.

The Past

See also History

Man is a history-making creature who can
neither repeat his past nor leave it
behind.   —W.H. Auden,
                    The Dyer's Hand: D.H. Lawrence
                                    (1962).

No matter what my birth may be,
    No matter where my lot is cast,
I am heir in equity
    Of all the precious Past.
                    —Abbie Farwell Brown
                    (1875–1927), *The Heritage*, i.

We may reject knowledge of the past as
the *end* of education and thereby only
emphasize its importance as a *means*.
When we do that we have a problem that
is new in the story of education: How
shall the young become acquainted with
the past in such a way that the acquaintance is a potent agent in appreciation of
the living present.   —John Dewey,
                    Experience and Education, i (1938).

The remembrance of the past is the
teacher of the future. —Kaibara Ekken,
                    Ten Kun (Ten Precepts), III.ii (1710).

The future is dark, the present burden-
some, only the past, dead and buried,
bears contemplation.   —G.R. Elton,
                    The Practice of History, preface (1967).

The past is never dead. It's not even past.
                    —William Faulkner,
                    Requiem for a Nun, I (1951).

The past is a foreign country: they do
things differently there. —L.P. Hartley,
                    The Go-Between, prologue (1953).

If the past cannot teach the present and
the father cannot teach the son, then
history need not have bothered to go on,
and the world has wasted a great deal of
time.   —Russell Hoban,
                    *The Lion of Boaz-Jachin and
                    Jachin-Boaz*, i (1973).

Life has to be lived forwards; but it can only be understood backwards.
— Aldous Huxley,
Mortal Coils, III (1922).

Nothing changes more constantly than the past; for the past that influences our lives does not consist of what actually happened, but of what men believe happened.   — Gerald White Johnson,
American Heroes and Hero-Worship,
i (1943).

Why doesn't the past decently bury itself, instead of sitting waiting to be admired by the present?   — D.H. Lawrence,
St. Mawr (1925).

I tell you the past is a bucket of ashes.
— Carl Sandburg,
Cornhuskers: Prairie (1918).

Those who cannot remember the past are condemned to repeat it.
— George Santayana,
The Life of Reason, 284 (1905–06).

What's past is prologue.
— William Shakespeare,
The Tempest, II.i.257 (1611).

The past has revealed to me the structure of the future.
— Pierre Teilhard de Chardin,
Letters from a Traveller (1962).

The past is only the present become invisible and mute; and because it is invisible and mute, its memoried glances and its murmurs are infinitely precious. We are tomorrow's past.   — Mary Webb,
Precious Bane, foreword (1924).

Patience

Patience is the companion of wisdom.
— St. Augustine,
On Patience (c.425).

There is however a limit at which forbearance ceases to be a virtue.
— Edmund Burke,
*Observations on a Late Publication
on the Present State of the Nation*
(1769).

Of all the virtues the virtue of patience is most foreign to youth.
— John Jay Chapman,
Memories and Milestones (1915).

Patience is a good nag, but she'll bolt.
— A.B. Cheales,
Proverbial Folk-Lore, 121 (1875).

Patience, and the mulberry leaf becomes a silk gown.   — Chinese proverb.

Patience is a necessary ingredient of genius.   — Benjamin Disraeli,
Contarini Fleming, IV.v (1832).

You have to have a lot of patience to learn patience.   — Stanislaw J. Lec,
Unkempt Thoughts,
tr. Jacek Galazka (1962).

Upon the heat and flame of thy distemper
Sprinkle cool patience.
— William Shakespeare,
Hamlet, III.iv.123 (1600–01).

How poor are they that have not patience!
What wound did ever heal but by degrees?   — William Shakespeare,
Othello, II.iii.371 (1604).

An impatient person is not fit to teach.
— *Talmud: Aboth*, 2.5 (before A.D. 500).

Patience is the art of hoping.
— Marquis de Vauvenargues,
Reflections and Maxims (1746).

Patriotism

For ourselves, we might be tempted to say that the deepest patriotism is best

engendered by giving unfettered scope to the most crochety beliefs.
— Felix Frankfurter, majority decision, U.S. Supreme Court, *Minersville School District v Gobitis*, 1940. The issue raised was whether the state may require all public school children to pledge allegiance to the flag.

The crazy combative patriotism that plainly threatens to destroy civilization is very largely begotten by the schoolmaster and the schoolmistress in their history lessons. They take the growing mind at a naturally barbaric phase and they inflame and fix its barbarism.   — H.G. Wells, *The Informative Content of Education* (1937).

Pedant

See also Intellectual; Pedantry

A man who has been brought up among books, and is able to talk of nothing else, is a very indifferent companion, and what we call a pedant.   — Joseph Addison, *The Spectator*, no.105, June 30, 1711.

I love the man who knows it all,
From east to west, from north to south,
Who knows all things, both great and small,
And tells it with his tiresome mouth.
— Robert Jones Burdette (1844–1914), *He Knows It All*, i.

With various readings stored his empty skull,
Learn'd, without sense, and venerably dull.   — Charles Churchill, *The Rosciad*, ln.591 (1761) [various = *variant*].

He conceits nothing in learning but the opinion, which he seeks to purchase without it, though it might with less labor cure his ignorance than hide it.
— John Earle, *Micro-cosmography: A Pretender to Learning* (1628) [conceits ... opinion = *values only the reputation of being learned*].

He is a great nomen-clator of authors, which he has read in general in the catalogue and in particular in the title, and goes seldom so far as the dedication.   — John Earle, *ibid*.

The pedant can hear nothing but in favor of the conceits he is amorous of, and cannot see but out of the grates of his prison.   — Joseph Glanvill, *The Vanity of Dogmatizing*, xxiii (1661).

The scholar reads in order to take thought; the pedant reads in order to take notes.   — Sydney Harris, syndicated column, *Detroit Free Press*, June 6, 1980.

A pedant is always throwing his system in your face, and applies it equally to all things, times, and places, just like a tailor who would make a coat out of his own head, without any regard to the bulk or figure of the person that must wear it.
— Mary Wortley Montagu, letter to Lady D., Jan. 13, 1716.

O, tis a precious apothegmaticall Pedant, who will finde matter inough to dilate a whole daye of the first invention of *Fy, fa, fum*, I smell the blood of an Englishman.   — Thomas Nashe, *Have with You to Saffron-walden*, III.43 (1596).

The bookful blockhead, ignorantly read,
With loads of learned lumber in his head,
With his own tongue still edifies his ears,
And always list'ning to himself appears.
All books he reads, and all he reads assails.   — Alexander Pope, *An Essay on Criticism*, III.612 (1711).

A man ...
    That hath a mint of phrases in his brain;
One who the music of his own vain tongue
    Doth ravish like enchanting harmony.
— William Shakespeare, *Love's Labour's Lost*, I.i.163 (1594).

The vacant skull of a pedant, generally furnishes out a throne and temple for vanity.   —William Shenstone, *Of Men and Manners* (1764).

The intellectual world is divided into two classes—dilettantes, on the one hand, and pedants, on the other.
          —Miguel de Unamuno, *The Tragic Sense of Life* (1912).

If a philosopher is not a man, he is anything but a philosopher; he is above all a pedant, and a pedant is a caricature of a man.   —Miguel de Unamuno, *ibid.*

Pedantry

See also Pedant

Where men shall not impose for truth and sense,
The pedantry of courts and schools.
          —George Berkeley, *Verses on the Prospect of Planting Arts and Learning in America* (1758).

Pedantry consists in the use of words unsuitable to the time, place, and company.
          —Samuel Taylor Coleridge, *Biographia Literaria*, x (1817).

Pedantry crams our heads with learned lumber, and takes out our brains to make room for it.   —Charles Caleb Colton, *Lacon*, 300 (1820–22).

Don't keep jingling in the course of your conversation any intellectual money you may have.   —Joseph Farrell, *Lectures of a Certain Professor* (1877).

Not All his Stock the Merchant's Window shows;
One should not make Display of All he knows.   —Arthur Guiterman, *A Poet's Proverbs* (1924).

There is nothing so pedantic as pretending not to be pedantic.
          —William Hazlitt, *The Plain Speaker* (1826).

Pedantry is the dotage of knowledge.
          —Holbrook Jackson, *The Anatomy of Bibliomania*, 150 (1930).

Pedantry is the unseasonable ostentation of learning.   —Samuel Johnson, *The Rambler*, no.173, Nov. 12, 1751.

Don't appear so scholarly, pray. Humanize your talk, and speak to be understood. Do you think a Greek name gives more weight to your reasons?
          —Molière, *La Critique de l'École des femmes*, vi (1663).

Pedantry only the scholarship of *le cuistre* [a waiter].   —Walter Pater, *Appreciations: Style* (1889).

Whoever interrupts the conversation of others to make a display of his fund of knowledge, makes notorious his own stock of ignorance.   —Saadi, *Gulistan (Rose Garden)*, viii (1258).

His mouth is full of particles.
          —William Scarborough, *A Collection of Chinese Proverbs*, no.488 (1875).

Pen

See also Writing

A good goose-quill is more dangerous than a lion's claw.   —H.G. Bohn, *Handbook of Proverbs*, 287 (1855).

Beneath the rule of men entirely great,
The pen is mightier than the sword.
          —Edward George Bulwer-Lytton, *Richelieu*, II.ii.307 (1838).

The pen is the tongue of the mind.
          —Miguel de Cervantes, *Don Quixote*, II.II.xvi (1615).

The pen is the interpreter of the heart.
          —Joseph Solomon Delmedigo, *Notes of Wisdom* (1631).

With pen of scribe the great man shall
attain
Ends that the warrior's sword can never
gain.   —Moses Ibn Ezra,
        Selected Poems, 92 (12th cent.).

The pen is a formidable weapon, but a
man can kill himself with it a great deal
more easily than he can other people.
        —George Dennison Prentice,
              Prenticeana (1860).

Perfection

See also Excellence

Don't ask me for perfection, ready-made;
That, my friend, is the pedant's stock in
trade.
        —Johann Wolfgang von Goethe
        (1749–1832), *Proverbs in Rhyme*.

Perfection has one grave defect: it is apt
to be dull.   —W. Somerset Maugham,
        The Summing Up, x (1938).

Trifles make perfection, and perfection is
no trifle.   —Michelangelo,
        in C.C. Colton, *Lacon* (1820–22).

Whoever thinks a faultless piece to see,
Thinks what ne'er was, nor is, nor e'er
shall be.   —Alexander Pope,
              An Essay on Criticism,
                      II.253 (1711).

You cannot get white flour out of a coal
sack, nor perfection out of human
nature.   —Charles Haddon Spurgeon,
        John Ploughman's Talks, x (1869).

Permissiveness

See also Child Rearing;
Teaching

The permissive fallacy is that children
learn good things from bad experiences.
                      —Donald Barr,
Who Killed Humpty Dumpty? (1971).

Do you know the surest way to make your
child miserable? Let him have everything
he wants; for as his wants increase in proportion to the ease with which they are
satisfied, you will be compelled, sooner
or later, to refuse his demands, and this
unlooked-for refusal will hurt him more
than the lack of what he wants.
        —Jean Jacques Rousseau,
              Émile, II (1762).

We have confused the free with the free
and easy.   —Adlai Stevenson,
        Putting First Things First
                      (1960).

Permissiveness is the principle of treating
children as if they were adults; and the
tactic of making sure they never reach
that stage.   —Thomas Szasz,
        The Second Sin: Childhood (1973).

Perseverance

Even the woodpecker owes his success to
the fact that he uses his head and keeps
pecking away until he finishes the job he
starts.   —Coleman Cox,
        Perseverance (c.1922–34).

Who persists in knocking will succeed in
entering.   —Moses Ibn Ezra,
        Shirat Yisrael, 113 (12th cent.).

Many strokes overthrow the tallest oaks.
        —John Lyly, *Euphues:
        The Anatomy of Wit* (1579).

By perseverance the snail reached the
Ark.   —Charles Haddon Spurgeon,
        Salt Cellars (1889).

Personality

I would call the personality of man the
gland of creativity.   —Sholem Asch,
        What I Believe, 173 (1941).

The entire world is nothing in comparison with human personality, with the

unique person of a man, with his unique destiny.   —Nickolai Berdyaev, *Slavery and Freedom* (1944).

Persuasion

More flies are taken with a drop of honey, than a tun of vinegar.   —H.G. Bohn, *Handbook of Proverbs*, 454 (1855).

If one word does not succeed, ten thousand are of no avail.
                    —Chinese proverb.

One may be confuted yet not convinced.
                    —Thomas Fuller (1654–1734), *Gnomologia*, no.3771 (1732).

Men may be convinced, but they cannot be pleased, against their will.
                    —Samuel Johnson, *Lives of the Poets: Congreve* (1779).

We may convince others by our arguments; but we can only persuade them by their own.   —Joseph Joubert, *Pensées*, no.106 (1810).

Yet hold it more humane, more heav'nly, first,
By winning words to conquer willing hearts,
And make persuasion do the work of fear.   —John Milton, *Paradise Regained*, I.222 (1671).

People are generally better persuaded by the reasons which they have themselves discovered than by those which have come into the mind of others.
                    —Blaise Pascal, *Pensées*, I.10 (1670).

Use a sweet tongue, courtesy, and gentleness, and thou mayest manage to guide an elephant with a hair.   —Saadi, *Gulistan (Rose Garden)*, iii (1258).

An infallible method of making fanatics is to persuade before you instruct.
                    —Voltaire, *Philosophical Dictionary: Oracles* (1764).

There is a danger in being persuaded before one understands.
                    —Thomas Wilson (1663–1755), *Maxims of Piety and of Christianity* (c.1755).

Philologist

See also Language

Philologists, who chase
A panting syllable through time and space,
Start it at home, and hunt it in the dark,
To Gaul, to Greece, and into Noah's Ark.
                    —William Cowper, *Retirement*, ln.691 (1782).

A philologist is a man who, horsed upon Grimm's law, chases the evasive syllable over umlauts and ablauts into the family echoing recesses of the Himalayas.
                    —Richard Grant White, *Words and Their Uses*, preface to 2nd ed. (1876).

Philosopher

See also Philosophy

I am weary of Philosophers, Theologians, Politicians, and Historians. They are immense Masses of Absurdities, Vices and Lies.   —John Adams, letter to Thomas Jefferson, June 28, 1812.

My definition [of a philosopher] is a man up in a balloon, with his family and friends holding the ropes which confine him to earth and trying to haul him down.   —Louisa May Alcott, in Ednah D. Cheney, *Louisa May Alcott, Her Life, Letters, and Journals*, x (1889).

The business of the philosopher is well done if he succeeds in raising genuine doubts.   —Morris Raphael Cohen, *A Dreamer's Journey*, 165 (1949).

What is the first business of the philosopher? To cast away conceit: for it is

impossible for a man to begin learning
what he thinks he knows.
                    —Epictetus,
        Discourses, II.xvii (c. A.D. 100).

Your philosopher will not believe what
he sees, and is always speculating about
what he sees not—which is a life, I think,
not much to be envied.
            —Bernard de Fontenelle,
        *Conversations on the Plurality
                of Worlds*, i (1686).

Perhaps it is the fate of philosophers to be
misunderstood.   —Edward C. Moore,
        William James, preface (1965).

To make light of philosophy is to be a
true philosopher.   —Blaise Pascal,
            Pensées, I.4 (1670).

Between the laughing and the weeping
philosopher there is no opposition: *the
same facts* that make one laugh make one
weep. No whole-hearted man, no sane
art, can be limited to either mood.
            —George Santayana,
        *Persons and Places, I: The
        Background of My Life*, x (1945).

For there was never yet philosopher
That could endure the toothache pa-
    tiently.   —William Shakespeare,
        Much Ado About Nothing,
            V.i.35 (1598–99).

The greater the philosopher, the harder it
is for him to answer the questions of common people.   —Henryk Sienkiewicz,
            Quo Vadis?, xix (1895).

There are nowadays professors of
philosophy, but not philosophers.
            —Henry David Thoreau,
        Walden, i: *Economy* (1854).

No sick man has ever dreamed of anything so absurd that one or another
philosopher has not said it.
            —Marcus Terentius Varro,
        Satires, frag.122 (1st cent. B.C.).

A philosopher of imposing stature
doesn't think in a vacuum. Even his most

abstract ideas are, to some extent, condi-
tioned by what is or is not known in the
time when he lives.
            —Alfred North Whitehead,
        Dialogues, as recorded by
            Lucien Price, 229 (1953).

Philosophy

    See also below; Metaphysics;
    Philosopher

What I have gained from philosophy is
the ability to feel at ease in any society.
        —Aristippus, apothegm (c.400 B.C.).
My beloved undergraduate professor of
philosophy, Dr. Orlando O. Norris, used
to define philosophy as "man's attempt
to feel at home in his world" [Ed.].

So if any man think philosophy and
universality to be idle studies, he doth
not consider that all professions are from
thence served and supplied.
            —Francis Bacon,
        The Advancement of Learning,
            II.8 (1605).

The philosophy of one century is the
common sense of the next.
            —Henry Ward Beecher,
            Life Thoughts (1858).

All philosophies, if you ride them home,
are nonsense.   —Samuel Butler,
        (1835–1902), *Note-Books* (1912).

The most practical and important thing
about a man is still his view of the
universe. We think that for a landlady
considering a lodger, it is important to
know his philosophy. We think that for
a general about to fight an enemy, it is
important to know the enemy's numbers,
but still more important to know the
enemy's philosophy. —G.K. Chesterton,
            Heretics, i (1905).

The philosophy of education is not a poor
relation of general philosophy even
though it is often so treated even by
philosophers. It is ultimately the most

significant phase of philosophy. For it is through the process of education that knowledge is obtained. —John Dewey, "The Relation of Science and Philosophy as a Basis of Education," *School and Society*, Apr. 1938.

In philosophy, it is not the attainment of the goal that matters, it is the things that are met with by the way.
— Havelock Ellis,
The Dance of Life, iii (1923).

Philosophy goes no further than possibilities, and in every assertion keeps a doubt in reserve.   —James Anthony Froude,
Short Studies on Great Subjects, Third Series: Calvinism (1877).

That's absurd in one philosophy which is worthy truth in another.
—Joseph Glanvill,
The Vanity of Dogmatizing, xx (1661).

Undoubtedly the study of the more abstruse regions of philosophy ... always seems to have included an element not very much removed from a sort of insanity.   —John Keble,
Lectures on Poetry, 1832–1841,
no.34 (1912).

A philosophic creed is impossible. The true function of philosophy is to educate us in the principles of reasoning and not to put an end to further reasoning by the introduction of fixed conclusions.
— George Henry Lewes,
The Biographical History of Philosophy
(1845–46).

The flour is the important thing, not the mill; the fruits of philosophy, not the philosophy itself. When we ask what time it is we don't want to know how watches are constructed.
— Georg Christoph Lichtenberg,
Reflections (1799).

Philosophy is such an impertinently litigious lady that a man had as good be engaged in lawsuits as have to do with her.   —Isaac Newton, letter to Edmund Halley, June 20, 1687.

The aim of a true philosophy must lie, not in futile efforts towards the complete accommodation of man to the circumstances in which he chances to find himself, but in the maintenance of a kind of candid discontent, in the face of the very highest achievement.
—Walter Pater,
Marius and Epicurean, xxv (1885).

For learning of every virtue there is an appropriate discipline, and for the learning of suspended judgment the best discipline is philosophy. —Bertrand Russell,
Unpopular Essays: Philosophy for Laymen (1950).

Philosophy ... molds and constructs the soul, guides our conduct, shows us what we should do and what we should leave undone; it sits at the helm and directs our course as we waver amid uncertainties. Without it, no one can live fearlessly or in peace of mind.   —Seneca,
Letters to Lucilius,
XVI.iii (c. A.D. 64).

Philosophy! the lumber of the schools,
The roguery of alchemy:
And we the bubbled fools
Spend all our present stock in hopes of
    golden rules.   —Jonathan Swift,
*Ode to the Honourable
Sir William Temple*, II (1692).

The proper method of philosophy consists in clearly conceiving the insoluble problems in all their insolubility and then in simply contemplating them, fixedly and tirelessly, year after year, without any hope, patiently waiting.
—Simone Weil, *First and Last Notebooks: London Notebook* (1943),
ed. Richard Rees (publ. 1970).

Philosophy begins in wonder. And, at the end, when philosophic thought has done its best, the wonder remains.
— Alfred North Whitehead,
Modes of Thought (1938).

Stumbling from thought to thought, falls headlong down

Into Doubt's boundless Sea, where like to
drown,
Books bear him up a while, and make
him try
To swim with Bladders of Philosophy.
—John Wilmot (2nd Earl of Rochester),
A Satyr against Mankind, ln.18 (1675).

Philosophy, Definition and Description of

See also Philosophy

Philosophy is common-sense in a dress
suit.   —Oliver S. Braston,
Philosophy.

Philosophy accepts the hard and hazardous task of dealing with problems not
yet open to the methods of science—
problems like good and evil, beauty and
ugliness, order and freedom, life and
death; so soon as a field of inquiry yields
knowledge susceptible to exact formula-
tion it is called science.
—Will Durant,
The Story of Philosophy (1926).

Philosophy—the thoughts of men about
human thinking, reasoning and imagining, and the real values in human
existence.   —Charles W. Eliot,
inscription on public library
in Warren, Pa.

Philosophy is the account which the
human mind gives to itself of the constitution of the world.
—Ralph Waldo Emerson,
Representative Men: Plato (1850).

Philosophical decisions are nothing but
the reflections of common life, method-
ized and corrected.   —David Hume,
*An Enquiry Concerning Human
Understanding* (1748).

Philosophy has often been defined as the
quest or the vision of the world's unity.
—William James,
Pragmatism (1907).

Our individual way of just seeing and
feeling the total push of and pressure of
the cosmos.   —William James,
ibid.

What am I? What ought I to do? What
may I hope to believe? All philosophy
may be reduced to this.
—Georg Christoph Lichtenberg,
Reflections (1799).

Philosophy consists very largely of one
philosopher arguing that all others are
jackasses. He usually proves it, and I
should add that he also usually proves
that he is one himself.
—H.L. Mencken,
Minority Report: Notebooks,
no.57 (1956).

Inertia rides and riddles me;
The which is called Philosophy.
—Dorothy Parker,
Enough Rope: The Veteran (1926).

Philosophy ... is not a presumptuous
effort to explain the mysteries of the
world by means of any superhuman insight or extraordinary cunning, but has
its origin and value in an attempt to give
a reasonable account of our own personal
attitude toward the more serious business
of life.   —Josiah Royce,
The Spirit of Modern Philosophy (1922).

Philosophy is not a theory but an activity.
—Ludwig Wittgenstein,
Tractatus Logico-Philosophicus,
iv.112 (1963).

Plagiarism

They lard their lean books with the fat of
others' works.   —Robert Burton,
*The Anatomy of Melancholy:
Democritus to the Reader* (1621).

If we steal thoughts from the moderns, it
will be cried down as plagiarism; if from
the ancients, it will be cried up as
erudition.   —Charles Caleb Colton,
Lacon, 254 (1820–22).

If every bird takes back its own feathers, you'll be naked.   —Henry Davidoff, *A World Treasury of Proverbs* (1946).

He that readeth good writers and pickes out their flowres for his own nose, is lyke a foole.   —Stephen Gosson, *The Schoole of Abuse: Loyterers* (1579).

'Tis cruel that critics should love to bela-
bour
Our plagiarist poet with stock and with stone,
For, if he has borrowed the thoughts of his neighbour,
'Tis harsh to assume that the faults are his own.   —Isaac ben Jacob (1801–63), epigram, in Lore and Maurice Cowan, *The Wit of the Jews* (1970).

Every generation has the privilege of standing on the shoulders of the generation that went before; but it has no right to pick the pockets of the first-comer.
—Brander Matthews, *Recreations of an Anthologist*, 20 (1904).

He liked those literary cooks
Who skim the cream of others' books;
And ruin half an author's graces
By plucking *bon-mots* from their places.
—Hannah More, *Florio*; and *The Bas Blue* (1786).

Steal!—to be sure they may; and egad, serve your best thoughts as gipsies do stolen children, disfigure them to make 'em pass for their own.
—Richard Brinsley Sheridan, *The Critic*, I.i (1779).

Poet

See also below; Writer

A poet is, before anything else, a person who is passionately in love with language.
—W.H. Auden, *New York Times*, Oct. 9, 1960.

Now comes the public and demands that we tell it what the poet desires to say. The

answer to this is: If we knew, he wouldn't be one.   —Hermann Bahr, *Studien zur Kritik der Moderne* (1894).

A great poet is the most precious jewel of a nation.   —Ludwig van Beethoven, letter to Bettina von Arnim, Feb. 10, 1811.

All poets are mad.
—Robert Burton, *The Anatomy of Melancholy: Democritus to the Reader* (1621).

A good poet is a kind of alchymist, who can turn the matter he prepares into the purest gold and an inestimable treasure.
—Miguel de Cervantes, *Don Quixote*, II.II.xvi (1615).

It is impossible to devise any scheme of education ... for promoting the develop-
ment of poetical genius.   —Julius Charles Hare and Augustus William Hare, *Guesses at Truth*, 194 (1827).

I Ask'd thee oft, what Poets thou hast read,
And lik'st the best? Still thou reply'st, The dead.
I shall, ere long, with green turfe cover'd be:
Then sure thou't like, or thou wilt envie me.   —Robert Herrick (1591–1674), epigram in reply to a detractor, in *Satire: A Critical Anthology*, ed. John Russell and Ashley Brown (1967).

Experience has taught me, when I am shaving of a morning, to keep watch over my thoughts, because, if a line of poetry strays into my memory, my skin bristles so that the razor ceases to act.... The seat of this sensation is the pit of the stomach.
—A.E. Housman, *The Name and Nature of Poetry* (1933).

O black and unknown bards of long ago,
How came your lips to touch the sacred fire?
How, in your darkness, did you come to know

The power and beauty of the minstrel's lyre?   —James Weldon Johnson, *O Black and Unknown Bards*, i, in J.W. Johnson, ed., *The Book of American Negro Poetry* (1931).

Perhaps no person can be a poet, or can even enjoy poetry, without a certain unsoundness of mind.
—Thomas Babington Macaulay, "Milton," *Edinburgh Review*, Aug. 1825.

I would advise no man to attempt the writing of verse except he cannot help it, and if he cannot it is in vain to dissuade him from it.   —Matthew Prior, *An Essay on Learning* (c.1715).

Many people like a poet just as they like their cheese: they find him good only when moldered by maggots.
—Moritz Gottlieb Saphir, *Humoristische Abende* (1830).

The poet's eye, in a fine frenzy rolling, Doth glance from heaven to earth, from earth to heaven;
And, as imagination bodies forth
The forms of things unknown, the poet's pen
Turns them to shapes, and gives to airy nothing
A local habitation and a name.
—William Shakespeare, *A Midsummer Night's Dream*, V.i.12 (1595).

That is what all poets do: they talk to themselves out loud; and the world overhears them.
—George Bernard Shaw, *Candida*, II (1895).

A Poet is a nightingale, who sits in darkness and sings to cheer its own solitude with sweet sounds.
—Percy Bysshe Shelley, *A Defence of Poetry*, I (1821).

Poetry

See also below; Literature; Poet; Rhyme; Writing

Poetry is not magic. In so far as poetry, or any other of the arts, can be said to have an ulterior purpose, it is, by telling the truth, to disenchant and disintoxicate.
—W.H. Auden, *The Dyer's Hand: Writing* (1962).

Were it not for poetry, life would be a constant bleeding. Poetry grants us what nature denies us: a golden age which never rusts, a spring which never fades, unbeclouded happiness and eternal youth.   —Ludwig Boerne, memorial address on Jean Paul, Dec. 2, 1825.

Good Sense is the Body of poetic genius. Fancy its Drapery, Motion its Life, and Imagination the Soul that is everywhere, and in each; and forms all into one graceful and intelligent whole.
—Samuel Taylor Coleridge, *Biographia Literaria*, xiv (1817).

The chief use of the "meaning" of a poem, in the ordinary sense, may be ... to satisfy one habit of the reader, to keep his mind diverted and quiet, while the poem does its work upon him: much as the imaginary burglar is always provided with a bit of nice meat for the house-dog. This is a normal situation of which I approve.   —T.S. Eliot, *The Use of Poetry and the Use of Criticism*, conclusion (1933).

Like a piece of ice on a hot stove the poem must ride on its own melting.
—Robert Frost, *Collected Poems*, preface: *The Figure a Poem Makes* (1949).

It [a poem] begins in delight and ends in wisdom.   —Robert Frost, *ibid.*

Then he asked the question that you are all itching to ask me: "How can you tell

good poetry from bad?"
    I answered: "How does one tell good
fish from bad? Surely by smell? Use your
nose." — Robert Graves,
        The Crowning Privilege:
    The Poet and His Public (1955).

The English method [of poetry] is to fill
the mind with beauty; the Greek method
was to set the mind to work.
            — Edith Hamilton,
        The Greek Way, iv (1930).

Even when poetry has a meaning, as it
usually has, it may be inadvisable to draw
it out.... Perfect understanding will
sometimes almost extinguish pleasure.
        — A.E. Housman, *The Name
        and Nature of Poetry* (1933).

I think Poetry should surprise by a fine
excess and not by Singularity — it should
strike the Reader as a wording of his own
highest thoughts, and appear almost a
Remembrance. — John Keats,
    letter to John Taylor, Feb. 27, 1818.

Poetry has nothing to do with the intellect: it is, in fact, a violent and irrecon-
cilable enemy to the intellect. Its purpose
is not to establish facts, but to evade
them. — H.L. Mencken,
    Prejudices, Sixth Series (1927).

If we may be excused the antithesis, we
should say that eloquence is *heard*,
poetry is *overheard*.
            — John Stuart Mill,
    Thoughts on Poetry and its varieties
                (1859).

Poetry atrophies when it gets too far from
music. — Ezra Pound,
        How to Read (1931).

More often than prose or mathematics,
poetry is received in a hostile spirit, as if
its publication were an affront to the
reader. — Michael Roberts,
    The Faber Book of Modern Verse,
        introd. to 1st ed. (1936).

The elegancy, facility, and golden cadence of poesy. — William Shakespeare,
    Love's Labour's Lost, IV.ii.126 (1594).

A great poem is for ages and ages in common and for all degrees and complexions
and for all departments and sects and for
a woman as much as a man and man as
much as a woman. — Walt Whitman,
    Leaves of Grass, preface to 1855 edition.

One should never talk of a moral or an
immoral poem — poems are either well
written or badly written, that is all.
            — Oscar Wilde,
    The English Renaissance of Art,
    lecture in New York City, Jan. 9, 1882.
    See also preface to *The Picture of
        Dorian Gray* (1891).

If English poetry is in danger ... what she
has to fear is not the fascination of dainty
metre or delicate form, but the predominance of the intellectual spirit over the
spirit of beauty. — Oscar Wilde,
    "A Note on Some Modern Poets,"
        Woman's World, Dec. 1888.

Poetry, Definition and Description of

See also Poetry

Poetry is simply the most beautiful, impressive and widely effective mode of saying things, and hence its importance.
            — Matthew Arnold,
        Essays in Criticism, I:
            Heinrich Heine (1865).

Poetry is the impish attempt to paint the
color of the wind.
    — Maxwell Bodenheim, quoted in
Ben Hecht's play, *Winkelberg* (1958?).

Poetry is man's rebellion against what he
is. — James Branch Cabell,
            Jurgen, xliv (1919).

Poetry, therefore, we will call musical
thought. — Thomas Carlyle,
        Heroes and Hero-Worship, III:
            The Hero as Poet (1840).

Poetry, or rather a poem, is a species of composition, opposed to science, as having intellectual pleasure for its object, and as attaining its end by the use of language natural to us in a state of excitement. —Samuel Taylor Coleridge, *Literary Remains* (1836–40).

[Poetry is the] expression of the hunger for elsewhere. —Benjamin De Casseres, *The Muse of Lies* (1936).

If I read a book and it makes my whole body so cold that no fire can ever warm me, I know *that* is poetry. If I feel physically as if the top of my head were taken off, I know *that* is poetry. These are the only ways I know it. Is there any other way? —Emily Dickinson, *Poems of Emily Dickinson*, ed. Helen Plotz (1964).

Poetry is the renewal of words forever and ever. Poetry is that by which we live forever and ever unjaded. Poetry is that by which the world is never old. —Robert Frost, letter to R.P.T. Coffin, Feb. 24, 1938, *Selected Letters of Robert Frost*, ed. Lawrance Thompson, 462 (1964).

Poetry is the language in which man explores his own amazement. —Christopher Fry, *Reader's Digest*, Apr. 1970.

I should define a good poem as one that makes complete sense; and says all it has to say memorably and economically, and has been written for no other than poetic reasons. —Robert Graves, *Steps: Talk on the Legitimate Criticism of Poetry* (1958).

Poetry is not the thing said but a way of saying it. —A.E. Housman, *The Name and Nature of Poetry* (1933).

Poetry is the art of uniting pleasure with truth, by calling imagination to the help of reason. —Samuel Johnson, *Lives of the Poets: Milton* (1779).

A poem should not mean
But be. —Archibald MacLeish, *Ars Poetica*, ln.23 (1926).

Poetry is what Milton saw when he went blind. —Don Marquis, *New York Sun*, "The Sun Dial" (1912–22).

Poetry is a comforting piece of fiction set to more or less lascivious music. —H.L. Mencken, *Prejudices, Third Series*, vii.150 (1922).

All poetry is of the nature of soliloquy. —John Stuart Mill, *What Is Poetry?* (1833).

A poem
Is a disease of the spirit
Caused by the irritation
Of a granule of Truth
Fallen into that soft gray bivalve
We call the mind.—Christopher Morley, *Translations from the Chinese: Bivalves* (1922).

Poetry is articulate painting, and painting is silent poetry. —Plutarch, *Moralia: How to Study Poetry*, 18A (A.D. c.95).

I would define, in brief, the Poetry of words as *The Rhythmical Creation of Beauty*. Its sole arbiter is Taste. —Edgar Allan Poe, *The Poetic Principle* (1845).

Poetry is the achievement of the synthesis of hyacinths and biscuits. —Carl Sandburg, "Poetry Considered," *Atlantic Monthly*, Mar. 1923.

Poetry is the opening and closing of a door, leaving those who look through to guess about what is seen during a moment. —Carl Sandburg, *Ten Definitions of Poetry*, in Louis Untermeyer, ed., *Modern American Poetry* (1936).

A poem is the image of life expressed in its eternal truth. —Percy Bysshe Shelley, *A Defence of Poetry*, I (1821).

Poetry is the search after, and the delineation, of the Ideal.
—Alexis de Tocqueville,
Democracy in America, II.xvii (1835).

Poetry is the spontaneous overflow of powerful feelings: it takes its origin from emotion recollected in tranquility.
—William Wordsworth,
Lyrical Ballads, preface to 2nd ed. (1802).

Poetry Writing

See also Poetry; Writing

Poetry, like schoolboys, by too frequent and severe correction, may be cowed into dullness! —Samuel Taylor Coleridge,
Anima Poetae (1895).

I never poetize save when I rheumatize.
—Ennius, *Satires*
(before 169 B.C.).

We all write poems; it is simply that poets are the ones who write in words.
—John Fowles,
The French Lieutenant's Woman,
xix (1969).

Writing free verse is like playing tennis with the net down. —Robert Frost,
address at Milton Academy, Mass.,
May 17, 1935.

A man who knows nothing of a ship fears to handle one; doctors undertake a doctor's work; carpenters handle carpenters' tools; but, skilled or unskilled, we scribble poetry alike. —Horace,
Epistles, II.i.114 (20 B.C.).

If Poetry comes not as naturally as the Leaves to a tree it had better not come at all. —John Keats,
letter to John Taylor, Feb. 27, 1818.

Ordering a man to write a poem is like commanding a pregnant woman to give birth to a redheaded child. You can't do it—it's an act of God. —Carl Sandburg,
Reader's Digest, Feb. 1978.

Point of View

The body travels more easily than the mind, and until we have limbered up our imagination we continue to think as though we had stayed home. We have not really budged a step until we take up residence in someone else's point of view.
—John Erskine,
The Complete Life, viii:
Foreigners (1943).

Two men look out through the same bars:
One sees the mud, and one the stars.
—Frederick Langbridge,
A Cluster of Quiet Thoughts (1896).

We might as well give up the fiction
That we can argue any view.
For what in me is pure Conviction
Is simple Prejudice in you.
—Phyllis McGinley,
Times Three: 1932–1960,
Note to My Neighbor (1960).

Pornography

The test of obscenity is this: whether the tendency of the matter charged as obscenity is to deprave and corrupt those whose minds are open to such immoral influences, and into whose hands a publication of this sort may fall.
—Alexander Cockburn,
Lord Chief Justice of England,
judgment in *Regina v Hicklin*,
1868.

Pornography is the attempt to insult sex, to do dirt on it. —D.H. Lawrence,
Phoenix: Pornography and
Obscenity (1936).

A sodomite got very excited looking at a zoology text. Does this make it pornography? —Stanislaw J. Lec,
Unkempt Thoughts, tr. Jacek Galazka
(1962).

There is no such thing as a dirty theme. There are only dirty writers.
— George Jean Nathan, *The Testament of a Critic*, 179 (1931).

Pornography is in the groin of the beholder. — Charles Rembar, *The End of Obscenity* (1968).

Obscenity has no objective existence. It is neither a quality that inheres in or emanates from a book, picture or play. On the contrary, obscenity is wholly an attitude or predisposition of the viewing and accusing mind, which is only delusionally read into, or ascribed to, that which is accused of being obscene.
— Theodore Schroeder, *A Challenge to Sex Censors* (1938).

Nothing is in itself absolutely sacred, or profane, and unclean, apart from the mind, but only relatively thereto.
— Baruch Spinoza, *Tractus Theologico-Politicus*, xii (1670).

The meaning of the word "obscene" as legally defined by the Courts is: tendency to stir the sex impulses or to lead to sexually impure and lustful thoughts.... Whether a particular book would tend to excite such impulses and thoughts must be tested by the Court's opinion as to its effect on a person with average sex instincts.... It is only with normal persons that the law is concerned.
— John M. Woolsey, Federal District Court decision, *United States v One Book Called "Ulysses,"* Dec. 6, 1933.

Potential

All the flowers of all the tomorrows are in the seeds of today. — Chinese proverb.

Might-have-beens can never be measured or verified; and yet sometimes it cannot be doubted that possibilities never realized were actual possibilities once.
— William James, *Letters*, II, introd., ed. by his son, Henry James (1920).

Canst thou prophesy, thou little tree, What the glory of thy bough shall be?
— Lucy Larcom, (1826–93), *Plant a Tree*, i, in J.G. Lawson, ed., *The World's Best-loved Poems* (1927).

We know what we are, but know not what we may be. — William Shakespeare, *Hamlet*, IV.v.43 (1600–01).

Every human being has some handle by which he may be lifted, some groove in which he was meant to run; and the great work of life, as far as our relations with each other are concerned, is to lift each one by his own proper handle, and run each one in his proper groove.
— Harriet Beecher Stowe, *Little Foxes*, v (1865).

Man's capacities have never been measured, nor are we judge of what he can do by any precedents, so little has been tried. — Henry David Thoreau, *Walden* (1854).

Practice

Practice makes — monotony.
— W. Burton Baldry (b.1888), *Stray Thoughts*.

Skill to do comes of doing.
— Ralph Waldo Emerson, *Society and Solitude: Old Age* (1870).

Every habit and every faculty is confirmed and strengthened by the corresponding acts, the faculty of walking by walking, that of running by running. If you wish to have a faculty for reading, read; if for writing, write. — Epictetus, *Discourses*, II.xviii (A.D. c.100).

Knowledge directeth Practice; but yet Practice increaseth Knowledge.
— Thomas Fuller (1654–1734), *Gnomologia*, no.3137 (1732).

Oft bend the bow, and thou with ease
shalt do,
What others can't with all their strength
put to.   — Robert Herrick,
Hesperides (1648).

Use maketh Masterie.
                    — Thomas Norton,
          The Ordinall of Alchimy,
                              vii (1477).

Who acquires knowledge and does not
practice it, resembles him who possesses
an ox but does not use him to plough or
to sow seed.   — Saadi,
          Gulistan (Rose Garden),
                    Maxim no.25 (1258).

For better or worse the beginner now
reads until he can read, and dances until
he can dance — or until it is perfectly clear
that he cannot.   — Wendell H. Taylor,
          in Jacques Barzun, *The Teacher
                    in America* (1944).

Practice What One Preaches

See also Example

Of right and wrong he taught
Truths as refin'd as ever Athens heard;
And (strange to tell!) he practis'd what he
preach'd.   — John Armstrong,
          The Art of Preserving Health,
                              IV.303 (1744).

He preaches well who lives well.
                    — Miguel de Cervantes,
          Don Quixote, II.II.xx (1615).

This noble ensample to his sheep he yaf
That first he wroughte, and afterward he
taughte.   — Geoffrey Chaucer,
          Canterbury Tales: Prologue, ln.498
          (c.1386) [ensample = *example*;
          wroughte ... taughte = *practiced what
                    he preached*].

He is a great teacher who practices what
he teaches.   — St. Columbanus,
          Carmen Monostichon, ln.23
                              (c. A.D. 600).

Like a beautiful flower full of color but
without scent are the fair words of him
who himself does not act accordingly.
          — *Dhammapada* (c.5th–3rd cent. B.C.).

Do not *say* things. What you *are* stands
over you the while and thunders so that
I cannot hear what you say to the contrary.   — Ralph Waldo Emerson,
          Journals, 1840; also *Letters and
          Social Aims: Social Aims* (1876).

I do think practising what one preaches is
an overrated virtue. Generally it means
that he who zealously practises what he
preaches is guilty of listening a little too
carefully to himself.   — Leon Garfield,
          Children's Literature in Education,
                              Winter, 1978.

I can easier teach twenty what were good
to be done, than be one of the twenty to
follow my own teaching.
                    — William Shakespeare,
          The Merchant of Venice, I.ii.1 (1596).

Never practice what you preach. If you're
going to practice it, why preach it?
                    — Lincoln Steffens,
                    Autobiography (1931).

Praise

See also Approbation

There is no such whetstone to sharpen a
good wit and encourage a will to learning
as is praise.   — Roger Ascham,
          The Schoolmaster, I (1570).

He that loveth to be praised for well-
doing at his father's or master's hand. A
child of this nature will earnestly love
learning, gladly labor for learning, willing learn of other, boldly ask any doubt.
                    — Roger Ascham, *ibid.*

Most people like praise.... Many people
have an unreasonable fear of administering it; it is part of the puritanical dislike
for anything that is agreeable — to others.
                    — Joseph Farrell,
          Lectures of a Certain Professor (1877).

It is more shameful to be praised faintly and coldly than to be censured violently.
—Favorinus,
apothegm (c. A.D. 110).

Praising all alike is praising none.
—John Gay, *Epistles*,
I.114 (1714).

Without some spurre of everlasting praise, fewe men would bee pricked forward to enterprise any thing worthie praise.   —Stefano Guazzo,
Civil Conversation, II.217 (1574).

True praise rootes and spreedes [spreads].
—George Herbert,
Outlandish Proverbs, no.638 (1640).

A child is fed with milk and praise.
—Mary Lamb,
The First Tooth (1809).

Praise a man at his back and not to his face, and he will really appreciate it when he hears about it.   —Shu Shuehmou,
Kueiyuyuan Chutan (16th cent.),
in Lin Yutang, *The Importance of Understanding*, 472 (1960).

The sweetest of all sounds is praise.
—Zenophon, *Hiero*,
I (c.373 B.C.).

Preciseness

Extreme exactness is the sublime of fools.
—Frederick Swartwout Cozzens,
Sayings, 56 (1870).

Her taste exact
For faultless fact
Amounts to a disease.
—W.S. Gilbert,
The Mikado, II (1885).

Ask to him of Jacob's ladder, and he would ask the number of steps.
—Douglas Jerrold,
Wit and Opinion of Douglas Jerrold: The Matter-of-Face Man (1859).

I have seldom found much good result from hypercritical severity, in examining the distinct force of words. Language is essentially defective in precision; more so, than those are aware of, who are not in the habit of subjecting it to philological analysis.   —William Johnson,
U.S. Supreme Court opinion,
Martin v Hunter, 1816.

To be exact has naught to do with pedantry or dogma.   —Leonora Speyer,
"On the Teaching of Poetry,"
Saturday Review of Literature, 1946.

Predecessor

I light my candle from their torches.
—Robert Burton,
The Anatomy of Melancholy,
III (1621).

The dwarf sees farther than the giant, when he has the giant's shoulders to mount on.   —Samuel Taylor Coleridge,
The Friend, I.viii (1809).

The merit belongs to the beginner should his successor do even better.
—Egyptian proverb.

Prejudice

See also Closemindedness;
Dogmatism

Prejudice, *n.* A vagrant opinion without visible means of support.
—Ambrose Bierce,
The Devil's Dictionary (1911).

Prejudices, it is well known, are most difficult to eradicate from the heart whose soil has never been loosened or fertilized by education; they grow there, firm as weeds among stones.— Charlotte Brontë,
Jane Eyre (1847).

Bigotry may be roughly defined as the anger of men who have no opinions.
—G.K. Chesterton,
Heretics, xx (1905).

Drive out prejudices by the door, they will come back by the window.
— Frederick the Great,
letter to Voltaire, Mar. 19, 1771.

Prejudice is never easy unless it can pass itself off for reason. — William Hazlitt,
Sketches and Essays: On Prejudice, (1839).

Prejudice is a raft onto which the ship-wrecked mind clambers and paddles to safety.   — Ben Hecht,
A Guide to the Bedevilled (1944).

But I hang on to my prejudices. They are the testicles of my mind. — Eric Hoffer,
Before the Sabbath (1979).

It is usual for people to defend their prejudices by calling them instincts.
— Joseph Kling,
Echoes (1920's).

One may no more live in the world without picking up the moral prejudices of the world than one will be able to go to hell without perspiring.
— H.L. Mencken,
Prejudices, Second Series, 174 (1920).

We all deprecate prejudice; but if all of us were not animated sacks of prejudices, and at least nine tenths of them were not the same prejudices so deeply rooted that we never think of them as prejudices but call them common sense, we could no more form a community than so many snakes.   — George Bernard Shaw,
The Intelligent Woman's Guide to Socialism and Capitalism, lxxxi (1928).

The Present

The present contains nothing more than the past, and what is found in the effect was already in the cause.
— Henri Bergson,
Creative Evolution, i (1907).

The ancients tell us what is best; but we must learn of the moderns what is fittest.
— Benjamin Franklin,
Poor Richard's Almanack, June 1738.

The only use of a knowledge of the past is to equip us for the present. No more deadly harm can be done to young minds than by depreciation of the present. The present contains all there is. It is holy ground; for it is the past, and it is the future.   — Alfred North Whitehead,
The Aims of Education, i (1929).

Principal

See also Administrator; Leader

Principal. Not to be confused with "principle," or with a person with principles.... As the head man, he has the power to lop off heads, make heads roll, etc., and is therefore known, in a private school, as the Headmaster.
— Richard Armour,
A Diabolical Dictionary of Education (1969).

Headmasters have powers at their disposal with which Prime Ministers have never yet been invested. — Winston Churchill,
My Early Life, ii (1930).

Principle

No rule is so general, which admits not some exception.   — Robert Burton,
The Anatomy of Melancholy,
I.ii.2.3 (1621).

Principles become modified in practice by facts.   — James Fenimore Cooper,
The American Democrat, xxix (1838).

You can't learn too soon that the most useful thing about a principle is that it can always be sacrificed to expediency.
— W. Somerset Maugham,
The Circle (1921).

Printing

The printing-press is either the greatest blessing or the greatest curse of modern times, one sometimes forgets which.
— James M. Barrie,
Sentimental Tommy (1896).

Th' printed wurrud! What can I do against it? I can buy a gun to protect against me inimy. I can change me name to save me fr'm the gran' jury. But there's no escape f'r good man or bad fr'm th' printed wurrud. — Finley Peter Dunne, "Mr. Dooley on the Power of the Press," *American Magazine*, Oct. 1906.

Every school boy and school girl who has arrived at the age of reflection ought to know something about the history of the art of printing.   — Horace Mann, "Printing and Paper Making," *The Common School Journal*, Feb. 1843.

Probability

A thousand probabilities do not make one fact.   — Italian proverb.

We can never achieve absolute truth but we can live hopefully by a system of calculated probabilities. The law of probability gives to natural and human sciences — to human experiences as a whole — the unity of life we seek.
— Agnes Meyer,
Education for a New Morality,
iii (1957).

Procrastination

Defer not till to-morrow to be wise,
To-morrow's sun on thee may never rise.
— William Congreve,
Letter to Viscount Cobham (1728).

What may be done at any time will be done at no time. — Thomas Fuller (1654–1734), *Gnomologia*, no.5500 (1732).

procrastination is the
art of keeping
up with yesterday   — Don Marquis,
archy and mehitabel: certain maxims of archy (1927).

The primrose path of dalliance.
— William Shakespeare,
Hamlet, I.iii.50 (1600–01)
[primrose path = *path of pleasure*].

Say not: 'When I shall have leisure I shall study;' perhaps thou wilt not have leisure.   — Talmud:
Aboth, 2.4 (before A.D. 500).

Procrastination is the Thief of Time.
— Edward Young,
Night Thoughts, I.392 (1742).

Profession

See also Vocation; Work

I hold every man a debtor to his profession; from the which as men of course do seek to receive countenance and profit, so ought they of duty to endeavour themselves by way of amends to be a help and ornament thereunto.   — Francis Bacon,
Rules and Maximes of the Law,
preface (1630).

The price one pays for pursuing any profession, or calling, is an intimate knowledge of its ugly side.
— James Baldwin,
Nobody Knows My Name: The Black Boy Looks at the White Boy (1961).

A profession is an occupation in which the service rendered is regarded, *by the worker*, more highly than the personal pecuniary rewards it brings. It is not some characteristic of the occupation itself that makes it professional; it is the attitude of the worker to the work.
— William C. Carr,
Collecting My Thoughts (1980).

With authority goes responsibility.... To whom is the professional person responsible? To the Chief for sure and to those to

whom the Chief reports.... To the academic community, to the state and to the public ... whom the University serves. But most of all, a professional is accountable to his profession, to its intellectual concerns, its ethics, its ideals.
— Lloyd Allen Cook,
Structuring the Wayne State Self-Study,
unpublished policy paper no.2, Wayne State University, Dec. 1956.

The best augury of a man's success in his profession is that he thinks it the finest in the world.   — George Eliot,
Daniel Deronda, II (1876).

Every profession does imply a trust for the service of the public. The artist's skill ought to be the buyer's security.
— Benjamin Whichcote,
Moral and Religious Aphorisms (1703).

Professor

See also Teacher; University

The professors laugh at themselves, they laugh at life; they long ago abjured the bitch-goddess Success, and the best of them will fight for his scholastic ideals with a courage and persistence that would shame a soldier. The professor is not afraid of words like *truth*; in fact he is not afraid of words at all.
— Catherine Drinker Bowen,
Adventures of a Biographer, v (1946).

A college professor is in the business of teaching. His business is not to give information.   — Bronson Cutting,
speech in U.S. Senate, June 14, 1934.

When eras die, their legacies
Are left to a strange police;
Professors in New England guard
The glory that was Greece.
— Clarence Day,
Thoughts Without Words (1928).

They were rather like great priests; famous cardinals might be closer to it. One felt, I felt, an awe in their presence.
— Joseph Epstein,
recollecting the great teachers at the University of Chicago in the mid-1950's, "A Class Act," *Quest*, Sept. 1981.

A Socrates in every classroom.
— A. Whitney Griswold,
president of Yale University, on his standard of a Yale faculty,
Time, June 11, 1951.

Take away paradox from the thinker and you have the professor.
— Søren Kierkegaard,
in *The University and the Modern World*, ed. Arnold S. Nash (1943).

Few professors, real ones, ever complete their work: what they give to the world is fragments. The rest remains. Their contributions must be added up, not measured singly. Every professor has his "life work" and sometimes does it, and sometimes dies first.   — Stephen Leacock,
Model Memoirs: On the Need for a Quiet College (1938).

The horse, the mass of human intelligence, draws along the cart of history in which stands the professor, looking backward and explaining the scenery.
— Stephen Leacock, *My Remarkable Uncle: Who Canonizes the Classics?* (1942).

Whenever the cause of the people is entrusted to professors it is lost.
— Nikolai Lenin,
Political Parties and the Proletariat (1917).

If the authority to which he [professor] is subject resides in the body corporate, the college, or university, of which he himself is a member, and in which the greater part of the other members are, like himself, persons who either are or ought to be teachers, they are likely to make a common cause, to be all very indulgent to one another, and every man to consent that his neighbour may neglect his duty,

provided he himself is allowed to neglect his own.   — Adam Smith,
The Wealth of Nations,
II.V.ii.247 (1776).

The discipline of colleges and universities is in general contrived, not for the benefit of the students, but for the interest, and more properly speaking, for the ease of the masters. Its object is, in all cases, to maintain the authority of the master, and whether he neglects or performs his duty, to oblige the students in all cases to behave to him as if he performed it with the greatest diligence and ability.
                — Adam Smith, *ibid.*,
II.V.ii.249.

Seven pupils, in the class
Of Professor Callias,
Listen silent while he drawls, —
Three are benches, four are walls.
                — Henry van Dyke,
Poems (1911): *The Professor.*

Perhaps there is something innate that in the first place disposes a man to become a University teacher or specialist. He is, I suspect, more often than not by nature and instinctively afraid of the uproar of things. Visit him in college and you will see that he does not so much live there as lurk.   — H.G. Wells,
The World of William Clissold (1926).

I consider it a monstrous presumption that university lecturers should think themselves competent to go on talking year after year to young men, students, while holding themselves aloof from the opportunity of learning from eager youths, which is one of the most valuable things on earth.
                — Alfred North Whitehead,
Dialogues, as recorded by
Lucien Price (1953).

To discharge the duties of a professor means to be willing to make ... ideas accessible to anyone, anywhere, at any time. It means to consider scholarship not as a property, but as a devotion, a sacrament.   — Norbert Wiener,
Boston Sunday Herald, Oct. 30, 1960.

Profundity

If this young man expresses himself in terms too deep for *me*,
Why, what a very singularly deep young man this deep young man must be!
                — W.S. Gilbert,
Patience, I (1881).

All that is necessary to raise imbecility into what the mob regards as profundity is to lift it off the floor and put it on a platform.   — George Jean Nathan,
"Profundity," *American Mercury*,
Sept. 1929.

It is easier to be impressed than to be instructed, and the public is very ready to believe that where there is noble language not without obscurity there must be profound knowledge.
                — George Santayana,
The Sense of Beauty (1896).

Where I am not understood, it shall be concluded that something very useful and profound is couched underneath.
                — Jonathan Swift,
A Tale of a Tub: Preface (1704).

Progress

I believe that education is the fundamental method of social progress and reform.
                — John Dewey,
"My Pedagogic Creed,"
The School Journal, Jan. 16, 1897.

Progress is man's ability to complicate simplicity.   — Thor Heyerdahl,
Fatu-Hiva (1974).

The history of progress is written in the lives of infidels.
                — Robert G. Ingersoll,
speech in New York City, May 1, 1881.

Not a change for the better in our human housekeeping has ever taken place that wise and good men have not opposed it — have not prophesied that the world would wake up to find its throat cut in consequence.   —James Russell Lowell, *Democracy and Other Addresses: Democracy* (1887).

New times demand new measures and new men;
The world advances, and in time out-grows
The laws that in our fathers' day were best;
And, doubtless, after us, some purer scheme
Will be shaped out by wiser men than we.   —James Russell Lowell, *A Glance Behind the Curtain*, ln.193 (1843).

All children know when they are progressing. Moreover, they're not allowed to forget it.   —Jean-Paul Sartre, *The Words* (tr. 1964).

Pronunciation

If you take care to pronounce correctly the words usually mispronounced, you may have the self-love of the purist, but you will not sell any goods.
—George Ade, *Fables in Slang* (1899).

Write with the learned, pronounce with the vulgar.   —Benjamin Franklin, *Poor Richard's Almanack*, Mar. 1738.

He pronounced some of his words as if they were corks being drawn out of bottles.   —Winston Graham, in *Reader's Digest*, Nov. 1981.

They spell it Vinci and pronounce it Vinchy; foreigners always spell better than they pronounce.   —Mark Twain, *The Innocents Abroad*, xix (1869).

The educated Southerner has no use for an *r*, except at the beginning of a word.
—Mark Twain, *Life on the Mississippi*, xliv (1883).

Proof

Proofe vppon practise, must take holde more sure
Than any reasonyng by gess can procure.
—John Heywood, *Proverbs*, I.vi (1546).

For when one's proofs are aptly chosen, Four are as valid as four dozen.
—Matthew Prior, *Alma: or, The Progress of the Mind*, I.515 (1718).

Prepare your proof before you argue.
—Samuel HaNagid, *Ben Mishle*, no.61 (11th cent.).

What was lately proved is now disproved.
—Terence, *Phormio*, ln.951 (161 B.C.).

No way of thinking or doing, however ancient, can be trusted without proof.
—Henry David Thoreau, *Walden*, i: *Economy* (1854).

Propaganda

Education by means of pre-fabricated ideas is propaganda.
—Mordecai M. Kaplan, *Reconstructionist*, Apr. 1950.

Much of what has been achieved by the art of education in the nineteenth century has been frustrated by the art of propaganda in the twentieth.
—Harold J. Laski, *A Grammar of Politics*, 147 (1925).

All great Art and Literature is propaganda.   —George Bernard Shaw, *On the Rocks*, preface (1934).

Proposition

See also Generalization; Hypothesis; Principle; Theory

General propositions do not decide concrete cases. The decision will depend on a judgment or intuition more subtle than any articulate major premise.
— Oliver Wendell Holmes, Jr., dissenting U.S. Supreme Court opinion, *Lochner v New York*, 1905.

It is more important that a proposition be interesting than that it be true.
— Alfred North Whitehead, *Adventures of Ideas*, III.xvi (1933).

Prophet

A prophet is not without honor except in his own country and in his own house.
— *Bible: Matthew* 13:57; also *Mark* 6:4.

The prophet and the martyr do not see the hooting throng. Their eyes are fixed on the eternities.
— Benjamin N. Cardoza, *Law and Literature* (1931).

He who anticipates his century is generally persecuted when living, and is always pilfered when dead. — Benjamin Disraeli, *Vivian Gray* (1826).

Prose

See also Writing

Whatever is not prose, is verse, and whatever is not verse, is prose.
— Molière, *The Merchant Gentleman*, II.vi (1670).

Good prose is like a window pane.
— George Orwell, *Collected Essays*, I (1968): *Why I Write*.

We have heard of the boy and his sister coming home from school to tell their mother, "We learned today we have been talking prose all our lives and we didn't know it." — Carl Sandburg, foreword to B.A. Botkin, ed., *A Treasury of American Folklore* (1944).

Proverb

See also Epigram; Maxim

A proverb is a racial aphorism which has been, or still is, in common use, conveying advice or counsel, invariably camouflaged figuratively, disguised in metaphor or allegory.— Selwyn Gurney Champion, *Racial Proverbs*, introd. (1938).

What is all wisdom save a collection of platitudes? Take fifty of our proverbial sayings—they are so trite, so threadbare, that we can hardly bring our lips to utter them. Nonetheless they embody the concentrated experience of the race, and the man who orders his life according to their teaching cannot go far wrong. How easy that seems! Has anyone ever done so? Never. — Norman Douglas, *South Wind* (1917).

The proverbs of all nations, which are always the literature of reason, are the statements of an absolute truth without qualification. Proverbs, like the sacred books of each nation, are the sanctuary of the intuitions. — Ralph Waldo Emerson, *Essays, First Series: Compensation* (1841).

Proverbs may not improperly be called the philosophy of the common people.
— James Howell, *English Proverbs* (1659).

Truth comes in a well rubbed-down state in the form of sayings of the ancestors.
— Khati, King of Egypt, *Teaching*, no.8 (c.2500 B.C.).

A proverb is an Instructive Sentence, in which more is generally Design'd than is Express'd, and which has pass'd into

Common Use and Esteem either among the Learned or Vulgar.
— Samuel Palmer,
Moral Essay on Proverbs (1710).

Almost every wise saying has an opposite one, no less wise, to balance it.
— George Santayana,
Little Essays, 237, ed. Logan Pearsall Smith (1920).

Psychology

It's a waste of time to read books on child psychology written by adults unless we are willing to check every page by what children know about the psychology of parents.   — John Erskine,
The Complete Life (1943).

Psychology, which explains everything,
Explains nothing,
And we are still in doubt.
— Marianne Moore,
Collected Poems: Marriage (1951).

The business of psychology is to tell us what actually goes on in the mind. It cannot possibly tell us whether the beliefs are true or false.   — Hastings Rashdall,
Philosophy and Religion (1909).

There is no psychology; there is only biography and autobiography.
— Thomas Szasz,
The Second Sin: Psychology (1973).

Publishing, Academic

The ambitious teacher can only rise in the academic bureaucracy by writing at complicated length about writing that has already been much written about.
— Gore Vidal,
Matters of Fact and Fiction (1977).

Pun

A pun is *prima facie* an insult to the person you are talking with. It implies utter

indifference to or sublime contempt for his remarks, no matter how serious.
— Oliver Wendell Holmes, Sr.,
The Autocrat of the Breakfast-Table,
i (1858).

A good pun deserves to be drawn and quoted.   — Ronald L. Holter,
quoted by L.M. Boyd, *Detroit Free Press*, Apr. 24, 1982.

The goodness of the true pun is in the direct ratio of its intolerability.
— Edgar Allan Poe,
Marginalia, i (1844–49).

Punctuation

See also Grammar

If you take hyphens seriously you will surely go mad.   — John Benbow,
Manuscript and Proof (1937).

A tired exclamation mark is a question mark.   — Stanislaw J. Lec, *Unkempt Thoughts*, tr. Jacek Galazka (1962).

A period is to let the writer know he has finished his thought and he should stop there if he will only take the hint.
— Art Linkletter, *A Child's Garden of Misinformation*, iii (1965).

A period is a stop sign. A semicolon is a rolling stop sign; a comma is merely an amber light.   — Andrew J. Offutt,
in *Writer's Digest*, July 1978.

Even where the sense is perfectly clear, a sentence may be deprived of half its force — its spirit — its point — by improper punctuation. For the want of merely a comma, it often occurs than an axiom appears a paradox, or that a sarcasm is converted into a sermonoid.
— Edgar Allan Poe,
Marginalia (1844–49).

Many writers profess great exactness in punctuation, who never yet made a point.   — George Dennison Prentice,
Prenticeana (1860).

Punishment

See also below; Discipline;
Punishment, Corporal

No teacher should ever punish a pupil when either is angry. — Edwin J. Brown, "Punishment: 14 Rules for Handing It Out," *Clearing House*, Feb. 1949.

Rewards and punishments are the lowest form of education.   — Chuang-tzu, *Philosophy*, xi (4th–3rd cent. B.C.).

A poor master ... relies almost wholly upon fear of punishment as the motive for work. To frighten one entire class is easier than to teach one boy properly; for the latter is, and always must be, a task as serious as it is honorable.... Do schoolmasters consider how many earnest, studious natures have been by treatment of this type — the hangman type — crushed into indifference? — Desiderius Erasmus, *Liberal Education of Boys* (1529).

To punish and not prevent, is to labour at the Pump, and leave open the Leak. — Thomas Fuller (1654–1734), *Gnomologia*, no.5216 (1732).

My object all sublime
I shall achieve in time —
To let the punishment fit the crime —
The punishment fit the crime.
                                  — W.S. Gilbert,
                                  The Mikado, II (1885).

Only the man who has enough good in him to feel the justice of the penalty can be punished; the others can only be hurt. — William Ernest Hocking, *The Coming World Civilization* (1956).

It [after-school detention] is, however, attended with one unpleasant circumstance. In order to confine the bad boys in the schoolroom after school hours, it is often needful the master, or some proper substitute, should confine himself in school to keep them in order. This inconvenience may be avoided by tying them to the desks, or putting them in logs,

etc., in such a manner that they cannot loose themselves.   — Joseph Lancaster, *Improvements in Education* (1803).

Nothing can be clearer than that, if you punish at all, you ought to punish enough. The pain caused by punishment is pure unmixed evil, and never ought to be inflicted except for the sake of some good. It is mere foolish cruelty to provide penalties which torment the criminal without preventing the crime. — Thomas Babington Macaulay, "Gladstone on Church and State," *Edinburgh Review*, Apr. 1839.

The object of punishment is, prevention from evil; it never can be made impulsive to good.   — Horace Mann, *Lectures and Reports on Education*, VII (1845).

Speaking generally, punishment hardens and numbs, it produces concentration, it sharpens the consciousness of alienation, it strengthens the power of resistance. — Friedrich Nietzsche, *The Genealogy of Morals*, ii.14 (1887).

This is what we really want to do — we want to be punitive in order to forget the stench of our own real neglect. — Fritz Redl, in reference to a "get-tough" policy in handling juvenile delinquency, in Eda J. LeShan, *The Conspiracy Against Childhood*, x (1967).

The reformative effect of punishment is a belief that dies hard, chiefly, I think, because it is so satisfying to our sadistic impulses.   — Bertrand Russell, *Unpopular Essays: Ideas That Have Harmed Mankind* (1950).

Human punishment is execrable even when just.   — Pope Sixtus I, *The Ring* (c. A.D. 120).

When you punish a pupil, only hit him with a shoe lace.   — *Talmud: Baba Bathra*, 21a (c. A.D. 500).

Punishment has in it the notion of a remedy, and has the place of a mean, not of an end.   —Benjamin Whichcote, *Moral and Religion Aphorisms* (1703).

Punishment, Corporal

See also below; Discipline; Punishment

A whipping never hurts so much as the thought that you are being whipped.
—Edgar W. Howe,
Country Town Sayings (1911).

One reason why corporal punishment is popular is that a big person can hit a little person with relative safety. Many parents, it seems, give up corporal punishment when their children are old enough to make a stiff defence or counter-attack.
—Arthur T. Jersild,
Educational Psychology,
ed. Charles E. Skinner (1942).

There is now less flogging in our great schools than formerly, but there is less learned there; so that what the boys get at one end they lose at the other.
—Samuel Johnson,
in James Boswell, *Life of Samuel Johnson*, xxix, 1775 (1791).

I chastise thee, not because I hate thee, but because I love thee.
—Latin saying of medieval schoolmasters flogging their pupils.

If you strike a child, take care that you strike it in anger, even at the risk of maiming it for life. A blow in cold blood neither can nor should be forgiven.
—George Bernard Shaw,
Maxims for Revolutionists (1903).

Corporal punishment, to be effective, must be cruel.
—George Bernard Shaw,
Sixteen Self Sketches, 41 (1949).

Punishment, Corporal (Con)

See also Discipline; Punishment

Many young wits be driven to hate learning before they know what learning is. I can be good witness to this myself, for a fond schoolmaster, before I was fully fourteen years old, drove me so with fear of beating from all love of learning.
—Roger Ascham,
The Schoolmaster, preface (1570).

"Spare th' rod an' spile th' child," said Mr. Hennessy.
"Yes," said Mr. Dooley, "but don't spare th' rod an' ye spile th' rod, th' child, an' the' child's father."
—Finley Peter Dunne,
Dissertations by Mr. Dooley: Corporal Punishment (1906).

We should abolish corporal punishment for many reasons, but if for no other reason than the fact that it causes more problems of vandalism and violence than it solves.   —William Glasser, "Disorders in Our Schools: Causes and Remedies," *Phi Delta Kappan*, Jan. 1978.

They use the Whip, the horse complains, Who have no Sense to use the Reins.
—Arthur Guiterman,
A Poet's Proverbs, 30 (1924).

Corporal Punishment is as humiliating for him who gives it as for him who receives it; it is ineffective besides. Neither shame nor physical pain have any other effect than a hardening one.
—Ellen Key,
The Century of the Child, viii (1909).

No master ought to be permitted to punish at his discretion.... If punishment be admitted, it should be delayed and considered. The very act of punishment, though begun in the most philosophic temper and coldest blood, excites anger by the habitual association of angry

feelings with inflicted blows, and the last stroke is always the severest.
—Benjamin H. Latrobe,
to Ferdinand Fairfax, May 28, 1798,
in *The Journal of Latrobe: Thoughts on the National System of Education* (1905).

Beating is the worst, and therefore the last means to be used in the correction of children; and that only in cases of extremity, after all gentler ways have been tried, and proved unsuccessful: which, if well observed, there will be very seldom any need of blows.   —John Locke,
Some Thoughts concerning Education (1693).

I have never observed other effects of whipping than to render boys more cowardly, or more willfully obstinate.
—Michel de Montaigne,
Essays, II.viii (1580): *Of the Affections of Fathers to Their Children*.

That boys should suffer corporal punishment ... I by no means approve; first, because it is a disgrace, and a punishment for slaves, ... an affront; secondly, because, if a boy's disposition be so abject as not to be amended by reproof, he will be hardened ... even to stripes; and lastly, because, if one who regularly exacts his tasks be with him, there will not be the least need of such chastisement.
—Quintilian,
Institutio Oratoria, I.iii.13
(A.D. 95 or 96).

The man who has graduated from the flogging block at Eton to the bench from which he sentences the garotter to be flogged is the same social product as the garotter who has been kicked by his father and cuffed by his mother until he has grown strong enough to throttle and rob the rich citizen whose money he desires.   —George Bernard Shaw,
Maxims for Revolutionists (1903).

In a really civilised state flogging would cease because it would be impossible to induce any decent citizen to flog another.
—George Bernard Shaw,
On the Rocks (1934).

Whipping and abuse are like laudanum; you have to double the dose as the sensibilities decline.
—Harriet Beecher Stowe,
Uncle Tom's Cabin, xx (1852).

I have ever been disposed to regard the cowhide as a nonconductor. Me thinks that, unlike the electric wire, not a single spark of truth is ever transmitted through its agency to the slumbering intellect it would address. I mistake, it may teach a truth in physics, but never a truth in morals.   —Henry David Thoreau,
after resigning his teaching position, held for two weeks, because a school board member complained to him that "the school would spoil" without the use of the ferule, in Myron C. Tuman, "Prometheus Bound: The Brief Teaching Careers of Great Writers," *Phi Delta Kappan*, Dec. 1980.

Punishment, Corporal (Pro)

See also Discipline; Punishment

Gold must be hammered, and the child must be beaten.
—*Alphabet of Ben Sira*,
no.4 (c.1000).

He who spares the rod hates his son, but he who loves him is diligent to discipline him.   —*Bible: Proverbs* 13:24. See also *Proverbs* 23:14.

Oh ye! who teach the ingenuous youth of nations,
Holland, France, England, Germany, or Spain,
I pray ye flog them upon all occasions,
It mends their morals, never mind the pain.   —Lord Byron,
Don Juan, II.i.1 (1819).

Beat your child once a day. If you don't know why, the child does.
—Chinese proverb.

The rod is only wrong in the wrong hands. —Joseph Gauld, *Time*, Aug. 9, 1976.

Some persons *will* plead for the rod as the partisans of Robespierre did for the guillotine, with an unrelenting fury. —Joseph Lancaster, *Improvements in Education* (1803).

Children are never too tender to be whipped: —like tough beefsteaks, the more you beat them the more tender they become. —Edgar Allan Poe, *"Fifty Suggestions," Graham's Magazine*, May/June, 1850.

There is nothynge that more displeaseth God
Than from theyr chyldren to spare the rod. —John Skelton, *Magnyfycence*, ln.1955 (1516).

Question

See also Inquiry; Questioning

Hypothetical questions get hypothetical answers. —Joan Baez, *Daybreak* (1966).

Every sentence I utter must be understood not as an affirmation, but as a question. —Niels Bohr, *New York Times Book Review*, Oct. 20, 1957.

That is the essence of science: ask an impertinent question, and you are on the way to the pertinent answer. —Jacob Bronowski, *The Ascent of Man*, 153 (1973).

Hasty questions require slow answers. —Dutch proverb.

Bromidic though it may sound, some questions *don't* have answers, which is a terribly difficult lesson to learn. —Katharine Graham, in Jane Howard, "The Power That Didn't Corrpt," *Ms.*, Oct. 1974.

A wise man's question contains half the answer. —Solomon Ibn Gabirol, *Choice of Pearls* (c.1050).

Any question can be made immaterial by subsuming all its answers under a common head. Imagine what college ball-games and races would be if the teams were to forget the absolute distinctiveness of Harvard from Yale, and think of both as One in the higher genus College. —William James, *The Principles of Psychology*, II (1890).

It is better to stir up a question without deciding it, then to decide it without stirring it up. —Joseph Joubert, *Pensées*, no.115 (1810).

If we would have new knowledge, we must get a whole world of new questions. —Susanne K. Langer, *Philosophy in a New Key* (3rd ed., 1957).

There is frequently more to learn from the unexpected questions of a child than the discourses of men, who talk in a road, according to the notions they have borrowed and the prejudices of their education. —John Locke, *Some Thoughts concerning Education*, 120 (1693).

It is not every question that deserves an answer. —Publilius Syrus, *Sententiae* (c.43 B.C.).

Good questions outrank easy answers. —Paul A. Samuelson, *Newsweek*, Aug. 21, 1978.

A question not to be asked is a question not to be answered. —Robert Southey, *The Doctor*, xii (1834–47).

But beyond the bright searchlights of science,
Out of sight the windows of sense,
Old riddles still bid us defiance,
Old questions of Why and Whence. —W.C.D. Whetham, *The Recent Development of Physical Science*, 10 (1904).

Questions are never indiscreet. Answers sometimes are.   — Oscar Wilde, *An Ideal Husband*, I (1895).

The sages say, Dame Truth delights to dwell
(Strange Mansion!) in the bottom of a well:
Questions are then the Windlass and the rope
That pull the grave ole Gentlewoman up.
— John Wolcot, *The Poetical Works of Peter Pindar* (1789): *Birthday Ode*.

Questioning

See also Curiosity; Doubt; Inquiry; Question; Wonder

The first key to wisdom is this — constant and frequent questioning ... for by doubting we are led to question and by questioning we arrive at the truth.
— Pierre Abélard, *Sic et Non*, prologue (c.1120).

Let your scholar be never afraid to ask you any doubt, but use discreetly the best allurements ye can encourage him to the same, lest his overmuch fearing of you drive him to seek some misorderly shift, as to seek to be helped by some other book, or to be prompted by some other scholar, and so go about to beguile you much and himself more.
— Roger Ascham, *The Schoolmaster* (1570) [shift = *subterfuge*].

He that questioneth much, shall learn much ... but let his questions not be troublesome, for that is fit for a poser.
— Francis Bacon, *Essays: Of Discourse* (1597) [poser = *one who tests or examines*].

He who asks a question is a fool for five minutes; he who does not ask a question remains a fool forever.
— Chinese proverb.

He who is afraid of asking is ashamed of learning.   — Danish proverb.

Better ask twice [ten times] than lose your way once.   — Danish proverb; also Yiddish proverb.

The interrogation of custom at all points is an inevitable stage in the growth of every superior mind.
— Ralph Waldo Emerson, *Representative Men: Montaigne* (1850).

He that nothing questioneth, nothing learneth.   — Thomas Fuller, *Gnomologia*, no.2241 (1732).

I keep six honest serving-men
(They taught me all I knew);
Their names are What and Why and When
And How and Where and Who.
— Rudyard Kipling, *Just So Stories: The Elephant's Child*, i (1902).

A teacher should not be asked any questions immediately upon his coming into the classroom, until he gets clear-minded. Nor should a student ask a question when he comes in until he sits down and is at ease. Two students should not ask questions at the same time. The teacher should not be asked questions about a different subject, but only about the subject in which they are engaged.
— Maimonides, *Mishneh Torah (Second Law)*, I.iv.6 (1180).

A fool may ask more questions in an hour than a wise man can answer in seven years.   — John Ray, *English Proverbs* (1670); also H.G. Bohn, *Handbook of Proverbs*, 286 (1855).

I will be a fool in question, hoping to be wiser by your answer.
— William Shakespeare, *All's Well that Ends Well*, II.ii.41 (1602).

We should never accept anything reverently without asking it a great many very searching questions.
—George Bernard Shaw,
The Apple Cart, preface (1929).

The wise man questions the wisdom of others because he questions his own, the foolish man because it is different from his own.   —Leo Stein,
Journey into the Self, 257 (1950).

I feel very strongly about putting questions; it partakes too much of the style of the day of judgment. You start a question, and it's like starting a stone. You sit quietly on top of a hill; and away the stone goes, starting others.
—Robert Louis Stevenson,
The Strange Case of Dr. Jekyll and Mr. Hyde (1886).

Quotation

One must be a wise reader to quote wisely and well.   —A. Bronson Alcott,
Table Talk: Quotation (1877).

There is not less wit nor invention in applying rightly a thought one finds in a book, than in being the first author of that thought.   —Pierre Bayle,
Historical and Critical Dictionary, II.1077 (1697).

With just enough of learning to misquote.   —Lord Byron,
English Bards and Scotch Reviewers,
ln.66 (1809).

I do not say a proverb is amiss when aptly and seasonably applied; but to be forever discharging them, right or wrong, hit or miss, renders conversation insipid and vulgar.   —Miguel de Cervantes,
Don Quixote, II (1615).

A quotation, like a pun, should come unsought, and then be welcomed only for some propriety of felicity justifying the intrusion.   —Robert William Chapman,
*The Portrait of a Scholar:
The Art of Quotation* (1920).

Quotation, like much better things, has its abuses. One may quote till one compiles.   —Isaac D'Israeli,
*Curiosities of Literature:
Quotation* (1791–1823).

Sometimes it seems the only accomplishment my education ever bestowed on me, the ability to think in quotations.
—Margaret Drabble,
The Summer Birdcage (1977).

It is the little writer rather than the great writer who seems never to quote, and the reason is that he is really never doing anything else.   —Havelock Ellis,
The Dance of Life (1923).

Next to the originator of a good sentence is the first quoter of it.
—Ralph Waldo Emerson,
Letters and Social Aims: Quotation and Originality (1876).

Quotation confesses inferiority.
—Ralph Waldo Emerson,
ibid.

I just want to know who said it. And also when he said it, and where he said it, and what it was he said, and whether he said it at all or whether I've merely imagined it.   —Michael Frayn,
Alphabetical Order, I (1977).

Quotations (such as have point and lack triteness) from the great old authors are an act of filial reverence on the part of the quoter, and a blessing to a public grown superficial and external.
—Louise Imogen Guiney,
in *Scribner's Magazine*, Jan. 1911.

A fine quotation is a diamond on the finger of a man of wit, and a pebble in the hand of a fool.   —Joseph Roux,
Meditations of a Parish Priest,
i.74 (1886).

Some, for renown, on scraps of learning dote,
And think they grow immortal as they quote.   —Edward Young,
Love of Fame, I.89 (1728).

Radical

See also Dissenter; Nonconformity

I never dared be radical when young
For fear it would make me conservative
when old.   — Robert Frost,
A Further Range: Precaution (1936).

The radical invents the views. When he
was worn them out the conservative
adopts them.   — Mark Twain,
Notebook, July 4, 1898 (1935).

Radicalism

See also Dissent; Noncon-
formity

A young man who is not radical about
something is a pretty poor risk for
education.   — Jacques Barzun,
The Teacher in America (1944).

It is love of candor that makes men
radical thinkers.   — Eric Bentley,
Thirty Years of Treason (1971).

Those who worry about radicalism in our
schools and colleges are often either reac-
tionaries who themselves do not bear allegiance to the traditional American principles, or defeatists who despair of the
success of our own philosophy in an open
competition.   — James Bryant Conant,
Education in a Divided World (1948).

Rationality

See also Logic; Reason

It takes a long time to realize that the rational is only a small segment of the
human complex, that the spirit of reason
is difficult to invoke, and that there are as
many dangers in the rational as in the
irrational.   — Anthony Burgess,
Urgent Copy (1968).

To begin with rationality in opinion: I
should define it merely as the habit of

taking account of all relevant evidence in
arriving at a belief.
          — Bertrand Russell,
The Will to Doubt: Can
Men Be Rational? (1958).

Reader

See also Reading

Some read to think, these are rare; some
to write, these are common; and some
read to talk, and these form the great
majority.   — Charles Caleb Colton,
Lacon, 258 (1820–22).

'Tis the good reader that makes the good
book.   — Ralph Waldo Emerson,
Society and Solitude: Success (1870).

The book-worm wraps himself up in his
web of verbal generalities, and sees only
the glimmering shadows of things reflected from the minds of others.
          — William Hazlitt,
Table-Talk: On the Ignorance
of the Learned (1821–22).

From one that reads but one book ... the
Lord deliver us.   — James Howell,
English Proverbs (1659).

He that reads and grows no wiser seldom
suspects his own deficiency, but complains of hard words and obscure sentences, and asks why books are written
which cannot be understood.
          — Samuel Johnson,
The Idler, no.70 (1758–60).

What a writer asks of his reader is not so
much to like as to listen.
          — Henry Wadsworth Longfellow,
letter to J.S. Dwight, Dec. 10, 1847.

A gentleman, one of the omnivorous
swallowers,
Who bolt every book that comes out of
the press,
Without the least question of larger or
less,
Whose stomachs are strong at the expense
of their head.   — James Russell Lowell,
A Fable for Critics (1848).

A reading-machine, always wound up
and going,
He mastered whatever was not worth the
knowing.		—James Russell Lowell,
ibid.

There are people who read too much: the
bibliobibuli. I know some who are constantly drunk on books, as other men are
drunk on whiskey or religion. They
wander through this most diverting and
stimulating of worlds in a haze, seeing
nothing and hearing nothing.
				—H.L. Mencken,
		Minority Report: Notebooks,
				no.71 (1956).

The soul that feeds on books alone—
I count that soul exceeding small
That lives alone by book and creed,—
A soul that has not learned to read.
		—Joaquin Miller, *Poetical Works*
		(1923): *The Larger College*, x.

Reading

See also below; Book; Reader

To read is to translate, for no two persons'
experiences are the same.
				—W.H. Auden,
		The Dyer's Hand: Reading (1962).

We'd be limited to very narrow and provincial lives if we depended upon direct
experience to familiarize ourselves with
the world in which we live.
			—Franklin Bobbitt,
		*The Curriculum of Modern
		Education*, 142 (1941).

Winter is good for reading the classics,
for one's mind is more collected. Summer
is good for reading history, for one has
plenty of time. The autumn is good for
reading the ancient philosophers, because of the great diversity of thought
and ideas. Finally, spring is suitable for

reading modern authors, for in spring
one's spirit expands.	—Chang Chao,
		Yumengying (before 1693), in Lin
			Yutang, *The Importance of
			Understanding*, 71 (1960).

Read proudly—put the duty of being
read invariably on the author. If he is not
read, whose fault is it? I am quite ready
to be charmed, but I shall not make-
believe I am charmed.
			—Ralph Waldo Emerson,
		address on the dedication of the
			library in Concord, May 1873.

Reading is an affirmation of the future by
an ability to use the past.
				—Harry Golden,
			*So What Else Is New?: How to
			read a book, and why* (1964).

If I had spent as much time in reading as
other men of learning, I should have
been as ignorant as they.
				—Thomas Hobbes,
		in Isaac D'Israeli, *Curiosities of
		Literature*, II.179 (1791–1834); also in
		John Aubrey, *Lives of Eminent Men:
			Life of Hobbes* (1813).

It is the noblest of arts, the medium by
which there still come to us the loftiest
inspirations, the highest ideals, the
purest feelings that have been allowed
mankind.... Reading itself as a psycho-
physiological process is almost as good as
a miracle.		—Edmund B. Huey,
		Psychology and Pedagogy of Reading,
				5 (1908).

What does it matter if we have a new
book or an old book, if we open neither?
				—Jesse Jackson,
			Time, July 10, 1978.

A man ought to read just as inclination
leads him; for what he reads as a task will
do him little good.	—Samuel Johnson,
		in James Boswell, *Life of Samuel
		Johnson*, xiv, July 14, 1763
				(1791).

What is reading but silent conversation?
—Walter Savage Landor,
Imaginary Conversations (1824–53):
Aristoteles and Callisthenes.

More true knowledge comes by meditation than by reading; for much reading is an oppression of the mind, and extinguishes the natural candle, which is the reason of so many senseless scholars in the world.   —William Penn,
Advice to His Children (1699).

It is not a spectator sport but a performing art.   —Peter S. Prescott,
Newsweek, Dec. 24, 1973.

Sir, he hath never fed of the dainties that are bred in a book.
He hath not eat paper, as it were; he hath not drunk ink: his intellect is not replenished; he is only an animal, only sensible in the duller parts.
—William Shakespeare,
Love's Labour's Lost, IV.ii.25 (1594).

Reading is seeing by proxy.
—Herbert Spencer,
The Study of Sociology (1873).

It's a continuous conversion.... The real question is what changes will be made in you as a result of really reading a book.
—Leo Stein,
Journey into the Self, 156 (1950).

Reading, Children's

Children read books, not reviews. They don't give a hoot about the critics.
—Isaac Bashevis Singer,
explaining why he writes for children,
in his acceptance statement for the
National Book award in 1970.

Children don't read to find their identity, to free themselves from guilt, to quench the thirst for rebellion or to get rid of alienation. They have no use for psychology. They detest sociology. They still believe in God, the family, angels, devils, witches, goblins, logic, clarity, punc-

tuation, and other such obsolete stuff....
When a book is boring, they yawn openly. They don't expect their writer to redeem humanity, but to leave to adults such childish illusions.
—Isaac Bashevis Singer,
address on receiving the Nobel
Prize for Literature, 1978.

I was never allowed to read the popular American children's books of my day, as my mother said, the children spoke bad English *without the author's knowing it.*
—Edith Wharton,
A Backward Glance, iii (1934).

Reading, Critical

Reading without thinking gives one a disorderly mind, and thinking without reading makes one flighty (or unbalanced).   —Confucius,
in Lin Yutang, ed., *The Wisdom of
China and India: The Aphorisms of
Confucius*, 841 (1942).

Comprehension is criticism, and criticism or judgment is a mere synonym for THOUGHT.   —Ernest Dimnet,
The Art of Thinking, III.ii.e (1928).

Reading without thinking is worse than no reading at all.   —Harry Golden,
For 2¢ Plain: The great books (1959).

Unless ... books are studied and understood, the whole thing is useless. If a man read only one book all his life, and it made him think, it would be worth more than having a smattering of a thousand works.   —Harry Golden,
ibid.

Those who have read of everything are thought to understand everything too; but it is not always so—reading furnishes our mind only with materials of knowledge; it is thinking makes what we read ours.   —John Locke,
*An Essay concerning Human
Understanding* (1690).

Who reads
Incessantly, and to his reading brings not
A spirit and judgment equal or superior,
(And what he brings what needs he else-
where seek?)
Uncertain and unsettled still remains,
Deep-versed in books and shallow in
himself.   —John Milton,
    Paradise Regained, IV.322 (1671).

What I mean by reading is not skim-
ming, not being able to say as the world
saith, "oh, yes, I've read that!," but
reading again and again, in all sorts of
moods, with an increase of delight every
time, till the thing read has become a
part of your system and goes forth along
with you to meet any new experience you
may have. —Charles Edward Montague,
A Writer's Notes on His Trade (1930).

Anyone who is too lazy to master the
comparatively small glossary necessary to
understand Chaucer deserves to be shut
out from the reading of good books for
ever.   —Ezra Pound,
    ABC of Reading, II (1934).

We must form our minds by reading
deep rather than wide. —Quintilian,
    Institutio Oratoria, X.i.26
    (A.D. 95 or 96).

Every book must be chewed to get out its
juice.   —William Scarborough,
    Chinese Proverbs, no.548 (1875).

If a man has read a great number of
books, and does not think things
through, he is only a bookcase.
                    —Shu Shuehmou,
    Kueiyuyuan Chutan, (16th cent.),
    in Lin Yutang, *The Importance of
    Understanding*, 469 (1960).

Books must be read as deliberately and
reservedly as they were written.
                —Henry D. Thoreau,
    Walden, iii: *Reading* (1854).

[Modern education] has produced a vast
population able to read but unable to
distinguish what is worth reading.
                    —G.M. Trevelyan,
    English Social History, XXX.iv (1942).

Nothing is worth reading that does not
require an alert mind.
                —Charles Dudley Warner,
    Backlog Studies: First Study (1873).

Reading, Effect of

Reading maketh a full man; conference a
ready man; and writing an exact man.
                    —Francis Bacon,
        Essays: Of Studies (1597)
    [conference = *discussion*; writing =
                    taking notes].

The benefit of reading varies directly with
one's experience in life. It is like looking
at the moon. A young reader may be
compared to one seeing the moon
through a single crack, a middle-aged
reader seems to see it from an enclosed
courtyard, and an old man seems to see it
from an open terrace, with a complete
view of the entire field. —Chang Chao,
    Yumengying (before 1693), in Lin
    Yutang, *The Importance of
    Understanding*, 71 (1960).

Give a man this taste [for reading] (and
the means of gratifying it) and you can
hardly fail to make him a happy man.
You place him in contact with the best
society in every period of history, with the
wisest and wittiest, the tenderest and
bravest who have adorned humanity.
You make him a denizen of all nations,
a contemporary of all ages.
                    —John Herschel,
        address at the opening of
        Eton Library, 1833.

The art of reading is in great part that of
acquiring a better understanding of life
from one's encounter with it in a book.
                —André Maurois,
        The Art of Living (1973).

Reading, Enjoyment of

Reading is a joy, but not an unalloyed joy. Books do not make life easier or more simple, but harder and more interesting.
— Harry Golden,
So What Else Is New?: How to read a book, and why (1964).

He ate and drank the precious Words —
His Spirit grew robust —
He knew no more that he was poor,
Nor that his frame was Dust.
— Emily Dickinson,
Complete Poems, no.1587 (c.1883),
ed. Thomas H. Johnson (1960).

Till I heard Chapman speak out loud and bold:
Then felt I like some watcher of the skies
When a new planet swims into his ken.
— John Keats,
On First Looking into Chapman's Homer, ln.8 (1816).

Until I feared to lose it, I never loved to read. One does not love breathing.
— Harper Lee,
To Kill a Mockingbird, I.ii (1960).

Love of reading enables a man to exchange the wearisome hours of life which come to every one, for hours of delight.
— Charles de Secondat Montesquieu,
Pensées Diverses (1853).

No man can read with profit that which he cannot learn to read with pleasure.
— Noah Porter,
Books and Reading, i (1871).

People say that life is the thing, but I prefer reading. — Logan Pearsall Smith,
Afterthoughts, vi: *Myself* (1931).

Reading — the nice and subtle happiness of reading.... This joy not dulled by Age, this polite and unpunished vice, this selfish, serene, life-long intoxication.
— Logan Pearsall Smith,
More Trivia: Consolation (1921).

If you cannot enjoy reading a book over and over again, there is no use reading it at all.   — Oscar Wilde,
Intentions: The Decay of Lying (1891).

Reading, New Books

Of all odd crazes, the craze to be forever reading new books is one of the oddest.
— Augustine Birrell,
Essays: Books Old and New (1899).

Somebody who reads only newspapers and at best books of contemporary authors looks to me like an extremely near-sighted person who scorns eyeglasses. He is completely dependent on the prejudices and fashions of his times, since he never gets to see or hear anything else.   — Albert Einstein,
Ideas and Opinions (1954).

If you would know what nobody knows, read what every body reads, just one year afterwards & you shall be a fund of new & unheard of speculations.
— Ralph Waldo Emerson,
Journals, June 26, 1835.

I cannot understand the rage manifested by the greater part of the world for reading new books.... If I have not read a book before, it is, to all intents and purposes, new to me, whether it was printed yesterday or three hundred years ago.
— William Hazlitt,
Sketches and Essays: On Reading New Books (1839).

What a sense of superiority it gives one to escape reading some book which everyone else is reading.
— Alice James,
Diary, ed. Leon Edel (1964).

The great drawback in new books is that they prevent our reading the old ones.
— Joseph Joubert,
Pensées (1810).

Reading, Old Books

In science read by preference, the newest works; in literature, the oldest. The classic literature is always modern.
— Edward George Bulwer-Lytton,
The Caxtons (1849).

It is more profitable to reread some old books than to read new ones, just as it is better to repair and add to an old temple than to build one entirely new.
— Chang Chao, *Yumengying* (before 1693), in Lin Yutang, *The Importance of Understanding*, 74 (1960).

When I take up a work that I have read before (the oftener the better) I know what I have to expect. The satisfaction is not lessened by being anticipated.
— William Hazlitt,
Sketches and Essays: On Reading Old Books (1839).

Reading, Purpose for

Read not to contradict and confute, nor to believe and take for granted, nor to find talk and discourse, but to weigh and consider.   — Francis Bacon,
Essays: Of Studies (1597).

The man who reads only for improvement is beyond the hope of much improvement before he begins.
— Jonathan Daniels,
Three Presidents and Their Books (1956).

Reading, to most people, means an ashamed way of killing time disguised under a dignified name.
— Ernest Dimnet,
The Art of Thinking, III.ii.c (1928).

Tell me why do you want to read? If you are drawn by the mere pleasure of reading, or by curiosity, you are a trifler, without perseverance: but if you judge it by the true standard, what is that but peace of mind? If reading does not win

you peace of mind, what is the good of it?   — Epictetus,
Discourses, IV.iv (A.D. c.100).

Do not read, as children do, to amuse yourself, or like the ambitious, for the purpose of instruction. No, read in order to live.   — Gustave Flaubert,
letter to Mlle de Chantepie, June 1875.

Reading is sometimes an ingenious device for avoiding thought. — Arthur Helps,
Friends in Council, II.i (1857–59).

The end of reading is not more books but more life.   — Holbrook Jackson,
The Reading of Books (1946).

[Reading] is a means whereby we may learn not only to understand ourselves and the world about us but whereby we may find our place in the world.
— Elizabeth Neterer,
This Is Reading (1949).

We always read for some purpose — unless some sad, bad, mad schoolteacher has got hold of us.   — I.A. Richards,
How to Read a Page, 20 (1942).

No one ever reads a book. He reads himself through books, either to discover or to control himself. And the most objective books are the most deceptive.
— Romain Rolland,
The Journey Within (1947).

There are two motives for reading a book: one, that you enjoy it; the other, that you can boast about it. — Bertrand Russell,
The Conquest of Happiness (1930).

And better had they ne'er been born,
Who read to doubt, or read to scorn.
— Walter Scott,
The Monastery: Answer of the Author of Waverly to the Letter of Captain Clutterbuck (1820).

Reading, Selective

The principle which has never failed to confer superiority on a man's thinking

activity is the well-worn precept: DO NOT READ GOOD BOOKS—life is too short for that—ONLY READ THE BEST.... ONLY READ WHAT GIVES YOU THE GREATEST PLEASURE.
— Ernest Dimnet,
The Art of Thinking, III.ii.c (1928).

Read only brief or systematic books, one at a time, and books beautifully written, on fine paper and attractively bound. Read in an attractive room, and from time to time let your eyes gaze upon beautiful objects so that you will come to love what you read. — Profiat Duran,
Maaseh Ephod (c.1400).

Because we all know how to read, we imagine that we know what we read. Enormous fallacy! — Aldous Huxley,
Music at Night (1931).

There is danger in reading bad books, but also greater danger in not reading good ones. — John Courtney Murray,
in *Upper and Lower Case*, Dec. 1982.

Life being very short, and the quiet hours of it few, we ought to waste none of them in reading valueless books.
— John Ruskin,
Sesame and Lilies, preface (1865).

Live always in the best company when you read. — Sydney Smith,
in Lady Holland, *A Memoir of the Rev. Sydney Smith* (1855).

Reading, Skill in

The art of reading, in short, includes all the same skills that are involved in the art of discovery: keeness of observation, readily available memory, range of imagination, and, of course, a reason trained in analysis and reflection.
— Mortimer J. Adler,
How to Read a Book, iii.4 (1940).

The art of reading is to skip judiciously.
— Philip G. Hamerton, *The Intellectual Life*, IV. let.iv (1873).

When you read, *read*! Too many students just half read. I never read without summarizing—and so understanding what I read. The art of memory is the art of understanding. — Roscoe Pound,
Reader's Digest, Feb. 1961.

The problem of learning to read may occupy a lifetime, and the acquirement of this ability is almost synonymous with education. — H.R. Ruse,
The Illiteracy of the Literate, 11 (1933).

Reading, Teaching of

See also Teaching

If we think of it, all that a university, or final highest school can do for us, is still what the first school began doing—teach us to *read*.... But the place where we are to get knowledge, even theoretic knowledge, is the books themselves! It depends on what we read, after all manner of professors have done their best for us.
— Thomas Carlyle,
Heroes and Hero-Worship, V: *The Hero as a Man of Letters* (1840).

The teaching of reading—all over the United States, in all the schools, in all the text books—is totally wrong and flies in the face of all logic and common sense. Johnny couldn't read ... for the simple reason that nobody ever showed him how. Johnny's only problem was that he was unfortunately exposed to an ordinary American school. — Rudolf Flesch,
Why Johnny Can't Read (1955).

[There is] growing agreement that there is no one and only orthodox way of teaching and learning this greatest and hardest of all arts, in which ear, mouth, eye, and hand, must in turn train the others to automatic perfection.
— G. Stanley Hall,
How to Teach Reading and What to Read in School (1887).

Teachers may say, "But reading must be difficult, or so many children wouldn't have trouble with it." I say it is *because* we assume that it is so difficult that so many children have trouble with it. Our anxieties, our fears, and the ridiculous things we do to "simplify" what is simple enough already, *cause* most of the trouble.   —John Holt, *How Children Learn* (1967).

Presenting the child with the alphabet is giving them what they never saw, heard, or thought before.... But the printed names of known things are the signs of sounds which their ears have been accustomed to hear, and their organs of speech utter. It can hardly be doubted therefore that a child would learn to name 26 familiar words sooner than the unknown, unheard-of and unthought of letters of the alphabet. —Horace Mann, *Annual Reports of the Secretary of the Board of Education of Massachusetts for 1837–1838.*

Reading was the most important subject in our early American schools, and it has continued to be the most important subject all through the years of our national growth.   —Nila Banton Smith, *American Reading Instruction*, p.iii (1934).

Reality

Unfortunately, we are inclined to talk of man as it would be desirable for him to be rather than as he really is.... True education can proceed only from naked reality, not from any ideal illusion about man, however attractive.
—Carl Gustav Jung, *Psychological Reflections*, ed. Jolande Jacobi and R.F. Hull (1970).

Ah! What avails the classic bent
And what the cultured word,
Against the undoctored incident
That actually occurred?
—Rudyard Kipling, *The Benefactors*, i (1912).

Reality is just itself, and it is nonsense to ask whether it be true or false.
—Alfred North Whitehead, *Adventures of Ideas* (1933).

Reason

See also Logic; Rationality; Reasoning

There are men who are bound by the chains of reason, and for such men there is no aerial soaring.   —Ahad HaAm, quoted by Joseph Leftwich, *Menorah Journal*, Spring 1952.

Reason is itself a matter of faith. It is an act of faith to assert that our thoughts have any relation to reality at all.
—G.K. Chesterton, *Orthodoxy*, iii (1908).

Reason cannot be forced into belief.
—Hasdai Crescas, *Or Adonai (Light of the Lord)* (1410).

I do not believe man possesses an avenue to truth which is superior to his reason.
—Roland B. Gittelsohn, *Man's Best Hope* (1961).

Reason has moons, but moons not hers
Lie mirrored on her sea,
Confounding her astronomers,
But O! delighting me.
—Ralph Hodgson, *Reason*, in Louis Untermeyer, ed., *Modern British Poetry* (1942).

Reason and free inquiry are the only effectual agents against error.
—Thomas Jefferson, *Notes on the State of Virginia* (1782).

All extremes does perfect reason flee,
And wishes to be wise quite soberly.
—Molière, *The Misanthrope*, I.i (1666).

The only authority that both sides to an argument must necessarily recognize will have to be an authority residing in the

very nature of humanity.... It is reason.
—James Bissett Pratt,
Religious Liberals Reply (1947).

Let reason be thy schoolmistress.
—Walter Ralegh (1552?–1618),
Instructions to His Son, sec.1 (1616).

Reason may introduce a belief to us but she seldom stays with it. The moment it is ours we become partisans and she has little or nothing to do with its defence.
—Mark Rutherford,
Last Pages from a Journal (1915).

Reason in my philosophy is only a harmony among irrational impulses.
—George Santayana,
Persons and Places, II: The Middle Span (1945).

Reason knows itself and its limitations. It knows that it is but a modest light in the dusk of infinitude, yet the only one at our disposal.   —Arthur Schnitzler,
Buch der Sprüche und Bedenken,
43 (1927).

His reasons are as two grains of wheat hid in two bushels of chaff: you shall seek all day ere you find them, and, when you have them, they are not worth the search.
—William Shakespeare,
The Merchant of Venice, I.i.116 (1596).

Logicians have but ill defin'd,
As rational, the human kind;
Reason, they say, belongs to man;
But let them prove it if they can.
—Jonathan Swift,
The Logicians Refuted (1731).

When a man's fancy gets astride on his reason, when imagination is at cuffs with the senses, and common understanding, as well as common sense, is kicked out of doors; the first proselyte he makes, is himself.   —Jonathan Swift,
A Tale of a Tub, ix (1704).

Reason, that which we call reason, reflex and reflective knowledge, the distin-

guishing mark of man, is a social product.   —Miguel de Unamuno,
The Tragic Sense of Life, ii (1912).

All the tools with which mankind works upon its fate are dull, but the sharpest among them is reason.   —Carl Van Doren, *Many Minds* (1924).

I can stand brute force, but brute reason is quite unbearable. There is something unfair about its use. It is hitting below the intellect.   —Oscar Wilde,
The Picture of Dorian Gray, iii (1891).

Thus whilst against false reas'ning I inveigh,
I owe right Reason, which I would obey;
That Reason, which distinguishes by Sense,
And gives us rules of good and ill from thence.   —John Wilmot
(2nd Earl of Rochester),
A Satyr against Mankind, ln.98 (1675).

Reasoning

See also Analysis; Consideration; Deliberation; Logic; Thinking

Reasoning draws a conclusion—but does not make the conclusion certain, unless the mind discovers it by the path of experience.   —Roger Bacon,
Opus Majus (1268).

Come now, let us reason together.
—*Bible: Isaiah* 1:18.

Reasoning with a child is fine, if you can reach the child's reason without destroying your own.   —John Mason Brown,
in *New York Times*, June 19, 1955.

When a man *reasoneth*, he does nothing else but conceive a sum total, from *addition* of parcels; or conceive a remainder, from *subtraction* of one sum from another.   —Thomas Hobbes,
Leviathan, I.v (1651).

What we call rational grounds for our beliefs are often extremely irrational attempts to justify our instincts.
— T.H. Huxley,
On the Natural Inequality of Man (1890).

A free activity of the mind, reaching conclusions under no compulsion save that of evidence.   — C.E.M. Joad,
Return to Philosophy (1936).

Those that differ upon reason may come together by reason.
— Benjamin Whichcote,
Moral and Religious Aphorisms (1703).

Reform

See also Change; Idea, New; Innovator

Seek not to reform every one's dial by your own watch.   — H.G. Bohn,
Handbook of Proverbs, 482 (1855).

Every reform, however necessary, will by weak minds be carried to an excess which will itself need reforming.
— Samuel Taylor Coleridge,
Biographia Literaria, i (1817).

For more than a hundred years much complaint has been made of the unmethodical way in which schools are conducted, but it is only within the last thirty that any serious attempt has been made to find a remedy for this state of things. And with what result? Schools remain exactly as they were.
— John Amos Comenius,
The Great Didactic (1628–32).

It is our American habit if we find the foundations of our educational structure unsatisfactory to add another story or wing. We find it easier to add a new study or course or kind of school than to recognize existing conditions so as to meet the need.   — John Dewey,
Characters and Events, II (1929).

We must destroy all which in the present school answers to the organization of constraint, the artificial surroundings by which children are separated from nature and life, the intellectual and moral discipline made use of to impose ready-made ideas upon them, beliefs which deprave and annihilate natural bent.
— Francisco Ferrer,
The Modern School (1909?).

Anyone who would attempt the task of felling a virgin forest with a penknife would probably feel the same paralysis of despair that the reformer feels when confronted with existing school systems.
— Ellen Key,
The Century of the Child, v (1909).

The first requisite for educational reform is the school as a unit, with its approved curriculum based on its own needs, and evolved by its own staff. It we fail to secure that, we simply fall from one formalism into another, from one dung-hill of inert ideas into another.
— Alfred North Whitehead,
The Aims of Education, i (1929).

Relaxation

Mentally, fallow is as important as seed-time. Even bodies can be exhausted by overcultivation. — George Bernard Shaw,
The Intelligent Woman's Guide to Socialism and Capitalism, lxxxi (1928).

There is one piece of advice, in a life of study, which I think no one will object to; and that is, every now and then to be completely idle, — to do nothing at all.
— Sydney Smith,
Lectures on Moral Philosophy (1804).

Religious Values

The parents have a right to say that no teacher paid by their money shall rob their children of faith in God and send

them back to their homes skeptical, or infidels, or agnostics, or atheists.
— William Jennings Bryan,
testimony at Scopes trial,
Dayton, Tenn., July 16, 1925.

Functionally viewed, American public education emancipated from sectarianism is indirectly the only universal teacher of religious values in the United States.
— Conrad Henry Moehlman,
School and Church:
The American Way (1944).

The religious element in public education is everything that promotes faith in the higher values of life. Religion is not something apart but a continuous part of our experience.
— Conrad Henry Moehlman,
ibid.

Repetition

It is repetition, like cabbage served at every meal, that wears out the schoolmaster's life.   — Juvenal,
Satires, III.vii.152 (c. A.D. 110).

A truth does not become greater by frequent repetition.   — Maimonides,
Tehiyat HaMethim: Responsa,
ii.9d (before 1204).

Repetition is the mother, not only to study, but also of education. Like the fresco-painter, the teacher lays colors on the wet plaster which ever fade away, and which he must ever renew until they remain and brightly shine.
— Jean Paul Richter,
Levana, ii (1807).

Report, School

Your elder boy gives me great satisfaction. His tone, character, and manners are all thoroughly good; and if only he was not so weak in composition he might really distinguish himself at Harrow.
— Letter from the housemaster at Harrow to the father of John Galsworthy (c.1881).

As we read the school reports upon our children, we realize with a sense of relief that can rise to delight that — thank Heaven — nobody is reporting in this fashion upon us.   — J.B. Priestley,
Delight (1949).

Reprimand

See also Child Rearing;
Discipline; Punishment

I never reprimand a boy in the evening — darkness and a troubled mind are a poor combination.
— Frank Boyden,
speech at Deerfield Academy,
Jan. 2, 1954.

He that chastens one, chastens 20.
— George Herbert,
Outlandish Proverbs, no.356 (1640).

A torn jacket is soon mended; but hard words bruise the heart of a child.
— Henry Wadsworth Longfellow,
Driftwood: Table Talk (1857).

Reprimand not a child immediately on the offence. Wait till the irritation has been replaced by serenity.   — Moses Hasid, *Iggeret HaMusar* (1717).

They have a right to censure, that have a heart to help: the rest is cruelty, not justice.   — William Penn,
Some Fruits of Solitude, I. no.46 (1693).

As we rate boys who, being mature in
  knowledge,
Pawn their experience to their present
  pleasure,
And so rebel to judgment.
— William Shakespeare,
Antony and Cleopatra, I.iv.31 (1607)
[rate = *scold*; mature in knowledge = *old*
enough to know; pawn ... pleasure =
gratify their desires against their
judgment].

Better a little chiding than a great deal of heart-break.   — William Shakespeare, *The Merry Wives of Windsor*, V.iii.11 (1599–1600).

I alone have a right to blame and punish, for he only may chastise who loves.
— Rabindranath Tagore, *The Crescent Moon: The Judge* (1913).

Research

See also Analysis; Experiment; Inquiry; Investigation

Inquiry is a duty, and error in research is not a sin.
— Benjamin ben Moses Nahawendi, *Sefer Dinim (Book of Rules)* (c.800).

The investigator should have a robust faith — and yet not believe.
— Claude Bernard, *Introduction to the Study of Experimental Medicine* (1865).

It often happens that an unsuccessful experiment may produce an excellent observation. There are, therefore, no unsuccessful experiments.   — Claude Bernard, *ibid.*

Wide research and steadfast purpose, eager questioning and close reflection, — all this tends to humanize a man.
— Confucius, *Analects*, XIX.vi (c.500 B.C.).

After all, the ultimate goal of all research is not objectivity, but truth.
— Helene Deutsch, *The Psychology of Women*, I (1944).

The way to do research is to attack the facts at the point of greatest astonishment.   — Celia Green, *The Decline and Fall of Science: Aphorisms* (1977).

Go and sit in the lounges of the luxury hotels and on the doorsteps of the flophouses; sit on the Gold Coast settees and in the slum shakedown.... In short, gentlemen, go get the seat of your pants dirty in real research.   — Robert E. Park, address to graduate sociology students, 1928.

The beginning of research is curiosity, its essence is discernment, and its goal truth and justice.   — Isaac Halevi Satanov, *Mishlê Asaf* (1789).

It is not worth the while to go round the world to count the cats in Zanzibar.
— Henry David Thoreau, *Walden*, xviii: *Conclusion* (1854).

The outcome of any serious research can only be to make two questions grow where only one grew before.
— Thorstein Veblen, *The Place of Science in Modern Civilization* (1919).

Respect

See also Teacher, Respect for

Respect a man, he will do the more.
— James Howell, *English Proverbs* (1659).

He that will have his son have a respect for him and his orders, must himself have a great reverence for his son.
— John Locke, *Some Thoughts concerning Education* (1693).

Just as the pupils are required to honor the teacher, so the teacher ought to be courteous and friendly toward his pupils. The sages said: "Let the honor of your student be as dear to you as your own."
— Maimonides, *Mishneh Torah (Second Law)*, I.v.12 (1180).

It is a duty to treat every scholar with respect, even though he is not one's teacher.   — Maimonides, *ibid.*, I.vi.1.

He who learns from his fellow one single section, or one single rule, or one single verse, or one single expression, or even one single letter, is under obligation to treat him with honor.   — *Talmud: Aboth*, 6.3 (before A.D. 500).

Rhetoric

See also Eloquence; Oratory

Rhetoric may be defined as the faculty of observing in any given case the available means of persuasion.   — Aristotle, *Rhetoric*, I.ii.1 (before 322 B.C.).

Rhetoric that rolls like a freight train over a bridge.   — David Brinkley, on oratory of unionist John L. Lewis, *Newsweek*, Mar. 13, 1961.

For rhetoric, he could not ope
His mouth but out there flew a trope.
        — Samuel Butler (1612–80), *Hudibras*, I.i.81 (1663) [trope = *figure of speech*].

For all a rhetorician's rules
Teach nothing but to name his tools.
        — Samuel Butler, *ibid.*, I.i.89.

That pestilent cosmetic, rhetoric.
        — T.H. Huxley, *Science and Morals* (1886).

Rhetoric without logic is like a tree with leaves and blossoms, but no root; yet more are taken with rhetoric than logic, because they are caught with fine expressions when they understand not reason.
        — John Selden, *Table Talk: Preaching* (1689).

I know them that think rhetoric to stand wholly upon dark words, and he that can catch an inkhorn term by the tail, him they count to be a fine Englishman and a good rhetorician.   — Thomas Wilson (c.1525–81), *The Arte of Rhetorique* (1553).

Rhyme

See also Poetry

This misliking of rhyming beginneth not now of any newfangle singularity, but hath been long misliked of many, and that of men of the greatest learning and deepest judgment.   — Roger Ascham, *The Schoolmaster*, II (1570).

Till barb'rous nations, and more barb'rous times,
Debas'd the majesty of verse to rhymes.
        — John Dryden, *To the Earl of Roscommon*, ln.11 (1684).

Rime being no necessary adjunct or true ornament of poem or good verse, in longer works especially, but the invention of a barbarous age, to set off wretched matter and lame metre. — John Milton, *Paradise Lost*, preface (1667).

The troublesome and modern bondage of riming.   — John Milton, *ibid.*

It is not riming and versing that maketh poesie. One may be a poet without versing, and a versifier without poetrie.
        — Philip Sidney, *An Apologie for Poetrie* (1595).

Ridicule

The talent of turning men into ridicule, and exposing to laughter those one converses with, is the qualification of little ungenerous tempers. — Joseph Addison, *The Spectator*, no.249, Dec. 15, 1711.

How comes it to pass, then that we appear such cowards in reasoning, and are so afraid to stand the test of ridicule?
        — Anthony Cooper, 3rd Earl of Shaftesbury, *Characteristicks*, I.i: A Letter Concerning Enthusiasm (1711).

Truth, 'tis supposed, may bear all lights; and one of those principal lights or natural mediums by which things are to be viewed in order to a thorough recognition is ridicule itself. — Anthony Cooper, *ibid.*, I.ii: *Essay on the Freedom of Wit and Humour.*

Rigidity

See also Closemindedness; Dogmatism

The uncompromising attitude is more indicative of an inner uncertainty than of deep conviction. — Eric Hoffer, *The Passionate State of Mind*, no. 63 (1954).

Too much rigidity on the part of teachers should be followed by a brisk spirit of insubordination on the part of the taught. — Agnes Repplier, *Points of View: Literary Shibboleths* (1891).

It is the rigid dogma that destroys truth; and, please notice, my emphasis is not on the dogma but on the rigidity. When men say of any question, "This is all there is to be known or said of the subject; investigation ends here," that is death. — Alfred North Whitehead, *Dialogues*, as recorded by Lucien Price (1953).

Routine

Routine is not organization, any more than paralysis is order. — Arthur Helps, *Organization in Daily Life* (1862).

Rule

The school should never lay down a rule without giving an adequate explanation as to why this rule is good for the pupil. —John B. Geisel, "Discipline Reconsidered," *School and Society*, Sept. 1945.

As you look at your youngsters, be sure that your standards of promptness, of attention, of quiet, of courtesy, are realistically geared to children, not idealistically geared to angels. —James L. Hymes, Jr., "The Old Order Changeth," *NEA Journal*, Apr. 1953.

How true it is that "complete legality is complete injustice." — St. Jerome, *Letters*, let.1, sec.14 (A.D. 370).

Salary, Teacher's

It is a pity that commonly more care is had, yea, and that amongst very wise men, to find out rather a cunning man for their horse than a cunning man for their children. They say nay in word, but they do so in deed. For to one they will gladly give a stipend of two hundred crowns by year and loathe to offer the other two hundred shillings. — Roger Ascham, *The Schoolmaster*, I (1570).

Twenty and five pounds in manner following: y^t is to say They have by bargin liberty to pay him ye one 3d part of s^d sum in Barley and no more: ye other two 3ds in other grain y^t is to say in indian corn: peas: or Rye in any or all of them: all these mentioned to be good and merchantable. — Contract to pay schoolmaster, 1703, Deerfield, Mass., in Clifton Johnson, *Old-Time Schools and School-books* (1904).

Now to the salaries of teachers. In a healthy society, every useful activity is compensated in a way to permit of a decent living. The exercise of any socially valuable activity gives inner satisfaction; but it cannot be considered as part of the salary. The teacher cannot use his inner satisfaction to fill the stomachs of his children. — Albert Einstein, message for Canadian Education Week, Mar. 2-8, 1952, *Ideas and Opinions* (1954).

Bring up your sons in the right way with gentleness. Their teacher must be constantly in your house, and you must pay him generously.
—Elijah ben Solomon Zalman, letter to his family, *Alim LiTerufa* (1836).

Modern cynics and skeptics ... see no harm in paying those to whom they entrust the minds of their children a smaller wage than is paid to those to whom they entrust the care of their plumbing.
—John F. Kennedy, address on 90th anniversary of Vanderbilt University, May 19, 1963.

For if we apply for a preacher or a School Master, we are told the price, So Much, & they cant go under, for it is agreed upon & they shall be disgrased if they take less.
—William Manning, *The Key of Libberty* (1798).

Many fathers reach such a pitch in their love for money as well as hatred of children that to avoid paying a larger stipend they choose as teachers for their children men worth nothing at all, shopping for ignorance at bargain prices.
—Plutarch, *Moralia: The Education of Children* (c. A.D. 95).

Aristippus on one occasion rebuked an empty-headed parent neatly and wittily. For being asked how much money a parent ought to pay for his son's education, he answered, "A thousand drachmae." And he replying, "Hercules, what a price! I could buy a slave for as much;" Aristippus answered, "You shall have two slaves then, your son and the slave you buy."   —Plutarch, *ibid*.

If it be true, that the teachers ... are insufficiently qualified for the task, the difficulty originates ... not in any deficiency of the means of obtaining ample qualifications, but in insufficiency of compensation. Those districts which are inclined to pay competent wages, can at all times be supplied with competent teachers.   —Report of the Committee on Education of the Massachusetts House of Representatives, March 7, 1840.

If you see cities uprooted, know that it came about because they did not maintain teachers' salaries.
—*Jerusalem Talmud: Hagigah*, 1.7 (before A.D. 400).

Satire

Satire is a lonely and introspective occupation, for nobody can describe a fool to the life without much patient self-inspection.   —Frank Moore Colby (1865–1925), *Simple Simon*.

The satire should be like the porcupine,
That shoots sharp quills out in every angry line,
And wounds the blushing cheek and fiery eye
Of him that hears and readeth guiltily.
—Joseph Hall (1574–1656), *Virgidemiarum*, V (1597–98).

Satires which censors can understand deserve to be suppressed.
—Karl Kraus, *Poems: Controversy* (1930).

Satire should, like a polished razor keen,
Wound with a touch that's scarcely felt or seen.   —Mary Wortley Montagu, *Verses Addressed to an Imitator of Horace* (c.1720).

Satire is moral outrage transformed into comic art.   —Philip Roth, *Reading Myself and Others* (1975).

The boldest way, if not the best,
To tell men freely of their foulest faults,
To laugh at their vain deeds and vainer thoughts.   —John Sheffield, *Essay on Satire* (c.1679).

Satire is a sort of glass, wherein beholders do generally discover everybody's face but their own; which is the chief reason for

that kind reception it merits in the world, and that so very few are offended with it.
— Jonathan Swift,
The Battle of the Books,
preface (1704).

Scholar

See also Student; Professor

Some scholars are like donkeys: they only carry a lot of books.
— ben-Joseph ibn Paquda Bahya,
Duties of the Heart (c.1080).

We can make majors and officers every year, but not scholars. — Robert Burton,
The Anatomy of Melancholy,
I (1621).

For him was levere have at his beddes heed
Twenty bookes, clad in blak or reed,
Of Aristotle and his philosophye,
Than robes riche, or fithele, or gay sautrye.
But al be that he was a philosophre
Yit hadde he but litel gold in cofre.
— Geoffrey Chaucer,
Canterbury Tales: Prologue,
ln.295 (c.1386) [levere = *would rather*;
fithele = *fiddle*; sautrye = *psaltery*].

The office of the scholar is to cheer, to raise, and to guide men by showing them facts amidst appearances.
— Ralph Waldo Emerson,
The American Scholar,
Phi Beta Kappa address at
Harvard, Aug. 31, 1837.

In this distribution of functions the scholar is the delegated intellect. In the right state he is *Man Thinking*. In the degenerate state, when the victim of society, he tends to become a mere thinker, or still worse, the parrot of other men's thinking.
— Ralph Waldo Emerson,
ibid.

Man Thinking.... Him nature solicits with all her placid, all her monitory pictures; him the past instructs; him the future invites. Is not indeed every man a student, and do not all things exist for the student's behoof? And finally, is it not the true scholar the only true master? But the old oracle said, "All things have two handles: beware of the wrong one."
— Ralph Waldo Emerson,
ibid. The quotation is from Epictetus,
Enchiridion, no.43: "Everything has two handles, one by which you can carry it, the other by which you cannot."

A scholar is a man with this inconvenience, that, when you ask him his opinion of any matter, he must go home and look up his manuscripts to know.
— Ralph Waldo Emerson,
Journals, 1855.

Every good Scholar is not a good Schoolmaster. — Thomas Fuller (1654–1734), *Gnomologia*, no.1417 (1732);
also H.G. Bohn, *Handbook of Proverbs*, 349 (1855).

The scholar is not The Intellectual. He is Man Thinking. Man Thinking is not the member of a race apart. He is the citizen performing the function appointed for all citizens in a civilized state, a function without which there would be no civilized state. He is Everyman purposefully apprehending the meaning of things.
— A. Whitney Griswold,
Liberal Education and the Democratic Ideal: Better Men and Better Mousetraps, 37 (1959).

It is the vice of the scholar to suppose that there is no knowledge in the world but that of books. — William Hazlitt,
Literary Remains: On the Conduct of Life (1836).

A mere scholar, who knows nothing but books, must be ignorant even of them.
— William Hazlitt,
Table-Talk: On The Ignorance of the Learned (1821–22).

The scholar digs his ivory cellar in the ruins of the past and lets the present sicken as it will. — Archibald MacLeish, *The Irresponsibles* (1940).

A man who knows a subject thoroughly, a man so soaked in it that he eats it, sleeps it and dreams it—this man can always teach it with success, no matter how little he knows of technical pedagogy.   — H.L. Mencken, *Prejudices, Third Series*, 13 (1922).

The ink of the scholar is more sacred than the blood of the martyr. — Mohammed, *Sunnah* (c.630 B.C.).

This is ever the test of the scholar: whether he allows intellectual fastidiousness to stand between him and the great issues of his time.   — John Morley, *Critical Miscellanies: Emerson* (1888).

Scholars who enter a field because of what it can do for them in career terms (rather than because of what they can do for it) often end up as members of intellectual blocs—gatekeepers insisting on tolls being paid to their fields and their preferred factors from any intellectual traffic.
                                        — David Riesman, *Constraint and Variety in American Education* (1956).

Scholars all too often move in a world as restricted as that in which their subjects lived or from which they escaped.
                                        — Alice Rossi, *The Feminist Papers*, I: *The Making of a Cosmopolitan Humanist* (1973).

He was a scholar, and a ripe and good one:
Exceeding wise, fair-spoken, and persuading;
Lofty and sour to them that lov'd him not,
But to those men that sought him sweet as summer.   — William Shakespeare, *Henry VIII*, IV.ii.51 (1612–13).

And one by one the solid scholars Get the degrees, the jobs, the dollars.
                                        — W.D. Snodgrass, *April Inventory*, ln.29 (1959).

A scholar takes precedence over a king of Israel, for if a scholar dies there is none to replace him.   — *Talmud: Horayoth*, 13a (before A.D. 500).

Scholars are wont to sell their birthright for a mess of learning.
                                        — Henry David Thoreau, *A Week on the Concord and Merrimack Rivers: Sunday* (1849).

An excellent scholar! One that hath a head filled with calves' brains without any sage in it.   — John Webster, *The White Devil*, I (1612).

It is the function of the scholar to evoke into life wisdom and beauty which, apart from his magic, would remain lost in the past.   — Alfred North Whitehead, *The Aims of Education*, vii (1929).

Scholarship

See also Research; Study

O scholar, if your scholarship affords no gain to men, you merit not admiration but contempt.   — Abu'l Ala, *Sakt al Zand (The Falling Spark of Tinder)*, no.16 (c.1000).

The ceaseless, senseless demand for original scholarship in a number of fields, where only erudition is now possible, has led either to sheer irrelevancy, the famous knowing of more and more about less and less, or the development of a pseudo-scholarship which actually destroys its object.   — Hannah Arendt, *Crises of the Republic: On Violence* (1972).

Originality is the essence of true scholarship. Creativity is the soul of the true scholar.   — Nnamdi Azikiwe, address, Lagos, Nigeria, Nov. 11, 1934.

That is the worst of erudition—that the next scholar sucks the few drops of honey that you have accumulated, sets rights your blunders, and you are superseded.
—A.C. Benson,
From a College Window (1906).

Scholars' pens carry farther, and give a louder report than thunder.
—Thomas Browne,
Religio Medici (1643).

That type of scholarship which is bent on remembering things in order to answer people's questions does not qualify one to be a teacher.   —Confucius,
in Lin Yutang, ed., *The Wisdom of China and India: The Aphorisms of Confucius*, 841 (1942).

Scholarship must be free to follow crooked paths to unexpected conclusions.
—Charles Frankel,
Time, May 14, 1979.

The history of scholarship is a record of disagreements. —Charles Evans Hughes, speech in Washington, May 7, 1936.

Scholarship is polite argument.
—Philip Rieff,
New York Herald Tribune,
Jan. 1, 1961.

School

See *also* below; Academy; High School; Schoolhouse; Schooling

I thank God there are no free schools nor printing, and I hope we shall not have these hundred years; for learning has brought disobedience and heresy and sects into the world, and printing has divulged them, and libels against the best government.... God keep us from both!   —William Berkeley,
Governor of Virginia, report to the English Committee for the Colonies, 1671.

Our schools are still set up as though every mother were at home all day and the whole family needed the summer to get the crops in.   —Sidney Callahan,
in *Reader's Digest*, Oct. 1972.

Any place that anyone young can learn something useful from someone with experience is an educational institution.
—Al Capp,
The Hardhat's Bedtime Story Book (1971).

Schools are now asked to do what people used to ask God to do.
—Jerome Cramer,
Time, June 16, 1980.

We might cease thinking of school as a place, and learn to believe that it is basically relationships between children and adults, and between children and other children. The four walls and the principal's office would cease to loom so hugely as the essential ingredients.
—George Dennison,
The Lives of Children (1969).

I believe that the school is primarily a social institution. Education being a social process, the school is simply that form of community life in which all those agencies are concentrated that will be most effective in bringing the child to share in the inherited resources of the race, and to use his own powers for social ends.   —John Dewey,
"My Pedagogic Creed," *The School Journal*, Jan. 16, 1897.

A school is a place through which you have to pass before entering life, but where the teaching proper does not prepare you for life.
—Ernest Dimnet,
The Art of Thinking, II.i.b (1928).

A school is a place or institution for teaching and learning.
Underneath this definition in every standard dictionary is another definition: School is a large number of fish of the

same kind swimming together in the same direction.   —Harry Golden,
*Ess, Ess, Mein Kindt
(Eat, Eat, My Child):
The meaning of "school"* (1966).

If there were no schools to take the children away from home part of the time, the insane asylum would be filled with mothers.   —Edgar W. Howe,
Country Town Sayings (1911).

Learned institutions ought to be favorite objects with every free people. They throw the light over the public mind which is the best security against crafty and dangerous encroachments on the public liberty.   —James Madison,
letter to W.T. Barry, Aug. 4, 1822.

Elementary teachers are appointed in each province, district and town. If a town is without an elementary school for children, its inhabitants are placed under a ban till they engage teachers for the young children. If they have failed to do so, the town is undone; for the world is maintained only by the breath of school children.   —Maimonides,
Mishneh Torah (Second Law),
I.ii.1 (1180).

What the school wants first from any child, whatever the psychologists say, is that he gets his work done—if only because children who don't work tend to employ their spare time by making mischief.   —Martin Mayer,
The Schools (1961).

They are called finishing-schools and the name tells accurately what they are. They finish everything.   —Olive Schreiner,
*The Story of an African Farm:
Lyndall* (1883).

Thou hast most traitorously corrupted the youth of the realm in erecting a grammar-school; and whereas, before, our forefathers had no other books but the score and the tally, thou hast caused printing to be used.
        —William Shakespeare,
II Henry VI, IV.vii.35 (1590–91).

Schools are prisons into which children are locked to prevent them from worrying their parents.   —George Bernard Shaw,
letter to Molly Tomkins, Feb. 19, 1931.

There is a grave defect in the school where the playground suggests happy, and the classroom disagreeable thoughts.
        —John Lancaster Spalding,
Aphorisms and Reflections (1902).

The schools of the country are its future in miniature.   —Tehyi Hsieh,
*Chinese Epigrams Inside Out
and Proverbs*, 22 (1948).

I've come to see that the real job of the school is to entice the student into the web of knowledge and then, if he's not enticed, to drag him in.
        —Mara Wolynski,
Newsweek, Aug. 30, 1976.

School, Criticism of

The school imprisons children physically, intellectually, and morally, in order to direct the development of their faculties in the paths desired. It deprives them of contact with nature, in order to model them after its own pattern.
        —Francisco Ferrer,
The Modern School (1909?).

A kind of state-supported baby-sitting service.   —Gerald Kennedy,
Time, Apr. 11, 1960.

If every day in the life of a school could be the last day but one, there would be little fault to find with it.
        —Stephen Leacock,
*College Days: Memories and
Miseries of a Schoolmaster* (1923).

Tell schools they want profoundness,
And stand too much on seeming.
        —Walter Ralegh (1552–1618),
The Lie, ln.63, in E.K. Chambers,
ed., *The Oxford Book of Sixteenth
Century Verse* (1932).

There is, on the whole, nothing on earth intended for innocent people so horrible as a school. To begin with, it is a prison. But it is in some respects more cruel than a prison. In prison, for instance, you are not forced to read books written by the warders and the governor.... In prison they may torture your body; but they do not torture your brains.
— George Bernard Shaw, *Parents and Children*, preface to *Misalliance* (1914).

It is not possible to spend any prolonged period visiting public school classrooms without being appalled by the mutilation everywhere — mutilation of spontaneity, of joy in learning, of pleasure in creating, of sense of self. — Charles E. Silberman, *Crisis in the Classroom* (1970).

The Founding Fathers ... in their wisdom decided that children were an unnatural strain on parents. So they provided jails called schools, equipped with tortures called an education. School is where you go between when your parents can't take you and industry can't take you.
— John Updike, *The Centaur*, iv (1963).

School, Financial Support for

See also Education, Financial Support for

I did not see why the schoolmaster should be taxed to support the priest, and not the priest the schoolmaster.
— Henry David Thoreau, *Resistance to Civil Government* (1849).

When I was a boy on the Mississippi River there was a proposition in a township there to discontinue public schools because they were too expensive. An old farmer spoke up and said if they stopped the schools they would not save anything, because every time a school was closed a jail had to be built.   — Mark Twain, address to Public Education Association, New York, Nov. 23, 1900, in Albert Bigelow Paine, ed., *Mark Twain's Speeches*, 212 (1923).

School, Function of

The school's obligation is to follow established principles and to uphold warranted knowledge as against the views commonly held in the marketplace. The competition is between scientific and critical beliefs, on the one hand, and popular emotional beliefs, on the other.
— I.B. Berkson, *The Ideal and the Community* (1958).

The school, from the present point of view, is simply a place which is specially designed to facilitate the business of securing the desired transformation of experience. It is a place where new experiences are provided in such form as to best promote that reconstruction or reorganization of experience which is identified with education.
— Boyd H. Bode, *How We Learn*, 245 (1940).

I believe that the school must present life — life as real and vital to the child as that which he carries on in the home, in the neighborhood, or on the playground.
— John Dewey, "My Pedagogic Creed," *The School Journal*, Jan. 16, 1897.

Educators can no longer assume that somebody else will do the educational job for them. With everybody going to school till adulthood, school has become the place for learning whatever one needs in order to be both human being and effective.   — Peter F. Drucker, *The Age of Discontinuity*, IV.xiv (1968).

School, Importance of

The classroom and teacher occupy the most important part, the most important position of the human fabric.... In the schoolhouse we have the heart of the whole society.   — Harry Golden, *So Long as You're Healthy: Teachers' revolution* (1970).

We can get along without burgomasters, princes, and noblemen, but we can't do without schools, for they must rule the world.   —Martin Luther,
                    Table Talk, 5247 (1566).

School, Public

The common schools bind together the people as they never can be bound together by exterior appliances. The nation must be held together by elective affinity, or else it will be disintegrated and scattered.   —Henry Ward Beecher,
                    Proverbs from Plymouth Pulpit: Political (1887).

The child learns more of the virtues needed in modern life—of fairness, of justice, of comradeship, of collective interest and action—in a common school than he can be taught in the most perfect family circle.   —Charlotte Perkins Gilman,
                    Women and Economics, xiii (1898).

Two institutions turned millions of immigrants into Americans within a single generation—the greatest miracle of human relations in the past century. These two institutions were the free public school and the free public library.
                    —Harry Golden,
                    So Long as You're Healthy: The library (1970).

The Common School is the greatest discovery ever made by man.
                    —Horace Mann,
                    inscription beneath his bust in the Hall of Fame.

The Public School is the chief vehicle for mutual love, forgiveness, and tolerance between races, classes, and creeds; it becomes an act of vandalism to attack it and an act of piety to work towards its improvement.   —Agnes Myer,
                    address to American Unitarian Association, 1954.

School Board

In the first place God made idiots. This was for practice. Then He made School Boards.   —Mark Twain,
                    Pudd'nhead Wilson's New Calendar,
                    II.xxv (1897). He made a similar observation about proofreaders,
                    Notebook, Sept. 29, 1893 (1935).

Schoolboy

See also Student

But to go to school in a summer morn,
O! it drives all joy away;
Under a cruel eye outworn,
The little ones spend the day
In sighing and dismay.—William Blake,
                    The Schoolboy, ii (c.1790).

The art of getting on at school depends on a mixture of enthusiasm with moral cowardice and social sense. The enthusiasm is for personalities and gossip about them, for a schoolboy is a novelist too busy to write.   —Cyril Connolly,
                    Enemies of Promise, xxi (1938).

I pay the schoolmaster, but 't is the schoolboys that educate my son.
                    —Ralph Waldo Emerson,
                    Journals, 1849.

They [British public schoolboys] go forth into it [the world] with well-developed bodies, fairly developed minds and underdeveloped hearts. An underdeveloped heart—not a cold one. The difference is important.   —E.M. Forster,
                    Abinger Harvest: Notes on the English Character (1936).

'Twas in the prime of summer time,
    An evening calm and cool,
And four-and-twenty happy boys
    Came bounding out of school.
                    —Thomas Hood,
                    The Dream of Eugene Aram,
                    i (1829).

Schoolboys are the reasonablest people in the world; they care not how little they have for their money.   —John Ray, *English Proverbs*, 81 (1670).

Schoolboys have no fear of facing life. They champ at the bit. The jealousies, the trials, the sorrows of the life of man do not intimidate the schoolboy.
      — Antoine de Saint-Exupéry, *Flight to Arras*, i (1942).

And then the whining schoolboy with his satchel
And shining morning face, creeping like snail
Unwillingly to school.
      —William Shakespeare, *As You Like It*, II.vii.145 (1600).

Schooldays

Some people say that their school days were the happiest of their lives. They may be right, but I always look with suspicion upon those whom I hear saying this.
      —Samuel Butler (1835–1902), *The Way of All Flesh*, xlv (1903).

School days, I believe, are the unhappiest in the whole span of human existence. They are full of dull, unintelligible tasks, new and unpleasant ordinances, brutal violations of common sense and common decency.   —H.L. Mencken, "Travail," *The Baltimore Evening Sun*, Oct. 8, 1928.

Show me the man who has enjoyed his schooldays and I will show you a bully and a bore.   —Robert Morley, *Robert Morley: Responsible Gentleman* (1966).

No one can look back on his schooldays and say with truth that they were altogether unhappy.   —George Orwell, *A Collection of Essays* (1970).

Schoolgirl

See also Student

Three little maids from school are we,
Pert as a school-girl well can be,
Filled to the brim with girlish glee,
Three little maids from school!
      —W.S. Gilbert, *The Mikado*, I (1885).

Schoolgirls we, eighteen and under,
From scholastic trammels free,
And we wonder—how we wonder!—
What on earth the world can be!
      —W.S. Gilbert, *ibid.*

Schoolhouse

This school was on top of a hill so that God could see everything that went on. It looked like a cross between a prison and a church and it was.   —Quentin Crisp, *The Naked Civil Servant*, ii (1966).

Beside yon straggling fence that skirts the way,
With blossom'd furze unprofitably gay,
There, in his noisy mansion, skill'd to rule,
The village master taught his little school.   —Oliver Goldsmith, *The Deserted Village*, ln.193 (1770).

No greater nor more affectionate honor can be conferred on an American than to have a public school named after him.
      —Herbert Hoover, at dedication of Herbert Hoover Junior High School, San Francisco, June 5, 1956.

The most significant fact in this world today is, that in nearly every village under the American flag, the school-house is larger than the church.
      —Robert G. Ingersoll, speech, Dec. 13, 1886.

In a green lane that from the village street
Diverges, stands the school-house; long
    and low
The frame, and blackened with the hues
    of Time.
Around it spreads the green with scat-
    tered trees;
Fenced fields and orchards stretching
    either hand,
And fronting.   — Alfred B. Street,
    The School-House, ln.1 (c.1886).

Within, the master's desk is seen,
    Deep scarred by raps official;
The warping floor, the battered seats,
    The jack-knife's carved initial.
                — John Greenleaf Whittier,
                In School-Days, ii (1870).

Schooling

See also Education; Instruction;
Learning; School

The chief wonder of education is that it
does not ruin everybody concerned in it,
teachers and taught. — Henry Adams,
    The Education of Henry Adams,
                iv (1907).

I'm forced to admit,
With some hesitation,
All I got out of school
Was an education.   — Richard Armour,
    A Diabolical Dictionary of Education,
                106 (1969).

What's a' your jargon o' your Schools,
Your Latin names for horns an' stools?
If honest Nature made you fools,
    What sairs your grammars?
Ye'd better ta'en up spades and shools,
    Or knappin'-hammers.
                — Robert Burns,
        Epistle to John Lapraik,
    ln.61 (1786) [sairs = *serves*; shools =
    shovels; knappin'-hammers = *hammers*
                for breaking stones].

Certainly the prolonged education indispensable to the progress of society is
not natural to mankind.
                — Winston Churchill,
                My Early Life, iii (1930).

The things taught in colleges and schools
are not an education, but the means of
education.   — Ralph Waldo Emerson,
                Journals, 1831.

We are students of words: we are shut up
in schools, and colleges, and recitation-
rooms, for ten or fifteen years, and come
out at last with a bag of wind, and a
memory of words, and do not know a
thing.   — Ralph Waldo Emerson,
        ibid., Sept. 14, 1839; also *Essays,*
    Second Series: New England Reformers
                (1844).

We don't educate our children at school;
we stultify them and then send them out
into the world half-baked. And why?
Because we keep them utterly ignorant of
real life. The common experience is
something they never see or hear.
                — Petronius,
        Satyricon, i.3 (c. A.D. 60).

And all the incoherent Jargon of the
Schools ... Contrive to chock your Minds,
with many a senseless doubt.
                — Jonathan Swift,
        Ode to the Athenian Society,
                ln.205 (1692).

Schoolmate

One of the problems of child education
which is not generally included in books
on the subject is the Visiting Schoolmate.
By this is meant the little friend whom
your child brings home for the holidays.
What is to be done with him, the Law
reading as it does? — Robert Benchley,
    The Stranger Within Our Gates,
        in *The Benchley Roundup*, ed.
        Nathaniel Benchley (1954).

Science

Science

See also below; Scientist

Science increases our power in proportion as it lowers our pride.
— Claude Bernard,
Introduction to the Study of Experimental Medicine (1865).

Science equips man, but does not guide him. It illumines the world for him to the region of the most distant stars, but it leaves night in his heart. It is invincible, but indifferent, neutral, unmoral.
— James Darmsteter,
Selected Essays, 6 (1895).

Putting on the spectacles of science in expectation of finding the answer to everything looked at signifies inner blindness.
— J. Frank Dobie,
The Voice of the Coyote, introd. (1949).

Every science begins as philosophy and ends as art.
— Will Durant,
The Story of Philosophy (1926).

Science is a first-rate piece of furniture for a man's upper-chamber, if he has common-sense on the ground floor.
— Oliver Wendell Holmes, Sr.,
The Poet at the Breakfast-Table, v (1872).

To a person uninstructed in natural history, his country or sea-side stroll is a walk through a gallery filled with wonderful works of art, nine-tenths of which have their faces turned to the wall.
— T.H. Huxley,
Lay Sermons, Essays, and Reviews: On the Educational Value of the Natural History Sciences (1870).

Addressing myself to you, as teachers, I would say, mere book learning in physical science is a sham and a delusion — what you teach, unless you wish to be impostors, that you must first know; and real knowledge in science means personal acquaintance with the facts, be they few or many.
— T.H. Huxley,
ibid.: On the Study of Zoology.

I often wish that this phrase, "applied science," had never been invented. For it suggests that there is a sort of scientific knowledge of direct practical use, which can be studied apart from another sort of scientific knowledge, which is of no practical utility, and which is termed "pure science." But there is no more complete fallacy than this.
— T.H. Huxley,
Science and Culture (1881).

Every science has been an outcast.
— Robert G. Ingersoll,
The Liberty of Man, Woman and Child (1877).

Science, like life, feeds on its own decay. New facts burst old rules; then newly divined conceptions bind old and new together into a reconciling law.
— William James,
The Will to Believe (1897).

Science should leave off making pronouncements: the river of knowledge has too often turned back on itself.
— James Jeans,
The Mysterious Universe, v (1931).

Science arises from the discovery of identity amidst diversity.
— W.S. Jevons,
The Principles of Science (1874).

The world of poetry, mythology, and religion represents the world as man would like to have it, while science represents the world as he gradually comes to discover it.
— Joseph Wood Krutch,
The Modern Temper (1929).

Science has promised us truth — an understanding of such relationships as our minds can grasp; it has never promised us either peace or happiness.
— Gustave Le Bon,
La Psychologie des Foules, introd. (1895).

Science, at bottom, is really anti-intellectual. It always distrusts pure reason, and demands the production of objective fact.   —H.L. Mencken,
Minority Report: Notebooks,
no.412 (1956).

The scientific spirit requires a man to be at all times ready to dump his whole cartload of beliefs, the moment experience is against them.
—Charles S. Peirce,
Philosophical Writings of Peirce,
ed. Justus Buchler, 46 (1955).

Traditional scientific method has always been at the very *best*, 20-20 hindsight. It's good for seeing where you've been.
—Robert M. Pirsig,
Zen and the Art of Motorcycle Maintenance, III.xxiv (1974).

We realize the absurdity of applying science to artistic or moral subjects if we try to speak of half a pound of beauty or two inches of courage.
—Arthur F. Smethurst, *Modern Science and Christian Beliefs* (1955).

Science is the great antidote of the poison of enthusiasm and superstition.
—Adam Smith,
The Wealth of Nations (1776).

Science has its being in a perpetual mental restlessness.   —William Temple
(1881–1944), *Essays and Studies by Members of the English Association*,
xvii (1932).

True science teaches, above all, to doubt, and to be ignorant.
—Miguel de Unamuno,
The Tragic Sense of Life,
v (1912).

Science, Aim and Function of

All science has one aim, namely, to find a theory of nature.
—Ralph Waldo Emerson,
Nature (1836).

Science has fulfilled her function when she has ascertained and enunciated truth.
—T.H. Huxley,
Man's Place in Nature,
ii (1863).

Though many have tried, no one has ever yet explained away the decisive fact that science, which can do so much, cannot decide what it ought to do.
—Joseph Wood Krutch,
*The Measure of the Man:
The Loss of Confidence* (1954).

The work of science is to substitute facts for appearances, and demonstrations for impressions.   —John Ruskin,
The Stones of Venice, iii (1851).

The task of science is to stake out the limits of the knowable, and to center consciousness within them.
—Rudolf Virchow,
Cellular Pathology (1858).

The aim of science is to seek the simplest explanation of complex facts. We are apt to fall into the error of thinking the facts are simple because simplicity is the goal of our quest. The guiding motto in the life of every natural philosopher should be, "Seek simplicity and distrust it."
—Alfred North Whitehead,
The Concept of Nature, 163 (1920).

Science, Definition and Description of

Science is a mode of conceiving universal and necessary truths.   —Aristotle,
Nicomachean Ethics, VI.vi.1
(before 322 B.C.).

By "scientific" is meant methods of control of formation of judgments.
—John Dewey,
Logical Conditions of a Scientific Treatment of Morality, in Reginald D. Archambault, *John Dewey on Education* (1964).

Science is the attempt to make the chaotic diversity of our sense-experience correspond to a logically uniform system of thought.   — Albert Einstein, *Out of My Later Years* (1950).

The whole of science is nothing more than a refinement of everyday thinking.   — Albert Einstein, *ibid.*, xiii: *Physics and Reality*.

Science is an imaginative adventure of the mind seeking truth in a world of mystery.   — Cyril Hinshelwood, address to Science Masters' Association, Oxford, England, 1953.

Equipped with his five senses, man explores the universe around him and calls the adventure Science.
    — Edwin Powell Hubble, *The Nature of Science* (1954).

Science is, I believe, nothing but *trained and organized common sense*, differing from the latter only as a veteran may differ from a raw recruit: and its methods differ from those of common sense only so far as the guardsman's cut and thrust differ from the manner in which a savage wields his club.   — T.H. Huxley, *Lay Sermons, Addresses, and Reviews: On the Educational Value of the Natural History Sciences* (1870).

Science is nothing but developed perception, interpreted intent, common sense rounded out and minutely articulated.
    — George Santayana, *The Life of Reason*, V: *Reason in Science* (1905–06).

Science is organised knowledge.
    — Herbert Spencer, *Education*, ii (1861).

Science, when well digested, is nothing but good sense and sound reason.
    — Stanislas I, King of Poland, *Oeuvres de Philosophe Bienfaisant* (1767).

The term *Science* should not be given to anything but *the aggregate of the recipes that are always successful*. All the rest is *literature*.   — Paul Valéry, *Moralités*, 41 (1932).

Science is the organisation of thought.
    — Alfred North Whitehead, *The Aims of Education*, viii (1929).

Science is the effort to find out what to do with the universe and what to do in the universe.   — Albert Edward Wiggam, *The New Decalogue of Science*, 115 (1923).

Science, Limitation of

Science can only ascertain what *is*, but not what *should be*, and outside of its domain value judgments of all kinds remain necessary.   — Albert Einstein, *Out of My Later Years*, viii: *Science and Religion* (1950).

Science, in the very act of solving problems, creates more of them.
    — Abraham Flexner, *Universities*, 19 (1930).

Existing scientific concepts cover always only a very limited part of reality.
    — Werner Heisenberg, *Physics and Philosophy* (1958).

Thou canst not tell where one drop of water or one grain of sand will be tomorrow noon; and yet with thy impotence thou insultest the sun! Science! Curse thee, thou vain toy. — Herman Melville, *Moby Dick* (1851).

Science will never be able to reduce the value of a sunset to arithmetic. Nor can it reduce friendship to a formula. Laughter and love, pain and loneliness, the challenge of accomplishment in living, and the depth of insight into beauty and truth: these will always surpass the scientific mastery of nature.   — Louis Orr, presidential address to the American Medical Association, June 6, 1960.

Science and Religion

To pursue science is not to disparage the things of the spirit. In fact, to pursue science rightly is to furnish a framework on which the spirit may rise.
— Vannevar Bush,
speech, Massachusetts Institute of Technology, Oct. 5, 1953.

Science without religion is lame, religion without science is blind.   — Albert Einstein, *Out of My Later Years,* viii: *Science and Religion*, II (1950).

The pursuit of science in itself is never materialistic. It is a search for the principles of law and order in the universe, and as such an essentially religious endeavor.   — Arthur Koestler, *Arrow in the Blue*, 52 (1952).

The thesis that there is an inherent conflict between science and our immortal souls is simply untrue.... Virtue does not of necessity go hand in hand with primitive plumbing, and nobility can be found in a skyscraper no less than in a log-cabin.
— David Sarnoff,
Youth in a Changing World,
June 12, 1954.

Scientist

See also Science

One may eat potatoes for forty years, yet that won't make one a botanist!
— Shemarya Levin,
at Zionist Congress, 1929.

The improver of natural knowledge absolutely refuses to acknowledge authority, as such. For him, scepticism is the highest of duties; blind faith the one unpardonable sin.   — T.H. Huxley, *Lay Sermons, Addresses, and Reviews: On the Advisableness of Improving Natural Knowledge* (1870).

Peeping Toms at the keyhole of eternity.
— Arthur Koestler,
The Roots of Coincidence (1972).

It is the proper role of the scientist that he not merely find new truth and communicate it to his fellows, but that he teach, that he try to bring the most honest and intelligible account of new knowledge to all who will try to learn.
— J. Robert Oppenheimer,
address at Columbia University, 1954.

Science rests itself not in the *world* the scientist beholds at any particular point in time, but in his mode of *viewing* that world. A man is a scientist not because of what he sees, but because of *how* he sees it.   — Theodore Roszak, *The Making of a Counter Culture* (1969).

Security, Sense of

It is difficult to give children a sense of security unless you have it yourself. If you have it, they catch it from you.
— William C. Menninger,
Self-Understanding (1951).

Seeing

See also Observation

The ear tends to be lazy, craves the familiar and is shocked by the unexpected; the eye, on the other hand, tends to be impatient, craves the novel and is bored by repetition.   — W.H. Auden, *The Dyer's Hand* (1962).

That which one sees, one learns.
— Selwyn Gurney Champion,
Racial Proverbs, 16 (1938).
A Basque proverb.

"I heard" is not as good as "I saw."
— Justus Doolittle, *A Vocabulary and Hand-Book of the Chinese Language*, ii. 280 (1872).

Segregation (Racial)

The chief sin of segregation is the distortion of human personality. It damages the soul of both the segregator and the segregated. —Benjamin E. Mays, *The Segregation Decisions* (1956).

To separate them from others of similar age and qualifications solely because of their race generates a feeling of inferiority ... that may affect their hearts and minds in a way unlikely ever to be undone.... We conclude that in the field of public education the doctrine of "separate but equal" has no place. Separate educational facilities are inherently unequal.
 —Earl Warren, unanimous U.S. Supreme Court decision, *Brown v Board of Education of Topeka*, May 17, 1954.

Self-Appraisal

See also Self-Knowledge

Seriously to contemplate one's abject personal triteness is probably the most painful act a man can perform.
 —Robert M. Adams, *Bad Mouth* (1977).

Self-Discipline

For an interest to be rewarding, one must pay in discipline and dedication, especially through the difficult or boring stages which are inevitably encountered.
 —Mirra Komarovsky, *Women in the Modern World*, iv (1953).

I hold that the only discipline, important for its own sake, is self-discipline, and that this can only be acquired by a wide use of freedom.
 —Alfred North Whitehead, *The Aims of Education*, iii (1929).

Self-Education

The only really educated men are self-educated. —Jesse Lee Bennett, *On Culture and a Liberal Education* (1922).

Every man who rises above the common level has received two educations: the first from his teachers; the second, more personal and important, from himself.
 —Edward Gibbon, *Memoirs of His Life and Writings* (1796).

Learn to know yourself to the end that you may improve your powers, your conduct, your character. This is the true aim of education and the best of all education is self-education. —Rutherford B. Hayes, *Diary*, Oct. 4, 1892.

Very few men are wise by their own counsel; or learned by their own teaching. For he that was only taught by himself, had a fool to his master.
 —Ben Jonson, *Explorata: Consilia* (1641).

The better part of every man's education is that which he gives himself.
 —James Russell Lowell, *My Study Windows: Abraham Lincoln* (1871).

A whaleship was my Yale College and my Harvard. —Herman Melville, *Moby Dick*, xxiv (1851).

Self-education is fine when the pupil is a born educator. —John A. Shedd, *Salt from My Attic*, 28 (1928).

Self-Esteem

Identity. Finding out who you are. This is difficult for your children who do not have credit cards, a Social Security number, or even a driver's license.
 —Richard Armour, *A Diabolical Dictionary of Education* (1969).

Our culture impedes the clear definition of any faithful self-image—indeed, of any clear image whatever. We do not break images; there are few iconoclasts among us. Instead, we blur and soften them. —Edgar Z. Friedenberg, *The Vanishing Adolescent: The Vanishing Adolescent* (1959).

One of the most important things a teacher can do is to send a pupil home in the afternoon liking himself just a little better than when he came in the morning.   —Ernest Melby, in Eda LeShan, *The Conspiracy Against Childhood*, vi (1967).

Think of yourself as you wish others to think of you.   —Dagobert D. Runes, *Treasury of Thought*, 329 (1966).

As the internal-combustion engine runs on gasoline, so the person runs on self-esteem: if he is full of it, he is good for a long run; if he is partly filled, he will soon need to be refueled; and if he is empty, he will come to a stop.
        —Thomas Szasz, *The Second Sin: Personal Conduct* (1973).

Public opinion is a weak tyrant compared with our own private opinion. What a man thinks of himself, that it is which determines, or rather indicates, his fate.
        —Henry David Thoreau, *Walden*, i: *Economy* (1854).

And, above all, never think that you're not good enough yourself. A man should never think that. My belief is that in life people will take you very much at your own reckoning.   —Anthony Trollope, *The Small House at Allington*, xxxii (1864).

Self-Knowledge

See also Self-Appraisal

O wad some Power the giftie gie us
To see oursels as ithers see us!
It wad frae monie a blunder free us,
    An' foolish notion.   —Robert Burns, *To a Louse*, viii (1785) [giftie = *gift*].

At nineteen I was a stranger to myself. At forty I asked: Who am I? At fifty I concluded I would never know.
    —Edward Dahlberg, *The Confessions of Edward Dahlberg* (1971).

It is not enough to understand what we ought to be, unless we know what we are; and we do not understand what we are, unless we know what we ought to be.
        —T.S. Eliot, *Religion and Literature* (1935).

We can see through others only when we see through ourselves.   —Eric Hoffer, *The Passionate State of Mind*, no.158 (1954).

Knowing others is wisdom.
Knowing the self is enlightenment.
    —Lao-tse, *Tao Te Ching*, sec.33 (c.550 B.C.), tr. Gia-Fu Feng and Jane English.

And all our Knowledge is, OURSELVES TO KNOW.   —Alexander Pope, *An Essay on Man*, concluding line, IV.396 (1734).

When you want to recognize and understand what takes place in the minds of others, you have first to look into yourself.   —Theodor Reik, *Listening with the Third Ear* (1948).

It is much more difficult to judge oneself than to judge others.
        —Antoine de Saint-Exupéry, *The Little Prince*, x (1943).

Ah, heavily weighs death on him
Who, known to others all too well,
Dies to himself unknown.   —Seneca, *Thyestes*, ln.401 (before A.D. 65).

Know thyself.
    —Inscription on the temple to Apollo at Delphi, ascribed to Solon, Pythagorus, or Chilon of Thales (c.6th cent. B.C.).

Self-Reliance

Every man must scratch his head with his own nails.   —Arab proverb.

No bird soars too high if he soars with his own wings.   —William Blake, *The Marriage of Heaven and Hell: Proverbs of Hell* (1790).

The first thing that education teaches you is to walk alone.   —A.A. Horn, *Trader Horn* (1927).

And don't consult anyone's opinions but your own.   —Persius (A.D. 34–62), *Satires*, i.7.

Whate'er your lot may be, Paddle your own canoe.   —Edward P. Philpots, *Paddle Your Own Canoe* (1854).

Senses

The eye, which is called the window of the soul, is the chief means whereby the understanding may most fully and abundantly appreciate the infinite works of Nature; and the ear is second, inasmuch as it acquires its importance from the fact that it hears the things which the eye has seen.   —Leonardo da Vinci, *Notebooks* (c.1500).

Sense-impression of Nature is the only true foundation of human instruction, because it is the only true foundation of human knowledge.   —Johann Pestalozzi, report in 1800 to a Society of Friends of Education, published as *The Method* (1828).

Severity

See *also* Child Rearing; Discipline; Punishment

I would never follow those austere maxims which cause children to count the days of their fathers.   —Molière, *The School for Husbands*, I.ii (1661).

Nothing comes of severity if there be no leanings towards a change of heart. And if there be natural leanings towards a change of heart, what need for severity?   —Antoine de Saint-Exupéry, *The Wisdom of the Sands*, xliii (1950).

Sex

See *also* below

One of the unwritten laws of contemporary morality, the strictest and best respected of all requires adults to avoid any reference, above all any humorous reference, to sexual matters in the presence of children. This notion was entirely foreign to the society of old.   —Philippe Ariès, *Centuries of Childhood* (1960).

The effort to inhibit all sex curiosity and pleasure in the child is quite useless; one succeeds only in creating repressions, obsessions, neuroses.   —Simone de Beauvoir, *The Second Sex* (1953).

Sex Differences

This is a boy, sir. Not a girl. If you're baffled by the difference it might be as well to approach both with caution.   —Joe Orton, *What the Butler Saw*, II (1969).

As to the qualities of mind peculiar to each sex, I agree with you that sprightliness is in favor of females and profundity of males. Their education, their pursuits would create such a quality even tho' nature has not implanted it.   —Eliza Southgate, *Letters from Eliza Southgate to Her Cousin Moses Porter*, in Nancy F. Cott, ed., *Root of Bitterness* (1972).

Sex Discrimination

No person in the United States shall, on the basis of sex, be excluded from participation in, be denied the benefits of, or be subjected to discrimination under any educational program or activity receiving federal financial assistance.
— Title IX of the Education Amendments of 1972.

Sex Education

Far too common is the error of those who with dangerous assurance ... propagate a so-called sex-education, falsely imagining they can forearm youth against the dangers of sensuality by means purely natural.   — Pope Pius XI, *On the Christian Education of Youth*, Dec. 31, 1929.

There is nothing more damaging to adequate sex instruction than timidity, shame, embarrassment, or a general hyper-emotionalism regarding matters of sex. The attitude that sex is shameful, disgusting, immoral, and so on, makes it *impossible* for anyone to deal adequately with the problem.
— Alexander A. Schneiders, *The Child and Problems of Today* (1952).

Silence

God has given to man a cloak whereby he can conceal his ignorance, and in this cloak he can enwrap himself at any moment, for it always lies near at hand. This cloak is silence.   — Bhartrihari, *The Niti Sataka* (c.625).

Teach your child to hold his tongue, he'll learn fast enough to speak.
— Benjamin Franklin, *Poor Richard's Almanack*, July 1734.

'Tis easier to know how to speak than how to be silent.   — Thomas Fuller (1654– 1734), *Gnomologia*, no.5075 (1732).

Sometimes you have to be silent to be heard.   — Stanislaw J. Lec, *Unkempt Thoughts*, tr. Jacek Galazka (1962).

Better to remain silent and be thought a fool than to speak out and remove all doubt.   — Abraham Lincoln, *Golden Book*, Nov. 1931.

The perversion of the mind is only possible when those who should be heard in its defense are silent.
— Archibald MacLeish, *The Irresponsibles* (1940).

I regret often that I have spoken; never that I have been silent.
— Publilius Syrus, *Sententiae* (c.43 B.C.).

The world would be happier if men had the same capacity to be silent that they have to speak.   — Baruch Spinoza, *Ethics*, II (1677).

Simplicity

It is not at all simple to understand the simple.   — Eric Hoffer, *The Passionate State of Mind*, no.230 (1954).

There often comes a meaning home
    Through simple verse and plain,
While in the heavy, bulky tome
    We find of truth no grain.
— Santob de Carrion, *Proverbios Morales* (c.1355–60).

The art of art, the glory of expression and the sunshine of the light of letters is simplicity. Nothing is better than simplicity ... nothing can make up for excess or for the lack of definiteness.
— Walt Whitman, *Leaves of Grass*, preface to 1855 edition.

Skeptic

See also Skepticism

A scoffer seeks wisdom in vain, but knowledge is easy for a man of understanding.   — *Bible: Proverbs* 14:6.

I am too much of a sceptic to deny the possibility of anything. — T.H. Huxley, letter to Herbert Spencer, Mar. 22, 1886.

Seek wisdom from sceptics.
          — Solomon Ibn Gabirol, *Choice of Pearls*, no.49 (c.1050).

Skeptic always rhymes with septic; the spirit died of intellectual poisoning.
          — Franz Werfel, *Realism and Inwardness* (1930).

Skepticism

See also Cynicism; Doubt; Skeptic

What has not been examined impartially has not been well examined. Skepticism is therefore the first step toward truth.
          — Denis Diderot, *Pensées Philosophiques*, 31 (1746).

The civilized man has a moral obligation to be skeptical, to demand the credentials of all statements that claim to be facts.
          — Bergen Evans, *The Natural History of Nonsense*, xix (1946).

A wise scepticism is the first attribute of a good critic.   — James Russell Lowell, *Among My Books: Shakespeare Once More* (1870).

What do I know? What does it matter? (Que sais-je? Qu'importe?)
          — Michel de Montaigne (1533–92), motto on his seal.

The path to sound credence is through the thick forest of skepticism.
          — George Jean Nathan, *Materia Critica*, 5 (1924).

Scepticism, riddling the faith of yesterday, prepares the way for the faith of tomorrow.   — Romain Rolland, *Jean Christophe* (1904–12).

Scepticism is the chastity of the intellect.
          — George Santayana, *Scepticism and Animal Faith* (1923).

Skill

See also Ability; Competence; Talent

Let each man exercise the art he knows.
          — Aristophanes, *The Wasps*, ln.1431 (422 B.C.).

Skilled hands eat trout.
          — Henry Davidoff, *A World Treasury of Proverbs* (1946).

Learne thou an art, and lay it aside, for tyme will come thou shalt haue neede of it.   — John Florio, *Firste Fruites*, fo.31 (1578).

Skill is a superb and necessary instrument but it functions at its highest level only when it is guided by a mature mind and an exalted spirit.
          — Richard H. Guggenheimer, *Creative Vision*, 107 (1950).

Where there is the necessary technical skill to move mountains, there is no need for the faith that moves mountains.
          — Eric Hoffer, *The Passionate State of Mind*, no.12 (1954).

Skill without imagination is craftsmanship and gives us many useful objects such as wickerwork picnic baskets. Imagination without skill gives us modern art.   — Tom Stoppard, *Artist Descending a Staircase* (1973).

Slang

See also Jargon; Language

Slang is a conventional tongue with many dialects, which are as a rule unintelligible to outsiders.   —Albert Barrère,
A Dictionary of Slang, Jargon and Cant, preface (1889).

Slang has no country, it owns the world .... It is the voice of the god that dwells in the people.   —Raley Husted Bell,
The Mystery of Words (1924).

All slang is metaphor, and all metaphor is poetry.   —G.K. Chesterton,
The Defendant: A Defence of Slang (1901).

Correct English is the slang of prigs who write history and essays. And the strongest of all is the slang of poets.
—George Eliot,
Middlemarch, ii (1872).

The language of the street is always strong. What can describe the folly and emptiness of scolding like the word *jawing?*   —Ralph Waldo Emerson,
Journals, 1840.

Slang is ... vigorous and apt. Probably most of our vital words were once slang; one by one timidly made sacrosanct in spite of ecclesiastical and other wraths.
—John Galsworthy,
Castles in Spain and Other Screeds (1927).

Slang is a poor-man's poetry.
—John Moore,
You Englsh Words (1961).

Slang, profoundly consider'd, is the lawless germinal element, below all words and sentences, and behind all poetry, and proves a certain perennial rankness and protestantism in speech.
—Walt Whitman, *November Boughs: Slang in America* (1888).

Slang ... is the wholesome fermentation or eructation of those processes eternally active in language, by which froth and specks are thrown up, mostly to pass away; though occasionally to settle and permanently chrystallize.
—Walt Whitman, *ibid.*

Snobbery

In the old days snobs constituted an aristocracy of taste.... But now there is a new phenomenon: mass snobbism. People buy paper backs exactly as they buy sardines. They have 2,000 books at home and they've read none of them.
—Jean Cau, in Israel Shenker,
Words and Their Masters,
37 (1974).

What intellectual snobs we have become! Virtue is now in the number of degrees you have—not in the kind of person you are or what you can accomplish in real-life situations.   —Eda J. LeShan,
The Conspiracy Against Childhood,
viii (1967).

Your learning's made you a snob.
—Petronius,
Satyricon, v.44 (c. A.D. 60).

We educate one another; and we cannot do this if half of us consider the other half not good enough to talk to.
—George Bernard Shaw,
The Intelligent Woman's Guide to Socialism and Capitalism,
lxxxi (1928).

Social Class

The association only with men of one's own class, such as the organization of college life today fosters, is simply fatal to any broad understanding of life. The refusal to make the acquaintance while in college of as many as possible original, self-dependent personalities, regardless of race and social status, is morally suicidal.   —Randolph Bourne,
Youth and Life (1913).

In teaching there should be no class distinctions.   — Confucius, *Analects*, XV.xxxviii (c.500 B.C.).

Sociologist

Those academic accountants who think that truth can be shaken from an abacus.
— Peter S. Prescott,
Newsweek, Apr. 14, 1972.

Sociology

The illumination of experience.
— Paul Starr,
New York Times, Oct. 31, 1976.

Son

Not by chance are son and book named in Latin by the same word, *liber*.
— Joseph Solomon Delmedigo,
Notes of Wisdom (1631).

Your son at five is your master, at ten your slave, at fifteen your double, and after that, your friend or foe, depending on his bringing up. — Abraham Hasdai,
Ben HaMelek VeHaNazir, vii (1230).

I taught thee sounds and words and soothed thy complainings and thy hidden hurts, and as thou didst crawl on the ground, I stooped and lifted thee to my kisses, and lovingly on my bosom lulled to sleep thy drooping eyes, and bade sweet slumber take thee. — P.P. Statius,
lament for his son, *Silvae*,
V.v.81 (before A.D. 96).

What is the duty of the son to his father? It is to make the world ask, "For what austerities of his faith has he been blessed with such a son?"   — Tiruvalluvar,
Kural, vii (c.100 B.C.–A.D. 300).

Specialist

See also Expert

To have one favourite study and live in it with happy familiarity, and cultivate every portion of it diligently and lovingly, as a small yeoman proprietor cultivates his own land, this, as to study at least, is the most enviable intellectual life.
— Philip G. Hamerton,
The Intellectual Life (1873).

Do not be bullied out of your common sense by the specialist; two to one, he is a pedant. — Oliver Wendell Holmes, Sr.,
Over the Teacups, vii (1891).

Wherever learning breeds specialists, the sum of human culture is enhanced thereby. That is the illusion and consolation of specialists. — Antonio Machado,
Juan de Mairena, i (1943).

The incessant concentration of thought upon one subject, however interesting, tethers a man's mind in a narrow field.
— William Osler,
Aphorisms from His Bedside Teachings and Writings, ed.
William Bennet Bean (1950).

The specialist who is trained but uneducated, technically skilled but culturally incompetent, is a menace.
— David B. Truman,
address in Chicago to Columbia University alumni, Apr. 15, 1964.

Speech

See also Eloquence; Oratory; Voice

One may have a right to speak, but that does not mean that he is right when he speaks.   — Charles L. Aarons,
The Lawyer Out of Court,
Oct. 23, 1950.

To speak as the common people do, to think as wise men do. —Roger Ascham, *Taxophilus: Dedication to All the Gentlemen and Yeomen of England* (1545).

It is not enough to know *what* we ought to say; we must also say it *as* we ought. —Aristotle, *Rhetoric*, III.i.2 (before 322 B.C.).

If you in a tongue utter speech that is not intelligible, how will any one know what is said. For you will be speaking into the air. —*Bible: I Corinthians* 14:9.

Deliver your words not by number but by weight. —H.G. Bohn, *Handbook of Proverbs*, 343 (1855).

If a thing goes without saying, let it. —Jacob M. Braude, *Treasury of Wit and Humor* (1964).

One never repents of having spoken too little, but often of having spoken too much. —Philippe de Commynes, *Memoires*, I.xiv (1524).

Let thy speech be better than silence, or be silent. —Dionysius the Elder, extant fragment (4th cent. B.C.).

Blessed is the man who, having nothing to say, abstains from giving us wordy evidence of the fact. —George Eliot, *The Impressions of Theophrastus Such*, iv (1879).

The true use of speech is not so much to express our wants as to conceal them. —Oliver Goldsmith, *The Bee* (1759).

Speak clearly, if you speak at all; Carve every word before you let it fall.... And when you stick on conversation's burrs, Don't strew your pathway with those dreadful *urs*. —Oliver Wendell Holmes, Sr., *A Rhymed Lesson*, ln.408 (1846).

The PROFESSOR, whose scholastic phrase At every turn the teacher's tongue betrays, Trying so hard to make his speech precise The captious listener finds it overnice. —Oliver Wendell Holmes, Sr., *Readings Over the Teacups: To My Old Readers* (1891).

Usage, in which lies the decision, the law and the norm of speech. —Horace, *Ars Poetica*, ln.71 (20 B.C.).

Speech has no value unless it can be translated into action, and action has no value unless it cannot be retranslated into speech. —Jacob Klatzkin, *In Praise of Wisdom*, 310 (1943).

A people's speech is the skin of its culture. —Max Lerner, *America as a Civilization* (1957).

Speak properly, and in as few words as you can, but always plainly: for the end of speech is not ostentation, but to be understood. —William Penn, *More Fruits of Solitude*, II. no.122 (1718).

If thou thinkest twice before thou speakest once, thou wilt speak twice the better for it. —William Penn, *Some Fruits of Solitude*, I. no.131 (1693).

I would argue that a man or woman who cannot speak or write clearly cannot think and reason cogently either. —John C. Sawhill, *Higher Education in the 80's: Beyond Retrenchment*, address to American Association of Higher Education, Washington, D.C., Mar. 6, 1980.

There was a flavour of pleasure in his speech, like a teacher who is confident and precise upon some difficulty his class has raised. —C.P. Snow, *Strangers and Brothers*, 300 (1940).

Every man is born with the faculty of reason and the faculty of speech, but why should he be able to speak before he has anything to say? — Benjamin Whichcote, *Moral and Religious Aphorisms* (1703).

Spelling

See also Orthography

Who cares about spelling? Milton spelt *dog* with two *g's*. The American Milton, when he comes, may spell it with three, while all the world wonders, if he is so minded. — Augustine Birrell, *Essays about Men, Women and Books* (1894).

I take a very old-fashioned view of the importance of spelling and grammar. I don't care tuppence for imaginative stories that are badly spelt in poorly constructed sentences with no observable punctuation. — Robert Burchfield, "A Conversation with Robert Burchfield," *U.S. News & World Report*, Dec. 15, 1980.

Take care that you never spell a word wrong. Always before you write a word consider how it is spelt, and if you do not remember it, turn to a dictionary. It produces great praise to a lady to spell well. — Thomas Jefferson, letter to his eldest daughter Martha, aged eleven, Nov. 28, 1783.

I hold that the man who regards an intelligibly spelt or prettily uttered word as "wrong" because it does not conform to the dictionary is a congenital fool. — George Bernard Shaw, *Our Theatres in the Nineties*, II: *Another Failure*, Feb. 8, 1896.

I don't see any use in spelling a word right, and never did. I mean I don't see any use in having a uniform and arbitrary way of spelling words. We might as well make all our clothes alike and cook all dishes alike. — Mark Twain, speech in Hartford, Conn., May 1875.

It is a pity that Chawcer, who had geneyus, was so unedicated. He's the wuss speller I know of. — Artemus Ward, *Artemus Ward in London, iv: At the Tomb of Shakespeare* (1867).

The spelling of words is subordinate. Morbidness for nice spelling and tenacity for or against some one letter or so means dandyism and impotence in literature. — Walt Whitman, *An American Primer* (c.1856).

State Responsibility for Education

See also Education, State Responsibility for

No one will doubt that a lawgiver should direct his attention above all to the education of youth, or that the neglect of education does harm to states. The citizen should be molded to suit the form of government under which he lives.... Democracy creates democracy, and ... oligarchy creates oligarchy. — Aristotle, *Politics*, VIII.i.1 (before 322 B.C.).

The first duty of government, and the surest evidence of good government, is the encouragement of education. A general diffusion of knowledge is the precursor and protector of republican institutions; and in it we must confide as the conservative power that will watch over our liberties, and guard them against fraud, intrigue, corruption and violence. — DeWitt Clinton, message to the New York legislature, 1826, *State of New York. Messages from the Governors*, ed. Charles Z. Lincoln, 114 (1909).

The first duty of a republic, is to provide for the instruction of its citizens; the next, to exact evidences of it. The most useful, the most charitable of all contributions, is the contribution of knowledge. — Thomas Cooper, *Lectures on the Elements of Political Economy*, 264 (1826).

Statistics

Statistics are the triumph of the quantitative method, and the quantitative method is the victory of sterility and death.   —Hilaire Belloc,
The Silence of the Sea (1941).

Statistics, which first secured prestige here by a supposedly impartial utterance of stark fact, have enlarged their domain over the American consciousness by becoming the most powerful statement of the "ought"—displacers of moral imperatives, personal ideals, and unfulfilled objectives.   —Daniel J. Boorstin,
The Decline of Radicalism (1973).

Statistically, today, there are more and more people who read, but statistics, as you know, is the most exact of the false sciences.   —Jean Cau,
in Israel Shenker, *Words and Their Masters*, 37 (1974).

Statistics are like alienists—they will testify for either side.
—Fiorello H. La Guardia,
"The Banking Investigation,"
Liberty, May 13, 1933.

He uses statistics as a drunken man uses lamp-posts—for support rather than illumination.   —Andrew Lang,
in Alan L. Mackay, *Scientific Quotations: The Harvest of the Quiet Eye* (1977).

Statistics is the art of lying by means of figures.   —Wilhelm Stekel,
Marriage at the Crossroads (1931).

There are three kinds of lies—lies, damned lies and statistics.
—Mark Twain,
Autobiography, V.i (1906?).

Stereotype of Teacher

Educational institutions mirror the stereotypes of the larger society. The fact that education has become known as a

"woman's field" stems from at least in part from the identification of child-care and child-rearing as woman's work.
—Carol Polowy,
"Sex Discrimination: The Legal Obligations of Education Institutions,"
Vital Speeches, Feb. 1, 1975.

Student

See also below; Schoolboy; Schoolgirl

The scholar teacheth his master.
—John Clark,
Paromiologia Anglo-Latina, 4 (1639).

I behaved in school like a half-wild animal who comes up to the common trough to get food, but sneaks off with it to his own den where he has gamier morsels of his own and his own ways of devouring them.   —Max Eastman,
Enjoyment of Living (1948).

A diligent Scholler, and the Master's paid.   —George Herbert,
Outlandish Proverbs, no.183 (1640).

Poor is the pupil who does not surpass his master.   —Leonardo da Vinci,
Notebooks (c.1500).

I have been filled through the ears, like a pitcher, from the well-springs of another.
—Plato, *Phaedrus*,
sec.235D (c.375–368 B.C.).

With song elate we celebrate
The struggling Student wight,
Who seeketh still to pack his pate
With treasures erudite.
—James Whitcomb Riley,
Complete Poetical Works (1937):
The Poor Student.

You don't have too talk too hard when you talk to a teacher.   —J.D. Salinger,
The Catcher in the Rye (1951).

For every person wishing to teach there are thirty not wanting to be taught.
—W.C. Sellar and R.J. Yeatman, *And Now All This* (1932).

I could undertake to be an efficient pupil if it were possible to find an efficient teacher. —Gertrude Stein, *Q.E.D.: Adele*, I (1903).

There are four types of characters among those who sit before the sages...: a sponge, which absorbs all; a funnel, which lets in at one end and lets out at the other; a strainer, which lets out the wine and retains the lees; a sieve, which lets out the course meal and retains the choice flour. —*Talmud: Aboth*, 5.15 (before A.D. 500).

The world endures only for the sake of the breath of school children.
—*Ibid.: Shabbath*, 119b.

He most honors my style who learns under it to destroy the teacher.
—Walt Whitman, *Leaves of Grass*, III: *Song of Myself*, sec. 47 (1855).

Student, College (University)

See also Student

Undergraduates owe their happiness chiefly to the consciousness that they are no longer at school. The nonsense which was knocked out of them at school is all put gently back at Oxford or Cambridge. —Max Beerbohm, *More: Going Back to School* (1899).

He wants to feel that the instructor is not simply passing on dead knowledge in the form that it was passed on to him, but that he has assimilated it and has read his own experience into it, so that it has come to mean more to him than almost anything in the world.
—Randolph Bourne, *Youth and Life* (1913).

A set o' dull, conceited hashes
Confuse their brains in college-classes,
They gang in stirks, and come out asses.
—Robert Burns,
Epistle to John Lapraik, ln.67 (1786) [hashes = *oafs, dunderheads*; stirks = *young bullocks*].

It was a formidable criticism when a student said, "They do not know I am here." In fact no teacher or official does, in most cases, become aware of the student as a human whole; he is known only by detached and artificial functions.
—Charles Horton Cooley, *Life and the Student* (1931).

The college undergraduate is lots of things—many of them as familiar, predictable, and responsible as the bounce of a basketball, and others as startling (and occasionally as disastrous) as the bounce of a football.
—John Sloan Dickey, "Conscience and the Undergradute," *Atlantic*, Apr. 1955.

Ye can lade a man up to th' university, but ye can't make him think.
—Finley Peter Dunne, *Mr. Dooley's Opinions: Mr. Carnegie's Gift* (1901).

Would I send a boy to college? Well, at the age when a boy is fit to be in college I wouldn't have him around the house.
—Finley Peter Dunne, *Observations by Mr. Dooley* (1902).

My tutors ... observed indeed, that I was a little dull; but at the same time allowed, that I seemed to be good-natured, and had no harm in me. —Oliver Goldsmith, *History of the Man in Black*. Goldsmith graduated from Trinity College in 1749 last on the list, as he had been when he entered in 1744.

When first the College Rolls receive his Name,
The young Enthusiast quits his Ease for Fame;
Thro' all his Veins the Fever of Renown

Burns from the strong Contagion of the
    Gown.   — Samuel Johnson,
        The Vanity of Human Wishes,
                    ln.135 (1749).

The scramble to get into colleges is going
to be so terrible that students are going to
put up with almost anything, even an
education.   — Barnaby C. Keeney,
        in Time, Aug. 29, 1955.

Four-fifths of our undergraduates feel inferior for life.   — Nathan M. Pusey,
        The Age of the Scholar:
    Observations on Education in a
        Troubled Decade (1963).

What a blessed place this would be if
there were no undergraduates!... No
waste of good brains in cramming bad
ones.   — Leslie Stephen,
    in Jacques Barzun, The American
        University, iii (1968).

Students, to you 'tis given to scan the
    heights
Above, to traverse the ethereal space,
And mark the systems of revolving
    worlds.   — Phillis Wheatley,
        To the University of Cambridge,
in New England [Harvard], ln.7 (1773).

Studies

See also Curriculum

Studies serve for delight, for ornament,
and for ability. Their chief use for delight
is in privateness and retiring; for ornament, is in discourse; and for ability, is in
the judgment and disposition of business; for expert men can execute and perhaps judge of particulars one by one; but
the general counsels and the plots and
marshalling of affairs, comes best from
those that are learned. — Francis Bacon,
    Essays: Of Studies (1597) [ability =
to make able; expert men = who have
learned from experience, not study].

To spend too much time in studies is
sloth; to use them too much for orna-

ment is affectation; to make judgment
wholly by their rules is the humor of a
scholar.   — Francis Bacon,
        ibid. [humor = peculiarity].

Histories make men wise; poets, witty;
the mathematics, subtile; natural philosophy, deep; moral, grave; logic and rhetoric, able to contend.... Nay, there is no
strand or impediment in the wit, but may
be wrought out by fit studies.
                — Francis Bacon,
    ibid. [witty = ingenious, imaginative].

The languages, especially the dead,
The sciences, and most of all the ab-
    struse,
The arts, at least all such as could be said
To be the most remote from common
    use,
In all these he was much and deeply read.
                — Lord Byron,
        Don Juan, I.xl.313 (1819).

These [literary] studies are the food of
youth, and consolation of age; they adorn
prosperity, and are the comfort and
refuge of adversity; they are pleasant at
home, and are no incumbrance abroad;
they accompany us at night, in our
travels, and in our rural retreats.
                — Cicero,
        Pro Archia, VII (62 B.C.).

This short life of ours has more than
enough to occupy it, even if we do not
waste it on worthless studies. Schools
must therefore be organized in such a
way that the scholars learn nothing but
what is of value.
                — John Amos Comenius,
        The Great Didactic (1628–32).

The proper study of mankind, the poet
tells us, is man. The proper study. He did
not say that it was the proper subject to
hold dogmatic and utterly unfounded
opinions about.   — Aldous Huxley,
    Essays New and Old: The
    Importance of Being Nordic (1925).

He who wishes to attain perfection must
first study logic, next the various branches

of mathematics in their proper order, then physics, and lastly metaphysics.
— Maimonides,
Guide for the Perplexed, I.xxxiv (1190).

The quiet and still air of delightful studies. —John Milton,
The Reason of Church Government Urged against Prelaty, II.i, introd. (1642).

Students who store themselves so amply with literature or science, that no room is left for determining the respective relations which exist between their acquisitions, one by one, are rather said to load their minds than to enlarge them.
—John Henry Newman,
Oxford University Sermons (1870).

Nothing is more useful to man than those arts which have no utility. —Ovid,
Epistulae ex Ponto, I.v (c. A.D. 5).

Pedagogues ... what do they teach their pupils? Words, words, words. Among all their boasted subjects, none are selected because they are useful.
—Jean Jacques Rousseau,
Émile (1762).

Balk logic with acquaintance that you have
And practise rhetoric in your common talk.
Music and poesy use to quicken you;
The mathematics and the metaphysics,
Fall to them as you find your stomach serves you.
No profit grows where is no pleasure tane;
In brief, sir, study what you must affect.
—William Shakespeare,
The Taming of the Shrew, I.i.34 (1596) [balk logic = *bandy arguments, use dialectic*; quicken = *stimulate*; stomach = *inclination*; tane = *taken*].

Study

Review your lesson twice the next day, for each time you will discover something

you did not know before.
—Israel ben Joseph Alnaqua,
Menorat HaMaor, iii.317 (14th cent.).

[Grandmother] fell silent again, then lowered her head and began to cry. "Study!" she suddenly said with great vehemence. "Study and you will have everything—wealth and fame! You must know *everything*. The whole world will fall at your feet and grovel before you."
—Isaac Babel,
You Must Know Everything (1915).

When night hath set her silver lamp on high,
Then it is time for study.
—Philip James Bailey,
Festus: A Village Feast (1839).

Some study shows the need for more.
—Selwyn Gurney Champion,
Racial Proverbs, 378 (1938).
A Chinese proverb.

Swallow all your learning in the morning, but digest it in company in the evenings.
—Lord Chesterfield,
Letters to His Son, May 10, 1751.

Those who do not study are only cattle dressed up in men's clothes.
—Chinese proverb.

Errors like straws upon the surface flow;
He who would search for pearls must dive below. —John Dryden,
All for Love, prologue (1677).

In truth man is made rather to eat ices than to pore over old texts.
—Anatole France,
The Crime of Sylvestre Bonnard, I (1881).

Studeration beats education.
—Jamaican proverb.

Some men study so much, they don't have time to know. —Jewish saying.

One must not pass all the time in study; one must also seek intercourse with people. —Jacob Joseph Katz,
Toldot Jacob Joseph (1780).

We enter new studies not so much from weariness of the old, or desire for change, as from a desire to be admired by those who are wiser than we, and a hope of gaining advantage over those who are not. —François de La Rochefoucauld, *Maxims*, no.178 (1665).

Real study, real learning must, for the individual, be quite valueless or it loses its value. —Stephen Leacock, *Model Memoirs: On the Need for a Quiet College* (1938).

Just as eating against one's will is injurious to health, so study without a liking for it spoils the memory, and it retains nothing it takes in. —Leonardo da Vinci, *Notebooks* (c.1500).

As turning the logs will make a dull fire burn, so changes of studies, a dull brain. —Henry Wadsworth Longfellow, *Driftwood: Table Talk* (1857).

Study depends on the good will of the student, a quality that cannot be secured by compulsion. —Quintilian, *Institutio Oratoria*, I.iii.8 (A.D. 95 or 96).

Just as we suffer from excess in all things, so we suffer from excess in literature; thus we learn our lessons not for life, but for the lecture room. —Seneca, *Letters to Lucilius*, CVI.xii (c. A.D. 64).

What is the end of study? Let me know?
Why, that to know, which else we should not know.
Things hid and barr'd, you mean, from common sense?
Ay, that is study's god-like recompense.
—William Shakespeare, *Love's Labour's Lost*, I.i.55 (1594).

Study is like the heaven's glorious sun,
That will not be deep-search'd with saucy looks:
Small have continual plodders ever won,
Save base authority from others' books.
—William Shakespeare, *ibid.*, I.i.84 [small = *little*].

He that repeated his chapter a hundred times is not to be compared with him who repeated it a hundred and one times. —*Talmud: Hagigah*, 9b (before A.D. 500).

My son, do not sit and study at the highest point of the town;[1] do not dwell in a town whose leaders are scholars.[2] —*Ibid: Pesahim*, 112a [[1]Many pass there, and they will disturb your studies. [2]Intent on their studies, they neglect the affairs of the town!].

Forasmuch as many people study more to have knowledge than to live well therefore ofttimes they err and bring forth little fruit or none. —Thomas à Kempis, *The Imitation of Christ*, I.iii (1426).

Many a bit we passed in our ignorance, in the days when we could see no metal but what glittered on the surface; and many a good time we went back again, long afterward, and broke our rejected lump with great exultation to find it fat with the riches of the mind.
—Susan Warner, *The Law and the Testimony*, foreword (1853).

Stupidity

See also Fool; Ignorance; Ignorant Person

The good Lord set definite limits on man's wisdom, but set no limits on his stupidity—and that's not fair! —Konrad Adenauer, *The Churchman*, Jan. 15, 1957.

To a senseless man education is fetters on his feet, and like manacles on his right hand. —*Apocrypha: Ecclesiasticus* 21:19 (c.180 B.C.).

When a finger points at the moon, the imbecile looks at the finger. —Chinese proverb.

The quickest of us walk well-wadded with stupidity. — George Eliot, *Middlemarch* (1872).

The hardest thing to cope with is not selfishness or vanity or deceitfulness, but sheer stupidity. — Eric Hoffer, *The Passionate State of Mind*, no.210 (1954).

Stupidity is no excuse for not thinking. — Stanislaw J. Lec, *Unkempt Thoughts*, tr. Jacek Galazka (1962).

Nothing sways the stupid more than arguments they can't understand. — Cardinal de Retz, *Mémoires* (1717).

Against stupidity the very gods
Themselves contend in vain. — Friedrich von Schiller, *The Maid of Orleans*, III.vi (1801).

Dumb enough to chew on the stick instead of sucking the lollipop. — Rex Stout, *The Broken Vase* (1941).

There is no sin except stupidity. — Oscar Wilde, *Intentions: The Critic as Artist*, II (1891).

Style, Writing

See also Grammar; Writing

Style in writing is something like style in a car, a woman, or a Greek temple—the ordinary materials of this world so poised and perfected as to stand out from the landscape and compel a second look, something that hangs in the reader's mind, like a vision. — Sheridan Baker, *The Practical Stylist*, 3rd ed. (1973).

Au author arrives at a good style when his language performs what is required of it without shyness. — Cyril Connolly, *Enemies of Promise*, iii (1938).

Style! style! why all writers will tell you that it is the very thing which can least of all be changed. A man's style is nearly as much a part of him as his physiognomy, his figure, the throbbing of his pulse—in short, as any part of his being which is at least subjected to the action of the will. — François Fénelon, *Dialogues on Eloquence* (tr. 1760).

Which, of all defects, has been the one most fatal to a good style? The not knowing when to come to an end. — Arthur Helps, *Companions of My Solitude* (1852).

A strict and succinct style is that, where you can take away nothing without loss, and that loss to be manifest. — Ben Jonson, *Explorata: Consuetudo* (1636).

Many intelligent people, when they set about writing books, force their minds to fit some notion that they have about style, just as they screw up their faces when they sit for their portraits. — Georg Christoph Lichtenberg, *Reflections* (1799).

Obscurity and affection are the two greatest faults of style. Obscurity of expression generally springs from confusion of ideas; and the same wish to dazzle at any cost which produces affectation in the manner of a writer is likely to produce sophistry in his reasonings. — Thomas Babington Macaulay, "Michiavelli," *Edinburg Review*, Mar. 1827.

A good style should show no sign of effort. What is written should seem a happy accident. — W. Somerset Maugham, *The Summing Up*, xiii (1938).

To the man with an ear for verbal delicacies—the man who searches painfully for the perfect word, and puts the way of saying a thing above the thing said—there is

in writing the constant joy of sudden discovery, of happy accident.
                            —H.L. Mencken,
     A Book of Prefaces, ii. sec.2 (1917).

Style might be described as that aspect of a piece of writing that we *perceive* but do not *observe*, what we respond to in writing without being aware of it.
                    —Louis T. Milic, *Stylists on Style: Introductory Essay*, 1 (1969).

Great style, which, if I may say so, is also modest style, is never blotchy and bloated. It rises supreme by virtue of its natural beauty.   —Petronius,
                    Satyricon, ii (c. A.D. 60).

A vile conceit in pompous words express'd,
Is like a clown in regal purple dress'd.
                    —Alexander Pope,
     An Essay on Criticism, II.320 (1711).

True ease in writing comes from art, not chance,
As those move easiest who have learn'd to dance.
'Tis not enough no harshness gives offence,
The sound must seem an Echo to the sense.   —Alexander Pope,
                              ibid., II.362.

Care should be taken, not that the reader *may* understand, but that he *must* understand.   —Quintilian,
     Institutio Oratoria (A.D. 95 or 96).

In a style, to be sure, of remarkable fullness,
But which nobody reads on account of its dullness.   —John Godfrey Saxe,
                    Poetical Works (1887):
                    Pyramus and Thisbe.

Long sentences in a short composition are like large rooms in a little house.
                    —William Shenstone,
     On Writing and Books (1764).

But why wasn't I born, alas, in an age of Adjectives; why can one no longer write

of silver-shedding Tears and moon-tailed Peacocks, of eloquent Death, of the Negro and star-enamelled Night?
                    —Logan Pearsall Smith,
          More Trivia: Adjectives (1921).

In composing, as a general rule, run your pen through every other word you have written; you have no idea what vigor it will give your style.   —Sydney Smith,
     in Lady Holland, *A Memoir of the Rev. Sydney Smith* (1855).

In general, writing should be like sailing clouds and flowing water. It has no definite [required] form. It goes where it has to go and stops where it cannot but stop. One has thus a natural style, with all its wayward charms.   —Su Tungpo,
     letter to Shieh Minshih, 11th cent.,
     in Lin Yutang, *The Importance of Understanding*, 321 (1960).

Proper words in proper places, make the true definition of a style.
                    —Jonathan Swift,
          letter to a young clergyman,
                              Jan. 9, 1720.

Success

See also Achievement

There are few successful adults who were not first successful children.
                    —Alexander Chase,
                    Perspectives (1966).

Success is counted sweetest
By those who ne'er succeed.
To comprehend a nectar
Requires sorest need.
                    —Emily Dickinson,
     Complete Poems, no.67 (c.1859),
          ed. Thomas H. Johnson (1960).

Nothing succeeds like success.
                    —Alexandre Dumas père,
               Ange Pitou, I.72 (1853).

By teaching at the child's level, the teacher takes advantage of one of the

most potent interest factors available to him—success. Nothing contributes to interest in an activity to as great an extent as does legitimate success.
—G. Orville Johnson,
Education for the Slow Learners (1963).

Suppression

See also Censorship

Persecution is the first law of society because it is always easier to suppress criticism than to meet it.
—Howard Mumford Jones,
Primer of Intellectual Freedom, introd. (1949).

You have not converted a man, because you have silenced him. —John Morley,
On Compromise, iii (1874).

Whoever persecutes a disagreeing person, armes all the world against himselfe, and all pious people of his owne perswasion, when the scales of authority return to his adversary, and attest his contradictory; and then, what can he urge for mercy for himselfe, or his party that sheweth none to the other. —Jeremy Taylor,
The Liberty of Prophesying, xiii:
Of the Deportment to Be Used Towards Persons Disagreeing (1647).

Talent

See also Ability; Genius; Skill

There are two kinds of talent, man-made talent and God-given talent. With man-made talent you have to work very hard. With God-given talent, you just touch it up once in a while. —Pearl Bailey,
Newsweek, Dec. 4, 1967.

In this world people have to pay an extortionate price for an exceptional gift whatever. —Willa Cather,
The Old Beauty and Others, iv (1948).

Hide not your Talents, they for Use were made.
What's a Sun-Dial in the Shade!
—Benjamin Franklin,
Poor Richard's Almanack, Oct. 1750.

Talent is best nurtured in solitude; character is best formed in the stormy billows of the world.
—Johann Wolfgang von Goethe,
Torquato Tasso, I.ii.66 (1790).

Gift, like genius, I often think only means an infinite capacity for taking pains. —Jane Ellice Hopkins,
Work Amongst Working Men (1870).

There is no substitute for talent. Industry and all the virtues are of no avail.
—Aldous Huxley,
Point Counter Point, xiii (1928).

There is the same difference between talent and genius that there is between a stone mason and a sculptor.
—Robert G. Ingersoll,
Shakespeare (1891).

I think this is the most extraordinary collection of talent, of human knowledge, that has ever been gathered together at the White House—with the possible exception of when Thomas Jefferson dined alone. —President John F. Kennedy,
at a dinner for 49 American Nobel Prize laureates, Apr. 29, 1962.

Talent is that which is in a man's power; genius is that in whose power a man is.
—James Russell Lowell,
Among My Books, I: *Rousseau and the Sentimentalists* (1870).

If the talent or individuality is there, it should be expressed. If it doesn't find its way out into the air, it can turn inward and gnaw like the fox at the Spartan boy's belly. —Shirley MacLaine,
Don't Fall Off the Mountain, iv (1970).

The teaching profession should hang its official head at the way the superior child has been neglected.
—Karl A. Menninger,
The Human Mind (1930).

Here is how I define talent: a gift which God has presented to us secretly, and which we reveal without perceiving it.
— Charles de Secondat Montesquieu,
Pensées Diverses (1853).

A great talent fares like a paper kite: the higher it rises, the more the street-arabs gather to pull it down.
— Moritz Gottlieb Saphir Shriften (1880):
Warum giebt es kein Narrenhaus.

You cannot define talent. All you can do is build the greenhouse and see if it grows.
— William P. Steven,
Time, Aug. 23, 1963.

Talent repeats; Genius creates. Talent is a cistern; Genius a fountain.... Talent jogs to conclusions to which Genius takes giant leaps.... Talent is full of thoughts, Genius of thought.
— Edwin Percy Whipple,
Literature and Life: Genius (1871).

If a man has a talent and cannot use it, he has failed. If he has a talent and uses only half of it, he has partly failed. If he has a talent and learns somehow to use the whole of it, he has gloriously succeeded, and won a satisfaction and triumph few men ever know. — Thomas Wolfe,
The Web and the Rock, xxix (1937).

Teacher

See also below; Professor;
Salary, Teacher's

My belief is that the last thing a good teacher wants to do is teach outside the classroom; certainly my own vision of bliss halfway through a term is solitary confinement in a soundproof cell.
— Jacques Barzun,
The Teacher in America (1944).

Sir Thomas More: Why not be a teacher? You'd be a fine teacher. Perhaps — a great one.
Richard Rich: And if I was, who would know it?

More: You, your pupils, your friends, God. Not a bad public, that.
— Robert Bolt,
A Man for All Seasons, I (1960).

Teachers are largely a meek, downtrodden, unappreciated body of men. To know that others believe in them, consider them capable of high thinking and doing, and are willing to help them out — may enable them to accomplish more than even they think possible.
— Louis D. Brandeis, letter to Frederick Wehle, Nov. 19, 1924.

Here lie Willie Michie's banes:
O Satan, when ye tak him,
Gie him the schulin o' your weans,
For clever deils he'll mak them!
— Robert Burns, Poetical Works (1974):
For Mr. William Michie, Schoolmaster
of Cleish Parish, Fifeshire [weans =
children; deils = devils].

Now honest William's gaen to Heaven,
I wat na gin't can mend him:
The fauts he had in Latin lay,
For nane in English kent them.
— Robert Burns, ibid.:
For William Cruickshank, A.M.,
classical master in Edinburgh High
School [wat = know; fauts = faults;
kent = knew].

It is forbidden for a teacher to be up at night and attend school in the daytime, or to fast at the time of teaching, or to overeat, because these things impair his health and result in neglect in teaching children. — Joseph Caro,
Code of Jewish Law: Yoreh De'ah,
245.8 (1567).

And gladly wolde he lerne, and gladly teche. — Geoffrey Chaucer,
Canterbury Tales: Prologue,
ln.310 (c.1386).

Monday. Went to board at Mr. B's; had a baked gander for dinner; suppose from its size, the thickness of the skin and other venerable appearances it must have been one of the first settlers of Vermont;

made a slight impression on the patriarch's breast. Supper—cold gander and potatoes.   —Diary of a schoolmaster, Vermont, early 19th cent., in Clifton Johnson, *Old-Time Schools and School-books* (1904).

To have been a schoolmaster or college professor thirty years only too often makes a man an unsafe witness in matters of education: there are flanges on his mental wheels which will only fit one gauge.   —Charles W. Eliot, "The New Education: Its Organization," *Atlantic Monthly*, 1869.

There's more guts in the li'l ole brick schoolhouse, less intimidation. The teachers are professionals. Doctors and lawyers don't take any guff—why should teachers?   —Harry Golden, *So Long as You're Healthy: Teachers' revolution* (1970).

If I can teach you something, it may mean that I can count at least somewhere.   —Hannah Green, *I Never Promised You a Rose Garden*, xvii (1964).

One of the things that is manifestly wrong with our school system is our thoughtless practice of hiring and assigning the youngest and the least experienced teachers for the lowest classes, when it should be quite the other way around.   —Sydney Harris, syndicated column, *Detroit Free Press*, July 15, 1981.

The child is not there for you, but you are there for the child.
          —Samson Raphael Hirsch, *Choreb* (1837).

Everyone who remembers his own educational experience remembers teachers, not methods and techniques. The teacher is the kingpin of the educational situation. He makes or breaks programs.
          —Sidney Hook, *Education for Modern Man* (1946).

Child, give me your hand
That I may walk in the light
of your faith in me.   —Hannah Kahn, *Haiku*, in Haim G. Ginott, *Teacher and Child*, frontispiece (1972).

Teachers are the most cynical people I know—which is sad, ironic, and unnatural, because no one ever became a teacher without believing he could change things for the better.
          —Ralph J. Kane, "The Mindless Box: The Case Against the American Classroom," *Phi Delta Kappan*, Mar. 1979.

The educator must above all understand how to wait; to reckon all effects in the light of the future, not of the present.
          —Ellen Key, *The Morality of Woman and Other Essays: The Conventional Woman* (1911).

For ten years I was a schoolmaster. About thirty years ago I was appointed to the staff of a great Canadian school. It took me ten years to get off it. Being appointed to the position of a teacher is like being hooked up through the braces and hung up against a wall. It is hard to get down again.   —Stephen Leacock, *College Days: Memories and Miseries of a Schoolmaster* (1923).

For him the Teacher's chair became a throne.—Henry Wadsworth Longfellow, *Parker Cleaveland* (1875).

God sends his teachers unto every age,
To every clime, and every race of men,
With revelations fitted to their growth
And shape of mind, nor gives the realm
of Truth
Into the selfish rule of one sole race.
          —James Russell Lowell, *Rhoecus*, i (1843).

For him who fain would teach the world
The world holds hate in fee—
For Socrates, the hemlock cup;
For Christ, Gethsemane.
          —Don Marquis, *The Wages*, in J.D. Morrison, ed., *Masterpieces of Religious Verse* (1948).

The teacher's life should have three periods—study until 25, investigation until 40, profession until 60, at which age I would have him retired on a double allowance.   —William Osler, speech in Baltimore, Feb. 22, 1905.

But where's the man, who counsel can bestow,
Still pleas'd to teach, and yet not proud to know?   —Alexander Pope, *An Essay on Criticism*, III.631 (1711).

The inexperienced teacher, fearing his own ignorance, is afraid to admit it. Perhaps that courage only comes when one knows to what extent ignorance is almost universal.   —Ezra Pound, *ABC of Reading*, I.viii (1934).

You've become silly from teaching children! You give them what little sense you have, and they give you all their stupidity.   —Joseph Roth, *Job: The Story of a Simple Man* (1931).

Teachers should unmask themselves, admit into consciousness the idea that one does not need to know everything there is to know and one does not have to pretend to know everything there is to know.   —Esther P. Rothman, *Troubled Teachers* (1977).

Schoolmasters will I keep within my house,
Fit to instruct her youth....
To cunning men
I will be very kind, and liberal
To mine own children in good bringing up.   —William Shakespeare, *The Taming of the Shrew*, I.iii.94 (1596) [cunning = *well-trained, able*].

I'm not a teacher: only a fellow-traveller of whom you asked the way. I pointed ahead—ahead of myself as well as of you.   —George Bernard Shaw, *Getting Married* (1908).

Good teachers are costly, but bad teachers cost more.   —Bob Talbert, *Detroit Free Press*, Apr. 5, 1982.

I am a teacher of young children and I teach the children of the poor as well as those of the rich; I take no fees from any who cannot afford to pay; further, I have a fishpond and any boy who is reluctant [to learn] I bribe with some of the fishes from it and thereby appease him so that he becomes eager to learn.   —*Talmud: Ta'anith*, 24a (before A.D. 500).

Of all the professions this world has known,...
The worst for care and undeserved abuse,
The first in real dignity and use,
(If skilled to teach, and diligent to rule)
Is the learned master of a little school.   —Alexander Wilson, *Poetical Works* (1844): *The Schoolmaster*, ln.1 (before 1813).

Teacher, Attributes of

A schoolmaster should have an atmostphere of awe, and walk wonderingly, as if he was amazed at being himself.   —Walter Bagehot, *Literary Studies*, I (1879).

Benevolence alone will not make a teacher, nor will learning alone do it. The gift of teaching is a peculiar talent, and implies a need and craving in the teacher himself.   —John Jay Chapman, *Memories and Milestones* (1915).

Teaching is the only major occupation of man for which we have not yet developed tools that make an average person capable of competence and performance. In teaching we rely on the "naturals," the ones who somehow know how to teach. Nobody seems to know, however, what it is the "naturals" do that the rest of us do not. No one knows what they do not do that the rest of us do.   —Peter F. Drucker, *The Age of Discontinuity*, IV.xv (1968).

Not any profane man, not any sensual, not any liar, not any slave can teach, but only he can give, who has; he only can create, who is.   —Ralph Waldo Emerson, An Address Delivered before the Senior Class in Divinity College, Cambridge, Sunday Evening, July 15, 1838.

I have never heard anyone whom I consider a good teacher claim that he or she *is* a good teacher—in the way that one might claim to be a good writer or surgeon or athlete. Self-doubt seems very much a part of the job of teaching: one can never be sure how well it is going.
—Joseph Epstein,
"A Class Act," *Quest*, Sept. 1981.

My teacher, Miss G., is very gifted. By that I mean she is young and beautiful.
—Robert Fontaine,
That's a Good Question (1960).

No one should teach who is not a bit awed by the importance of the profession.
—George W. Frasier,
An Introduction to the Study of Education, 18 (1951).

The most successful teachers, those in whose classes student achievement is greatest, are the ones who accept their students as worthwhile individuals and make the students conscious of this acceptance.
—Norma Furst and Marciene S. Mattleman,
"Classroom Climate," *NEA Journal*,
Apr. 1968.

Only those teachers are worthy of their calling, or vocation, who have a profound respect not only for truth, in all its inexhaustible breadth and depth, but for the equally unfathomable personalities of their students and of all men everywhere. This respect is, in moments of heightened awareness, so tinged with awe as to be very close to authentic religious reverence.
—Theodore Meyer Greene,
"Religion and the Philosophies of Education," *Religious Education*,
Apr. 1954.

A good teacher is one who helps you become who you feel yourself to be. A good teacher is also one who says something you won't understand until 10 years later.
—Julius Lester,
"College Teachers," *Quest*,
Sept. 1981.

Since I would rather make of him an able man than a learned man, I would also urge that care be taken to choose for him a guide with a well-made rather than a well-filled head; that both these qualities should be required of him, but more particularly character and understanding than learning; and that he should go about his job in a novel way.
—Michel de Montaigne,
Essays, I.xxvi (1580):
Of the Education of Children.

What constitutes the teacher is the passion to make scholars.
—George Herbert Palmer,
The Teacher, Essays and Addresses on Education: The Ideal Teacher (1908).

For the job of establishing good discipline and maintaining it, ... the personality of the teacher is the most essential factor. Under ordinary circumstances the teacher can get along with a few technical considerations if this one factor of personality is strongly represented.
—Fritz Redl,
When We Deal with Children,
303 (1966).

Teacher, Description of

'Twas an old pedagogue, long ago,
Tall and slender, and sallow and dry;
His form was bent, and his gait was slow,
His long thin hair was white as snow.
—George Arnold,
The Jolly Old Pedagogue (1867).

A man severe he was, and stern to view,
I knew him well, and every truant knew;
Well had the boding tremblers learn'd to trace
The day's disasters in his morning face.
—Oliver Goldsmith,
The Deserted Village, ln.197 (1770).

Grave is the Master's look; his forehead wears
Thick rows of wrinkles, prints of worrying cares;

Uneasy lie the heads of all that rule,
His most of all whose kingdom is a
school.—Oliver Wendell Holmes, Sr.,
        The Iron Gate and Other Poems:
        The School-Boy (1878).

Her cap, far whiter than the driven snow,
Emblem right meet of decency does
    yield:
Her apron dy'd in grain, as blue, I trowe,
As is the hare-bell that adorns the field.
                —William Shenstone,
        The School-Mistress, ln.46 (1737).

Teacher, Dispraise for

Nothing is more tiresome than a superan-
nuated pedagogue.   —Henry Adams,
        The Education of Henry Adams,
                        xxiii (1907).

[Many a teacher] will chill the fire in a
January stove ... and will furrow the brow
of a happy, barefoot boy.... She rings the
bell, calls the roll, and hears the spelling
and arithmetic with the same spirit in
which she counts the linen for the wash.
At best her brow wears the gloom of
forced duty.   —Frederic Burk,
    "The Withered Heart of the Schools,"
    Educational Review, Dec. 1907.

Arrogance, pedantry, and dogmatism are
the occupational diseases of those who
spend their lives directing the intellects of
the young.   —Henry Seidel Canby,
                Alma Mater (1936).

It is remarkable that Rabelais, Montaigne, Locke, Fenelon, Rousseau, as well
as most of the numerous educators who
appeared during the nineteenth century
are *against* teachers. It may be because
most of these theorists never had any experience of that wild unbroken thing, a
class, and imagine that what they are now
they already were at twelve or fourteen.
                —Ernest Dimnet,
    The Art of Thinking, II.i.b (1928).

Lorde God, howe many good and clene
wittes of children, be nowe a dayes
perisshed by ignorant schole maisters.
            —Thomas Elyot, *The Boke*
        Named the Governour (1531).

Grammarians..., a generation of men
than whom nothing would be more
miserable, nothing more perplext,
nothing more hated of the Gods, did I
not allay the troubles of that pittiful Profession with a certain kind of pleasant
madness ... as being ever hunger-starv'd,
and slovens in their Schools—Schools,
did I say? Nay, rather Cloisters, Bridwells
or Slaughter-houses.
            —Desiderius Erasmus,
        The Praise of Folly (1509).

I was, but am no more, thank God—a
school teacher—I dreamed last night I
was teaching again—that's the only bad
dream that ever afflicts my sturdy
conscience.   —D.H. Lawrence,
Selected Letters, ed. Diana Trilling (1958).

The truth is that the average schoolmaster, on all the lower levels, is and
always must be ... next door to an idiot,
for how can one imagine an intelligent
man engaging is so puerile an avocation?
                —H.L. Mencken,
    Prejudices, Third Series, 244 (1922);
New York Evening Mail, Jan. 23, 1918.

It is when the gods hate a man with uncommon abhorrence that they drive him
into the profession of a school-master.
                    —Seneca,
        Letters to Lucilius (c. A.D. 64).

He who can, does. He who cannot,
teaches.   —George Bernard Shaw,
        Maxims for Revolutionists (1903).

I am a paid keeper of Society's un-
usables—the lame, the halt, the insane,
and the ignorant. The only incentive I
can give you, kid, to behave yourself is
this: if you don't buckle down and learn
something, you'll be as dumb as I am,
and you'll have to teach school to earn a
living.... I don't wish it on you, kid.
—John Updike, *The Centaur*, iv (1963).

Everybody who is incapable of learning has taken to teaching. — Oscar Wilde, *Intentions: The Decay of Lying* (1891).

Teacher, Education of

Be familiar with the ancient wisdom and become acquainted with the modern; then you may become a teacher.
— Confucius,
Analects, XIX.vi (c.500 B.C.).

In our efforts to supply enough teachers for the public schools we have sacrificed quality for quantity.
— Willard S. Elsbree,
The American Teacher, 334 (1939).

Which brings me to claim it as a duty incumbent on Statesmen and Churchmen alike to provide that there be a due supply of men qualified to educate the youth of the nation. It is a public obligation in no way inferior, say, to the ordering of the army. — Desiderius Erasmus,
The Argument ... That Children Should Straight Away from Their Earliest Years Be Trained in Virtue and Sound Learning (1529).

I believe it will be absolutely necessary that you should prevail on our future masters to learn their letters.
— Robert Lowe,
speech in the House of Commons,
July 15, 1867. Popularized as "We must educate our masters."

No teacher I of boys or smaller fry,
No teacher I of teachers, no, not I.
Mine was the distant aim, the longer reach,
To teach men how to teach men how to teach. — Allen Beville Ramsay,
in William Cole, ed.,
Pith and Vinegar (1969).

Teacher, Expectation from

Teachers are expected to reach unattainable goals with inadequate tools. The miracle is that at times they accomplish this impossible task. — Haim G. Ginott, *Teacher and Child*, preface (1972).

The modern schoolmaster is expected to know a little of everything because his pupil is required not to be entirely ignorant of anything. He must be superficially, if I may say so, omniscient.
— Charles Lamb,
The Essays of Elia: The Old and the New Schoolmaster (1823).

It is because of our unassailable enthusiasm, our profound reverence for education, that we habitually demand of it the impossible. The teacher is expected to perform a choice and varied series of miracles. — Agnes Repplier,
Times and Tendencies (1931).

Teacher, Function of

The teacher is not in the school to impose certain ideas or to form certain habits in the child, but is there as a member of the community to select the influences which shall affect the child and to assist him in properly responding to these influences.
— John Dewey,
"My Pedagogic Creed,"
The School Journal, Jan. 16, 1897.

I believe that the teacher's business is simply to determine, on the basis of larger experience and riper wisdom, how the discipline of life shall come to the child. — John Dewey,
ibid.

It is the supreme art of the teacher to awaken joy in creative expresssion and knowledge. — Albert Einstein,
motto for the Astronomy Building,
Pasadena Junior College.

A teacher is a mediator between the child and society. It is his job to be the guardian of the child's opportunity to grow in his own time, at his own rate; he secures for the child a kind of moratorium from the demands and expectations of society, during which the child learns what he must to develop a secure identity and in other ways mature until he can play the role of the adult.   —Aubrey Haan, *Education for the Open Society* (1962).

A teacher of young children is in a sense a travel agent. He helps a child go where the child wants to go. He counsels on the best way of getting there, indicating the kind of currency and the rate of exchange, the necessary "shots," the books that will help the traveler understand what he sees. He warns that some places are too dangerous or too difficult to visit just now.   —Allan Leitman, in introd. by John Holt to *Open Education: The Informal Classroom*, ed. Charle H. Rathbone, 5 (1971).

It is the mission of the pedagogue, not to make his pupils think, but to make them think *right*, and the more nearly his own mind pulsates with the great ebbs and flows of popular delusion and emotion, the more admirably he performs his function. He may be an ass, but that is surely no demerit in a man paid to make asses of his customers.   —H.C. Mencken, *Baltimore Evening Sun*, Mar. 12, 1923.

We teachers can only help the work going on, as servants wait upon a master.
        —Maria Montessori, *The Absorbent Mind* (1967).

The teacher is a kind of medical man whose purpose is to cure the patient of childishness.   —Bertrand Russell, *Unpopular Essays: The Functions of a Teacher* (1950).

The business of the American teacher is to liberate American citizens to think apart and act together.
        —Stephen S. Wise, in *New York Times Magazine*, Mar. 22, 1953.

Teacher, Importance of

We have spoken of the office of the education of human beings, as the noblest on earth, and have spoken deliberately. It is more important than that of the statesman.... We maintain that higher ability is required for the office of an educator of the young, than for that of a statesman.
        —William Ellery Channing (1780–1842), "Remarks on Education," *Christian Examiner*, Nov. 1833.

To regard teachers—in our entire educational system, from the primary grades to the university—as priests of our democracy is therefore not to indulge in hyperbole. It is the special task of teachers to foster those habits of open-mindedness and critical inquiry which alone make for responsible citizens, who, in turn, make possible an enlightened and effective public opinion.   —Felix Frankfurter, U.S. Supreme Court decision, *Wieman v Updegraff*, 1952.

Teachers of teachers! Yours the task,
Noblest that noble minds can ask.
        —Oliver Wendell Holmes, Sr., *Before the Curfew: To the Teachers of America*, poem read before the National Educational Association, Boston, Feb. 23, 1893.

I maintain, my friends, that every one of us should seek out the best teacher whom we can find, first for ourselves, who are greatly in need of one, and then for the youth, regardless of expense or anything.
        —Plato, *Laches*, sec.200B (before 389 B.C.).

Teachers are more than any other class the guardians of civilization.
        —Bertrand Russell, *Unpopular Essays: The Functions of a Teacher* (1950).

Teachers are greater benefactors than parents.   —Pope Sixtus I, *The Ring* (c. A.D. 120).

He who teaches a child is as if he had created it.   —*Talmud: Sanhedrin*, 19b (before A.D. 500).

Teacher, Influence of

Pledge not allegiance to a favorite master,
Nor let the scholar hold you by his love.
—Pierre Abélard,
Astrolabius (before 1142).

A teacher affects eternity; he can never tell where his influence stops.
—Henry Adams,
The Education of Henry Adams,
xx (1907).

The true teacher defends his pupils against his own personal influence. He inspires self-distrust. He guides their eyes from himself to the spirit that quickens him. He will have no disciple.
—A. Bronson Alcott,
Orphic Sayings: The Teacher (1840).

We lov'd the doctrine for the teacher's sake.   —Daniel Defoe,
Character of the Late Dr. S. Annesley (1697).

The measure of a master is his success in bringing all men round to his opinion twenty years later.
—Ralph Waldo Emerson,
The Conduct of Life: Culture (1860).

The influence that passes from a teacher to a student is probably best recollected and understood only in tranquility—that is to say, only in years to come.
—Joseph Epstein,
"A Class Act," *Quest*, Sept. 1981.

There is nothing which spreads more contagiously from teacher to pupil than elevation of sentiment: often and often have students caught from the living influence of a professor, a contempt for mean and selfish objects, and a noble ambition to leave the world better than they found it, which they have carried with them throughout life.
—John Stuart Mill,
inaugural address as Rector of University of St. Andrews, Feb. 1, 1867.

In truth, to express sufficiently how much I owe you were a work far greater than my strength.   —John Milton,
letter to Thomas Young,
his former tutor, Mar. 26, 1627.

In education, the closeness of students to a good and great man or woman is the finest we can offer our children.
—Seymour St. John,
"Hard Education or Soft?"
Vogue, Jan. 15, 1958.

And when I am forgotten, as I shall be,
And asleep in dull cold marble, where no mention
Of me must be heard of, say, I taught thee.   —William Shakespeare,
Henry VIII, III.ii.433 (1612–13).

And if any one should ask you now,
Where you got all your knowledge,
Jist tell them 'twas from Paddy Blake,
Of Bally Blarney College.
—James A. Sidey,
The Irish Schoolmaster, x,
in Carolyn Wells, ed., *The Book of Humorous Verse* (1936).

The influence of teachers on the rising generation is almost unlimited. Only father and mother have more, and theirs is largely by precept and example rather than instruction.   —Harry S Truman,
speech at a teachers' meeting in Independence, Mo., Aug. 30, 1957.

One good teacher in a lifetime may sometimes change a delinquent into a solid citizen.   —Phillip Wylie,
Generation of Vipers, vii (1942).

Teacher, Praise for

I am quite sure that in the hereafter she will take me by the hand and lead me to my proper seat. I always have a great reverence for teachers. For teachers, both lay and clerical, and for nurses. They are the most underpaid people in the world for what they do.   —Bernard Baruch, recalling one of his early teachers, Katherine Devereux Blake, in *The New York Times*, Aug. 29, 1955.

We must have teachers—a heroine in every classroom.   —Fidel Castro, *Time*, Jan. 26, 1959.

God's greatest gift is a Teacher, and when will he send me one full of truth and of boundless benevolence and of heroic sentiments?   —Ralph Waldo Emerson, *Journals*, 1833.

A load of books does not equal one good teacher.   —H.H. Hart, *Seven Hundred Chinese Proverbs*, no.167 (1937).

She teaches girls to be women and inspires our sons to deserve such ladies.   —Henry Luce, introducing Mary Bunting, president of Radcliffe College, *Time*, May 17, 1963.

They were all admirable scholars, the masters who taught in the cloisters of the old school.... They were, to a man, well-meaning and sweet-humored; and they were one in the belief that knowledge and good cheer are not mutually exclusive.   —Thomas Mann, *Buddenbrooks*, II.iii (1902).

Here teachers are the hours who open or close the gates of heaven.
              —Jean Paul Richter, *Levana*, preface (1807).

Those teachers were stray individuals; they had not yet been standardized by educational departments and pedagogy.... In a word, they were *cultivated* men.   —George Santayana, *Persons and Places, I: The Background of My Life*, x (1945).

Teacher, Respect for

See also Respect

Dear Lord,
Bless our dear Teacher,
Give her the brightest crown in heaven.
Give her the whitest robe that can be given.
Put golden sandals on her feet, and let her
Slip and slide up to the throne of Master Jesus.
    AMEN.   —Anon., in *The Book of Negro Folklore*, ed. Langston Hughes and Arna Bontemps (1958).

Teachers, who educate children, deserve more honor than parents, who merely gave them birth; for the latter provided mere life, while the former ensure a good life.   —Aristotle, in Diogenes Laërtius, *Lives and Opinions of Eminent Philosophers* (before A.D. 300).

To hold my teacher in this art equal to my own parents; to make him partner in my livelihood; when he is in need of money to share mine with him; to consider his family as my own brothers, and to teach them this art, if they want to learn it, without fee or indenture.
              —Hippocrates, *The Physician's Oath* (c.400 B.C.).

JOHNSON. I had no notion that I was wrong or irreverent to my tutor. BOSWELL. That, Sir, was great fortitude of mind. JOHNSON. No, Sir, stark insensibility.   —Samuel Johnson, in James Boswell, *Life of Samuel Johnson*, ii, Nov. 5, 1728 (1791).

If the teacher is not respected,
And the student not cared for,
Confusion will arise, however clever one is.   —Lao-tse, *Tao Te Ching*, sec.27 (c.550 B.C.), tr. Gia-Fu Feng and Jane English.

Just as a person is commanded to honor and revere his father, so it is his duty to honor and revere his teacher, even more than his father.... There is no honor higher than that which is due the teacher, no reverence more profound than that which should be bestowed on him.
— Maimonides,
Mishneh Torah (Second Law),
I.v.1 (1180).

We should honor our teachers more than our parents, because while our parents cause us to live, our teachers cause to to live well. — Philoxenus,
in Stobaeus, *Florilegium*, appendix,
260 (c. A.D. 450–500).

Teaching

See also below; Instruction; Interest; Language, Teaching of; Lesson Planning

When I teach people, I marry them.
— Sylvia Ashton-Warner,
Teacher (1963).

The older I get the more I realize that the only thing a teacher has to go on is that rare spark in a boy's eye. And when you see *that*, Brian, you're an ass if you worry where it comes from. Whether it's an ode of Horace or an Icelandic saga or something that goes bang in a laboratory.
— Louis Auchincloss,
The Rector of Justin, iii (1964).

When will the public cease to insult the teacher's calling with empty flattery? When will men who would never for a moment encourage their own sons to enter the work of the public schools cease to tell us that education is the greatest and noblest of all human callings?
— William C. Bagley,
Craftsmanship in Teaching (1911).

Teaching is not a lost art, but the regard for it is a lost tradition.
— Jacques Barzun,
in *Newsweek*, Dec. 5, 1955.

Any subject can be effectively taught in some intellectually honest form to any child at any stage of development.
— Jerome S. Bruner,
The Process of Education, iii (1960).

Not to enlighten one who can be enlightened is to waste a man; to endeavor to enlighten one who cannot be enlightened is to waste words. The intelligent man wastes neither his man nor his words. — Confucius,
Analects, XV.vii (c.500 B.C.).

One might as well say he has sold when no one has bought as to say he has taught when no one has learned.
— John Dewey, in
Readings in the History of Education,
ed. Edward A. Fitzpatrick (1936).

If a teacher have any opinion which he wishes to conceal, his pupils will become as fully indoctrinated into that as into any which he publishes.
— Ralph Waldo Emerson,
*Essays, First Series:
Spiritual Laws* (1841).

There is no teaching until the pupil is brought into the same state or principle in which you are; a transformation takes place; he is you and you are he; then is a teaching, and by no unfriendly chance or bad company can he ever quite lose the benefit. — Ralph Waldo Emerson,
ibid.

Teaching is, in one of its aspects, a performing art. — Joseph Epstein,
"A Class Act," *Quest*, Sept. 1981.

The whole art of teaching is only the art of awakening the natural curiosity of young minds for the purpose of satisfying it afterwards. — Anatole France,
The Crime of Sylvestre Bonnard,
II.iv (1881).

If he is indeed wise he does not bid you enter the house of his wisdom, but rather leads you to the threshold of your own mind. — Kahlil Gibran,
The Prophet: On Teaching (1923).

To reach a child's mind a teacher must capture his heart. Only if a child feels right can he think right.
　　　　　　　　—Haim G. Ginott,
　　　　　　　Teacher and Child, 81 (1972).

Good teaching is one-fourth preparation and three-fourths theatre.
　　　　　　　　—Gail Godwin,
　　　　　　　The Odd Woman (1974).

And, as a bird each fond endearment tries,
To tempt its new-fledged offspring to the skies;
He tried each art, reproved each dull delay,
Allured to brighter worlds, and led the way.　　　　　—Oliver Goldsmith,
The Deserted Village, ln.167 (1770).

The right to impart instruction, harmless in itself or beneficial to those who receive it, is a substantial right of property.
　　　　　　　　—John Marshall Harlan,
　　　　　　U.S. Supreme Court decision,
　　　　　　　Berea v Kentucky, 1908.

It is a luxury to learn; but the luxury of learning is not to be compared with the luxury of teaching.
　　　　　　　　—Roswell D. Hitchcock,
　　　　　　　The Eternal Atonement:
　　　　　　Receiving and Giving (1888).

Psychology is a science; teaching is an art, and sciences never generate arts directly out of themselves. An intermediary inventive mind must make the application, by use of its originality.
　　　　　　　—William James, *Talks*
　　　　to Teachers on Psychology (1899).

Nobody can be taught faster than he can learn.... Every man that has ever undertaken to instruct others can tell what slow advances he has been able to make, and how much patience it requires to recall vagrant inattention, to stimulate sluggish indifference, and to rectify absurd misapprehension.　　　—Samuel Johnson,
　　　　　Lives of the Poets: Milton
　　　　　　　　　(1779).

They [students] got nothing from me in the way of intellectual food but a lean and perfunctory banquet; and anything that I gave them in the way of sound moral benefit I gave gladly and never missed. But schoolboys have a way of being grateful. It is the decent thing about them.　　　　　—Stephen Leacock,
　　College Days: Memories and Miseries
　　　　　of a Schoolmaster (1923).

Teachers are overworked and underpaid. True. It is an exacting and exhausting business, this damming up the flood of human potentialities. What energy it takes to make a torrent into a trickle, to train that trickle along narrow, well-marked channels! —George B. Leonard,
　　　　　Education and Ecstasy, 1 (1968).

I offer them as what I believe, not what is to be believed. I aim here only at revealing myslf, who will perhaps be different tomorrow, if I learn something new which changes me. I have no authority to be believed, nor do I want it, feeling myself too ill-instructed to instruct others.　　—Michel de Montaigne,
　　　　　Essays, I.xxvi (1580): *Of*
　　　　　the Education of Children.

I have sometimes wondered whether my pupils realized the intensity of feeling which underlay a decorous classroom manner of dealing with certain books and men. Perhaps I gave myself away when I read poetry aloud.　　　—Bliss Perry,
　　　　　And Gladly Teach (1935).

If we value independence, if we are disturbed by the growing conformity of knowledge, of values, of attitudes, which our present system induces, then we may wish to set up conditions of learning which make for uniqueness, for self-direction, and for self-initiated learning.
　　　　　　　　—Carl R. Rogers,
　　　　　On Becoming a Person (1961).

If you send somebody to teach somebody, be sure that the system you are teaching is better than the system they are practicing.　　　　—Will Rogers,
　　　　　Autobiography (1926).

The well-meaning people who talk about education as if it were a substance distributable by coupon in large or small quantities never exhibit any understanding of the truth that you cannot teach anybody anything that he does not want to learn. —George Sampson, *Seven Essays* (1947).

Teaching occurs when two people enter into symbolic exchange with one another about some other thing. The otherness of that "thing" is important: the two do not talk about one another. The two can be children, adults, or an adult and a child. In symbolic exchange at its best, both of them learn. The most familiar such exchange in education is, of course, the one between teacher and student.
—Joseph J. Schwab, "Teaching and Learning," *The Center Magazine*, Nov./Dec. 1976.

In the last analysis, every mental act—including teaching and learning—is a mystery—one which psychologists and philosophers can only speculate about. Hence, at bottom, in the depths of the mind, teaching is a mystery.
—Joseph J. Schwab, *ibid.*

Unless one has taught ... it is hard to imagine the extent of the demands made on a teacher's attention.
—Charles E. Silberman, *Crisis in the Classroom* (1970).

Delightful task! to rear the tender thought,
To teach the young idea how to shoot,
To pour the fresh instruction o'er the mind,
To breathe the enlivening spirit, and to fix
The generous purpose in the glowing breast. —James Thomson, *The Seasons: Spring*, ln.1152 (1746).

I can give you no theoretical advice in pedagogy, but I'll tell you one thing from experience. It will frequently happen when you are holding forth that some boy in the class will disagree. He will probably shake his head violently. You will be tempted to go after him and convert him then and there. Don't do it. He is probably the only one who is listening.
—William Peterfield Trent, to John Erskine at the beginning of the latter's teaching career, c.1903.

I'll learn him or kill him.
—Mark Twain, *Life on the Mississippi*, viii (1883). A veteran pilot's philosophy of teaching.

"I understand you have had no previous experience?"
"No, sir, I am afraid not."
"Well, of course, that is in many ways an advantage. One too easily acquires the professional tone and loses vision."
—Evelyn Waugh, *Decline and Fall*, I.i (1928).

Teaching, Aim of

Education, other than self-education, lies mainly in the shaping of men's interests and aims. If you convince a man that another way of looking at things is more profound, another form of pleasure more subtle than that to which he has been accustomed—if you make him really see it—the very nature of man is such that he will desire the profounder thought and the subtler joy.
—Oliver Wendell Holmes, Jr., oration, Harvard Law School Association, Cambridge, Nov. 5, 1886, on the 250th anniversary of Harvard University, in M.D. Howe, *Occasional Speeches of Justice Oliver Wendell Holmes* (1962).

Then take him to develop, if you can,
And hew the Block off, and get out the Man. —Alexander Pope, *The Dunciad*, IV.269 (1743).

The close observer soon discovers that the teacher's task is not to implant facts but to place the subject to be learned in front of the learner and, through sympathy,

emotion, imagination, and patience, to awaken in the learner the restless drive for answers and insights which enlarge the personal life and give it meaning.
— Nathan M. Pusey,
in *The New York Times*,
Mar. 22, 1959.

Therefore I summoned the teachers before me and I said to them:....
You shall not fill them with hollow formulas, but with visions that are the portals of creative action.
Nor must you begin by imparting the dry bones of knowledge, but you shall impart to them a mode of thought enabling them to grasp the Here and Now.
— Antoine de Saint-Exupéry,
The Wisdom of the Sands, xxv (1950).

No man can better display the power of his skill and disposition, than in so training men, that they come at last to live under the domination of their own reason.   — Baruch Spinoza,
Ethics, IV. Appendix ix (1677).

Teaching kids to count is fine, but teaching them what counts is best.
— Bob Talbert,
Detroit Free Press, Apr. 5, 1982.

Teaching, Criticism of

Better untaught than ill taught.
— H.G. Bohn,
Handbook of Proverbs, 330 (1855).

A schoolmaster spends his life telling the same people the same things about the same things.   — Greek proverb.

According to the proverbe, I went about to fil your mouth, with an empty spoone. That is, seeme to teach, not to teach.
— Stefano Guazzo,
Civil Conversation, III.86 (1574).

If, as is our custom, the teachers undertake to regulate many minds of such different capacities and forms with the same lesson and a similar amount of

guidance, it is no wonder if in a whole race of children they find barely two or three who reap any proper fruit from their instruction.
— Michel de Montaigne,
Essays, I.xxvi (1580):
Of the Education of Children.

Certain mental habits are commonly instilled by those who are engaged in educating: obedience and discipline, ruthlessness in the struggle for wordly success, contempt towards opposing groups, and an unquestioning credulity, a passive acceptance of the teacher's wisdom. All these habits are against life.
— Bertrand Russell,
Principles of Social Reconstruction:
Education (1916).

I want simply this world better taught.
— H.G. Wells,
The Undying Fire, 182 (1919).

We, in our educational system, have burdened the memory with a load of unconnected facts, and laboriously striven to impart our laboriously-acquired knowledge. We teach people how to remember, we never teach them how to grow.   — Oscar Wilde,
Intentions: The Critic as Artist (1891).

Teaching, Dispraise of

It were better to perish than to continue schoolmastering.   — Thomas Carlyle,
in D.A. Wilson, *Life of Carlyle*
(1923–34): *Carlyle till Marriage*.

School-keeping is a dreary task, only relieved by the pleasure the teacher takes in two or three bright and beautiful pupils.   — Ralph Waldo Emerson,
Journals, 1863.

Do you teach? Bowels of iron is what a teacher needs when each pupil stands up in turn and recites the self-same things in the self-same way. The same daily fare again and again — it is death to the wretched master. "What would I not give," he cries, "that the boy's father might listen to him as often as I do." And you live in a hole no blacksmith would put up with.   —Juvenal, *Satires*, VII (c. A.D. 110).

The lust to teach—a passion apparently analogous to concupiscence or dipsomania, and, in the more extreme varieties of pedagogues, maybe quite as strong.   —H.L. Mencken, *Heathen Days, 1890–1936: The Educational Process* (1943).

The teacher's life is painfull and therefore would be pityed: it wrastles with unthankfulnesse above all measure.... Our calling creepes low and hath pain for companion.   — Richard Mulcaster, *Positions* (1581).

The vanity of teaching often tempteth a man to forget he is a blockhead.   — George Savile, Marquis of Halifax, *Maxims* (1693).

Teaching, Effect of

In teaching you cannot see the fruit of a day's work. It is invisible and remains so, maybe for twenty years.   —Jacques Barzun, *The Teacher in America*, 301 (1944).

Teaching may hasten learning; it may also block it or kill it outright, or sometimes just render it comatose for years.   —James Harvey Robinson, *The Human Comedy as Devised and Directed by Mankind Itself* (1937).

Teaching, Importance of

Much as we respect the ministry of the gospel, we believe that it must yield in importance to the office of training the young.   —William Ellery Channing, (1780–1842), "Remarks on Education," *Christian Examiner*, Nov. 1833.

What greater or more beneficial service can I render the republic than to teach

and train the youth, considering how far astray our young men have gone because of the prevailing moral looseness. The greatest effort will be needed to restore them and point them in the right direction.   —Cicero, *De Devinatione*, II.ii.6 (44 B.C.?).

I think that saving a little child
And bringing him to his own,
Is a derned sight better business
Than loafing around the Throne.
          —John Milton Hay, *Little Breeches* (1871).

What office is there which involves more responsibility, which requires more qualifications, and which ought, therefore, to be more honourable, than that of teaching?
          —Harriet Martineau, *Society in America*, III: *Women* (1837).

Teaching, Lack of Knowledge for

How are you to impart to them what you do not possess yourself?   —Epictetus, *Discourses*, III.xxi (c. A.D. 100).

Of what he knows nothing, nobody can teach anything.   —Ovid, *Tristia*, II.348 (c. A.D. 9).

Teaching, Learning by

It is by teaching that we teach ourselves, by relating that we observe, by affirming that we examine, by showing that we look, by writing what we think, by pumping that we draw water into the well.   —Henri Frédéric Amiel, *Journal*, Oct. 27, 1853.

Teaching of others, teacheth the Teacher.
          —Thomas Fuller (1654–1734), *Gnomologia*, no.4323 (1732).

Whatever thou hast learned from me or from thy teachers, impart it again

298   Teaching, Learning by; Teaching Method

regularly to worthy pupils, so that thou mayest retain it, for by teaching it to others thou wilt know it by heart, and their questions will compel thee to precision, and remove any doubts from thine own mind.   —Judah Ibn Tibbon, to his son, *Ethical Will* (c.1190).

To teach is to learn twice over.
—Joseph Joubert,
Pensées (1810).

While we teach, we learn.   —Seneca,
Letters to Lucilius,
VII.viii (c. A.D. 64).

I have learnt much from my teachers, and from my colleagues more than from my teachers, but from my disciples more than from them all.   —*Talmud: Ta'anith*, 7a (before A.D. 500).

Teaching Method

To know how to suggest is the great art of teaching. To attain it we must be able to guess what will interest; we must learn to read the childish soul as we might a piece of music.   —Henri Frédéric Amiel, *Journal*, Nov. 16, 1864.

Beat a child if he dance not well and cherish him though he learn not well, ye shall have him unwilling to go to dance and glad to go to his book. Knock him always when he draweth his shaft ill and favor him again though he fault at his book, ye shall have him very loath to be in the field and very willing to be in the school.   —Roger Ascham, *The Schoolmaster*, I (1570).

But if the child miss, either in forgetting a word, or in changing a good with a worse, or misordering the sentence, I would not have the master either frown or chide with him, if the child have done his diligence and used no truantship therein. For I know by good experience that a child shall take more profit of two faults gently warned of than of four things rightly hit.   —Roger Ascham, *ibid.*

How then do you pour a little bit of what you feel and think and know into another's mind?... To help children visualize, to convince them, the teachers use maps, charts, diagrams, they write words on the board, they gesture, admonish, orate. Hence the fatigue and hence the rule that good teaching is a matter of basal metabolism. Some teachers have the facts but not the phosphorescence of learning.   —Jacques Barzun, *The Teacher in America*, 31 (1944).

For it is precept upon precept, precept upon precept, line upon line, line upon line, here a little, there a little.
—*Bible: Isaiah* 28:10.

Not only is there an art in knowing a thing, but also a certain art in teaching it.
—Cicero,
De Legibus, II.xix.47 (c.46 B.C.).

A good teacher, like a good entertainer first must hold his audience's attention. Then he can teach his lesson.
—John Henrik Clarke,
"A Search for Identity,"
Social Casework, May 1970.

Therefore, those who drive boys to their studies, do them great harm. For what result can they expect? If a man have no appetite, but yet takes food when urged to do so, the result can only be sickness and vomiting, or at least indigestion and indisposition. On the other hand, if a man be hungry, he is eager to take food, digests it readily, and easily converts it into flesh and blood.
—John Amos Comenius,
The Great Didactic (1628–32).

Let the main object of this, our Didactic, be as follows: To seek and find a method of instruction, by which teachers may teach less, but learners learn more; by which schools may be the scene of less noise, aversion, and useless labour, but more of leisure, enjoyment, and solid progress.   —John Amos Comenius, *ibid.*

I do not open up the truth to one who is not eager to get knowledge, nor help out anyone who is not anxious to explain himself. When I have presented one corner of a subject to anyone, and he cannot from it learn the other three, I do not repeat my lesson. — Confucius, *Analects*, VII.viii (c.500 B.C.).

Seek to delight, that they may mend mankind.
And, while they captivate, inform the mind. — William Cowper,
Hope, ln.367 (1781).

Everything the teacher does, as well as the manner in which he does it, incites the child to respond in some way or other, and each response tends to set the child's attitude in some way or other.
— John Dewey,
How We Think: The Influence of the Habits of Others (1933).

Let not the teacher impose his yoke heavily on them [children], for instruction is only efficient when it is conveyed easily and agreeably. Give the children small presents of money and the like, to please them — this helps their studies.
— Elijah ben Solomon Zalman,
letter to his family,
Alim LiTerufa (1836).

We put all the pleasure on one side, and all the irksomness on the other; all the irksomness in study, and all the pleasure in amusement.... Let us endeavor then to change this order: let us render study agreeable, let us conceal it under the appearance of liberty and pleasure; let us allow children sometimes to interrupt their studies with little flights of amusement; they have need of these distractions in order to rest their minds.
— François Fénelon,
The Education of Girls (1687).

Teaching youngsters isn't much like making steel ... and essential as good technique is, I don't think education is basically a technological problem. It is a problem of drawing out of each young-

he has to give and of helping him to see the world he is involved in clearly enough to become himself — among other people — in it, while teaching him the skills he will need in the process.
— Edgar Z. Friedenberg,
The Dignity of Youth and Other Atavisms (1965).

A good teacher feels his way, looking for response. — Paul Goodman,
Growing Up Absurd (1960).

Children are simple — loving — true;
'Tis Heaven that made them so;
And would you teach them — to be so too —
And stoop to what they know.
— Samuel Griswold Goodrich (1793–1860), *The Teacher's Lesson*, ln.25.

Why may not one be telling truth while one laughs, as teachers sometimes give little boys cakes to coax them into learning their letters? — Horace,
Satires, I.i.24 (c. 35 B.C.).

Education in the long run is an affair that works itself out between the individual student and his opportunities. Methods of which we talk so much, play but a minor part. Offer the opportunities, leave the student to his natural reaction on them, and he will work out his personal destiny, be it a high one or a low one. — William James,
Stanford's Ideal Destiny,
address at Stanford University
on Founders' Day, 1906.

It is no matter what you teach them first, any more than that what leg you shall put into your breeches first.... You may stand disputing which is best to put in first, but in the meantime your breech is bare.... While you are considering which of two things you should teach your child first, another boy has learnt them both.
— Samuel Johnson,
in James Boswell,
Life of Samuel Johnson,
xv, July 26, 1763 (1791).

How should a class be taught? The teacher sits at the head of the table and the pupils surround him as a wreath, so that all can see the teacher and hear what he says. The teacher must not sit on a chair while his pupils sit on the ground; either they all sit on the floor or they all occupy chairs.   —Maimonides,
Mishneh Torah (Second Law),
I.iv.2 (1180).

If a teacher has taught a subject and the pupils failed to understand it, he must not be angry with them nor get excited, but should review the lesson with them many times until they finally grasp it. Neither should a pupil say *I understand* when he does not, but should keep on asking questions repeatedly.
—Maimonides,
ibid., I.iv.4.

There is only one sound method of moral education. It is teaching people to think.
—Everett Dean Martin,
The Meaning of a Liberal Education
(1926).

I maintain, in truth,
That with a smile we should instruct our youth,
Be very gentle when we have to blame,
And not put them in fear of virtue's name.   —Molière,
The School for Husbands (1661).

This method of education ought to be carried on with a severe sweetness, quite contrary to the practice of our pedants, who, instead of tempting and alluring children to letters by apt and gentle ways, do in truth present nothing before them but rods and ferrules, horror and cruelty. Away with this violence! away with this compulsion! than which, I certainly believe nothing more dulls and degenerates a well-descended nature.
—Michel de Montaigne,
Essays, I.xxvi (1580):
Of the Education of Children.

Let the tutor demand an account not only of the words of his lesson, but of their

meaning and substance, and let him estimate the profit he has gained, not by the testimony of his memory, but of his life. Let him show what he has just learned from a hundred points of view, and adapt it to as many different subjects, to see if he has rightly taken it in and made it his own.
—Michel de Montaigne,
ibid.

Let the tutor make him pass everything through a sieve and lodge nothing in his head on mere authority and trust.... Let variety of ideas be set before him; he will choose if he can; if not, he will remain in doubt. Only the fools are certain and assured.   —Michel de Montaigne,
ibid.

He who wishes to teach us a truth should not tell it to us, but simply suggest it with a brief gesture, a gesture which starts an ideal trajectory in the air along which we glide until we find ourselves at the feet of the new truth.   —José Ortega y Gasset,
*Meditations on Quixote:
Preliminary Meditation* (1914).

A teacher should give his pupil opportunity for independent practice without suggestions from himself, and thus set upon him the stamp of indelible memory in its purest form.   —Philo,
On the Change of Names,
xlvii (before A.D. 54).

Knowledge which is acquired under compulsion obtains no hold on the mind.... Then ... do not use compulsion, but let early education be a sort of amusement; you will then be better able to find out the natural bent.   —Plato,
Republic, VIII (c.375 B.C.).

Children ought to be led to honorable practices by encouragement and reasoning, and most certainly not by blows or ill-treatment, for these are fitting rather for slaves than for free-born.
—Plutarch,
Moralia: The Education of Children,
xii (c. A.D. 95).

Men must be taught as if you taught
them not,
And things unknown propos'd as things
forgot.   — Alexander Pope,
An Essay on Criticism, III.574 (1711).

Let him [teacher] ... adopt a parental attitude to his pupils, and regard himself as
the representative of those who have
committed their children to his charge....
Let him be strict but not austere, genial
but not too familiar: for austerity will
make him unpopular, while familiarity
breeds contempt.   — Quintilian,
Institutio Oratoria, II.ii (A.D. 95 or 96).

Let him [teacher] often question his
pupils about the lecture, and insist on
repetition. But after the lecture let him
remain in or near the school, that his
hearers may be able to question him.
        — Society of Jesus (Jesuit Order),
        Ratio Studiorum (1599).

One should always teach his pupil in concise terms.   — *Talmud:*
        Pesahim, 3b (before A.D. 500).

Let us now ask how in our system of
education we are to guard against mental
dryrot. We enunciate two educational
commandments, "Do not teach too many
subjects," and again, "What you teach,
teach thoroughly."
        — Alfred North Whitehead,
        The Aims of Education, i (1929).

Textbook

THE SCHOOLMASTER: Or plain and
perfect way of teaching children, to
understand, write, and speak the Latin
tongue, but specially purposed for the
private bringing-up of youth in gentlemen's and noblemen's houses, and com-
modious also for all such as have forgot
the Latin tongue, and would, by themselves, without a schoolmaster, in short
time, and with small pains, recover a
sufficient ability to understand, write,
and speak Latin.   — Roger Ascham,
        title page of *The Schoolmaster* (1570).

The textbook remains the essential part
of the American educational technique,
and the work of the school is still closely
identified with book-learning.
        — George S. Counts,
        The American Road to Culture,
        129 (1930).

Dear little child, this little book
    Is less a primer than a key
To sunder gates where wonder waits
    Your "Open Sesame!"
        — Rupert Hughes, *With a First
    Reader*, in B.E. Stevenson, ed., *The
    Home Book of Modern Verse* (1925).

It is one of the great pleasures of a student's life to buy a heap of books at the
beginning of the autumn. Here, he fancies, are all the secrets. — Robert Lynd,
        Solomon in All His Glory (1922).

It is a pity therefore that books have not
been composed for youth, by some
curious and careful naturalists, and also
mechanicks, in the Latin tongue to be
used in schools, that they might learn
things with words: things obvious and
familiar to them; and which would make
the tongue easier to be obtained by
them.   — William Penn,
        Some Fruits of Solitude,
        I. no.15 (1693).

A text-book is no place for anything that
could be interpreted or even misinter-
preted as a personal grievance.
        — Ezra Pound,
        ABC of Reading, I.i (1934).

When you teach your son, teach him
from a corrected scroll [carefully edited
text].   — *Talmud:*
        Pesahim, 112a (before A.D. 500).

Theater

See also Tragedy

The *Theatres* — those *Cages of Uncleanness*, and publick Schools of Debauchery.
        — St. Augustine, *De Consensu
        Evangelistarum* (publ. 1473).

Spending time in the theatre produces fornication, intemperance, and every kind of impurity.
　　　　　　－St. John Chrysostom,
　　　　　Homilies, XV (c. A.D. 388).

Farce is the essential theatre. Farce refined becomes high comedy: farce brutalized becomes tragedy. But at the roots of all drama farce is to be found.
　　　　　　－Edward Gordon Craig,
　　　　　Index to the Story of My Days
　　　　　　　　　　　　(1981).

The most alarming thing about the contemporary American theater is the absolute regularity of its march toward extinction.　　　　－Walter Kerr,
　　　　How Not to Write a Play,
　　　　　　　　introd. (1955).

In all ages the drama, through its portrayal of the acting and suffering spirit of man, has been more closely allied than any other art to his deeper thoughts concerning his nature and his destiny.
　　　　　　－Ludwig Lewisohn,
　　　　　The Modern Drama (1915).

Great drama is the reflection of a great doubt in the heart and mind of a great, sad, gay man.　　－George Jean Nathan,
　　　　　Materia Critica (1924).

Drama—what literature does at night.
　　　　　　－George Jean Nathan,
　　　　　The Testament of a Critic,
　　　　　　　　179 (1931).

Drama is no mere setting up of the camera to nature: it is the presentation in parable of the conflict between Man's will and his environment: in a word, of problem.　　　　－George Bernard Shaw,
　　　　　Mrs. Warren's Profession,
　　　　　　　　preface (1902).

Theory

See also below; Hypothesis

Throw theory into the fire; it only spoils life.　　　　－Mikhail A. Bakunin,
　　letter to his sisters, Nov. 4, 1842.

Purely theoretic studies seem to me to be of those fine flowers which relieve the drabness of our existence and help to make the human scene worth while.
　　　　　　－Morris Raphael Cohen,
　　　　　The Faith of a Liberal, 86 (1946).

In the sphere of speculation there is no influence which hinders us from following what we are taught, but in life there are many influences which drag us to the contrary way.　　　　－Epictetus,
　　　　Discourses, I.xxvi (c. A.D. 100).

All theory, dear friend, is grey, but the golden tree of actual life springs ever green. －Johann Wolfgang von Goethe,
　　　　　Faust, I: *Study* (1808).

First ... a new theory is attacked as absurd; then it is admitted to be true, but obvious and insignificant; finally it is seen to be so important that its adversaries claim that they themselves discovered it.　　　　－William James,
　　　　Pragmatism: Lecture VI (1907).

The moment a person forms a theory, his imagination sees, in every object, only the traits which favor that theory.
　　　　　　－Thomas Jefferson,
　　　　letter to Charles Thompson,
　　　　　　　Sept. 20, 1787.

The theory of our modern technic shows that nothing is as practical as theory.
　　　　　　－J. Robert Oppenheimer,
　　　　　　　Reflex, July 1927.

Theory helps us to bear our ignorance of facts.　　　　－George Santayana,
　　　The Sense of Beauty: The Average Modified in the Direction of Pleasure
　　　　　　　　　　　　(1896).

People prefer theory to practice because it involves them in no more real responsibility than a game of checkers, while it permits them to feel they're doing something serious and important.
　　　　　　　　－Leo Stein,
　　　　　Journey into the Self,
　　　　　　　　107 (1950).

Theory in Education

See also Theory

Unless education marches on both feet—theory and practice—it risks going astray.   —Henry Adams, *The Education of Henry Adams*, xxviii (1907).

Perhaps I should,
As certain educators would,
Content myself with the conclusion;
In theory there is no solution.
          —W.H. Auden,
Collected Poetry: Labyrinth (1945).

A theory of instruction must concern itself with the relationship between how things are presented and how they are learned. Though I myself have worked hard and long in the vineyard of learning theory, I can do no better than to start by warning the reader away from it. Learning theory is not a theory of instruction. It describes what happened. A theory of instruction is a guide to what to do in order to achieve certain objectives.
          —Jerome S. Bruner,
address, "Educational Leadership,"
          May 1963.

The history of education is full of stillborn theories; the literature on the subject is largely made up of theorizing; whoever reads it much will turn with infinite relief to the lessons of experience.
          —Charles W. Eliot,
"The New Education: Its Organization,"
          Atlantic Monthly, 1869.

A theory of education is a glorious ideal, and it matters little, if we are not able to realize it at once. Only we must not look upon the idea as chimerical, nor decry it as a beautiful dream, though difficulties stand in the way of its realization.
          —Immanual Kant,
Pedagogy (1803).

Theories are more common than achievement in the history of education.
          —Richard Livingstone,
On Education (1944).

Thesis

The average Ph.D. thesis is nothing but a transference of bones from one graveyard to another.   —J. Frank Dobie, *A Texan in England*, i (1945).

It is not for nothing that the scholar invented the Ph.D. thesis as his principal contribution to literary form. The Ph.D. thesis is the perfect image of his world. It is work done for the sake of doing work—perfectly conscientious, perfectly laborious, perfectly irresponsible.
          —Archibald MacLeish,
The Irresponsibles (1940).

At the University every great treatise is postponed until its author attains impartial judgment and perfect knowledge. If a horse could wait as long for its shoes and would pay for them in advance, our blacksmiths would all be college dons.
          —George Bernard Shaw,
Maxims for Revolutionists (1903).

Thinker

See also Thinking

A "new thinker," when studied closely, is merely a man who does not know what other people have thought.
          —Frank Moore Colby,
The Margin of Hesitation (1921).

Although the proportion of those who *do* think be extremely small, yet every individual flatters himself that he is *one* of the number.   —Charles Caleb Colton, *Lacon*, I, preface (1820).

Beware when the great God lets loose a new thinker on this planet.
          —Ralph Waldo Emerson,
Journals, 1840; also *Essays, First Series: Circles* (1841).

Thinking

See also Freedom of Thought;
Thinker; Thought

It takes longer to think clearly than it
takes to learn rifle-shooting, round-arm
bowling, or piano-playing. The great
masses of people (of all classes) cannot
think at all. That is why the majority
never rule. They are led like sheep by the
few who know that they cannot think.
— Robert Blatchford,
God and My Neighbor (1903).

To think hard and persistently is painful.
— Louis D. Brandeis,
Business — A Profession (1914).

To most people nothing is more troublesome than the effort of thinking.
— James Bryce, *Studies in History
and Jurisprudence*, II.8 (1901).

Thinking means connecting things, and
stops if they cannot be connected.
— G.K. Chesterton,
Orthodoxy, iii (1908).

By freethinking I mean the use of the
understanding in endeavoring to find out
the meaning of any proposition what-
soever, in considering the nature of the
evidence for or against, and in judging of
it according to the seeming force or
weakness of the evidence.
— Anthony Collins,
A Discourse of Freethinking (1713).

To think is to differ.
— Clarence Darrow,
from the court records of the Scopes
trial, Dayton, Tenn., July 13, 1925.

It would be as wise and reasonable to say
that it does not matter which way the
rudder swings as the ship moves, as to say
that it does not matter what a man
thinks.   — W.J. Dawson,
The Making of Manhood (1895).

The more a man thinks the better
adapted he becomes to thinking, and
education is nothing if it is not the

methodical creation of the habit of
thinking.   — Ernest Dimnet,
The Art of Thinking, II.i.b (1928).

What was once thought can never be
unthought.   — Friedrich Dürrenmatt,
The Physicists, II (1962)

There is no expedient to which a man will
not go to avoid the real labor of thinking.
— Thomas A. Edison, motto posted
throughout his laboratories (c.1895).

In this world, if a man sits down to think,
he is immediately asked if he has the
headache?   — Ralph Waldo Emerson,
Journals, 1833.

We must dare to think about "unthinkable things," because when things
become "unthinkable," thinking stops
and action becomes mindless.
— J. William Fulbright,
address in U.S. Senate, Mar. 26, 1964.

The proper method for hastening the
decay of error is ... by teaching every man
to think for himself.
— William Godwin, *An Enquiry
concerning Political Justice* (1793).

Most men think dramatically, not quanti-
tatively. — Oliver Wendell Holmes, Jr.,
Speeches: Law and the Courts (1913).

To think correctly is the condition of
behaving well. It is also in itself a moral
act; those who would think correctly must
resist considerable temptations.
— Aldous Huxley, *The Olive Tree:
Words and Behavior* (1937).

The stream of thinking is only a careless
name for what, when scrutinized, reveals
itself to consist chiefly of the stream of my
breathing.   — William James,
Essays in Radical Empiricism, i (1912).

You may derive thoughts from others;
your way of thinking, the mould in which
your thoughts are cast, must be your
own.   — Charles Lamb,
*The Essays of Elia: The Old and
the New Schoolmaster* (1823).

Think before you think!
— Stanislaw J. Lec,
Unkempt Thoughts, tr. Jacek Galazka
(1962).

It is so much easier to assume than to prove; it is so much less painful to believe than to doubt; there is such a charm in the repose of prejudice, when no discordant voice jars upon the harmony of belief; there is such a thrilling pang when cherished dreams are scattered, and old creeds abandoned, that it is not surprising that men close their eyes to the unwelcome light.
— William E.H. Lecky,
A History of Rationalism (1900).

If men are for a long time accustomed only to one sort or method of thoughts, their minds grow stiff in it, and do not readily turn to another.... I do not propose ... a variety and stock of knowledge, but a variety and freedom of thinking ... an increase of the powers and activity of the mind, not ... an enlargement of its possessions.   — John Locke,
An Essay concerning Human Understanding (1690).

To think is to meander from highway to byway, and from byway to alleyway, till we come to a dead end. Stopped dead in our alley, we think what a feat it would be to get out. That is when we look for the gate to the meadows beyond.
— Antonio Machado,
Juan de Mairena, xviii (1943).

Thinkin' is cheap, but thinkin' wrong is expensive.   — Van Wyck Mason,
The Sulu Sea Murders, 43 (1933).

The fatal tendency of mankind to leave off thinking about a thing when it is no longer doubtful, is the cause of half their errors. A contemporary author has well spoken of "the deep slumber of a decided opinion."   — John Stuart Mill,
On Liberty, ii (1859).

Thinking is the endeavor to capture reality by means of ideas.
— José Ortega y Gasset,
The Dehumanization of Art (1925).

Man is but a reed, the most feeble thing in nature; but he is a thinking reed.
— Blaise Pascal,
Pensées, VI.347 (1670).

One of the worst diseases to which the human creature is liable is its disease of thinking. If it would only just *look* at a thing instead of thinking what it must be like, or *do* a thing, instead of thinking it cannot be done, we should all get on far better.   — John Ruskin,
The Political Economy of Art (1857).

At Learning's fountain it is sweet to
   drink,
But 't is a nobler privilege to think.
— John Godfrey Saxe,
The Library, ln.31 (1860).

There is nothing either good or bad but thinking makes it so.
— William Shakespeare,
Hamlet, II.ii.251 (1600–01).

There are few things more irritating than the glibness with which people tell us to think for ourselves when they know quite well that our minds are mostly herd minds, with only a scrap of individual mind on top. — George Bernard Shaw,
The Intelligent Woman's Guide to Socialism and Capitalism, v (1928).

Though man a thinking being is defined,
Few use the grand prerogative of mind.
How few think justly of the thinking few!
How many never think, who think they do!   — Jane Taylor,
Essays in Rhyme: On Morals and Manners: Prejudice, I.xlv (1820).

You would think that there was a tariff on thinking and originality.
— Henry David Thoreau,
Autumn, Nov. 25, 1858.

"I don't know that I care so much about going far," he said at last, "but I should like to go *deep* where I go."
— Agnes Sligh Turnbull,
The Rolling Years, epilogue (1936).

To think is to dig and to measure with a plummet. Many have no strength to dig; others have not the courage to let the plummet sink into the depths.
— Rahel Levin Varnhagen,
Diary, Apr. 10, 1806.

In order to draw a limit to thinking, we should be able to think both sides of this limit. — Ludwig Wittgenstein, *Tractatus Logico-Philosophicus*, preface (1922).

If the power of reflecting on the past and darting the keen eyes of contemplation into futurity, be the grand privilege of man, it must be granted that some people enjoy this prerogative in a very limited degree. — Mary Wollstonecraft,
A Vindication of the Rights of Women, ix (1792).

Thought

See also Freedom of Thought; Thinker; Thinking

Who can mistake great thoughts?
They seize upon the mind — arrest, and search,
And shake it. — Philip James Bailey,
Festus: A Village Feast (1839).

A thought which does not result in an action is nothing much, and an action which does not proceed from a thought is nothing at all. — Georges Bernanos,
The Last Essays of Georges Bernanos: France Before the World of Tomorrow,
tr. Joan and Barry Ulanov (1955).

Stung by the spendour of a sudden thought. — Robert Browning,
Dramatis Personae: A Death in the Desert, ln.59 (1864).

Thought is valuable in proportion as it is generative. — Edward George Bulwer-Lytton, *Caxtoniana*, XIV (1863).

All great deeds and great thoughts have a ridiculous beginning.
— Albert Camus, *The Myth of Sysyphus: Absurd Walls* (1955).

Thought once awakened does not again slumber. — Thomas Carlyle,
Heroes and Hero Worship, I:
The Hero as Divinity (1840).

As the fletcher makes straight his arrow, a wise man makes straight his trembling and unsteady thought, which is difficult to guard, difficult to hold back.
— *Dhammapada*, iii (c.450–250 B.C.).

This then is the final triumph of thought — that it distintegrates all societies, and at last destroys the thinker himself. — Will Durant,
On the Meaning of Life (1932).

As certainly as water falls in rain on the tops of mountains and runs down into the valleys, plains and pits, so does thought fall first on the best minds, and run down, from class to class, until it reaches the masses, and works revolutions. — Ralph Waldo Emerson,
Lectures and Biographical Sketches: The Man of Letters (1884).

Thought is the seed of action.
— Ralph Waldo Emerson,
Society and Solitude: Art (1870).

Even knowledge has to be in the fashion.... Thought and taste change with the times. Do not be old-fashioned in your ways of thinking, and let your taste be in the modern style.
— Balthasar Gracián, *The Art of Worldly Wisdom*, cxx (1647).

Thought precedes action as lightning does thunder.
— Heinrich Heine, *History of Religion and Philosophy in Germany* (1834).

Every real thought on every real subject knocks the wind out of somebody or other. — Oliver Wendell Holmes, Sr.,
The Autocrat of the Breakfast-Table, v
(1858).

Thought must be divided against itself before it can come to any knowledge of itself. —Aldous Huxley, *Do What You Will: Wordsworth in the Tropics* (1929).

Thoughts, like fleas, jump from man to man. But they don't bite everybody. —Stanislaw J. Lec, *Unkempt Thoughts*, tr. Jacek Galazka (1962).

Though old the thought and oft exprest, 'T is his at last who says it best. —James Russell Lowell, *Under the Willows and Other Poems: For an Autograph* (1868).

Pain makes man think. Thought makes man wise. Wisdom makes life endurable. —John Patrick, *The Teahouse of the August Moon* (1954).

We find it hard to believe that other people's thoughts are as silly as our own, but they probably are. —James Harvey Robinson, *The Mind in the Making* (1921).

He who cannot change the very fabric of his thought will never be able to change reality. —Anwar el-Sadat, *In Search of Identity* (1978).

A thought by thought is piled, till some great truth
Is loosened, and the nations echo round, Shaken to their roots. —Percy Bysshe Shelley, *Prometheus Unbound*, II (1820).

Second thoughts oftentimes are the very worst of all thoughts. Indeed, second thoughts are too frequently formed by the love of novelty, of showing penetration, of distinguishing ourselves from the mob, and have consequently less of simplicity, and more of affectation. —William Shenstone, *Of Men and Manners* (1764).

The world is not so much in need of new thoughts as that when thought grows old and worn with usage it should, like current coin, be called in, and from the mint of genius, reissued fresh and new. —Alexander Smith, *Dreamthorp: On the Writing of Essays* (1863).

Thought is born of failure. —L.L. Whyte, *The Next Development in Man* (1944).

Time

Time as he grows old teaches many lessons. —Aeschylus, *Prometheus Bound*, ln.981 (c.490 B.C.).

The grand Instructor, Time. —Edmund Burke, *Second Letter to Sir Hercules Langrishe on the Catholic Question*, May 26, 1795.

The years teach much which the days never know. —Ralph Waldo Emerson, *Essays, Second Series: Experience* (1844).

Ordinary people think merely how they will *spend* their time; a man of intellect tries to *use* it. —Arthur Schopenhauer, *Aphorisms on the Wisdom of Life* (c.1845).

O Time! thou tutor both to good and bad. —William Shakespeare, *The Rape of Lucrece*, ln.995 (1594).

Tolerance

See also Closemindedness; Dogmatism; Openmindedness; Rigidity

Toleration is good for all, or it is good for none. —Edmund Burke, *Speech on the Relief of Protestant Dissenters*, House of Commons, 1773.

The peak of tolerance is most readily achieved by those who are not burdened with convictions.   — Alexander Chase, *Perspectives* (1966).

I have seen gross intolerance shown in support of toleration.
— Samuel Taylor Coleridge,
Biographia Literaria (1817).

The only true spirit of tolerance consists in our conscientious toleration of each other's intolerance.
— Samuel Taylor Coleridge,
The Friend, 56 (1809).

Tolerance always has limits—it cannot tolerate what is itself actively intolerant.
— Sidney Hook,
Pragmatism and the Tragic Sense of Life (1975).

The highest result of education is tolerance.   — Helen Keller,
Optimism, ii (1903).

Those wearing Tolerance for a label Call other views intolerable.
— Phyllis McGinley,
"In Praise of Diversity,"
The American Scholar, 1954.

Pray you use your freedom,
And, as far as you please, allow me mine.
To hear you only; not to be compelled
To take your moral potions.
— Philip Massinger,
The Duke of Milan, IV (1623).

Toleration is not the *opposite* of intoleration, but is the *counterfeit* of it. Both are despotisms. The one assumes to itself the right of withholding liberty of conscience, and the other of granting it.
— Thomas Paine,
The Rights of Man, I (1791).

It is easy to be tolerant when you do not care.   — Clement F. Rogers,
Verify Your References, 11 (1938).

The degree of tolerance attainable at any moment depends on the strain under which society is maintaining its cohesion.
— George Bernard Shaw,
Saint Joan, preface (1924).

Tradition

See also Custom

Tradition is a guide and not a jailer.
— W. Somerset Maugham,
The Summing Up, lx (1938).

You cannot walk the middle of the road holding hands with tradition on one side and modernism on the other. You have to make a choice. — Alvin E. Rolland,
School and Community, May 1962.

There is nothing sacred about convention: there is nothing sacred about primitive passions or whims; but the fact that a convention exists indicates that a way of living has been devised capable of maintaining itself. — George Santayana,
*Persons and Places, II:
The Middle Span*, iii (1945).

The young cannot teach tradition to the old.   — Yoruban proverb.

Tragedy

See also Theater

Tragedy is an imitation of an action that is serious, complete, and of a certain magnitude, effecting through pity and fear the proper katharsis or purgation, of emotions.   — Aristotle,
Poetics, vi (c.330 B.C.).

True tragedy may be defined as a dramatic work in which the outward failure of the principal personage is compensated for by the dignity and greatness of his character. — Joseph Wood Krutch,
introd. to *Nine Plays by
Eugene O'Neill* (1932).

First, tragedy always involves the manful struggle of a personality in the pursuit of some end, at the cost of suffering,

perhaps of death and failure.... Second, it is part of the essence of tragedy that the conflict should be recognized as necessary and its issue as inevitable.
—DeWitt H. Parker,
The Principles of Aesthetics (1946).

Training

See also Teaching

Teaching gives ideas, training reduces ideas to habits. Teaching gives knowledge, training reduces it to character.
—Henry Ward Beecher,
Proverbs from Plymouth Pulpit:
The Human Mind (1887).

Training is everything. The peach was once a bitter almond; cauliflower is nothing but cabbage with a college education. —Mark Twain,
Pudd'nhead Wilson's Calendar,
v (1894).

Translation

All translation is commentary.
—Leo Baeck,
The Pharisees, 35 (1947).

Translation is at best an echo.
—George Borrow,
Lavengro, xxv (1851).

Translations (like wives) are seldom faithful if they are in the least attractive.
—Roy Campbell,
Poetry Review, June/July 1949.

Nor ought a genius less than his that writ Attempt translation. —John Denham (1615–69), *To Sir Richard Fanshawe* (c.1650).

I should as soon think of swimming across Charles River, when I wish to go to Boston, as of reading all my books in originals, when I have them rendered for me in my mother tongue.
—Ralph Waldo Emerson,
The Conduct of Life:
In Praise of Books (1860).

There are few efforts more conducive to humility than that of the translator trying to communicate an incommunicable beauty. Yet unless we do try, something unique and never surpassed will cease to exist except in the libraries of a few inquisitive book lovers. —Edith Hamilton,
Three Greek Plays, introd. (1937).

The translation of a book which is a triumph of style in its own language, is always a piece of effrontry.
—H.T. Lowe-Porter,
translator's note (1924) to Thomas Mann,
Buddenbrooks (1902).

True, translation may use the value terms of its own tongue in its own time; but it cannot force these on a truly alien text.
—Josephine Miles,
Poetry and Change, xii (1974).

If the translator is a good poet, he substitutes his verse for that of the original; —I don't want his verse, I want the original; if he is a bad poet, he gives us bad verse, which is intolerable.
—George Moore,
Confessions of a Young Man,
vii (1888).

No literal translation can be just to an excellent original in a superior language; but it is a great mistake to imagine (as many have done) that a rash paraphrase can make amends for this general defect.
—Alexander Pope,
preface to translation of Homer's *Iliad*
(1715).

A translation is no translation, unless it will give you the music of a poem along with the words of it.
—John Millington Synge,
The Aran Islands (1907).

An idea does not pass from one language to another without change.
—Miguel de Unamuno,
The Tragic Sense of Life (1912).

It is impossible to translate poetry. Can you translate music? —Voltaire, letter to Mme. de Deffand, May 19, 1754.

Travel

The traveled mind is the catholic mind educated from exclusiveness and egoism.
— Amos Bronson Alcott,
Table Talk: Travel (1877).

Travel, in the younger sort, is a part of education; in the elder, a part of experience. He that travelleth into a country before he hath some entrance into the language, goeth to school, and not to travel. — Francis Bacon,
Essays: Of Travel (1625).

Many shall run to and fro, and knowledge shall increase. —*Bible: Daniel* 12:4.

If an ass goes traveling he'll not come home a horse. — Thomas Fuller
(1654–1734), *Gnomologia* (1732).

The young fellows of this age profit no more by their going abroad than they do by their going to church.
— John Vanbrugh,
The Relapse, I (1696).

He travelled here, he travelled there;—
But not the value of a hair
Was head or heart the better.
— William Wordsworth,
Peter Bell, ln.238 (1798).

Trust

All a child's life depends on the ideal it has of its parents. Destroy that and everything goes—morals, behaviour, everything. Absolute trust in some one else is the essence of education.
—E.M. Forster,
Where Angels Fear to Tread, v (1905).

The only way to make a man trustworthy is to trust him; and the surest way to make him untrustworthy is to distrust him and show your distrust.
— Henry Lewis Stimson,
"The Bomb and the Opportunity,"
Harper's Magazine, Mar. 1946.

Truth

See also below

The truth is often a terrible weapon of aggression. It is possible to lie, and even to murder, with the truth. — Alfred Adler,
Problems of Neurosis (1929).

The truth that makes men free is for the most part the truth which men prefer not to hear. — Herbert Agar,
A Time for Greatness (1942).

All truth is equilibrated. Pushing any truth out very far, you are met by a counter-truth. — Henry Ward Beecher,
Proverbs from Plymouth Pulpit: Truth (1887).

Nobody ever sees truth except in fragments. — Henry Ward Beecher,
ibid.

Crushing truths perish by being acknowledged. — Albert Camus,
The Myth of Sysyphus, 122 (1955).

Truths turn into dogmas the moment they are disputed. — G.K. Chesterton,
Heretics, xx (1905).

The "truths" that come down the ages are like a long string of grasshoppers standing in single file who jump over one another's backs. They continue without pause, always "moving ahead," until they arrive over and over again at the point where they began. And where was that?
— Benjamin De Casseres,
Fantasia Impromptu (1933).

Whoever undertakes to set himself up as judge in the field of Truth and Knowledge is shipwrecked by the laughter of the gods. — Albert Einstein,
Ideas and Opinions (1954).

Truth has rough flavours if we bite it through. — George Eliot,
Armgart, ii (1871).

Truth is to be accepted from any man. Its touch-stone is not the rank or position of its professor, but its intrinsic worth.
— Shem Tob Falaquera,
Sefer HaMaalot (13th cent.).

Truth always lags last, limping along on the arm of Time. — Balthasar Gracián, *The Art of Worldly Wisdom*, cxlvi (1647).

The cause of truth counts not the number of adherents. — Samson Raphael Hirsch, *Nineteen Letters*, no.18 (1836).

Truth is tough. It will not break, like a bubble, at a touch; nay, you may kick it about all day, like a foot-ball, and it will be round and full at evening.
— Oliver Wendell Holmes, Sr., *The Professor at the Breakfast-Table*, v (1860).

All truths cannot be equally important. It is true that a finite whole is greater than any of its parts. It is also true, in the common-sense use of the word, that the New Haven telephone book is smaller than that of Chicago. The first truth is infinitely more fertile and significant than the second. — Robert M. Hutchins, *The Higher Learning in America* (1936).

Absolute truth is incompatible with an advanced state of society.
— Joaquim Maria Machado, *Epitaph of a Small Winner* (1881).

But it is not enough to possess a truth; it is essential that the truth possess us.
— Maurice Maeterlinck, *The Treasure of the Humble: The Deeper Life* (1896).

Truth and reason are common to everyone, and no more belong to the man who first said them than to the man who says them later. — Michel de Montaigne, *Essays*, I.xxvi (1580): *Of the Education of Children*.

One's belief in truth begins with a doubt of all the truths one has believed hitherto. — Friedrich Nietzsche, *Human, All Too Human* (1878).

The old faiths light their candles all about,
But burly Truth comes by and puts them out. — Lizette Reese (1856–1935), *Truth*.

Truths may clash without contradicting each other. — Antoine de Saint-Exupéry, *The Wisdom of the Sands*, xxii (1950).

For truth is truth
To th' end of reck'ning.
— William Shakespeare, *Measure for Measure*, V.i.45 (1604).

The truth sticks in our throats with all the sauces it is served with: it will never go down until we take it without any sauce at all. — George Bernard Shaw, *Saint Joan*, preface (1924).

Truth generally lies in the coordination of antagonistic opinions.
— Herbert Spencer, *Autobiography* (1904).

There would seem to be a law operating in human experience by which the mind once suddenly aware of a verity for the first time immediately invents it again.
— Agnes Sligh Turnbull, *The Golden Journey*, x (1955).

Truth is mighty and will prevail. There is nothing the matter with this, except that it ain't so. — Mark Twain, *Notebook*, July 4, 1898 (1935).

All truths wait in all things,
They neither hasten their own delivery nor resist it,
They do not need the obstetric forceps of the surgeon. — Walt Whitman, *Leaves of Grass*, III: *Song of Myself*, sec. 30 (1855).

Truth, Changing

What late was Truth, now turn'd to
Heresie.   — Michael Drayton,
           Legends, iv. 909 (1596).

No truth so sublime but it may be trivial
to-morrow in the light of new thoughts.
                   — Ralph Waldo Emerson,
       Essays, First Series: Circles (1841).

Most of the change we think we see in life
Is due to truths being in and out of favor.
                        — Robert Frost,
     North of Boston: The Black Cottage,
                        ln.109 (1914).

The truth may be one, final, determined,
but my apprehension of it can never be
anything of the kind; it is changing
continuously.   — Bede Jarrett,
       Meditations for Layfolk (1915).

What everybody echoes or in silence
passes by as true to-day may turn out to
be falsehood to-morrow, mere smoke of
opinion, which some had trusted for a
cloud that would sprinkle fertilizing rain
on their fields. — Henry David Thoreau,
              Walden, i: *Economy* (1854).

Truth, Definition of

Truth is an ideal expression of the
Universe, at once coherent and com-
prehensive. It must not conflict with
itself, and there must be no suggestion
which fails to fall inside it. Perfect truth
in short must realize the idea of a systematic whole. And such a whole ...
possesses essentially the two characters of
coherence and comprehensiveness.
              — Francis Herbert Bradley,
         *Essays on Truth and Reality:
         On Truth and Coherence* (1914).

That what guides us truly is true—
demonstrated capacity for such guidance
is precisely what is meant by truth.... The
hypothesis that works is the *true* one; and
truth is an abstract noun applied to a collection of cases, actual, foreseen, and
desired, that receive confirmation in their
consequences.   — John Dewey,
Reconstruction in Philosophy, 128 (1920).

The truth of an idea is not a stagnant
property in it. Truth *happens* to an idea.
It *becomes* true, is *made* true by events.
Its verity *is* in fact an event, a process: the
process namely of its verifying itself, its
veri-*fication*. Its validity is the process of
its valid-*ation*.   — William James,
         Pragmatism: Lecture VI (1907).

Truth is the object of Knowledge of
whatever kind; and when we inquire
what is meant by Truth, I suppose it is
right to answer that Truth means facts
and their relations, which stand towards
each other pretty much as subjects and
predicates in logic.
                   — John Henry Newman,
              The Idea of a University,
                   Discourse III (1873).

A belief is *true* when it corresponds to a
certain associated complex, and *false*
when it does not.   — Bertrand Russell,
              *The Problems of Philosophy:
              Truth and Falsehood* (1912).

Truth, New

See also Idea, New

Every great scientific truth goes through
three stages. First, people say it conflicts
with the Bible. Next, they say it has been
discovered before. Lastly, they say they
have always believed it.
                        — Louis Agassiz,
     in Bennett Cerf, *The Laugh's on Me*
                        (1959).

History warns us that it is the customary
fate of new truths to begin as heresies and
to end as superstitions. — T.H. Huxley,
              Science and Culture, xii:
              *The Coming of Age of "The
              Origin of Species"* (1881).

All the durable truths that have come into the world within historic times have

been opposed as bitterly as if they were so many waves of smallpox, and every individual who has welcomed and advocated them, absolutely without exception, has been denounced and punished as an enemy of the race.
—H.L. Mencken,
in *Smart Set*, June 1920.

Truth ... never comes into the world, but like a Bastard, to the ignominy of him that brought her forth. —John Milton,
The Doctrine and Discipline of Divorce, dedicatory address to Parliament (1644).

All great truths begin as blasphemies.
—George Bernard Shaw,
Annajanska (1917).

As a rule people are afraid of truth. Each truth we discover in nature or social life destroys the crutches on which we used to lean.   —Ernst Toller,
in *Saturday Review of Literature*,
May 20, 1944.

Heaven knows what seeming nonsense may not tomorrow be demonstrated truth.   —Alfred North Whitehead,
Science and the Modern World,
vii (1925).

Truth, Search for

Chase after the truth like all hell and you'll free yourself, even though you never touch its coat-tails.
—Clarence Darrow,
Voltaire (1916).

Truth, sir, is a profound sea, and few there be that dare wade deep enough to find out the bottom on't.
—George Farquhar,
The Beaux' Stratagem, V.i (1707).

Believe those who are seeking the truth; doubt those who have found it.
—André Gide,
So Be It (1959).

Follow not truth too near the heels, lest it dash out thy teeth.
—George Herbert,
Jacula Prudentum, no.1138 (1651).

The way of truth is like a great road. It is not difficult to know; the evil is only that men will not seek it.   —Mencius,
Discourses, VI.II.vii.7 (c.300 B.C.).

The essential thing is not to find truth but to investigate and search for it.
—Max Nordau,
Paradoxes, preface (1885).

He who sets out in search of Truth must leave Superstition forever and wander down into the land of Absolute Negation and Denial. He must then go ... where the mountains of Stern Reality will rise before him. *Beyond* them lies Truth.
—Olive Schreiner,
The Story of an African Farm (1883).

Truth, Tentative

If men can ever learn to accept their truths as not final, and if they can ever learn to build on something better than dogma, they may not be found saying, discouragedly, every once in so often, that every civilization carries in it the seeds of decay.   —Clarence Day,
This Simian World, xviii (1920).

If more men accept a doctrine than reject it, and those who accept it are more intelligent than its opponents, it is as near the truth as we can get at present.
—Edgar W. Howe,
Country Town Sayings (1911).

It is neither possible for man to know the truth fully nor to avoid the error of pretending that he does.
—Reinhold Niebuhr,
Human Destiny (1943).

No human being is constituted to know the truth, the whole truth, and nothing but the truth; and even the best of men must be content with fragments, with

partial glimpses, never the full fruition.
— William Osler,
Aequanimitas (1904).

There are no whole truths; all truths are
half-truths. It is trying to treat them as
whole truths that plays the devil.
— Alfred North Whitehead,
Dialogues, as recorded by Lucien Price,
16 (1953).

Uncertainty

See also Certainty

We are not certain; we are never certain.
If we were, we could reach some conclusions, and we could, at last, make others
take us seriously.   — Albert Camus,
The Fall (1957).

The quest for certainty blocks the search
for meaning. Uncertainty is the very condition to impel man to unfold his
powers.   — Erich Fromm,
Man for Himself, iii (1947).

If we will disbelieve everything because
we cannot certainly know all things, we
shall do much-what as wisely as he who
would not use his legs, but sit still and
perish because he had no wings to fly.
— John Locke,
*An Essay concerning Human
Understanding*, introd., sec.5 (1690).

We are most likely to get angry and excited in our opposition to some idea
when we ourselves are not quite certain of
our own position, and are inwardly tempted to take the other side.
— Thomas Mann,
Buddenbrooks, VIII.ii (1902).

Understanding

See also below; Knowledge

I will light in your heart the lamp of
understanding, which shall not be put
out.   — *Apocrypha:
II Esdras* 14:25 (c. A.D. 100).

The human understanding is of its own
nature prone to suppose the existence of
more order and regularity in the world
than it finds. And though there be many
things in nature which are singular and
unmatched, yet it devises for them
parallels and conjugates and relatives
which do not exist.   — Francis Bacon,
Novum Organum, I. Aphor. 45 (1620).

The healthy Understanding, we should
say, is not the Logical, argumentative,
but the Intuitive; for the end of Understanding is not to prove and find reasons,
but to know and believe.
— Thomas Carlyle,
Characteristics (1831).

It takes a long time to understand
nothing.   — Edward Dahlberg,
*Reasons of the Heart: On Wisdom
and Folly* (1965).

No man thoroughly understands a truth
until he has contended against it.
— Ralph Waldo Emerson,
Essays, First Series: Compensation
(1841).

The growth of understanding follows an
ascending spiral rather than a straight
line.   — Joanna Field,
A Life of One's Own (1934).

Whenever truth stands in the mind unac-
companied by the evidence upon which it
depends, it cannot properly be said to be
apprehended at all. — William Godwin,
*An Enquiry concerning Political
Justice* (1793).

Men hate what they cannot understand.
— Moses Ibn Ezra,
Shirat Yisrael, 96 (12th cent.).

Sir, I have found you an argument; but
I am not obliged to find you an understanding.   — Samuel Johnson,
in James Boswell, *Life of Samuel
Johnson*, lvi, June 19, 1784 (1791).

It is dangerous and presumptuous,
besides the absurd temerity that it

implies, to disdain what we do not comprehend. —Michel de Montaigne, *Essays*, 1.xxvii (1580): *It Is Folly to Measure the True and False by Our Own Capacity.*

Much was believed, but little understood,
And to be dull was constru'd to be good.
—Alexander Pope,
An Essay on Criticism, III.689 (1711).

Give it an understanding, but no tongue.
—William Shakespeare,
Hamlet, I.ii.249 (1600–01).

Look, he's winding up the watch of his wit. By and by it will strike.
—William Shakespeare,
The Tempest, II.i.12 (1611).

Men credit most easily the things which they do not understand. They believe most easily things which are obscure.
—Tacitus,
Histories, I.xxii (c. A.D. 104).

Where there is no understanding there is no knowledge; where there is no knowledge there is no understanding.
—*Talmud: Aboth*,
3.17 (before A.D. 500).

I wish to understand in such a way that everything that is inexplicable shall present itself to me as *necessarily* inexplicable. —Leo Tolstoy,
My Confession (1887).

To know a little less and to understand a little more: that, it seems to me, is our greatest need. —James Ramsey Ullman,
The White Tower (1945).

Understanding, Limited

Man, being the servant and interpreter of Nature, can do and understand so much only as he has observed in fact or in thought of the course of nature: beyond this he neither knows anything nor can do anything. —Francis Bacon,
Novum Organum, I. Aphor.1 (1620).

He neither knew anything, nor wished to know anything. His instinct told him that it was better to understand little than to misunderstand a lot. —Anatole France,
The Revolt of the Angels, i (1914).

Between
Our birth and death we may touch understanding
As a moth brushes a window with its wing. —Christopher Fry,
The Boy with a Cart (1945).

We have learnt that nothing is simple and rational except what we ourselves have invented; that God thinks in terms neither of Euclid nor of Riemann; that science has "explained" nothing; that the more we know the more fantastic the world becomes and the profounder the surrounding darkness. —Aldous Huxley,
Essays New and Old: Views of Holland (1925).

And what did I see I had not seen before?
Only a question less or a question more.
—Edna St. Vincent Millay,
Second April (1921): *White Swans.*

Understanding Others

To understand another human being you must gain some insight into the conditions which made him what he is.
—Margaret Bourke-White,
in Anne Tucker, *The Woman's Eye* (1973).

You must look into people, as well as at them. —Lord Chesterfield,
Letters to Son, Oct. 4, 1746.

Understanding a person does not mean condoning; it only means that one does not accuse him as if one were God or a judge placed above him. —Erich Fromm,
Man for Himself (1947).

I have made it my earnest concern not to laugh at, nor deplore nor detest, but to understand the actions of human beings.
—Baruch Spinoza,
Tractatus Politicus, I.iv. (1677).

Uneducated Person

See also Ignorant Person

Education is a fine thing and doubtless deserves the high reputation it enjoys, particularly with the uneducated.
— George E. Allen,
Presidents Who Have Known Me (1950).

A people uneducated is like an iron mountain whose ore is unwrought.
— Henry Ward Beecher,
Proverbs from Plymouth Pulpit:
Education (1887).

A man with a little learning is like the frog who thinks its puddle a great sea.
— Burmese proverb.

The man who does not learn is dark, like one walking in the night.
— Chinese proverb.

It may very truely be saide, that it is not so muche commendation to a man to bee learned, as it is shame to be unlearned.
— Stefano Guazzo,
Civil Conversation, II.216 (1574).

Prola. It is dangerous to educate fools. *Pra.* It is still more dangerous to leave them uneducated.
— George Bernard Shaw,
The Simpleton of the Unexpected Isles (1934).

Illiteracy is a form of curable blindness.
— Humbert Wolfe,
in Lore and Maurice Cowan,
The Wit of the Jews (1970).

University

See also below; Dean; Degree, Academic; Professor; Student, College

Predictable demography has caught up with the university empire builders.... To keep their mammoth plants financially solvent, many institutions have begun to use hard-sell, Madison-Avenue tech-niques to attract students. They sell college like soap.
— Caroline Bird,
The Case Against College (1975).

I am not impressed by the Ivy League establishments. Of course they graduate the best — it's all they'll take, leaving to others the problem of educating the country. They will give you an education the way the banks will give you money — provided you can prove to their satisfaction that you don't need it.
— Peter De Vries,
The Vale of Laughter, I.iv (1967).

The trouble with some Christian colleges is that they exist as promotional or maintenance institutions of the Church, and are not, in a high and holy sense, educational.
— Nels F.S. Ferré,
Christian Faith and Higher Education (1954).

The university must be a tributary to a larger society, not a sanctuary from it.
— A. Bartlett Giamatti,
Time, Oct. 2, 1978.

The actual benefit of college does not come so much from curriculum as from the change of environment. New people, new scenes, new conditions with which to cope — these are the things that work for growth.
— Elbert Hubbard,
Note Book, 89 (1927).

Any attempt to reform the university without attending to the system of which it is an integral part is like trying to do urban renewal in New York City from the twelfth storey up.
— Ivan D. Illich,
Deschooling Society, iii (1970).

A college doesn't need students: it's the students who need the college.
— Stephen Leacock,
Model Memoirs: On the Need for a Quiet College (1938).

The idea that going to college is one of the inherent rights of man seems to have

obtained a baseless foothold in the minds of many of our people.
— Abbott Lawrence Lowell, address at Haverford College, Apr. 17, 1931.

Universities are full of knowledge; the freshmen bring in a little and the seniors take none away; and the knowledge accumulates. — Abbott Lawrence Lowell, in Herbert R. Mayes, *An Editor's Treasury*, 2099 (1968).

Helping your eldest to pick a college is one of the greatest educational experiences of life — for the parents. Next to trying to pick his bride, it's the best way to learn that your authority, if not entirely gone, is slipping fast.
— Sally and James Reston, *Saturday Evening Post*, May 5, 1956.

College is always on the road to somewhere else.   — Tom Robbins, interview in *Bookviews*, Feb. 1978.

If our universities would exclude everybody who had not earned a living by his or her own exertions for at least a couple of years, their effect would be vastly improved.   — George Bernard Shaw, *Parents and Children*, preface to *Misalliance* (1914).

I give and bequeath in perpetuity the fifty shares which I hold in the Potomac Company ... towards the endowment of a university to be established within the limits of the District of Columbia, under the auspices of the general government, if that government should incline to extend a fostering hand towards it.
— George Washington, last will and testament, July 9, 1799. This stipulation was never fulfilled.

I asked W.: "What would you say of the university and modern life?" "I wouldn't say anything; I'd rather be excused."
— Walt Whitman, in Horace L. Traubel, *With Walt Whitman in Camden*, iv (1914).

University, Aim of

The course of instruction which is given to the undergraduates in the college is not designed to include *professional* studies. Our object is not to teach that which is peculiar to any one of the professions but to lay the foundation which is common to them all.   — Jeremiah Day and James Kingsley, *Yale Report of 1828*.

Under an intelligible program of general education, the student would come to the end of the sophomore year with a solid knowledge of the foundations of the intellectual disciplines. He would be able to use language and reason. He would have some understanding of man and of what connects man with man. He would have acquired some degree of wisdom.
— Robert M. Hutchins, *The Higher Learning in America*, 91 (1936).

What the colleges ... should at least try to give us is a general sense of what, under various disguises, *superiority* has always signified and may still signify. The feeling for a good human job anywhere, the admiration of the really admirable, the disesteem of what is cheap and trashy and impermanent — this is what we call the critical sense, the sense for ideal values. It is the better part of what men know as wisdom.   — William James, *Memories and Studies* (1911).

A university anywhere can aim no higher than to be as British as possible for the sake of the undergraduates, as German as possible for the sake of the public at large — and as confused as possible for the preservation of the whole uneasy balance.
— Clark Kerr, lecture at Harvard on "The Uses of the University," *New York Times*, Apr. 26, 1963.

The aim of the college, for the individual student, is to eliminate the need in his life for the college; the task is to help him become a self-educating man.
— C. Wright Mills, *Power, Politics and People: Mass Society and Liberal Education* (1963).

It is our task not to produce "safe" men, in whom our safety can never in any case lie, but to keep alive in young people the courage to dare to seek the truth, to be free, to establish in them a compelling desire to live greatly and magnanimously, and to give them the knowledge and awareness, the faith and the trained facility to get on with the job. Especially the faith.   — Nathan M. Pusey, *Time*, Mar. 1, 1954.

The use of a university is to make young gentlemen as unlike their fathers as possible.   — Woodrow Wilson, address in Pittsburgh, Oct. 24, 1914.

University, Definition of

The true university of these days is a collection of books.   — Thomas Carlyle, *Heroes and Hero-Worship*, V: *The Hero as a Man of Letters* (1840).

A university—an institution consciously devoted to the pursuit of knowledge, the solution of problems, the critical appreciation of achievement, and the training of men at a really high level.
— Abraham Flexner, *Universities*, 42 (1930).

My definition of a University is Mark Hopkins at one end of a log and a student on the other.   — James A. Garfield, address to Williams College Alumni in New York, Dec. 28, 1871.

If Carlyle could define a university as a collection of books, Socrates might have defined it as a conversation about wisdom.   — A. Whitney Griswold, *Essays on Education* (1954).

A university is a place that is established and will function for the benefit of society, provided it is a center of independent thought and criticism that is created in the interest of the progress of society, and the one reason that we know that every totalitarian government must fail is that no totalitarian government is prepared to

face the consequences of creating free universities.   — Robert M. Hutchins, testimony before House of Representatives committee, 1952.

A university is a community of scholars. It is not a kindergarten; it is not a club; it is not a reform school; it is not a political party; it is not an agency of propaganda.... Freedom of inquiry, freedom of discussion, and freedom of teaching—without these a university cannot exist.... The university exists only to find and to communicate the truth. If it cannot do that it is no longer a university.
— Robert M. Hutchins, address, in David Fellman, "Academic Freedom in American Law," *1961 Wisconsin Law Review*.

Colleges are places where pebbles are polished and diamonds are dimmed.
— Robert G. Ingersoll, *Abraham Lincoln* (c.1894).

If it is not prepared for the free competition of ideas, it is not, in the true sense, a university.   — Harold J. Laski, *I Believe* (1939).

A University ... [is] a place of instruction, where universal knowledge is professed.
— John Henry Newman, *The Idea of a University*, Discourse II (1873).

A place to learn how to learn.
— Henry M. Wriston, *New York Times*, June 11, 1975.

University, Dispraise for

Doctors without doctrine, masters without art, and graduates more suited to drink than to honor.
— Christopher Anstey, speech (c.1745) which offended authorities of King's College, Cambridge, and prevented him from receiving his M.A.

O Granta! sweet Granta! where studious of ease

I slumbered seven years, and then lost my
degrees.　　—Christopher Anstey,
The New Bath Guide, epilogue (1766).
Refers to the preceding quotation.

Universities incline wits to sophistry and
affectation.　　—Francis Bacon,
*Valerius Terminus of the Interpretation
of Nature*, xxvi (1603).

Universities where individualism is
dreaded as nothing else, wherein manu-
factories of patent drama, business
schools and courses for the propagation of
fine embroidery are established on the
order of the monied.　　—Thomas Beer,
The Mauve Decade (1926).

How sad a spectacle, so frequent
nowadays, to see a young man after ten
years of college education come out,
ready for his voyage of life,—and to see
that the entire ship is made of rotten,
honeycombed, traditional timber without so much as an inch of new plank in
the hull.　　—Ralph Waldo Emerson,
Journals, 1839.

Universities are fit for nothing but to
debauch the principles of young men, to
poison their minds with romantic notions
of knowledge and virtue.
　　—Henry Fielding,
The Temple Beau, I (1730).

I enjoy learning things, but a university is
the last place in the world to learn
anything.　　—Charles Kowal,
Time, Oct. 27, 1975.

Alas! university chairs are better for the
unreasoning end of the human organism
than for the reasoning one.
　　—George Bernard Shaw,
What I Really Wrote About the War,
appendix (1914).

A sanctuary in which exploded systems
and obsolete prejudices find shelter and
protection after they have been hunted
out of every corner of the world.
　　—Adam Smith,
The Wealth of Nations (1776).

Places of Learning should not be Places of
Riot and Pride.... 'Tis not worth the
while for persons to be sent to the *Colledge* to learn to Complement men and
Court Women.　　—Solomon Stoddard,
sermon in Boston, 1703. Reference
is to Harvard College.

University, Function of

See also University, Aim of

In its relation to society, a free university
should be expected to be, in a sense,
"subversive." We take for granted that
creative work in any field will challenge
prevailing orthodoxy.—Noam Chomsky,
*The Function of the University in
a Time of Crisis*, in R.M. Hutchins
and M.J. Adler, eds., *The Great
Ideas of Today 1969*.

The function of the university is not
simply to teach bread-winning, or to furnish teachers for the public schools or to
be a centre of polite society; it is, above
all, to be the organ of that fine adjustment between real life and the growing
knowledge of life, an adjustment which
forms the secret of civilization.
　　—W.E.B. Du Bois,
The Souls of Black Folks, v (1903).

The college was not founded to give
society what it wants. Quite the contrary.
　　—May Sarton,
The Small Room (1961).

The business of the university then is to
finish the education of students, in the
sense that when they leave it, permanently or temporarily, they are fitted to continue and test their education in greater
independence of it. But "finish" must
then of course, mean to bring to some
climactic point, rather than, as at present, finish off.　　—John R. Seeley,
The University as Slaughterhouse,
in R.M. Hutchins and M.J. Adler,
eds., *The Great Ideas Today* (1969).

The function of a University is to enable you to shed details in favour of principles.　—Alfred North Whitehead, *The Aims of Education*, ii (1929).

The justification for a university is that it preserves the connection between knowledge and the zest of life, by uniting the young and the old in the imaginative consideration of learning.... A university which fails in this respect has no reason for existence.
　—Alfred North Whitehead, *ibid.*, vii.

University, Praise of

He who enters a university walks on hallowed ground.
　—James Bryant Conant, *Notes on the Harvard Tercentenary* (1936).

Glory we owe in no small part to the all-embracing influence of our colleges and universities. They have wrought mightily in the making of America. They stand like mighty fortresses within whose protection the truth is secure. Against them no enemy shall prevail.
　—Calvin Coolidge, address at Amherst College alumni dinner, New York City, Nov. 27, 1920.

There are few earthly things more beautiful than a university ... a place where those who hate ignorance may strive to know, where those who perceive truth may strive to make others see.
　—John Masefield, quoted by President J.F. Kennedy, commencement address, American University, June 10, 1963.

I wonder anyone does anything here but dream and remember; the place is so beautiful one expects the people to sing instead of speaking.
　—William Butler Yeats, referring to Oxford University, letter to Katherine Tynan Hinkson, c.1925.

University Education

See also University Education, Effect of

It takes most men five years to recover from a college education, and to learn that poetry is as vital to thinking as knowledge.　—Brooks Atkinson, *Once Around the Sun: August 31* (1951).

University education cannot be handed out complete like a cake on a tray. It has to be fought for, intrigued for, conspired for, and sometimes simply stolen. If it had not, it would scarcely be education.
　—Arnold Bennett, *How to Make the Best of Life* (1923).

Anybody who gets out of college having his confidence in the perfection of existing institutions affirmed has not been educated. Just suffocated.　—Al Capp, in Lore and Maurice Cowan, *The Wit of the Jews* (1970).

I learned three important things in college—to use a library, to memorize quickly and visually, to drop asleep at any time given a horizontal surface and fifteen minutes. What I could not learn was to think creatively on schedule.
　—Agnes De Mille, *Dance to the Piper* (1952).

Hanging around until you've caught on.
　—Robert Frost, defining a college education, *Philadelphia Inquirer*, Jan. 30, 1963.

If you feel that you have both feet planted on level ground, then the university has failed you.　—Robert Goheen, baccalaureate address, Princeton University, *Time*, June 23, 1961.

A college education is a taste for knowledge, a taste for philosophy, a capacity to explore, question and perceive relationships between fields of knowledge and experience.　—A. Whitney Griswold, on revising Yale's curriculum, *New York Times*, Apr. 20, 1963.

A fool's brain digests philosophy into folly, science into superstition, and art into pedantry. Hence University education.
— George Bernard Shaw,
Maxims for Revolutionists (1903).

It is possible to get an education at a university. It has been done; not often, but the fact that a proportion, however small, of college students do get a start in interested, methodical study, proves my thesis.   — Lincoln Steffens,
Autobiography, xvii (1931).

University Education, Effect of

See also University Education

College ain't so much where you been as how you talk when you get back.
— Ossie Davis,
Purlie Victorious, I.i (1961).

"D'ye think th' colledges has much to do with th' progress iv th' wurruld?" asked Mr. Hennessy.
"D'ye think," said Mr. Dooley, "'tis th' mill that makes th' water run?"
— Finley Peter Dunne,
Mr. Dooley's Opinions: Colleges and Degrees (1901).

One of the benefits of a college education is to show the boy its little avail.
— Ralph Waldo Emerson,
The Conduct of Life: Culture (1860).

A girl out of a village or nursery [is] more capable of receiving instruction than a lad just set free from the university. It is not difficult to write on blank paper, but 'tis a tedious if not impossible task to scrape out nonsense already written.
— Mary Wortley Montagu,
letter to James Steuart, Apr. 7, 1760.

I believe that college makes complete fools of our young men.   — Petronius,
Satyricon, i (c. A.D. 60).

A small-town boy who goes to college may be lifted by that encounter into the wild blue yonder of the mind: a discipline with its national and even international market of ideas, can free him from the ethnocentric nest of home and parish, give him a new past (the traditions of "his" field) and a new identity.
— David Riesman,
Constraint and Variety in American Education, 103 (1956).

Unknown

See also Knowledge, Limited

Whoever starts out toward the unknown must consent to venture alone.
— André Gide,
Journals, May 12, 1927.

There is a lurking fear that some things are "not meant" to be known, that some inquiries are too dangerous for human beings to make.   — Carl Sagan,
Broca's Brain (1979).

Unlearning

See also Learning

We may prevent people from learning, but we cannot make them unlearn.
— Ludwig Boerne,
Aphorismen und Fragmente,
no.103 (1840).

We do but learn to-day what our better advanced judgements will unteach us tomorrow.   — Thomas Browne,
Religio Medici, II (1643).

He knows not how to know who knows not how to un-know.
— Richard Burton, *The Kasîdah of Hâjî Abdû el-Yazdî*, I.ii (1880).

Everyone should keep a mental wastepaper basket and the older he grows the more things he will consign to it — torn up to irrecoverable tatters.
— Samuel Butler (1835–1902),
Note-Books: Higgledy-Piggledy (1912).

It is almost as difficult to make a man unlearn his errors, as his knowledge. Malinformation is more hopeless than noninformation; for error is always more busy than ignorance. Ignorance is a blank sheet, on which we may write; but error is a scribbled one, from which we must first erase.   —Charles Caleb Colton, *Lacon*, 17 (1820–22).

Learn to unlearn.
—Benjamin Disraeli, *Contarini Fleming*, I (1832).

That which any one has been long learning unwillingly, he unlearns with proportionate eagerness and haste.
—William Hazlitt, *The Plain Speaker: On Personal Character* (1826).

For only by unlearning Wisdom comes.
—James Russell Lowell, *The Parting of the Ways*, vi (1849).

The mind is slow in unlearning what it has been long in learning.   —Seneca, *Troades*, ln.633 (c. A.D. 60).

The latter part of a wise man's life is taken up in curing the follies, prejudices, and false opinions he had contracted in the former.   —Jonathan Swift, *Thoughts on Various Subjects* (1706).

Verbosity

A plurality of words does not necessarily represent a plurality of things.
—Joseph Albo, *Sefer ha-Ikkarim (Book of Principles)*, 2.9 (1428).

He multiplies words without knowledge.
—*Bible: Job* 35:16.

A barren superfluity of words.
—Samuel Garth, *The Dispensary*, II.95 (1699).

Amplification is the vice of the modern orator. Speeches measured by the hour die by the hour.   —Thomas Jefferson, letter to David Harding, Apr. 20, 1824.

A glouton of wordes.
—William Langland, *The Vision of Piers Plowman*, I.139 (14th cent.).

In general those who nothing have to say
Contrive to spend the longest time in doing it;
They turn and vary it in every way,
Hashing it, stewing it, mincing it, *ragouting* it.
—James Russell Lowell, *An Oriental Apologue*, xv (1849).

We shall probably have nothing to say, but we intend to say it at great length.
—Don Marquis, *The Almost Perfect State* (1927).

You say, to start with, you have laryngitis;
Stop right there, Maximus, and you'll delight us.   —Martial, *Epigrammata*, III.xviii (A.D. 93).

But there is one blanket statement which can be made about the world's schools: the teachers talk too much.
—Martin Mayer, *The Schools* (1961).

The unluckiest insolvent in the world is the man whose expenditure of speech is too great for his income of ideas.
—Christopher Morley, *Inward Ho!*, ix (1923).

He that useth many words for the explaining any subject, doth, like the cuttle fish, hide himself for the most part in his own ink.   —John Ray, *On Creation* (before 1705).

He draweth out the thread of his verbosity finer than the staple of his argument.
—William Shakespeare, *Love's Labour's Lost*, V.i.18 (1594). Sometimes incorrectly attributed to Richard Porson [staple = *fiber*].

Like a high hat crowning a low brow is a long preface to a short treatise.
— Zevi Hirsch Somerhausen,
Hitze Shenunim (1840).

Vocabulary

A person with a mind tidily stocked with a rich vocabulary feels adequate; and that sense of adequacy is the sense of power.
— Mauree Applegate,
Easy in English (1960).

One forgets words as one forgets names. One's vocabulary needs constant fertilizing or it will die.   — Evelyn Waugh,
Diaries, Dec. 25, 1962.

Vocation

See also Profession; Work

Blessed is he who has found his work; let him ask no other blessedness. He has a work, a life purpose. — Thomas Carlyle,
Past and Present (1843).

Jack of all trades and master of none.
— Maria Edgeworth,
Popular Tales (1800).

A man who is not in his place is like a dislocated bone; he suffers and he causes suffering.   — Joseph Roux,
Meditations of a Parish Priest (1886).

In order that people may be happy in their work, these three things are needed: They must be fit for it: They must not do too much of it: And they must have a sense of success in it.   — John Ruskin,
Pre-Raphaelitism (1850).

A skilful trade is better than an inherited fortune.   — Welsh proverb.

Vocational Education

See also Education

The only adequate training *for* occupations is training *through* occupations. The principle ... that the educative process is its own end, and that the only sufficient preparation for later responsibilities comes by making the most of immediately present life, applies in full force to the vocational phases of education. The dominant vocation of all human beings at all times is living — intellectual and moral growth.
— John Dewey,
Democracy and Education, xxiii (1916).

The antithesis between a technical and a liberal education is fallacious. There can be adequate technical education which is not liberal, and no liberal education which is not technical: that is, no education which does not impart both technique and intellectual vision. In simpler language, education should turn out the pupil with something he knows well and something he can do well.
— Alfred North Whitehead,
The Aims of Education, iv (1929).

Will

See also Achievement

If we cannot do what we will, we must will what we can.   — Hanan J. Ayalti,
Yiddish Proverbs (1949).

He who can will can always accomplish.
— Kaibara Ekken,
Ten Kun (Ten Precepts), II (1710).

Them ez will, kin.
— Edward Rowland Sill
(1841–87), *A Baker's Duzzen
of Wize Sawz*.

Wisdom

See also below; Knowledge; Learning; Wise Person

If a man has wisdom, what need has he of riches?   —Bhartrihari, *The Niti Sataka*, no.21 (c.625).

For wisdom will come into your heart, and knowledge will be pleasant to your soul; discretion will watch over you; understanding will guard you.
—*Bible: Proverbs* 2:10, 11.

People must not be wiser than the experience of mankind.
—Charles Synge Christopher Bowen, English judge, *Filburn v People's Palace & Aq. Co.*, 1890.

Mixing one's wines may be a mistake, but old and new wisdom mix very well.
—Bertolt Brecht, *The Caucasion Chalk Circle*, prologue from first script (1944).

Wisdom is greater than knowledge, for wisdom includes knowledge and the due use of it.   —Joseph Sevelli Capponi, *Ham and Dixie: The Five Pillars* (1895).

It is not enough to acquire wisdom, it is necessary to employ it.   —Cicero, *De Finibus*, I.1 (c.45 B.C.).

To have lived long does not necessarily imply the gathering of much wisdom and experience. A man who has pedaled twenty-five thousand miles on a stationary bicycle has not circled the globe. He has only garnered weariness.
—Paul Eldridge, *Horns of Glass* (1943).

Wisdom don't always speak in Greek and Latin.   —Thomas Fuller (1654–1734), *Gnomologia*, no.5762 (1732).

Knowledge can be communicated, but not wisdom. One can find it, live it, be fortified by it, do wonders through it, but one cannot communicate and teach it.
—Hermann Hesse, *Siddhartha: Govinda* (1923).

Every man is a damn fool for at least five minutes every day. Wisdom consists in not exceeding the limit.
—Elbert Hubbard, *Roycroft Dictionary and Book of Epigrams* (1923).

Wisdom is like fire: a little enlightens, much burns.   —Moses Ibn Ezra, *Shirat Yisrael*, 37 (12th cent.).

It requires wisdom to understand wisdom; the music is nothing if the audience is deaf.   —Walter Lippmann, *A Preface to Morals*, III.xv.2 (1929).

It is not wise to be wiser than is necessary.
—Phillippe Quinault, *Armide* (1686).

Wisdom never kicks at the iron walls it can't bring down.   —Olive Schreiner, *The Story of an African Farm: Lyndall* (1883).

Wisdom brings back the basic beliefs of eighteen.   —Karl Shapiro, *The Bourgeois Poet*, i.30 (1964).

Wisdom is ever a blessing; education is sometimes a curse.   —John A. Shedd, *Salt from My Attic*, 29 (1928).

The chief aim of wisdom is to enable one to bear with the stupidity of the ignorant.
—Pope Sixtus I, *The Ring* (c. A.D. 120).

Knowledge comes, but wisdom lingers.
—Alfred, Lord Tennyson, *Locksley Hall*, ln.141 (1842).

A man is wise with the wisdom of his time only, and ignorant with its ignorance. Observe how the greatest minds yield in some degree to the superstitions of their age.   —Henry David Thoreau, *Journal*, Jan. 31, 1853.

Wisdom ...

Though knowledge is one chief aim of intellectual education, there is another ingredient, vaguer but greater, and more dominating in its importance. The ancients called it "wisdom." You cannot be wise without some basic of knowledge; but you may easily acquire knowledge and remain bare of wisdom.
— Alfred North Whitehead,
The Aims of Education, iii (1929).

Wisdom is not finally tested in the schools,
Wisdom cannot be pass'd from one having it to another not having it,
Wisdom is of the soul, is not susceptible of proof, is its own proof.
— Walt Whitman,
Leaves of Grass, VII: *Song of the Open Road*, sec.6 (1855).

Wisdom is ofttimes nearer when we steep Than when we soar.
— William Wordsworth,
The Excursion, III.232 (1814).

Wisdom, Beginning of

The beginning of wisdom is this: Get wisdom, and whatever you get, get insight. Prize her highly, and she will exalt you; she will honor you if you embrace her. She will place on your head a fair garland; she will bestow on you a beautiful crown. — *Bible: Proberbs* 4:7–9.

He dares to be a fool, and that is the first step in the direction of wisdom.
— James G. Huneker,
Pathos of Distance (1913).

The beginning of wisdom is to desire it.
— Solomon Ibn Gabirol,
Choice of Pearls (c.1050).

The doorstep to the temple of wisdom is a knowledge of our own ignorance.
— Charles Haddon Spurgeon,
Gleanings among the Sheaves: The First Lesson (1864).

Wisdom, Search for

Wisdom is not to be obtained from textbooks, but must be coined out of human experience in the flame of life.
— Morris Raphael Cohen,
A Dreamer's Journey, 118 (1949).

The clouds may drop down titles and estates;
Wealth may seek us; but wisdom must be sought. — Edward Young,
Night Thoughts, VIII (1744).

Wisdom, Value of

The greatest good is wisdom.
— St. Augustine,
Soliloquies, I (c. A.D. 387).

Happy is the man who finds wisdom, and the man who gets understanding, for the gain from it is better than gain from silver and its profit better than gold. She is more precious than jewels, and nothing you desire can compare with her. Long life is in her right hand; in her left hand are riches and honor. Her ways are ways of pleasantness, and all her paths are peace. She is a tree of life to those who lay hold of her; those who hold fast to her are called happy. — *Bible: Proverbs* 3:13–18. See also *Job* 28:18; *Proverbs* 8:10; 16:16; 20:15.

Great is wisdom; infinite is the value of wisdom. It cannot be exaggerated; it is the highest achievement of man.
— Thomas Carlyle,
address in Edinburgh, Apr. 2, 1866.

Wisdom is never dear, provided the article be genuine. — Horace Greeley,
address in Houston, May 23, 1871.

Wisdom outweighs any wealth.
— Sophocles,
Antigone, ln.1050
(c.441 B.C.).

Wisdom—What It Is

Wisdom lies
In masterful administration of the un-
foreseen.   —Robert Bridges,
The Testament of Beauty (1929).

The invariable mark of wisdom is to see
the miraculous in the common.
—Ralph Waldo Emerson,
Nature, Addresses, and Lectures:
Prospects (1849).

Wisdom is knowing when you can't be
wise.   —Paul Engle,
Poems in Praise (1959).

Wisdom is that olive that springeth from
the heart, bloometh on the tongue, and
beareth fruit in the actions.
—Elizabeth Grymeston, *Miscellanea.*
Meditations. Memoratius (1604).

Wisdom is an affair of values, and of
value judgments. It is intelligent conduct
of human affairs.   —Sidney Hook,
"Does Philosophy Have a Future?"
Saturday Review, Nov. 11, 1967.

It is wit to pick a lock and steal a horse,
but it is wisdom to let them alone.
—James Howell,
English Proverbs, 3 (1659); John Ray,
English Proverbs, 30 (1670); Thomas
Fuller, *Gnomologia*, no.3031 (1732).

Wisdom denotes the pursuing of the best
ends by the best means.
—Francis Hutcheson,
An Inquiry into the Original of
Our Ideas of Beauty and Virtue,
I.v.18 (1725).

To know
That which before us lies in daily life,
Is the prime wisdom.   —John Milton,
Paradise Lost, VIII.192 (1667).

What is it to be wise?
'Tis but to know how little can be known;
To see all others faults, and feel our own.
—Alexander Pope,
An Essay on Man, IV.260 (1734).

True wisdom consists not in seeing what
is immediately before our eyes, but in
foreseeing what is to come.   —Terence,
Adelphi, III.iii.32 (160 B.C.).

Wise Person

See also Wisdom

It is of the highest advantage for one that
is wise not to seem to be wise.
—Aeschylus,
Prometheus Bound, ln.386 (c.490 B.C.).

Be wiser than other people if you can; but
do not tell them so.
—Lord Chesterfield,
Letters to His Son, Nov. 19, 1745.

There needs but one wise man in a company and all are wise, so rapid is the
contagion.   —Ralph Waldo Emerson,
Representative Men, I (1850).

Among wise men, the wisest knows that
he knows least; among fools, the most
foolish thinks he knows most.
—Antonio de Guevara,
Libro Llamado Relox de Principes
(1529).

Man is wise only while in search of
wisdom; when he imagines he has attained it, he is a fool.
—Solomon Ibn Gabirol,
Choice of Pearls, no.21 (c.1050).

Whoever is not too wise is wise.
—Martial,
Epigrammata, XIV.x.2 (A.D. 93).

Let thy house be a house of meeting for
the sages and suffer thyself to be covered
with the dust of their feet, and drink in
their words with thirst.   —*Talmud:*
Aboth, 1.4 (before A.D. 500).

Who is he that is wise? He who learns
from every man.   —*Ibid.*,
4.1.

Wit

See also Intellect; Intelligence

The mere wit is only a human bauble. He is to life what bells are to horses—not expected to draw the load, but only to jingle while the horses draw.
—Henry Ward Beecher,
Proverbs from Plymouth Pulpit:
Man (1887).

Wit is a treacherous dart. It is perhaps the only weapon with which it is possible to stab oneself in one's own back.
—Geoffrey Bocca,
The Woman Who Would Be Queen
(1954).

Wit is the salt of conversation, not food.
—William Hazlitt,
Lectures on the English Comic Writers:
On Wit and Humour (1819).

Wit, at its best, consists in the terse intrusion into an atmosphere of serene mental habit of some uncompromising truth.
—Philander Johnson,
"Colyumists' Confessional,"
Everybody's Magazine, May 1920.

It is not enough to possess wit. One must have enough of it to avoid having too much.   —André Maurois,
Conversation (1927).

Wit is a happy and striking way of expressing a thought.   —William Penn,
Some Fruits of Solitude,
I. no.168 (1693).

The delectable form which intelligence takes in its moments of surplus power—the form of wit.
—Stuart Pratt Sherman,
introd. to W.C. Brownell,
American Prose Masters (1923).

Somebody has said "Wit is the sudden marriage of ideas which before their union were not perceived to have any relation."   —Mark Twain,
Notebook, Aug. 6, 1885 (1935).

Woman

See also Girl; Women,
Education of

Who can measure the advantages that would result if the magnificent abilities of [women] ... could be devoted to the needs of government, society, home, instead of being consumed in the struggle to obtain their birthright of individual freedom?   —Susan B. Anthony,
"The Struggle of Women, Past, Present and Future,"*The Arena*, May 1897.

Woman is as intelligent as man, but less capable of emotion.   —Henri Bergson,
Two Sources of Morality and Religion,
36 (1935).

I hate a learned woman.   —Euripides,
Hippolytus, ln.640 (428 B.C.).

As for Western women, it seems to me that they have often had to struggle to obtain their own rights. That did not leave them much time to prove their abilities.   —Indira Gandhi, in José-Luis de Villallonga, "Conversation with Indira Gandhi," *Oui*, 1975.

That learning belongs not to the female character, and that the female mind is not capable of a degree of improvement equal to that of the other sex, are narrow and unphilosophical prejudices.
—Vicesimus Knox,
Essays, III.142 (1735).

The capacity of the female mind for studies of the highest order cannot be doubted, having been sufficiently illustrated by its works of genius, of erudition, and of science.... It merits an improved system of education.
—James Madison,
letter to Albert Picket, *et al.*, Sept. 1821.

Nobody objects to a woman being a good writer or sculptor or geneticist as long as she manages also to be a good wife, mother, good-looking, good-tempered, well-dressed, well-groomed, unaggressive.   —Marya Mannes, "New Bites by a Girl Gadfly," *Life*, June 1964.

Boys don't make passes at female smart-
asses.   —Letty Cottin Pogrebin,
Down with Sexist Upbringing, in
Francine Klagsbrun, ed., *The First
Ms. Reader* (1972).

I believe we must cope courageously and
practically, as women have always done,
with the here and now, our feet on this
ground where we now live. But nothing
less than the most radical imagination
will carry us beyond this place, beyond
the mere struggle for survival, to that
lucid recognition of our possibilities
which will keep us impatient and unre-
signed to mere survival.—Adrienne Rich,
On Lies, Secrets and Silence (1979).

Women are wiser than men because they
know less and understand more.
          —James Stephens,
          The Crock of Gold, ii (1912).

Women, Education of

See also Girls, Education of;
Woman

Woman must possess the means of the
highest development of which her nature
is capable. She must, equally with man,
have the opportunity of cultivating and
developing her intellect. In her labors for
freedom and happiness, she must possess
the same rights as man.
          —Fredrika Bremer,
The Homes of the New World (1853).

The acceptance of women as authority
figures or as role models is an important
step in female education.... It is this process of identification, respect, and then
self-respect that promotes growth.
          —Judy Chicago,
*Through the Flower: My Struggle
as a Woman Artist*, i (1975).

And this goddamned school is antife-
male, they look down on women, especially women my age. It's a goddamned monastery that's been invaded
by people in skirts and the men who run
it only hope that the people in skirts are

pseudomen, so they won't disturb things,
won't insist that feeling is as important as
thinking and body as important as mind.
          —Marilyn French,
          The Women's Room, IV.xii (1977).

That we have not made any respectable
attempt to meet the special educational
needs of women in the past is the clearest
possible evidence of the fact that our
educational objectives have been geared
exclusively to the vocational patterns of
men.   —Betty Friedan,
          The Feminine Mystique, xi (1963).

The true aim of female education should
be not a development of one or two, but
all the faculties of the human soul,
because no perfect womanhood is developed by imperfect culture.
          —Frances Ellen Watkins Harper,
          "The Two Offers," *The Anglo-
African Magazine*, Sept. 1859.

They braced my aunt against a board,
     To make her straight and tall;
They laced her up, they starved her
     down,
     To make her light and small;
They pinched her feet, they singed her
     hair,
They screwed it up with pins.
          —Oliver Wendell Holmes, Sr.,
               My Aunt (c.1830–36),
          describing a "stylish school."

What are we educating women for? To
raise this question is to face the whole
problem of women's role in society. We
are uncertain about the end of women's
education precisely because the status of
women in our society is fraught with contradictions and confusion.
          —Mirra Komarovsky,
     Women in the Modern World (1953).

College for women was a refinement
whose main purpose was to better prepare you for your ultimate destiny ... to
make you a more desirable product.
          —Pat Loud, with Nora Johnson,
     Pat Loud: A Woman's Story (1974).

The sum and substance of female education in America, as in England, is

training women to consider marriage as the sole object in life, and to pretend that they do not think so.
— Harriet Martineau,
Society in America, III: *Women* (1837).

When a woman turns to scholarship there is usually something wrong with her sexual apparatus.   — Friedrich Nietzsche,
Beyond Good and Evil,
iv. no.144 (1886).

Nothing can be more absurd than the practice ... of men and women not following the same pursuits with all their strength and with one mind, for thus the state ... is reduced to a half.   — Plato,
Laws, VII.805 (c.367–347 B.C.).

You ought not to educate a woman as if she were a man, or to educate her as if she were not.   — George Shuster,
The Ground I Walked On (1962).

A great part of the objections made to the education of women are rather objections made to human nature than to the female sex: for it is surely true, that knowledge, where it produces any bad effects at all, does as much mischief to one sex as to the other. — Sydney Smith,
Selections (1854): *Female Education*.

Why the disproportion in knowledge between the two sexes should be so great, when the inequality in natural talents is so small; or why the understanding of women should be lavished upon trifles, when nature has made it capable of higher and better things, we profess ourselves not able to understand.
— Sydney Smith, *ibid.*

If women knew more, men must learn more — for ignorance would then be shameful — and it would become the fashion to be instructed.
— Sydney Smith, *ibid.*

O, I wish
That I were some great princess, I would build

Far off from men a college like a man's,
And I would teach them all that men are taught.   — Alfred, Lord Tennyson,
The Princess: Prologue, ln.133 (1847).

There are some women who have no talent for learning, just as there are men; other women have such talent that they seem to have been born for learning, or at least it is not difficult for them. The former should not be urged to learn; the latter should not be hindered from learning, but should rather be coaxed and attracted to it and encouraged toward the virtue to which they are inclined.
— Juan Luis Vives,
*The Instruction of a Christian
Woman* (1524).

In all nations a good education is that which renders the ladies correct in their manners, respectable in their families, and agreeable in society. That education is always wrong which raises a woman above the duties of her station.... In America female education should have for its object what is useful.
— Noah Webster,
*On the Education of Youth
in America* (1790).

Contending for the rights of women, my main argument is built on this simple principle, that if she be not prepared by education to become the companion of man, she will stop the progress of knowledge, for the truth must be common to all, or it will be inefficacious with respect to its influence on general practice.   — Mary Wollstonecraft,
*A Vindication of the Rights
of Women* (1792).

Wonder

See also Curiosity

The man who cannot wonder ... is but a Pair of Spectacles behind which there is no Eye.   — Thomas Carlyle,
Sartor Resartus, I.x (1833).

Men love to wonder, and that is the seed of our science. — Ralph Waldo Emerson, *Society and Solitude: Works and Days* (1870).

Wonder, rather than doubt, is the root of knowledge.   — Abraham Heschel, *Man Is Not Alone*, 11 (1951).

Any genuine philosophy leads to action and from action back to wonder, to the enduring fact of mystery.
— Henry Miller, *The Wisdom of the Heart* (1941).

To be surprised, to wonder, is to begin to understand.   — José Ortega y Gassett, *The Revolt of the Masses*, i (1930).

The larger the island of knowledge, the longer the shore line of wonder.
— Ralph W. Sockman, *Now to Live!* (1946).

Word

See also below; Jargon; Language; Slang

Here therefore is the first distemper of learning, when men study words and not matter.   — Francis Bacon, *The Advancement of Learning*, I.iv.3 (1605).

You can taste a word.
— Pearl Bailey, *Newsweek*, Dec. 4, 1967.

All words are pegs to hang ideas on.
— Henry Ward Beecher, *Proverbs from Plymouth Pulpit: The Human Mind* (1887).

There is no means by which men so powerfully elude their ignorance, disguise it from themselves and from others as by words.
— Gamaliel Bradford, *Letters* (1934).

Weasel words are words that suck all the life out of the words next to them, just as a weasel sucks an egg and leaves the shell.
— Stewart Chaplin, "The Stained-Glass Political Platform," *Century Magazine*, June 1900.

Words are what hold society together.
— Stuart and Marian T. Chase, *Power of Words* (1954).

Words are the dress of thoughts, which should no more be presented in rags, tatters, and dirt, than your person would.
— Lord Chesterfield, *Letters to His Son*, Jan. 25, 1750.

Why shouldn't we quarrel about a word? What is the good of words if they aren't important enough to quarrel over? Why do we choose one word more than another if there isn't any difference between them?   — G.K. Chesteron, *The Ball and the Cross* (1909).

Science in the modern world has many uses; its chief use, however, is to provide long words to cover the errors of the rich. The word "kleptomania" is a vulgar example of what I mean.
— G.K. Chesterton, *Heretics*, xiii (1905).

Words, like men, grow individuality; their character changes with years and with use.   — Frederick E. Crane, Court of Appeals, New York, *Adler v Deegan*, 1929.

[A] source of our errors is, that we attach thoughts to words which do not express them with accuracy.   — René Descartes, *The Principles of Philosophy*, I (1644).

Spinning words, we are much like the spider spinning its web out of its own body. We, however, unlike the spider, may be enmeshed in our own web.
— Isaac Goldberg, *The Wonder of Words*, 298 (1938).

Words are not pebbles in alien juxtaposition. —Learned Hand,
U.S. Circuit Court decision, *NLRB v Federbush Co. Inc.*, 1941.

Every word or concept, clear as it may be, has only a limited range of applicability. —Werner Heisenberg, *Physics and Beyond* (1971).

A good catchword can obscure analysis for fifty years. —Johan Huizinga, *The Waning of the Middle Ages* (1924).

Words form the thread on which we string our experiences.
—Aldous Huxley, *The Olive Tree: Words and Behavior* (1937).

We should have a great many fewer disputes in the world, if words were taken for what they are, the signs of our ideas only. —John Locke, *An Essay concerning Human Understanding*, III.x.15 (1690).

Words have weight, sound and appearance; it is only by considering these that you can write a sentence that is good to look at and good to listen to.
—W. Somerset Maugham, *The Summing Up*, xiii (1938).

All words are in a sense tombs of a forgotten past. —Ben Morrison, *Wonderful Words* (1954).

Every word is a preconceived judgment. —Friedrich Nietzsche, *Human, All Too Human*, II (1878).

Let the truth be said outright: there are no synonyms, and the same statement can never be repeated in a changed form of words. —Walter Alexander Raleigh, (1861–1922), *Style* (1897).

The great disease of knowledge is that in which, starting from words, we end up with them. —I.A. Richards, *How to Read a Page*, 206 (1942).

We are all born with an original sin—a facility in repeating words without understanding them. Without this tendency we would never learn to talk, but, unless control is developed, there is no escape from infantilism. —H.R. Ruse, *The Illiteracy of the Literate*, 123 (1933).

What do you read, my lord?
Words, words, words.
—William Shakespeare, *Hamlet*, II.ii.191 (1600–01).

Words may varnish facts, they cannot alter them. —Harry James Smith, *Mrs. Bumpstead-Leigh*, III (1911).

Words should be clean and tough as cobble-stones,
That simple people, in the market-place,
Should grip them with their feet and never stumble. —Judah Stampfer, *Jerusalem Has Many Faces*, 89 (1950).

A great many people think that polysyllables are a sign of intelligence.
—Barbara Walters, *How to Talk with Practically Anybody About Practically Anything*, viii (1970).

His words leap across rivers and mountains, but his thoughts are still only six inches long. —E.B. White, *World Government and Peace* (1945).

Words ... conceal one's thought as much as they reveal it; and the uttered words of philosophers, at their best and fullest, are nothing but floating buoys which signal the presence of submerged unuttered thoughts. —Harry Austryn Wolfson, *Philo*, i.107 (rev. ed. 1962).

A word or a form of speech is not good because it is in the dictionary; it is in the dictionary because it was good before it was put there.
—Franscesco Maria Zanotti, *Opere* (1779–1802): *Paradossi*, xix.

Word, Beauty of

A word fitly spoken is like apples of gold in a setting of silver.   —*Bible: Proverbs* 25:11.

Winged words.   —Homer, *Iliad*, I (before 700 B.C.).

Words like winter snowflakes.
    —Homer, *ibid.*, III.

Words become luminous when the poet's finger has passed its phosphorescence over them.   —Joseph Joubert, *Pensées* (1810).

I love smooth words, like gold-enamelled fish
Which circle slowly with a silken swish,
And tender ones, like downy-feathered birds:
Words shy and dappled, deep-eyed deer in herds.   —Elinor Wylie,
Collected Poems (1932): *Pretty Words*.

Word, Meaning of

See also Meaning

No one means all he says, and yet very few say all they mean, for words are slippery and thought is viscous.
    —Henry Adams, *The Education of Henry Adams*, xxxi (1907).

You see it's like a portmanteau—there are two meanings packed up into one word.   —Lewis Carroll,
Through the Looking-Glass, vi (1872).

Words are chameleons, which reflect the color of their environment.   —Learned Hand, U.S. Circuit Court decision, *Commissioner v National Carbide*, 1948.

To say dogmatically that we "know what a word means" *in advance of its utterance* is nonsense. All we can know in advance is *approximately* what it *will* mean. After the utterance, we interpret what has been said in the light of both verbal and physical contexts, and act according to our interpretation.   —S.I. Hayakawa, *Language in Thought and Action* (1941).

A word is not a crystal, transparent and unchanged; it is the skin of a living thought and may vary greatly in color and content according to circumstances and the time in which it is used.
    —Oliver Wendell Holmes, Jr.,
    U.S. Supreme Court decision,
    Towne v Eisner, 1918.

The meaning of a word in general is determined, not by pundits, still less by official action of any kind, but by the people. It is the duty of the professional linguist to find out, by investigation, what the usage of the people is, in this particular matter, and to record his findings.   —Kemp Malone,
    On Defining Mahogany (1940).

Almost all compositions contain words, which, taken in their rigorous sense, would convey a meaning different from that which is obviously intended. It is essential to just construction, that many words which import something excessive, should be understood in a more mitigated sense—in that sense which common usage justifies. The word "necessary" is of this description. It has not a fixed character peculiar to itself.... A thing may be necessary, very necessary, absolutely or indispensably necessary.
    —John Marshall,
    Chief Justice of United States,
    M'Culloch v Maryland, 1819.

Words differently arranged have a different meaning, and meanings differently arranged have different effects.
    —Blaise Pascal, *Pensées*, I.23 (1670).

Word, Misuse of

Abuse of words has been the great instrument of sophistry and chicanery, of party faction, and division of society.
    —John Adams, *Dissertation on the Canon and the Federal Law* (1765).

Some of mankind's most terrible misdeeds have been committed under the spell of certain magic words or phrases.   —James Bryant Conant, baccalaureate address, Harvard University, June, 1934.

All our words from loose using have lost their edge.   —Ernest Hemingway, *Death in the Afternoon*, vii (1932).

Language makes culture, and we make a rotten culture when we abuse words.
—Cynthia Ozick,
We Are the Crazy Lady and Other Feisty Feminine Fables, in Francine Klagsbrun, ed., *The First Ms. Reader* (1972).

Against the misuse of words every editorial prejudice should be fixed in concrete.   —Ellery Sedgwick, *The Happy Profession*, xviii (1946).

How often misused words generate misleading thoughts.   —Herbert Spencer, *Principles of Ethics*, I.II.vii.152 (1892–93).

Word, Power of

The power of words is such that they have prevented our learning some of the most important events in the world's history.
—Norman Angell,
Let the People Know, vii: *Words That Are Assassins* (1943).

Don't talk to me of your Archimedes' lever.... Give me the right word and the right accent, and I will move the world.
—Joseph Conrad,
A Personal Record (1912).

He who wants to persuade should put his trust, not in the right argument, but in the right word. The power of sound has always been greater than the power of sense.   —Joseph Conrad, *ibid.*

Words are, of course, the most powerful drug used by mankind.
—Rudyard Kipling,
speech, Feb. 14, 1923.

They sing. They hurt. They teach. They sanctify. They were man's first, immeasurable feat of magic. They liberated us from ignorance and our barbarous past.   —Leo Rosten,
The Many Worlds of L*E*O R*O*S*T*E*N: The Power of Words (1964).

Syllables govern the world.
—John Selden,
Table Talk: Power (1689).

Word, Strange

Avoid a strange and unfamiliar word as you would a dangerous reef.   —Caesar, *De Analogia, Aulus Gellius*, I.x.4 (before 44 B.C.).

In words, as fashions, the same rule will hold;
Alike fantastic, if too new, or old;
Be not the first by whom the new are try'd,
Nor yet the last to lay the old aside.
—Alexander Pope,
An Essay on Criticism, II.333 (1711).

I love words but I dont like strange ones. You dont understand them, and they dont understand you. Old words is like old friends, you know em the minute you see em.   —Will Rogers,
Autobiography, xviii (1926).

Beware as long as thou livest of strange words, as thou wouldst take heed and eschew great rocks in the sea.
—Thomas Wilson (1525?–81),
The Arte of Rhetorique (1553).

Work

See also Profession; Vocation

Every man's work, whether it be literature or music or pictures or architecture or anything else, is always a portrait of himself, and the more he tries to conceal

himself the more clearly will his character appear in spite of him.
— Samuel Butler (1835-1902),
The Way of All Flesh, xiv (1903).

If it were desired to crush a man completely, to punish him so severely that even the most hardened murderer would quail, it would only be needed to make his work absolutely pointless and absurd.
— Fëdor Dostoevsky,
The House of the Dead, I.ii (1862).

The most important motive for work in the school and in life is the pleasure in work, pleasure in its result and the knowledge of the value of the result to the community. In the awakening and strengthening of these psychological forces in the young man, I see the most important task given by the school.
— Albert Einstein, *Out of My Later Years*, ix: *On Education* (1950).

The prevailing philosophy of education tends to discredit hard work.
— Abraham Flexner,
Universities, 47 (1930).

Every child should be taught that useful work is worship and that intelligent labor is the highest form of prayer.
— Robert G. Ingersoll,
How to Reform Mankind (1896).

Work spares us from three great evils: boredom, vice, and need. — Voltaire,
Candide, xxx (1759).

No race can prosper till it learns that there is as much dignity in tilling a field as in writing a poem.
— Booker T. Washington,
Up From Slavery, xiv: *The Atlanta Exposition Address*, Sept. 18, 1895 (1901).

Writer

See also Poet

When I am dead, I hope it may be said: "His sins were scarlet, but his books were read."
— Hilaire Belloc,
On His Books (c.1910).

The writer of art has in mind the psychology of his characters; the writer of trash, the psychology of his readers.
— Shlomo Bickel,
Detaln un Sach-Hakeln, 256 (1943).

There is probably no hell for authors in the next world — they suffer so much from critics and publishers in this.
— Christian Nestell Bovee,
Summaries of Thought: Authors (1862).

But in all circumstances of life … the writer can win the heart of a living community that will justify him, on the one condition that he will accept to the limit of his abilities the two tasks that constitute the greatness of his craft: the service of truth and the service of liberty.
— Albert Camus,
Nobel Prize acceptance speech,
Stockholm, 1957.

There are men that will make you books, and turn them loose into the world, with as much dispatch as they would do a dish of fritters. — Miguel de Cervantes,
Don Quixote, II.II.iii (1615).

In my opinion, any novelist who can't lure a reader away from a bad soap opera is wasting his time. — John Cheever,
"In Praise of Readers,"
Parade, Dec. 28, 1980.

Novelists, whatever else they may be besides, are also children talking to children — in the dark.
— Bernard De Voto,
The World of Fiction (1950).

Choose an author as you choose a friend.
— Wentworth Dillon,
Essay on Translated Verse, ln.96 (1684).

He [writer] must teach himself that the basest of all things is to be afraid; and, teaching himself that, forget it forever, leaving no room in his workshop for anything but the old verities and truths of

the heart, the old universal truths lacking which any story is ephemeral and doomed—love and honor and pity and pride and compassion and sacrifice.
—William Faulkner,
Nobel Prize acceptance speech,
Stockholm, Dec. 10, 1950.

The only impeccable writers are those who never wrote.   —William Hazlitt,
Table-Talk: On the Aristocracy of Letters (1821–22).

The simplest way to torture an author is to get his name wrong and forget what books he has written. —Gilbert Highet,
Explorations: How to Torture an Author (1971).

Great writers leave us not just their works, but a way of looking at things.
—Elizabeth Janeway,
in *New York Times Book Review*,
Jan. 31, 1965.

Writers aren't like mushrooms—you can't grow them.   —Simas Kaselionis,
Chicago, Aug. 1975.

Every compulsion is put upon writers to become safe, polite, obedient, and sterile.   —Sinclair Lewis, letter
declining the Pulitzer Prize, 1926.

A person who publishes a book willfully appears before the populace with his pants down. —Edna St. Vincent Millay,
Letters, ed. Alan R. Macdougall (1952).

A writer lives, at best, in a state of astonishment. Beneath any feeling he has of the good or evil of the world lies a deeper one of wonder at it all.
—William Sansom,
Blue Skies, Brown Studies (1961).

Thus great with child to speake, and helplesse in my throwes,
Biting my trewand pen, beating my selfe for spite,
Foole, said my Muse to me, looke in thy heart and write.   —Philip Sidney,
Astrophel and Stella, i (1591)
[throwes = *throes*; trewand = *truant*].

What I like in a good author is not what he says, but what he whispers.
—Logan Pearsall Smith,
Afterthoughts (1931).

Writing is so difficult that I often feel that writers, having had their hell on earth, will escape all punishment hereafter.   —Jessamyn West,
To See the Dream, i (1956).

Writing

See also Editing; Pen; Poetry
Writing; Style, Writing

With pen and pencil we're learning to say Nothing, more cleverly, every day.
—William Allingham,
Blackberries (1884).

It is like writing a cheque: it is easy to write if you have enough money in the bank, and writing comes more easily if you have something to say.
—Sholem Asch,
New York Herald Tribune,
Nov. 6, 1955.

I always have two things in my head—I always have a theme and the form. The form looks for the theme, theme looks for the form, and when they come together you're able to write.   —W.H. Auden,
in Israel Shenker, *Words and Their Masters*, 212 (1974).

The reason that so few good books are written is that so few people that can write know anything. —Walter Bagehot,
Literary Studies: Shakespeare (1879).

Creative writing is or pretends to be a course in originality, although crabbed English teachers assert that creative writing is just a composition course in which the spelling is not corrected.
—Morris Bishop,
"The Perfect University,"
The Atlantic, May 1966.

Writing is nothing more than a guided dream.   —Jorge Luis Borges, *Doctor Brodie's Report*, preface (1972).

The discipline of the writer is to learn to be still and listen to what his subject has to tell him.   —Rachel Carson, speech before American Association of University Women, June 22, 1956.

One's words must glide across the page like a swan moving across the waters. One must be conscious of the movement without a thought of what is causing it to move.   —Robert Crichton, *The Secret of Santa Vittoria* (1966).

People who want to write sociology should not write a novel.
—Ralph Ellison, *Newsweek*, Feb. 20, 1978.

You don't write because you want to say something; you write because you've got something to say. —F. Scott Fitzgerald, *The Crack-Up* (1936).

I've just found out what makes a piece of writing good...: it is making the sentences talk to each other as two or more speakers do in a drama. The dullness of writing is due to its being, much of it, too much like the too long monologues and soliloquies in drama.   —Robert Frost, letter to L.W. Payne, Mar. 12, 1936, in Lawrance Thompson, ed., *Selected Letters of Robert Frost*, 427 (1964).

A book, like a child, needs time to be born. Books written quickly—within a few weeks—make me suspicious of the author. A respectable woman does not bring a child into the world before the ninth month.   —Heinrich Heine, *Thoughts and Fancies* (1869).

When writing a novel a writer should create living people; people not characters. A *character* is a caricature.
—Ernest Hemingway, *Death in the Afternoon*, xvi (1932).

No man but a blockhead ever wrote, except for money.   —Samuel Johnson, in James Boswell, *Life of Samuel Johnson*, xxxii, Apr. 5, 1776 (1791).

To write is to inform against others.
—Violette Leduc, *Mad in Pursuit* (1971).

When once the itch of literature comes over a man, nothing can cure it but the scratching of a pen.   —Samuel Lover, *Handy Andy*, xxxvi (1842).

The p'int of good writing is knowing when to stop.
—Lucy Maud Montgomery, *Anne's House of Dreams*, xxiv (1917).

A people that grows accustomed to sloppy writing is a people in process of losing grip on its empire and on itself.
—Ezra Pound, *ABC of Reading*, I.iii (1934).

How hard it is to make your thoughts look anything but imbecile fools when you paint them with ink on paper.
—Olive Schreiner, *The Story of an African Farm: Lyndall* (1883).

Clean, fresh writing is like polished sandalwood where the wood grain shows its natural beauty. On the other hand, the writings of the hosts of imitators are like lacquer ware, which shine on the outside but do not wear well.
—Shu Shuehmou, *Kueiyuyuan Chutan* (16th cent.), in Lin Yutang, *The Importance of Understanding*, 470 (1960).

The profession of book-writing makes horse racing seem like a solid, stable business.   —John Steinbeck, Nobel Prize acceptance address, Stockholm, 1962.

Blot out, correct, insert, refine,
Enlarge, diminish, interline;
Be mindful, when invention fails,
To scratch your head, and bite your nails.
—Jonathan Swift, *On Poetry* (1712).

A sentence should be read as if its author, had he held a plough instead of a pen, could have drawn a furrow deep and straight to the end.
— Henry David Thoreau,
A Week on the Concord and Merrimack Rivers: Sunday (1849).

With sixty staring me in the face, I have developed inflammation of the sentence structure and a definite hardening of the paragraphs. — James Thurber,
in *New York Post*, June 30, 1955.

As to the Adjective: when in doubt, strike it out. — Mark Twain,
Pudd'nhead Wilson's Calendar,
xi (1894).

By increasing the size of the keyhole, to-day's playwrights are in danger of doing away with the door. — Peter Ustinov,
in *Christian Science Monitor*,
Nov. 14, 1962.

Youth

See also Adolescence; Adolescent; Boy; Boyhood; Childhood; Girl; Youth and Age

The young have no depth perception in time. Ten years back or 10 years forward is an eternity. — Robert C. Alberts,
New York Times, Nov. 17, 1974.

They think they know everything, and are quite sure about it. — Aristotle,
Rhetoric, II.xii.14 (before 322 B.C.).

Youth has the resilience to absorb disaster and weave it into the pattern of his life, no matter how anguishing the thorn that penetrates its flesh.
— Sholem Asch,
East River, I (1946).

I never felt that there was anything enviable in youth. I cannot recall that any of us, as youths, admired our condition to excess or had a desire to prolong it.
— Bernhard Berenson,
Rumor and Reflection (1952).

It is one of the surprising things about youth that it can so easily be the most conservative of all ages.
— Randolph Bourne,
Youth and Life (1913).

The young do not know enough to be prudent, and therefore they attempt the impossible — and achieve it, generation after generation. — Pearl S. Buck,
The Goddess Abides (1972).

To me it seems that youth is like spring, an overpraised season — delightful if it happen to be a favoured one, but in practice very rarely favoured and more remarkable, as a general rule, for biting east winds than genial breezes.
— Samuel Butler (1835–1902),
The Way of All Flesh, vi (1903).

The egoism and turbulence of youth — is it not too often merely the need of a worthy cause to absorb the first violence of a responsible will? — Joyce Cary,
Except the Lord, xxxiv (1953).

The excesses of our youth are drafts upon our old age, payable with interest, about thirty years after date.
— Charles Caleb Colton,
Lacon, 55 (1820–22).

I remember my youth and the feeling that never came back any more — the feeling that I could last forever, outlast the sea, the earth, and all men.
— Joseph Conrad,
Youth (1898).

It is better to waste one's youth than to do nothing. — Georges Courteline,
La Philosophie de G. Courteline (1917).

Anybody that tries to do anything before he's an uncomfortable risk for the life insurance company is snubbed for youthful impertinence. — Finley Peter Dunne,
*Mr. Dooley Remembers:
Youth and Age* (1963).

If youth is a fault, one soon gets rid of it.
—Johann Wolfgang von Goethe,
Proverbs in Prose (1819).

Their intolerance is breath-taking. Do your thing means do their thing.
—Paul Goodman,
New Reformation (1970).

Never tell a young person that anything cannot be done. God may have been waiting for centuries for someone ignorant enough of the impossible to do that very thing.—John Andrew Holmes,
Wisdom in Small Doses (1927).

It does not matter one whit whether you lack wisdom teeth if you only possess wisdom.   —Earnest Albert Hooton,
Twilight of Man, 224 (1939).

A majority of young people seem to develop arteriosclerosis forty years before they get the physical kind.
— Aldous Huxley,
in Malcolm Cowley, ed., *Writers at Work, Second Series* (1963).

Youth is a continual intoxication; it is a delirium of the reason.
—François de La Rochefoucauld,
Maxims, no.271 (1665).

The elbowing self-conceit of youth.
—James Russell Lowell, *My Study Windows: A Good Word for Winter* (1871).

It is an illusion that youth is happy, an illusion of those who have lost it; but the young know they are wretched, for they are full of the truthless ideals which have been instilled into them, and each time they come in contact with the real they are bruised and wounded.
— W. Somerset Maugham,
Of Human Bondage, xxix (1915).

Each youth is like a child born in the night who sees the sun rise and thinks that yesterday never existed.
— W. Somerset Maugham,
A Writer's Notebook (1949).

My salad days,
When I was green in judgment.
—William Shakespeare,
Antony and Cleopatra, I.v.73 (1607)
[salad days = *inexperienced youth*].

The morn and liquid dew of youth.
—William Shakespeare,
Hamlet, I.iii.41 (1600–01).

The nervous agonies of the young have caused more discomfort in the world than the torments of the Inquisition.
—George Bernard Shaw,
Our Theatres of the Nineties, I: The Chili Widow, Oct. 12, 1895.

Don't laugh at a youth for his affections: he's only trying on one face after another till he finds his own.
—Logan Pearsall Smith,
Afterthoughts, 2 (1931).

Youth is wholly experimental.
—Robert Louis Stevenson (1850–94),
Letter to a Young Gentleman.

For God's sake give me the young man who has brains enough to make a fool of himself.   —Robert Louis Stevenson,
Virginibus Puerisque: Crabbed Age and Youth (1881).

To assume that the young will inevitably be both wiser and better than their elders is a forlorn hope, hardly justified by historic experience.
—Harold Blake Walker,
Prairie Farmer, Jan. 3, 1970.

Youth and Age

See also Age, Old; Generation Gap; Youth

Young men have a passion for regarding their elders as senile.   —Henry Adams,
The Education of Henry Adams,
xi (1907).

The old repeat themselves and the young have nothing to say. The boredom is mutual.   —Jacques Bainville, *Lectures: Charme de la Conversation* (1937).

Your old men shall dream dreams, and your young men shall see visions.
—*Bible: Joel* 2:28.

Is education of the young the whole of life? I hate the young—I'm worn out with them. They absorb you and suck you dry and are vampires and selfish brutes at best. Give me some good old rumsoaked club men—who *can't* be improved and make no moral claims—and let me play chequers with them and look out of the Club window and think about what I'll have for dinner.   —John Jay Chapman, *John Jay Chapman and His Letters*, ed. M.A. DeWolfe Howe (1937).

When I was young my teachers were the old....
I went to school to age to learn the past.
Now I am old my teachers are the young....
I go to school to youth to learn the future.   —Robert Frost, *West Running Brook: What Fifty Said* (1928).

When a man is young he is so wild he is insufferable. When he is old he plays the saint and becomes insufferable again.
—Nikolai Gogol, *The Gamblers* (1842).

Young men think old men fools, but old men know the young men are.
—John Grange, *The Golden Aphroditis* (1577); George Chapman, *All Fools*, V.1.292 (1605). Also slightly different, Royall Tyler, *The Contrast*, V.ii (1787).

A man of 60 who upbraids a young of 20 for being imprudent has forgotten far more than he has learned in the last 40 years.   —Sydney Harris, syndicated column, *Detroit Free Press*, May 29, 1980.

I suppose it's difficult for the young to realize that one may be old without being a fool.   —W. Somerset Maugham, *The Circle* (1921).

Youth, which is forgiven everything, forgives itself nothing: Age, which forgives itself everything, is forgiven nothing.   —George Bernard Shaw, *Maxims for Revolutionists* (1903).

The denunciation of the young is a necessary part of the hygiene of older people, and greatly assists in the circulation of their blood.
—Logan Pearsall Smith, *Afterthoughts* (1931).

Age may have one side, but assuredly Youth has the other. There is nothing more certain than that both are right, except perhaps that both are wrong.
—Robert Louis Stevenson, *Virginibus Puerisque: Crabbed Age and Youth* (1881).

Youth is a noisy stream
  Chattering over the ground,
But the sad wisdom of age
  Wells up without sound.
—Sara Teasdale, *Strange Victory: Age* (1933).

Zeal

See also Enthusiasm

Zeal without knowledge is a runaway horse.   —Henry Davidoff, *A World Treasury of Proverbs* (1946).

ZEAL *n*. Quality seen in new graduates—if you're quick. —Graham Storr, "A (Fairly) Concise Science Dictionary," *New Scientist* (London), Dec. 23, 1982.

Violent zeal for truth hath an hundred to one odds to be either petulancy, ambition, or pride.   —Jonathan Swift, *Thoughts on Religion* (1728).

Author Index

Saadi ben Joseph 116
Sabatier, Auguste 92
Sadat, Anwar el- 307
Sagan, Carl 321
Saint-Exupéry, Antoine de 5, 9, 56, 122, 188, 193, 261, 268, 269, 296, 311
St. John, Seymour 291
Saki [*pseud. of* H(ector) H(ugh) Munro] 130
Salinger, J(erome) D(avid) 48, 277
Sallust 103
Sampson, George 295
Samuel, Harold 198
Samuel, *Sir* Herbert Louis 184
Samuel HaNagid 231
Samuelson, Paul A. 237
Sand, George [*pseud. of* Amandine Aurore Dupin] 201
Sandburg, Carl 31, 61, 192, 211, 222, 223, 232
Sansom, William 335
Santayana, George 21, 28, 61, 112, 117, 131, 142, 143, 156, 165, 183, 198, 207, 211, 216, 230, 233, 248, 265, 271, 292, 302, 308
Santob de Carrion 270
Saphir, Moritz Gottlieb 220, 284
Sapir, Edward 172
Sapirstein, Milton R. 52, 88, 209
Sarnoff, David 163, 266
Sarton, (Eleanor) May 110, 319
Sartre, Jean-Paul 28, 231
Satanov, Isaac Halevi 251
Savile, *Sir* George (Marquis of Halifax) 169, 297
Sawhill, John C. 274
Saxe, John Godfrey 64, 184, 282, 305
Sayers, Dorothy L. 115
Scammon, Richard M. 95
Scarborough, William 31, 213, 243
Schechter, Solomon 25
Schelling, Felix Emmanuel 151
Schiller, (Johann Christoph) Friedrich von 281
Schneiders, Alexander A. 270
Schnitzler, Arthur 132, 248
Schopenhauer, Arthur 2, 3, 20, 307
Schreiner, Olive [*pseud.*: Ralph Iron] 50, 258, 313, 324, 336
Schroeder, Theodore 224
Schubert, William Henry 137
Schwab, Joseph J. 295
Scogan, John 73
Scott, *Sir* Walter 26, 48, 245
Scott-Maxwell, Florida 207
Scudder, Vida Dutton 31
Sedgwick, Ellery 25, 333
Seeley, John R. (1913–) 319
Seeley, *Sir* John Robert (1834–) 136

Sefer Hasidim (Book of the Righteous) 36, 77, 209
Selden, John 177, 203, 252, 333
Seldes, Gilbert 56
Sellar, Watler Carruthers 277
Seneca, Lucius Annaeus 78, 112, 125, 170, 176, 181, 217, 268, 280, 288, 298, 322
Seuss, Dr. [*pseud. of* Theodor Geisel] 8
Sexton, Anne 117
Shakespeare, William 4, 7, 10, 17, 19, 23, 31, 33, 35, 41, 52, 64, 79, 83, 103, 113, 118, 130, 146, 150, 172, 173, 177, 180, 181, 186, 196, 201, 203, 206, 211, 212, 216, 220, 221, 225, 228, 238, 242, 248, 250, 251, 256, 258, 261, 279, 280, 286, 291, 305, 307, 311, 315, 322, 331, 338
Shannon, James P. 72
Shapiro, Karl 324
Sharpe, Tom 163
Shaw, George Barnad 5, 10, 25, 28, 31, 39, 44, 48, 52, 56, 64, 65, 72, 74, 83, 85, 86, 87, 89, 99, 104, 107, 110, 112, 124, 125, 130, 138, 142, 148, 168, 173, 176, 181, 199, 200, 202, 205, 209, 220, 224, 227, 231, 235, 236, 239, 249, 258, 259, 272, 275, 286, 288, 302, 303, 305, 208, 311, 313, 316, 317, 319, 321, 338, 339
Shedd, John Augustus 206, 267, 324
Sheffield, John 254
Shelley, Mary Wollstonecraft 60, 306, 329
Shelley, Percy Bysshe 220, 222, 307
Shenstone, William 213, 282, 288, 307
Sheridan, Richard Brinsley 127, 185, 190, 219
Sheridan, Thomas 36
Sherman, Stuart Pratt 327
Shu Shuehmou 226, 243, 336
Shuster, George Nauman 329
Sidey, Hugh 42
Sidey, James Archibald 291
Sidney, *Sir* Philip 23, 252, 335
Sienkiewicz, Henryk 216
Sigismund I. 130
Silberman, Charles E. 259, 294
Sill, Edward Rowland 323
Simeon ben Lakish 166, 178
Simpson, Alan 86
Singer, Isaac Bashevis 25, 188, 242
Sitwell, *Sir* Osbert 21
Sixtus [*also* Xystus] I, *Saint* 234, 290, 324
Skelton, John 237
Skinner, B(urrhus) F(rederic) 87, 92
Smethhurst, Arthur F. 264
Smith, Adam 229, 230, 264, 319
Smith, Alexander 307
Smith, Bernard 87
Smith, Betty 17
Smith, Harry James 331
Smith, Horace 10, 149

Subject Index

The arrangement of this book is alphabetical by over 600 topics.
See the Table of Contents. This index to subjects is supplemental
and bears both "see" and "see also" references to the Table of Contents.